Jesus

according to Scripture

Jesus

according to Scripture

Restoring the Portrait from the Gospels

Darrell L. Bock

Baker Academic
A Division of Baker Book House Co
Grand Rapids, Michigan 49516

APOLLOS

© 2002 by Darrell L. Bock

Published by Baker Academic
a division of Baker Book House Company
P.O. Box 6287, Grand Rapids, MI 49516-6287

and

Apollos (an imprint of Inter-Varsity Press)
38 De Montfort Street
Leicester LE1 7GP England
e-mail: ivp@uccf.org.uk
web site: www.ivpbooks.com

Second printing, July 2003

Printed in the United States of America

Library of Congress Cataloging-in-Publication Data

Bock, Darrell L.
    Jesus according to Scripture : restoring the portrait from the Gospels / Darrell L. Bock.
       p.   cm.
    Includes bibliographical references and index.
    ISBN 0-8010-2370-X (cloth : alk. paper)
    1. Jesus Christ—Biography—Textbooks. 2. Bible. N.T. Gospels—Textbooks.
    I. Title.
    BT301.3 .B63 2002
    232.9′01—dc21   2002066584

British Library Cataloguing in Publication Data
A catalogue record for this book is available from the British Library.
Apollos ISBN 0-85111-288-9

For information about Baker Academic, visit our web site:
                    www.bakeracademic.com

Contents

Gospel References by Unit

The following table identifies the main passages discussed in each unit. To find all the places a particular verse or passage is mentioned, refer to the Scripture index in the back of the book.

Unit	Page	Matthew	Mark	Luke	John
1	53			1:1–4	
2	55	1:1–17			
3	57			1:5–25	
4	59			1:26–38	
5	61			1:39–56	
6	62			1:57–80	
7	64	1:18–25			
8	66			2:1–7	
9	66			2:8–20	
10	68			2:21–38	
11	69	2:1–12			
12	71	2:13–21			
13	72	2:22–23		2:39–40	
14	74			2:41–52	
15	78		1:1		
16	79	3:1–6	1:2–6	3:1–6	
17	81	3:7–10		3:7–9	
18	82			3:10–14	
19	83	3:11–12	1:7–8	3:15–18	
20	85	14:3–4	6:17–18	3:19–20	
21	86	3:13–17	1:9–11	3:21–22	
22	88			3:23–38	
23	89	4:1–11	1:12–13	4:1–13	
24	93	4:12–17	1:14–15	4:14–15	
25	95	13:53–58	6:1–6a	4:16–30	
26	98	4:18–22	1:16–20		
27	99		1:21–22	4:31–32	
28	100		1:23–28	4:33–37	
29	103	8:14–15	1:29–31	4:38–39	
30	104	8:16–17	1:32–34	4:40–41	
31	105		1:35–38	4:42–43	
32	106	4:23	1:39	4:44	

Unit	Page	Matthew	Mark	Luke	John
33	106			5:1–11	
34	107	8:1–4	1:40–45	5:12–16	
35	109	9:1–8	2:1–12	5:17–26	
36	112	9:9–13	2:13–17	5:27–32	
37	114	9:14–17	2:18–22	5:33–39	
38	115	12:1–8	2:23–28	6:1–5	
39	118	12:9–14	3:1–6	6:6–11	
40	120	4:24–25; 12:15–16	3:7–12	6:17–19	
41	121	10:1–4	3:13–19a	6:12–16	
42	126	5:1–2		6:20a	
43	127	5:3–12		6:20b–26	
44	130	5:13	9:49–50	14:34–35	
45	130	5:14–16	4:21	8:16	
46	131	5:17–20		16:17	
47	133	5:21–26		12:57–59	
48	134	5:27–30	9:43, 45, 47		
49	135	5:31–32		16:18	
50	136	5:33–37			
51	136	5:38–42		6:29–30	
52	137	5:43–48		6:27–28, 32–36	
53	138	6:1–4			
54	139	6:5–6			
55	139	6:7–15		11:1–4	
56	141	6:16–18			
57	141	6:19–21		12:33–34	
58	142	6:22–23		11:34–36	
59	143	6:24		16:13	
60	144	6:25–34		12:22–32	
61	144	7:1–5	4:24–25	6:37–42	
62	146	7:6			
63	146	7:7–11		11:9–13	
64	147	7:12		6:31	
65	148	7:13–14		13:23–24	
66	149	7:15–20		6:43–45	
67	150	7:21–23		6:46; 13:25–27	
68	152	7:24–27		6:47–49	
69	153	7:28–29	1:22		
70	153			6:20–49	
71	158	8:1–4	1:40–45	5:12–16	
72	158	8:5–13		7:1–10	
73	160			7:11–17	
74	160	8:14–15	1:29–31	4:38–39	
75	161	8:16–17	1:32–34	4:40–41	
76	161	8:18–22		9:57–62	
77	163	8:23–27	4:35–41	8:22–25	
78	164	8:28–34	5:1–20	8:26–39	
79	166	9:1–8	2:1–12	5:17–26	
80	166	9:9–13	2:13–17	5:27–32	
81	166	9:14–17	2:18–22	5:33–39	
82	167	9:18–26	5:21–43	8:40–56	

Unit	Page	Matthew	Mark	Luke	John
83	169	9:27–31; 20:29–34	10:46–52	18:35–43	
84	169	9:32–34; 12:22–24	3:22	11:14–15	
85	170	9:35–38	6:6b, 34	8:1; 10:2	
86	171	10:1–16	3:13–19a; 6:7–11	6:12–16; 9:1–5; 10:3	
87	173	10:17–25	13:9–13	6:40; 12:11–12; 21:12–19	
88	175	10:26–33		12:2–9	
89	176	10:34–36		12:51–53	
90	176	10:37–39		14:25–27; 17:33	
91	177	10:40–42	9:41	10:16	13:20
92	178	11:1			
93	178	11:2–6		7:18–23	
94	179	11:7–19		7:24–35	
95	181	11:20–24		10:12–15	
96	182	11:25–27		10:21–22	
97	183	11:28–30			
98	183	12:1–8	2:23–28	6:1–5	
99	184	12:9–14	3:1–6	6:6–11	
100	184	12:15–21	3:7–12	6:17–19	
101	185	26:6–13	14:3–9	7:36–50	12:1–8
102	187			8:1–3	
103	188		3:19b–21		
104	188	12:22–30	3:22–27	11:14–15, 17–23	
105	191	7:16–20; 12:31–37	3:28–30	6:43–45; 12:10	
106	192	12:38–42; 16:1–2a, 4	8:11–12	11:16, 29–32	
107	193	12:43–45		11:24–26	
108	194	12:46–50	3:31–35	8:19–21	
109	199	13:1–9	4:1–9	8:4–8	
110	200	13:10–15	4:10–12	8:9–10	
111	202	13:16–17		10:23–24	
112	202	13:18–23	4:13–20	8:11–15	
113	204		4:21–25	8:16–18	
114	205		4:26–29		
115	205	13:24–30			
116	206	13:31–32	4:30–32	13:18–19	
117	207	13:33		13:20–21	
118	207	13:34–35	4:33–34		
119	208	13:36–43			
120	209	13:44–46			
121	209	13:47–50			
122	210	13:51–52			
123	210	12:46–50	3:31–35	8:19–21	
124	211	8:23–27	4:35–41	8:22–25	
125	211	8:28–34	5:1–20	8:26–39	
126	211	9:18–26	5:21–43	8:40–56	
127	212	13:53–58	6:1–6a	4:16–30	
128	213	9:35; 10:1, 7–11, 14	6:6b–13	9:1–6	
129	213	14:1–2	6:14–16	9:7–9	
130	214	14:3–12	6:17–29	3:19–20	
131	215		6:30–31	9:10a	
132	216	14:13–21	6:32–44	9:10b–17	6:1–15

Unit	Page	Matthew	Mark	Luke	John
133	217	14:22–33	6:45–52		6:16–21
134	218	14:34–36	6:53–56		
135	219	15:1–20	7:1–23		
136	221	15:21–28	7:24–30		
137	222	15:29–31	7:31–37		
138	223	15:32–39	8:1–10		
139	224	12:38–39; 16:1–4	8:11–13	11:16, 29; 12:54–56	
140	225	16:5–12	8:14–21	12:1	
141	226		8:22–26		
142	230	16:13–20	8:27–30	9:18–21	
143	232	16:21–23	8:31–33	9:22	
144	233	16:24–28	8:34–9:1	9:23–27	
145	234	17:1–9	9:2–10	9:28–36	
146	235	17:10–13	9:11–13		
147	236	17:14–21	9:14–29	9:37–43a	
148	238	17:22–23	9:30–32	9:43b–45	
149	238	17:24–27			
150	239	18:1–5	9:33–37	9:46–48	
151	241	10:42	9:38–41	9:49–50	
152	241	18:6–9	9:42–50	14:34–35; 17:1–2	
153	242	18:10–14		15:3–7	
154	243	18:15–18		17:3	
155	244	18:19–20			
156	245	18:21–22		17:4	
157	245	18:23–35			
158	249			9:51	
159	250			9:52–56	
160	250	8:18–22		9:57–62	
161	251	9:37–38; 10:7–16, 40; 11:20–24	6:8–11	10:1–16	
162	252			10:17–20	
163	253	11:25–27; 13:16–17		10:21–24	
164	254	22:34–40	12:28–34	10:25–37	
165	256			10:38–42	
166	257	6:9–13		11:1–4	
167	257			11:5–8	
168	258	7:7–11		11:9–13	
169	259	12:22–30	3:22–27	11:14–23	
170	259	12:43–45		11:24–26	
171	260			11:27–28	
172	260	12:38–42	8:11–12	11:29–32	
173	261	5:15	4:21	8:16–18; 11:33	
174	261	6:22–23		11:34–36	
175	262	15:1–9; 23:4, 6–7, 13, 25–26, 27–28, 29–32, 34–36	7:1–9	11:37–54	
176	263	16:5–6	8:14–15	12:1	
177	264	10:26–33		12:2–9	
178	265	12:31–32	3:28–30	12:10	
179	266	10:19–20	13:11	12:11–12; 21:14–15	
180	266			12:13–15	
181	267			12:16–21	

Unit	Page	Matthew	Mark	Luke	John
182	267	6:25–34		12:22–32	
183	268	6:19–21		12:33–34	
184	269	24:42–51	13:33–37	12:35–48	
185	270	10:34–36	10:38	12:49–53	
186	271	16:2–3		12:54–56	
187	272	5:25–26		12:57–59	
188	272			13:1–9	
189	274			13:10–17	
190	274	13:31–32	4:30–32	13:18–19	
191	275	13:33		13:20–21	
192	275	7:13–14, 22–23; 8:11–12; 19:30		13:22–30	
193	276			13:31–33	
194	276	23:37–39		13:34–35	
195	277			14:1–6	
196	277			14:7–14	
197	278	22:1–14		14:15–24	
198	279	10:37–38		14:25–33	
199	280	5:13	9:49–50	14:34–35	
200	280	18:12–14		15:1–7	
201	281			15:8–10	
202	281			15:11–32	
203	283			16:1–9	
204	284			16:10–12	
205	284	6:24		16:13	
206	284			16:14–15	
207	285	5:18, 32; 11:12–13		16:16–18	
208	286			16:19–31	
209	288	18:6–7	9:42	17:1–3a	
210	288	18:15		17:3b–4	
211	289	17:19–21	9:28–29	17:5–6	
212	289			17:7–10	
213	290			17:11–19	
214	290			17:20–21	
215	291	24:17–18, 23, 26–27, 28, 37–39, 40–41	13:14–16, 19–23	17:22–37	
216	293			18:1–8	
217	294			18:9–14	
218	298	19:1–2	10:1		
219	299	19:3–12	10:2–12	16:18	
220	301	19:13–15	10:13–16	18:15–17	
221	302	19:16–22	10:17–22	18:18–23	
222	304	19:23–30	10:23–31	18:24–30	
223	305	20:1–16			
224	306	20:17–19	10:32–34	18:31–34	
225	308	20:20–28	10:35–45	22:24–27	
226	309	20:29–34	10:46–52	18:35–43	
227	310			19:1–10	
228	311	25:14–30	13:34	19:11–27	
229	313	21:1–9	11:1–10	19:28–40	12:12–19
230	315			19:41–44	

Unit	Page	Matthew	Mark	Luke	John
231	318	21:10–19	11:11–17	19:45–46	2:13–17
232	321		11:18–19	19:47–48	
233	322	21:20–22	11:20–26		
234	323	21:23–27	11:27–33	20:1–8	
235	324	21:28–32			
236	325	21:33–46	12:1–12	20:9–19	
237	327	22:1–14		14:15–24	
238	328	22:15–22	12:13–17	20:20–26	
239	329	22:23–33	12:18–27	20:27–40	
240	331	22:34–40	12:28–34	10:25–28	
241	331	22:41–46	12:35–37a	20:41–44	
242	333	23:1–36	12:37b–40	6:39; 11:39–41, 42, 43, 44, 46, 47–48, 49–51, 52; 20:45–47	
243	337	23:37–39		13:34–35	
244	337		12:41–44	21:1–4	
245	338	24:1–2	13:1–2	21:5–6	
246	340	24:3–8	13:3–8	21:7–11	
247	341	24:9–14	13:9–13	21:12–19	
248	342	24:15–22	13:14–20	21:20–24	
249	344	24:23–28	13:21–23	17:23–24	
250	345	24:29–31	13:24–27	21:25–28	
251	346	24:32–36	13:28–32	21:29–33	
252	347		13:33–37	12:40; 21:34–36	
253	348	24:37–44		12:39–40; 17:26–36	
254	349	24:45–51		12:41–46	
255	349	25:1–13			
256	351	25:14–30		19:11–27	
257	352	25:31–46			
258	354			21:37–38	
259	354	26:1–5	14:1–2	22:1–2	
260	355	26:6–13	14:3–9		12:1–8
261	356	26:14–16	14:10–11	22:3–6	
262	357	26:17–20	14:12–17	22:7–14	
263	358	26:21–25	14:18–21	22:21–23	13:21–30
264	359	26:26–29	14:22–25	22:15–20	
265	362	26:21–25	14:18–21	22:21–23	
266	362	19:28; 20:24–28	10:41–45	22:24–30	
267	363	26:30–35	14:26–31	22:31–34	13:36–38
268	365			22:35–38	
269	366	26:36–46	14:32–42	22:39–46	
270	368	26:47–56	14:43–52	22:47–53	18:2–12
271	370	26:57–75	14:53–72	22:54–71	18:13–28
272	377	27:1–2	15:1	23:1	
273	377	27:3–10			
274	378	27:11–14	15:2–5	23:2–5	18:29–38
275	380			23:6–12	
276	380			23:13–16	
277	381	27:15–23	15:6–14	23:17–23	18:39–40
278	383	27:24–26	15:15	23:24–25	
279	384	27:27–31a	15:16–20a		19:2–3
280	384	27:31b–32	15:20b–21	23:26–32	19:17a

Unit	Page	Matthew	Mark	Luke	John
281	385	27:33–37	15:22–26	23:33–34	19:17b–27
282	387	27:38–43	15:27–32a	23:35–38	
283	389	27:44	15:32b	23:39–43	
284	389	27:45–54	15:33–39	23:44–48	19:28–30
285	392	27:55–56	15:40–41	23:49	
286	393	27:57–61	15:42–47	23:50–56	19:38–42
287	393	27:62–66			
288	394	28:1–8	16:1–8	24:1–12	20:1–13
289	397	28:9–10			20:14–18
290	398	28:11–15			
291	398			24:13–35	
292	400			24:36–43	20:19–29
293	401	28:16–20			
294	402			24:44–53	
J1	410				1:1–18
J2	416				1:19–34
J3	419				1:35–51
J4	424				2:1–12
J5	426				2:13–25
J6	430				3:1–21
J7	433				3:22–36
J8	434				4:1–42
J9	438				4:43–54
J10	440				5:1–18
J11	442				5:19–47
J12	446				6:1–15
J13	448				6:16–21
J14	449				6:22–59
J15	453				6:60–71
J16	455				7:1–13
J17	456				7:14–52
—	461				7:53–8:11
J18	464				8:12–59
J19	469				9:1–41
J20	473				10:1–21
J21	476				10:22–42
J22	478				11:1–54
J23	482				11:55–12:11
J24	484				12:12–19
J25	486				12:20–50
J26	492				13:1–20
J27	495	26:21–25	14:18–21	22:21–23	13:21–30
J28	497				13:31–38
J29	498				14:1–14
J30	502				14:15–26
J31	504				14:27–31
J32	506				15:1–8
J33	508				15:9–17
J34	509				15:18–25
J35	511				15:26–27
J36	511				16:1–4
J37	512				16:5–15
J38	514				16:16–22
J39	516				16:23–28

Unit	Page	Matthew	Mark	Luke	John
J40	517				16:29–33
J41	519				17:1–26
J42	525				18:1–12
J43	527				18:13–28
J44	530				18:29–19:16
J45	535				19:17–30
J46	538				19:31–42
J47	542				20:1–18
J48	545				20:19–29
J49	548				20:30–31
J50	549				21:1–25

Preface

This textbook is designed for students taking classes in the Gospels or on the life of Christ and for pastors who wish to study the life and teaching of Jesus. However, it is not a standard life of Christ in that it works directly with a synopsis and separates the examination of the Synoptics from that of John. It pays special attention to the similarities and differences within the Gospel accounts. This material has been used over the last several years in classes at Dallas Theological Seminary, Talbot Theological Seminary, and Trinity Evangelical Divinity School. I have benefited greatly from the feedback that students and pastors have given to me about this material. Some students spent extra time with the material, giving full and direct feedback. They include Greg Herrick, Jim Samra, Brittany Burnette, and Carol Kahil.

Many thanks go to Baker Book House, which proposed that I undertake this work years ago. Special appreciation goes to Jim Weaver, Jim Kinney, and Wells Turner for their encouragement and aid in structuring the book for publication. I also thank the administration of Dallas Theological Seminary, whose creative design of a research professorship for me has allowed me to work on this project while teaching a limited amount of hours in the classroom. So my gratitude goes to Chuck Swindoll, Mark Bailey, John Grassmick, and Harold Hoehner.

My family deserves special mention. Sally, my dear wife, and my children, Elisa, Lara, and Stephen, have sacrificed time with me so that I could complete this responsibility. Elisa also read through the pages with an editor's eye and a student's interest to help me shape the volume for the right audience.

This work is dedicated to my full-time colleagues in the New Testament department. Their willingness to free me up to write has made this project possible. More importantly, their fellowship and encouragement has been one of the great joys of my life. I wish that everyone could have the blessing of working alongside such fine people. So my dedication goes out to them with deep appreciation: Harold Hoehner, Buist Fanning, John Grassmick, David Lowery, W. Hall Harris, Dan Wallace, and Jay Smith. Most of us have worked side by side for almost twenty years. Effective ministry takes a team. They have been exceptional partners.

My hope is that this work will help students of Jesus to appreciate even more the message of the four Gospels—in sum and in some of its detail. It is written with the conviction that knowing what God has done through Jesus is life-changing in the fullest sense. No amount of pages or words can convey the depth of what his life meant and means. However, if this work helps to convey even a small token of that truth in an age that needs to embrace Jesus' message and person, then this labor will be worth every invested hour.

Darrell L. Bock
June 18, 2002

Introduction

There is no doubt that Jesus of Nazareth is one of the most important historical and religious figures of all time. Today, numerous attempts are under way to search for the "historical Jesus" in an effort to determine who he really claimed to be and what he actually did. Many of these efforts are quite skeptical about what Scripture tells us about Jesus. Yet it is a fact that the Jesus who has so impacted our world is the one we find presented mainly in these four Gospel portraits of him. This book is not a technical historical Jesus study. It seeks rather to argue that a coherent portrait of Jesus emerges from the canonical Gospels that is both rooted in history and yet has produced its own historical, cultural impact because of the portrait these four Gospels give of him.

The premise of this textbook is that too few people, much less students of the Gospels, are familiar enough with the Gospel accounts as they stand. Nor are they sufficiently aware of the Gospels' first-century roots to fully appreciate their message. So this study initially works through the Gospels systematically. The text is designed to be used with a Bible near at hand so that one can see the relationships between parallel texts. We begin with the Synoptists and then proceed to John. In the final section, we discuss the major themes of Jesus' ministry, pointing out the highlights emerging from the full survey of the Gospels.

Before we assess a Jesus reconstructed by various approaches to the historical-critical method, we would do well to understand how the Gospels present him. At least in this case we all are working with the same textual data, even if differing worldviews cause us to respond to that data differently. One argument made throughout the book is that the reader of the Gospels needs to respect the documents' claims to present Jesus as a figure making unique claims of authority tied to his unique relationship to God. It is especially at this point that the Gospel portraits cohere, even in the midst of their diversity. Rather than seeing difference as evidence of contradiction and inauthenticity, I hope to show that the very diversity in the Gospels underscores an inherent unity in their claims that adds depth to

17

the account of Jesus in a way that simply overlapping accounts would not. Just as a three-dimensional portrait gives depth to an image in a way that two dimensions cannot, so these four Gospels reveal a many-sided Jesus whose fundamental claims still challenge us today. Thus, such a look at Jesus according to Scripture gives us a glimpse of how unique a figure Jesus was.

Abbreviations

General

ℵ	Codex Sinaiticus
A	Codex Alexandrinus
AB	Anchor Bible
ABRL	Anchor Bible Reference Library
Aland	Kurt Aland, *Synopsis Quattuor Evangeliorum,* 13th ed. (Stuttgart: Deutsche Bibelgesellschaft, 1985); idem, *Synopsis of the Four Gospels,* 2d ed. (Stuttgart: United Bible Societies, 1975)
Ant.	Josephus, *Jewish Antiquities*
b.	Babylonian Talmud
B	Codex Vaticanus
BAGD	W. Bauer, W. F. Arndt, F. W. Gingrich, and F. W. Danker, *A Greek-English Lexicon of the New Testament and Other Early Christian Literature,* 2d ed. (Chicago: University of Chicago Press, 1979)
BDAG	W. Bauer, F. W. Danker, W. F. Arndt, and F. W. Gingrich, *A Greek-English Lexicon of the New Testament and Other Early Christian Literature,* 3d ed. (Chicago: University of Chicago Press, 2000)
BDF	F. Blass, A. Debrunner, and R. W. Funk, *A Greek Grammar of the New Testament and Other Early Christian Literature* (Chicago: University of Chicago Press, 1961)
BECNT	Baker Exegetical Commentary on the New Testament
Byz	Byzantine manuscript tradition
D	Codex Bezae
DJG	*Dictionary of Jesus and the Gospels,* ed. J. B. Green and S. McKnight (Downers Grove, Ill.: InterVarsity, 1992)
Eccl. Hist.	Eusebius, *Ecclesiastical History*
Huck-Greeven	Albert Huck and Heinrich Greeven, *Synopse der Drei Ersten Evangelien, mit Beigabe der Johanneischen Parallelstellen* (Synopsis of the first three Gospels, with the addition of the Johannine parallels), 13th ed. (Tübingen: Mohr, 1981)
Itala	Old Latin manuscript tradition
IVPNTCS	IVP New Testament Commentary Series
JSNTSup	Journal for the Study of the New Testament: Supplement Series
LXX	Septuagint
m.	Mishnah (the spelling of tractate names follows *The SBL Handbook of Style* and differs occasionally from that of older works, such as Danby's *Mishnah*)
MM	J. H. Moulton and G. Milligan, *The Vocabulary of the Greek Testament: Illustrated from the Papyri and Other Non-literary Sources* (repr., Grand Rapids: Eerdmans, 1976)

MT	Masoretic Text
NEB	New English Bible
NICNT	New International Commentary on the New Testament
NIV	New International Version
Orchard	John Bernard Orchard, *A Synopsis of the Four Gospels, in a New Translation: Arranged according to the Two-Gospel Hypothesis and Edited by John Bernard Orchard* (Macon, Ga.: Mercer University Press, 1982); idem, *A Synopsis of the Four Gospels in Greek: Arranged according to the Two-Gospel Hypothesis and Edited by John Bernard Orchard* (Edinburgh: Clark, 1983).
𝔓	papyrus
par.	parallel(s)
PGM	*Papyri graecae magicae: Die griechischen Zauberpapyri,* ed. K. Preisendanz (Berlin: Teubner, 1928)
RSV	Revised Standard Version
SNTSMS	Society for New Testament Studies Monograph Series
t.	Tosefta
TDNT	*Theological Dictionary of the New Testament,* ed. G. Kittel and G. Friedrich, trans. and ed. G. W. Bromiley, 10 vols. (Grand Rapids: Eerdmans, 1964–76)
Trypho	Justin Martyr, *Dialogue with Trypho*
v(v).	verse(s)
War	Josephus, *Jewish War*
WBC	Word Biblical Commentary
WUNT	Wissenschaftliche Untersuchungen zum Neuen Testament
y.	Jerusalem (Yerushalmi) Talmud

Biblical and Extrabiblical

Old Testament

Gen.	Genesis	Neh.	Nehemiah	Hos.	Hosea
Exod.	Exodus	Esth.	Esther	Joel	Joel
Lev.	Leviticus	Job	Job	Amos	Amos
Num.	Numbers	Ps.	Psalms	Obad.	Obadiah
Deut.	Deuteronomy	Prov.	Proverbs	Jon.	Jonah
Josh.	Joshua	Eccles.	Ecclesiastes	Mic.	Micah
Judg.	Judges	Song	Song of Songs	Nah.	Nahum
Ruth	Ruth	Isa.	Isaiah	Hab.	Habakkuk
1–2 Sam.	1–2 Samuel	Jer.	Jeremiah	Zeph.	Zephaniah
1–2 Kings	1–2 Kings	Lam.	Lamentations	Hag.	Haggai
1–2 Chron.	1–2 Chronicles	Ezek.	Ezekiel	Zech.	Zechariah
Ezra	Ezra	Dan.	Daniel	Mal.	Malachi

Old Testament Apocrypha

1–4 Macc.	1–4 Maccabees
Sir.	Sirach
Tob.	Tobit
Wis.	Wisdom of Solomon

New Testament

Matt.	Matthew	1–2 Thess.	1–2 Thessalonians
Mark	Mark	1–2 Tim.	1–2 Timothy
Luke	Luke	Titus	Titus
John	John	Philem.	Philemon
Acts	Acts	Heb.	Hebrews
Rom.	Romans	James	James
1–2 Cor.	1–2 Corinthians	1–2 Pet.	1–2 Peter
Gal.	Galatians	1–3 John	1–3 John
Eph.	Ephesians	Jude	Jude
Phil.	Philippians	Rev.	Revelation
Col.	Colossians		

Qumran Texts

1QapGen	Genesis Apocryphon
1QH	Thanksgiving Hymns/Psalms (*Hôdāyôt*)
1QM	War Scroll (*Milḥāmâ*)
1QpHab	Commentary (*Pesher*) on Habakkuk
1QS	Manual of Discipline (*Serek Hayyaḥad,* Rule/Order of the Community)
1QSa	Rule of the Congregation (1Q28a, appendix A to 1QS)
3Q15	Copper Scroll
4Q181	Ages of Creation[b]
4QFlor	Florilegium (4Q174)
4QMMT	Halakhic Letter (*Miqsāt Maʿăśê Tôrâ*)
4QpIsa[d]	Commentary (*Pesher*) on Isaiah[d] (4Q164)
4QPrNab	Prayer of Nabonidus (4Q242)
11QMelch	Melchizedek text (11Q13)
11QTemple[a]	Temple Scroll[a] (11Q19)
CD	Damascus Document

Part 1

The Four Gospels: Distinctive Voices

For as there are four quarters of the world in which we live, and four universal winds, and as the church is dispersed over all the earth, and the gospel is the pillar and base of the church and the breath of life, so it is natural that it should have four pillars, breathing immortality from every quarter and kindling the life of men anew. Whence it is manifest that the Word, the architect of all things, who sits upon the cherubim and holds all things together, having been manifested to men, has given us the gospel in fourfold form, but held together by one Spirit.[1]

The writers of the Gospels make no attempt to develop the life of Christ historically or chronologically. They make no attempt to provide a biography of Christ. The writers, using the same extant material, select and arrange according to their individual emphasis and interpretation that which presents the particular portrait of Christ they desire to convey. The Gospels present the life of Christ thematically and thus are to be viewed as complementary and supplementary rather than contradictory.[2]

The forming of the fourfold Gospel canon probably took place around the middle of the second century. At about the same time, the apologist Justin Martyr was referring to these church scriptures as "memoirs of the apostles." He tells us that they were being read as scriptures in the worship services of the church.[3]

All four [Gospels] agree that in his deeds and words Jesus acts and speaks for God. He is not just a prophet, nor even the human agent of the kingdom of

1. Irenaeus, *Against Heresies* 3.11.8 (ca. A.D. 180).
2. J. Dwight Pentecost, *The Words and Works of Jesus Christ: A Study of the Life of Christ* (Grand Rapids: Zondervan, 1981), 24.
3. William R. Farmer, *The Gospel of Jesus: The Pastoral Relevance of the Synoptic Problem* (Louisville: Westminster/John Knox, 1994), 187.

God; for the extraordinary response is that of worship, worship which may only be given properly to God himself. There may be four gospels, but there is only one Jesus, and he is God.[4]

The Scripture does not give us one story of Jesus, but four Gospels. Following this introductory unit, I will present the work of Jesus in a twofold structure, one part reflecting the Synoptics' portrait of Jesus from the earth up and the other working with John's presentation from heaven down. The present unit sets each Gospel in its context; it also overviews each Gospel. It is the briefest unit of the book, consisting of only one chapter, which surveys the structure, themes, authorship, setting, and date of each Gospel as a way of helping to summarize and set out each Gospel's contribution to the canonical portrait of Jesus. Much more complete presentations of this material can be found in the technical commentaries on each Gospel and in specialized introductions to the New Testament. Such an overview will help orient us to the emphases of each Gospel before we examine how they work together to present Jesus.

None of the Gospels names its author. What we do often have is a rich tradition that describes authorship. However, that tradition sometimes is inconsistent in its details. Issues of date and setting are difficult to resolve. In all of these areas, attention also should be paid to internal evidence from the texts. The problem is that the significance of these internal details is debatable when it comes to making judgments about implications for setting and authorship. Often inferences, not hard facts, are what we are considering. So we will have to go with probabilities in the judgments we make about some of the roots of each Gospel. The combination of external and internal evidence suggests that two Gospels are rooted in apostolic origins (Matthew, John), while two others have close connections with the apostolic tradition (Mark through Peter, Luke through Paul and others).

When it comes to outline and themes, we are on slightly more solid ground, because we are working with the textual data. But outlines also are a construct, a way of trying to map the structure of a Gospel. Such outlines are another useful tool in trying to see the main movements within a Gospel. The outlines presented here are set forth merely with such a suggestive intent. This unit has almost a listlike feel to it, since the details are found either in the Gospels themselves or in technical treatments more fully dedicated to such questions. Nonetheless, such an overview begins to reveal both how similar to and distinct from one another the Gospels are. It is this mix of continuity and diversity in the Gospels that gives their portrait of Jesus its richness and that opens the door to a fresh appreciation of who Jesus is in light of the Gospels studied as a unit.

4. Richard A. Burridge, *Four Gospels, One Jesus?* (Grand Rapids: Eerdmans, 1994), 171.

ONE

Overviews of Matthew, Mark, Luke, and John

The evangelists, I have argued, did not write for specific churches they knew or knew about, not even for a very large number of such churches. Rather drawing on their experience and knowledge of several or many specific churches, they wrote *for any and every church* to which their Gospels might circulate. No more than almost any other author, at their time or most other periods, could they know which specific readers and hearers their work would reach. Thus, to ask, for example, if Luke knew whether there were any Christian churches in Gaul at the time when he wrote, and, supposing he knew there were, if he intended to address them in his Gospel is to ask altogether the wrong sort of question. His intended audience was an *open category*—any and every church to which his Gospel might circulate—not a specified audience in which he had consciously either to include churches in Gaul or not.[1]

That the Gospels were written ultimately for a broad audience is important in approaching the Gospels and how they work.[2] Many details about the original audience of each Gospel are unclear. A common consensus, which the preceding quotation correctly challenges, is that the Gospels were written in each case for one community or set of local communities. The consensus argument is that each Gospel's stories are told in such a way that the account

---

1. Richard Bauckham, "For Whom Were Gospels Written?" in *The Gospels for All Christians: Rethinking the Gospel Audiences,* ed. Richard Bauckham (Grand Rapids: Eerdmans, 1998), 46.

2. A shorter version of this overview appears in my *Studying the Historical Jesus* (Grand Rapids: Baker, 2002). This chapter fills out some of the debated points noted in that earlier overview as well as setting forth more developed outlines for each Gospel. There, I make the point that certainly the Gospels have circulated far more broadly than the original evangelists could have foreseen.

would be relevant to a narrow community. That view gradually is being rejected. Rather, the Gospel writers wrote for the church at large through what one author called "the holy Internet."[3]

The implication of their intention to address the church at large means that what we do not know for certain about the specifics of each Gospel's setting—and there is quite a lot we do not know about such details—has little impact on our appreciation of the basic message of these Gospels. Intimate knowledge of the original community to which each Gospel was addressed is not required to understand a Gospel's message, though such knowledge, when it can be determined, does help us appreciate certain nuances of detail.

Appreciating the structure of each Gospel as well as being aware of what we do and do not know about its origin does enhance our ability to interact with each Gospel's message. So we consider the structure, themes, authorship, date, and setting of each of these works. Doing so helps us to see how the Gospels are both similar to and distinct from each other, one of the most fundamental characteristics about the Gospel portrait of Jesus.

Matthew

Matthew's Gospel is the one most focused on Jewish issues and concerns. Also important to his Gospel is the key role that Jesus' discourses play in the development of the argument. Although it is often said that Matthew contains five discourse units, it is important to note that the last unit is particularly large and combines two distinct discourses: the condemnation of the leadership followed by the eschatological discourse (Matt. 23–25). Other discourse units cover blessing, law, righteousness and the walk with God (Matt. 5–7), instructions for mission (Matt. 10), the kingdom (Matt. 13), and remarks about community—accountability and forgiveness (Matt. 18).

A look at a working outline of Matthew reveals much about its concerns:

  I. Prologue: "God with Us," "King of the Jews," "Born of God" according to Promise in the Midst of Conflict from Israel and Gentile Adoration (1:1–2:23)
  II. Introduction: John the Baptist Prepares the Way for the Beloved Son, Who Overcomes Temptation (3:1–4:11)
  III. Messiah Confronts Israel in Galilee and Meets Rejection (4:12–12:50)
      A. Introduction and Summary (4:12–25)
      B. Discourse: Call to Genuine Righteousness (5:1–7:29)

---

3. Michael B. Thompson, "The Holy Internet: Communication between Churches in the First Christian Generation," in Bauckham, ed., *Gospels for All Christians*, 49–70.

    C. Ministry of Nine Miracles and Teaching for Disciples (8:1–
        9:35)
    D. Discourse: Mission to Israel—A Shepherd for the Sheep (9:36–
        11:1)
    E. Rejected by Jewish Leaders, Call for Disciples to Rest in the Just
        Servant for the Nations (11:2–12:50)
 IV. Responses: Kingdom, Provision-Acceptance-Call for Disciples, and
      Rejection by Israel (13:1–20:34)
    A. Discourse: The Mysteries of the Kingdom (13:1–53)
    B. Rejection Intensified by Many in Israel, Provision for and Ac-
        ceptance by Disciples, and Call for Discipleship (13:54–17:27)
    C. Discourse: Community—Accountability and Forgiveness
        (18:1–35)
    D. To Jerusalem: Instruction on Faith Commitment and Grace
        (19:1–20:34)
  V. Messiah Inaugurates Kingdom through Rejection and Vindication
      (21:1–28:20)
    A. Messiah Confronts Israel in Jerusalem (21:1–22:46)
    B. Discourses: Pharisees and Scribes Condemned, Messiah Predicts
        the Judgment of Unbelieving Israel and His Return (23:1–
        25:46)
    C. Messiah Is Rejected in Crucifixion, but Vindicated in Resurrec-
        tion as a Basis for Commission (26:1–28:20)

For Matthew, Jesus' relationship to Israel and explaining Israel's rejection are
major concerns. Matthew wishes to point out that those who are Christian
did not seek a break with Judaism but have been forced to be distinct because
the nation rejected the completion of the divine and scriptural promise that
Jesus brought and offered. However, that rejection did not stop the arrival of
promise. What rejection did was raise the stakes of discipleship and lead to
the creation of a new entity, the church. Their message not only continued to
appeal to Israel but also went out as part of a mission to all the world. Five
discourse units comprising six discourses (the fifth unit contains two discourses) are the backbone of the book. As with all the Gospels, there is an interaction and interchange between Jesus' words and deeds. What Jesus does
supports what he preaches. Jesus' death was an act of the divine plan that led
to his vindication and mission. Disciples are those who come to him and set
upon the task of reflecting the righteousness that God so graciously offers.
    A brief listing of major Matthean themes shows the variety of his interests.
Italics identify the key themes, which in some cases overlap with other Gospels and in other cases are unique. Matthew's Christology presents fundamentally a *royal, messianic understanding of Jesus,* who as *Son of God* comes to be
seen as the revealer of God's will and the bearer of divine authority. As the

promised king of the Jews, Jesus heals, teaches *the real meaning of Torah in all its dimensions,* calls for a *practical righteousness,* inaugurates the kingdom, and teaches about the *mystery* elements of God's promise. This is all part of what Matthew associates with a program that involves what he calls the *kingdom of heaven.*[4] This kingdom is both present and yet to come (12:28; 13:1–52; 24:1–25:46). John the Baptist announces the approach of this kingdom. Jesus proclaims its hope throughout the nation to the lost sheep of *Israel.* He *calls on them to repent, challenges their current practices, expresses his authority over sin and Sabbath,* and *calls them to read the law with mercy.* Most of Israel rejects the message, but the mystery is that the promise comes despite that rejection. One day that kingdom will encompass the entire world (parables of Matt. 13). At the consummation, the authority of Jesus in that kingdom will be evident to all in a *judgment* rendered on the entire creation (Matt. 24–25). Thus, the kingdom program, eschatology, and salvation history are bound together for Matthew.

God is seen as the *Father* who has a *sovereign and abiding presence* over the world. That presence is seen in the way that Jesus' program is a realization of God's promises. His presence is also seen in the way that Jesus exercises judgment over Israel in the promise of the judgment of the temple. God's sovereignty over the world emerges through the Messiah, who bears responsibility at the final judgment. Disciples have the benefit of calling on God as Father.

Most of the *scriptural fulfillment* that Matthew cites helps us understand who Jesus is and how he is realizing God's plan. Scripture is fulfilled as Jesus (1) is conceived of a virgin, (2) is born in Bethlehem, (3) emerges from Egypt, (4) comes to life in a period of suffering for the nation, (5) is called a "Nazarene" (Matt 1–2), (6) goes to Galilee of the Gentiles, (7) bears our sicknesses, (8) is a shepherd sent to a shepherdless people, and (9) is the *servant who brings justice to Gentiles* (4:14–16; 9:36; 12:18–21). All of these promises underscore the deliverance and mission that Jesus brings for Israel. Israel's promised one has been sent to bring the people back to God, just as the prophets earlier had tried to do. Yet, now and then there are hints that the story circulates beyond Israel. A centurion and a Syrophoenician woman have exemplary faith (8:5–13; 15:21–28). Gentiles as well as Jews hear the Sermon on the Mount. As Israel's rejection becomes more intense, Jesus is sent as a servant who brings justice in hope to the nations.

The final *commission* sends disciples into the entire world (28:16–20). All of this takes place through a new community to be called the *church,* which Jesus will build (16:16–20; 18:15–20). Matthew is the only Gospel to speak directly of the church. Those disciples who compose the church are called to a *demanding discipleship* that puts following Jesus first; is grounded in *spiritual*

---

4. Matthew refers to the kingdom as the kingdom of heaven in all but four uses (12:28; 19:24; 21:31, 43 are the exceptions).

accountability, mercy, and *forgiveness;* pursues righteousness as a calling; and goes out into the world to make more disciples (16:24–28; 18:1–35).

Introductory Issues. The issues of authorship, date, and setting are debated. The association of this Gospel with the apostle Matthew dates back to a remark from Papias about Matthew having collected sayings of Jesus in a Hebrew dialect (Eusebius, *Eccl. Hist.* 3.39.16). Much about this citation is disputed. Is Papias referring to the Gospel or to something else? If something else, what is the relationship between our Greek Gospel and what Papias describes? The answers to these questions are not clear.[5] On the other hand, the superscripts that accompany manuscripts of this Gospel uniformly refer to Matthew as the author. The roots for these go back to the early-to-mid–second century.[6] In addition, this Gospel was widely accepted and the most popular in the early period. The likelihood is high that its roots were well known.

Still, some question the apostolic association. Arguments, often dependent on Markan priority, include the idea that as an apostle, Matthew would not have used a Gospel by a nonapostle. However, this criticism ignores the real likelihood that Mark has roots in Peter's preaching and was associated with this key apostle. Others argue that the nature of the Greek used in Matthew makes it unlikely that a Jewish author wrote it. However, a figure who was a tax collector in a highly Hellenistic region very likely would have been bilingual. The most important argument is the one tied to the date of Mark. If Mark is the first Gospel and is supposedly a work of the late A.D. 60s or 70s (which is not certain, as we will see), then some time is needed for Matthew's release. The later this goes, the less likely that Matthew is the author. Those who reject Matthew as author usually see the author as a Jewish Christian.[7]

As one can see, the arguments surrounding authorship are a matter of tradition versus certain judgments about internal evidence. This often will be the case as we consider these issues for each Gospel. The balance of the argument, especially given the quick and widespread acceptance of the Gospel, favors that its roots do go back to the apostle. That conclusion best explains its rapid and wide use in the early church.

Determining the book's date also is difficult. The earliest citations of Matthew come in the early second century with Ignatius (*To the Smyrnaeans* 1.1; *To Polycarp* 2.2), who died about A.D. 107. Some of the instruction is given

---

5. Scot McKnight, "Matthew," *DJG*, 527–28. However, his explanation that the passage is merely about Hebrew style is less likely than that Papias may be describing a Hebrew work that preceded the Gospel we now have.

6. Martin Hengel, *Studies in the Gospel of Mark* (Philadelphia: Fortress, 1985), 65–67. He notes that this process was distinct from that which led to the recognition of the four Gospels as canonical.

7. W. D. Davies and D. C. Allison, *A Critical and Exegetical Commentary on the Gospel according to Saint Matthew,* 3 vols., International Critical Commentary (Edinburgh: Clark, 1988–97), 1:33, 58.

in a form that makes it look as if the temple still is in service (5:23–24; 17:24–27). The problem is that this teaching reaches back into the life of Jesus, when the temple was present. The argument is that retaining such instruction about sacrificial practice and the temple tax makes more sense if a temple still existed, to make the examples still practical. Irenaeus claimed that the Gospel was written while Paul and Peter were still in Rome founding that church, placing it in the early-to-mid-60s at the latest and suggesting that it was even earlier (*Against Heresies* 3.1.1; cf. Eusebius, *Eccl. Hist.* 5.8). The picture of intense conflict with Judaism could fit any period in the mid–first century, especially that tied to Nero in the mid-60s, because he applied pressure to the Christians in a way that distinguished them from Jews. In A.D. 62 the Jews stoned James, Jesus' brother, in an incident that even Jews worried about in regard to Roman reaction because they did not have authority to execute (Josephus, *Ant.* 20.9.1 §§197–203).[8] All of this evidence appears to point to a date in the 60s.

Those who reject this date and prefer an earlier one argue again on the basis that Matthew's Gospel preceded Mark's or that an apostle would not rely on a nonapostolic Gospel. We noted above the responses to these arguments.

Those who argue for a date after the 60s contend that texts such as Matt. 24:1–29 (the prediction of Jerusalem's destruction) and Matt. 22:6–7 (the prediction about a burning of "their" city) indicate a Gospel written after A.D. 70. Here is someone, so they argue, who has separated himself from a Jewish perspective, as the use of "their" city indicates. However, any Jew arguing that Israel had been unfaithful to God could foresee a destruction of Jerusalem as a judgment along the lines of the fall to Babylon, which precipitated the exile. By the 60s a break in perspective for some was emerging, as James's death shows. So again we are faced with the tension between external evidence and internal judgments. Most who see some merit in these arguments place Matthew after A.D. 70, usually somewhere in the 80s.[9]

Determining the setting for this Gospel is the most uncertain exercise of all. It involves inference alone. Matthew's heavy emphasis on Jewish concerns points either to a setting in Israel or to a locale with a major Jewish population. The previously cited evidence from Irenaeus indicates a setting "among the Hebrews." The use of Greek suggests a racially mixed setting. The best candidate for a community outside of Israel is Antioch of Syria. But no one really knows. As we have noted, this determination is not crucial to appreciating the message, because certainly the Gospel was intended to circulate beyond this one community.

8. Everett F. Harrison, *Introduction to the New Testament,* rev. ed. (Grand Rapids: Eerdmans, 1971), 176.

9. For example, Davies and Allison, *Matthew,* 1:138. Harrison opts for anywhere between the 60s and 80s.

It is often said that Matthew is the Gospel most concerned with Jewish issues, and that certainly is true. But this Gospel also shows wider concerns tied to Christology, community, discipleship, and mission. More than anything else, this Gospel explains that despite his death, Jesus was the promised Messiah sent from God, calling people back to following God and pursuing the kingdom.

We also should note why the Gospels appear in our canon in the order they do. Matthew is first because when the church came to establish the canon, Matthew was believed to be the first Gospel written and the one with the most developed connection to the Old Testament. In the early centuries of the church, it was the most popular Gospel among the Synoptics because it had a direct tie to the apostles that Mark and Luke did not, given that the second and third Gospels were written by nonapostles. John assumed the fourth position because his story differed enough from the first three Gospels. His Gospel probably was the last written of the four as well.

Mark

Today, Mark's Gospel generally is regarded as the first one written. Thus, its outline of Jesus' ministry has become the basic structure through which his life has been traced, even though sections of it probably are given not in chronological order but in topical arrangement (e.g., the conflicts of Mark 2–3). Here is a basic working outline:

I. Prologue on the Beginning of the Gospel (1:1–15)
II. Jesus' Public Ministry (1:16–8:26)
    A. Calling of Disciples and Conflicts Leading to Rejection (1:16–3:12)
    B. Teaching on the Mystery-Filled Kingdom and Miracles of Power Still Yield Rejection (3:13–6:6)
    C. Challenge and Misunderstanding up to Confession (6:7–8:26)
III. To Jerusalem, Passion, and Vindication (8:27–16:8)
    A. Passion Predictions and Discipleship Teaching (8:27–10:52)
    B. Conflict in Jerusalem and Prediction of Judgment (11:1–13:37)
    C. King of the Jews Executed for Blasphemy, Confessed as Son, and Vindicated by God (14:1–16:8)

The first major section of this Gospel cycles through a consistent structure in each of its three parts. There is a story about disciples at the start (1:16–20; 3:13–19; 6:7–13) and a note about rejection or a summary at the end (3:7–12; 6:1–6; 8:22–26).[10] The turning point of the Gospel is the confession in

10. R. A. Guelich, "Mark," *DJG,* 516.

8:27–31 that Jesus is the Christ. Before this confession a miracle appears that pictures Jesus giving sight. After the confession comes the repeated instruction that the one confessed will suffer. Half of the Gospel treats the movement toward the final week of Jesus' ministry, while a full quarter of it is on the last week alone. For Mark, the events of the final week are central to the story.

The key themes are also evident in how the account proceeds. It begins with a note that what is being told is *the gospel.* Though to a lesser degree than Matthew or Luke, Mark also traces the *kingdom of God* as a theme. For Mark, it has elements that indicate its initial presence, while the bulk of the emphasis is that it will come in fullness one day in the future. Kingdom entry, available now, requires one to be like a child. The parables look to a day when it will be like a place where birds nest. The *mystery of the kingdom* is that it starts out small but still will accomplish all that God has called it to be. It will grow into a full harvest.

Another theme that is present but less developed than in Matthew or Luke is that *the time of fulfillment has come.* Mark opens with this theme (1:15), and it appears here and there.

Mark is more a Gospel of *action* than teaching. Things happen *immediately*—one of Mark's favorite expressions. Mark has only two discourses, one involving the parables of the kingdom (4:1–33) and the other being an eschatological discourse (13:1–37). Miracles abound. Mark has twenty *miracle accounts.* Combined with healing summaries, these units comprise a third of the Gospel and nearly one-half of the first ten chapters.[11] These pictures of Jesus' authority are important to Mark; he presents Jesus as one who teaches with authority, but a key part of that authority is seen in his activity, not just in his pronouncements. The authority underscores that Jesus is the *Christ, the Son of God* (1:1; 8:29; 15:39). Mark's Christology presents Jesus as this promised figure. Jesus' claims of authority over sin, relationship, and practices tied to purity, Sabbath, and temple get him into trouble with the Jewish leaders, who early on determine they must stop him. This *conflict that Jesus' claims raise* is also a central feature of the Gospel.

However, Jesus' authority is not one of raw power. In terms of proportion, Mark highlights Jesus as *the suffering Son of Man and Servant* more than the other Gospels. In fact, nine of thirteen uses of this language look to Jesus' suffering. Although Isa. 53 is not cited, the descriptions of Jesus clearly parallel the portrait of this figure, especially the claim that his mission is to come and give his life as *a ransom for many* (10:45). The importance of understanding the suffering role probably explains the *commands to silence* given in Mark to those, including demons, who confess Jesus as the Messiah (1:44; 5:43; 9:9).

---

11. Graham H. Twelftree, *Jesus the Miracle Worker: A Historical and Theological Study* (Downers Grove, Ill.: InterVarsity, 1999), 57.

Without an appreciation of his suffering, Jesus' messianic calling is not understood. Some have called this the "messianic secret," but it is not so much that his messiahship is to be kept a secret as that it is not to be shared until it is more fully understood. Only as the cross draws near does the full scope of divine promise and calling emerge. The disciples are not in a position to preach Jesus until they appreciate this aspect of his mission, as the subsequent mission of the church makes clear.

The servant Jesus is an example of how to walk with God in a world that rejects those sent by God. It is here that the pastoral *demands of discipleship* appear as well (10:35–45). Mark is like Matthew here. After the suffering comes glory and vindication. The same Son of Man will return one day to render judgment, as the eschatological discourse reveals. The need for discipleship and really listening to Jesus is clear as Mark notes without hesitation *the failures of the disciples.* Their instincts will not take them in the right direction. Trust in God and his ways is what is required. Alongside of this, Mark notes *the emotions of Jesus and the disciples* more than do any of the other Gospels.

In sum, Mark addresses the church under duress, suffering a rejection like that of their teacher. Yet the call to serve, to rest in God's plan, and to look to Jesus as the example provides the antidote for their stressful situation.

Introductory Issues. As with the other Gospels, discussions about authorship, date, and setting for Mark revolve around external testimony and inferences about internal features of this Gospel. As with the other Gospels, the author does not name himself in his work. The association of the Gospel with Mark comes to us through early church testimony.[12] Mark is described as Peter's interpreter by Papias in a reference given by Eusebius (*Eccl. Hist.* 3.39.15).[13] The Anti-Marcionite Prologue (ca. A.D. 180), Irenaeus (*Against Heresies* 3.1.1–2), and Clement of Alexandria (as reported in Eusebius, *Eccl. Hist.* 6.14) confirm this identification.[14] Justin suggests that Mark is the author as well in an allusion in *Trypho* 106. The evidence of the superscriptions also confirms this connection.[15] There is no external evidence for any other author.[16] For many, Mark refers to John Mark, known as an assistant to Peter, Paul, and Barnabas (Acts 12:12, 25; 13:13; 15:37–39; 1 Pet. 5:13; Philem. 24; Col. 4:10; 2 Tim. 4:11). The name Mark was common, so this conclusion

---

12. Vincent Taylor, *The Gospel according to St Mark,* 2d ed. (New York: Macmillan, 1966), 1–8.

13. Papias dates to about A.D. 140. Papias notes that his remark goes back to John the Elder, reaching back another generation.

14. The Anti-Marcionite Prologue contains the now famous reference to Mark as "stump fingered."

15. Hengel, *Gospel of Mark,* 74–81.

16. Taylor (*St Mark,* 26) writes, "There can be no doubt that the author of the Gospel was Mark, the attendant of Peter." He argues that the conclusion that this was John Mark "may be accepted as sound."

also is dependent to some degree on early church testimony and the association of Mark with both Peter and Paul. No good alternative options exist.[17] It is this Gospel's close connection to Peter that explains its acceptance and circulation in the church. It must have had apostolic links for the church to welcome it into the basic fourfold Gospel collection even though the church readily acknowledged that a nonapostle wrote it.

Determining Mark's date is slightly more difficult because the external testimony is not in agreement. Irenaeus places the composition after the death of Peter and Paul, a date that looks to the late 60s, while Clement of Alexandria looks to a date during Peter and Paul's time in Rome. This could push the date back into the 50s. Most commentators opt for a date in the A.D. 65–70 range, while others place Mark just after A.D. 70. Those opting for the late date argue, unpersuasively, that Mark 13 has a post–A.D. 70 perspective. However, if one accepts the testimony tied to Clement of Alexandria that Peter ratified Mark's work (Eusebius, *Eccl. Hist.* 2.15.2), then a date in the late 50s to mid-60s is possible.[18] The possibility of a date in the early 60s is good. As is the case with each Gospel, the discussion revolves around what part of the external testimony one accepts as well as one's view of the order of composition among the Gospels.

The same text from Clement gives the Gospel's setting as Rome. Later tradition claims a setting as far away as Egypt (John Chrysostom, *Homilies on Matthew* 1.3). However, the evidence of Latinisms in the book suggests that the traditional association is the best candidate for a locale. That the Christian community in Rome had to endure pressure from Rome and from Jews may well explain the Gospel's emphasis on suffering. One can look to Roman pressure on the Jews in A.D. 49 and to Nero's persecution of Christians in A.D. 64. The Gospel itself suggests the tension that existed between the disciples and the Jews, especially those holding positions of authority in Judaism.

Luke

The third Gospel is the longest of the four Gospels. It has a mix of teaching, miracle, and parable. Luke gives us more parables than any other Gospel. Fully half of the material in Luke is unique to his Gospel. Where Matthew presents teaching in discourse blocks, Luke scatters teaching throughout his Gospel, usually in smaller units. Many key discourses in Luke happen in meal scenes (7:36–50; 11:37–52; 14:1–24; 22:1–38; 24:36–49), which recall Greek symposia where wisdom is presented.

17. Craig Blomberg, *Jesus and the Gospels* (Nashville: Broadman & Holman, 1997), 124.
18. A date in the mid-to-late 60s argues that although Mark got his material from Peter, he took some time to compile and compose his Gospel.

A working outline of Luke shows his concern for geography in the progression of the Jesus account:

I. Introduction of John the Baptist and Jesus (1:1–2:52)
 A. Preface: Luke Builds on Precedent (1:1–4)
 B. Infancy Narrative: Forerunner and Fulfillment (1:5–2:40)
 C. Jesus' Revelation of His Self-Understanding (2:41–52)
II. Preparation for Ministry: Jesus Anointed as Messianic Son-Servant (3:1–4:13)
 A. John the Baptist: One Who Goes Before (3:1–20)
 B. Jesus: One Who Comes After (3:21–4:13)
III. Galilean Ministry: The Revelation and Teaching of Jesus (4:14–9:50)
 A. Overview of Jesus' Ministry (4:14–44)
 B. Gathering of Disciples (5:1–6:16)
 C. Jesus' Call to Love (6:17–49)
 D. Calls to Faith and Christological Questions (7:1–8:3)
 E. Faith and Christological Revelation (8:4–9:17)
 F. Christological Confession and Instruction on Discipleship (9:18–50)
IV. Jerusalem Journey: Jewish Rejection and the New Way of True Discipleship with God (9:51–19:44)
 A. Blessing of Decision: Privilege, Mission, and Commitment (9:51–10:24)
 B. Discipleship: On One's Neighbor, Jesus, and the Father (10:25–11:13)
 C. Controversies, Corrections, and Calls to Trust (11:14–54)
 D. Discipleship: Trusting God (12:1–48)
 E. Knowing the Nature of the Time: Israel Rejects, but Blessing Still Offered (12:49–14:24)
 F. Discipleship in the Face of Rejection (14:25–35)
 G. Pursuit of Sinners: Heavenly Examples (15:1–32)
 H. Generosity: Handling Money and Possessions (16:1–31)
 I. False Teaching, Forgiveness, and Service (17:1–10)
 J. Faithfulness in Looking to the King, the Kingdom, and the Kingdom's Consummation (17:11–18:8)
 K. Humbly Entrusting All to the Father (18:9–30)
 L. Turning to Jerusalem: Messianic Power and Warnings (18:31–19:44)
V. Jerusalem: The Innocent Slain and Raised in Preparation for Disciple Empowerment (19:45–24:53)
 A. Controversy in Jerusalem (19:45–21:4)
 B. Jerusalem's Destruction and the End (21:5–38)

    C. Betrayal and Farewell (22:1–38)
    D. Trials and Death of Jesus (22:39–23:56)
    E. Resurrection and Ascension of Jesus (24:1–53)

Luke's Gospel proceeds from Galilee to Jersualem. The first half of the Gospel is structured much like Mark. The distinctive section of this Gospel is the journey of divine destiny that Jesus takes as he draws near to Jerusalem in Luke 9–19. This key section juxtaposes two central themes: the rejection of Jesus by the leadership and the preparation of disciples for ministry without Jesus. As in Mark and Matthew, the disciples must learn that Jesus suffers as the Messiah, but in Luke the scope of discipleship in relationships and values is given much more development. In the final week, Jesus dies unjustly as an innocent, but it is all according to a divine plan (Luke 23). Luke also goes to great lengths to prepare his disciples for his departure, as the journey section of the Gospel shows. John's Gospel does a similar thing with the upper-room discourse (John 13–17).

Key themes center around that activity of *God's plan.* Things "must be" (δεῖ) in Luke (2:49; 4:43; 9:22; 24:7, 26, 44–47). God has designed a plan by which he will reach and deliver *the poor, oppressed, and those caught in Satan's oppressive grip* (4:16–19; 11:14–23). The plan reflects a *promise and fulfillment* structure, in which scriptural realization of the plan is expressed through the words of the key figures in the account (7:28; 16:16). The opening infancy section does this through the use of hymns decorated in scriptural language, underscoring the note of *joy* that works through the Gospel. Things also happen with an immediacy; many texts speak of what is happening "today" (σήμερον) (2:11; 4:21; 5:26; 19:9; 22:34; 23:43). The Gospel marches forward, as indicated by the *geographic progression* in the story.

Jesus appears as the *Messiah-Servant-Lord.* The basic category is his messianic one (1:31–35; 3:21–22; 4:16–30; 9:18–20), but as the story proceeds, it is clear that this role is one of great authority that can be summarized by the image of the *judging Son of Man* or by the concept of Lord (5:24; 20:41–44; 21:27; 22:69). All of these connections reflect what Scripture has said about the plan. Jesus also functions as a *prophet,* but as one promised like Moses, a ruler-prophet who is to be heard (4:20–30; 9:35). Jesus brings the *kingdom,* with the miracles evidencing its inaugurated presence and the *defeat of Satan,* which ultimately is what the kingdom brings with its deliverance (11:14–23; 17:20–21). Yet there also is a future to that kingdom, which will see Jesus return to reign over both Israel and the nations, visibly expressing the sovereignty he now claims (21:1–38). Thus, Jesus' deliverance looks to the realization of covenantal promises made to Abraham, David, and their nation (1:45–55).

The national leadership is steadfast in its rejection of the message. The plan proceeds nonetheless. *Israel* will experience judgment for being unfaithful

(19:41–44; 21:20–24). Jerusalem will be destroyed as a picture of what final judgment is like and as an assurance that God's program is taking place. Efforts to call Israel to faithfulness continue despite their refusal to embrace God's care and promised one.

In the meantime, Jesus forms a *new community*, which in the Book of Acts is called "the Way." This community is made up of those who *turn* to embrace Jesus' message and follow in *faith*. Luke likes to speak of this response in terms of *repentance*, looking back to the change of direction that faith brings (5:32). Surprisingly, it is *tax collectors and sinners* who are most responsive, while the *Jewish leadership* is steadfast in rejection (7:29–30; 18:9–14). *Women* also abound in Luke as examples of spiritual responsiveness (2:38–39; 7:36–50; 8:1–3). Jesus wants the community to take the initiative in reaching out to all of these fringe groups, including the *poor and oppressed* (4:16–19; 6:20–23).

Jesus' work brings intense rejection and will lead to *persecution* one day. This means that disciples must *persevere* in their walk in the face of great pressure (21:7–19). However, enemies should be loved, God should be trusted, *prayer* should abound, and *watchfulness* for God's remaining work should continue (6:27–36; 11:1–13; 12:22–31; 18:1–8). The two great obstacles to discipleship are the pressure that this persecution produces and excessive attachment to the world, especially through *possessions* (8:11–15; 18:8 raises the question of whether anyone will stay faithful until Jesus returns). Thus, Luke challenges the wealthy with regard to their stewardship of what God gives to them.

Luke seeks to reassure his readers that rejection by the world is not a sign of the Gospel's inauthenticity. Such rejection was at the heart of the plan all along. So readers can be assured of the truth concerning the things they have heard about Jesus (1:1–4). *Reassurance* is the key motive for this Gospel.

What Jesus gives through his work is *deliverance, forgiveness,* and ultimately *enablement.* For this evangelist, the "power from on high" of the *Spirit* is to be given now that Jesus is raised (3:15–16; 24:49). His *ascension* will allow disciples to accomplish all that God has for them. For Luke, this hope stands at the core of the Gospel, alongside the *eternal life* God gives.

Introductory Issues. Issues of authorship, date, and setting parallel the preceding discussions that have involved a mix of evidence from tradition and from the Gospel itself. As with the other Gospels, the author of the third Gospel does not name himself in the work. However, external evidence again is consistent in naming Luke as the author (Justin [*Trypho* 103.19] notes that this "memoir of Jesus" was written by a follower of the apostles).[19] Allusions to Luke's Gospel appear as early as *1–2 Clement* (ca. A.D. 95 and 100). The Muratorian Canon also attributes the Gospel to Luke, a doctor. Irenaeus (*Against Heresies* 3.1.1; 3.14.1) also ties the Gospel to Luke, a follower of Paul,

---

19. Darrell L. Bock, *Luke 1:1–9:50,* BECNT 3A (Grand Rapids: Baker, 1994), 5–6.

and notes the evidence of the "we" sections of Acts as pointing to one who knew Paul. Tertullian (*Against Marcion* 4.2.2; 4.5.3) calls Luke's Gospel a "digest of Paul's gospel." Eusebius (*Eccl. Hist.* 3.4.7) notes that Luke is a native of Antioch. What makes this evidence impressive is the large list of possible companions of Paul who might have filled in the blank of the "we" sections had the author not been known. The unanimity of the tradition on authorship is important.[20] If Luke is the figure included in Col. 4:10–14, which is likely, then he was a non-Jew and a doctor. Given the use and knowledge of the Old Testament present in this Gospel, it may well be that Luke was a God-fearer or former Jewish proselyte. It should be noted that in Acts, Luke is not a constant companion of Paul, but an occasional one. Thus, claims about his association with Paul should not be exaggerated.

The date of Luke is related in part to three issues: the relationship to Mark's date, the ending of Acts, and whether allusions to Jerusalem's destruction in A.D. 70 occur in Luke 21. Those who see the ending of Acts as key argue that the events narrated there take us to about A.D. 62. The Gospel would have to have been written before Acts, making a date in the late 50s or early 60s plausible.[21] Those who see allusions to Jerusalem's destruction in Luke 21 argue that a date sometime after that event is required. The allusions in *1–2 Clement* make the 90s the latest possible date. It is also argued that time would be needed for Paul to emerge as a hero and that the theology of some degree of church structure points to a consolidation that suggests the 80s.

Evidence for a late date in the 80s or 90s is thin, relying heavily on a claim that there is a direct allusion to Jerusalem's fall in A.D. 70 in a small set of texts. First, the allusions to Jerusalem in Luke 21 are not clear enough to establish an "after the event" claim. What such a "prophecy after the fact" view often reflects is a denial that Jesus could predict an event like this. Even if A.D. 70 is alluded to, however, it is not clear that a significantly later date is required. Second, Paul developed a reputation early on. It did not take so long for the church to recognize his important role. Third, the assumption that church organization and consolidation emerged only after the 60s is not what the evidence of Acts actually suggests.[22]

Those who prefer a date in the mid-60s to 70s rely in part on Luke's relationship to Mark. It seems likely that the author of Luke knew Mark's Gospel. What is impossible to know is how long Mark had to exist for Luke to make use of it.

20. Joseph A. Fitzmyer, *The Gospel according to Luke,* 2 vols., AB 28, 28A (Garden City, N.Y.: Doubleday, 1981–85), 1:40.

21. Such arguments assume that the writer of Luke also wrote Acts, which is a common view in light of how the end of Luke and the beginning of Acts connect thematically, as well as the recognition of a narrative thematic unity extending through the two volumes.

22. Those who contend otherwise argue that Acts reflects issues of its "later" time and does not give a real historical look at the earlier period it describes.

A date in the 60s seems likely. For Luke, the outcome of the trial of Paul was not as important as that the Gospel was shared openly there. In favor of a 60s date are factors that emerge mostly from Acts. There is next to nothing about the Roman community, which is against a later date. Nor is there an explicit reference to A.D. 70, even where it could have been inserted as a narrative note (as would have been possible in presenting Stephen's speech about the temple). The degree of uncertainty about Jewish-Gentile relations also fits better with an earlier period. The communities portrayed in Acts are largely racially mixed, a better match with the earlier period. More difficult is specifying when in the 60s Luke appeared. A good candidate, given Mark, is the mid-60s.

The setting of Luke is not known. Candidates abound, including the traditions for Antioch and for Achaia in Greece, as well as suggestions for Rome in light of the ending of Acts. However, the fact is that the Gentile concerns in the book could fit a host of settings. The absence of a clear indication in the external tradition means that we do not know the exact setting. Issues that dominate involve a mixed Jewish-Christian and Gentile-Christian community. Beyond that, we can say little.

John

The Fourth Gospel's account emphasizes Jesus as the one sent from God, who acts in unity with the Father. In fact, they work so closely together that Jesus is presented as God taking on flesh. From the declaration of the incarnation through a narration of seven signs and multiple interactive discourses, John highlights Jesus' uniqueness. This Gospel's explicit portrayal of Jesus gives it its literary power.

A working outline of John goes as follows:

    I. Prologue (1:1–18)
   II. The Book of Signs: Before the Hour (1:19–12:50)
      A. John the Baptist's Witness (1:19–34)
      B. The First Disciples (1:35–51)
      C. Sign 1: Water to Wine (2:1–12)
      D. The Cleansing of the Temple (2:13–25)
      E. What Do the Signs Show? Jesus and Nicodemus (3:1–21)
      F. John the Baptist: "He Must Increase" (3:22–36)
      G. True Worship: Jesus and the Samaritan Woman (4:1–42)
      H. Sign 2: Healing the Royal Officer's Son (4:43–54)
      I. Sign 3: Sabbath Healing Controversy (5:1–18)
      J. Sabbath Defense: The Son Does Nothing on His Own (5:19–47)

John's themes focus on *Christology*. Unlike the Synoptics, John speaks little of the kingdom. Rather, *eternal life* is the key theme used to express what the Synoptics call the kingdom promise. The emphasis in the term "eternal life" is not merely the duration of the life (eternal), but also its quality (i.e., *real, unending life*). Thus, to know the Father and Jesus Christ, whom the Father sent, is eternal life (17:3). This life is available now (5:24–26). In the opportunity is also the prospect of judgment for those who refuse it (3:16–21, 36).

It is the *Word/Logos* sent from God in the form of human flesh that brings this promise. The various ways in which Jesus represents the way of God are developed in the *"I Am" sayings.* He is the light of the world, the resurrection and the life, the good shepherd, the bread of life, and the vine. Each image specifies some central role that belongs to Jesus. As *Son,* Jesus does only what the *Father* shows him. It is Jesus' *unity with the Father* in mission that John highlights. Jesus is the hoped-for *Messiah.* This is expressed in the hope of others. And Jesus is the *Son of Man,* who ascends and descends between earth and heaven. In this role, he will judge (5:27), be lifted up (3:14), and serve in mediating salvation (3:13; 6:27). Even when Jesus is seen as a *prophet,* it is his role as a *leader-prophet* like Moses that this identification highlights (6:14; 7:40).

Obviously, the role of *signs* for John is crucial to his work. Seven signs dominate the first two-thirds of the Gospel. The response to them covers the range from rejection (12:37–40) to openness (9:25). Interestingly, unlike the Synoptics, there are *no exorcisms* in John. He focuses on acts of healing, restoration, and provision. What these signs highlight above all is *Jesus' superiority to Jewish institutions or its leadership* (1:17; 2:19–21; 7:37–39; 9:28–41; 10:1–18). Most of the miracles take place in settings of Jewish celebrations and underscore how Jesus provides what the feasts celebrate. At the end of the Gospel, blessing comes to those who have faith without the need for signs (20:29).

Jesus is seen as the *revelator* of God. It is he who makes the Father and his way known (1:14–18). This is part of Jesus' function as light. Jesus' death shows the love of the Father for his own people and is an example to disciples of how they should love (13:1, 11–17). Jesus' death also serves to gather God's people together (10:1–18) and is a means by which the Son and Father are glorified as life is made available though him (3:14–16). His ministry takes place in both Judea and Galilee.

Also of great importance to John is the *Spirit,* also called the *Paraclete.* This encourager-enabler will come after Jesus' death as one sent by the Son to lead the disciples into the truth, empower them for ministry and mission, and convict the world of sin, righteousness, and judgment (14:25–31; 16:8–11). Here is the one who sustains life (4:8–10; 7:37–39).

The new community that Jesus forms is to be characterized by *love and unity.* The love and unity have their model in Jesus' offering of himself and in the Son's relationship to the Father (13:31–35; 17:1–26). To function effectively, the community must stay rooted in its relationship to Jesus, who is the vine (15:1–6).

John declares that his *purpose* is to write a Gospel so that the reader might believe and in doing so have life in Jesus' name (20:30–31). John supports the point by continuously showing how central relationship to Jesus is both for establishing eternal life and for maintaining its quality in a hostile world. In this fundamental goal, John is like the other three Gospels.

Introductory Issues. When it comes to authorship, date, and setting, once again we encounter a discussion that rotates around internal versus external evidence. As with the other Gospels, the fourth evangelist does not name himself. We start with external evidence. The earliest indications of authorship come from the Anti-Marcionite Prologue to John and the Muratorian Canon in the second part of the second century. The Prologue indicates that the Gospel was for the churches in Asia. The Canon speaks of the input of other apostles, a detail that most scholars today reject as an elaboration on the tradition. Irenaeus, Tertullian, and Clement of Alexandria agree that John the apostle is the author. Irenaeus is important because he stood in a line that was only one generation away from John. He knew Polycarp and Pothinus, who had been with John. In his *Epistle to Florinus,* Irenaeus has John writing his Gospel after the other Gospels, while he lived in Ephesus (Eusebius, *Eccl. Hist.* 5.20.6). In *Against Heresies* 3.1.2, he states that the author was John, the one who leaned on Jesus' breast, and that the book was written in Ephesus.

Some critics challenge this external testimony, but without solid rationale.[23] Some efforts to sever the tie to John involve an examination of internal evidence. These claims often have to do with what John lacks: the parables, the transfiguration, the bread and cup of the Last Supper, and other such accounts. It appears, however, that John has chosen to write a Gospel that concentrates on material distinct from the tradition found in the other Gospels.[24] At the least, he knew what already had been in broad circulation for some time. John is consciously undertaking a fresh angle on things, so a lack of repetition is not surprising.

The well-known argument from internal evidence seeks to identify the author, working into increasingly narrow points of identification.[25] The author was (1) a Jew, (2) of Palestine, (3) an eyewitness of what he describes, (4) an apostle, and (5) John. The linking of the argument with the "beloved disciple" (13:23; 19:26; 20:2; 21:7, 20) is key and shows up in Irenaeus's remark about the one who leaned on Jesus' breast. The best candidate for this identification is John the son of Zebedee, especially given the frequent pairing of John and

23. Harrison, *Introduction to the New Testament,* 218–25, has a solid overview of the discussion, as does G. R. Beasley-Murray, *John,* WBC 36 (Waco: Word, 1987), lxvi–lxx, though he distinguishes John the evangelist from John the prophet who wrote Revelation.

24. There is a finely balanced debate over whether or not the writer of the Fourth Gospel had direct knowledge of the other Gospels. C. K. Barrett argues for such knowledge, while R. E. Brown often argues that John is working with independent but overlapping tradition. For a treatment of this debate, see D. Moody Smith, *John among the Gospels: The Relationship in Twentieth-Century Research* (Minneapolis: Fortress, 1992).

25. The argument goes back to B. F. Westcott in 1881 and reappears with more detail in his commentary on John.

Peter in the Synoptics and the beloved disciple and Peter in the Fourth Gospel. Despite other challenges, this still is the best option.[26]

The setting of this Gospel seems more solidly established than the settings for the other Gospels, given the strong association with an Asian context tied to Ephesus. In regard to date, the generally recognized view is that John comes after the other Gospels, following the external evidence. Some, however, make a case for John in the 60s or 70s, given the lack of reference to Jerusalem's destruction in A.D. 70 and the nonuse of the Synoptics.[27] The external evidence, however, seems to suggest a date in the 80s or 90s, near the end of the apostle's life. But the question of date remains somewhat open, with any period from about the mid-60s to the 90s being possible. Older efforts to date the Gospel to the second century were refuted when two fragments appeared that indicated that the Gospel circulated in Egypt in the early second century. The tie of the Gospel to Ephesus is strong. However, this does not preclude the use of traditions whose origins go back to Palestine, not to mention the Jewish roots of the author.[28]

Conclusion

This survey of the roots of the four Gospels shows two with apostolic origins (Matthew and John) and two with apostolic connections (Mark-Peter; Luke-Paul). They are four different works. While Matthew is concerned with Jewish response, Mark treats the issue of suffering and persecution. Luke provides reassurance by making clear how the message went from Jew to Gentile through divine direction—although the completion of this theme required a second volume, Acts. John goes his own way, highlighting the unique sending of the unique Son. All four present Jesus as a messianic claimant who challenged the Jewish leadership while offering deliverance to any who would embrace him and his message as the unique, anointed one sent from God. This is why he is called Jesus Christ. So we turn now to a detailed look at the Synoptics and John to see how these themes emerged.

---

26. Gary Burge, *Interpreting the Gospel of John* (Grand Rapids: Baker, 1992), 37–54.

27. Leon Morris, *The Gospel according to John,* rev. ed., NICNT (Grand Rapids: Eerdmans, 1995), 25–30, leans toward an early date but argues that it is not proved.

28. See Beasley-Murray, *John,* lxxv–lxxxi, for the plausible option of the account having connections with Palestine, Antioch, and Ephesus.

Part 2

Jesus according
to the Synoptists

Jesus of Nazareth, a man attested to you by God with deeds of power, wonders, and signs that God did through him in your midst, as you yourselves know—this man, delivered up by the predetermined plan and foreknowledge of God, you crucified and killed by the hands of those without the law. But God raised him up, having loosed the pangs of death, because it was impossible for him to be held by it.[1]

This apostolic summary of Jesus' life presents all the key elements about Jesus. He was a man attested by God as the consummate representative of what God is all about. That attestation came through a ministry rich with demonstrations that God stood behind him and his teaching. That teaching brought Jesus to his death under the Romans at the instigation of some in Israel. But death was a weak opponent, because God stood behind him. Exaltation followed in a resurrection. What followed the empty tomb revealed the importance and authority of this one who is unique in history.

The story of this ministry is told not once, but four times in Scripture. Three of those stories—Matthew, Mark, and Luke—share the same basic narrative line, portraying Jesus from his start on earth, even though each one begins with a different emphasis. They are rightly described as "synoptics," accounts that look at things together. The fourth story, John, stands alone at the start by highlighting that Jesus, the Word become flesh, was sent from above. So we examine the story first from the earth up, before turning our attention to how John supplements that account. I will cite the numbering of some standard synopses of the Gospels. A synopsis is helpful when we want to compare the flow and wording of events as set forth in the Synoptics. It traces the wording of the Gospels in parallel columns and sets out charts showing the

---

1. Acts 2:22–24, the apostle Peter in his speech at Pentecost.

order of various events in the Gospels. I will cite the numbering of the synopses of Aland, Orchard, and Huck-Greeven, as well as introduce my own numerical system.[2]

We seek to read the story with its basic narrative lines intact. Though I combine the Synoptics here within the sequence, each time an account appears, it is placed in its context within that Gospel, even if it is a repeat of a parallel in another Gospel. This way, its contribution can be noted both internally to that Gospel and in terms of what it shares with its parallels. This combination of reading vertically through a Gospel while paying attention to reading horizontally across the Gospels helps us gain fresh insight into the canonical portrayal of Jesus' life and ministry. Thus, this approach is not strictly like a harmony, which seeks to reconstruct a chronological flow to Jesus' ministry. Nor is it like a typical "life of Christ," which often builds off of a harmony. Rather, we seek to stay within the various narrative lines that each Gospel sets for us without claiming that we necessarily are proceeding chronologically.

We will consider the story of Jesus' infancy, then shift our focus briefly to John the Baptist. Next follows a description of the ministry in Galilee up to the confession of Peter. After the confession, Jesus turns his attention to preparing the disciples for his death, before starting his slow journey of destiny to Jerusalem. In the last week of Jesus' life, the conflict over the issue of his authority that slowly raged and grew leads to his death and the great act of divine vindication that we call the resurrection. Here God showed his commitment to Jesus—and his commitment to us. The life and ministry of Jesus was too extraordinary to be contained in one account. His significance was too great to be overcome by death. The rationale for his victory is displayed in these Gospel accounts. From the earth up summarizes the direction of Jesus' ministry in the Synoptics' narrative movement. The story starts in categories that the readers can identify with and then pushes the envelope of their un-

2. Kurt Aland's two synopses—one presenting only the Greek text of the Gospels and the other giving Greek and English on facing pages—are the ones most commonly used today. The numbering system is the same in both. The Greek-only version is *Synopsis Quattuor Evangeliorum,* 13th ed. (Stuttgart: Deutsche Bibelgesellschaft, 1985). It uses the Nestle-Aland 26th edition of the Greek text, and it includes citations from the early church fathers on the passages, making it valuable to those who can work with Greek. The diglot Greek-English version is *Synopsis of the Four Gospels,* 2d ed. (Stuttgart: United Bible Societies, 1975). It uses the Nestle-Aland 26th edition of the Greek text and the RSV for the English. The synopsis compiled by John Bernard Orchard also comes in two forms: *A Synopsis of the Four Gospels, in a New Translation: Arranged according to the Two-Gospel Hypothesis and Edited by John Bernard Orchard* (Macon, Ga.: Mercer University Press, 1982); and *A Synopsis of the Four Gospels in Greek: Arranged according to the Two-Gospel Hypothesis and Edited by John Bernard Orchard* (Edinburgh: Clark, 1983). The synopsis compiled by Albert Huck has undergone subsequent revision by Heinrich Greeven. It is essentially Greek-only, with explanatory comments in German and English: *Synopse der Drei Ersten Evangelien, mit Beigabe der Johanneischen Parallelstellen* (Synopsis of the First Three Gospels, with the Addition of the Johannine Parallels), 13th ed. (Tübingen: Mohr, 1981).

derstanding to have them realize that Jesus is more than an extraordinary man. Jesus goes to God's side on behalf of those who respond to and trust in him.

The general outline of the story in the Synoptics is fairly consistent. Matthew and Luke both note Jesus' unique birth, but from differing perspectives. Matthew, concentrating on conflict and Joseph's perspective, notes the fulfillment of Scripture by citing specific texts in his narrative notes. Luke, concentrating on celebration and Mary's perspective, points to fulfillment through the language of the characters. Each leaves no doubt that Jesus' origins rest in God's creative initiative and plan.

Mark joins the story at this point with John the Baptist preparing the way, also featuring the fulfillment of Scripture at the start of his account. John the Baptist points the way to the invasion of God's promise for his people Israel. Jesus, equipped with a confirmatory baptism and victory over demonic temptation, turns to minister to Israel. His ministry focuses on Galilee, to the north. That ministry involves teaching, healing, exorcism, disciple gathering, and mission. Jesus draws attention from some Gentiles, but his ministry concentrates on Israel and the realization of its promised redemption. To understand Jesus, one must appreciate his Jewish roots and goals. Jesus' assertion of uniquely personal authority leads him into controversy. The conflict emerges from several elements: his interpretation of the law, his Sabbath activity, his nonuse of Jewish cleansing tradition, his association with sinners, and ultimately his challenge of Jewish and temple authority in the forming of a new community. Meanwhile, the poor, the fringe, and sinners are attracted to him and his mission. His outreach involves rather ordinary, everyday people. His acceptance of them and initiation of outreach to them also is controversial. The disciples who follow him struggle to make sense of his ministry, even after they have identified his mission as messianic. Much of the early part of the story drives toward this confession, though once it is given, there is still much more for disciples to learn about Jesus and following him. It is the suffering and sacrificial aspects of his destiny that the disciples struggle to appreciate. Also, the exact identity of Jesus consistently eludes them until his resurrection. In the meantime, as Jesus draws near to Jerusalem to complete his calling, he is preparing these disciples for the days when he will no longer be physically present with them. All the while, Jesus continues to challenge the leadership, giving rise to their increasingly strident opposition. Those already in a position of power reject his claim that he brings the kingdom. They seek to bring him to an end. Jesus warns that such opposition will bring his death. Disciples will face the same persecution.

In the midst of this conflict, Jesus enters Jerusalem and cleanses the temple, a final assault on the leadership's claims to have authority over Israel. The leadership reacts. Judas's betrayal brings the opportunity to arrest Jesus. Meanwhile, Jesus has warned that the nation of Israel stands judged before God for its covenantal unfaithfulness. That judgment, which will destroy the second temple and lead to the nation being overrun, is but a picture of the ultimate authority that Jesus possesses as the Son of Man to render final judgment. In the various investigations of Jesus during his final night, his prosecutors consider both religious and political charges. The leadership finally brings the messianic claimant before Pilate with a combination of charges rooted in blasphemy, portrayed as deception of Israel, and the claim to be an alternative king. Jesus claims before his Jewish interrogators that he is their judge. He predicts that God will vindicate him and that one day he will render judgment from God's right hand. The issue of the nature and source of Jesus' authority is central to their conflict. This charge of blasphemy is translated into a political charge about kingship when Jesus comes before Pilate. The Roman ruler finds Jesus innocent of any crime worthy of death but succumbs to the pressure of the leaders and crowds. Jesus dies as an innocent on behalf of people, with creation and the temple indicating that something is amiss in his death, even as the fulfillment of promise takes place. However, God takes this gross injustice and triumphs over it. With an empty tomb and resurrection, Jesus calls his followers to complete his mission; he is raised to continue the exercise of the authority that his ministry revealed him to possess. In doing so, he reminds the disciples that he has power over life and death. He also makes clear that in them his ministry continues. That is the outline of the Synoptic story. The details follow. No detailed outline of these chapters appears as we simply proceed through the narrative.

Strictly speaking, this study is not one conducted in the context of historical Jesus studies. There is no effort in this work to enter into the critical debates about which portions of these Gospels do or do not go back directly to Jesus. My contention is that the final form of the text is important to study and appreciate in and of itself, for this is the story that the church has worked with throughout its history. It is often the case that this story is not as well known as it should be. Recent criticism, picking the story apart, has only made matters worse in this regard. At points, I will note how the details sit well in Jesus' cultural context or that a detail makes good historical sense. However, it should be clear to the reader that *Jesus according to Scripture* is not intended as a technical study of the historical Jesus but a presentation of the canonical Jesus—that is, Jesus as the historic canon of Scripture has presented him. My basic contention is that the coherence of this portrait emerges and commends itself as one that gives unique insight into who Jesus is and was.

The Structure of the Synoptic Survey

This Synoptic survey has two goals: (1) to present a summary of the events recorded in the Gospels, noting key features of background or significance;

(2) to keep a sense of how each Gospel account develops those events. Thus, this is not a survey in the usual sense of simply trying to construct a detailed chronological sequence of Jesus' life and ministry. As will become evident, the nature of the material will allow this only in the case of some event sequences, not all of them. Thus, the placement of events is dictated by where they fall within the Gospel accounts, not through an attempt on my part always to argue for a strict chronological order. The placement, however, often does indicate where events fell in the general outline of Jesus' ministry, even if we cannot always know the specific sequence. In addition, I have chosen not to go through each Gospel sequentially, but rather to juxtapose them by keeping an eye on their narrative order and interrelationship, much as a synopsis does.

This juxtaposition of events between Gospels sometimes requires some redundancy in presentation to keep an event's location within a particular Gospel clear. In some cases this is an indication that some of Jesus' teaching was repeated on different occasions. In other cases it means a distinct kind of topical grouping by a Gospel writer. My goal is to present each event in relation to where it is placed within a given Gospel. Such an approach means that in a few cases the same event will be discussed more than once because two or more Gospels have placed it in a different location. The juxtaposition also means that the story line of any given Gospel will not always remain clear as we proceed. This is why a separate section earlier in the book treats each Gospel individually for its structure and emphases.

This juxtaposition also breaks up the natural narrative sequence within a Gospel at certain points because material from another Gospel seemingly fits into the gap. In one sense this move is artificial because it brings accounts together into a proposed sequence that does not exist within the documents themselves. On the other hand, to the extent these documents do complement one another, such a procedure is justified in showing Jesus' ministry and the connections that exist between the events that the Gospels cover. Judgments about sequence are determined by the literary flow and notes about setting that the Gospels provide. However, in some cases the text does not give enough information for us to be certain of sequence. In these cases I am only suggesting a general locale for the event. It is important to remember that Jesus taught far more than the Gospels record, and that what we have is only a representative portion of that whole. In some cases they record events, especially teaching, that would have been typical of Jesus' teaching throughout his ministry. Thus, chronology often is not important to the Gospel writers. They tend to focus on the general character of Jesus' ministry and teaching—especially as it relates to his fundamental emphases about the coming of the divine promise and the call to a faithful walk with God—and how opposition arose against him.

My goal is not to "merge" the Gospels into one story, although that is a by-product of this approach. Rather, I seek to help readers to appreciate the Gospels' relationship to one another, both in terms of uniqueness and overlapping concerns. Many current discussions highlight the differences and difficulties between the Gospel accounts so that one gets the misimpression that the accounts are not very united. This is the way that some liberal critics read the texts. They "divide and conquer," leaving the false impression that different, even contradictory, stories are being told among the Gospels. On the other hand, conservatives tend to merge the accounts so entirely that the themes of the individual books are swallowed up in setting forth the combined story. In my presentation of a narrative for the Synoptic story, I hope to trace both the fundamental, unified story of Jesus and to keep an eye on the unique aspects of each Gospel. A flowing sequence like this one can reveal how much agreement there is within this tradition, where the distinct emphases are, as well as how much of the material does connect in describing the broad character and development of Jesus' life and ministry. This survey aims to show both the unity and diversity that reside within the Synoptic Gospels.

Finally, I note once again that this work is not an effort aimed at historical Jesus studies, although at points it does respond to issues raised in such study. My goal is to suggest that the coherence and complexity of the scriptural portrayal of Jesus do address how historical Jesus study sometimes overplays the differences between accounts. Sometimes, themes absent in some texts show up in other contexts as the evangelists pursue their accounts through their own choices and points of emphasis. One of the problems in the pursuit of historical Jesus questions is that a knowledge of the scriptural story is either lost or greatly devalued, even though it is the Gospel portraits of Jesus that have been the real source of historical impact. It is this story that I seek to trace with some sense of how the Synoptics and John work individually and together to present Jesus.

The numbering of units is my own, but I also track the numbering of standard synopses now in use. I diverge from their order wherever I think it appropriate to do so. Keeping an eye on the differences between myself, Aland, Orchard, and Huck-Greeven will give clues as to where discussions about order become significant, even though I do not enter into that debate in any detail. In cases where section numbers are accompanied with a letter, I have divided what the synopsis has as a larger unit. I also note key ancient texts that discuss these events or that raise points of background. This way, we can keep an ear to how these Gospel texts may have been heard in the ancient world. Those interested in the details of these texts can follow up the references or examine many of these texts in a sequel volume, *The Jesus Reader*.

TWO

The Birth and Childhood of Jesus

The Hope of Promise (Matt. 1–2; Luke 1–2)

Matthew's accounts of Jesus' childhood set the stage for Jesus' ministry depicted in the rest of the gospel, "defining his origin and goal." Matthew builds almost every paragraph following the genealogy and preceding the Sermon on the Mount around at least one text of Scripture. He thus invites us to read Jesus in light of Scripture and Scripture in light of Jesus—to recognize that the person and work of Jesus are central to Scripture's character. Some have suggested that Matthew made up the infancy stories to fit Scripture texts about Jesus, but the evidence suggests that he chose the Scripture texts to fit the stories. Matthew hardly cites the most obvious messianic texts here; he probably depends on earlier traditions for these stories.[1]

The story of Jesus' birth and childhood is a celebration of God's love for Israel, and, indeed, for all humanity. This love is manifest most brilliantly in the repeated declaration of the eschatological fulfillment of God's promise of redemption. One of the primary features of this section is its elegant intertwining of the stories of John and Jesus, presenting the two in parallel fashion.[2]

These quotations stress how the beginnings of Matthew and Luke introduce us to celebratory themes associated with Jesus' birth and childhood. It is significant that only two of the four Gospels treat this topic at all. Mark begins his Gospel with John the Baptist's ministry, while John begins with a grand prologue reaching back to the beginning of time and the creation, before the

1. Craig Keener, *Matthew*, IVPNTCS 1 (Downers Grove, Ill.: InterVarsity, 1997), 55.
2. Joel Green, *The Gospel of Luke*, NICNT (Grand Rapids: Eerdmans, 1997), 47.

Word came to earth. Therefore, it is possible to tell the story of Jesus' life and ministry without discussing his birth or childhood, but the descriptions of Jesus' birth that come to us from Matthew and Luke enrich our understanding of Jesus and why he came.

Although Matthew and Luke both present Jesus' birth, they do so from different angles. Matthew tells the story from the perspective of Joseph, with a strong emphasis on the fulfillment of Scripture. Luke gives the account from a perspective that highlights Mary. The Lukan characters sing to us through the language of Scripture of God's love for humanity. In both accounts, many from every walk and station of life are enthralled by what is taking place. Thus, we see the complementary relationship of Matthew and Luke as they present their story of Jesus' birth in their own unique ways.

Traditionally, we have used these accounts at Christmas to present how Jesus "came" to earth. In some ways this reading gets ahead of the story. It reads the beginning of the story in light of what we will learn about Jesus by the end of the story. Yet Matthew and Luke do not disclose everything about Jesus at the beginning of their stories (John does take more of that approach). What Matthew and Luke give instead is an announcement, an arrival that is intimately connected to God's design to deliver humanity and work out the promises he made in Scripture. When the birth story is read as a developing one or as events experienced at the time, the reader and those closest to the events had no idea how much was involved in Jesus' birth. These tasted of events whose full richness they would come to appreciate only after more of the story had passed. So the infancy material sets the stage for what will follow, planting the seeds of themes that will grow to fruition as the accounts proceed. This is why Scripture is so prominent in both accounts. Scripture explains what apparently was initially surprising and lacking in explanation. Therefore, it is important to keep in mind that these opening accounts both introduce the story rather than conclude it, and anchor it firmly within the plan and purpose of God throughout history.

As we study the accounts of Jesus' birth, the tendency is to become ensnared in questions about the supernatural elements and miss the emphasis of the message in the process. The modern world has no place for virgin births, angelic announcements, prophetic fulfillments, and guiding stars. But reading the Gospels is tricky business. Some who read these accounts see only what they want to see or what they already have decided is possible, excluding the rest. They see only the natural things that they believe are common to all births and ignore the supernatural. This modernistic reading reduces the Jesus presented here largely to a metaphor whose experience is much like our own. Tragically, an active God doing unusual things to point out the unusual nature of this birth is ruled out before one even engages the text. But this is not the reading that the evangelists provide. They emphasize the unusual nature of the birth because of the unusual nature of the one being born. In fact, Matthew and Luke, as well as Mark, take the rest of their Gospels to show how unusual he really is.

For those of us who do believe that the miraculous events of the account did occur, there still exists the danger that our efforts to defend the historicity of the accounts will distract us from a real reading of the text. We may miss the account's emerging messages with the emphases that the evangelists gave to it. Our apologetic to defend the more miraculous aspects of these texts can deflect us from reading and hearing the account's actual story. It is like watching a movie and debating whether the events in the movie are possible rather than focusing on the actual story the director tells. While it is true that Jesus came with an array of divine signs to indicate who he was, signs that included his unique birth, the focus of these accounts is never simply upon who Jesus is or how he was born. In the infancy material, who Jesus is and how he was born are never separated from declaring what he will do on behalf of humanity. It is his anticipated action on behalf of those in need that is celebrated in the two infancy accounts. This is why a mood of awe and worship accompanies the description of these unique events.

1. The Prologue to Luke (Luke 1:1–4) (Aland §1; Orchard §1; Huck-Greeven §5)

Only one Gospel writer tells us why he is writing before giving us his Gospel. While John saves his explanation for the end of his Gospel (John 20:30–31), Mark simply gives his Gospel a short introduction identifying his opening as the "beginning of the gospel of Jesus Christ, the Son of God." Matthew launches into his account with Jesus' genealogy.

Luke's opening with a prologue is a very formal, literary way to begin his Gospel.[3] It is a common ancient literary form. Works, both Jewish and Greco-Roman, often begin with prefaces to prepare readers for what follows. One can read 2 Macc. 2:19–32, Josephus's *Ant.* preface 1–4 §§1–26, and *Letter of Aristeas* 1–8 to see how ancient prologues worked and how they varied in length.[4]

Luke notes that he is not the first to write, but that others, who remain unnamed, went before him (Luke 1:1). What these predecessors wrote were "narrative reports about the things that have been fulfilled among us." But

3. Loveday Alexander, "Luke's Preface in the Context of Greek Preface Writing," *Novum Testamentum* (1986): 48–74.

4. Although not technically a prologue, Lucian of Samosata's explanation of history writing in *How to Write History* 53–55 shows how the ancients viewed this task. It can be compared to Thucydides' remarks in *History of the Peloponnesian War* 1.21–22 to show how ancient historians were concerned about the accuracy of what they communicated.

there was a stage of reporting that came before the recording of these events. That stage involved the oral "delivery" of the presentation of these events by "eyewitnesses and ministers of the word." Here is the tradition base, grounded in eyewitness reports made to the church. They stood at the base of the accounts that Luke notes in v. 1 and at the base of his own work as well. Luke seeks to join this tradition of reporting about Jesus. He does so as an innovator, because only he will produce a sequel that connects this story to that of the early church (Acts 1:1–2). To that extent, Luke felt that the previous accounts needed supplementing. So in the Book of Acts he will show the inherent connection between the ministry of Jesus and that of the early church.

In Luke 1:3, the evangelist highlights that he was careful about his work. He sought to follow these things closely. There is some question whether Luke next discusses the length of his research (so RSV, "followed all things closely for some time past") or the starting point of his Gospel (so NIV, "investigated everything from the beginning"). Either view is grammatically and conceptually possible. The nature of the narrative, starting as it does with John the Baptist, and the idea of tracing back contextually may favor the option of going back to the beginning, but the choice here is not certain.

What Luke seeks to write is an orderly account. This need not mean ordering the account chronologically. Luke can speak of order in various ways. For example, in the Jerusalem journey section, Jesus is in the north at its start in Luke 9:51–52 as he sets his face to go to Jerusalem. Then in Luke 10:38–42, he eats at Martha and Mary's home, which John appears to place in Bethany in the south (John 12:1–2). Then in Luke 17:11, Jesus is traveling along the Samarian-Galilean border, back in the north again. It seems clear that Luke does not mean here a straight-line, geographic journey to Jerusalem but intends a journey of divine destiny for Jesus to meet his appointed death. Another example is Jesus' Nazareth synagogue sermon in Luke 4:16–30, which refers to past ministry at Capernaum in 4:23, even though Jesus has not yet been to Capernaum in that Gospel. Rather, he goes there in the following passage in 4:31–44. Thus, this synagogue event seems to be placed where it is for purposes of summarizing what this period of ministry was like by way of a representative scene. These examples suggest that the orderliness may have more to do with general development of the ministry than strict chronology. Luke will tell the account in an orderly way so that the development of God's plan for salvation is clearly evident.

Luke's account is to reassure Theophilus of the things that he has been taught. That Theophilus is addressed with the respectful "most excellent" shows that he likely is a man of some social standing, possibly a major official. That Theophilus has been taught previously indicates that he is not one seeking to become a Christian, but one who needs encouragement for his Christian walk. The numerous themes in the Gospel about discipleship and holding on to one's faith to the end also suggest this conclusion. Thus, Luke's prologue explains that his Gospel is written to reassure someone for whom the pressure surrounding the faith is becoming great. Luke's hope appears to be that a reading of the Gospel will strengthen the faith of the recipient of his account by showing how Jesus did fulfill the promise of God.

2. Matthew's Genealogy of Jesus (Matt. 1:1–17) (Aland §6; Orchard §4; Huck-Greeven §1)

We could proceed with the account of Luke here because he turns in Luke 1:5–25 to the announcement of John the Baptist's birth, an event that precedes Jesus' birth. However, we turn first to Matthew's beginning because of the narrative point it makes. Matthew starts with Jesus' genealogy before treating his birth. Here we begin to point out how Matthew and Luke, even though they both begin with Jesus' infancy, do so in distinct ways. Matthew stays focused on the story of Jesus' origins, while Luke steps back and places Jesus in the context of the forerunning ministry and preparatory role of John. Luke argues that John's role started even before he ministered publicly. Interestingly, Mark will begin where Luke does, with John, but he will do it in a distinct way, picking up the story years later at the point of preparation for Jesus' actual ministry.[5] Even the way the Gospels open show their complementary character.

Matthew 1–2 is structured around notes of fulfillment, both through Scripture and through the genealogical list. His first chapter explains who Jesus is (descendant of David and Abraham, Emmanuel [that is, God with us]; and ruler and shepherd in chapter 2), while chapter 2 explains how Jesus' geographical connections (Bethlehem in Judea, Egypt, Ramah, Nazareth) also point to fulfillment of Old Testament promises.

Matthew's genealogy is important culturally. Genealogies are significant because they communicate a person's social standing and status. A person's family line, if it is prominent, conveys his or her importance. Thus, the fact that the Matthean line travels through figures such as Solomon, David, Judah, Jacob, Isaac, and Abraham connects Jesus to the greats of the nation. Matthew's genealogy differs in direction and scope from Luke's. Matthew starts from the ancestors and works to the present, while Luke works from the present to the past. Matthew starts with Abraham, highlighting the line as it relates to Israel; Luke goes back to Adam, stressing the universality of Jesus and connecting Adam's creation to God's generation of humanity. This em-

---

5. When John the evangelist turns in his account to pick up Jesus' life, he will start similarly to Mark, with John the Baptist's ministry. However, his prologue introduces Jesus in the most explicit style as the Word become flesh.

phasis on the shared origin of humanity lays the foundation for Luke's concern for all nations, indicating the basic unity of humanity as God's children.

Matthew's genealogy has a clear structure. As with most genealogies, it is laid out with a patriarchal focus. The term "begat" or "was the father of" need not refer to the most recent ancestor, but can skip generations. Abraham's genealogy is laid out with rhetorical balance because there is a structure of fourteen generations: Abraham to David, David to the deportation, and the deportation to Christ (v. 17). The last listing gives thirteen names, while the first two lists are compressed to fourteen each.[6] The significance of this number is debated. It might be an example of *gematria,* where a number based on Hebrew letters points to a name, because the Hebrew for "David," דוד (4 + 6 + 4 = 14), adds up to fourteen. Those who object to this point argue that it is too subtle for any Greek readers, but it is possible, given the Jewish concerns of the book. Other suggestions are that the balance is rhetorical and suggests that Jesus came at the proper time, or that the list is balanced for reasons of memorization, or that the balance is more general. A final option is that the Davidic house rose to power at the first division, fell at the end of the second division, and now reappears at the third.[7] Some type of connection to David is likely, and a combination of the first and last explanations is very possible.

Matthew's genealogy has a couple of important twists that make significant theological points about God. First, although the lists are patriarchal, at four key points they diverge to mention women: Tamar, Rahab, Ruth, and the wife of Uriah (= Bathsheba). These women either were involved in questionable sexual relationships (Tamar with Judah [Gen. 38]; Rahab by vocation [Josh. 2]; Bathsheba with David [2 Sam. 11]) or represent the surprising presence of Gentile women (Rahab; Ruth [Ruth 3]). They all have a connection to rumors about illegitimacy.[8] The conscious pointing out of these dimensions show that God's work includes people of all sorts of backgrounds and races. Thus, even though the genealogy is national and Davidic, the suggestion that the story has a broader scope is present in these surprising inclusions—not just of some women, but of women with this diverse background.

6. For example, the list appears to skip Joash, Amaziah, and Azariah (= Uzziah). Matthew may be following in part lists that appear in the Greek Old Testament. Jews claimed to tenaciously keep their ancestry records, as books such as Genesis and 1 Chronicles show. See the remarks by Josephus in *Life* 1 §§1–6 about the availability of records for his own family line. Note also the report by Eusebius from Julius Africanus in *Eccl. Hist.* 1.7, where he attempts to explain the differences between Matthew and Luke, as well as how some families kept private family records.

7. Keener, *Matthew,* 52; W. C. Allen, *A Critical and Exegetical Commentary on the Gospel according to St. Matthew,* 3d ed., International Critical Commentary (Edinburgh: Clark, 1912), 2, 6.

8. C. L. Blomberg, "The Liberation of Illegitimacy," *Biblical Theological Bulletin* 21 (1991): 145–50.

Second, Matthew presents Joseph's genealogy as the legal right that Jesus has to the Davidic throne. In part, that right comes through his presence in Joseph's house. Nevertheless, Matthew also is clear that Jesus' biological connection to the family comes only through Mary. In v. 16, Matthew says, "Mary, *from whom* [ἧς, a feminine relative pronoun in Greek] Jesus was born who is called the Christ." This note is the first hint that Matthew affirms the unusual, divinely wrought character of Jesus' birth.[9] Matthew's listing, with its many surprises, shows that the story possesses an important and unusual character.

3. The Announcement of John the Baptist's Birth
(Luke 1:5–25) (Aland §2; Orchard §9; Huck-Greeven §6)

For Luke, the announcement of John the Baptist's birth begins a parallelism in presentation that runs through Luke 2:52. Here there are alternating scenes between John and Jesus on seven topics, with Jesus always being described in a way that shows his superiority to John. Those topics are introduction of parents (1:5–7/1:26–27), annunciation (1:8–23/1:28–38), the mother's response (1:24–25/1:39–56), the birth (1:57–58/2:1–20), circumcision/dedication = faithfulness (1:59–66/2:21–24), prophetic response (1:67–79/2:25–39), and growth of the child (1:80/2:40–52, with two such notes in vv. 40, 52). Luke's goal involves treating the relationship of John to Jesus as one contrasting the preparer of the way to the way itself.

The start of the account begins in the most sacred site of the nation, the temple. Zechariah is serving in the days of King Herod. John's parents are marked out as righteous but barren. Zechariah and Elizabeth have lived piously and faithfully (cf. Deut. 6:25; 24:13; Isa. 33:15), but now on in years, they have no progeny. In the later Jewish midrash, *Genesis Rabbah* 38.14 (23c) on Gen. 11:29–30, Rabbi Levi remarked that when Scripture says "she had not," God gave her a child.[10] The resultant child always is a person of signifi-

---

9. A naturalist suggestion about Jesus' birth comes from Jane Schaberg, *The Illegitimacy of Jesus* (San Francisco: Harper & Row, 1987). Schaberg argues, based on Deut. 22:22–25, that Jesus' birth has roots in a sexual violation of Mary by someone other than Joseph. Thus, the birth in the original traditions was explained as a triumph of God's grace. This explanation is a naturalist one, must import the rape backdrop, and must deny the textual claims that Mary was sexually inexperienced at the point of the Lukan birth announcement. The debate over Jesus' unusual birth is old, as Origen (*Against Celsus* 1.28, 32, 33, 39) discusses claims that Jesus' birth came from suspect roots. It is hard to explain why Christians would invent such an event, as culturally a supernatural birth was not required to get a "divine" imprimatur on a ruler, especially a Jewish one.

10. H. Freedman and M. Simon, eds., *Midrash Rabbah*, 3d ed., 10 vols. (London and New York: Soncino, 1983), 1:312.

cance. So it was with Isaac, Samson, and Samuel (Gen. 18:11; Judg. 13:2, 5; 1 Sam. 1–2). The parallel is not accidental. It points out that God is acting again in ways that recall the days of old.

The nation was required to offer corporate sacrifice and prayer twice a day, once at about nine in the morning, and then again at three in the afternoon. An order of about seven hundred priests would serve two weeks out of the year, but only once in any priest's career would he be allowed to have a role in presenting the national sacrifice. Estimates place the number of priests during this time at several thousand.[11] This was to give the opportunity to as many priests as possible to have this honor. Details of how such sacrifices were offered, as described by analogy with the high priestly offerings, are found in *m. Tamid* 5–7. So at this most sacred moment in Zechariah's career, God moves to deal with both the nation's hope and this family's disappointment.

The literary form of what follows constitutes a birth announcement common in the Old Testament, including the aforementioned figures who come forth from barrenness. Gabriel appears to Zechariah and tells him that his prayer has been answered. In a beautiful ambiguity—because the reference to prayer is singular—the national prayer, which would have included a request for national deliverance, and the long-abandoned desire for a child are fused into one. The child will be given the name John. His birth will lead many to rejoice. This is because he will be great before God, live piously, and be filled with the Spirit from his conception. As a classic prophet, his role will be to bring spiritual reconciliation to the nation, turning many of the people of Israel to the Lord their God. He will operate in the power and spirit of Elijah, a reference to John's preaching and to his role within the eschaton; the hope was that Elijah would be part of the events of restoration at the end, a hope intimated in Mal. 3:1 and stated explicitly in Mal. 4:5–6. This reconciliation to God also will involve other relationships, as parents and children are brought together and the disobedient are turned into the just. This language recalls hopes expressed in the intertestamental period. Sirach 48:10 says of Elijah, "At the appointed time, it is written, you are destined to calm the wrath of God before it breaks out in fury, to turn the heart of the father to the son, and to restore the tribes of Jacob." Thus, Luke's account evokes major hopes. John will "make ready for the Lord a people prepared." This language about a prepared people comes from Isa. 43:7. It refers to Israel as an elect people, set apart for God. John's job is to get Israel ready for what God (the Lord, in this context) is about to do. So besides explaining how John relates to Jesus, this account shows that God is back at work on behalf of his people.

11. See *Letter of Aristeas* 95. See also Joachim Jeremias, *Jerusalem in the Time of Jesus: An Investigation into Economic and Social Conditions during the New Testament Period,* trans. F. H. Cave and C. H. Cave (Philadelphia: Fortress, 1969), 200. Jeremias places the estimate at eighteen thousand (twenty-four orders times seven hundred and fifty).

Besides the announcement, there is a lesson to be learned about how God works. When Zechariah raises the question about how all of this can happen, given his age, the priest indicates that he understands normal biology! He and his wife, advanced in years, are past the age of childbearing. Gabriel notes, in effect, that a confirmatory sign will be given to underscore what has been announced as well as to show God's hand in these events. Zechariah will be silent, which means deaf and mute (see Luke 1:62–63), until these things come to pass. The sign is one of temporary judgment for not believing what God had announced. These events will be fulfilled in their time. So Luke underscores a second theme in this unit: God will do what he promises, even when appearances suggest otherwise.

The initial fulfillment and initiation of the sign were immediate. When Zechariah emerges from the temple, he is unable to utter a blessing. He returns home silent, left to contemplate what God has told him in that silence. Fulfillment also is noted when the text reports that Elizabeth did conceive. She withdraws to wait out the realization, but there is a note of relief in how the Lord has "taken away my reproach." In language that echoes Rachel's words upon conceiving Joseph (Gen. 30:23), Elizabeth adds a third note to the scene. These events mean the removal of a painful burden.

4. The Birth Announcement to Mary (Luke 1:26–38) (Aland §3; Orchard §10; Huck-Greeven §7)

Gabriel is also sent to Mary in Nazareth, who is described as a virgin betrothed to Joseph. He is of the house of David.[12] The note about betrothal means that the marriage probably would be consummated within a year. In all likelihood, Mary is in her early teens, as this is when Jewish girls usually would marry.

Once again, the form of the passage is a birth annunciation, only this time there will be a unique difference in the source of conception. The angel announces that Mary has found favor from God as the recipient of an act of grace. She, too, will conceive and bear a son, whose name will be Jesus. This child will be great, as John was, but the description here is unqualified versus that of John in 1:15, which described John as "great before the Lord." Jesus will be Son of the Most High. This title then is explained in terms of kingship. Probably the announcement initially was understood as describing the king of Israel, not as a clear reference to ontological sonship associated with the Trin-

---

12. It appears that the genealogies both go through Joseph. Nonetheless, there is early church tradition in both the church fathers and in other works that also associates Mary with the house of David (Justin, *Trypho* 43, 45, 100; Irenaeus, *Against Heresies* 3.21.5; Tertullian, *Against the Jews* 9; *Martyrdom and Ascension of Isaiah* 11.2; *Gospel of the Nativity of Mary* 1.1).

ity, for the child is associated with the throne of his ancestor David. The reference to throne is a description of that fact that he will rule as a Davidic king (thrones are where kings sit and rule). It describes an authoritative function that God gives to Jesus. Authority is a major theme of the Jesus Gospel tradition. In this eschatological context, where John is shown to be like Elijah, the reference to Jesus describes a messianic function. Jesus will reign over Israel ("the house of Jacob") forever. His kingdom will have no end. Thus, the announcement is of the arrival of the eschatological age of deliverance in the promised ruler. It is the long-awaited hope of the nation. The nationalistic language resembles *Psalms of Solomon* 17–18, where a regal, national deliverer is anticipated. The language is not "Christianized" here, but fits the original Jewish setting. What Jesus' messiahship looks like and whom he battles are themes Luke's narrative account will develop.

Mary obviously takes the announcement not in terms of what the future marriage will bring but in terms of something that will happen in the near future, for she notes that currently she has no husband. The answer is simple. The promise will take place, and it is the Spirit of God that will come upon her and overshadow her. Therefore, this child will be called holy—that is, regarded as set apart. He will be the Son of God. Exactly what all of this meant—and much is suggested here but not spelled out—is what Luke wishes to explain in his Gospel. Here Luke affirms the creative work of God within Mary, doing so without any Old Testament citation, in contrast to Matt. 1:23.[13]

Mary also receives a sign: the pregnancy of her kinswoman Elizabeth. We are never told the exact relationship here. However, it is noted that Elizabeth already is six months along. The announcement and the sign are an indication that "nothing is impossible with God." Just as God had shown Zechariah, so also Mary can know that God will perform what he promises.

Mary's response is exemplary, even though her situation will be a cause of embarrassment. The narrative does not develop the plight into which this circumstance places Mary, but those contemplating what the narrative anticipates can see the awkwardness of her situation in this seemingly "premature" birth. (Narratives often expect us "to fill in gaps" with what we know culturally. John 8:41 explicitly traces the innuendoes that emerged from Jesus' birth, that he was a child of fornication.) Nonetheless, she responds with trust:

13. For two significant periodical studies on the virgin birth, see C. E. B. Cranfield, "Some Refections on the Subject of the Virgin Birth," *Scottish Journal of Theology* 41 (1988): 177–89; H. Douglas Buckwalter, "The Virgin Birth of Jesus Christ: A Union of Theology and History," *Evangelical Journal* 13 (1995): 3–14. The classic study on the virgin birth is J. Gresham Machen, *The Virgin Birth of Christ* (New York: Harper, 1930). Cranfield's article points out that the testimony to this event is not limited to Matthew and Luke; its implications are present in several other New Testament texts (Rom. 1:3; Gal. 4:4; Phil. 2:7; Mark 6:3; John 1:13; 6:41–42).

"Behold, I am a handmaid of the Lord; let it be to me according to your word." In this response Mary becomes an example of trust, a willing vessel in God's hands to do God's will as he has instructed. The note of piety serves to commend this member of Jesus' family. His roots stem from people who followed God.

5. Mary's Visit to Elizabeth (Luke 1:39–56) (Aland §4; Orchard §11; Huck-Greeven §8)

This unit actually consists of two parts: the visit (1:39–45) and the hymn known as the *Magnificat* (1:46–56) (this name comes from the first word of the hymn in its Latin version). The visit works like a bridge for the narrative. Characters representing John and Jesus finally meet. As the two greet one another, John, still in the womb, serves as a witness and leaps within Elizabeth (vv. 41, 44). This act reflects the initial fulfillment of the remark that John would be filled with the Spirit from his mother's womb (1:15). It represents another indication that God's word will come to pass. Elizabeth, filled with the Spirit, extends a blessing to Mary and to her child. She also expresses amazement that she can participate in this momentous event. Luke loves to revel in the joy of these events. Elizabeth's submission surfaces in her addressing Mary as "the mother of my Lord." Thus, she acknowledges Jesus' superior position. Luke emphasizes that blessing has come because Mary is one who "believed that there would be a fulfillment of what was spoken to her from the Lord." The stress for the reader is to believe what God has promised, as Mary did.

Mary's song of praise comes in two parts (1:46–49; 1:50–56). The first portion describes the reason for praise in terms of Mary's personal experience, while the second portion explains the broader theological principles at work for Israel and God's people. The hymn is another Lukan notation of the mood and the emotion that belong with these events. The hymn is a standard praise psalm, where one issues a call to praise God and then explains why such praise is appropriate. The dependence on Old Testament praise language suggests that these events parallel great events of old. The language recalls several expressions from the Old Testament, while its role is like that of Hannah's song in 1 Sam. 2:1–10. (Note how often the Old Testament is alluded to in this hymn: v. 48, 1 Sam. 1:11; v. 49, Ps. 111:9; v. 50, Ps. 103:13, 17; v. 51, Ps. 89:10 [a royal psalm]; 2 Sam. 22:28; v. 52, Job 12:19; 5:11; v. 53, 1 Sam. 2:5; Ps. 107:9; v. 54, Isa. 41:8; v. 55, Mic. 7:20; Gen. 17:7; 22:17; 2 Sam. 22:51.)

Mary declares that she will be blessed because future generations will appreciate how God reached out to this humble bond servant. God is holy—

that is, unique—because he has exercised power on her behalf that no one else could.

Not only is God's power at work, but also his mercy is that which God extends to all who fear him from generation to generation. Now the hymn describes how God works in general, and it does so using past-tense verbs (Greek aorist tenses) to describe events that are still future. The accomplishment of God's word and promise is that certain. God's power extends to humanity in a particular pattern. He scatters the proud and puts down the mighty. Those of "low estate" are exalted. The hungry are filled, while the rich are sent away empty. Luke also will develop this theme of God's ultimate vindication for the pious who are taken advantage of in the world. The "eschatological reversal" present in the hymn, where the poor end up exalted, will show up in the hope of Jesus' synagogue sermon in Luke 4:16–30 and in the blessings and woes of the Sermon on the Plain (6:20–26). The activity is rooted in God's special relationship to his servant Israel. His mercy extends to them and is rooted in ancient promises given to Abraham and his posterity forever. God acts out of his covenant commitments, promises made that he will bring to pass. Mary expresses the heart of a pious believer in Israel's God. What God is doing is part of a heritage established long ago. Mary remains with Elizabeth for three months, apparently until just before John's birth, before returning home.

6. The Birth of John the Baptist and Praise for His Arrival
(Luke 1:57–80) (Aland §5; Orchard §12; Huck-Greeven §9)

This section, in which Luke returns to John the Baptist, also contains two units (1:57–66; 1:67–80). In the first unit Zechariah goes against cultural convention and obeys the angelic instruction to name the child John. The child's birth is seen as an act of God's mercy, given the parents' age. When Zechariah and Elizabeth bring the child for circumcision, showing themselves to be pious Jews, Elizabeth chooses the name John. The crowd turns to the father to make sure that this name is correct, because no relatives bear this name. Zechariah, still deaf and mute, writes on a wax tablet that John is to be the name, surprising all. One thing Zechariah has learned in his period of enforced silence is that he should believe God's word and obey it. Immediately, his tongue is freed. He begins praising God. The matter leaves an impression on those in the region, who are said to respond with fear. The events raise the issue that Luke's narrative seeks to resolve: "What, then, is this child going to be? For the hand of the Lord is with him." The hymn that follows, known as the *Benedictus* (from its opening word in the Latin version), begins to answer that question with a second note of formal praise in this infancy material.

The hymn is a praise psalm in form and also, like the *Magnificat,* comes in two sections (1:68–75; 1:76–79). The first section is the general call to praise, while the second section directly addresses the child and tells of his role in God's plan. Zechariah, like Elizabeth earlier in 1:41, speaks while "filled with the Holy Spirit." His prophetic word involves an expression of praise. Again, Old Testament hope is prominent. The Lord God of Israel receives blessing for visiting and redeeming his people (v. 69). The language recalls 1 Kings 8:15, where Solomon offers thanks at the fulfillment of God's promise to have the nation build a house for God (cf. 1 Kings 1:48; Ps. 41:13; 72:18; 106:48). There is a figure of power, a horn of salvation, who will arise from within the house of David, God's servant (Ps. 89:24; 1 Chron. 17:4 has this description of David). What God is doing fulfills his word through the prophets to give salvation to Israel from their enemies and from the hands of all who hate them. Exactly who is included in this great battle over God's people is what the rest of the narrative details, where ultimately both spiritual and material opponents are in view.[14] Zechariah sees God as keeping sacred covenantal commitments by what God is about to do. The language recalls Ps. 106:10, 45–46. God's action also reflects his "mercy," a term that appears five times in this chapter (1:50, 54, 58, 72, 78). In seeing God's mercy to the fathers as grounded in the oath to Abraham, the hymn makes the point that God keeps his word, even when it takes a long period of time for the realization to come (Ps. 105:8–9; Gen. 17:7). Such a rescue is exciting to Zechariah because it will free him and those like him to serve God without fear in holiness and righteousness for all of their days. This desire to serve reveals the heart of an exemplary follower of God.

So who is John? The second section reveals that this child is a prophet of the Most High who prepares the way before the Lord. The language here recalls Isa. 40:3–5, which the evangelist cites in Luke 3:4–6. The effect of John's ministry is to give knowledge of salvation to God's people in the forgiveness of their sins. This work describes John's labor and teaching, not that of Jesus, for whom he sets the stage. John's entire ministry is grounded in God's merciful compassion. Part of that compassion will send the "the dawn from heaven."[15] The Greek term for "dawn" here could be a double entendre, as its Semitic root can mean "branch" or "sprout" as well as "light," but in this context the light imagery is dominant. The Messiah to come is light whose "visit" (see v. 68) represents the coming of illumination to a people seated in darkness and death. His work will guide them into the path of peace. Peace is another major Lukan theme (Luke 2:14; 7:50; 8:48; 10:6; 19:38, 42; Acts

---

14. For the hermeneutics involved in this hymn, viewed from the standpoint of the text as part of Luke's introductory section, see Darrell L. Bock, "The Son of David and the Saints' Task: The Hermeneutics of Initial Fulfillment," *Bibliotheca Sacra* 150 (1993): 458–78.

15. See BAGD, 62 §3 under ἀνατολή; also BDAG, 74 §3.

10:36). Thus, this hymn is a commentary on the way in which John prepares for God's work that will be mediated through the coming promised one, who himself functions as a light guiding the people into peace.

7. Joseph's Concern over Mary's Condition and the Announcement to Him (Matt. 1:18–25) (Aland §7; Orchard §5; Huck-Greeven §2)

Matthew 1:18–2:23 consists of a presentation of the infancy of Jesus in relationship to five Old Testament texts. In each case, Matthew, as narrator, points out the way in which the event fulfills Scripture. The fulfillment formulas differ: 1:22 (Isa. 7:14), "All this took place to fulfill what the Lord had spoken by the prophet"; 2:5 (Mic. 5:2), "For so it is written by the prophet"; 2:15 (Hos. 11:1), "This was to fulfill what the Lord had spoken by the prophet"; 2:17 (Jer. 31:15), "Then was fulfilled what was spoken by the prophet Jeremiah"; and 2:23 (no specific text, but probably a theme about someone from a despised place), "that what was spoken by the prophets might be fulfilled." In each case, however, what is said is declared to come "through" (διά) the prophet(s), so that the ultimate author of what is said is seen to be God. Each text tells something about Jesus or the mood of his coming: "God with us," shepherd for Israel, "my son," senseless suffering for the nation in rejection, the (rejected) "Nazarene." Matthew ultimately is arguing that Jesus recapitulates the pattern of Israel's experience while also presenting him as Israel's hope.

It is in this context of fulfillment that we are to see the announcement to Joseph and the angel's instruction to him not to put Mary away. The very fact that this text presents this dilemma in terms of how "shameful" the situation appeared to Joseph is significant. "She was with child *before* they had come together." On the one hand, Joseph is a sensitive man who does not wish to shame her; on the other hand, honor, so important in this culture, virtually would require that he look for a more faithful potential wife. He wished to spare her a shameful public trial like that described in *m. Sotah* 1.1, 5; 5.1.[16] His preference was to do something quietly. These details tell us something of the character of Joseph and are part of the Matthean narrative portrayal of him.

Joseph's plans are stopped by a dream. This is one of several such direct interventions in these two chapters (2:12, 19, 22). God is at work in these events to lead and to guide. An unnamed angel instructs Joseph to take Mary as his

---

16. A. Tosato, "Joseph, Being a Just Man," *Catholic Biblical Quarterly* 41 (1979): 547–51. See also Keener, *Matthew*, 60–61. On the process of divorce, see *m. Gittin* 2.5; 9.3–4, 8.

wife. The explanation is that she has conceived "by the Holy Spirit" (the phrase ἐκ πνεύματος . . . ἁγίου is repeated from 1:18). Joseph is addressed explicitly as the son of David, highlighting the Davidic theme already mentioned in the genealogy. Then follows a standard birth announcement, similar in form to the one in Luke with the announcements to Zechariah and Mary. Matthew, however, has one added feature, an explanation of the name Jesus: "for he will save his people from their sins." In this context the remark may well have been heard by Joseph as a promise of political deliverance, for the Jewish belief was that their exile was the result of their sin and covenant unfaithfulness as a people. We noted previously *Psalms of Solomon* 17–18, where a political redeemer comes to bring victory and to cleanse the nation from unfaithfulness. Matthew's story will go on to show how there is much more to Jesus than what had been expected. This certainly is how Zechariah understood an earlier similar announcement.

Matthew closes the section by noting how this event fulfills Scripture. The text from Isa. 7:14 has become controversial in our day. This is because in the original setting there appears to be no prediction of a virgin birth. Rather, the reference in that context seems to be about a child designated as a sign for Ahaz. This child will come to maturity only after certain judgments have taken place for Ahaz. But the text is appropriate for two reasons. First, Matthew is appealing to a pattern like that of old. Jesus is a sign child, like this child of the past. As happened in the original setting, God would give the sign and yet preserve the line of David. Second, this child will be Emmanuel, not in the literal sense of this being his given name, but in the sense that Jesus is "God with us," exactly as the text explains. Jesus' presence represents God's presence and activity on their behalf, as the events of the birth indicate. Thus, the citation reveals more than just Jesus' miraculous birth through a virgin (ἡ παρθένος). The appeal to Isa. 7:14 points to God's renewal of activity within the Davidic line in a way that demonstrates how God is "God with us." Here, Matthew says what Zechariah said in different words when he offered praise for the fact that "God has visited us and made redemption for his people and has raised up a horn of salvation for us in the house of his servant David" (Luke 1:68–69). In other words, although they say it in different settings and in complementary ways, Matthew and Luke make much the same point about Jesus' birth.

As he closes the unit, Matthew notes Joseph's obedience. Here is a complementary parallel to Luke's picture of Mary's obedience. Joseph took Mary to be his wife despite appearances. He withheld consummating the marriage until the child was born. The child was named Jesus, as the angel had instructed in Matt. 1:21.

8. The Birth of Jesus in Bethlehem (Luke 2:1–7) (Aland §7; Orchard §13a; Huck-Greeven §10a)

Luke reports that what brought Jesus to Bethlehem was a census ordered by Augustus Caesar. This census has been the source of much controversy because many regard Luke as having erred in mentioning a census under Quirinius, which most have dated in A.D. 6, too late for Jesus' birth. But the options concerning the census and the amount of time it would have taken to complete are factors that may well allow Luke's remarks to be accurate.[17] So Joseph and Mary, as law-abiding citizens, journey to Bethlehem to be counted in a census that asked each Jew to be registered in his or her traditional home. This sent Joseph into the city of David, Bethlehem, because "he was from the house and family of David." Once again, Luke stresses the royal roots of this child's family.

However, the birth is hardly one that we would associate with a king. What is important about the birth is its absolute lack of fanfare. The child, despite all the unusual circumstances surrounding his birth, is placed in an animal stall, probably born in a room on the fringe of an already crowded residence where animals and families stayed. He is placed in a feeding trough after the birth.[18] No one could imagine a more humble birth, one that hardly would be created from imagination if one were making up the details of this birth. Thus, the very humility built into the scene points to the account's credibility.

9. The Adoration by the Shepherds (Luke 2:8–20)
(Aland §8; Orchard §13b; Huck-Greeven §10b)

The Lukan account of Jesus' birth is filled with notes of joy and celebration. In this passage, creation and humanity celebrate together. Shepherds

17. See the detailed excursus on this census in Darrell L. Bock, *Luke 1:1–9:50*, BECNT 3A (Grand Rapids: Baker, 1994), 903–9. Note also these remarks by C. E. B. Cranfield, "Some Reflections on the Subject of the Virgin Birth," *Scottish Journal of Theology* 41 (1988): 182: "A far-reaching reform of the administration of the empire was certainly carried out under Augustus. And it certainly did involve censuses or taxation-assessments of a very thorough and comprehensive kind. Plenty of evidence for them has survived. The work of assessment took varying amounts of time according to the circumstances obtaining in particular areas: it could take several decades. It could be objected that, since at the time of Jesus' birth Judaea was a client state and not part of the empire, a tax-assessment by Augustus' authority could not have taken place there. But a Roman tax-assessment was carried out in the autonomous city-state of Apamea by Quirinius, and the fact that towards the end of his life Herod was not in high favour with Rome makes it far from improbable that a Roman tax-assessment was instituted in Judaea."

18. See the remarks in Green, *Gospel of Luke*, 128–29. Green notes that Bethlehem probably was too small to have had a formal inn for travelers.

represent humanity, and probably not the despised, although commentators often claim the latter. The evidence of shepherds as being despised comes from later Jewish sources. What shepherds do represent are the lowly and humble, as notes in 1:38, 52, and 4:16–18 about who this message benefits suggest. Present here is yet another annunciation scene, although not of an impending birth but of one that already has taken place. Although an angel appears, there is no need to fear. The angelic commentary tells us that the shepherds serve as representative witnesses on behalf of humanity, for the angel says, "I bring you good news of great joy for all the people." The announcement is that there "was born for all of you today in the city of David a Savior, who is Christ the Lord." The announcement uses several titles for which Luke has prepared us. The idea that Jesus is the Christ emerges from Luke 1:31–33, while the picture of him as Savior is the theme noted in Luke 1:68–69, 78–79. The one title that we are not entirely prepared for in terms of any previous explanation is "Lord." This title will be a key one for Luke; in Acts 2:36 it appears as the key title in Peter's Pentecost address. Its meaning is fully defined there. Filling out its meaning is one of the goals of Luke's Gospel.

The shepherds also get a sign: a baby wrapped in swaddling clothes and lying in a manger. This is hardly where we would expect the promised one to reside. It is an initial note that this Messiah will not match expectations.

Praise rings out from heaven as glory is given to God. As God is honored in heaven, so declarations of peace ring out for the earth (see 1:79), at least for people whom God favors. The last part of this heavenly praise often is translated in a way that obscures its meaning. It is not a general promise of peace to all humanity, but rather is specifically focused on those who are the objects of God's goodwill. This is a way to refer to the people of God, those who fear him because he has worked graciously in their lives. In the first century the expression "people with whom he is pleased" was a technical phrase for the elect of God (1QH 4.32–33 [= col. 12]; 11.9 [= col. 19]; *Shemoneh Esreh,* benediction 17, where the people of God are those who have received the gracious acts of God's mercy).

The shepherds journey to see what the angel announced. They find things exactly as the angel said: Joseph and Mary along with the baby lying in a manger. God's word comes to pass, as the signs indicate. The shepherds share what the angel had told them about the child. The people "marvel." This expression in Luke denotes contemplation of what is taking place but need not indicate belief or understanding. Mary also pondered these things. The Lukan account is told from her perspective. It may well be that the roots of what is described here come ultimately from her, whether directly or through someone such as James. The unit ends with a note of joy and praise to God as the shepherds return with a sense that they have been a part of something very special, events that have occurred just as they had been told. Throughout the

infancy material, Luke highlights scriptural language and teaching by presenting it as something that explains the significance of events, supplies the words
of praise, or offers a promise that will be fully realized one day. Given the examples of the divine Word's realization within the birth events, we can expect
his remaining promises to be fulfilled.

10. A Word to Obedient Parents at the Temple (Luke 2:21–38)
(Aland §9; Orchard §14; Huck-Greeven §11a)

Jesus' parents were faithful Jews. They had him circumcised on the eighth
day, giving him the name that the angel had said he should have. They followed purification laws after the birth (see Lev. 12:2–4), so they went up to
the temple thirty-three days after the circumcision to offer sacrifices. The text
is explicit that the sacrifices are for both of them, possibly because Joseph may
have helped in the delivery, rendering him ceremonially unclean as well. They
also appeared at the temple because the law required that a firstborn be dedicated to the Lord (Exod. 13:2, 12, 15). Everything they did reflects their piety
and faithfulness to God in following his law. Jesus' parents were not renegade
Jews.

During their time at the temple, the family meets another pious Jew, Simeon. We are told nothing about him except that he was righteous and devout,
looking for the deliverance of Israel, and that the Spirit was on him. It is likely
that he is old, because the Spirit told him that he would not see death until he
had "seen the Lord's Christ." It is Jesus' messianic status that Luke again un-
derlines here. By the Spirit's direction, Simeon finds himself at the temple, the
most sacred national religious site. Taking the child in his arms, he utters the
third hymnic piece of this introductory section of Luke. The hymn is known
as the *Nunc Dimittis* (from its beginning words in the Latin version).

The mission of Jesus is set forth, much as Zechariah had done for John the
Baptist in 1:69–77. The note of acceptance of what God is doing serves to introduce the reader to what Luke's Gospel as a whole will be about: seeing
God's will and design in the life and career of this child. Simeon's eyes "have
seen your salvation, which you have prepared in the presence of all peoples"
(Luke 2:30–31). The plural λαῶν ("peoples") is significant. Jesus' work is for
the whole of humanity, made up as it is of various nations. Jesus is "light,"
remark that emphasizes the picture of him as the breaking dawn in 1:78–79.
For the nations, he is "for revelation," while for Israel, God's special people at
the center of the plan from the start, he is "glory." Jesus' work will bring honor
to the chosen nation. Thus, a note of the broad scope of salvation arises here.

There is more to Simeon's remarks. As the parents again are marveling at
unsolicited commendation of the child, he gives a blessing to the parents and

warns Mary that it will not be painless. The child will divide the nation because he "is set for the fall and rising of many in Israel." He will be a sign spoken against, because although he has come for the nation, many in the nation will reject him. Simeon compares the effect of the nation's response to a sword piercing Mary's soul. In it all, the condition of people's hearts will be exposed before God. Here is Luke's first note that suffering and pain come with the bestowal of salvation.

Along with the pious old man who thanks God for Jesus' coming, a pious old woman appears who balances out the passage. This prophet, Anna, had been married for seven years. The text may well suggest that she was a widow for eighty-four years (see the NIV margin), in which case she would be more than a hundred, like Judith, immortalized in Judaism for her piety (see the Book of Judith). Her devotion in widowhood was directed to worship at the temple, fasting, and prayer. She also thanked God for what was taking place, although no content of what she said is noted other than she "spoke of him to all who were looking for the redemption of Jerusalem." So here is a second note that this child comes to bring the promise of the nation Israel to the world.

11. The Visit of the Magi to Bethlehem (Matt. 2:1–12) (Aland §8; Orchard §6; Huck-Greeven §3)

The Christmas scene familiar to most of us has shepherds and wise men gathered together around the manger, but it is very unlikely that this is what Scripture portrays. This Matthean scene seems to fall some time after Jesus' birth, even though Jesus is described as a παιδίον, a diminutive form of the word for "child." This term can refer to a newborn (LXX Gen. 17:12, an eight-day-old), but when Herod determines to kill the child, he makes a two-year window to ensure that he gets the child. This suggests that the magi came to him after the child was born and some time had passed.

More important to the story is that the magi are sensitive to the testimony in the creation, while "the king" in Jerusalem is not. In fact, he is hostile. A major goal of this unit sets forth this contrast. The trigger for events in this section is not the magi per se but a sign coming from the creation, a star that appears to them in the east and leads these outsiders to want to find the one born "king of the Jews" and offer him worship. This announcement certainly would strike Herod as a threat. All we are told about the magi is that they come from the east. It is not clear whether Arabia, Babylon, or Persia is meant. "Magi" is a term whose roots are in Persia, while giving attention to the stars was associated with Babylon. If there is an allusion to Isa. 60:6, then perhaps Arabia is in view. We also are not sure what is meant by the term "magi." Apparently, it indicates astrologers, given their attention to the stars. Less well supported is the idea that they are sages.[19] The contents of their gifts point to Arabia. Determining where they are from is not as important as realizing that they come from outside Israel. What is clear is that their initiative stands in contrast to the indifference or secret hostility of Israel's leaders. Here, Matthew hints that those outside Israel are sensitive to what God is doing through Jesus.

When Scripture is used as a guide, it is Bethlehem in Judea that is identified as the place of Jesus' birth. Micah 5:2 points to Bethlehem as the source of a "ruler who will be a shepherd of my people Israel." Skeptics challenge this identification as motivated only by a post facto, early-church apologetic concern; the church simply wished to make Jesus' birth fit with messianic Scripture.[20] However, if the Bethlehem of Judea claim were false, it would have been easy to challenge it by pointing out the real site of Jesus' birth, whether one pointed to the alleged locales of Nazareth or Bethlehem of Galilee. But these Gospels were written early enough that such facts could not be manufactured without meeting the challenge of someone who might have known the "real" facts. Despite claims to the contrary, there is no solid evidence for Jesus having been born anywhere else but in Bethlehem of Judea.

The citation of Mic. 5:2 is the most straightforward of all of Matthew's citations. One point that it makes dramatically is that the current king, whose roots are in Idumea, is not the one mentioned in the ancient text. Herod responds to the threat with a ruse: once the magi find Jesus, they should let him know, and he will join those who honor the child. However, as subsequent events show, Jesus' rejection from within official circles starts early.

The magi do go and offer their worship. We are not told how many of them there are. Many have assumed that there were three because they honor the child with gold, incense, and myrrh. They honor him as a king whose arrival has been signaled by the God of the heavens. The contrastive responses of the "outsider" magi and the Jewish "insider" Herod are also an important introductory note to the opening of this Gospel. It parallels what Simeon suggested in Luke 2:30–32: Jesus' coming will impact far more than Israel, even though he came to be their king.

Just as God superintends the events at the start of this scene, so also he acts now to protect the child. The magi are warned in a dream that Herod should

19. For a discussion of this text and the way magi were perceived, see W. D. Davies and D. C. Allison, *A Critical and Exegetical Commentary on the Gospel according to Saint Matthew*, 3 vols., International Critical Commentary (Edinburgh: Clark, 1988–97), 1:228–32.

20. Other efforts to identify Bethlehem with a locale in Galilee also must be regarded as failed, but so Bruce Chilton, *Rabbi Jesus: An Intimate Biography* (New York: Doubleday, 2000). The move is based on a reference to such a locale in the Talmud. Against it is the entire thrust of Matthew's claim for a Judean locale for Jesus' birth, supported independently by Luke's census claim. A Galilean origin also would leave no rationale for Herod's massacre of the babies in Bethlehem of Judea and Jesus' flight to Egypt only to return to Nazareth as a major change in locale tied to Archelaus's role as ruler. In addition, Chilton's theory that Jesus grew up conscious of being illegitimate (a Hebrew *mamzer*) trips over the problem that in the Talmud a *mamzer* is a child of a heathen father or one who is a slave, neither of which describes Joseph (*b. Qiddušin* 70ª).

not be told of the child. So they exit without revisiting the current king, an act that eventually will lead Herod to show his true attitude toward the child.

12. A Reenactment of Israel's Journey: Jesus to Egypt and Back alongside Unjust Suffering (Matt. 2:13–21) (Aland §10; Orchard §§7–8a; Huck-Greeven §4)

Two of the five infancy Old Testament citations of Matthew appear in this unit. The literary bracket of the unit is the parallel instructions in vv. 13 and 20 to "rise up and take this child and his mother and flee to Egypt/go to Israel." In this act Jesus recapitulates the history of the nation itself, when it came into Israel by way of Egypt in the original journey of redemption. In both cases where Joseph receives direction, the instruction comes from an angel in the midst of a dream, as God is seen protecting his special child. The reasons for the family's journey to and from Egypt likewise are parallel: v. 13, "for Herod is about to search for the child to destroy him"; v. 20, "for those who sought the child's life are dead." Similarly, Joseph's obedience in each case is noted in virtually identical language in v. 14 and in v. 21: "And he rose and took the child and his mother."

The journey back from Egypt is anticipated with the notation of the historical parallel of the original call of the nation out of Egypt from Hos. 11:1. This historical exodus event is now paralleled in a redeeming pattern that Jesus undertakes as the nation's representative. As such, he fulfills the passage by repeating the pattern, a repetition that points to God's design in the recognizable pattern of his saving activity. Two other points about the passage are worthy of note: (1) the location, Egypt, is part of a pattern in Matt. 2 of noting key locales (as Bethlehem in vv. 5–6 and Nazareth in v. 23); (2) the title given to Jesus in the citation is "my son," expressing the special, chosen relationship between God and Jesus.

In between the journeys to and from Egypt stands Herod's reaction to being "tricked by the wise men." The failure to get the exact location of the child caused Herod to fly into a rage and command that all children two years of age and younger in the Bethlehem region be slain.[21] The injustice here recalls the suffering of former days as expressed in Jer. 31:15, where the matriarch of the nation, Rachel, is described as weeping for her children as she sees Israel and Judah fall into captivity. As in the days of the original exile, the na-

---

21. The history of Herod's murderous tendency to defend his throne through executing even members of his own family is well known (Josephus, *Ant.* 15.7.4 §§218–231; 16.5.4. §151). Thus, these acts fit his character. Because Bethlehem was a small town, the number of small children to have been executed would not be large, certainly not as large as the few hundred sometimes proposed in popular exposition.

tion suffers at the hands of those who do not trust in God. What is interesting is that in Jeremiah, right after the verse that Matthew cites, comes the promise that the weeping will cease because the people will return from the land of the enemy, "so there is hope for your future" (Jer. 31:16–17). Thus, these events, as gruesome as they are and as unjust as the suffering is, also point in pattern to a sequence that opens up opportunity for hope after the suffering. The pattern of suffering followed by hope also will end the Gospel. The fact that rejection and the cause of suffering come from within the nation is another tragic point throughout this Gospel. Jesus' coming to Israel from Egypt points to both salvation and return. He encompasses Israel's history and hope.

13. To Nazareth in Galilee (Matt. 2:22–23; Luke 2:39–40)
   (Aland §11; Orchard §§8b, 15; Huck-Greeven §§4b, 11b)

Here is one place where Matthew and Luke overlap. They both have Jesus going to Nazareth. However, there is a significant difference. Luke describes a return to Nazareth, while Matthew appears to have Joseph contemplating a return to Judea, and he is stopped only when a dream causes him to "withdraw to the district of Galilee" because Archelaus is chosen to rule after his father, Herod. The resolution of this difference may reside with Luke, for reasons to be noted below.

Joseph had reason to be nervous about Archelaus. Secular history confirms that many Jews did not want Archelaus to rule over Judea (Josephus, *Ant.* 17.11.1–5 §§299–323). Nonetheless, he was given the demoted role of ethnarch, in comparison to his father, the king. He was seen as a cruel and incompetent leader who eventually was removed from office in A.D. 6. Once again, it is God's direction and protection through a dream that is noted as the driving factor in the action. Joseph's withdrawal to Nazareth leads to the final Old Testament citation by Matthew in the infancy material (2:23). It appears that here Matthew cites not a passage but a theme. This is first indicated by the plural reference to the "prophets," in contrast to three of the other references where the singular, "prophet," appears. (Only Matt. 2:17 names the prophet Jeremiah in making a citation.) If this observation about a reference to an idea is correct, then it is the mention of "Nazarene" that is key. However, that term does not appear in either the Hebrew or the Greek text of the Old Testament. Still, the mention of Nazareth is important regardless of how this is the point of the citation. The Jewish view was that nothing good comes from there (John 1:46), but God is full of surprises.

Three suggestions about the citation are made. (1) Given that "Nazirite" sounds like "Nazarene," some see an allusion to the Nazirite vow through a play on sound. In addition, some point out that in the LXX there is an interchange between the ideas of Nazirite and holy one (Judg. 13:7; 16:17 [Codexes A and B]). So this may be an indirect way to say that Jesus is the holy one. This seems unlikely, since there is no contextual indication that a reference to the Nazirite is present.[22] (2) There is a wordplay involving *nezer*, which in Semitic languages can mean either "branch" or "light." The term has messianic overtones because of its use in texts such as Isa. 11:1. The suggestion is subtle because "Nazareth" does not have any etymological connection to this term. However, sometimes Hebrew wordplays employ a variety of sounds, whether etymologically connected or not.[23] (3) Nazareth is to be associated with its locale in Galilee and thus with a region of Israel that was viewed with disrespect. So the name "Nazarene" points to a note of rejection of Jesus' claims because he comes from a distant, rural locale (cf. John 1:46; 7:41). This view was noted by Jerome in his comments on Isa. 11:1. If this third reading is in view, then Matthew picks up this theme again more positively in Matt. 4:12–16, where Galilee, a region formerly in darkness, now receives a great light. Matthew's remark is so subtle that it is hard to choose between the second and third options, especially because either view makes good sense contextually. Perhaps the theme of rejection, which is so prominent in Matt. 2, favors the third option. It is also possible that a combination of the second and third views works; an epithet and an obscure town express the very lowliness from which the Messiah would emerge.

Luke gives no indication of an Egyptian sojourn for the family or of Joseph's intent to return to Judea before being warned and directed to Galilee. Luke simply notes that, after performing everything according to the law, "they returned into Galilee, into their own city." This is followed by a note about Jesus' growth in strength, wisdom, and the favor of God. This difference from Matthew troubles some people, especially in light of the fact that Matthew gives no indication that Joseph and Mary came originally from Galilee. But it is clear that each writer is being selective in what he narrates. If Matthew and Luke are working independently here, as most of those who hold to Markan priority would maintain or those who hold to the independence of these Gospels would argue, then what is present is a difference in the selection of details about the early life of Jesus. Even if Matthew is the first Gospel, then we may be dealing only with Matthew's choices versus the emphasis that Luke chooses to have. Matthew focuses on what will help him present five notes of fulfillment and the contrast between the Gentile welcome and the official rejection of Jesus as king. This rejection they still needed to

22. For more against this view, see Robert Gundry, *The Use of the Old Testament in St. Matthew's Gospel with Special Reference to the Messianic Hope,* Supplements to Novum Testamentum 18 (Leiden: Brill, 1975), 98–100.

23. See, for example, the rabbinic wordplay in the *Midrash Psalms,* §8 on Ps. 2:6. See William G. Braude, trans., *The Midrash on Psalms,* 2 vols., Yale Judaica Series 13 (New Haven, Conn.: Yale University Press, 1959), 1:40.

fear under Archelaus. Luke focuses on the parents' faithful temple piety. Given Matthew's normal Jewish concerns, a reader might expect that the temple account and Luke's Jerusalem focus would be found also in Matthew. However, each Gospel writer has chosen what to highlight, sometimes in ways that defy prediction. The point is that selectivity should not be confused with contradiction or historical error. There is nothing that prevents us from seeing Luke 2:39 as a literary collapse of time that simply gets us to his next event, the pilgrimage journey from Nazareth back to the temple, when Jesus was twelve. The choice does allow Luke to stay focused on temple scene events without anything intervening. Such topical coupling may be a simple explanation for this difference, and such topical arrangement is typical of ancient works.

14. Jesus at the Temple (Luke 2:41–52) (Aland §12; Orchard §16; Huck-Greeven §12)

Up to this point in Luke, everyone has spoken about Jesus. Now it is time for him to speak. This unit is important because it concludes the infancy section with Jesus as an emerging young man who is thinking for himself. As such, this technically is not an infancy story. However, the account is transitioning to Jesus taking a more direct role in the account. Jesus' first words in Luke express themselves with a sense of divine direction and destiny. The account is designed to underscore respect for Jesus, who is seen dialoguing with the teachers of the faith in a way that leaves those around him "amazed at his understanding and his answers." In another sense, the text is a pronouncement account, because the clear key to the passage is the saying in 2:49.

The occasion is the pilgrimage from Galilee to Jerusalem, which every pious Jew sought to make at least once a year. Although this trip was commanded to take place three times a year (Exod. 23:14–17; 34:22–23; Deut. 16:16), in the first century it was regarded as common to make the trip once a year from Galilee. The Passover took place on the fifteenth of Nisan, which falls in our calendar either in March or April. As they return, Jesus' parents discover that he has not accompanied them. Returning to Jerusalem, they find him in the temple, engaged with the teachers. The discovery leads to an encounter where Mary is once again the focal figure in Luke's account. She questions Jesus as to why he has treated his parents so insensitively and left them anxious. The commonness and predictability of the parental reaction is what makes the story so easy to identify with in terms of its emotion.

Jesus' reply is ambiguous in the Greek, reading literally, "Did you not know that I must be in/about the [things] of my Father?" (ἐν τοῖς τοῦ πατρός μου [note the lack of a noun for the plural definite article]). Three elements of the reply are important. (1) The use of "must" (δεῖ) points to a divine necessity in what Jesus does. He is destined to do this. Luke often will highlight key points with this term, which itself underscores the note about the divine design within events that he narrates. (2) The lack of a noun in Greek with the definite article leaves the meaning of the verse ambiguous and disputed. A noun needs to be supplied contextually. Three options are commonly given: (a) among those of my Father's house, (b) about my Father's business, or (c) in my Father's house. Idiomatically, the best option is the last one.[24] However, the point is not so much about a place as what it represents. The temple was the place of God's presence. It was only appropriate that Jesus would be engaged in discussion about God in a place where his presence is highlighted. (3) Whatever the reply means exactly, it recognizes that ultimately Jesus' unique relationship to God will be a priority over any familial duty or custom. It is specifying Jesus' unique relationship to "my Father" that is the topic of much of the rest of Luke's Gospel. Jesus' strong sense of identity with and relationship to God is foreshadowed here. His sense of mission expresses itself early on. Luke makes it clear that what Jesus meant was not initially understood by his parents. This is not the only time in the Gospel that those close to Jesus will fail to understand him.

This leads Luke to note that an obedient Jesus returned with his parents to Nazareth, as Mary pondered these things in her heart (Luke 2:51). Luke closes with a second note about Jesus' growth (Luke 2:52), versus only one such note about John (Luke 1:80). Wisdom, stature, and favor with both God and people reveal Luke's very human portrait of Jesus.

Conclusion

The infancy material sets the tone for both Matthew and Luke. Each goes his own way to highlight how Jesus fulfills promises of old. Matthew does it through five Old Testament citations that point to Jesus as the promised Davidic son-king. Luke uses the style of Old Testament historical narrative and employs hymns to make his points about Jesus in language that recalls the Old Testament. In both accounts God is highly active. Each account suggests that suffering is associated with the presence of Jesus. Matthew does this in the slaying of the innocents, while Luke has the note predicted in Simeon's remarks to Mary. Each account also notes that Jesus comes as king of the Jews, although what he does also will involve the nations. Matthew's picture of magi responding to the testimony of creation shows that Gentiles will be sensitive to Jesus' coming. In Luke it is Simeon's note that Jesus is a light of revelation to the Gentiles that makes the point. Thus, for all their distinct details, the beginnings of both accounts share some basic themes.

24. BAGD, 552 §II.7; BDAG 689 §2.g.

Differences between the accounts also emerge. Luke focuses on how John prepares for Jesus but is inferior to him. The hymns in Luke 1 highlight how Jesus' coming will lift up those on the fringe of society, the humble and hungry, as well as rescue God's people so they may serve him. Luke uniquely presents one incident of Jesus' adolescence to indicate how young he was when he understood that God's work would be his priority. In a real way, Jesus is the climactic witness in Luke's infancy account.[25] Matthew explains that Jesus is Israel's legitimate king while focusing on Herod's horrific rejection of Jesus. Matthew also shows how Jesus recapitulates patterns of association in Israel's history tied to the exodus deliverance and suffering. The combination of similarity and diversity between Luke and Matthew shows how complementary the Gospel accounts can be as each Gospel lays the groundwork for its developing narrative about Jesus.

25. For a significant study of Luke's narrative, see Mark Coleridge, *The Birth of Lucan Narrative: Narrative as Christology in Luke 1–2*, JSNTSup 88 (Sheffield: Sheffield Academic, 1993).

THREE

The Backdrop to Jesus' Ministry

John the Baptist, Jesus' Baptism and Temptations
(Matt. 3:1–4:11; Mark 1:1–13; Luke 3:1–4:13)

The story begins with a voice offstage, reading from Scripture. While John [the Baptist] and Jesus may seem to appear out of the blue, this citation of Scripture [from Mark 1:2–3] makes it clear that they appear out of the blueprint of God's plan. This story is the beginning of the good news, but every beginning is a consequence. By cross-referencing Scripture Mark makes it clear that the gospel is bound fast to the promise of God in the Old Testament and is a continuation of the story of God's saving activity. Long before the promise-filled preaching of John the Baptizer, there was the promise-filled preaching of Isaiah, which shows that God had planned things out long before John appeared on the scene. God initiates the action. The prophets' hope was not a pipe dream; their prophecy still rings forth, and it will be fulfilled by God.[1]

This quotation highlights how Mark begins. Just as Matthew and Luke began looking back to Scripture and hope, so also Mark begins his Gospel with a note about divine promise in Scripture. To understand Jesus, one also must appreciate the ministry of John the Baptist and its connection to promised deliverance. Matthew and Luke would agree. It is a prepared people who benefit from the coming of divine hope.

According to the Synoptic evangelists, the backdrop to Jesus' ministry is rooted in hope expressed in the Hebrew Scripture. Making sense of the events that immediately preceded Jesus' ministry means understanding the background of certain promises, rituals, and events. This chapter considers the

---

1. David Garland, *Mark,* NIV Application Commentary (Grand Rapids: Zondervan, 1996), 43.

preministry phase of Jesus' career. It presents the ministry of John the Baptist, Jesus' baptism by John, one of the Synoptic genealogies, and the temptation accounts. Figures from the Old Testament such as Elijah and Adam are invoked to help us explain what we see—sometimes in comparison and other times in contrast. An understanding of certain Jewish rituals and symbols also is important to appreciating John's ministry. Just as the infancy materials proclaimed the arrival of promise tied to Jesus, so also does the preministry period. Jesus did not preach in a vacuum. John the Baptist already had engaged Israel with a message that the nation could understand because his actions were couched in rituals and idioms of prophetic warning and national hope. It was a message that Jesus identified with before he launched out on his own.

15. The Introduction to Mark (Mark 1:1) (Aland §1; Orchard §2; Huck-Greeven §13a)

Mark does not begin where his Synoptic partners do. He begins with John the Baptist. That the story of Jesus' ministry began with John was the common view of the church (Acts 1:21–22; 10:37). However, before Mark points to the scriptural fulfillment that John the Baptist represents, Mark 1:1 gives his work a brief title. This practice had precedent. Hosea 1:2a in the Greek translation reads, "The beginning of the Word of the Lord to Hosea" (see also the LXX of Prov. 1:1; Eccles. 1:1; Song 1:1). Mark 1:1 serves as the introduction to the whole work and not just of John's ministry because the concept of "gospel" had a broad meaning in the church, the term "beginning" lacks an article in Greek, and Mark fails to give a title to any other subsection of his Gospel. Mark relates the start of a story that continues to unfold. That Mark refers to the "beginning" of the sequence of Gospel events as opposed to the "origin" of the gospel, as some suggest, is made clear by the scriptural indicators Mark presents that show God unfolding a plan previously noted in Scripture. For Mark and for the early church, the origins of the gospel are found in God's plan as set forth in these texts. Thus, Mark is noting the start of the arrival of divine acts of "good news" (gospel) that previously had only been announced in the ancient Scripture.

The term "gospel" has its background in the Hebrew Scripture, where the verb בשׂר is employed to picture the announcement of important, positive news, like a birth, a victory, or the coming of God's deliverance (1 Sam. 31:9; Jer. 20:15; Isa. 40:9; 41:27; 52:7; 61:1; Nah. 1:15). Many of these texts appear in settings where God's presence and redeeming power are proclaimed. The term "gospel" in the present context is not a reference to the literary genre of Mark, but characterizes what the events and message of Jesus entail.[2]

---

2. The first recorded use of the term "gospel" as a literary genre comes from Justin Martyr in the mid–second century. See *First Apology* 66.

The topic of that good news and its source is Jesus Christ, the Son of God. It is debated whether the reference to the "gospel of Jesus Christ" is more accurately understood as "the gospel *about* Jesus Christ" or "the gospel *from* Jesus Christ."[3] In this context, the distinction may be a false one, although the former idea is more pronounced because not everything that concerns the gospel comes from Jesus, as John the Baptist's ministry shows.

The title "Son of God" also is significant for Mark (Mark 1:11; 3:11; 5:7 [in a vocative]; 9:7; 12:6; 13:32; 14:36 [God addressed as "Father"], 61; 15:39).[4] Mark is concerned to show how the "Son of God" relates to the recognition that Jesus is the Christ, the designated, anointed agent of God, who brings good news. As all the Synoptics show, it took a while for the disciples to appreciate all that was entailed in designating Jesus as God's son. Explaining this is one of the major concerns of the Synoptics; the story reveals how one who was expected to be a delivering figure came to die and be resurrected into God's presence so deliverance could occur.

16. John the Baptist and Scripture (Mark 1:2–6; Matt. 3:1–6; Luke 3:1–6) (Aland §13; Orchard §17; Huck-Greeven §13b)

Mark opens his portrait of John with a citation credited to Isaiah (40:3), although the citation actually has been combined with Mal. 3:1. The introductory formula refers only to Isaiah because in the exposition that follows it is the portion from Isaiah that is cited for special comment. The link words "in the wilderness" (ἐν τῇ ἐρήμῳ) connect the citation from Isaiah to the exposition that follows the citation. In Judaism, link words are a common way to expound Scripture. The citation makes two points. (1) Malachi describes John as a divinely appointed prophet-messenger whose responsibility is to prepare the people for God's coming. The references to "you" ("your face," "your way") may reflect influence from Exod. 23:20, as Malachi speaks of the preparation of "my" (God's) way. John is a prophetic figure like the expected Elijah of the end, the person to whom the image in Malachi alludes (see Mal. 4:5; Sir. 48:10). (2) The call in the wilderness is a repetition of the pattern of the call to escape the exile and experience the decisive deliverance that Isaiah declared centuries earlier. Such hope of ultimate deliverance was also noted at Qumran via Isa. 40 (1QS 8.12–16; 9.17–20). So the text was established in Jewish hope. The wilderness is the locale associated with a new exodus and deliverance. In Judaism

---

3. The question is whether the phrase is an objective or subjective genitive in Greek.
4. This title is disputed text-critically in Mark 1:1, so some suggest that it is not a part of this verse. However, although the title is missing in the original reading in Codex Sinaiticus and some other versions, such as editions of the Sahidic, it is attested in many excellent manuscripts, such as Codices Vaticanus and Bezae and the Old Latin.

of this period, the wilderness spawned many movements that challenged the political leadership (Josephus, *War* 2.13.4–5 §§259–261). This theme explains why John located himself where he did. The association was tied to salvation and suggested the need for a change of direction among God's people, a change that Isaiah suggests God will bring. One author has noted that Isa. 40:1–5 "was a classic statement of the consolation that comes from God and was understood specifically in the context of God's eschatological comfort."[5]

Mark notes that John preached a baptism. This washing was directed at repentance for the forgiveness of sins. The point is not that the baptism provided forgiveness, but that the attitude of a person seeking baptism indicated a ready heart, to which God responded by granting forgiveness ("a baptism that has reference to forgiveness," reading εἰς in a more general sense). In the eschatological context of deliverance that Isaiah evokes, this forgiveness refers not merely to a personal or private cleansing, but to a corporate preparation by people for the approach of God's way. While most Jewish washings were self-administered, John performed these baptisms, suggesting their uniqueness. They appear to function as a way of declaring a person's readiness for the new era as the one being baptized submits to a washing that pictures cleansing from sin.[6] Though the association with Isaiah is something that the evangelist makes, it indicates the end-time deliverance context in which John's acts should be seen.

Mark also notes that people from Judea and Jerusalem went out to the Jordan River to be baptized as they confessed their sins. Sin often was seen as the cause for exile and judgment that the people had experienced (Lam. 1:8–22). Unfaithfulness had forced God to act, as shown by the message of the prophets from Isaiah through Jeremiah. The roots for this concept of repentance are in the prophetic call to "turn."

John was an ascetic. He wore clothing that resembled Elijah's wardrobe (2 Kings 1:8).

5. Klyne Snodgrass, "Streams of Tradition Emerging from Isaiah 40:1–5 and Their Adaptation in the New Testament," *Journal for the Study of the New Testament* 8 (1980): 31.

6. For a thorough study of the background of John's work, see Robert L. Webb, *John the Baptizer and Prophet: A Socio-Historical Study*, JSNTSup 62 (Sheffield: Sheffield Academic Press, 1991). Recently, some have challenged the idea that John's baptism was nonrepeatable. They argue on the basis that John's washing is like other acts of Jewish purification or that John saw himself as a prophet. Webb's study correctly argues otherwise. For alternative views, see Joan Taylor, *The Immerser: John the Baptist within Second Temple Judaism* (Grand Rapids: Eerdmans, 1997); Bruce Chilton, "John the Purifier," in *Judaic Approaches to the Gospels* (Atlanta: Scholars, 1994), 1–37. The touch of unique features about his washing, namely, his administration of it and the reference to his baptism in the singular (not baptisms), point to a single eschatological washing that was a preparatory, one-time act. Josephus (*Ant.* 18.5.2 §§116–119) also describes the work of the Baptist in purification terms and as a call to righteousness. The New Testament imagery and that of Josephus complement each other. For the washings that were a part of Judaism and John's relationship to these, see Webb, *Baptizer and Prophet*, 95–216.

Matthew's portrayal adds one more feature. John's message involved the declaration that the kingdom of heaven—the inbreaking of the promised eschatological rule of God from heaven—was "at hand." Matthew repeats the identification of John with Isa. 40 and his Elijah-like clothing. Matthew adds further that people from all the region of the Jordan also came out to John, alongside those from Judea and Jerusalem.

Luke has three more important features. First, he locates John's ministry in the framework of larger world history, showing his more universal concern. How this discussion of rulers from Tiberius Caesar up to the high priestly family of Annas and Caiaphas fits chronologically was treated in chapter 2 of my *Studying the Historical Jesus*.[7] Second, he notes that it was "the word of God" that came to John in the wilderness. So his prophetic role is highlighted. Third, the citation from Isa. 40 is expanded to include vv. 4–5. This means that the citation ends by noting that "all flesh shall see the salvation of God." Luke indicates that John's message has implications for people from every nation. Unlike Matthew and Mark, he never notes from where the people who heard John came. For Luke, John's importance extends beyond the people of Israel. Luke also lacks a description of John's clothing, although he does suggest knowledge of it in Luke 7:24–26, 33. For Luke, John is foremost a prophetic messenger of God who warns of accountability to God and proclaims the approach of God's salvation.

17. John's Preaching of Repentance (Matt. 3:7–10; Luke 3:7–9)
(Aland §14; Orchard §18; Huck-Greeven §14)

This passage, once it gets to John's speech, has almost exact agreement between Matthew and Luke (sixty of sixty-four words in Greek). There is one significant difference between Matthew and Luke: the audience. Matthew notes that it is "Pharisees and Sadducees coming for baptism," while Luke refers only to "the multitudes who were coming out to be baptized by him." The Matthean account, by the directness of John's address and the absence of any positive query about what John commands, suggests that the leadership also was scrutinizing John. In fact, the tone of the account is startling, regardless of the audience. John is portrayed as proclaiming the approach of the day of judgment. His remarks stress that the situation is serious. Judgment is very near, and those who engage in the baptism had better take it seriously.

The passage has three elements. First, there is the warning, given almost in biting sarcasm, that those who come for baptism should not take lightly the warning to flee wrath. This is not a mere rite to perform with indifference or as a matter of course. In the context of Judaism, which had many rituals, some of

7. Grand Rapids: Baker, 2002.

which took place regularly, this was not merely another rite to add to the list. John compares his audience to snakes fleeing the fire in the wilderness, forced out of their protective holes by the heat. Regardless of who told them that they needed to prepare to flee God's wrath, they had better understand what God seeks. John sees the person who accepts baptism as needing a heart committed to the pursuit of righteousness with a recognition that what was needed was the forgiveness that God would provide as the era of judgment and blessing approached. The remarks fit in with a challenging prophetic declaration.

Second, there is a call to bear fruit that befits repentance and not to rely on mere ancestry as a way into blessing. Merely claiming a relationship to Abraham does not give an automatic birth into life. John warns that God can create his children out of anything, even stones.

Finally, John portrays judgment as imminent, like an axe aimed at the base of a tree. That axe will swing against anyone who does not bear fruit. For those who lack fruit, there is only the prospect of being removed and cast into the fire of judgment. John apparently expected this judgment in the near future. However, it must be understood that in another sense blessing or judgment in that future comes with the decision that one makes today about John, for in that decision was either an opening up of the heart toward God and his work or the prospect of judgment. In this call to respond to God and his approaching coming, John prepared the way for God's work.

18. What, Then, Shall We Do? (Luke 3:10–14) (Aland §15; Orchard §19; Huck-Greeven §15)

Only Luke gives the ethical content of John's preaching, by noting the crowd's reaction and John's response. In each case John responds with a relational thrust that looks to how considerately one treats another. The remarks illustrate what one must do to bear fruit. They also fit with the announced work of John in Luke 1:16–17. To turn to God means changing how one relates to others. Also significant is who responds: the crowd, the toll collectors, and the soldiers.[8] The religious leadership is conspicuously absent (Luke 7:29–30). Toll collectors and soldiers present two highly political groups whose potential to abuse their authority is great. John specifically advises that this is not what they should do; the toll collector is to collect only what is due,

8. On the role and controversy surrounding toll collectors and the taxes they exacted, see unit 36 in chapter 4. For ancient texts showing how toll collectors were seen, see Josephus, *Ant.* 12.4.2–9 §§160–222, showing the work of Joseph, a crafty collector for the Ptolemies. The emperor Tiberius is reported to have said to his governors about tax collection, "A good shepherd shears his flock; he does not flay them" (Suetonius, *Tiberius* 32). See also Dio Cassius, *Roman History* 57.10.5, which addresses the same tradition about Tiberius.

and the soldier is not to rob or make false accusations. In Greek, the latter injunction contains a strong picture: the Greek word for "rob" means "to shake someone," matching the English expression "to shake someone down." Nor is the soldier to complain that he is not paid enough by the state. These soldiers either were from Antipas's army in Perea, which means they could have non-Jews among them, or were the Judean "police" tasked with helping toll collection. As for the multitude, they are to be generous, offering a coat or food to the person who needs it.

There is probably a word link in this text built around the idea of "doing/ making" (ποιέω). In the citation of Isa. 40, Luke notes the call to make straight one's path (Luke 3:4). The verb ποιέω is used in this verse, and the idea of making, using the same verb, reappears in v. 8 with the exhortation "to make fruit worthy of repentance." In v. 9, the one "not making fruit" is cut down. This forces the issue: "What, then, shall we do?" In each case, the verb reappears. Each of the three groups raises this question, in vv. 10, 12, 14. This kind of word link is common in Judaism. In this case it unifies the Lukan scene. It shows that repentance has a practical and relational focus. It is manifested in how we treat others and how we do not seek to exercise authority inappropriately. Luke is drawing his reader into the story to ask similar types of questions for personal reflection. The spirit of John's reply is not unusual; it follows the exhortations of the prophets of old (Isa. 1:16–17; 58:7–8; Mic. 6:8; also in Jewish texts, such as Sir. 4:1, 4, 8; 7:32; 10:23; 11:12; 34:21). The reply shares their explicitly practical tone and emphasis.

19. The Mightier One to Come (Matt. 3:11–12; Mark 1:7–8; Luke 3:15–18) (Aland §16; Orchard §20; Huck-Greeven §16)

This event is fascinating to trace in each Gospel. Mark's account is the most concise, and Luke's is the most expansive. Mark simply notes that John preached about one coming after him who is mightier than he is. John is not worthy to untie the thong of his sandal. This detail is important because in Judaism it was a dishonor to be a slave, since that recalled the period in Egypt before the exodus. According to the rabbis, even if one was a slave, the task of loosening the sandal was beneath a Jew and was an act not to be performed (*Mekilta de Rabbi Ishmael, Nezikin* 1 on Exod. 21:2). So John sees himself as not worthy of even the most humiliating of tasks for a slave. John then contrasts his baptism of water with a coming baptism of the Spirit. This probably evokes themes tied to the era of realization and new covenant (Jer. 31:31–33; Ezek. 36:24–27). The roots of this promise reach back into Torah and stretch forward into the prophets (Deut. 30:1–6; Joel

2:28–32; Ezek. 11:17–21). The stress was that the Spirit would bring a deliverance and an internal obedience to God. Although Jewish expectation did not necessarily tie this baptism to any particular eschatological figure, it was regarded as a key act of God in the era of fulfillment (although Ezek. 34–36 juxtaposes the Messiah as new shepherd and the Spirit as agents who belong to the same era). It is this connection that both Matthew and Luke note.

Matthew makes the same contrast while noting that John's baptism was specifically for repentance. Matthew adds that the baptism involves not just the Spirit but also fire. This adds a note of judgment and warning to the passage, as does the additional remark that this coming figure will have a winnowing fork in his hand, clear the threshing floor, and gather wheat into the granary while burning the chaff with unquenchable fire.[9] Fire is a consistent Old Testament image for judgment (Isa. 29:6; 66:15; Ezek. 38:22; Amos 1:4; 7:4; Zeph. 1:18; 3:8; Mal. 3:2; 4:1). Numerous passages from other Jewish writings also use this image (*Jubilees* 9.15; 36.10; *1 Enoch* 10.6; 54.6; 90.24–27; *4 Ezra* [= 2 Esdras] 7:36–38; 13:4; *Psalms of Solomon* 15.4–7; 1QH 3.28–31 [= col. 11]; 1QS 2.8, 15; 4.13). Thus, the baptism to come purges as well as blesses. John is portrayed as preaching the advent of a decisive judgment that the coming figure brings.

Luke is similar to Matthew but with one important addition. Luke uniquely gives the context that triggered these remarks: the crowd's speculation that John might be the Christ. Luke, like Matthew, says that the baptism is one of Spirit and fire. He also presents the winnowing-fork image. However, only Luke notes that John preached many other exhortations and good things to the people.

So John preached the approach of a day of blessing and decision when a sent agent of God will distribute the Spirit in a way that divides humankind. Another crucial point emerges from Luke's description. John is not the Christ, but the way that this coming agent of God will be identified is by the Spirit baptism that this stronger agent will bring. If the Spirit comes, then a person can know that the Christ has been present. Luke will make much of this point in his Gospel and its sequel, the Book of Acts.

---

9. The exact force of the Spirit and fire imagery is debated. Some have tied the language to Pentecost in Acts 2 as the realization, but the language of fire there does not match the judgment imagery of this context or the parallel in Luke 3. Others speak of two baptisms: one for salvation and one for judgment. This is unlikely, however, because the description is tied to a singular reference to baptism and has only one group as the object. So the most likely reading is to see a purging and dividing of humanity in the baptism, with the background in Isa. 4:4–5, the only Old Testament text where baptism and fire appear together. See Darrell L. Bock, *Luke 1:1–9:50*, BECNT 3A (Grand Rapids: Baker, 1994), 322–23.

20. John's Imprisonment (Luke 3:19–20; noted later in Matt. 14:3–4; Mark 6:17–18) (Aland §17; Orchard §21; Huck-Greeven §17)

This brief, uniquely Lukan note explains how John ended up in jail. Luke does not record the death of John the Baptist, described in Matt. 14:3–12 and Mark 6:17–29. This account works as a substitute for it, explaining why Herod arrested John. This difference allows Luke to finish discussing John before turning his attention completely to Jesus.

Luke notes that John reproved the leader for his marriage to Herodias, who had been the wife of his half brother, Philip, also called Herod by Josephus (*Ant.* 18.5.1 §§109–115).[10] In addition, Herod himself had been married to the daughter of King Aretas IV of Nabatea. He divorced her to marry his brother's wife, who also got a divorce to make the union possible. The divorces and the marriage to the spouse of a brother violated Lev. 18:16 and 20:21. Then John also challenged the leader on other evil things, so that Herod finally locked him up.

Josephus argues that the destruction of Herod's army by Aretas in A.D. 36 was seen by many as God's judgment for this marriage (*Ant.* 18.5.2 §§116–119). Josephus notes that John was slain even though he was a good man. John simply had commanded the Jews to exercise virtue, both in terms of righteousness to others and piety toward God.[11] He also offered a baptism that was not to put away sin (i.e., not to replace sacrifices), but for purification. Josephus notes that many were moved by John's teaching. So Herod locked John up at the fortress of Machaerus before executing him. The summary from Josephus parallels the Gospel portrait and supplements it. Josephus lacks mention of a forerunner motif from John and any note of eschatology in his teaching, but that may well be because he is trying to placate the Romans

10. On issues surrounding this identification and the views tied to it, see Harold Hoehner, *Herod Antipas: A Contemporary of Jesus Christ,* SNTSMS 17 (Cambridge: Cambridge University Press, 1972), 131–39. He argues that the difference between Josephus and the Gospels is simply that the figure in question had two names, with each source using one of them. Chapter 7 of his book works through this passage in detail.

11. References to "virtue" put John's teaching in a Greek light, because that is a popular summary term in Greek wisdom for a call to ethical living. Josephus is sensitive to his audience here. This fits the historian's emphases (*Ant.* 16.2.4 §42; 7.14.2 §§338, 342; 7.14.5 §356; 7.14.10 §374; 7.15.1 §384; 9.11.2 §236; *War* 2.8.7 §139). See Steve Mason, *Flavius Josephus on the Pharisees: A Composition-Critical Study,* Studia Post-biblica 39 (Leiden: Brill, 1991), 85–89. That Josephus and the Gospels parallel each other is noted by Mason, *Josephus and the New Testament* (Peabody, Mass.: Hendrickson, 1992), 154–55, although Mason seems to question excessively whether John really pointed to Jesus as his forerunner. Mason's position is quite common among those who study John the Baptist, especially John's doubt about Jesus as seen in Luke 7:18–23. However, the rationale for questioning whether John pointed to Jesus as forerunner seems to underestimate how people can move to moments of doubt when events do not go as they expected.

about the Jews and thus omits the mention of these potentially disturbing ideas.

21. Jesus' Baptism (Matt. 3:13–17; Mark 1:9–11; Luke 3:21–22)
(Aland §18; Orchard §22; Huck-Greeven §18)

Mark describes Jesus' baptism with minimal detail. He simply relates that John baptized Jesus in the Jordan and notes the testimony of the heavenly voice. But one point of the detail is quite significant. Mark makes it clear that it was Jesus who saw the heavens open and the Spirit descend like a dove. In other words, the evangelist portrays Jesus having a private experience. Mark is the only Gospel writer who makes this clear. There is no indication of a crowd reaction in any of the Synoptics, also suggesting a private event. John's Gospel adds the note that John the Baptist saw this testimony to Jesus, but by making him a unique witness, the Gospel also seems to exclude it as a wider public event (John 1:32–34). The "opening of the heavens" depicts how God is actively crossing into acting in history in a way unlike how he normally operates. The Greek in Mark is unique, using σχίζειν to speak of a ripping open of heaven. The background here may well be Isa. 63:11, 14, and 64:1, which, looking back at the exodus, extol God's saving power through Moses by means of God's Spirit. The connection suggests hope for something similar in the final deliverance.[12] The additional association of the dove and the Spirit may evoke "new creation" imagery based on possible but disputed background from Gen. 1:2.[13]

The divine voice from heaven explains who Jesus is. In both Mark and Luke, the voice says, "You are my beloved Son; with you I am well pleased." The mixture of first and second persons in the remarks here supports the view that this was a private experience. God is affirming Jesus' role to him as God identifies with John's call that the era of fulfillment comes. In effect, then, the baptism pictures an affirmation of Jesus' role and call by God through the Spirit.[14] It also represents Jesus' endorsement of John's message for the nation. That God's confirmation comes during John's baptism connects Jesus and John. John's message of approaching divine deliverance is embraced by Jesus.

12. Joel Marcus, *The Way of the Lord: Christological Exegesis of the Old Testament in the Gospel of Mark* (Louisville: Westminster/John Knox, 1992), 49–50.

13. Dale Allison, "The Baptism of Jesus and a New Dead Sea Scroll," *Biblical Archaeology Review* 18 (1992): 58–60. He appeals to a text known as the "messianic vision" fragment. The text itself is presented by R. H. Eisenman in *Biblical Archaeology Review* 17 (1991): 65.

14. Craig Blomberg, *Jesus and the Gospels* (Nashville: Broadman & Holman, 1997), 222, rightly speaks of an incipient Trinitarianism residing in the event.

The language of "beloved Son" and one with whom "God is pleased" recalls two ancient texts. One is Ps. 2:7, which attributes sonship to the chosen king of the nation. The other is Isa. 42:1, which highlights God's acceptance and election of a servant to represent him and show the way to his deliverance. Exactly what type of kingship we have and whom he battles remain to be seen.

Luke's portrayal is a virtual match to Mark, with a few important differences. (1) Luke notes that Jesus' baptism took place in a setting where "all the people were baptized." Jesus was doing what many others were doing when the affirmation was made. He was like them. However, the divine voice makes it clear that Jesus also is unique. He shares in the baptism as the one who is called to lead the people John calls to repent. (2) Luke virtually removes John as a character in the event; his name is lacking in the summary of this event. Luke simply notes that Jesus "had been baptized." It is obvious contextually that John is implied here, but his role is less prominent. Luke emphasizes the event as totally divinely wrought. (3) Luke associates the moment of baptism with Jesus praying. Luke often will be alone in highlighting how certain events took place in the context of prayer. (4) Luke will offer commentary on this anointing by the Spirit later in his Gospel. For Luke, Jesus' giving of the Spirit represents a key eschatological blessing that begins an era of the realization of promise. So the one who will give the Spirit is pictured as having received the Spirit directly from heaven. The anointing enables him for the task and points to the launching of a new era—at least that is how Jesus explains it in a subsequent synagogue sermon as he notes the fulfillment of Isaianic promise there in referring back to this baptism (Isa. 61:1–2; Luke 4:16–19).

Matthew is both similar to and distinct from his fellow evangelists. He also notes how Jesus came from Galilee to be baptized by John. However, before Jesus is baptized, Matthew notes a discussion that the two have as John seeks to prevent Jesus from submitting to his baptism. John expresses his need to be baptized by Jesus. Clearly, Matthew wishes to suggest that John had some awareness of the greater role that Jesus has, pointing to the stronger one to come, whom Matthew had just mentioned in 3:11. Also, this implies that John did not sense that Jesus needed to engage in the baptism, because perhaps such an act by Jesus would be perceived as a declaration of the personal need for forgiveness of sins. Perceptions aside, Jesus saw a more important need to press ahead with the baptism. Whatever the objection that John had, Jesus retorted that he needed to engage in the baptism to "fulfill all righteousness." Jesus seems to be suggesting here a need to identify with John's ministry and call to the nation before he goes out to complete what John has started. Jesus' connection to Israel as a whole compelled him to respond to John's call and the nation's need for preparatory cleansing. Matthew also notes the descent of the Spirit like a dove, but he relates the voice from heaven slightly differently. The voice says, "This is [not 'you are'] my beloved son, with whom [not 'you'] I am well pleased." Matthew relates the point for his readers as a time when God marked out Jesus for the task. Matthew gives the historical effect of the event.[15]

When we look at John's ministry and Jesus' baptism together, we see a prophet of God in John, who heralds the approach of a new era of deliverance from God. The drawing near of this time points to a need that God's people be morally prepared. Thus, John's unique baptism expressed a person's acceptance of this call to be ready morally for the new era, an act that would express itself in an ethical and considerate lifestyle with one's neighbors. Not surprisingly, John expected a greater figure to come after him who would bring either blessing or judgment as the eschatological agent of God. This one John called "the stronger one to come." Judaism had long anticipated such a dominating figure to bring in the promised blessing. John noted that this figure would identify himself by baptizing not with water but with the Spirit. So when Jesus is baptized, the Spirit falls upon him, and the voice confirms the call to Jesus (and to the readers of the Gospels) by identifying Jesus as the beloved Son, in whom God is pleased. Jesus' submission to John's baptism represents Jesus' identification with the approach of the special time that John preaches about and an acceptance of the fact that people prepare for this time by seeking forgiveness in the context of repentance. John's baptism, given uniquely to this period, makes that preparatory statement until the arrival of the greater baptism from the stronger one to come, signaling the arrival of a new era of fresh blessing.

22. Luke's Genealogy of Jesus (Luke 3:23–38) (Aland §19; Orchard §23; Huck-Greeven §19)

The form of this genealogy is unique to Luke; he traces the line of Jesus back to Adam, the son of God. This highlights Luke's universal perspective, in contrast to Matthew's genealogy, which goes back only to Abraham to highlight a connection to Israel's patriarch. Luke's ending also sets up the temptation of the Son of God as an act by the one who represents humanity, succeeding where the previous son of God, Adam, failed. The line passes through Nathan as the descendant of David, also in contrast to Matthew, who runs the line through Solomon. Some argue that this is to give Jesus a prophetic mantle over a messianic one, but this is unlikely in light of the messianic stress in Luke's infancy account. Depending on how one reads some textual variants, the list can be cast in eleven groups of seven in contrast to Matthew's three groups of fourteen.

15. Robert H. Stein, *Jesus the Messiah: A Survey of the Life of Christ* (Downers Grove, Ill.: InterVarsity, 1996), 99. Stein also notes how the *Gospel of the Nazareans* records a discussion between Jesus and his family in which Jesus suggests that there is no need for him to accept this baptism, unless perhaps it is for sins of ignorance. See fragment 2 as reported by Jerome, *Against Pelagius* 3.2. The Synoptics lack any kind of statement like this from Jesus.

Luke also notes the timing of Jesus' ministry by pointing out that Jesus began his ministry at about thirty years of age. He also affirms the virgin birth again here by noting that Joseph was the "supposed" father of Jesus. The remark indicates that the genealogy is Joseph's. However, the line is merely a "legal" one, tracing the roots of his earthly "father." In Jesus' patriarchal society, his legal status would come through his father.[16]

23. The Temptations of Jesus (Matt. 4:1–11; Mark 1:12–13; Luke 4:1–13) (Aland §20; Orchard §24; Huck-Greeven §20)

Immediately following the baptism, Jesus is directed into the desert, an act that both prepares him for his ministry and sets up a test of his qualifications for it. This experience was a private one. It must have been passed on to the disciples at a later date, as most spiritual experiences of such intensity would be. Each Gospel is clear that Jesus ended up in the wilderness as a result of the Spirit's direction. Alone except for his God and the animals of creation, Jesus was tempted by Satan.

Mark's account is the shortest of the three, mentioning only the Spirit's direction, the duration of the temptations as forty days, and the presence of the wild beasts. The forty days recall the period that Moses spent before receiving the law (Deut. 9:9). A new era has a parallel introduction. The wild beasts may suggest both a note of potential danger and of Jesus' ability to survive alone in that hostile environment.[17] The *Testament of Naphtali* 8.4 reads, "If you achieve the good, my children, men and angels will bless you; and God will be glorified through you among the gentiles. The devil will flee from you; wild animals will be afraid of you, and the angels will stand by you."[18] This extra-biblical text looks to the eschaton, but it well expresses the idea that righteousness ultimately is protected from all that threatens it. The tone of the temptation accounts is the same.

Matthew and Luke present more detail, though in a differing sequence. Matthew's order of temptations is turning stone to bread, protection in a leap from the temple, and worshiping Satan in exchange for the kingdoms of the world. Luke's order reverses the second and third temptations. Matthew has the tighter temporal markers in 4:5, 10, 11. Luke uses only "and" (καί) as well

16. For a detailed consideration of the relationship between the genealogies of Matthew and Luke, see Bock, *Luke 1:1–9:50*, 918–23.

17. Jeffrey Gibson, "Jesus' Wilderness Temptation according to Mark," *Journal for the Study of the New Testament* 53 (1994): 3–34; idem, *The Temptations of Jesus in Early Christianity*, JSNTSup 112 (Sheffield: Sheffield Academic, 1995).

18. H. C. Kee, trans., "Testaments of the Twelve Patriarchs," in *The Old Testament Pseudepigrapha*, ed. James H. Charlesworth (Garden City, N.Y.: Doubleday, 1983–85), 1:813.

as "but" or "and" in a thematic sense (δέ).[19] In addition, Matthew has a clear dismissal of Satan at the account's end. Thus, it is likely that Luke has rearranged the order because he wants to highlight the temple confrontation, given the way that he highlights Jerusalem as the place of the key conflict in 9:51 to the end of his Gospel.

Each temptation challenges Jesus' faithfulness. Will he provide for himself independently of God's direction and draw on his power in self-interest (bread)? Will he insist that God protect him by putting God to the test of his protection of the Son (temple)? Will the Son defect from the Father and worship someone else for his own gain (kingdoms)? In each text Jesus stresses his loyalty to the Father as he cites Deuteronomy. There is more to life than bread; obedience is more important than food (Deut. 8:3—bread; only Matthew's version cites the whole verse; Luke leaves the note about obedience unexpressed but implied). Testing God's faithfulness implies a doubt of him and should not be done (Deut. 6:16—temple). Worship and service should be given only to God (Deut. 6:13—kingdoms). Honoring God drives Jesus, not self-interest or self-benefit. In this way Jesus succeeds against Satan where the previous representative of humanity (Adam) failed.

Satan addresses Jesus as "Son of God," a title that appropriately follows the baptism. Luke's fresh placement of the two events in juxtaposition is no accident. Luke places the account after Adam is named as "son of God" in the genealogy to highlight Jesus' representational role. Thus, Luke's use of the title carries an additional nuance that it lacks in Matthew. Sonship is important here because the cosmic battle indicates that more than Jesus' messianic status is under challenge. Satan seeks to undermine the intimate connection between Jesus as Son and the Father. Jesus will not do it, because for him the Father functions as "the Lord God." Two of the replies use this title for God. In showing how God is seen, Jesus underscores that an appreciation of God's unique position and the loyalty that that position demands are the grounds for resisting temptation. Jesus shows himself fully qualified to represent humanity and exemplify the way to victory. His faithfulness is the model held up to disciples under pressure for their choice to walk in God's way. The devil departs, having failed to deter the Son. The ministry of angels tangibly shows heaven's support, as even the text quoted above from the *Testament of Naphtali* indicates.

Conclusion

Jesus enters into ministry through the door opened for him by John the Baptist calling people to recognize that a new era approaches for which their

---

19. The particle δέ can indicate either a contrast or simply a transition to a new unit. It is a looser term than καί.

hearts must be ready. God seeks a prepared people to walk in his paths. That requires a heart turned in faithfulness to him and expressing itself in concern for others. Jesus enters into ministry with the heavens opened to him by God in the provision of the Spirit. It is only right that the beloved Servant-Son would be endowed with heavenly enablement, for the new era itself will come with a similar baptism that he, as the stronger one to come, will provide. Jesus enters into ministry with the temptations in the wilderness behind him and the snares of Satan overcome. Jesus, in his faithful, unswerving focus on the Father, shows himself capable of representing humanity in a way that an earlier "son of God" had dismally failed to do. The forerunner has pointed the way, God has opened the way, and the devil has failed to block the way as Jesus embarks on his ministry to proclaim and bring the promise of God.

FOUR

The Initial Portrait of Jesus' Galilean Ministry

Teaching, Healing, and Controversy
(Matt. 4:12–25; Mark 1:14–3:19a; Luke 4:14–6:16)

Jesus did things that got him into trouble and caused controversy. His choice to participate in table fellowship with the unlikely, his choice to do things on the Sabbath that were considered by others to be sacrilegious, and especially his act of turning tables upside down in the temple courts during a holy festival— each, in its own way, provoked heated controversy, accusations, and exchange, not to mention questionings, plots, and machinations on the part of the establishment. Alongside these acts we should note his choice of the twelve, surely a symbol for the restoration of the twelve tribes of Israel and the end-time reconstitution of Israel. These deeds are to be understood in the category of "prophetic symbolic acts" and not simply as "acts of compassion" performed by one who, in needing and wanting to reach out to people in mercy, could not comprehend what all the fuss was about. In each of these acts, Jesus knew what he was doing and what others would say—and he did them because of what others *would* do and say! These acts reveal Jesus, at least in his mission and self-understanding of his relation to God, as one who had a mission to Israel.[1]

Looming large in the Gospels and no doubt in his actual ministry, Jesus' miracle-working activity played an integral part in his being able to attract attention, both positive and negative. His miracle-working activity not only supported but also dramatized and actualized his eschatological message, and it may have contributed to some degree to the alarm felt by the authorities who

---

1. Scot McKnight, *A New Vision for Israel: The Teachings of Jesus in National Context* (Grand Rapids: Eerdmans, 1999), 7.

finally brought about his death. Any historian who seeks to portray the historical Jesus without giving due weight to his fame as a miracle-worker is not delineating this strange, complex Jew, but rather a domesticated Jesus reminiscent of the bland moralist created by Thomas Jefferson.[2]

These two statements, the first by an evangelical scholar and the second by a critical scholar, summarize the character of Jesus' ministry and typify key elements of the Synoptics' portrayal of his early ministry. Jesus' actions and his miracles created both interest in himself and controversy about him. His actions recalled the prophets, yet they suggested that something more than just another prophet was present. They represented a mission to Israel in line with prophetic hope and evoked the arrival of a special time of God's activity. These events set the tone for all that follows in the Synoptics.

We consider Jesus' ministry up to the point where Matthew recounts the Sermon on the Mount and Luke has its equivalent, the Sermon on the Plain. Most of the passages follow a sequence given in Mark and Luke, while Matthew places many of these controversial miracles after the Sermon on the Mount.[3] I will suggest that there are reasons to see some topical groupings here in the sequence of controversies traced in Mark 2:1–3:6 and Luke 5:17–6:11. Still, it is just as important to note that these groupings bring to the surface why Jesus' ministry became so controversial. That role justifies the narrative placement given to them in these Gospels. As such, they serve well in exactly the role that Mark and Luke give to them. These controversies introduce us to the character of Jesus' actions and how those actions prompted the opposition of the Jewish leadership to him. What Jesus did was so directed toward Israel that it demanded the attention of Israel's religious leadership. This conflict over authority is one of the key narrative lines of argument in the Synoptics' portrait of Jesus. Each of the Synoptics follows the temptations with a short summary about Jesus' ministry in Galilee. It is here that we pick up the story again.

24. Jesus' Preaching in Galilee (Matt. 4:12–17; Mark 1:14–15; Luke 4:14–15) (Aland §§30, 32; Orchard §§36, 39; Huck-Greeven §21)

Each Gospel introduces and summarizes the Galilean ministry uniquely. Matthew notes that it was the arrest of John the Baptist that leads Jesus to with-

---

2. John Meier, *A Marginal Jew: Rethinking the Historical Jesus,* 2 vols., ABRL (New York: Doubleday, 1994), 2:970.

3. In these chapters where we survey events shared by the various Gospels, the Gospel whose order we are following is listed first. In this section Mark is often the lead, although where he and Matthew overlap exactly, Matthew is listed first.

draw to Galilee. This suggests that he was elsewhere first. Matthew does not tell the story behind the arrest and death of John until Matt. 14:3–12. The interval may suggest that John was in prison for some time. Matthew then goes on to note that Jesus moved from Nazareth, which was his home, to Capernaum by the sea, a larger village in the region of Zebulun and Naphtali. Matthew closes the overview by noting that this act fulfilled Isa. 9:1–2, a section where the prophet sets forth the promise of a delivering king. The important feature of the citation is that it describes the area as "Galilee of the Gentiles—the people who sat in darkness have seen a great light, and for those who sat in the land of the shadow of death light has dawned." The picture of the promise of light associated with a delivering figure is how Luke begins his Gospel in Zechariah's *Benedictus* (Luke 1:78–79). There, Luke also brings in concern for the Gentiles.

For Matthew, the light is both Jesus and the message he heralds, "Repent, for the kingdom of heaven is at hand." The rule of God draws near in this figure. It is a rule that comes from heaven. The reader should not miss the point of juxtaposing Isa. 9 to the call to repent and the announcement of the kingdom. Jesus calls for Israel to prepare for restoration and deliverance, a salvation promised long ago. Although it is Israel that is called to recognize its approach, the message is heralded in a Gentile region, showing the mixed ethnic focus that will emerge in Jesus' ministry.

Mark is similar to Matthew. Jesus came into Galilee after John was arrested. In Galilee, Jesus preached the gospel. Mark lacks any specific location, unlike Matthew, but the content of the message is similar, "The time is fulfilled, and the kingdom of God is at hand; repent, and believe in the gospel." By sandwiching the remark between two uses of the term "gospel," Mark is identifying this message about the approach of God's rule as the gospel. This idea is reinforced by the fact that the term "gospel" appears three times in Mark 1:1–15. To believe the gospel means to prepare for the kingdom's coming as the sent one announces it. This text also suggests that what Matthew means by the kingdom of heaven (or, possibly better, from heaven) equals what Mark calls the kingdom of God. Matthew prefers the reference to heaven in all likelihood to show respect for the person of God by avoiding naming him. This reflects typical Jewish custom. The different name also highlights this promised rule's origin as residing in heaven, a rule distinct from that which originates on the earth.

One other point is significant. Jesus' message in Mark 1:15 is very similar to John's in Mark 1:4, but there is significant intensification. Fulfillment is noted here, where it was not present with John. The term "gospel" is associated with Jesus but is not mentioned with John. In this way Mark elevates Jesus' message over John's and also suggests that what John merely had announced was now drawing very near indeed.[4]

---

4. Larry W. Hurtado, *Mark,* New International Biblical Commentary 2 (Peabody, Mass.: Hendrickson, 1989), 21–22.

Luke, in line with his characteristic emphasis on the Spirit, has Jesus directed into Galilee by God's Spirit and has no mention of John's arrest, having already noted it in 3:19–20. It is the Spirit-enabled Jesus who ministers to the people. Luke does not mention the kingdom of God or repentance here, as he chooses to summarize Jesus' message in the synagogue scene that follows. Somewhat enigmatically, Luke notes that a report about Jesus went throughout the surrounding country. Luke leaves the details about what Jesus did to generate such a report for later. He simply notes that Jesus taught in the synagogues and was being "glorified" (i.e., praised) by all. Luke follows this note with his first summary of Jesus' teaching, a sample of his message from a synagogue in Nazareth. This event typifies his Galilean ministry as a whole and serves as a developed equivalent of Matthew and Mark's summary that Jesus preached repentance and the nearness of the kingdom. What Matthew and Mark say in words, Luke shows in actions.

25. Jesus Preaches in Nazareth (Luke 4:16–30; Matt. 13:53–58 and Mark 6:1–6a place this incident later) (Aland §33; Orchard §38; Huck-Greeven §22)

Jesus' preaching in the synagogue at Nazareth is significant for three reasons. First, Luke has placed the event in a setting entirely different from that in Matthew and Mark. Luke's relocating the event is suggested by the allusion in 4:23 to Jesus doing work in Nazareth like that which the crowd had heard about him doing in Capernaum, even though in Luke there has not yet been a ministry in Capernaum. (In fact, the Capernaum events follow right after this scene.) Thus, this event is a good example of a redactional choice by an evangelist to order things for reasons other than chronology.[5] This event typifies Jesus' ministry, both in his proclamation of his role in a key new time of God's work and in the hostile reaction that his claim generates.

Second, the text represents how Jesus fused together the claims about himself with claims about the nature of the time of which he is a part. In the Synoptics, this fusion often is how Jesus explains who he is. The appeal to texts from the second portion of Isaiah, namely, Isa. 61:1–2 and 58:6, associates Jesus' ministry with the story of the promised deliverance of the Jewish nation from sin and exile. In part, Jesus is important because with him

---

5. It seems likely that Matthew and Mark contain the event's approximate, temporal location. Matthew and Mark are sufficiently similar in depicting the crowd's reaction to Jesus to equate this event with Luke's account. Another point is that Luke's disclosure of Jesus' synagogue message probably should be seen at a literary level as representative of what he preached in other synagogues, although the claims are most poignant in Nazareth, where they knew him so well.

comes the hope of promised deliverance. Thus, the citation from the Old Testament stresses his mission and what he brings as much as or more than who he is. It is God's actions that Jesus carries out. It is his program that is being proclaimed and realized. Jesus portrays himself as an anointed agent who declares release, making an analogy with the year of Jubilee (Lev. 25:8–13). However, unlike the Old Testament, which merely proclaimed the release, Jesus effects that deliverance. Those in need, the poor, the blind, and the captive are the beneficiaries of his work. Forgiveness of sins, which is what is required to reverse such captivity, is at the center of his work. Jesus' work seeks to restore God's people to their proper place. When Jesus says, "Today this scripture is fulfilled in your hearing," he is declaring an end to the nation's judgment and that the promise of God's long-expected deliverance has come in his message and acts. God's Spirit has enabled him for this task. The implication of this declaration, when it is placed alongside the call that will be a part of the mission of the disciples in Luke 9–10, is that Jesus calls for the people to embrace the approaching kingdom program of God. This message of kingdom arrival is Jesus' gospel (see Luke 9:2, 6). Thus, although Luke does not use the terminology here of the shorter summaries in Matt. 4 and Mark 1, conceptually he is presenting in more explicit detail the same fundamental message. The one difference is that Luke more prominently displays Jesus' central role as the proclaiming and effecting figure. In contrast, the other Synoptics merely set forth the basic call to respond to the kingdom.

Third, this text pulls together Luke's story at the literary level. When in Luke 4:18 Jesus describes himself as anointed, there is a potential ambiguity unless we pay attention to Luke's story up to this point. If we were to take this scene simply as its own independent unit, we might conclude that Jesus merely is making a prophetic claim to be a prophet who announces the eschaton. From this limited perspective, the scene itself stresses God's act as Jesus' primary concern, not Jesus' own identity. After all, the passage highlights the preaching of a message with Jesus identifying himself as a prophet (vv. 18–19 [3x], 24, and the examples are prophetic in vv. 25–27 [Elijah, Elisha]). God has enabled Jesus to bring this message. But if from a narrative standpoint we ask when the anointing that Jesus describes in 4:18 took place, immediately we are driven back in Luke's story to Jesus' baptism. There, a heavenly voice identified Jesus not merely as a prophet but as "my beloved Son, in whom I am well pleased." The fusion of language from Ps. 2 and Isa. 42 points to a royal and proclaiming figure, the messianic servant. This figure will both represent his people and proclaim God's will to them, even as he leads and delivers them. Thus, Luke's initial presentation of Jesus' teaching highlights both the activity of God and Jesus' messianic role within that activity, directing us to recall who the voice from heaven identified him to be. The point of Luke's placement is not to focus on any one of these ideas but to present all of them together.

Jesus' mission and identity are not all that makes this passage so significant. In citing both Isa. 61 and 58, Jesus juxtaposes two distinct contexts.[6] In one there is the hope of the proclamation of deliverance (Isa. 61), but in the other there is the naming of Israel's failure. Isaiah 58 describes how the people of the nation fast. The people stand rebuked because they fast without really honoring God by their life even as they engage in this seeming act of worship. The call in Isa. 58 is to do a better job of responding to God— in other words, to repent. The passage is typical of a prophetic denunciation of the failure of the nation. When Jesus claims to release the captives described in the language of Isa. 58, he is claiming to take on a responsibility that the nation itself had been called to perform but had failed to execute. His task is to follow the lead that John the Baptist already had taken. The Baptist had called on the people to respond properly to God. To effect this turn, they now must respond properly to Jesus, the anointed messenger who follows John.

This theme of the nation's failure carries right through the passage. When in 4:22 the crowd reacts to Jesus initially with some hesitation because he is the son of Joseph, Jesus presses the point to show how telling their hesitancy is. He notes that they will challenge him to do what he has done elsewhere, while pointing out that a prophet does not receive honor in his own country. He then appeals to two examples from the past, Elijah and Elisha. They ministered in another low period of Israel's history, as is indicated by the fact that Elijah was a prophet during a three-and-a-half-year drought. That drought was a judgment for Israel's failure. In addition, Jesus highlights that the only people ministered to by these two prophets were a widow from Sidon and a leper from Syria, both Gentiles. In other words, only those outside the nation were blessed. Jesus' remarks make a shaming comparison and imply a warning that the present period is potentially one of Israel's lowest spiritual moments. That in part explains why Jesus must come and preach release. Their captivity is not merely the one that Rome has imposed on them, as these synagogue attendees thought, but one of their own doing. The ideas that God's people are in such need out of their own doing and that a messianic ministry may end up extending blessing to outsiders produced anger in the crowd. Jesus had called those in the nation sinners and had suggested that God might even reach out to those they hated, to Gentiles.

In turning the tables on these expectant people, Jesus confronted them with a choice even as he offered them great hope. To accept him and his

---

6. For a full discussion of the Christology and debate surrounding this text, see Darrell L. Bock, *Luke 1:1–9:50,* BECNT 3A (Grand Rapids: Baker, 1994), 404–13.

message was to acknowledge their failure and need. To share in the opportunity of deliverance, a person had to acknowledge his or her own unrighteousness and distance from God. Grace comes not to those who deserve it but to those who know they have no right to it. The message of hope also held out a prospect of judgment if one did not respond. Those in Jesus' audience found this challenging of their status hard to accept, so they sought to take him out and toss him over the edge of a cliff. This is the first Lukan glance at rejection during Jesus' ministry; it will become a consistent theme throughout his account. Jesus walks away because it is not yet time for rejection to play its full hand. There is both opportunity and risk in the message of Jesus.

26. The Calling of the Disciples (Matt. 4:18–22; Mark 1:16–20)
(Aland §34; Orchard §40; Huck-Greeven §23)

This account is very similar in Matthew and Mark and comes very early in the presentation of Jesus' ministry. It highlights that Jesus sought followers, those dedicated to his mission, from the earliest moments of his ministry. Jesus' work never was going to be a "loner" operation.

The selection of fishermen among the followers is significant. Jesus was choosing people from everyday walks of life. Fishing was a major industry in Galilee. These men even had "hired servants" (Mark 1:20), showing that they were among the closest thing to a middle class that existed at the time. The nets being cast in Mark and Matthew are "circular casting nets," typical of the region.[7] Around the nets were attached stones that caused them to sink, so they could be dragged and catch the fish.

Jesus challenges the fishermen with a call to follow him and be fishers of people. The remark is typical of Jesus' teaching style. He takes an everyday element and makes a metaphorical image from it that depicts a deeper theological call or reality. Luke 5:1–11 makes a similar conceptual play around a miracle tied to fishing. Many think that the "fishers of people" image comes from Jer. 16:16, where clearly it refers to judgment before God does his restoring work in Israel and among the nations.[8] The goal is to deal with sin and show that God is Lord. On the other hand, the image in Ezek. 47:10 is more positive. Here, in the new work that God will do in the end, the water will swarm with fish. Fish in the river flowing by the temple will be as plentiful as those in the Mediterranean. It perhaps is best to see a mix here, as the image of Matt. 13:47–50 suggests, because the invitation to grace also is an occasion to face

7. BAGD, 47; BDAG, 55.
8. David Garland, *Mark,* NIV Application Commentary (Grand Rapids: Zondervan, 1996), 69, also notes Ezek. 29:4; 47:10; Amos 4:2; Hab. 1:14–17.

judgment if it is rejected.[9] The call to be a part of the kingdom will extend to all people, but how they relate to it depends on their response.

Jesus' call to follow him is not really like the call of the rabbis or the prophets. This call is unlike the way Elisha followed after Elijah in 1 Kings 19:19–21.[10] Elisha followed and served Elijah, but not because Elijah "called" him. Discipleship became possible only after Elisha delayed following in order to meet family obligations. In contrast to those who followed rabbis and continued a trade, Jesus' specially chosen disciples leave everything to dedicate themselves fully to following the call (Luke 9:61). Also in contrast to the rabbinic model, the one being followed chooses them, whereas students of rabbis chose whom they would follow. In the remark about following him, Jesus personalizes the model of discipleship. They do not go after law or teaching in abstraction, but rather, learn to model themselves after a person. The call to follow Jesus was more demanding and urgent than anything that preceded it. Both accounts highlight that discipleship meant leaving behind the former primary commitment to family as well as abandoning the family's vocation.

27. Teaching in the Synagogue at Capernaum (Mark 1:21–22; Luke 4:31–32) (Aland §35; Orchard §41; Huck-Greeven §24a)

At this point Matthew leaves the sequence of events as he summarizes the activity of Jesus' ministry after giving a full sample of his teaching in the Sermon on the Mount. Thus, many of the events that Mark and Luke present now, Matthew saves for portions of Matt. 8–9.

One of the details in Jesus' ministry that shows his ongoing tie to Judaism is that he continued to participate in the synagogue. In fact, as this passage notes, he taught there on the Sabbath. Mark adds that Jesus went immediately to Capernaum. This city was located on the lakefront, just west of where the Jordan River enters the Sea of Galilee. It was known for its lush environment (Josephus, *War* 3.10.8 §§516–519). It appears to have housed a Roman garrison, which is why a later passage will discuss a centurion (Matt. 8:5–13; Luke 7:1–10). The city also collected taxes for Herod. Its population probably was one to two thousand.[11]

9. Robert Gundry, *Mark: A Commentary on His Apology for the Cross* (Grand Rapids: Eerdmans, 1993), 72. See also 1QH 5.7–8 (= col. 13), where the image is likewise associated with judgment.

10. Gundry, *Mark*, 66, 70.

11. Richard Horsley, *Galilee: History, Politics, and People* (Valley Forge, Pa.: Trinity Press International, 1995), 193–94.

Luke also gives his first summary of the scope of Jesus' ministry while discussing events in Capernaum. Luke does not mention the synagogue but does note that the teaching took place on the Sabbath. The locale is the synagogue, as the next Lukan scene opens there (see 4:33).

Both Mark and Luke stress the authority inherent in Jesus' teaching.[12] Mark specifically contrasts that teaching with the scribes. Matthew 7:29, at the end of the Sermon of the Mount, has a similar emphasis. Authority—both its presence in Jesus and the claim for it in his teaching and action—is a major theme of all the Synoptics. Whereas Jewish teaching frequently appealed to outside authorities such as Scripture or tradition or both, often with explicit appeal to rabbis who had gone before, Jesus addressed topics directly without such appeal, except occasionally when he appealed to Scripture. But there may be something more implied here, as the following accounts will specify. Teaching is one key element of Jesus' ministry. The second element, his acts, is noted next. Both come with authority. That authority points to a cosmic struggle and a new age.

28. The Healing of the Demoniac in the Synagogue
(Mark 1:23–28; Luke 4:33–37) (Aland §36; Orchard §42; Huck-Greeven §24b)

Jesus' actions were a decisive part of his ministry. Among the key acts of Jesus were his miracles. Among the miracles, exorcisms are particularly significant. It is no accident that in both Mark and Luke the first miracle that Jesus performs is the healing of a demoniac. (For Matthew, the first miracle is a leper cleansing, and the first exorcism involves the Gadarene demoniacs.) For

12. For the importance of this text to Mark, see Robert Stein, "The 'redactionsgeschichtlich' Investigation of a Marcan Seam (Mc 1:21ff.)," *Zeitschrift für die neutestamentliche Wissenschaft und die Kunde der älteren Kirche* 61 (1970): 70–94. This article also appears in his *Gospels and Tradition: Studies on Redaction Criticism of the Synoptic Gospels* (Grand Rapids: Baker, 1991), 69–96. Stein seeks to discover Mark's emphases by how he links passages together by means of these seams. He notes that although Mark has little discourse material, his Gospel does use the term "teacher" twelve times to describe Jesus' work. R. T. France, "Mark and the Teaching of Jesus," in *Gospel Perspectives: Studies of History and Tradition in the Four Gospels*, vol. 1, ed. R. T. France and David Wenham (Sheffield: JSOT, 1980), 101–36, notes that Mark is filled with numerous pronouncement accounts. One pronouncement from Jesus often is all that is needed (p. 106). As France says, "A 'new teaching' was apparently to be part of the messianic age, so that the Messiah would be expected to accomplish his mission in word as well as deed, and this Mark shows Jesus doing. . . . The kingdom is established as much in his teaching as in his works" (p. 111). France argues that teaching is more important to Mark than is thought to be the case by those who have argued that Mark tends to focus on the recording of deeds. As France rightly notes, absence of teaching blocks does not equal absence of teaching. Jesus' teaching is highlighted in Mark through the many key, decisive pronouncements.

example, Mark contains thirteen miracle accounts, and four of them are exorcisms (Mark 1:23–28; 5:1–20; 7:24–30; 9:14–29).[13] Exorcism is the most frequently occurring type of healing in Mark. Exorcism accounts have a clear form: (1) initial dramatic confrontation, (2) the words of the demons, (3) the words of exorcism, (4) the demon's plea, and (5) the (violent) cure.[14] In some accounts far more detail about the condition of the possessed person is added to set the scene (see esp. Mark 5:1–20). A comparison of the exorcisms of Jesus with accounts of other ancient exorcists shows that Jesus is not that unusual in how he went about performing exorcism, although he did introduce a dimension of unique personal authority that seems to make the confrontation one between him and the demon.[15] In most cases a word from him was all that was needed, in contrast to more involved actions from a normal healer or exorcist.

The exorcism in view here is very similar in Mark and Luke. It has a similar role in each Gospel. The event portrays the authority and cosmic battle in which Jesus is engaged as he declares that fulfillment has come. The setting of the event in the synagogue adds a note of sanctity to the confrontation. The battle takes place in a location where the people of promise pray and worship. Two features are significant in the "words of the demons." First, they seek to gain control of Jesus by asking what Jesus of Nazareth has to do with them.

13. Graham H. Twelftree, *Jesus the Exorcist: A Contribution to the Study of the Historical Jesus* (Peabody, Mass.: Hendrickson, 1993), 3. This is the first miracle account in our sequence. Two excellent treatments of the issues tied to miracles are (evangelical) Twelftree, *Jesus the Miracle Worker: A Historical and Theological Study* (Downers Grove, Ill.: InterVarsity, 1999), and (critical) Meier, *A Marginal Jew*, 2:509–1038. Meier's chapter 18 on ancient parallels is particularly valuable in pointing out the differences between biblical and Greco-Roman miracle accounts, while chapter 17 explains how many critics regard miracles as being outside the sphere of demonstrable historical documentation, speaking strictly historically. In the end, miracles are a matter of worldview and theology. For one who believes that God exists and acts in history, they are possible. For those who discount God's presence or believe that he does not act within history, other explanations for such phenomena will be sought. What both Twelftree and Meier stress is that no strand of the Jesus tradition is as well attested for its presence as the belief that Jesus performed miracles in the eyes of his audience. I would note as well that this reputation even leaves traces in the traditions that come from Jesus' opponents (see chapter 1 of my *Studying the Historical Jesus* [Grand Rapids: Baker, 2002] and the traditions tied to arguing that Jesus was a deceiver and sorcerer). As such, Jesus' reputation as a miracle worker is not easily dismissed.

14. Graham H. Twelftree, "ΕΙ ΔΕ . . . ΕΓΩ ΕΚΒΑΛΛΩ ΤΑ ΔΑΙΜΟΝΙΑ . . . ," in *Gospel Perspectives: Studies of History and Tradition in the Four Gospels,* vol. 6, ed. David Wenham and Craig Blomberg (Sheffield: JSOT, 1986), 361–400, esp. 368–87.

15. Twelftree, "ΕΙ ΔΕ," 383–87. Twelftree notes numerous parallels in his summary. He notes especially in magical papyri the habit of naming that goes on between the demon and the exorcist, appeals to the Most High, and calls for the demon to be "bound" as a way of calling for its silence. See *PGM* 4.1068, 1243–45, 3019; 5.46; 8.6–7, 13; 9.9; 36.164; P.London 121.396, 967 (*Greek Papyri in the British Museum,* vol. 1, ed. F. G. Kenyon [London: British Museum, 1893]).

This kind of remark has precedent in Judg. 11:12; 2 Sam. 19:16–23; 1 Kings 17:18 (= LXX 3 Kingdoms). The "what are you and I?" appears in confrontation contexts and is a way of suggesting that one should have nothing to do with the other. The claim to know who Jesus is, which follows this challenge, represents an attempt to assert this control over a spiritual enemy.[16]

Second, the confession of Jesus as "Holy One" should not be exaggerated as some type of high christological confession. The title "Holy One" is used in the Old Testament of a variety of figures and simply means one who is set apart to serve God (Aaron, Ps. 106:16 [= LXX 105]; Sir. 45:6; Samson, Judg. 16:17 [LXX Codex B]). It is not entirely clear how the demons see Jesus other than that they recognize him to possess an authority that is a threat to them. Working out his exact function is something that Mark is in the process of telling. In all likelihood the confession here could have messianic overtones within the narrative, since already at the baptism Mark has identified Jesus as the Son in royal terms. Regardless, Jesus' call for the demon to be silent has nothing to do with any attempt at keeping his identity secret, but rather is part of the ritual of telling a demon to be bound and thus silent. Although Twelftree calls Jesus' command an "incantation-restriction," it is hard to see an "incantation" in a simple, direct command to come out.[17] Incantations tend to come in some type of formulaic appeal, including the invocation of an external authority.[18] Jesus performs exorcisms in ways that connect to past practice. However, his practice differs in a few details that point to something "new" as present. One example is the idea that he "rebuked" (or better, "commanded") the demon. This term may have roots in parallel Semitic terms at Qumran (גער) that mean "the commanding word, uttered by God or his spokesman," by which evil powers are brought into submission so that the way is prepared for God's righteous rule in the world. It is unattested in Hellenistic contexts, suggesting a Jewish backdrop to this tradition.[19]

The cure is effected with some violence, as this depicts the struggle for the man and his well-being. Mark notes only the violence, while Luke adds that the exorcism resulted in no harm to the man.

The reaction is significant. Mark notes that the crowd calls it "new teaching," while Luke expresses it in terms of what kind of "word" this is.

---

16. Twelftree, "EI ΔE," 374–75.

17. Ibid., 378. For the debate that swirls around this text and a few other Markan texts as part of the debate over Wrede's proposal of a messianic secret in Mark, see Ben Witherington III, *The Christology of Jesus* (Minneapolis: Fortress, 1990), 263–65.

18. The qualification by Edwin Yamauchi is appropriate here: "Magic or Miracle? Diseases, Demons and Exorcisms," in Wenham and Blomberg, eds., *Gospel Perspectives,* vol. 6, 132–33.

19. Howard Clark Kee, "The Terminology of Mark's Exorcism Stories," *New Testament Studies* 14 (1967–69): 232–46, esp. 235. See Zech. 3:2 (of Satan); Ps. 68:31 (= 68:30 Eng.); 106:9; 1QapGen 20.28–29; Joseph A. Fitzmyer, *The Gospel according to Luke,* 2 vols., AB 28, 28A (Garden City, N.Y.: Doubleday, 1981–85), 1:546.

The key is that the action is seen as communicating a powerful message that points to Jesus' authority over cosmic forces of evil. Both Gospels note that he commands the unclean spirits. Mark says that they obey him, while Luke reports the result, that they come out. Jesus is announcing that deliverance has come, and his acts of deliverance are aimed at the unseen forces that bring suffering to the creation. The connection is no accident. So reports begin to spread throughout the whole region, which Mark specifies as Galilee.

29. The Healing of Peter's Mother-in-Law (Mark 1:29–31; Luke 4:38–39; Matt. 8:14–15, in a later context in which he has chosen first to discuss Jesus' miraculous activity) (Aland §37; Orchard §43; Huck-Greeven §25)

The healing of Peter's mother-in-law is the first of several healings noted in Jesus' ministry. Jesus' miracles are multiply attested, appearing in every level of source material about his career. Looking at the miracles as a whole, we see four miracles that deal with some form of paralysis, three that involve blindness with one summary note, two cases of leprosy plus a summary, one of epilepsy (also an exorcism), one of deafness, one replaced ear, and five other individualized miracles (fever, dropsy, sickness [at least twice, one tied to an unclean spirit], hemorrhage).[20] Finally, there are three cases of raising someone from the dead along with one summary note. The miracles as a group show Jesus' work of restoration and point to the arrival of a special time of God's deliverance (Luke 7:22–23 = Matt. 11:4–6).

The healing itself leads us into a discussion that has produced much debate. It often is said that the ancients did not distinguish between disease and demonic possession and that the evangelists take the same approach.[21] However, it seems that occasionally some distinction was made, although in many cases the two do overlap. Thus, in Mark 1:32 two classes of people were brought to Jesus: those who were sick and those who were possessed. The same distinction applies in Mark 1:34 and 6:13. Luke and Matthew also have this distinc-

20. This count from all the Gospels is from Twelftree, *Jesus the Miracle Worker*, 328–29. Twelftree has seventeen miracles plus three raisings from the dead. Meier, *A Marginal Jew*, 2:678, has a total of seventeen miracles including raisings from the dead. Meier's number excludes two Matthean accounts that he regards as doublets. The question of whether the centurion's son is also recounted in John 4 may yield a different number of total healings, reducing the total by one if it is seen to equal Matt. 8 and Luke 7. By contrast, the Gospels note four exorcisms (synagogue demoniac, Gadarene demoniac[s], Syrophoenician daughter, epileptic boy), none of them appearing in John.

21. Note the discussion in Gerd Theissen, *Miracle Stories of the Early Christian Tradition* (Edinburgh: Clark, 1983), 85–90.

tion (Luke 7:21; 9:1–2; 13:32; Acts 5:16; 8:7; Matt. 4:24; 8:16; 10:8).[22] Only in some cases does Luke seem to overlap the two, with the healing of Peter's mother-in-law being one of the possible examples when Jesus "rebukes" the fever in 4:39 with a remark that recalls the rebuke of 4:36 (also Acts 10:38). The rebuke remark is unique to Luke's presentation of this account. There also is the epileptic boy who has an unclean spirit (Luke 9:37–43; Mark 9:14–29; Matt. 17:14–20). The healing of the Syrophoenician daughter is of the same combined type (Mark 7:24–30; Matt. 15:21–28), as is the crippled woman of Luke 13:10–17.

The healing is part of a swirl of events that Mark and Luke record as part of the same day in Capernaum. As is common with a miracle account, the event proceeds in a form that includes (1) the condition described, (2) the approach or request to heal, (3) the act or words of healing, (4) the healing demonstrated, and (5) the reaction. Mark has more detail of the event. He alone notes that Andrew, James, and John are with them. The Lukan omission is simple to explain: he has not yet described how they came to be part of the disciples. Only Luke describes the condition as a "high" fever. Matthew and Mark simply note that the healing took place as Jesus "touched her" (Matthew) or "took her by the hand and lifted her up" (Mark). Thus, only Luke, with his rebuke, notes that anything was said. Luke alone notes how the healing was immediate. The proof of the healing came in her immediate service. Matthew and Luke, using different Greek verbs, say that she "rose up," but they both use the same verb to say she "served them." The picture of the following service is not accidental. As we will see, when we consider Luke 5:1–11, the miracles are not merely events but often are metaphors of deeper realities. In this case, the point is that healing and restoration lead to a grateful response in service.

30. The Sick Healed in the Evening (Mark 1:32–34; Luke 4:40–41; Matt. 8:16–17, in a later context in which he introduces Jesus' activity) (Aland §38; Orchard §44; Huck-Greeven §26)

This summary closes out the day in Capernaum. All the Synoptics distinguish between Jesus' healing the sick and his exorcisms. Mark details that the "whole city" was gathered at the door, showing how Jesus' activity had spread across Capernaum. Only Luke notes the laying of hands on the sick, while only Matthew notes that demons were cast out with a word from Jesus. Jesus was successful, as healing was experienced by "all" (Matthew), "many" (Mark), or "everyone" (Luke). Mark and Luke relate how Jesus prevented the

22. Twelftree, "EI ΔΕ," 362–63.

demons from speaking. Mark's vague "because they knew him" is specified in Luke as "because they knew that he was the Christ." Luke already had uniquely noted the demons' confession of Jesus: "You are the Son of God." This confession was a vain attempt to gain control of the situation by naming the role that Jesus had, one that Luke explains as tied to his "anointed," messianic status. So Luke continues to underline the messianic emphasis of his account that reaches back into the infancy material and the baptismal scene. Matthew identifies Jesus' work as part of the representation he undertakes as the "Servant," citing fulfillment of Isa. 53:4. Jesus takes their diseases and bears their infirmities, which in this context stresses how he delivers them from these maladies, not that he is a sacrificial substitute on their behalf. Many in the church today defend healing miracles on the basis of this text, but ultimately Jesus' work moves beyond this physical healing to full spiritual restoration. In doing so, Isa. 53 becomes a key text for showing how physical healing points to a more significant spiritual healing, a theme that the healings as a whole develop in the Gospels. Thus, these summaries in Matthew and Luke explain the significance of Jesus' activity, whereas in Mark they simply describe his work.

31. Jesus Leaves Capernaum (Mark 1:35–38; Luke 4:42–43)
(Aland §39; Orchard §45; Huck-Greeven §27)

This summary results in a pronouncement about Jesus' mission and comes after Jesus withdrew from the crowds to a lonely place. Mark adds the detail that he was praying, something that Luke lacks even though he often highlights Jesus praying.

The differences between Mark and Luke largely are reflecting the fact that Luke has not yet mentioned the gathering of disciples. So in Mark the suggestion is for "us" to go on to the next towns, while in Luke the pronouncement is put strictly in the first person and becomes a mission statement about Jesus' need to preach the good news of the gospel of the kingdom of God. Mark speaks only of preaching, with no specific content mentioned, although this point already was made in Mark 1:15.

The pronouncement comes in response to Jesus' being "pursued" (Mark) or the attempt to keep Jesus "from leaving them" (Luke). Jesus' mission is not limited in scope to one locale, nor does he desire that the focus be on his miracles, which are drawing the attention. His calling is to proclaim the arrival of the promised rule of God. Just as Mark juxtaposed kingdom and gospel in Mark 1:15, so Luke here does the same in v. 43. The stress on what Jesus preached is significant, for Mark especially spends much time on Jesus' miraculous works, but in doing so he makes it clear that this is not Jesus' primary task.

32. Summary: Jesus' Tour of Galilee (Matt. 4:23; Mark 1:39; Luke 4:44) (Aland §40; Orchard §46; Huck-Greeven §28)

Jesus carries out the program he proposes. Matthew has the fullest summary and notes that Jesus went about all of Galilee, teaching in the synagogues, preaching the gospel of the kingdom, and healing every disease and infirmity. So here Matthew juxtaposes gospel and kingdom as the other Synoptic writers had done earlier. Mark also highlights preaching in the synagogues through all of Galilee, but he notes the act of casting out demons. Word and work are side by side, functioning together in Jesus' ministry. Luke simply notes that Jesus was preaching in the synagogues of Judea. Some say that Luke is guilty of a geographical slip here, but he is simply using the term "Judea" in its broadest sense (Luke 1:5; 6:17; 7:17; 23:5; Acts 10:37).[23] What Matthew and Mark say in summary, Luke has portrayed in Luke 4:16–44, where preaching is followed by acts of exorcism and healing. Preached word and supporting deed are a capsule of the nature of Jesus' ministry.

33. Jesus' Miracle Leads to a Discipleship Call (Luke 5:1–11) (Aland §41; Orchard §47; Huck-Greeven §29)

This text is important for several reasons. First, for Luke it functions as the equivalent of the call to the four disciples in Mark 1:16–20 (= Matt. 4:18–22).[24] It repeats the imagery of being "fishers of people" from that passage. So after overviewing Jesus' ministry of word and deed, Luke now shows that Jesus gathered followers around him. The task of ministry will be a gathering of humanity that also will separate them into two classes. As is often the case, the pronouncement becomes the key to the passage.

Second, the miracle of the great catch of fish serves as a backdrop to the call to be fishers of people. An important mirroring takes place within this miracle when real fishing points to another type of fishing. Such mirroring highlights a fundamental characteristic of Jesus' miracles. They are more than simply events of power and authentication. These miracles picture some type of significant

23. Note how a few of these passages mention what is happening in Judea, beginning or starting in Galilee. I. H. Marshall, *Luke: Historian and Theologian* (Grand Rapids: Zondervan, 1971), 71 n. 3, points out that Pliny the Elder, *Natural History* 5.70 (specifying Galilee as part of Judea); Strabo, *Geographica* 16.21; and Dio Cassius, *Roman History* 37.15.2–17.3 (esp. 37.16.5–17.1) attest to this "wide" use of the term. So also Rom. 15:31; 2 Cor. 1:16; 1 Thess. 2:14; see W. Gutbrod, "Ἰσραήλ," *TDNT*, 3:382.

24. Attempts have been made to equate this text with the miraculous text in John 21 and to call it an epiphany, but these events and their settings are too distinct to equate. See Bock, *Luke 1:1–9:50*, 448–49.

"deeper" reality to which Jesus' power relates. This claim neither interprets these miracles as allegories nor views them as mere literary depictions of this reality. The miracles are portrayed as real events, but as events with illustrative teaching power. Thus, it is no accident that a catch of fish leads to a pronouncement about being fishers of people. This historical miracle serves as a metaphor of Jesus' call to mission and ministry for those Jesus draws to himself.

Third, there is the important interaction between Peter as a representative of the disciples and Jesus. Peter exercises much trust in Jesus when the initial request comes to "let down your nets." Peter, an experienced fisherman, replies that they had tried to make a catch all last evening, when conditions would have been more favorable, but had failed. Nonetheless, Peter gives the order, showing an element of trust in Jesus. When the catch is overwhelmingly successful, Peter stops what he is doing, falls down before Jesus out of respect, and asks him to leave, saying, "Depart from me, for I am a sinful man, O Lord." Peter's view was that a sinner never could be so close to someone through whom God obviously was working. This very humility is what Jesus affirms when he tells Peter not to fear, that "from now on" he will be catching people. It is precisely those who understand their position and who respond in trust whom God can and does use. So this text not only describes a call to the disciples, but also reveals characteristics about the heart of God's disciples.

What are we to make of the combination of call scenes that appear in Mark (which equals Matthew) and Luke? Luke's text appears to be an affirmation of that which Mark and Matthew affirmed as an earlier event. This Lukan event confirms the earlier call of Mark-Matthew, even down to repeating the "mission" statement. On any approach to the Synoptic problem, Luke knows either Mark or Matthew, so his choice to present the call in this manner serves to supplement that initial call. The exchange between Peter and Jesus is a key element that gives a new dimension to the sequence of events describing Jesus' call to the disciples. This observation shows how the Gospels do not merely repeat events but sometimes supplement each other with fresh information.

34. The Cleansing of the Leper (Mark 1:40–45; Luke 5:12–16; Matt. 8:1–4 initiates his later, initial summary of Jesus' activity) (Aland §42; Orchard §48; Huck-Greeven §57)

The Markan sequence, which Luke follows at this point, continues with Jesus' cleansing of a leper, a miracle that Matthew uses later to introduce his survey of Jesus' miraculous activity. The miracle shows Jesus' "cleansing" power and that God is giving him an authority distinct from any that the priests possess.

In Mark, the account precedes a series of five controversies and suggests that this miracle was a key one in getting the attention of the leadership to what Jesus was doing. The leper initiates the event by kneeling before Jesus in respect and noting that if Jesus so wished, he could cleanse him.[25] Jesus' compassion for the leper is noted, a remark unique to Mark that reflects his tendency to record Jesus' emotions. With a word and a touch, Jesus cleanses the man. This is a reversal of the normal pattern, where touching an unclean person normally would make the clean person unclean. However, where healing occurs, there is no uncleanness, only the grace and authority of God. Again, the miracle provides a picture of how God's presence in Jesus reverses a person's dire condition. Having leprosy caused one to be ostracized and isolated from any association, so Jesus' act would free this man to return to a normal life.

Jesus commands the man to say nothing about this to anyone except the priest, an act that fulfills what Lev. 13:49 required for a healed leper to be recognized. This command "to say nothing" has been the cause of much discussion.[26] Would not the reversal be obvious? Was it realistic to expect nothing to be said? Why this command? As events showed, the man could not remain silent, so the news of Jesus' acts spread. Mark notes the effect. Jesus no longer could enter a town and teach; he had to move to the country to deal with the multitudes. This very reaction may well provide the reason for Jesus' attempt to silence the man. Jesus seems to have anticipated that if the man did go about giving testimony, Jesus would be overwhelmed by those seeking healing, with the risk that miracles, rather than what they embodied, would become the focus of people's attention. Luke makes a similar point in presenting a "great crowd" gathering to hear Jesus and be healed by him. Jesus' reaction is to withdraw and pray, a point that Luke often makes uniquely, as he does here. Matthew's account is the shortest of the three versions and lacks any discussion of the reaction, leaving that to the impression that his sequence of miracles gives as a whole.

All three versions are quite similar otherwise. A key part of the passage is the idea of the leper going to the priest, with the act serving as a "testimony

25. The request is expressed in Greek as a class three condition, so the leper neither indicates how he thinks nor presumes how Jesus will respond. For an overview of Greek conditional sentences and their classification, see Daniel B. Wallace, *Greek Grammar beyond the Basics* (Grand Rapids: Zondervan, 1996), 679–712.

26. One thing that this command does not indicate is a "messianic secret" created by Mark to conceal a nonmessianic ministry of Jesus in the face of the early church's confession of him as the Messiah. William Wrede argued that the "secret" was a way for Mark to portray the ministry as messianic when the reality was otherwise. But Wrede's argument is poorly conceived because the man's reaction and disobedience show that the "secret" was not very well kept, thus seriously undercutting what is supposed to be a motif created after the fact. A better explanation for the command is Jesus' nervousness about the attention that his acts would draw, as Mark suggests.

for/against them."[27] What the act would be is a double-edged sword. On the one hand, the leper would be a witness of God's gracious act toward the leper, but on the other hand, that act was accomplished through Jesus. Thus, the report would raise the question of what God was doing. Jesus' preaching earlier, in Luke 4:16–19, suggested the answer. Those who were captive by any means, physical or spiritual, were experiencing release in acts that pointed to God's work of deliverance through the one whom God had anointed. Here is where the edge of the testimony was. The healing forced a recognition that God was at work through Jesus, so what would they do? The testimony then could work for or against the priests, depending on how they responded to it. That both Mark and Luke follow this event with five consecutive controversies shows where things will be heading. The leaders will challenge Jesus, not embrace him.

35. The Healing of the Paralytic (Mark 2:1–12; Luke 5:17–26; Matt. 9:1–8, in later summary section) (Aland §43; Orchard §51; Huck-Greeven §64)

This event constitutes the first controversy in Mark and is part of an account that contains both a miracle story and a pronouncement. Luke already has noted a controversy in the synagogue scene of Luke 4 but uses the paralytic to lead into a sequence of five controversies, as Mark does. Mark's placement is based on a chiasm (an ABCB'A' pattern) where the gospel is the subject. So the next five scenes proceed:

A healing
  B eating
    C fasting and pietistic practices
  B' eating
A' healing

The gospel is illustrated in action that meets people's needs and is open to all types of association for its sake. Matthew's placement is distinct. This healing is the final part of a second triad of healings (out of three triads total) that he narrates in Matt. 8:1–9:34 to introduce Jesus' ministry.[28] Each triad is broken up with some type of summary or teaching unit. Thus, Matthew has this miracle

27. The plural translated "them" here is sometimes translated "people," as in the RSV. But this probably makes the text say too much. It is the priest and his circle who would hear the testimony and accept the joyful sacrifice that came with it. Thus, in following the law, the priests would hear about what God was doing among the people.

28. W. D. Davies and D. C. Allison, *A Critical and Exegetical Commentary on the Gospel according to Saint Matthew*, 3 vols., International Critical Commentary (Edinburgh: Clark, 1988–97), 1:67–69. They note how Matthew uses numerous triads in Matt. 1–12; see also 86–87.

follow two miracles that Mark and Luke save for later in their accounts: the stilling of the storm and the curing of demoniacs (Matt. 8:23–34 mentions two demoniacs, not just one; Mark 4:35–5:20; Luke 8:22–39). What this difference indicates is that the evangelists sometimes felt free to arrange events rather than attempting to give a chronological sequence. Interestingly, this event is the first controversy account in Matthew's Gospel as well, although Matthew introduces controversy far later in sequence than Mark does. For Matthew, it is simply part of a cycle in which the evangelist is focused on Jesus' miraculous acts and the attention they are drawing. Matthew's major section highlighting confrontation comes in Matt. 11:2–12:50. In their own ways, Mark and Luke are topical here, highlighting controversy, with this event as a key. For Matthew, the event is also part of another topical focus on Jesus' miraculous activity.

Looking at the event, we see that Matthew and Mark locate the healing in Capernaum ("his own city" [Matthew]; "Capernaum," "at home" [Mark]). Mark notes that the audience is made up of many, while Luke specifies that "Pharisees and teachers of the law were sitting by, who had come from every village of Galilee and Judea and from Jerusalem." Thus, Luke notes the spread of attention that Jesus has gained in ways that the other Gospels do not. Luke also uniquely notes that the "power of the Lord was with him to heal." So Luke reaffirms his description of Jesus as an anointed agent of God (see Luke 4:18). Mark and Luke detail the size of the crowd and the difficulty that those who bore the paralytic had in getting him before Jesus by lowering him down through the roof. In other words, Matthew tells the story with his usual brevity, getting right to the dialogue.

The key to this event is the dialogue. Presented with a lame man, Jesus opts to declare his sins forgiven and do nothing initially about his condition. This seemingly was an odd response to what obviously was a request to heal the man. The move to forgive was immediately of theological significance to the theologians present. It is here that Matthew and Mark say that scribes are present, with each writer noting that their questions were expressed in private ("to themselves" [Matthew]; "questioning in their hearts" [Mark]). The objection is stated with some variation: "This man is blaspheming" (Matthew); "Why does this man speak thus? It is blasphemy! Who can forgive sins but God alone?" (Mark); "Who is this that speaks blasphemies? Who can forgive sins but God alone?" (Luke). Once again, Matthew is briefest, but the point in each Gospel is the same. Jesus has assumed a prerogative that belongs uniquely to God. Although some precedent for this type of declaration exists in Nathan's address to David in 2 Sam. 12:13 and in a Qumran text, 4Q242 (Prayer of Nabonidus), it is not stated there with the directness that Jesus seems to use here.[29]

---

29. In the Nabonidus text, the king had an inflammation for seven years that was cleared up when he prayed to God and an "exorcist forgave my sin." No such acknowledgment or preparation is indicated in Jesus' encounter with the paralytic. Jesus does use the passive voice ("your sins are forgiven"), which indicates that God is the source of the forgiveness. However, the controversy arises because Jesus walks directly and uninvited into this area.

Each evangelist notes that Jesus knew what his questioners were thinking, indicating that Jesus acted with some type of special enablement. So he speaks. Matthew notes that Jesus accuses them of thinking evil in their hearts, adding an element of confrontation. Mark and Luke simply show Jesus asking why they raise questions. Jesus' remarks set up his real reply to their questions, which comes in his actions. He raises a dilemma about what is easier. Is it easier to forgive sin or to declare that one rise up and walk? The answer, which never is stated, is that it depends. If one is looking for evidence that something has taken place, then to say "Get up and walk" is harder because then the lame man would have to walk. If one is thinking about what forgiving sins really requires, then that is harder because one must have the authority to really do it even though it is not seen. So how will Jesus resolve the dilemma? He will link the two together so that he invokes God's power and thus reveals that God has delegated forgiving authority to him in the process: "But that you may know that the Son of Man has authority on earth to forgive sins. . . ." Jesus tells the paralytic to arise. The man's response is framed by Jesus' remarks, to illustrate the authority he possesses to forgive sins. If the man can get up, it is because God has given Jesus, as Son of Man, the authority to forgive sin *and* has healed the lame man as authentication. In other words, the theological authorities challenged Jesus concerning his claim to be able to forgive sins; the healing of the lame man is his response, expressed in terms of God's powerful reply.

The reaction of the rest of the observing crowd to the healing is variously expressed. In Matthew, they fear and yet glorify God that such authority had been given to human beings. The plural shows that for the crowd, there was no particularity of the act as one tied exclusively to Jesus, but simply amazement that God would do such a thing through human agents. In Mark, they are amazed and glorify God noting, "We never saw anything like this!" Mark is stressing the "newness" and "authority" in Jesus' teaching that he noted for the reader in 1:22, 27. Something really new is at work, so that even religious practice is different. Luke is similar. Having uniquely noted that the man was praising God as he walked (!) home, the crowd is also amazed and glorifies God. For them, what is seen are "strange" things. This is not a crowd given to accept a miracle on every corner, but they recognize that what is happening through Jesus is unusual. It is something that needs explanation and reflection.

In sum, Jesus' act is controversial because the claim to forgive sin is controversial. The pronouncement is far more important here than the miracle itself, for the miracle itself speaks in the way that Jesus set it up. Though the background for Jesus' description of himself as the Son of Man is not yet explained, the point is that such great authority resides in him and his declarations.[30] That authority extends even to forgiveness and also is pictured in the reversal of a condition of lameness that allows this paralytic now to walk in newness of life. The act forces a choice on the observers and thus on readers: do they believe that Jesus has such authority?

36. The Calling of Levi/Matthew (Mark 2:13–17; Luke 5:27–32; Matt. 9:9–13, in a later summary section) (Aland §44; Orchard §52; Huck-Greeven §65)

A second area of controversy was the company Jesus kept. This event also comes in two parts. First, there is the call of the tax collector called "Levi" in Mark and Luke and "Matthew" in the first Gospel.[31] Second comes the account of a banquet where Jesus is scandalously present, at least in the eyes of the religious leaders. The second part of the event sequence leads to another key pronouncement of Jesus.

All the Synoptics have this event in the same sequence, following the healing of the paralytic. So in Mark and Luke it is the second controversy in the sequence of five. In Matthew it is one of the teaching units that falls between the second and third triad of grouped miracles in Matt. 8–9. In this position, it explains how the note of controversy is rising before it breaks out in full in Matt. 11–12.

The call to the tax collector recalls the "call narrative" of Mark 1:16–20 and parallels. The tax collector is sitting at a booth when Jesus says to him, "Follow me." So he rose and followed him. In typical Lukan style, the third evangelist uniquely notes that this meant that he "left everything." The choice of a tax collector is significant because he was seen as an agent of a foreign state, Rome, a vivid reminder that Israel was not free. As such, tax collectors were despised. Their constant contact and association with Gentiles and potential fraud (see Luke 3:12–13; cf. 19:8) made their reputation as sinners a natural conclusion.

As Matthew and Mark note, Jesus willingly engaged in such associations, even sharing table fellowship with them. Luke refers to the triggering event as a "great feast." The whole scene is disturbing to those scribes and Pharisees

30. The roots of this title reside in a description of a human figure who is given divine authority in Dan. 7:13–14. That figure is described as "one like a son of man." In Daniel, the phrase is not yet a title, although in later Judaism the image came to describe a figure of eschatological judging authority (see *1 Enoch* 37–71; *4 Ezra* [= 2 Esdras] 14). The biblical roots of the title and its explicit association with Dan. 7 do not emerge until later in Jesus' ministry, making its use here somewhat cryptic. For a fuller treatment of the complexity behind the usage of Son of Man, because it also is an Aramaic idiom meaning "some human," see Darrell L. Bock, "The Son of Man in Luke 5:24," *Bulletin for Biblical Research* 1 (1991): 109–21.

31. People known by two names are not uncommon in this period—Saul/Paul and Simon/Peter, for example. Thus, it is likely Levi and Matthew are the same person.

aware of it, and they complain to the disciples about Jesus eating (and drinking [Luke only]) with tax collectors and sinners.[32] Jesus' reply involves a proverb and has a mission statement ("I come to") as an explanation in Mark and Luke. Those who are well do not need a physician, but the sick do. Jesus' mission is to serve those in need. So his mission is not to call the righteous but to call sinners. Luke's slightly longer version notes that the mission is to call sinners to repentance.[33] Matthew also uses the proverb and the mission statement. However, between the proverb and the mission statement is added a scriptural note: "Go and learn what this means, 'I desire mercy, and not sacrifice.'" This remark of prophetic rebuke comes from Hos. 6:6.[34] Thus, Matthew shows how the leadership's question represents a failure to understand God's will and a failure to heed God's prophetic call to understand the priority of the pursuit of relationships in such a way that people are restored. The effect of the rebuke is that the leadership itself is exposed as being sick, even if they do not realize it. The additional remark also heightens the note of confrontation in a way that is missing in the parallels from Mark and Luke. In this honor and shame culture, to castigate the leadership for lack of understanding Scripture would be almost shocking. The Jewish leadership knew the principle, so Jesus' complaint is about a lack of practice.[35]

Jesus pursues relationships with sinners, not a separation from them. In seeking God's will, he pursues the display of God's mercy, not as a way of denying sin, but in a way that allows it to be profitably treated, because it is *sinners* whom he seeks to cure, as shown by the previous controversy. As controversial as it is, Jesus is at table, fellowshiping with those whom the religious leadership has shunned. Two different styles of relating are placed before the reader of the Gospels, forcing a choice in how one engages in relationships. Jesus' mission is successful when a sinner comes to the physician seeking to be cured, a picture that Luke describes with the term "repentance." To come to the doctor is to realize that one has a disease that someone else must treat. God in his mercy will treat those who turn to him.[36] Jesus' relationships are designed to make this point. Reform of God's people is possible only in a context

32. The charge including drinking is something that Luke will return to in Luke 7:34.

33. "Repentance" is a favorite term of Luke. He uses it as a noun or in its verbal form in his Gospel fourteen times, as compared to Mark's three times and Matthew's seven times.

34. Matthew will cite this text again in 12:7.

35. Craig Keener, *Matthew,* IVPNTCS 1 (Downers Grove, Ill.: InterVarsity, 1997), 189–90. Keener notes how the principle is stated in texts such as Sir. 35:1–7 and Prayer of Azariah 16–17. The Sirach passage explains how activity that honors God and shows kindness is like a worthy offering at the altar. Keener also notes that the physician image is common, citing a later example from Diogenes Laertius (*Lives of Eminent Philosophers* 6.1.6), who responds to a criticism of philosophers' associations with "Physicians are in attendance on their patients without getting the fever themselves."

36. "Turning" is the basic meaning of repentance in the Old Testament. Jesus later will note that the preaching of repentance is something rooted in the Old Testament (Luke 24:47).

where mercy can be granted. Once again, Jesus' actions are designed to teach these theological values and even display them in his actual practice.

37. The Question about Fasting (Mark 2:18–22; Luke 5:33–39; Matt. 9:14–17, in a later setting) (Aland §45; Orchard §53; Huck-Greeven §66)

The third controversy in the Markan-Lukan sequence is over the disciples' lack of fasting. Matthew also has the event after the call of the tax collector as part of his break between the second and third triad of miracles in Matt. 8–9. For Matthew, the note about the nature of the time is almost as significant as the dispute itself because it serves as a commentary on the ministry activity that is being described. Jesus is doing things now with his presence that do not require any reason for fasting. The account itself is very similar in all three Gospels.

The issue is a specific act of pious practice. In contrast to both the Pharisees and John the Baptist's followers, Jesus' disciples do not fast.[37] The Pharisees appear to have had a tradition of fasting twice a week (Luke 18:12; *Didache* 8.1).[38] Judaism had certain fasts associated with key holidays such as the Day of Atonement and the memorial to Jerusalem's fall (Lev. 16:29, 31; Zech. 7:3, 5; 8:19). They were viewed as expressions of serious worship. Jesus' seeming lack of concern for this would have been disturbing, and his lack of spiritual sensitivity was implied by those raising the question.

Jesus' reply is important not only because he explains his followers' practice, but also because the imagery he uses of a wedding feast is so full of significance. Jesus describes fasting as inappropriate because the current period is like the celebration of a wedding feast with the groom present. The celebratory mood of a wedding captures the tone of what the arrival of good news should mean. However, things will change. Days will come, Jesus notes, when the groom is removed, and that will make fasting appropriate again. This reference to the groom's removal appears to allude to his rejection and death, but what is significant is that Jesus equates himself with the groom, an Old Testament image for God (Isa. 61:10; 62:5; Jer. 2:2, 32).[39] Also important is the implied backdrop of God's marital relationship to his people (Isa. 54:4–5;

---

37. Note how Luke again includes the issue of drinking as part of the complaint—a unique note, as in Luke 5:30.

38. The *Didache* passage is fascinating. It notes a twice-a-week fast for Christians on Wednesdays and Fridays, but the exhortation is not to fast on the same two days as do the "hypocrites," that is, Mondays and Thursdays. Clearly, then, the practice being defended is not one motivated by early church practice, a point of dissimilarity that argues for the dispute's authenticity. See Gundry, *Mark,* 133.

39. Craig Blomberg, *Jesus and the Gospels* (Nashville: Broadman & Holman, 1997), 237.

62:4–5; Ezek. 16; Hos. 2). Judaism did not have a concept of the Messiah as a bridegroom, so the imagery is unique. The remark is cryptic but suggests how closely Jesus is identified with God's cause and plan. His presence is its key. Mark makes the point most emphatically by adding uniquely, "As long as they have the bridegroom with them, they cannot fast."

To this basic pronouncement come additional proverbial images, two in Matthew and Mark and three in Luke. The point of these images is that simply adding what Jesus brings onto what was done before will not work. He brings something new that will require a distinct receptacle. One does not fasten a new, unshrunken piece of cloth on an old, shrunken piece. What often is missed is the assumption in the figure, at least in its Matthean and Markan forms, that there is a tear in the cloth that needs patching. The saying ends with a note that if new and old cloths are mixed, the subsequent tear is made worse than the implied one that previously existed. So the point is that Jewish practice (both Judaism of the Old Testament type and the Second Temple practice that grew from it) has a rip and needs repair. That repair requires something fresh, not mere patchwork. The Lukan version points simply to the damage that the wrong mix does (it tears) and the lack of a match between the old and new parts, a point that only Luke makes.

The second image uses the imagery of wineskins. Here the point is that new wine makes old wineskins break because the old wineskins are worn and inelastic. The result of attempting this mixture of old and new is the loss of both the wineskins and the new wine. Therefore, new wine must go in new wineskins. Thus, the good news that Jesus brings is like a new era. It is like the arrival of a marriage and a new family with new customs. It involves a fresh approach to drawing near to God. The "new" teaching requires "new" ways of looking at religious practice. Fresh wine comes in new wineskins, so both the wine and the skins are preserved. This final point is made explicitly only in Matthew.

Only Luke has the third image. It reflects on why some do not try the "new" wine. It is simply that they are satisfied with the old. They say, "The old is good." Thus, Jesus here recognizes that when he challenges the nation and argues for the need for something new, some will remain satisfied with what they have. So Luke's additional illustration anticipates that some will not want any change, setting the basis for future opposition.

38. The Dispute over the Disciples' Plucking of Grain on the Sabbath (Mark 2:23–28; Luke 6:1–5; Matt. 12:1–8, in a later section in which controversy is highlighted) (Aland §46; Orchard §54; Huck-Greeven §81)

The fourth and fifth controversies in the Markan-Lukan sequence involve activity on the Sabbath. Matthew places this event later in a section where confrontation and invitation fall side by side. After discussing John the Baptist and issuing woes alongside an invitation, Matthew turns to this event, followed by a second Sabbath controversy, while noting Jesus' ministry as "Servant of God," a ministry not just for Israel but also for Gentiles. For Matthew, these controversies with Israel will not derail God's plan for humanity.

The background of this event is rooted in the sacred day of rest that is the Sabbath in Judaism.[40] The disciples' plucking of grain and winnowing it to eat are seen as multiple violations of Sabbath practice, if *m. Šabbat* 7.2 is any guide. There, the "forty less one" acts prohibited on this day include reaping, threshing, and winnowing. Food preparation was done a day earlier so that the Sabbath day could be properly honored. Failing to observe such a holy day was seen as completely disrespectful of the law because Sabbath rest was one of the Ten Commandments. This incident was a major dispute.

The account is fairly similar in the three Gospels, although Matthew has two important elements of additional material. As it stands, the account is another controversy ending with a pronouncement by Jesus. The response is triggered by the complaint and question about why his disciples are doing what is not permitted on the Sabbath.[41]

Jesus begins, as he did in the dispute over his personal associations in the Matthean version, with a challenge from Scripture. Here it is the example of David and his men eating from the shewbread, which was for the priests only (Lev. 24:9; 1 Sam. 21:1–6). Some have complained that the parallel is not relevant, as it does not involve an act on the Sabbath. But that objection misses the point. David was permitted to do something that the law explicitly had prohibited. In fact, all three Synoptics highlight this point with the remark "which is not permitted for them to eat," with all noting that this bread was for the priests only. Jesus apparently suggests, as one of his arguments, that there are times when a law, like that of the Sabbath, could be "broken," as in the case of the shewbread.[42] At the base of the analogy may be the issue of basic human need, because all the accounts note that he and those with him were hungry. This type of relational concern fits with the general ethical thrust of Jesus' teaching about being concerned for one's neighbor.

Jesus' argument does not stop there. Matthew and Luke conclude with the remark that "the Son of Man is Lord of the Sabbath." Here Jesus makes a comprehensive personal claim of authority over the sacred day that God insti-

---

40. See Emil Schürer, *The History of the Jewish People in the Age of Jesus Christ* (*175 B.C.– A.D. 135*), vol. 2, ed. Geza Vermes, Fergus Millar, and Matthew Black, rev. ed. (Edinburgh: Clark, 1979), 467–75.

41. Each Gospel addresses the culprits differently and yet makes the same charge: "your disciples" (Matthew), "they" (possibly inclusive of Jesus [Mark]), and "you all" (Luke).

42. The quotation marks with "broken" are intentional. Jesus' remark here is that what appears to be a violation need not be one in fact. Jesus will go on to present additional arguments to make his full case.

tuted, a day governed by one of the commandments. As with his substitution of himself for the groom and the claim to forgive sins, this associates Jesus with Yahweh. In other words, Jesus is making a series of claims in these controversies that intimately link him with God. Rather than making the explicit identification or confession of being a certain figure, Jesus argues that his actions help to define who he is.

It probably is no accident that this account follows the "new wineskins" discussion in Luke and Mark, for Jesus' attitude about the Sabbath shows how different Jesus' way is from current practice. Luke's account is the shortest, as he wishes only to make the basic point about the identity of the one who reigns over even the Sabbath.

Mark has one other unique remark. It is that "the Sabbath was made for humankind, and not humankind for the Sabbath." In other words, this is a countercomplaint by Jesus that Sabbath law never was intended to restrict a person from meeting basic needs. David and his men were hungry, so they ate shewbread without experiencing God's judgment (and the priests at the temple apparently let them do it!). Therefore, Jesus' disciples can pluck the grain left on the edge of a field for the needy (Deut. 23:25). Jesus' statement that the Son of Man is Lord of the Sabbath follows this point in Mark, making some wonder if Jesus' remark in that Gospel is more generic, pointing to authority for people in general. However, Jesus is not making a remark about humanity's authority over the Sabbath. Nothing else like that exists in his teaching. Rather, the one who is the Son of Man and who has received eschatological judging authority from God possesses such a right. The new time points to the presence of the key figure who brings the new era. Thus, an eschatological claim serves as a clinching argument alongside an illustration permitting exception. Jesus' explanation argues that the Sabbath law was designed not to be an obstacle for people.

Matthew's argument, possibly because he is most concerned with Jewish issues, is even more detailed. In between the David example and the closing eschatological remark come two fresh points. First, Matthew appeals to another example: priests working on the Sabbath in the temple. They "labor" on the Sabbath over sacrifices and "profane" the day while being "guiltless." Jesus' point seems to be that the Sabbath law is not as absolute a law as tradition suggests. It may have exceptions. But in making this point, he raises the stakes by arguing that something greater than the temple is here. In other words, if priestly labor in the temple is not covered by Sabbath restrictions, neither is his activity! This is another way to make the eschatological claim just noted. If Jesus has a value that is greater than the temple—note how shocking that would be to Jewish ears, because the temple was viewed as the dwelling place of God!—then Sabbath issues are exempt for him and those working with him, even more than for the priests in the temple.

Matthew's second unique appeal is again to cite Hos. 6:6, as was done in Matt. 9:13. Here is Jesus' relational argument. God desires mercy, not sacrifice. He desires that people be treated in a way that puts a premium on mercy rather than on mandated ritual. As such, their implied condemnation of the "guiltless" is wrong even by prophetic standards. Matthew desires to show that whether his reader looks at Israel's history, worship, or prophets, what Jesus has done more accurately reflects the values of God.

The argument that Jesus makes works at many levels: scriptural, legal, relational, and eschatological. Almost no matter which way the question is considered, the right of the disciples to take grain on the Sabbath as they travel should not have been challenged. The "new" way brings controversy with "old" practices. No violation of law has occurred, although on the surface it looks like it might have. Rather, it honors the relational desire God had that mercy be displayed and that the Sabbath be for people's good. Even if those arguments do not persuade, one final factor applies. The Son of Man, the representative human being, has received authority from God even over the Sabbath. In the end, all the controversies force a choice about who Jesus is.

39. Synagogue Sabbath Healing: The Man with the Withered Hand (Mark 3:1–6; Luke 6:6–11; Matt. 12:9–14, in the later controversy section) (Aland §47; Orchard §55; Huck-Greeven §82)

The final controversy in the Markan and Lukan sequence has the feel of a setup. In form, the account is another mixed "controversy" account and healing, but in this case, the healing clearly is subservient to detailing the dispute. Almost no attention is given to the man healed or to any crowd reaction. It is Jesus versus the leadership.

Into the synagogue comes a man having a withered right hand, a condition that probably prevents him from working. Under normal circumstances people would have viewed such a healing with great respect (1 Kings 13:6; *Testament of Simeon* 2.12–13). However, the Pharisees are said to be "watching" Jesus to see if he will heal the man on the Sabbath.[43] All three accounts note the opponents' motive: they seek to accuse him. Matthew's location of the event also follows the previous Sabbath healing as part of his section on confrontation in Matt. 11–12. In Matthew, Jesus is directly challenged as to whether it is lawful to heal on the Sabbath. The test seems to equate healing

43. The Greek term for "watching" can have a malicious meaning of "lying in wait for someone" (see BAGD, 622; BDAG, 771). The remark apparently assumes that he is capable of performing the healing! All the accounts have Pharisees on the watch (Matt. 12:14 and Mark 3:6 look back to the "they" of 12:10 and 3:2 respectively).

with labor. For someone who was not in danger of dying, the leaders' view was that such acts of healing could wait for a day.

The later Mishnah did discuss what could and could not be done on the Sabbath. For many, medicine could be applied only if life was in danger or there was some other urgent need (*m. Yoma* 8.6: "Further did R. Mattiah b. Harash say, 'He who has a pain in his throat—they drop medicine into his mouth on the Sabbath, because it is a matter of doubt as to danger to life'"; *m. Šabbat* 22.6: one should not even set a broken bone; see also *m. ʿEduyyot* 2.5), although attempts to get around this restriction existed, especially if the medicine had been prepared before the Sabbath (*m. Šabbat* 14.4; 19.2). The sectarians at Qumran were even stricter; they prohibited any significant activity (CD 11.5–18: one is not allowed to pasture an animal beyond a length of one thousand cubits).[44]

Jesus, knowing their thoughts, according to Luke, tells the man to come to him. At this point, Matthew has a unique detail, pointing to an inconsistency in Jewish practice and adding a note of additional confrontation like the previous account on plucking grain on the Sabbath. He notes that if one of their sheep was suffering after falling into a pit on the Sabbath, they would take hold of it and lift it out. But a human being is of more value than a sheep, so the implication is that human suffering also should be alleviated on the Sabbath. At this point, all the accounts note this conclusion: to do good on the Sabbath is "lawful." In Mark and Luke, Jesus uses the same term for "lawful" (ἔξεστιν) that his opponents use in the question present in Matthew's version. In these Gospels, Jesus presses the issue with his own ironically loaded question: "Is it lawful on the Sabbath to do good or do harm, to save a life or to destroy it [Luke]/to kill [Mark]?" Jesus is pointing to motive. On a day when God is to be honored, the Pharisees are looking to see if they can catch Jesus and make an accusation against him. In contrast, Jesus will perform a deed that restores a man to complete health. Now which is better? The query raises a genuine question about who is doing a better job of honoring the Sabbath!

Jesus acts. Mark alone notes that he does so in a combination of anger and grief at the hardness of heart that they display. Jesus "labors." He simply tells the man to stretch out his hand. In doing so, he presents the evidence that his hand had been restored. Unlike the previous Sabbath controversy, in which Jesus and his disciples had taken the initiative to act on the Sabbath, this event showed a display of authority that seemingly proved that God had acted on Jesus' behalf. In turn, the Pharisees' reaction is swift. In Matthew it is said that they "took counsel against him, how to destroy him." Mark reports that they

---

44. Keener, *Matthew*, 226–27; Craig Blomberg, *Matthew*, New American Commentary 22 (Nashville: Broadman, 1992), 197–99. Keener notes that the issue was debated among Jews; some did at least permit prayer for the sick on the Sabbath (if a tradition in the Tosefta is old: *t. Šabbat* 16.22).

held a counsel with the Herodians "against him, how to destroy him."[45] Luke is more vague: they discussed what they "might do to Jesus."

Thus, all three Synoptics see a line being crossed for the leadership in this final Sabbath challenge. The series of controversies has yielded a choice to resist Jesus. His Sabbath activity is a key turning point in the dispute. Jesus brings "new" ways, but those who like the old ways do not want his reforms.

40. Summary: Jesus Heals by the Sea (Mark 3:7–12; Luke 6:17–19, following the choosing of the Twelve, reversing Mark's order; Matt. 4:24–25 and 12:15–16) (Aland §48; Orchard §57; Huck-Greeven §84a)

This Markan-Lukan summary caps off the controversy section, although in Luke this summary follows the pericope on the choosing of the Twelve, whereas in Mark it precedes it. Both summaries in Matthew are noted because one (Matt. 4) precedes his next great block of teaching, the Sermon on the Mount, which in Luke is paralleled by the Sermon on the Plain, which also follows shortly. The Matt. 12 summary is what follows that Sabbath incident. It also is very similar in thrust to Mark 3:9–12. Here is another case where distribution varies between the Gospels and some themes even seem to be repeated. The summary in Matt. 12 is part of a longer unit that cites Isa. 42:1–4 as being fulfilled in Jesus.

The major feature of these summaries is that they attest to the widening influence of Jesus. Great crowds are coming. Luke notes Judea, Jerusalem, Tyre, and Sidon. Thus, those both in and outside of Israel are coming. They come to hear, be healed, and have unclean spirits exorcized. The crowds sought to touch him because they knew that "power came forth from him and healed them all." Jesus is portrayed as enabled and empowered by God to bring healing.

Mark speaks of Jesus withdrawing to the sea and of a great many coming from Galilee. But also there are people from Judea, Jerusalem, Idumea, from beyond the Jordan, and from Tyre and Sidon. Mark's inclusion of Idumea, the homeland of Herod, is interesting. It links up with Mark's earlier unique note in 3:6 about Herodian opposition. So there is political opposition to Jesus as well as curiosity about him from Herod's homeland. As a look at an ancient map will show, word about Jesus spread in all directions. The crowd was becoming a crush as they sought him, so he had a boat prepared for himself. He also performed exorcisms. The demons would attempt to name him,

---

45. This detail about the Herodians suggests that this is an early tradition because by the time Mark wrote, the Herodians were gone. The Herodians did not want any instability in the current situation where there was religious and political cooperation in which the Herodians shared. This reaction also shows how there was no separating the religious from the political in this first-century setting.

probably as a means of controlling him.[46] However, their naming Jesus as "Son of God" brings an order of silence from him, much as Luke 4:41 already had noted. Jesus will not permit a demonic source for this confession. Yet again, the point is ironic, because what evil spiritual forces recognize has been rejected by many who should have been expected to see God's hand at work.

The Matt. 4 summary is the most fascinating. Even though this evangelist is most concerned with issues related to Israel, as seen in his detail on the Sabbath disputes, he notes that Jesus' fame has spread into places like Syria, the Decapolis, and beyond the Jordan. These locales were predominately non-Jewish, so the Gentiles, along with people from Galilee and Judea, brought him their sick. Matthew even specifies all the classes: "those afflicted with various diseases and pains, demoniacs, epileptics, and paralytics." Jesus healed them, so great crowds came to him. What is significant is that the Sermon on the Mount is presented to these crowds despite their mixed ethnicity. Thus, Jesus' ethical message about the discipleship and hope for the kingdom went out to all, without ethnic discrimination, even though Israel was the primary concern. The summary in Matt. 12 simply notes that Jesus healed and at the same time ordered those healed "not to make him known." Jesus was concerned about what was said about him and how many people were being drawn to the healing aspect of his ministry. Matthew 12:15 notes how he had just been forced to withdraw because of the attention his teachings drew.

These summaries indicate the spreading popularity of Jesus and curiosity about him. His healings and exorcisms drew much attention. Matthew and Luke will note Jesus' teaching as well when Matthew relates the Sermon on the Mount and Luke presents the Sermon in the Plain.

41. The Choosing of the Twelve (Mark 3:13–19a; Luke 6:12–16; Matt. 10:1–4, in a later section in which mission is the topic) (Aland §49; Orchard §58; Huck-Greeven §85)

The final event to examine before we turn to consider Jesus' teaching is the selection of the Twelve. From within the wider group of his followers came those around whom Jesus especially would build his "new" way of reform. That Jesus would choose a group of disciples in the face of opposition, as the placement in Mark and Luke indicates, shows that Jesus' rejection by key strands of Judaism will not stop him.

The Synoptics have different emphases. Matthew's placement at the beginning of a section on mission is fitting. Jesus gathers the Twelve to help him get out his message of the kingdom's approach. Only Luke notes that the se-

46. See unit 28 above.

lection followed a full night of prayer. He also is the only one to call them "apostles" at this point and to specify that the selection emerged from a larger group. His account also is the briefest, simply naming the Twelve, starting with Peter and ending with the one who ultimately will betray Jesus, as all three Synoptic lists of the Twelve do.[47] Not every list is in the same order. One disciple appears to have had two names (Thaddaeus = Judas son of James). The first four always are Peter, Andrew, James, and John, but they do not always appear in the same order.[48] Mark describes their mission in threefold terms: to be with him, to preach, and to have authority to cast out demons. Matthew highlights the granting of authority to cast out demons and heal every disease. The call to preach is saved for the following description of the mission.

The significant element of the selection is that there are twelve chosen for this special role. They serve as a parallel to the structure of Israel with its twelve tribes. Jesus' prophetic call to reform will have its own structure and leadership.[49] As Luke shows later when a larger mission is sent out in Luke 10, they are the nucleus of a more significant group of emissaries. One final point is that these men come from a variety of backgrounds emerging from everyday life. We know that several of them were fishermen. In the group is a tax collector and a "Zealot," two people who would have started out on opposite ends of the political spectrum, one serving Rome and the other seeking to overthrow it. The variety in the selection indicates how Jesus brought people of diverse perspectives together. It also shows that he wanted "everyday folk" to take the message to their peers.

Conclusion

The beginning of Jesus' activity entails three elements: his teaching, his activity of healing and exorcism, and the controversies that his claims to authority raised. Jesus was challenged for his claim to forgive sin, his associations with sinful or politically suspect people, his lack of attention to details of pious tradition, and his handling of the Sabbath. His healings and exorcisms indi-

---

47. A listing of the Eleven in Acts 1:13 lacks Judas, who had killed himself by that time.

48. Luke and Matthew agree here, while Mark and Acts go their own way. But Matthew and Luke diverge in that Matthew has Thaddaeus while Luke lists Judas son of James. Their ordering of the names also differs. All these differences suggest that the names of the Twelve circulated widely and in slightly divergent forms. For details, see Bock, *Luke 1:1–9:50*, 540–47.

49. This call surely is historical. The early church would not invent a gathering of these twelve when many of those named are not heard from and especially in light of the choice of Judas Iscariot. Who would create the detail that one of the inner circle betrayed Jesus? See C. E. B. Cranfield, *The Gospel according to Saint Mark*, Cambridge Greek Testament Commentary (Cambridge: Cambridge University Press, 1959), 127.

cated the presence of unusual power, and his practices made many officials in Judaism nervous. His call to reform also challenged the spiritual state of the nation. But most disturbing of all was his declaration of authority and the nature of the era that he declared as being present. It was an era of fulfillment, and he was its central, triggering figure. His teaching with authority was both a new way and a claim to bring to realization what had been promised. The tensions of continuity and discontinuity in his teaching brought their own tensions as Jesus both fulfilled and superseded the Old Testament. People were confronted with the need to decide about him, as well as to consider their own spiritual state. This physician had a mission to preach the kingdom and call the sick to repent. His role in the plan was a central element in the program. The doctor's prescription pointed to him as the key to obtaining healing. Thus, Jesus' ministry in Galilee forced his audience to make a choice about God's plan and the one who represented it. Would he be embraced or repelled? The Gospels' reporting of that ministry compels the same choice from readers today. Those who embrace the call to share in God's era of promise and realization face the question "What does the call to participate involve?" Key elements of the answer surface in one of Jesus' most famous discourses as recorded in Matthew, the Sermon on the Mount. Luke's version, the Sermon on the Plain, is a digest of that teaching, lacking some of the Jewish-oriented legal elements. Luke's concise form shows how this teaching was presented to a predominantly non-Jewish audience. This is where our story goes next.

FIVE

Jesus' Teaching on Relating to God and Others

The Sermon on the Mount and the Sermon on the Plain
(Matt. 5:1–7:29; Luke 6:20–49)

Not all of Jesus' hearers could literally follow him on his travels. But all could practice his way of life, a way of forgiveness and prayer, a way of jubilee, a way which renounced xenophobia toward those outside Israel and oppression of those inside. This is the context, I suggest, within which we should understand the material in what we call the Sermon on the Mount. It is not simply a grand new moral code. It is, primarily, the challenge of the kingdom: the summons to Israel to be Israel indeed at the critical junction of her history, the moment when, in the kingdom announcement of Jesus, the living God is at work to reconstitute his people and so fulfill his long-cherished intentions for them and for the whole world.[1]

The depth of the sermon has produced a variety of views. Beyond the recognition that it reflects Jesus' ethical standards for his disciples, the sermon defies classification. But most of the sermon reflects a proper response to God's invitation to enter humbly into the blessing of kingdom relationship as offered in the Beatitudes. In short, if one is in the Light, then one should be light (Matt. 5:14–16; Col. 1:9–14). The sermon's focus causes disciples to look to God and to look within, so that they live in a way that honors God and loves his fellow humans. Only by accepting God's grace and justice can one live in the way Jesus calls disciples to live. The sermon is an ethic that leaves justice and retribution to God, while one rests in his grace and love. . . . [The sermon] is a

1. N. T. Wright in *The Meaning of Jesus: Two Visions,* by Marcus J. Borg and N. T. Wright (San Francisco: HarperSanFrancisco, 1999), 39.

124

warning against a selfish focus in approaching God, life, and ethics. It is a warning against loving with strings attached, loving for self-gain, or ignoring the call to true righteousness. Indeed, the sermon is a call to exhibit the type of forgiveness, giving, grateful and compassionate love that is like God (Luke 6:36 = Matt. 5:48), which the sermon describes as a righteousness that exceeds that of the Pharisees (Matt. 5:20).[2]

Perhaps no portion of Jesus' teaching is as widely known as the Sermon on the Mount. Here Matthew details a sample of Jesus' teaching for those who are considering him; Jesus makes both an invitation and sets forth how those who follow him should live. The Lukan version is a far more compact presentation of the same theme.[3] It lacks mostly those portions that relate to issues associated with the law. The fact that Luke has such a reduced version shows that the core ethic of the sermon transcends issues related to Israel and questions raised about how Jesus related to Torah, a major concern in the first portion of Matthew's version. For Matthew, this material is the first block of five major blocks of teaching that he presents (Matt. 5–7 [ethics]; 10 [mission]; 13 [kingdom parables]; 18 [the new community]; 24–25 [eschatological discourse]). Matthew's sermon is complex in structure. After an introduction involving beatitudes and a basic call for disciples to be salt and light (Matt. 5:1–16), the first major section deals with Jesus' call for disciples to truly fulfill the law, including six antitheses (5:17–48). Then follow treatments of acts of piety such as almsgiving, prayer, and fasting (6:1–18). Next, Matthew has a section of themes tied to having the right kind of treasure as well as trusting God (6:19–34). Various themes related to judging, prayer, knowing a tree by its fruit, and warnings about false relationship to Jesus (7:1–23) precede a final illustration about heeding Jesus' teaching (7:24–27). For Luke, the sermon introduces very early in his Gospel the key ethical requirement for disciples: that they love in a manner that exceeds the love that sinners give to people. Luke's sermon consists of three parts: a short section on blessing and woes setting forth God's standards (Luke 6:20–26), a call to love even at self-risk (6:27–36), and a warning about judgment and the need to heed Jesus' wisdom (6:37–49).

The sermon is representative of Jesus' teaching, because much of what Matthew has in the sermon Luke scatters throughout his Gospel as distinct units of teaching.[4] In fact, thirteen sayings of the sermon show up elsewhere in Luke. In

2. Darrell L. Bock, *Luke 1:1–9:50*, BECNT 3A (Grand Rapids: Baker, 1994), 943.

3. For details on the relationship of these two sermons to one another and the many views surrounding this question, see Bock, *Luke 1:1–9:50*, 931–44. Matthew has 107 verses to Luke's 30.

4. Parts of thirty-seven verses of Matthew show up elsewhere in Luke (some sayings take up more than one verse). This means that about a third of the passages have contact with other portions of Luke. In the Matthean version, forty-six verses lack parallels in Luke. That represents 43 percent of the sermon.

its Matthean form, then, the sermon operates as a kind of anthology of some of Jesus' most basic teaching.[5] The sermon's influence in the earliest church is obvious from a look at James and 1 Peter. There are conceptual contacts with James at eighteen points of his epistle, while Peter has five such overlaps.[6] The sermon contains several highly rhetorical expressions that have made it the subject of great debate concerning how "literally" one should apply the sermon. Recognizing the presence of this stylistic trait of Jesus is important to appreciating the sermon's message. I proceed through the sermon in its Matthean order, noting how Luke has handled the material along the way at the relevant points. At the end of the chapter, I will focus on Luke's presentation as a whole to give a better sense of Luke's use of this material.

42. The Occasion of the Sermon (Matt. 5:1–2; Luke 6:20a)
(Aland §50b; Orchard §§58a, 59a; Huck-Greeven §30)

The setting is briefly noted in each Gospel. In fact, the summary noted in unit 40 above provides the context for this event. Crowds from an array of locales are gathered, with Jesus performing healings and exorcisms. Even the Markan summary in 3:13a has Jesus in a mountain setting at this point. Matthew simply has Jesus ascend a mountain, with the disciples then coming to him. At that point he begins to teach. Luke, as a part of the previous summary, has Jesus on a level place, facing a great crowd. After summarizing the ministry, Jesus lifts up his eyes to teach. The difference in geographical terrain between Luke and Matthew may reflect a difference in literary compression because the "level" locale in Luke really describes the summary he uses to introduce the sermon. Another possible explanation is that Jesus is at a level plateau in the mountain setting.[7]

It is likely that we are dealing with the same sermon. In favor of this conclusion are the agreement in the event's relative placement between Matthew

5. Such a literary function is the case whether one sees distinct historical settings for the Matthean and Lukan versions (i.e., two distinct sermons), one sees Luke as summarizing the same sermon more compactly, or one believes that Matthew pulled together this teaching into a topical grouping that puts all of it in one locale. The power of the exposition is related to the order given to it in Matthew. This unity is especially important in those units unique to Matthew and his presentation of the antitheses of the law and its relationship to Matt. 5:17–20. This section of the sermon (Matt. 5:17–48) is compactly constructed and should be read as a whole to be fully understood.

6. Bock, *Luke 1:1–9:50*, 938 n. 11; J. Hartin, *James and the Q Sayings of Jesus*, JSNTSup 47 (Sheffield: JSOT, 1991), 140–72, analyzes the James parallels.

7. D. A. Carson, "Matthew," in *The Expositor's Bible Commentary*, vol. 8, ed. Frank E. Gaebelein (Grand Rapids: Zondervan, 1984), 129. BAGD, 638, and BDAG, 790, note that Luke's term for "plain" can be a plateau on a mountain (Jer. 21:13; Isa. 13:2).

and Luke in the flow of their Gospels and the fact that virtually all of Luke's version is contained in Matthew's, with virtually the same order (only Luke 6:24–26 has no Matthean parallel; only Luke 6:31 is radically "out of order" within the Sermon on the Plain).

43. The Beatitudes (Matt. 5:3–12; Luke 6:20b–26, with beatitudes and woes) (Aland §51; Orchard §59; Huck-Greeven §31)

The blessings represent an announcement of who is or will be "happy" because of experiencing the acceptance of God.[8] In considering the function of the Beatitudes, it is important to consider them as a unit. Four features stand out. First, these blessings are tied to association with the kingdom of God as Jesus preached it. This means that there is a tension between the kingdom as it is being offered and what it one day will be. This explains why the poor are said to possess the kingdom of God (5:3), while many of the remaining Beatitudes treat what will be when the fullness of the eschaton reverses what is occurring currently (5:4–9).[9] Second, the issue of persecution is assumed, which means that Jesus is preaching that the kingdom's presence is meeting stiff resistance (5:10, 12). Followers had better understand that and be ready. A key to the Beatitudes is that they have a kind of sandwich structure in which the kingdom "is" (vv. 3, 10, 12), yet the realization of blessing tied to it "will be" (vv. 4–9). This raises the third feature: the connection between eschatological reversal and the kingdom. Although the kingdom is within reach now, being possessed by the poor in spirit and those who suffer persecution for righteousness' sake, the more complete blessing arrives in the reversal to come. One day, what presently has the look of suffering and defeat will become blessing and reward through God's grace. Eschatology and the hope that accompanies it have invaded the present even as it awaits its full expression in the future. Fourth, the Beatitudes work from the inside out. They start with attitudes of heart and spirit (poor in spirit, mourn, meek, hunger and thirst for righteousness, merciful, pure) and then move to actions either by disciples or against them (peacemakers, persecuted, reviled). Spirituality starts from within and then shows itself in action, often resulting in a hostile reaction by a world that does not understand it.

Thus, the Beatitudes announce who it is that God will bless and reward in the forthcoming era when God removes the current opposition to the kingdom. In that day, mourners will be comforted, the meek will inherit the land,

---

8. On the term "blessed," see μακάριος, BAGD, 486–87; BDAG, 610–11.

9. The shift from present tense in 5:3 to future tenses in 5:4–9 is significant. The reader should not interpret the first present tense as if it were future, especially because the present tense returns in 5:10 and 12.

those hungering and thirsting for righteousness will be satisfied, the merciful will obtain mercy, the pure in heart will see God, and the peacemakers will be called children of God. The implication of all of this is clear: if you desire to receive God's blessing, then respond to the announcement of blessing, identify with it, and seek to reflect these characteristics even though you may know that many in the world will persecute and revile you as a result. More than that, however, the Beatitudes function as words of comfort and assurance. God will bless those who in trying to be responsive to him suffer for their effort to honor him and pursue righteousness. To be faithful in the face of such opposition is a cause for rejoicing because disciples join a great line of godly people who preceded them ("for so they persecuted the prophets who were before you"). In other words, these characteristics are *not* the requirements for entry into the kingdom or conditions for blessedness; instead, they reflect those who have identified with God in the face of a hostile world that is going in the other direction and leaving them alienated and out of step in the midst of that world.

Conceptually, the Beatitudes appear to draw on Isa. 61 for background. A look at Isa. 61 in the Greek shows that the poor, the mourners, the meek, the brokenhearted, and those who rejoice all are noted in 61:1–11.[10] In addition, the idea of righteousness is prevalent. In the New Testament, Isa. 61 is of great significance (Matt. 11:5 = Luke 7:22; Luke 4:18–19; Acts 10:38). In ancient Judaism, this was one of the great texts of hope (11QMelch 2.4, 6, 9, 13, 17, 20; *Targum Pseudo-Jonathan* to Num. 25:12; *Midrash Ekhah* on Lam. 3:5). Thus, the imagery of this text and the period it evokes were familiar.

Just as significant is the implication of Isa. 61 in the background: the text with its promises affirms a time when a herald of God's good news will be anointed and present. If the promises of Isa. 61 are at work, then the figure of Isa. 61 must be present. In this way, Matt. 5:3–12 overlaps christologically with Luke 4:16–30. The first teaching block of Matthew then ends up with a christological element similar to that in the first teaching block of Luke even though they narrate very different events and make the point in different ways. Thus, the sermon begins with a time of announcement and assurance: blessing will come no matter how difficult things become for those who are allied with God today. Why? Because the agent who brings God's blessing and promise has come and assures those who follow him that God will accept their alliance with God and his ways.

The backdrop of Isa. 61 is important for another reason. It shows who is being discussed when "the poor in spirit" are named. It is the Old Testament figure of the *anawim*, the "pious poor." These are people who suffer because they have

10. W. D. Davies and D. C. Allison, *A Critical and Exegetical Commentary on the Gospel according to Saint Matthew*, 3 vols., International Critical Commentary (Edinburgh: Clark, 1988–97), 1:436–39. This unit is indebted to their discussion of the background.

walked in humility with their God, so they are meek, mourning, and broken-hearted now. Mercy, purity of heart, and a desire for righteousness and peacemaking drive them. Jesus promises that God will recognize and reward that pursuit, not because they have performed meritorious works of law, but because they have sought to walk in his steps and reflect his character as his children.

Luke opens the sermon with a shorter list of blessings and a corresponding list of woes. Just as the genre of beatitudes indicates God's acceptance, woes indicate rejection.[11] Luke's listing describing the beneficiaries of blessing is more compact; he refers to the "poor," "the hungry," and "those who weep now." The persecution context is shared with Matthew; Luke speaks of those who hate, exclude, revile, and cast out those who are blessed. Luke's rendering appears less interpretive and less expansive, although the backdrop is the same. The persecution context makes it clear that those who are poor suffer because they are reviled "on account of the Son of Man."[12] Thus, we are not dealing with the abstract poor here, although poverty is the material consequence and condition of those addressed. We know that Luke has a material focus because the context goes on to pronounce a woe on the rich, and they *cannot* be seen as the "rich in spirit." He goes on to note that these rich, who are full and laugh now, will hunger, mourn, and weep in that day to come. Their seeking of approval now is like the line of false prophets who were popular long ago. Thus, although Luke's language is more sociologically descriptive of a person's social status, it is not lacking a spiritual dimension.[13] Here is someone who gives up what the world has to offer (safety, security, comfort, laughter) to choose the way of God. Seen in this light, Luke and Matthew are not as diverse as they initially might appear. What does differ with the presence of the woes is that the cost for going the way of the world is more explicit in Luke's version. In Jesus' Lukan proclamation, there are both winners and losers, those who are and will be accepted and those who face rejection. Thus, a note of warning as well as comfort opens the Sermon on the Plain.

The Beatitudes, as they assure and announce hope, also serve to set forth the disciple's character. These descriptions do not reflect an abstract, ethical category of human character and attainment, so that this blessing is earned. Rather, they are part of a spiritual commitment to walk in God's ways in the pursuit of his character, which results in rejection and suffering from those who do not understand God's character (Matt. 5:48; Luke 6:35–36). The children of God will reflect the character of the God they follow. God will honor them for drawing near to him and his messenger. Thus, a description of the calling and the task follows.

11. On the term "woe," see οὐαί, BAGD, 591; BDAG, 734.

12. Matthew has "on my account."

13. The Lukan contrast of the rich and the poor is a major theme in his Gospel, starting conceptually with Mary's words in Luke 1:50–53 and extending to texts such as 12:13–21; 18:18–30; and 19:1–10.

44. The Salt of the Earth (Matt. 5:13; conceptual:[14] Mark 9:49–50; Luke 14:34–35) (Aland §52; Orchard §61; Huck-Greeven §32a)

Those who would consider the calling of God need to understand their role. They are the salt of the earth. It is significant that this calling looks at the world, not just Israel. Exactly how they are salt is debated, but it seems that salt serves in some type of enhancing role, given the association with taste in the next phrase.[15] Disciples are useful as servants to impact the world and influence it for good. A life of character and integrity as well as a different way of relating reflect being light.

What follows is a warning. Salt that ceases to function as designed is useless. There is only one thing that can be done with it: toss it out and let it be trampled. There is no specificity here as to the penalty, and that probably is intentional. The point is to warn, not to give specific consequences. Disciples who care about following God would not want to risk being considered useless by him. The warning thus becomes an exhortation to respond positively to God's calling.[16]

45. The Light of the World (Matt. 5:14–16; conceptual: Mark 4:21; Luke 8:16) (Aland §53; Orchard §62; Huck-Greeven §32b)

In contrast to the potentially negative warning using salt, the next image of light is positive and describes the mission. Those who follow Jesus' call are to be light for the world. Again, the scope of the mission is to all. Disciples, like light, are not designed to be concealed. Like a lit city on a hill, God's people are to be seen. Like a lamp, they are not to be placed under a bushel basket but out on a stand to shine for the entire house.

14. The description "conceptual" means that a similar image is found in a clearly distinct context, so that a true parallel is not present. The noting of these helps us see where the Gospels attribute similar imagery to Jesus in multiple contexts. Some of these are the subject of judgment and dispute, and a look at various synopses shows differences of opinion.

15. Davies and Allison, *Matthew*, 1:472–73, note eleven different ancient uses of the salt metaphor. They rightly remark that the association cannot be limited to one point of contact. Fundamentally, salt is an enhancer or a catalyst. That is the best way to see the metaphor. To be salt for the world is an image of beneficial service.

16. The other uses of salt imagery differ. Mark 9:49–50 comes in a context where salt is a figure for relationships within the community. Members are to be salt and be at peace with one another, not a cause for sin. Luke 14:34–35 is similar to Matthew. It comes as a warning at the end of a section on counting the cost of discipleship. "When saltiness is lost, how can it be restored? It is fit neither for the land nor for the dunghill; people throw it away." This is followed by Jesus' common exhortation "Those who have ears to hear, let them hear." Thus, Jesus gives a warning about being discarded by God and then says, "Pay attention."

"Light for the world" was a common image in Judaism, although often the sun was the point of comparison. It was used of the intertestamental high priest Simon son of Onias (Sir. 50:6–7 [compared to the sun]), Abraham (*Testament of Abraham* 7.8 [compared to the sun]), the Messiah (*1 Enoch* 48.4 [light of the Gentiles and the hope of those who are sick in their hearts]), and Israel (Sir. 17:19 [compared to the sun]). The roots of the imagery predate Jesus and are significant. The Old Testament often used this image (Isa. 42:6 [of the task of the servant as a light to the nations, to open the eyes of the blind, to bring out prisoners from the dungeon, from the prison of those who sit in darkness]; 49:6 [of Israel as a light to the nations, salvation to the ends of the earth]; Dan. 12:3 [those who are wise shine like the brightness of the sky]). Thus, the picture of being light often had in mind a call to guide the nations. A simple exhortation concludes the unit: "Shine before people, that they may see your good works and give glory to your Father who is in heaven." As the metaphor makes clear, the role of light is to illumine the way, just as light does in an otherwise dark house. The light performs a service, a ministry that allows others to see how life that is a credit to God should be lived. That is the mission of those who would follow God. That call is directed far beyond Israel to the world.[17]

46. On the Law and the Prophets (Matt. 5:17–20; conceptual: Luke 16:17) (Aland §54; Orchard §63; Huck-Greeven §33)

This unit serves as an introduction to six examples involving the law that follow in Matt. 5:21–48. Those six examples have often been called the six "antitheses," but the problem with that label is that Jesus introduces the unit not as a contrast to the law but as a realization of it. Thus, that label misstates Jesus' most fundamental point: he came to fulfill the law. It seems likely that here Jesus is dealing with the charge of being antinomian since his controversies suggested an approach to the law that was different from traditional thinking. His reply shows that he seeks a standard that looks at the law from an internal, not an external, perspective. The issue is not murder but anger. The issue is not adultery but lust. The issue is not divorce but unfaithfulness to a vow and its effect on another. The issue is not oaths but integrity. The issue is not retaliation but nonretaliation and a willingness to go an extra step. The issue is not hate, even toward enemies, but love. The issue is not a set of rules but a response from within. That response is not self-produced but is a reflec-

---

17. The conceptual parallels in Mark 4 and Luke 8 follow the parable of the sower. These two texts, which seem parallel to each other, apparently view God's word as an exposing lamp that will disclose. Light functions in a context of warning in these two texts.

tion of a faith that trusts and follows in God's way. Alfred Plummer perhaps has said it most concisely:

> It is not obvious at first sight what Christ means by "fulfilling (πληρῶσαι) the Law." He does not mean taking the written Law as it stands, and literally obeying it. That is what he condemns, not as wrong, but as wholly inadequate. He means rather, starting with it as it stands, and bringing it on to completeness; working out the spirit of it; getting at the comprehensive principles which underlie the narrowness of the letter. These Messiah sets forth as the essence of the revelation made by God through the Law and Prophets.[18]

The goal seems to be a greater conformity to God's standard by asking not what is the least that can be done or the most that can be permitted but what is best from the standpoint of the inner person and his or her attitude. It is crucial that this unit not be seen or understood as distinct from what follows it, for the examples that follow are the commentary on what is meant here.

Jesus' mention of the law and the prophets also is significant. Jesus has more than the Pentateuch in mind. A look at his ministry shows how important a lens the prophets were for his understanding of what God's will entailed for his people. So it is God's revelation as a whole that is addressed. In addition, Jesus fulfills the law, not only in explaining its true force, as Plummer suggests, but also by pointing to its completion and realization in a fresh way of packaging its thrust. This is the "new wineskin" that Jesus will mention later, in Matt. 9:17 (a passage already treated with Mark 2:22 and Luke 5:37–38). Such a view of the law was not without Jewish precedent s1ince   there was a belief that the future would bring a better understanding of the law (in 1 Macc. 4:46 a prophet will come and tell them what to do concerning covenant requirements).[19] By placing a discussion of law in the context of God's assuring promise, as noted in the Beatitudes, Jesus can appeal to a lack of retaliation in light of the certainty of God's reward, an act that takes consummate faith. Thus, there is an eschatological dimension to Jesus' exhortation. The law will achieve its goal of creating a people set apart to God and trusting in him. That goal will be reached before creation passes away, a remark that reflects Jesus' rhetorical, hyperbolic flair.[20]

Greatness in the kingdom of heaven is defined by those who teach others this standard, while those who relax this demand to follow the law at an inner

18. Alfred Plummer, *An Exegetical Commentary on the Gospel according to S. Matthew* (London: Robert Scott, 1909), 76.

19. Davies and Allison, *Matthew,* 1:492. Such an idea may stand behind the image of Jesus as a "prophet like Moses."

20. A variation of this image appears in a distinct context in Luke 16:17, but even here Jesus is affirming that in the kingdom's arrival and overtaking of the period of the law and prophets, the goal of the entire law will be reached; it is easier for creation to pass away than for one part of the law to be voided.

level will be least in the kingdom. This verse also is integrated into the whole unit, because the standard is that the disciple's kingdom righteousness must exceed that of the scribes and the Pharisees. That standard is not the mere external attaining of a legal standard, but a reworking of the heart from within that seeks to honor God with a renewed spirit and seeks to follow the relational goal of the law. Here is where the contrast that Jesus introduces lies—not with the law, but with a traditional reading of the law that does not look at how the soul and spirit relate to its penetrating standards. Jesus' remarks show that he expects disciples to be a contrast to what the scribes and the Pharisees are. Here is another challenge by Jesus: Israel needs reform and repentance, even among the religious leadership. It is another reason why they rejected him.

47. On Murder and Wrath (Matt. 5:21–26; conceptual: Luke 12:57–59) (Aland §55; Orchard §§64–65; Huck-Greeven §34)

The first example treats the prohibition to murder from Exod. 20:13 and Deut. 5:17, one of the Ten Commandments.[21] Immediately Jesus speaks with an expository "But I say to you" and raises the issue of anger. What is significant is not just that anger is raised, but also that it is specified in various forms, because insults and addressing another as a fool are included.[22] Attitude and subsequent action are linked. Such a violation of the human dignity of another is subject to a judgment equal to murder ("liable to the Gehenna of fire"). That the punishment is stated so severely makes the point that the crime is the equal of murder, a rhetorical way of saying how serious the offense is. However, the one who has been angry is not to remain so and be headed for judgment. The way out is to see that anger is symptomatic of a deeper problem and that contempt and disrespect are dangerous expressions of lingering anger.

Jesus gives the solution in what follows: seeking reconciliation. Even before worshiping at the altar, the one with a brother or sister who "has something against you" should go and make things right with that person. Be reconciled and then worship. The order is significant because worshiping God normally would be seen as a top priority. Thus, reconciliation is so important that wor-

21. A translation of "murder" for this text is better than "kill," for the issue involves a form of intentionality separate from self-defense, participation in war, capital punishment, and manslaughter (e.g., Exod. 21:12–27).

22. The Greek, *raka,* means "empty-head." "Numskull" might be closest to this in English (see BAGD, 733–34; BDAG, 903). This is but one example of a host of such remarks. It should be noted that Jesus sometimes labeled people as fools (Matt. 23:17), so the issue is not the uttering of the words themselves but the attitude that underlies it. Jesus addresses anger and alienation that express themselves in such utterances.

ship is to be put on hold, because true worship takes place when accounts with others are clean.[23] Here we see how relational the intent of the law is. We also see how much stress God places on genuine and healthy community. Real worship is not possible without it. The opportunity comes with a warning. Failure to make things right will leave the disciple liable. Jesus uses the picture of a debtor's court in which one is remanded until full restitution is paid.[24] Thus, the law as Jesus opens it up to us shows that we are accountable not only for murder, but also for anger toward and slander of others, which is like murdering the person. So people are called to be mindful of how they relate to others.

48 On Adultery (Matt. 5:27–30; conceptual: Mark 9:43, 45, 47)
(Aland §56a; Orchard §66; Huck-Greeven §35)

The second example comes from Exod. 20:14 and Deut. 5:18 and is another of the Ten Commandments (the seventh). The topic is adultery, which legally could produce a death penalty, reflecting the seriousness of the unfaithfulness that the act represents (Deut. 22:22–24). Jesus' "but I say to you" retort raises the standard from adultery to lust, alluding to the last of the Ten Commandments, about coveting. The connection is not an accident. To lust after someone dehumanizes that person and turns that person into an object of self-indulgence. Once again, what Jesus says here is not morally new, but he does intensify the point. Jesus argues that this *is* the law, while Judaism tended to exhort in a way that applied the law this way. Judaism contained warnings against lust. Sirach 9:8 reads, "Turn away your eyes from a shapely woman, and do not gaze at beauty belonging to another; many have been seduced by a woman's beauty, and by it passion is kindled like a flame."[25] Note how the Jewish exhortation is concerned about the damage to the one doing the lusting, while Jesus' instruction considers how the other is impacted through the establishment of a damaged relationship. In Jesus' view, lust is not a private affair. Here is where adultery starts. It is committed first in the heart. Culpability rests not with the woman who is beautiful. Nor does Jesus urge her to be veiled. Responsible behavior involves not indulging one's eyes, hands, or even the mind. So the remedy is to separate oneself from the cause of the desire and not use one's senses and person for such endeavors. Jesus ex-

---

23. Judaism did teach this, as *m. Yoma* 8.9 reads, "For transgressions done between man and man, the Day of Atonement atones, only if the man regains the goodwill of his friend." So in one sense what Jesus says here reinforces what already was known. See Craig Keener, *Matthew,* IVPNTCS 1 (Downers Grove, Ill.: InterVarsity, 1997), 114–16.

24. This image is used in a conceptually distinct context in Luke 12:57–59 to argue that we had better settle accounts with God or we will pay to the last penny.

25. Note also Sir. 41:20–21; 1QS 1.6, which condemns "lecherous eyes"; CD 2.16, which contrasts "lascivious eyes" with a pleasing walk with God.

presses this idea rhetorically as plucking out the right eye, cutting off the right hand, or losing one's members versus having the whole body end up in Gehenna. Gehenna describes the place of final judgment. It was named after the Valley of Hinnom, a place of slaughter and consuming child sacrifice in the Old Testament (2 Kings 16:3; 2 Chron. 28:3).[26] The image evokes a frightful tone.

49. On Divorce (Matt. 5:31–32; conceptual: Luke 16:18) (Aland §56b; Orchard §67; Huck-Greeven §36)

The third example discusses Deut. 24:1. It is the briefest of the contrasts. Here Jesus deals with the effect of an action. The one who divorces transforms the divorced spouse into an adulterer. The remark presupposes that a remarriage will follow, because a divorce is designed to free one up for remarriage as well as untie one's possessions from the spouse. In addition, marrying a divorced woman in effect ratifies the divorce and results in adultery. Jesus is being rhetorical here as he has been in the previous contexts.[27] His major point is that the renouncing of a vow, which is what divorce is, has destructive and catastrophic consequences. It is not a private matter, but has public consequences. Marriage commitments should be honored; divorce should be shunned.

Judaism also debated this issue and had three approaches (*m. Giṭṭin* 9.10). Hillel argued that a wife could be dismissed for "any good cause," which included something as trivial as burning the food. Shammai limited such a dismissal to "unchastity." Akiba even permitted it for finding "someone else prettier than she."[28] For Jesus, the issue is staying in a marriage, not seeking how to get out. An illegitimate divorce is no divorce at all and has consequences for promoting unfaithfulness.

The role of the exception that Jesus makes on the grounds of immorality always has been controversial because only Matthew notes it. Yet Jewish background is relevant here. The assumption in Judaism is that immorality required divorce (*m. Yebamot* 2.8F–H [Neusner numbering; divorce is required]; *m. Soṭah* 5.1 [she is not allowed to marry her lover]).[29] Jesus apparently leaves this option open but does not require it.[30]

26. Mark 9:43, 45, and 47 have a more generic use of this imagery to apply separating oneself from the cause of any sin.

27. On this point, see Keener, *Matthew*, 124.

28. See also Josephus, *Ant.* 4.8.23 §253, who notes that many causes for divorce existed. Josephus divorced his wife because he was "not pleased with her behavior" (*Life* 76 §426).

29. This intense disapproval of immorality is what made Hosea's action so exceptional.

30. On the exception clause issue, see Carson, "Matthew," 413–18. He rejects other options, such as the clause applying to unfaithfulness in betrothal or incestuous marriages. The term for immorality is too generic to be a technical term here. The parallel in Luke 16:18 comes in a distinct context where divorce is the example for a high standard that Jesus urges be maintained in the face of the arrival of the era of promise. The Lukan discussion is not an exhaustive treatment of the issue.

50. On Oaths (Matt. 5:33–37) (Aland §57; Orchard §68; Huck-
Greeven §37)

The fourth example comes from Lev. 19:12, although related ideas appear in Num. 30:3–4 and Deut. 23:21. Jesus' "but I say to you" reply resembles Deut. 23:22, which reads, "But if you refrain from vowing, you will not incur guilt." So he urges not making any vows at all. Do not invoke heaven, earth, or Jerusalem, because they are God's throne, footstool, and great city, respectively. Nor should one swear by one's head, because people have no ability to create life. The solution is to have integrity. Yes should mean yes. No should mean no. The very need for a vow is evil because it suggests that something more than one's word is required. Again, the rhetorical thrust that emphasizes integrity should not be missed. Vows were approved of in Scripture (Num. 5:19–22; 6:2). Jesus' point is that oaths should not replace integrity or become a means of manipulation by how they are made. Jesus' exhortation is not without precedent in Judaism; the Essenes also shunned oaths, with the possible exception of when they joined the new community (Josephus, *War* 2.8.6–7 §§135–142; 1QS 5.8; Philo, *Every Good Man Is Free* 12 §84). However, once again the intensity of Jesus' exhortation is worth noting. Integrity should make oath-taking unnecessary.

51. On Retaliation (Matt. 5:38–42; Luke 6:29–30) (Aland §58;
Orchard §69; Huck-Greeven §38)

The fifth example involves the question of legal, equal retaliation, "an eye for an eye and a tooth for a tooth." This standard of equal retribution for loss appears in Exod. 21:24, Lev. 24:20, and Deut. 19:21 and is known as the *lex talionis*. By the first century, monetary reparations had replaced physical maiming as the penalty for physically injuring another.[31] The context of each passage involves legal claims. The remarks deal with personal relationships and are not an issue of how political states function (cf. Rom. 13:1–7). Jesus' "but I say to you" urges nonresistance to evil. Three specific examples appear: turning the other cheek, giving one's cloak in a lawsuit as well as one's coat, and going the extra mile in the case of a military conscription.[32] Background helps us appreciate the first illustration. The slap was a common Jewish insult that could express rejec-

---

31. Keener, *Matthew*, 127.

32. A legal setting is in view for the second example of the taking of the coat. Generally, a cloak was protected, so that the person retained some covering (Exod. 22:26–27; Deut. 24:12–13). See BAGD, ἱμάτιον, 376 §2; BDAG, 475 §2; R. A. Horsley, "Ethics and Exegesis: 'Love Your Enemies' and the Doctrine of Non-Violence," *Journal of the American Academy of Religion* 54 (1986): 3–31. Generosity and sensitivity mean going beyond the minimum.

tion. The "offering of the other cheek" pictures a willingness to remain vulnerable in the face of such rejection. Finally, the willingness to give to those who beg or borrow is affirmed. The examples stress that rather than exacting an equal payment, mercy and even generosity should be the response. The point is to reverse a tendency for keeping score and a response that often only fosters ill will. The willingness to give without considering a payback or even to suffer without payback is urged here. In fact, that spiral should be reversed by a trend to be generous to those who have genuine need.[33] An example of the application of this principle is found in 1 Cor. 6:1–9.

The Lukan parallel follows a general exhortation to love your enemies, to do good to those who hate you, bless those who curse you, and pray for those who abuse you. The examples come in Jesus' praying for his executors from the cross and Stephen's prayer for his persecutors (Luke 23:34; Acts 7:60). In Luke the coat-cloak image is slightly different in that the image is reversed and appears in a context where stealing is involved. The issue here seems to involve not being overly zealous in defending one's possessions so that the situation escalates.

52. On Loving One's Enemies (Matt. 5:43–48; Luke 6:27–28, 32–36)
(Aland §59; Orchard §71; Huck-Greeven §39)

The sixth example involves the exhortation to "love your neighbor and hate your enemy." The positive exhortation reflects Lev. 19:18, while elements of the negative can be seen in texts such as Ps. 139:21–22; 137:7–9. These texts are rooted in a kind of righteous indignation for real wrongs done. Jesus' "but I say to you" asks that one transcend that understandable reaction. Judaism sometimes made this point as well: "For a good man does not have a blind eye, but he is merciful to all, even though they may be sinners" (*Testament of Benjamin* 4.2).[34] Jesus' call intensifies this perspective. In loving enemies and praying for persecutors, the disciple becomes an example that reflects being a child of the heavenly Father, for he provides sun and rain for the just and unjust alike. To love only those who love you and to salute only friends is to do what sinners and Gentiles do.[35] The impli-

33. Much debate exists as to whether Jesus urges giving to all who beg. The assumption in the remark about the one who begs is that the need is legitimate. As with the rest of this section, there is an element of rhetorical hyperbole present to show that simply responding in kind or showing no concern is what should not be done. On how begging was viewed in Judaism, see Sir. 40:28–30. It truly was to be a last resort, because being a beggar was considered worse than dying. Only among the shameless is begging sweet.

34. H. C. Kee, trans., "Testaments of the Twelve Patriarchs," in *The Old Testament Pseudepigrapha*, ed. James H. Charlesworth (Garden City, N.Y.: Doubleday, 1983–85), 1:826.

35. Although Jesus sought out sinners and Gentiles, here they are alluded to as a representation of what unspiritual people might do, a figure that appears elsewhere in Matthew (6:7; 18:17; 20:25). Why let the standard be set by the unspiritual?

cation here is that disciples are not to live by the standards of the average person. The relational response of the disciple is not to mirror the average standard of the world but to reflect the character of the Father. Thus, it calls for a "perfection," or completeness, of maturity that matches that of God. This is precisely how the disciple's response will exceed the standard of the righteousness of the scribes and Pharisees that Jesus mentioned in introducing these six examples in 5:20. So Jesus' exhortation begins and ends by noting the overarching goal that one pursues in these relationships: surpassing the seemingly pious, surpassing the average person, and reflecting the character of God. The walk seeks to reach for the highest standard of love and giving.

It is this portion of the sermon that forms the center of the Lukan version. Both in Luke 6:27–28 and in 32–36, Luke highlights the call to love one's enemy. The refrain in the examples is this: if you do what sinners do, what credit is that to you? So we are to love beyond those who love us and to do good beyond those who do good to us. Lending should extend beyond those who surely will repay. Doing so and expecting nothing in return leads to great reward from heaven and reflects that we will be "children of the Most High," following God's example to the ungrateful and selfish. Luke notes a standard other than the perfection stated in Matthew. Luke speaks of being "merciful, even as your Father is merciful." The refusal to keep score and to seek retribution is the exercise of mercy.

These six examples show Jesus not rejecting the law but intensifying it. He shows how he has come to fulfill it. Not only does he call on us to look at the law from the standpoint of the heart (murder-anger; adultery-lust), but also he asks for integrity and generosity that reflect mercy and love toward all (marriage vows, oaths, lack of retaliation, love for enemies). Living this way means maintaining relationships as the Father does, demonstrating to all that we are his children, reflecting his character.

53. On Giving Alms (Matt. 6:1–4) (Aland §60; Orchard §72; Huck-Greeven §40)

In 6:1–18, three acts of piety, which Matthew calls "righteousness," receive attention: alms, prayer, and fasting. In each case disciples are to serve quietly, not drawing attention to themselves. The passage opens with the fundamental premise that acts of piety performed to be seen by other people have no reward before the Father. Religious practice should not be like that of the hypocrites (vv. 2, 5, 16).[36] In Matt. 5:16, Jesus makes a point that religious acts should be noticed by others, but Jesus' point here is that the attention they draw should come naturally. The Jewish *Letter of Aristeas* 168 reads, "Practice righteousness before all

36. The term "hypocrite" refers to a "pretender" or "stage actor" (ὑποκριτής, BAGD, 845; BDAG, 1038). The actions are a big show.

men, being mindful of God." The context of the letter is significant, as it looks at Jewish relationships with Gentiles. Jesus' exhortation is not unprecedented. The giving of alms was seen as a fundamental religious practice (Deut. 15:11; Sir. 29:8 [do not make the needy wait for alms]; Tob. 4:7, 16 [give some food and clothing to the needy, and one's surplus as alms]; 12:8; 14:10; *Testament of Job* 9.7–8 [an example of giving without seeking attention and encouraging those who need help to come]; *m. ʾAbot* 5.13 [the saint is the one who gives and wishes that others give as well]). Jesus' descriptions are rhetorical. One should not blow a trumpet like the hypocrites do when they give in such a way as to draw attention to themselves. Rather, a disciple should give with the right hand while the left does not know what is happening. The act should be secret, and the reward will be the same (see also Matt. 6:6, 18).

54. On Prayer (Matt. 6:5–6) (Aland §61; Orchard §73a; Huck-Greeven §41)

Similar is the exhortation about prayer. One is not to pray while standing in the synagogue or street so as to be seen by others. Jewish prayer could be done while standing (1 Sam. 1:26; Neh. 9:4) or while kneeling to prostrate oneself (1 Kings 8:54; Ezra 9:5). Kneeling generally was reserved for solemn occasions or to show exceptional distress.[37] The reward of those who pray ostentatiously is only that others see them. Rather, prayer is to take place in secret in the "inner room" with the door shut.[38] Jesus is speaking rhetorically again, for when he prayed, he often withdrew to a remote place to do so. Jesus' point is neither that one should go into a particular room nor that prayer should never be public (for Jesus did pray publicly on occasion). Rather, the act should be done for God, as prayer should reflect what it is: a discussion between the disciple and God. The divine reward will be the same, between God and the disciple. Again, the point is not to prohibit public prayer (Matt. 15:36; 18:19–20; 1 Tim. 2:8), but that praying in order to be seen by others is not "godly."

55. The Disciples' Prayer (Matt. 6:7–15; conceptual: Luke 11:1–4) (Aland §62; Orchard §§73b–75; Huck-Greeven §42)

Jesus gives advice about prayer before setting forth an example. He suggests that one should not use empty phrases (cf. Luke 18:11–12). This probably is

37. Davies and Allison, *Matthew*, 1:585.
38. For this term, see ταμεῖον, BAGD, 803; BDAG, 988. This is the inner room of a house, into which no one outside can see.

a reference to the names of multiple deities and a listing of deeds, almost as if the petitioner had to persuade the gods to act. Numerous magical papyri give evidence of this kind of repetition. Ecclesiastes 5:2 reasoned, "Do not be rash with your mouth, nor let your heart be hasty to utter a word before God, for God is in heaven, and you upon the earth; therefore let your words be few." Sirach 7:14 urged, "Do not repeat yourself when you pray." So Jesus sounds like the voice of wisdom literature. The disciple need not linger repetitively in prayer, because God knows what is needed before one asks. A point underlying the remark is that God responds with reference to our needs, not our desires.

So Jesus gives a sample prayer, which, because it comes from him, is known as the Lord's Prayer. However, it actually is the disciples' prayer. Jesus gives it for disciples to pray as a community. When Jesus says to pray like this, he probably is not giving specific wording to be repeated, but a sample form of prayer in theme and attitude.

Two characteristics stand out. First, the prayer is exceedingly brief. Judaism used a corporate prayer, the *Shemoneh Esreh,* which was quite long.[39] It treated eighteen topics, with a few sentences given to each topic. It is likely that some form of this prayer goes back to this period, although it also is quite possible that it was substantially shorter. Nevertheless, in contrast, Jesus' example prayer is very short. It contains an address to God as Father, three requests tied to God's actions, and then four petitions put in personal terms. Disciples address God with an intimate term that also appears in Rom. 8:15. They call God "Father." The disciples ask that God's name remain set apart, that is, that God show his unique character. The disciples also look for the day when God will bring his kingdom, showing the fullness of his justice and authority. The disciples also seek that God's will be accomplished. The point in each of these three petitions is that disciples express a common submission to God's character, plan, and instruction. The prayer also reflects an eschatological perspective. When God's kingdom and will on earth receive attention, the desire is that God's presence and authority fully disclose themselves. So second, the prayer is saturated with the disciples' submission and dependence on the Father. Even the personal requests take on this emphasis. Whether the disciple thinks of daily needs such as bread, or of the need to seek forgiveness, or of the need for protection from temptation and evil, he or she seeks God's provision and protection.

There is also the recognition that a request for mercy in seeking God's forgiveness implies the disciple's readiness to forgive. The disciple as follower is

---

39. It is possible that a Jewish prayer similar to this is the short *Kaddish,* which followed the synagogue sermon. It asked that God's name be exalted, that his kingdom rule show itself soon, and that his name be praised. See Davies and Allison, *Matthew,* 1:595–97, who also note the *Shemoneh Esreh.*

reflected in virtually every aspect of the prayer. Thus, there is the assurance that with our forgiving comes God's readiness to forgive. On the other hand, a failure to forgive on our part results in God treating us in similar terms. Once again, relationship to God is tied to how we relate to others. One relationship should define the other.

The Lukan version of the prayer occurs in a separate context where the disciples asked to be taught to pray, as John so taught his disciples. What Luke has as private instruction, Matthew presents as a more public prayer with a liturgical flair. Luke uses the occasion to make several remarks about prayer afterward. The lack of agreement within the tradition on the wording—Luke's version is shorter—may well confirm that Jesus did not seek to teach specific wording as much as a type of prayer. Luke's version has an address to the Father, two affirmations that God's name be set apart and his will be done, and three requests. The requests are for daily bread, for forgiveness, and not to be led into temptation. This last request shows that the disciples recognize that if temptation is to be avoided, God must lead the way. The spirit of the two versions of the prayer is similar. The Lukan prayer will be treated in detail later in Luke's context.

56. On Fasting (Matt. 6:16–18) (Aland §63; Orchard §76; Huck-Greeven §43)

Jesus' word about fasting parallels his advice about alms and prayer. Fasting is not to follow the example of the hypocrites, who disfigure their faces in order to make their suffering obvious to other people. Luke 18:12 suggests that some fasted twice a week. Some rabbis instructed that those who fast should not bathe (which suggests not wash their faces) when fasting (*m. Yoma* 8.1 forbids bathing; the only exception is a king and his bride). Jesus teaches that the reward of those who broadcast their fasting is simply the attention they draw to themselves. Rather, fasting that God honors requires only an anointing of the head with washing of the face. God observes it in secret and will reward the effort of those who do it before him. Thus, in this section, Jesus consistently urges that our practice and service to God be directed to him and not be done to draw attention to ourselves.

57. Treasures in Heaven (Matt. 6:19–21; Luke 12:33–34) (Aland §64; Orchard §77; Huck-Greeven §44)

This unit in Matthew begins a concentration on wealth that extends to Matt. 6:34. The pursuit of wealth is the issue until Matt. 6:24, while the relationship of wealth to worry is the topic to the end of Matt. 6. The discussion on the pursuit of wealth has three parts: seeking treasure, the eye as lamp, and the two masters.

One should pursue treasure in heaven, not on earth. Earthly treasure has limits and eventually is consumed by moths or rust. Also, such goods can be stolen. The Greek behind the English translation "rust" actually refers to rot and how clothes are wasted by consumption or wear. A variation on this theme is found in Luke 12:15–21, where possessions cannot be taken to heaven, while James 5:2–3 speaks of moth-eaten garments. Sirach 29:10–11 reads, "Lose your silver for the sake of a brother or a friend, and do not let it rust under a stone and be lost. Lay up your treasure according to the commandments of the Most High, and it will profit you more than gold." Once again Jesus recalls the Jewish wisdom tradition. What Jesus precludes here is the accumulation of massive amounts of treasure as a life goal.

In contrast is the pursuit of heavenly treasure. Here, nothing is consumed or stolen. Again, Jewish wisdom tradition speaks similarly. Discussing giving, Tobit 4:9 says, "So you will be laying up a good treasure for yourself against the day of necessity." *Psalms of Solomon* 9.5 says, "He that does righteousness lays up for himself life with the Lord." *Second Baruch* 24.1 speaks of the treasures of righteousness being stored in the reckoning of the end.

The issue for Jesus is one's heart. Is it set on heaven or on earth? So he notes that where one's treasure is, that is, what one values and seeks after, will guide and direct the heart's actions. This is precisely why a focus on heaven and its values is so important. In effect, Jesus' discourses are treasures of heaven, wisdom that is worth more than pearls (Prov. 3:13–18).

The Lukan parallel comes in a distinct context where Jesus exhorts disciples to sell their possessions and give alms. Doing so provides purses that do not grow old and heavenly treasure that does not fail, because here there is no moth or thief. The parallel closes with the declaration that where one's treasure is, there will be the heart. This kind of proverb is not beyond repetition in Jesus' teaching, so it appears in multiple settings.

58. The Sound Eye (Matt. 6:22–23; Luke 11:34–36) (Aland §65; Orchard §78; Huck-Greeven §45)

In speaking about the heart, one also must consider the eye. This proverb is so short that it is hard to be certain what is referred to in the eye image. Is it what comes in through the eye that makes for light or darkness? Or is it what comes out through the eye that reflects light or darkness? Again, ancient texts may help. *Testament of Job* 18.3 states, "My eyes, acting as lamps, searched out." Here, eyes do not receive but act. In fact, all six ancient Jewish uses of the image do not have light coming into a dark place inside the person but coming out from the eye.[40] So in Dan. 10:6, the eyes of the heavenly figure are like "flaming torches." The lamps in Zech. 4 are the eyes of the Lord roaming the earth. We noted the *Testament of Job* passage previously. Eyes are the expression of the soul, not its intake, although certainly the two ideas are related. What Jesus stresses in this saying is that a good eye acts in a healthy way. It is the sign of a healthy soul. If it acts otherwise, then an unhealthy soul is present. Stress is on the risk of a lack of health. For if darkness is present, that darkness is great. Here is another reason why one's heart must be inclined to heavenly treasure, righteousness, and values. Such a focus produces the right quality of life.

The Lukan parallel occurs in a distinct context after several texts where the need to respond to Jesus' message is urged.[41] In contrast to the Matthean example, it ends with a note on the positive example: if the body is full of light, having no dark part, it will be wholly bright, like a lamp with its rays giving light. The image is of light going out. Thus, it confirms the imagery as one of action, not reception. The proverbial character of this image also makes it capable of repetition in multiple settings.

59. On Serving Two Masters (Matt. 6:24; Luke 16:13) (Aland §66; Orchard §79; Huck-Greeven §46)

The exhortation concerning treasure closes with a warning about loyalty. One cannot serve God and mammon. Mammon is not merely a reference to money; it refers to possessions in any form. At Qumran, one of Belial's three nets that entrap Israel is wealth (CD 4.17; 6.15 speaks of a wicked wealth that defiles). The contrast between love and hate has to do with the priority of making a choice when one has to decide (on this contrast, see Gen. 29:30, 33; Jer. 8:2). One will opt for possessions or for God. One has a choice in 6:19–24 of two types of treasure, two types of seeing, and two types of loyalty.

The parallel in Luke 16:13 concludes the parable of the dishonest steward. It is worded almost exactly like Matt. 6:24. Much of Luke 16 handles the issue of possessions. Luke reports that the Pharisees scoffed at Jesus' teaching on this topic. The prophets also made complaints about wealth, as Jesus does here (Amos 5:10–12; Isa. 1:22–23; 5:8–10) and as did later Judaism (*1 Enoch* 92–105).[42]

40. Davies and Allison, *Matthew*, 635–36.

41. Note that this Lukan parallel (Luke 11:34–36) falls earlier than the previous passage's Lukan parallel (Luke 12:33–34), so that Luke's parallels do not all fall in the same order as they appear in Matthew.

42. On this parallel, see George Nickelsburg, "Riches, the Rich, and God's Judgment in 1 Enoch 92–105 and the Gospel according to Luke," *New Testament Studies* 25 (1978–79): 324–44.

60. Do Not Worry (Matt. 6:25–34; Luke 12:22–32) (Aland §67; Orchard §80; Huck-Greeven §47)

This well-known text calls for complete trust in God's care and appeals to the example within creation to show that God does care. The exhortation makes sense in the Matthean context because not being concerned about possessions raises the question of how the disciples will have their needs met. One should not be anxious about food, drink, or clothing—the necessities of life. Is not life more than these? The Greek interrogative chosen shows that the expected answer is positive: life is more than food and clothing. Whether one looks at the birds, who get fed, or the grass and flowers, which are clothed, one sees that God cares for the creation.[43] Besides, worry cannot add to one's life span. So such worry is fruitless.

People are more important than the birds, grass, or even flowers. Again, Matthew's version has the remark as a question that expects a positive answer. This "how much more" style of argument is known as *qal wahomer*. If it is true of the lesser, then it is even more true of the greater. The only hint of critique comes when Jesus calls his audience people of little faith. The Gentiles seek such things, but the Father knows what is needed (Ps. 127:2; Isa. 32:17; 1 Pet. 5:7; even for animals: Job 38:41; Ps. 147:9). The implication is that the caring Father can be trusted.

The basic exhortation is to continually seek God's kingdom and pursue his righteousness—really the topic of this entire sermon. The promise is that these basics will be taken care of, so that one need not be anxious. The exhortation closes with a call to realize that each day has enough worry of its own.

The Lukan parallel in 12:22–32 comes in a distinct context, following the parable of the rich fool, yet a second context outside of Luke 16 where riches, seen in terms of possessions, is the key topic. The wording is fairly similar to Matthew's. The most significant difference comes at the end of the exhortation, where disciples are told not to fear, because the Father's pleasure is to give them the kingdom. For Luke, the stress is that the kingdom alone is sufficient.

61. On Judging (Matt. 7:1–5; Luke 6:37–42; conceptual: Mark 4:24–25) (Aland §68; Orchard §81; Huck-Greeven §48)

The sermon now proceeds with a series of more randomly arranged topics, beginning with judgment in Matt. 7:1–5. By "random" I mean that the ser-

---

43. The idea that flowers are better clothed than Solomon refers to one who was exceedingly well attired (1 Kings 9:26–10:29).

mon now moves more quickly from topic to topic with a less clear connection between the units. The first portion of the exhortation treats the issue of not judging. The risk here is to overinterpret the scope of the passage by arguing that it is a comprehensive prohibition against judging. Against this view, so well known in the world's frequent citing of this passage, stands Matt. 7:5, which shows that this comprehensive meaning cannot be intended. Correction can be pursued once one is careful to cure one's own errors. Thus, Jesus is condemning harsh and insensitive judgment in which one assumes immunity from the risk of failing. The warning is that our standard of judgment is what God will apply to us. The premise is shared in Jewish wisdom. Sirach 28:2–4 teaches, "Forgive your neighbor the wrong he has done; and then your sins will be pardoned when you pray. Does anyone harbor anger against another, and expect healing from the Lord? If one has no mercy toward another like himself, can he then seek pardon for his own sins?" The appeal really is for a merciful spirit, even in the midst of moral faults. Galatians 6:1 is similar in tone.

An illustration makes the point concrete, showing its intention. One should not tinker with a speck in another's eye when one has a log in one's own eye. The rhetorical exaggeration fits with Jesus' style in the sermon as a whole. Disciples are not to be so quick in judging the little sins of others when their own sin is so great. Priority goes to our own spiritual welfare and correction. Having learned from our mistakes and having removed the log from our own eye, we are in a better position to help another. Rabbi Hillel is reported to have said, "Do not judge your brother until you have come to his place" (*m. 'Abot* 2.4). Relating to others, even in correction, requires self-reflection and sensitivity.

The Lukan parallel in 6:37–42 forms part of the third portion of his sermon, which treats judgment as well. Luke emphasizes in addition the issue of reward, because he has additional exhortations to be giving and forgiving. Jesus explains that what is given will be given back in full measure to overflowing. These additions show and explain well the point of Jesus' teaching. Luke also adds a note about being discerning by asking if a blind person can lead another blind person, while noting that a disciple will be like his or her teacher. The implication is that they should judge carefully whom they choose to follow. Luke then has the speck-log teaching. In this Lukan context, the additional point emerges that one should be careful to assess one's own instruction properly before offering to help others. An implication about being responsive to Jesus' teaching emerges more clearly in Luke's version, something that both versions make explicit at the end of the discourse.

62. On Profaning the Holy (Matt. 7:6) (Aland §69; Orchard §82; Huck-Greeven §49)

This short proverb probably is laid out in an ABB'A' pattern; it discusses dogs (A) and pigs (B), and then pigs who trample (B') and dogs who turn to attack (A').[44] In the Old Testament, a dog was often a figure of reproach (1 Sam. 17:43; 24:14; Prov. 26:11; also in 2 Pet. 2:22). Pigs were ceremonially unclean animals. So the point is that one does not give what is precious (holy things or pearls) to those who will not respond appreciatively. As with other parts of Jesus' teaching, the point is not an absolute prohibition, because then the disciple could not share the gospel with those who are not responsive. Rather, the point is that the disciple is not obligated to share with those who are hard-hearted. These people are like pigs that trample what is precious and like dogs that turn and attack the one seeking to feed them. Using discernment is the point here. The sentiment recalls Prov. 23:9: "Do not speak to a fool, for he will scorn the wisdom of your words." A contrast in attitude is suggested in Prov. 9:8: "A scoffer who is rebuked will only hate you; the wise, when rebuked, will love you." The discerning follower of Jesus can tell when a scoffer is present, and so remains quiet.

63. On Asking God (Matt. 7:7–11; Luke 11:9–13) (Aland §70; Orchard §83; Huck-Greeven §50)

In Matthew, Jesus turns his attention to how God relates to us. Although the passage encourages the disciple to ask, the passage's focus is on how God responds. God's character is to give us what we need as an expression of his generosity. Thus, the disciple can ask confidently. Whether this is expressed as asking, seeking, or knocking, the disciple can ask with a confidence that God will give what is needed. The stress on God's character is evident from the illustrations, which focus not on the one who asks, but on the attitude of the one who responds. The key illustration is the example of a father and all the care that role implies. A series of questions indicates the theme. A son who asks for bread does not get a stone; nor does a request for fish yield a serpent. No father in his right mind would respond this way. The illustrations treat some basic elements of life, just as the earlier exhortation about worry in Matt. 6:25–34 did. However, the "good gifts" look to things beyond possessions; Luke's reading of the prayer sees the Spirit as the key gift. The conclusion says it all: "If you, being evil, know how to give good gifts to your children, how much more will your Father in heaven give good things

---

44. Davies and Allison, *Matthew,* 677.

to those who ask him." Here we see a "how much more" argument, as we did between the creation and humankind in 6:25–34. Humankind is more valuable than the creation, so here our heavenly Father will respond with more sensitivity than earthly fathers do and give disciples what they really need for their good.

The other key point is that what is given is related to the good things of wisdom and life. James 1:5–8 touches on this theme in a similar way. It is a standard theme of wisdom. Proverbs 8:17 says, "I [Wisdom] love those who love me, and those who seek me diligently find me." Wisdom of Solomon 6:12 notes that Wisdom is found by those who diligently seek her. Ecclesiastes 7:23–29 illustrates the point in a short narrative. Jeremiah 29:13 argues, "You will seek me and find me, when you seek me with all your heart." The theme's frequency and consistency reveal that Jesus is addressing the good things associated with the wise walk, which is the topic of the sermon.

The Lukan parallel in 11:9–13 comes in a context where prayer is the issue. The point is fundamentally the same, but Luke narrows the focus. Rather than speaking of good gifts, he notes that the Holy Spirit is given. Since the Spirit is the consummate gift of God and also is a source of enablement and wisdom, the difference is not that great. Luke's illustrations also differ in order and content: a fish and an egg are requested, and a serpent and a scorpion are given. The point made is the same, even though the illustrations differ: no parent would give in such a manner.

The disciple can ask for wisdom in prayer and should do so knowing that God is better than a caring parent and will grant the request. The passage does not show God signing a blank check of requests for disciples to fill out. It involves the basic needs for a healthy walk.

64. The Golden Rule (Matt. 7:12; Luke 6:31) (Aland §71; Orchard §84; Huck-Greeven §51)

This passage sums up the relational thrust of the whole sermon. The allusion back to the law and the prophets recalls 5:17–20. All that they teach relationally is summed up in "So whatever you wish that people would do to you, so do to them." This has been known for the last few centuries as the Golden Rule. It is not unprecedented, in that this idea was expressed in one way or another in the ancient world as another basic piece of wisdom.[45] What makes Jesus' presentation unique is that he does express it in the most emphatic way possible, because there is no note of reciprocity in the motivation. In contrast stands *Letter of Aristeas* 207, which reads, "As you wish that no evil

45. For a host of ancient parallels, see Bock, *Luke 1:1–9:50*, 595–98.

shall befall you, but to be a partaker of all good things, so you should act on the same principle towards your subjects and offenders." More typical of wisdom material is Sir. 31:15, which says, "Judge your neighbor's feelings by your own, and in every matter be thoughtful." *Testament of Naphtali* 1.6 (late Hebrew ed.) reads, "None should do to his neighbor what he does not like for himself."[46] Jesus' summary is drawing on another popular theme that represents the best of the wisdom tradition.

Luke's parallel in 6:31 is also a part of his sermon. As in Matthew, it comes at a key point of the discourse because it occupies a pivotal role in the central part of the sermon treating love for others, including enemies. It is the only remark of the sequence within the speech that deviates from the Matthean order of the material that Luke also has in his sermon. However, what is interesting is that within the alteration, its central role has remained. In the section where Jesus has urged love for enemies (6:27–36), this rule stands at the center as the core principle of the exhortation. Luke does not allude to the law and the prophets because he has presented his version of Jesus' teaching without mentioning issues tied to the law.

So Jesus' "Golden Rule" really is his core relational rule when it comes to how people should interact with others. It is appropriate that this remark follows the example of the considerate Father in Matt. 7:7–11, because the exhortation has a model for it. Concern for the feelings of others mirrors God's care of us.

65. The Two Ways (Matt. 7:13–14; Luke 13:23–24) (Aland §72; Orchard §85; Huck-Greeven §52)

The doctrine of the two ways was also well known in Judaism. Deuteronomy 11:26 sets forth the choice between opting for blessing or for cursing, something reinforced in Deut. 30:15, which reads "See, I have set before you this day life and good, death and evil." Jeremiah 21:8 refers to the two ways directly as "the way of life and the way of death," while Ps. 1 contrasts the way of the blessed and of the wicked. Extrabiblical texts also raise the theme. *Testament of Asher* 1.3–5 notes two ways, two inclinations, two kinds of action, two modes of action, and two issues before humanity. *Second Enoch* 30.15 argues that Adam was shown two ways, light and darkness. Mishnah *'Abot* 2.9 contrasts a good way with an evil way, and Qumran document 1QS 3.14–4.26 contrasts the ways of the sons of light and of the sons of darkness. So the motif was well known.

46. See R. H. Charles, ed., *The Apocrypha and Pseudepigrapha of the Old Testamant in English*, 2 vols. (Oxford: Clarendon, 1913), 2:361.

Jesus' exhortation stresses that the way to life is through the narrow gate and is not easily or automatically obtained. The way is easy that leads to destruction; that gate is wide and many enter it. This theme also has roots in Judaism. Sirach 21:10 discusses the wicked: "The way of a sinner is paved with smooth stones, but at its end is the pit of Hades." Wickedness comes easy, says wisdom; righteousness must be pursued, as Prov. 2:1–4 argues. So Jesus explains that the gate to life is narrow and its way is hard. It goes against the grain and is not popular in the larger culture. Those who find it are few. In other words, wisdom that leads to life has to be searched for; it does not come naturally. Again, Jesus' teaching stands within the Jewish wisdom tradition. What is unique is that he brings it into such a compact focus.

The Lukan parallel in 13:23–24 really is a distinct use of the same image. It comes in response to a question from the crowd about whether few will be saved. Apparently, someone listening to Jesus deduced this from his teaching. Rather than answer the question, Jesus exhorts that a person should strive, or better, continually labor to enter through the narrow door.[47] Then he warns that many will seek to enter and not be able to do so. Later in the same text, Jesus does note that people will come from east and west, north and south, to recline at table in the kingdom. This suggests that many will make it in, but not necessarily those who originally seemed to have the inside track—a reversal theme that Jesus often uses. Jesus turns the question around here from how many will be saved to whom the saved will include. That is why one must look for and journey through the narrow door. Luke 13:25–27 makes the issue whether the Lord knew the seeker, an issue that Matthew's sermon also will raise shortly.

66. Fruit and False Prophets (Matt. 7:15–20; Luke 6:43–45)
(Aland §73; Orchard §86a; Huck-Greeven §53)

Discernment and judgment have been the theme since Matt. 7:13. Jesus now gives a major hint about how to recognize the genuine from the dangerous. There is a threat of which they must beware. Matthew 7:15–20 warns the disciples, while 7:21–23 will warn of the fate of those who mistakenly thought they knew Jesus.

Disciples should beware of false prophets, who look like docile sheep but in fact are devouring wolves. To discern their presence, a disciple need only check their fruit. Job 14:4 says, "Who can bring a clean thing out of an unclean?" Grapes will not come from thorns, nor figs from thistles. James 3:11–12 uses similar imagery in regard to what speech reveals about the

---

47. Note the present tense ἀγωνίζεσθε, which looks to ongoing effort.

heart.[48] A sound tree yields good fruit, just as a bad tree bears evil fruit. In fact, a good tree will not bear evil fruit, nor will a bad tree give good fruit. A tree not bearing good fruit is cut down and burned. There possibly is an allusion to the Jewish leadership here in Jesus' context, but the danger is constant and not limited to Jesus' setting alone. The subsequent passage in 7:21–23 seems to address those who attached themselves to the Lord in some way. Thus, the warning seems better suited to take heed of those who appear to be inside the camp but really are not.[49] Disciples always must keep careful watch. Jesus' advice is that these false disciples can be identified by their fruit. A simple claim to be attached to Jesus or even the use of his name in ministry is not enough.

The Lukan parallel in 6:43–45 is less clearly connected to the context of a false prophet. It appears as a more general warning about any person whom one chooses to follow because it comes after the warning about the blind being unable to lead the blind and the speck-log illustration. At this point Luke and Matthew overlap conceptually. Luke has only the example about a good tree not being able to bear bad fruit and a bad tree not being able to produce good fruit. Fruit reveals a tree's quality. So figs do not come from thorns, nor grapes from a bramble bush. At this point the overlap ends. Following these remarks, Luke alone has a note that the good person produces good, while the evil person produces evil. In both the good and evil cases, it is from the abundance of the heart that the mouth (i.e., the teaching) speaks. Thus, the Lukan context is slightly more generic, while Matthew's point is a more narrow application of the same imagery. This difference fits Luke's less specific engagement of the themes in his version of this teaching, given the more concise form of the address.

67. Calling Out "Lord, Lord" and the Reply "I Never Knew You" (Matt. 7:21–23; Luke 6:46; conceptual: Luke 13:25–27)
(Aland §74; Orchard §§86b–87; Huck-Greeven §54)

The sermon closes on a somber note. The warning indicates the fate of some who have claimed to minister in the name of the Lord. Jesus' authority

---

48. This distinct topical use of this imagery for speech is also in Sir. 27:6: "Its [speech's] fruit discloses the cultivation of a tree; so a person's speech discloses the cultivation of his mind." In contrast, Gal. 5:19–23 makes a point similar to Jesus', except that here the stress looks to the fruit of the righteous, who have the benefit of the presence of God's Spirit to enable them. John 15 places the key to fruitfulness in abiding in Jesus—a proper development of the image that Jesus raises here, as Matt. 7:24–27 will suggest.

49. The mixed character of the community is something that Matthew develops in the kingdom parables (see 13:24–30, 36–43). See also Davies and Allison, *Matthew*, 701–3. They note that the description of a hypocrite also would apply to those criticized here, beyond its earlier association with the practices of the apparently pious. This theme is one that Matthew repeats in 7:22 and 24:5, 12, 24, 48–51. The language recalls 3:8, 10, John's warning to his Jewish audience.

stands out in this scene; he is the judge at the final judgment "on that day." The moment of judgment is the arrival of the kingdom at the time of consummation. The emotional double address of Jesus as "Lord, Lord" is not a mantra that guarantees entry into the kingdom. Rather, entry comes from doing the will of the Father who is in heaven. Lest this be read as pure law, the remarks that follow are exceedingly important. Many will claim to have done the Father's work in the Lord's name, but the truth of the association is not a given (cf. Jer. 14:14; 27:15; 29:9). They will claim to have prophesied, exorcised demons, and done other mighty works, yet none of that activity will matter. Claiming to know the one who has authority over judgment is not what counts; actually knowing him is. The exclusion is noted with the phrase "I never knew you; depart from me, you evildoers." The remark about not knowing is a renunciation phrase (cf. John 10:14; 1 Cor. 8:3; 2 Tim. 2:19). Psalm 6:9 (= 6:8 Eng.) addresses the wicked with this phrase: "Depart from me, all you workers of evil." The righteous one in the psalm looks forward to God's vindication in being separated from the wicked. So here the judge utters words of exclusion for some who had been active in his name but did not know him. Their lawlessness has exposed them (Matt. 7:20).

The Lukan parallel in 6:46 is less specific. Here there is no explicit note of judgment, nor is there any detail about the claim. There is only rebuke about invoking the name of the Lord and not doing what he says. As in Matthew, Jesus is seen as occupying an authoritative position. His teaching is not an option to be lightly regarded; it is to be embraced.

A second parallel comes in Luke 13:25–27. Here the context is the same as the Lukan parallel to Matt. 7:15–20, where the question is raised about whether only a few will be saved. Alongside the exhortation to strive to enter the narrow door comes an illustration of people standing at the door seeking entry. The reply comes twice. First, the Lord replies, "I do not know where you are from." This produces the objection that those at the door had eaten and drunk in the Lord's presence and that he had taught in their streets. The claim is that acquaintance with Jesus is enough. The reply comes a second time, "I tell you, I do not know where you come from; depart from me, all you workers of unrighteousness." The effect of the reply is that entry is not granted. Weeping and gnashing of teeth will result from the rejection as they recognize that they are thrown out, which in this context means being denied entry. They are excluded and judged, left on the outside. Rather, as the passage goes on to say, entry will come to many others from the north, south, east, and west. So in this context, as in Matthew, the passage describes exclusion from the kingdom of some who had contact with Jesus. Luke simply is more generic in his description, while Matthew has in mind those who claimed an association with Jesus without ever coming to know him.

68. Houses Built on Rock or Sand (Matt. 7:24–27; Luke 6:47–49)
(Aland §75; Orchard §88; Huck-Greeven §55)

In both Matthew and Luke, the sermon closes with the same basic illustration. Only details differ. The picture is of the construction of two kinds of houses. One has its foundation on rock, while the other is set precariously on sand. As with other portions of the sermon, the imagery has roots in wisdom literature. Proverbs 10:25 reads, "When the tempest passes, the wicked is no more, but the righteous is established forever." Proverbs 12:7 is similar: "The wicked are overthrown and are no more, but the house of the righteous will stand." Proverbs 14:11 argues, "The house of the wicked will be destroyed, but the tent of the righteous will flourish."[50] However, the most interesting text is Isa. 28:16–17, because it was used so frequently in the early church. God lays a precious cornerstone in Zion, a foundation stone, so that "one who trusts will not panic." Those who have made a covenant of death will be swept away when the waters overwhelm the shelter. The Isaiah text is a warning to scoffers that judgment comes to those who do not heed the Lord. Jesus sees his teaching *and* the association to him as the rock. That both Jesus and his teaching are in view is clear from the previous passage about exclusion being grounded in the judge not knowing the one excluded. So Jesus argues that one who hears this teaching and does it is like the one who builds with a solid foundation that will withstand the waters of assessment. Judgment pictured as a flood is common in the Old Testament (Gen. 6–7; Isa. 28:2, 17; 30:28; Ezek. 13:10–16).[51] The teaching in view is that of the sermon. In contrast, the one who hears but does nothing is a fool because his house has no base to survive the torrent.

The Lukan parallel makes the same point, but the fool builds his house without a foundation, not on sand. The good house has its foundation dug deep—an additional detail. In Luke, the torrents result from rivers that overflow, whereas heavy rains cause the torrents in Matthew. The image, however, is the same; both accounts stress the tragedy of failing to heed Jesus' teaching through the collapsing house of a foolish man. A falling house and torrents that can destroy are Old Testament images (Job 8:15; Ps. 11:6; 83:15; Prov. 14:11). So the sermon ends with a challenge not to ignore responding to Jesus and his teaching. Jesus is a figure who is not plac-

---

50. In later Judaism, in *'Abot de Rabbi Nathan* 24, Elisha ben Abuyah is said to have taught that the one who studies Torah and has good works is like a man who built his house with stones and bricks, and it withstood the waters against the house. In contrast, the one who studies Torah but has no good works is like a man who built his house of a similar substance, but even a little water overturns the house. What is so important about Jesus' illustration is that he does not appeal to doing the law but to following his teaching, and thus he points to his comprehensive authority.

51. Davies and Allison, *Matthew*, 721.

ing his teaching forward because it is a recommended way of life. He represents far more than that. His teaching is a call to an allegiance that means the difference between life and death, between blessing and woe. Jesus is more than a prophet.

69. The Reaction to the Sermon (Matt. 7:28–29; conceptual: Mark 1:22) (Aland §76; Orchard §89; Huck-Greeven §89a)

As Matthew does at the end of each of the major discourses of Jesus, he notes that Jesus "finished these sayings" (Matt. 11:1; 13:53; 19:1; 26:1). The crowds are left in astonishment and fear. Matthew saves the term ἐκπλήσσω for the response to Jesus' teaching (Matt. 13:54; 19:25; 22:33). The mix of emotion is appropriate because Jesus' statements, even though they are grounded in familiar images of wisdom, are attached to a personal claim of authority that is unprecedented. So Matthew notes that Jesus taught as one with authority, not as one of their scribes. The remark is like Mark 1:22, but here the issue is tied exclusively to the way in which Jesus presented the issues of a disciple's walk.

70. The Lukan Version of the Sermon (Luke 6:20–49) (Aland §§77–83; Huck-Greeven §§86–91)[52]

Luke's sermon has three parts: the blessings and woes (6:20–26), a call to love one's enemies and show mercy (6:27–36), and closing remarks about judgment and caution about whose teaching one follows (6:37–49). Jesus' authority is highlighted at the sermon's end. The fact that Luke presents a version of this teaching minus its legal aspects, which were not a concern to his Gentile audience, shows that this teaching was intended to guide the life of disciples in the current community. It is not that here we have an ideal relevant only for another time, nor is the teaching to be seen as too idealistic to be applied. The closing insistence that this teaching is to be done excludes such a reading or any reading that in effect denies the sermon's applicability. Luke's basic point is similar to one of Matthew's fundamental points. Love for the enemy and the showing of mercy are signs that we have genuine filial relationship with God, living and relating to others as God does in showing mercy even to the unrighteous. Our response to God's graciousness to us is to

52. Orchard's synopsis does not go back through the Lukan sermon in its sequence. Our discussion only overviews the Lukan emphases and approach to the sermon as a unit. Detailed differences between the Lukan and Matthean passages were noted in the treatment of Matthean units.

reflect that graciousness to others. Any judgment or vindication of righteousness that is to come must come from the Father. Although Luke's version
speaks of judgment far less than Matthew's, it is present in both the woes and
in Jesus' closing remarks. One thing the Sermon on the Plain emphasizes is that
the disciple's way of relating demands more than the standard set by sinners.

Summary

This sermon about the heart is to be taken to heart.[53] It is not law in the
sense of giving rules, but it does show that God wants those who follow him
to keep close accounts of how they respond to him and to others. In tracing
the sermon, we have paid special attention to how much of this teaching existed already in the biblical wisdom tradition. Jesus drew on the known, but
he did so with an authority about his own understanding and judging role
that was unprecedented. Jesus is not merely a rabbi here in Matthew, nor is
he a teacher of ethics for Luke. He is a teacher-prophet who also speaks as the
judge of the eschaton. If anyone understands what God is asking from those
who desire blessing, it is Jesus.

One disturbing aspect of the sermon is the seemingly unattainable standard
it sets in a context where judgment is also discussed. Jesus seems to make it
sound as if works save. But that misinterprets the sermon. Jesus is saying that
a transformed heart relating in a healthy way to God (and as a result, to others)
is what yields an approved righteousness. It is not the self-attained keeping of
works that earns salvation; it is a humble and responsive heart that seeks what
God provides. Jesus offers the power of God's presence and an enablement
that yields a knowledge of God that changes a person's direction. Such an internal change by God's grace is precisely what Paul calls the gospel and the
power of God in Romans (Rom. 1:16–17 as an entry way into Rom. 1–8).
For in Romans, the problem of sin and condemnation is resolved by the gifts
of adoption into God's family and the indwelling Spirit. The Spirit, in turn,
is received by faith apart from works of the law. The result is a filial allegiance
to God that brings the effective presence of God's Spirit and an ability to re-

---

53. For a fine exposition of the sermon, see Dallas Willard, *The Divine Conspiracy: Rediscovering Our Hidden Life with God* (San Francisco: HarperSanFrancisco, 1998). I disagree with
Willard that the Beatitudes are not about the kind of heart that God honors and that the kingdom discussed is strictly one about the present era, as he argues citing C. H. Dodd. The kingdom in the present is connected to and based upon what it ultimately will be in fullness. In a
sense, the kingdom now is God in strength working through Christ pulling the future into the
present and giving us a powerful preview of his transforming power. On this point, the current
consensus is correct about the future-present tension in Jesus' kingdom teaching. Nonetheless,
Willard's exposition of Matt. 5:13–7:27 is as fine a walk through the sermon as anyone could
hope to read.

spond to God that previously were lacking. Those who know God are drawn to him and his ways. They rest as well in the benefits that his forgiveness provides. The sermon presents the ideal character that God asks disciples to possess through his calling. The graphic, even rhetorical nature of the sermon highlights how comprehensive the standard is, but not by giving a "new" law. Rather, it shows that the commitment to God also yields a commitment to relate well to others. Thus, the sermon is a call to righteousness. It is neither a theoretical righteousness nor a righteousness only for a future time. Rather, it is a righteousness that seeks the kingdom and seeks to love as God does. In relating with responsiveness to God and to Jesus, the one whom God has sent, the sermon calls disciples to be merciful, considerate, and generous to others in ways unlike the walk of the world.

SIX

More Galilean Ministry

Miracles, Mission to the Outcasts, and Discipleship in the Face of Opposition (Matt. 8:1–12:50; Luke 7:1–8:3; Mark 3:19b–35)

Despite the differences in where they place these various events, Matthew, Mark and Luke all demonstrate widespread agreement about the types of things Jesus did early in his Galilean ministry: he called men and women to repent, gathered disciples, exorcised and healed, challenged conventional Jewish wisdom with the radical newness of the gospel, created a new family out of those who would follow him, and engendered considerable hostility among at least a handful of his nation's leaders. All of this demonstrated a new and vibrant presence of God's reign.[1]

This chapter covers two more key passage units describing Jesus' Galilean ministry: Matt. 8:1–12:21 and Luke 7:1–8:3. In addition, I note a couple of passages from Mark 3:19b–35, plus the remainder of Matt. 12. This brings us to the point where the kingdom parables are introduced in each Gospel. That unit begins the next chapter. As the variation suggests, the Synoptic Gospels are each going their own way at this point as they review the Galilean ministry. In fact, Matt. 8–9 is the first evangelist's initial description of the activity of that ministry. The balanced grouping gives the impression that Matthew has topically arranged this material to present it in this sequence, especially given the variation he has in contrast to Mark and Luke. Thus, it draws on some events that I already treated in chapter 4, on the early Galilean ministry. For those cases where an event is repeated, I mostly refer back to the earlier discus-

1. Craig Blomberg, *Jesus and the Gospels* (Nashville: Broadman & Holman, 1997), 244.

sion and note only some additional points that emerge from the Gospel that now is the point of focus.

Three themes are key to this unit. First are the miracles. Matthew 8–9 consists of three triads of miracles, although one miracle is a double miracle, making the total number of miracles in the unit ten. Each triad is separated by a unit of teaching that discusses the other key theme of discipleship and deals with issues of mission and the opposition that Jesus' outreach is raising. Thus, mission and discipleship in the midst of developing opposition are the second and third key themes.

Mission and how to pursue it are major topics in Matt. 10, while Matt. 11–12 deals with the question of who Jesus is and how Jesus' authority is forcing choices, including a significant rejection of him. This combination of themes also is prevalent in Luke 7:1–8:3. In both Gospels, how Jesus reaches out to those on the fringe is highlighted.

Of the next four events in Matt. 8:1–17, three were treated in Mark and Luke (cleansing of the leper [Matt. 8:1–4 = Mark 1:40–45 = Luke 5:12–16]; healing of Peter's mother-in-law [Matt. 8:14–15 = Mark 1:29–31 = Luke 4:38–39]; healing of the sick at evening [Matt. 8:16–17 = Mark 1:32–34 = Luke 4:40–41]). The only event not yet presented in any Gospel is the healing of the centurion's servant (Matt. 8:5–13 = Luke 7:1–10 = possibly John 4:46b–54). The healing of Peter's mother-in-law and the summary about the healing of the sick are part of the events in the Capernaum ministry. The locale of Jesus' healing of the leper is specified only as in Galilee, inasmuch as it is connected to the aftermath of the sermon. What Matthew details here is, in effect, his first survey of Jesus' Galilean ministry, a role that parallels how these events functioned in Mark and Luke.

Matthew 8–9 contains mostly miracle material (ten pericopes out of fourteen) that serves to underscore Jesus' authority. In particular, 8:1–17 shows Jesus healing the excluded, including a leper, a Gentile's servant, the sick, and the possessed. Three more events in these two Matthean chapters also were treated earlier: healing the paralytic (Matt. 9:1–8 = Mark 2:1–12 = Luke 5:17–26), the calling of Levi (Matt. 9:9–13 = Mark 2:13–17 = Luke 5:27–32), and the question on fasting (Matt. 9:14–17 = Mark 2:18–22 = Luke 5:33–39). In this section issues of controversy are coming to the fore as Jesus shows his power and authority. What is important is that the healing of the centurion's servant involves a Gentile whose faith is commended as an example for Israel. His introduction as an example of faith is almost a shock in what to this point has been a Gospel that has concerned itself with calling Israel back to faithfulness as a response to the arrival of promise.

71. The Healing of the Leper (Matt. 8:1–4; Mark 1:40–45;
Luke 5:12–16 [see unit 34 above]) (Aland §84; Orchard §§89b–90;
Huck-Greeven §57)

Most of the development of this event was treated earlier. Matthew's placement makes it the first of several examples in which Jesus reaches out to those
excluded from society and restores them. The first triad of miracles in Matthew covers the fringe and the common people. Here Jesus instructs the
cleansed leper to follow the law supporting a theme that his sermon also raised
(Matt. 5:17–20). Jesus is not an antinomian. Unlike Mark and Luke, Matthew does not note the outcome of the healing in terms of a spreading report
about him. Matthew often is more concise in his rendering of material that he
shares with Mark.

72. The Healing of the Centurion's Servant (Matt. 8:5–13;
Luke 7:1–10) (Aland §85; Orchard §91; Huck-Greeven §58)

This miracle is told with some significant variation between Matthew and
Luke. In Matthew, Jesus and the centurion meet face to face, while Luke describes the event as involving Jewish emissaries representing the centurion,
who never actually sees Jesus. The conversation is mediated through the emissaries. This seeming discrepancy probably results from two factors.[2] First is
the ability of an emissary to represent another, much like the White House
press secretary speaks for the president. Second is Matthew's tendency to con-
dense and simplify accounts, as shown even in the previous passage. Thus, it
is likely that Luke has the full detail here, while Matthew has condensed the
account because the key statement of faith about Jesus' authority still is
sourced in the centurion's remarks.

Luke's version does allow the issue of the potential for Jewish-Gentile cooperation to come out far more explicitly. Here are Jews beseeching Jesus to
come to the aid of someone seemingly excluded from blessing. In this case,
these emissaries are an example beyond the issues of the centurion's faith and
Jesus' authority. Luke loves to make this kind of point. He also shows some
sympathy for those Gentiles who respect Israel's God. The very fact that Jewish emissaries "recommend" the Gentile indicates an underlying assumption
about the nature of Jesus' ministry. Jesus was so occupied with Israel that a
special appeal was needed for him to consider this outsider. Of course, those
very familiar with his ministry also would have known that his outreach could

2. Craig Blomberg, *Matthew,* New American Commentary 22 (Nashville: Broadman,
1992), 140.

extend that far (Luke 4:25–27). Matthew makes nothing of any of this because his account lacks the emissaries.

Three elements dominate this event, although the third point is unique to Matthew. First is the humility and the understanding that the centurion has, which cause Jesus to marvel at the man and commend his faith as unlike anything he had seen in Israel. There is a combination of key elements to his faith. The man reflects humility in his approach to Jesus. He understands that he is not worthy of Jesus' help but that this agent of God may choose to help him anyway. He also understands that this authority neither is magical in quality nor demands his physical presence. Jesus' will and word are sufficient. There also may be a cultural sensitivity in the Gentile's remark (although he says nothing about it), because it was considered problematic for a Jew to enter a Gentile's home, and so Jesus might become ceremonially unclean (*m. Pesaḥim* 8.8 discusses other rulings and restrictions that relate to Passover; *m. ʾOhalot* 18.7). Finally, he has come to this understanding of Jesus fairly quickly. For those whose eyes and ears are open, appreciating Jesus' authority is not hard.

So the second theme is Jesus' authority, but it is handled differently in the two Gospels. In Luke, this represents an expansion of the portrait of Jesus' authority as it takes on a new expanded scope beyond what was raised in Luke 4–5 (Jesus can work from a distance and need not be physically present!). For Matthew, this is the opening salvo in describing the active authority of Jesus at work. It is an exclamation point next to the authority of his words in the sermon, showing how comprehensively from the start God was at work through him.

The third theme is unique to Matthew. It also is a seeming surprise in light of the Gospel's "Jewishness." Jesus concludes the healing by noting that many will come from east and west to sit at the table with the patriarchs Abraham, Isaac, and Jacob in the kingdom of heaven.[3] Thus, the first miracle series in Matthew makes the point that Gentiles will be present at the table of blessing. But there is more. Others will be missing. The "heirs of the kingdom," which is an allusion to some excluded from the promised people of God, will be thrown into outer darkness, where there will be weeping and gnashing of teeth, a consistent Matthean image for the pain of rejection (13:42, 50; 22:13; 24:51; 25:30). The darkness imagery clearly pictures rejection and exclusion from blessing, because in God there is nothing but light (Matt. 4:15–16; 5:14–16; cf. 1 John 1:5–2:2, 8–11). Matthew is explaining that neither rejection from within the nation nor Gentile inclusion should be a surprise. The inheritance of kingdom blessing is not a matter of heredity, but faith.

---

3. Luke 13:28–29 has this image in another context, when Jesus is asked whether the saved will be few. For the background, see 4 Macc. 13:17; *1 Enoch* 70.4.

73. The Healing of the Widow of Nain's Son (Luke 7:11–17)
(Aland §86; Orchard §92; Huck-Greeven §93)

The extent of Jesus' authority is now expanded in the Lukan account to meeting the need of a woman tragically left to fend for herself. Luke gives this account after narrating the account of the centurion. A widow in the little village of Nain has lost her only son. Having no male in the house in an ancient patriarchal society, she not only has lost a son but also is isolated in terms of family and provision. She is left to subsist on the kindness of relatives and friends. They weep for her now, but the question is whether they will be there for her in the future. Her mourning, which traditionally would last thirty days, is only the beginning of her plight (*m. Berakot* 3.1 notes that those who bear the dead do not have to recite the Shema until after burial, nor do women who only recite blessings tied to the Shema). The healing focusing on a woman in need is coupled with the story of the centurion, thus giving a male-female pairing, which Luke likes to note, as with Zechariah and Mary in Luke 1 and Simeon and Anna in Luke 2.

Jesus enters the scene. Filled with compassion, he tells her not to weep and touches the bier, an open backboard, on which the corpse lies. According to custom, the funeral procession indicates that the son has just died, because most burials took place on the same day as death (*m. Šabbat* 23.4–5; *m. Sanhedrin* 6.5). Touching the bier does not render Jesus unclean, as would normally be the case (Num. 19:11, 16; Sir. 34:30), because of what happens next. Jesus tells the dead man to arise, and as the text declares almost ironically, "The dead man sat up, and began to speak." The son is returned, and the crowd is seized with fear.

The conclusion is that a great prophet has arisen, and that God is visiting his people, a theme Luke raised in 1:68. This is not without cause, because the miracle replicates what Elijah had done in 1 Kings 17:17–24.[4] Luke likes to note the prophetic aspects of Jesus' work (Luke 7:39; 9:8, 19; 24:19), but he eventually will show that this assessment of Jesus is inadequate. Jesus' action points to God's amazing power and activity, extending even over death. So a report went out throughout Judea and the countryside. This is the latest in a series of summaries, including Luke 5:17 and 6:17.

74. The Healing of Peter's Mother-in-Law (Matt. 8:14–15;
Mark 1:29–31; Luke 4:38–39 [see unit 29 above]) (Aland §87; Orchard §109; Huck-Greeven §59)

In Matthew, the next miracle involves Peter's mother-in-law and a summary that follows. She arises and continues to serve them, as the imperfect

4. Elisha also performed such a miracle in 2 Kings 4:32–37.

tense (διηκόνει) portrays the ongoing nature of her service. Service is what naturally follows God's grace.

75. The Sick Healed at Evening (Matt. 8:16–17; Mark 1:32–34; Luke 4:40–41 [see unit 30 above]) (Aland §88; Orchard §110; Huck-Greeven §60)

In the summary tied to this miracle, Matthew mentions the exorcisms and healings in agreement with the parallels in Mark and Luke, but he adds two notes. First, he observes that the exorcisms took place "with his word," not with magical incantations or elaborate rituals often associated with such acts (Tob. 6:7–8; 17–18; Josephus, *Ant.* 8.2.5 §§45–49). Second is the remark about fulfilling what Isaiah had proclaimed in 53:4, where the Servant, who performs God's call, engages sickness and disease on behalf of the people. The effects of sin are being reversed.[5] Isaiah 53 appears again in the New Testament in Luke 22:37, Acts 8:26–40, and 1 Pet. 2:22–25. Matthew completes the first triad of miracles (the leper, the paralyzed servant, and the ill mother-in-law) with this explanatory summary that God's promised work is being done.

76. Warning on Following Jesus (Matt. 8:18–22; Luke 9:57–62, in a later context) (Aland §89; Orchard §111; Huck-Greeven §61)

The priority of following Jesus is part of a Matthean scene in which Jesus is preparing to cross the sea. In contrast, Luke gives no setting, although the account does follow some events occurring in Samaria. Matthew notes that the first remark comes from a scribe who says that he is willing to follow wherever Jesus goes and addresses Jesus with appropriate respect, calling him "Teacher." The reply indicates that Jesus wants him to appreciate what this prospective disciple is in for if he follows him. Jesus warns him that foxes and birds have it better than Jesus does because they have holes and nests, respectively. In contrast, the Son of Man has nowhere to lay his head. This is Matthew's first use of the title "Son of Man."[6] It is the Son of Man as rejected that is introduced here. The note almost comes as a shock because Jesus is perform-

---

5. On the issue of whether there is a promise of physical healing for today in Jesus' work, see Douglas Moo, "Divine Healing in the Health and Wealth Gospel," *Trinity Journal*, n.s., 9 (1988): 191–209; Craig Keener, *Matthew*, IVPNTCS 1 (Downers Grove, Ill.: InterVarsity, 1997), 178.

6. In contrast, Mark's first use is in Mark 2:10, the healing of the paralytic, as is Luke's in Luke 5:24.

ing powerful ministry, yet it will not mean that he is welcomed. Jesus ministered out of Capernaum, but here he is referring to the fact that his mission has him out in the region, and many will oppose him. Sometimes people do not acknowledge and welcome the presence of God. To follow Jesus means to follow in that path of possible rejection. Jesus warns him to be prepared.

The second query comes from "another disciple," which again suggests that the scribe also had been seeking to follow Jesus. This disciple asks if he can delay his following of Jesus until he has performed a basic obligation for his family: burying his father. Such care was seen as fundamental in Judaism (*Letter of Aristeas* 228; Josephus, *Against Apion* 2.27 §206; Tob. 4:3–4 [a father tells his son to bury him and to make sure that his mother is not abandoned]; 6:14–15 [Tobias worries that if he dies by connecting himself to a demonic woman, no one will be around to bury his mother and father]). There is debate as to the setting. Most suggest that a burial, which took place on the day of death (see unit 73 above), is not in view, for things would be too hectic to stop and raise this issue with Jesus. The suggestion is that the disciple is either waiting for his father to die one day or that he wants to wait until the official mourning period, up to a year, is over, because this meant taking care of his father's bones after the body has decomposed.[7] Regardless of what the setting is, Jesus' reply is strong and shocking: "Follow me, and leave the dead to bury their own dead." What does Jesus mean? Is he saying "Let the spiritually dead take care of burying the physically dead?" Or is he speaking with irony, arguing satirically that the actual dead can do that (which they cannot)?— meaning, of course, that this familial concern is not as important as following him. Either way, the reply is shocking culturally. Jesus makes the point that following him takes precedence over the most basic of family priorities. Taking Jesus' responses together, we see the teacher warning the overly eager and naïve of the real commitment that he requires of disciples. Jesus also challenges those who do not give following him a high enough priority.

The Lukan parallel comes later in his Gospel as part of the discipleship instruction at the beginning of the Jerusalem journey section in Luke 9:57. It has a few differences from Matthew. Jesus takes the initiative with the one who wants to bury his father, calling him to follow. Matthew seems to have condensed this account. When the request comes, Luke has an additional note at the end of Jesus' response, about going and proclaiming the kingdom of God. The importance of the call and the topic of the preaching create the urgency and priority. Luke also has a third figure, who asks to say farewell to those at home. Jesus' reply is curt. No one who looks back is fit for the kingdom of God. Again, the priority of the kingdom is the driving point in Jesus'

7. Kenneth E. Bailey, *Through Peasant's Eyes: More Lucan Parables* (Grand Rapids: Eerdmans, 1980), 26–27; B. R. McCane, "Let the Dead Bury Their Own Dead: Secondary Burial and Matthew 8:21–22," *Harvard Theological Review* 83 (1990): 31–43.

remark. An excessive attachment and loyalty to home and the "old life" does not lead to worthy service for the kingdom.

77. The Stilling of the Storm (Matt. 8:23–27; Mark 4:35–41, in a later context; Luke 8:22–25, in a later context) (Aland §90; Orchard §112; Huck-Greeven §62)

The second Matthean triad of miracles treats Jesus' authority over the fallen creation, whether it be the elements (8:23–27), the demons (8:28–34), or sin present in the world (9:1–8). The first miracle is the stilling of the storm on the Sea of Galilee. Matthew's version, as usual, is the most concise. As the storm appears, Jesus is asleep in the boat even as it is being swamped with waves. Sleep often is used to picture someone at peace (Ps. 3:5; 4:8). The disciples are in a panic, so they wake him and ask him to save them because they are at risk of perishing. After Jesus rebukes them for having little faith in God's care or presence, he rebukes the wind. The language of rebuke matches that of exorcisms in other Gospels, using ἐπιτιμάω (Mark 1:25; 9:25; Luke 4:41). In the next moment, there is great calm. So those present marvel and query, "What sort of man is this, that even winds and sea obey him?" The remark serves in the narrative to leave the question to be pondered by the reader. Those familiar with the Old Testament would recognize that God has such authority (Ps. 65:5–6; 89:8–9; 104:7; 107:23–32) and that such authority is alluded to for the ideal king (Ps. 89:25). The setting also recalls the story of Jon. 1–2. The point of the miracle stresses that the disciples can trust in Jesus' care because of who he is. The fact that the question closes the account shows what the emphasis is: to ponder who Jesus is.

Mark adds the note that the instruction to cross to the other side had precipitated the event. He also gives more detail in describing the danger of the storm and that Jesus is asleep on a cushion. The disciples, when they awaken Jesus, ask him whether he cares if they perish. The question is asked with a Greek interrogative, suggesting that they know he does care, but the inquiry could be seen as backing Jesus into a corner. Jesus rebukes the wind and speaks to the sea, telling it, "Peace. Be still!" Jesus then rebukes them for their fear and absence of faith. The account closes with the question "Who then is this, that even the wind and the sea obey him?" The disciples are beginning to sense that they are dealing with an extraordinary figure.

Luke's version is close to Mark's. He describes the storm in a little less detail but notes that they were in danger. Here the disciples cry out, "Master, Master, we are perishing!" Jesus rebukes the wind and the waves, but Luke does not report what is said. When things are calm, Jesus asks the disciples, "Where is your faith?" They are both afraid and marvel as they ask the question about who can command the wind and water so that they obey him. Luke's framing of the question in terms of commanding creation heightens the sense of authority that the event raises.

78. The Gadarene/Gerasene Demoniac(s) (Matt. 8:28–34; Mark 5:1–20, in a later context; Luke 8:26–39, in a later context) (Aland §91; Orchard §113; Huck-Greeven §63)

This exorcism again is told most concisely in Matthew, while it is rendered in great detail in Mark. Nevertheless, it is the first exorcism that Matthew notes as he treats Jesus' authority over creation and the forces in it.[8] The locale differs between Matthew (Gadarenes [five miles southeast of the sea]), Mark (Gergesenes [on the sea] or Gerasenes [thirty miles southeast of the sea]), and Luke (Gergesenes or Gerasenes).[9] Various solutions are proposed, none of which is the clear choice. One is that Gergesa is an alternative to Khersa (= Kursi) and has been variously rendered or confused in the subsequent textual tradition.[10] Another is that Mark and Luke, in choosing the more distant Gerasa, are naming not the exact locale but the region's most prominent locale. Regardless, the point is that Jesus is on the east side of the Sea of Galilee in the Decapolis region, which was predominantly Gentile, although it had a substantial Jewish population (Josephus, *War* 1.7.7 §155).

In this setting, two demoniacs emerging from the tombs meet Jesus. This is one of three places in which Matthew notes two of something present instead of one, as in Mark and Luke (see also Matt. 9:27; 20:30).[11] Blomberg suggests a Matthean appeal to truth through multiple witnesses here (cf. Deut. 19:15), a point of value for Jewish audiences only. The linking of demoniacs with the tombs is not unusual; cemeteries were viewed as unclean places (*m. Nazir* 3.5; 7.3) and often associated with demons (*PGM* 101.1–3). All the features of exorcisms are in play here. The danger to others is real; "no one could go that way." The demons name Jesus as a way to try to control him and confess his authority because they know that the end is not yet present. They sense danger because Jesus' presence gives evidence of the presence of

---

8. On exorcisms, see unit 28 above.

9. Mark and Luke present a difficult textual problem here, so the reading is uncertain. For discussion, see Robert Gundry, *Mark: A Commentary on His Apology for the Cross* (Grand Rapids: Eerdmans, 1993), 255–57; Darrell L. Bock, *Luke 1:1–9:50*, BECNT 3A (Grand Rapids: Baker, 1994), 782–84.

10. On this option, see Craig Blomberg, *Matthew*, 150–51. Others challenge this equation, among them Alfred Plummer, *A Critical and Exegetical Commentary on the Gospel according to St. Luke*, International Critical Commentary (Edinburgh: Clark, 1896).

11. See Blomberg, *Matthew*, 151.

God's rule and Jesus' potential to defeat the great enemy (cf. Matt. 12:28). The demons ask permission to go into a swine herd feeding at some distance from them. It is hard to know the rationale for the request from Matthew, but Luke notes that they did not wish to be sent immediately to the abyss. Jesus' granting of the request lets an important set of events take place. The entry of the demons into the pigs causes them to run over the cliff and drown. Thus, the reality of the exorcism is seen and the destructive effect of these demons is manifested. The destruction of property, the pigs, not the healing of the two men, seems to be the crowd's priority, and those in the region ask Jesus to leave. Jesus' power over demons is observed but not appreciated. Other, material issues matter more.

The Markan account falls in a context in which a series of miracles occurs, as the stilling of the storm precedes and the double healing of Jairus's daughter and the woman with a hemorrhage follows. Luke also follows this order. Mark and Luke, rather than placing the miracles in a "nature" context as Matthew, have a sequence that moves from nature to demons to disease to death. Thus, the threat becomes more intense and more internal as it proceeds.

Both accounts add unique details, allowing the development of additional points. Luke alone notes that the man was naked, adding a theme of shame. Mark details the strength of the possessed man, who could not be bound in any kind of restraint. He continually injured himself on the stones. The scene is described in full detail and paints a tragic picture of self-destruction. Both accounts note that Jesus also extracted the name of the demons, "Legion," indicating that he was significantly outnumbered. On the surface it is an uneven fight, but Jesus' authority is confirmed when they enter the swine, which Mark numbers at about two thousand. This helps us appreciate the extent of the economic impact of what the demons did to the swine. Unlike Matthew, Mark and Luke point out how part of what created the fear was seeing the man in a sane condition! Mark notes that the destruction of the swine was part of the witnesses' retelling of the account, while Luke notes only that they report the healing of the demon-possessed man. Both accounts relate that upon Jesus' departure, the man asked to accompany Jesus but was refused. Instead, he was to testify to the Lord's work and mercy (Mark), which Luke describes as God's work. The freedom given to the healed man in Mark to discuss Jesus' work is interesting, given the earlier instructions for silence. The likely explanation is that in a Gentile region there was less chance of a misunderstanding of what Jesus was doing. In both accounts, the restored man responds and tells how much Jesus had done for him. He could not discuss God's work without consideration of Jesus' role. So Mark and Luke end the account by highlighting the testimony of the man to the linkage between God's work and Jesus' work. Mark notes that this testimony spread through the Decapolis. The event ends on a positive note in contrast to Matthew.

79. The Healing of the Paralytic (Matt. 9:1–8; Mark 2:1–12, in an earlier context; Luke 5:17–26, in an earlier context [see unit 35 above]) (Aland §92; Orchard §114; Huck-Greeven §64)

This event is treated in full above, but one point needs attention here. This is the second consecutive miracle in Matthew that contains a negative note. The powerful evidence of God working through Jesus is not leading to complete acceptance. Here, an explanation is supplied for why the Son of Man has no place to lay his head and why followers need to be ready to face that same lot (cf. Matt. 8:19–20). His claim to forgive sin, including evidence for such authority in a miraculous act of God, is not well received by all, just as his exorcisms were not. Others do respond with awe and by giving glory to God, but in generic terms. What is affirmed is that God has given such authority to men. They do not yet see Jesus as the point. The Matthean ending makes this distinct point in contrast to the declaration of "unusual things" in Mark and Luke.

80. The Calling of Matthew/Levi (Matt. 9:9–13; Mark 2:13–17, in an earlier context; Luke 5:27–32, in an earlier context [see unit 36 above]) (Aland §93; Orchard §115; Huck-Greeven §65)

This event is covered in detail above. One contextual factor is unique to Matthew. In the last teaching unit that broke up the triad of miracles, there were warnings about the appropriate response to Jesus (Matt. 8:18–22). This was followed by a series of miracles in which notes of rejection are mixed with reactions of amazement. This account of the calling of Matthew and the following remark about fasting indicate that some are responding appropriately by viewing Jesus' presence positively. It also explains how his outreach to the rejected and to sinners is purposeful as well as appropriate.

81. The Question about Fasting (Matt. 9:14–17; Mark 2:18–22, in an earlier context; Luke 5:33–39, in an earlier context [see unit 37 above]) (Aland §94; Orchard §116; Huck-Greeven §66)

This account is treated fully above. The explanation of Jesus' different ways fits in a context in which opposition is rising. Jesus brings the needed new wine for new wineskins. In Matthew, the special point is that the claim for authority also involves an era that involves new things.

82. Jairus's Daughter and the Woman with a Hemorrhage

(Matt. 9:18–26; Mark 5:21–43, in a later context; Luke 8:40–56, in a later context) (Aland §95; Orchard §117; Huck-Greeven §67)

This miracle is a part of the last Matthean triad of miracles, which covers various diseases, including one that is demon induced (9:33), and a resuscitation from the dead (a new topic for Matthew; Luke 7:11–17, treated above in unit 73, is the first such miracle in Luke). Matthew will summarize this activity in 11:5. In this section, the faith of those who are helped is an important point (Matt. 8:10; 9:2). The motif of this miracle section is Jesus' comprehensive ability to deliver people and his compassion for them, as the comment in Matt. 9:35–38 makes clear. For Mark and Luke, the miracle culminates a sequence of four miracles of differing need—danger in nature, demons, disease, and death—also emphasizing Jesus' comprehensive ability to deliver people. His authority extends to the whole of creation and life.

This is the only intertwined set of miracles in the Gospels. Mark tells us that Jesus has returned to the western side of Galilee, while Luke simply says that he returned. Matthew, as is his custom, tells the story with brevity. A synagogue leader, one with responsibility for the organization of local worship, comes humbly before Jesus. Matthew notes that he knelt, while Mark and Luke speak of his falling before Jesus. Matthew's conciseness leads to Jairus saying that his daughter has died, but that Jesus' laying on of hands can reclaim her to life. Mark and Luke note that she is dying. Their details will pinpoint the time of death as occurring in the midst of Jesus' dealings with the bleeding woman. The leader has faith in Jesus' capability; the level of his faith will be examined by what happens next.

As they move through the crowd, a woman, who has been hemorrhaging for twelve years, seeks to touch Jesus. Her condition is not only an uncomfortable one, but also it has forced her to live detached from society, because anyone coming in contact with her would become unclean until evening—and someone touching her could inquire if she were unclean (Lev. 15:19–33; *m. Toharot* 5.8; *m. Zabim,* esp. 5.6; by contrast, touching the dead left one unclean for a week, Num. 19:11–12). The result would be complete social isolation, possibly extending to being unable to marry or being subject to divorce. Despite this cultural pressure to stay away, she seeks Jesus out. Her desperation is detailed in Mark, who notes that she had sought so much help from doctors that all her resources were depleted. Luke simply notes that the condition had not been healed by anyone. However, the fact that her condition had lasted twelve years shows that there is no immediacy here. Her life is not in danger. This healing could have waited. On the surface, getting to Jairus's daughter was more urgent.

The woman reasons that simply touching Jesus' garment is good enough. She possibly is trying to avoid the public embarrassment of rendering Jesus unclean in front of many people. Both Matthew and Mark render the phrase "If I only touch the fringe of his garment" as a class three condition in Greek. This means, in effect, "perhaps if." Her faith, though present, is feeble.

Mark and Luke both develop the scene in lingering detail, all the while leaving the reader to remember that Jairus is waiting for Jesus to help his dying daughter. The woman touches Jesus. Jesus senses that power has gone out from him. He asks, "Who touched me?" Peter is amazed at this response, given the crush of the crowd. Imagine how Jairus viewed the delay that the woman and now Peter's interaction had caused! The entire delay causes the woman to come forward and confess her healing. Jesus affirms that it is her faith that has led to her "saving."

At this point in Mark and Luke, a messenger comes to report that Jairus's daughter has died, so there is no need to bother Jesus anymore. Imagine now how Jairus must have felt about the opportunity lost because of a healing that could have waited! This is the time for a second lesson about faith and Jesus' authority. The woman needed her feeble faith affirmed. Jairus and his household needed to understand God's sovereign timing and the extent of Jesus' power, so Jesus tells Jairus not to fear but only to believe. Jesus then takes Peter, James, John, and the girl's parents with him into the house.

At the home, the obligatory mourners already are playing the dirge (*m. Ketubbot* 4.4 notes that even the poorest of families had mourners wail upon the death of even a woman). This man's status probably made it an affair for the entire town. Jesus dismisses these mourners, even rebuking them in Mark, because the girl only sleeps. They respond by laughing, because, as Luke explains, they knew that "she was dead." Jesus goes into the house and tells her to arise. Mark and Luke note the details, while Matthew only summarizes. The resuscitation leaves her parents amazed.

In summarizing the aftermath, Mark and Luke note that Jesus told the parents not to say anything. It is a strange request as, given the crowds, those present surely must know what took place. But the point is that Jesus does not want excessive attention drawn to this aspect of his work, so he directs them not to talk about it. In contrast, Matthew notes that the report went out into all the district. This also is not surprising, for it involved a prominent synagogue figure. Whether facing disease or death, both the woman and Jairus learned important things about faith and Jesus' power.

Mark in particular likes to sandwich events as he has done here. He will do it again in Mark 11 with the fig tree and temple interaction and again in Mark 14 at Jesus' examination by the Jews and Peter's denials. The movement back and forth, much like shifting settings in a movie, adds to the drama.

83. Two Blind Men Healed (Matt. 9:27–31; a similar miracle appears in a later context in Matt. 20:29–34; Mark 10:46–52; Luke 18:35–43) (Aland §96; Orchard §118; Huck-Greeven §68)

This miracle often is called a doublet because of a very similar account later in Matthew, Mark, and Luke. But this is not the same event told twice. What the repetition shows is that Jesus repeatedly performed healings of the blind. The locations are different. Here, he is on the western shore of Galilee; there, he is in Jericho. Here, the healing occurs in a house; there, it takes place in the open. Here, he tells them to say nothing; there, the miracle is public. So the present account is unique to Matthew.

What stands out is the sensitivity, one might even say the insight, of the blind men.[12] They appeal to the "Son of David" for mercy. They recognize his royal power and status, which in turn they connect to his ability to heal. They understood that the messianic age would be a period when restoration would come with the promised one (Isa. 35:5–6). Once again, it is those on the fringe who understand. It is hard to know where this insight would have come from. Did they just put it together on the basis of what they had heard? Or were they aware of an association in Judaism with Solomon as "Son of David," who was so full of wisdom and power that he could overcome demons and disease (Josephus, *Ant.* 8.2.5 §§44–45)? Regardless of the origin of this idea, the example of faith is evident here with great depth.

Jesus acts in private. When he enters the house, Jesus asks the blind men if they believe that he can heal them. Their positive reply leads him to touch their eyes as he says, "Let it be in response to your faith." Their spiritual ability to see through faith has led to their physical ability to see. Jesus charges them not to say anything. However, it proves to be a difficult request, because anyone who knew the men would know that they had been blind. Something must have happened. Matthew notes that his fame spread through the entire district. What the command seems to be about is that the healing should not be broadcast, because the healing is only an indication of a more important restoration that Jesus brings.

84. The Mute Demoniac (Matt. 9:32–34; a similar miracle appears in a later context in Matt. 12:22–24; Mark 3:22; Luke 11:14–15) (Aland §97; Orchard §119; Huck-Greeven §69)

This miracle completes the third triad of Matthean miracles. It is one of the few miracles in which the reaction is as important as the narration of the heal-

---

12. Matthew attributes such insight to the blind and to Gentiles, as the magi account in Matt. 2 showed. See J. M. Gibbs, "Purpose and Pattern in Matthew's Use of the Title 'Son of David,'" *New Testament Studies* 10 (1963–64): 446–64.

ing (Matt. 8:14–17; Luke 11:14–23). Here a possessed man is mute, which can mean that he cannot hear or speak (Luke 1:20–22, 62–63). After Jesus has cast out the spirit, the man speaks, causing the crowd to marvel. They then observe what was obvious: "Never was anything like this seen in Israel." The remark is not that the miracles were unique, for many of the greats of old, such as Moses, Joshua, Elijah, and Elisha, had performed miracles. The key was the scope and frequency of Jesus' miraculous activity. This is what was unprecedented. Matthew made the point vivid by piling miracle upon miracle in this section. A reader of the Gospel might think that Jesus' being embraced would automatically follow this unprecedented display of divine power, but the next remark makes it clear that success is not guaranteed.

The Pharisees come to a decision as well. They cannot deny that something is happening. They also reject one option that modernists give: it all never happened. They acknowledge that something supernatural is taking place, but they conclude that it is by the ruler of the demons that these demons are expelled. Thus, the explosion of miraculous activity ends in opposition and rejection of the claim that it is rooted in God's work. There is an irony here. Who really is unperceptive? It is not those on the fringe who are open to Jesus, but the religious leadership.

This account, like the previous miracle, has very similar parallels in Matt. 12:22–24 and Luke 11:14–15, while Mark 3:22 notes this conclusion about the devil's work in another context. Although some see this Matt. 9 incident as a doublet, it really is an event distinct from that in Matt. 12. The repetition surely is intentional, showing that what is present is a persistent opposition based on a settled assessment of Jesus' work (cf. John 7:20; 8:48, 52; 10:20).

85. Summary (Matt. 9:35–38; conceptual: Mark 6:6b, 34; Luke 8:1; 10:2) (Aland §98; Orchard §121; Huck-Greeven §70a)

This unit contains a summary and a saying. They form a transition into the mission that Jesus will send out despite the rise of opposition. Many in the crowd are impressed, but the work is too great for one person.

The summary describes Jesus journeying through cities and villages. He teaches in the synagogues, preaches the gospel about the kingdom, and heals every disease and infirmity. The content of what the preaching included has been illustrated in the Sermon on the Mount. Matthew stops to discuss Jesus' motivation. Jesus acts out of compassion. He sees the multitudes as torn and thrown down. The image is of sheep left to fend for themselves in the wild. Shepherds who should protect and provide for them are nowhere to be found. The expression "sheep without a shepherd" appears in the Old Testament (Num. 27:17; 1 Kings 22:17 = 2 Chron. 18:16). Nowhere is it as prominent as in the rebuke that Ezekiel gave to the nation and its leaders in Ezek. 34:1–10 (esp. v. 5). The leaders' failure to embrace their role as shepherd meant that God would have to become the nation's shepherd (34:15). He would do this by raising up a ruler to be the true shepherd, one who would provide and protect (34:23–24). The image is full of messianic and eschatological import. In contrast to the evaluation by the Pharisaic leadership that the prince of the demons is behind the scenes in Jesus' work, Matthew argues that Jesus' ministry shows that God's promise is at work. John 10 makes the same observation, using the same imagery.

The new shepherd will not work alone, and the task is great. So he tells his disciples that they need to pray for more laborers to work in a field that is ready for harvesting but has few laborers to reap it. The kind of labor that the field requires is the topic of Matt. 10.

Luke 10:2 is parallel and verbally exact. The third evangelist ties it to the mission of the seventy. Matthew 10 is the equivalent scene for the first Gospel.

86. The Commissioning of the Twelve and the Mission Instruction (Matt. 10:1–16; Mark 3:13–19a; Luke 6:12–16; conceptual: Mark 6:7–11; Luke 9:1–5; 10:3 [see unit 41 above]) (Aland §99; Orchard §122–25a; Huck-Greeven §70b)

This unit actually has several elements and introduces the second major discourse in Matthew. The passage includes the calling of the Twelve (v. 1), the naming of the Twelve separated into groups of two ([unlike Mark and Luke] vv. 2–4), and instruction about where to go (vv. 5–6). In addition, exhortation about what to do follows: to preach and heal without charging (vv. 7–8) and to travel simply (vv. 9–10). There is also teaching about how to enter and stay in a town, including how to handle rejection (vv. 11–14), warning of the fate of towns that reject them (v. 15), and direction about the need to be both wise and innocent (v. 16). The issue of how to deal with persecution and rejection follows in vv. 17–25. Then come exhortations about whom to really fear and confessing Jesus (vv. 26–33). Jesus assures his disciples that his mission will be a cause of division (vv. 34–39). Then he promises that those who respond will receive reward (10:40–11:1).

This initial unit is the only place where Matthew calls the Twelve "apostles." That name reflects the idea of being a commissioned agent for another, so it is entirely appropriate in this context. Jesus sets forth a ministry of service and compassion just like his own, as noted in 9:35. They are to cast out demons and heal the sick. The listing of the Twelve was discussed earlier, but Matthew saves the listing until he explains what role Jesus gave them. They are the first of the "laborers," of which many are to be added through prayer and their witness (9:37–38). The two-by-two (Mark 6:7) listing shows how they are to go "in teams" to support each other.

The initial restriction to Israel is not permanent, as 8:11–13, 24:14, and 28:18–20 show. Nonetheless, Jesus' initial call is to Israel because they were the original recipients of the promise. The "lost sheep" image also connects with 9:36 (see Luke 15). These people need pursuing because they are straying, as Ezek. 34 also had noted. It is the approach of the promised kingdom that is preached. It is "at hand," as John and Jesus already had noted (3:2; 4:17). It is at hand, so one must "come home" from the straying. That is the apostles' message. Evidence of God's grace appears in the healing, cleansing, and exorcising that they will do. Their ministry replicates Jesus' own work (Matt. 8–9). In a sense, this ministry allows Matthew to summarize his Gospel up to this point.

The messengers' lives are to be generous and simple. They are not to be paid for their work, unlike many others, such as the Cynics, who had an itinerant ministry. They also are to travel with only the barest provisions of money, food, and clothing. Their provisions will be supplied by those who welcome their ministry. It is almost as if support for them is an indication that those to whom they have ministered appreciate what they have done. So they stay in one "worthy" home in a given village. An unworthy home will forfeit their blessing.

All of these instructions assume God's care and watch over what takes place in people's responses to the messengers. A rejected message means that one should move on in this early period, a key period that later included the practice of Paul (Acts 13:51). A town that rejects their message determines its own fate. In fact, even the worst of towns of the old era, Sodom and Gomorrah, will do better than these towns in the judgment because more is being offered to these rejecting towns now than what was offered then to those wicked cities. It is serious to contemplate the nature of a judgment worse than what Sodom received!

Jesus suggests that the effort will be dangerous, like exposing sheep to preying wolves.[13] The only way to survive is to be both wise and innocent. Wisdom means being aware of where the dangers are and the risks, while innocence speaks of unmixed motives for actions. They must appreciate what their call to serve might entail.

Mark has a note about mission in 6:7–11 with instructions similar to parts of this text (authority over spirits, traveling light, staying at one place,

13. Sheep was a common figure for the pious, or the people of God, when the picture is of those who need guidance and protection (Ezek. 34; *1 Enoch* 90.6–17). Here these sheep are sent forth at risk in a seemingly dangerous situation. The only assurance they have in this discourse is that the Spirit will help them, and eventually they will be vindicated for their testimony. God will be their shepherd and provide for them a shepherd to guide and protect them, as Ezek. 34 promised.

and shaking the dust from the feet). Luke notes two missions in 9:1–6 and 10:1–23. The instructions are similar in each Lukan passage. The Markan instructions also have some elements different from what we see in Matthew (missing a reference to preaching the kingdom and healing). Two themes appearing in Matt. 10 are split across the two Lukan scenes (shake the dust [Luke 9]; lambs to wolves [Luke 10]). In Luke 10, Luke repeats the instruction from Luke 9 on remaining at one house and the return of peace from the rejecting house. The commissioned group in Luke 10 is larger than the original twelve of Luke 9. What this shows is that Jesus' mission did expand. More laborers were sent, but they had the same fundamental instructions each time. Matthew's note about going only to Israel is not made in the parallels, although it is obvious from Acts that this is what took place. So Matthew's warning about a harder judgment for the rejecting towns than for Sodom is unique. Jesus is clear that declaring the approach of the kingdom to the lost sheep will not be easy. The reality of rejection must be faced.

87. The Fate of the Disciples (Matt. 10:17–25; conceptual: Mark 13:9–13; Luke 12:11–12; 6:40; 21:12–19) (Aland §100; Orchard §125; Huck-Greeven §71)

The mission and what it represents will not be popular. Jesus tells the story of mission not only in terms of this current mission for the Twelve, but also as an example of what preaching the kingdom will be like beyond this mission. Persecution will be a part of the testimony, so he urges them to beware. These missionary laborers will be delivered up to "sanhedrins" and synagogues. Thus, Jews will examine them, but they also will find themselves before governors and kings, giving their testimony before Gentiles. All of this is "for my [Jesus'] sake." The Book of Acts is filled with examples that show the fulfillment of these expectations. The fact that it is in this future context that these predictions are realized shows that Jesus here, by his predictions of suffering, is addressing more than this initial mission of the Twelve.

The predicted resistance will become an opportunity to testify about Jesus. They should not be nervous or anxious about what to say, because a proper reply will be given to them by God. The Spirit of the Father will speak through them. The rejection will be painful because families will be divided, with brothers handing over brothers, parents handing over children, and children handing over parents. Some even will be put to death. During the persecution others could end up being beaten like those described in *m. Makkot* 3.10–12. Beatings can be up to thirty-nine lashes with a belt made of leather straps. The leaders estimate when the striking on the back (two-thirds of the lashes) and front (one-third of the lashes) is enough, up to the total of thirty-nine.[14] All striking takes place with the recipient bent over. Actions like these possibly are in Jesus' mind when he tells them, "You will be hated by all for my name's sake." The "all" here denotes all kinds of people, even relatives (Mic. 7:6). Deliverance comes to those who endure to the end, whether that refers to the end that comes with vindication or through death. The earlier mention of death makes it clear that something other than physical deliverance is in view here.[15]

They are not to seek suffering and martyrdom, however, as some later during the time of the early church tried to do. If persecution surfaces, they may flee to the next city. Vindication will come, because the Son of Man will come before they finish going through all the towns of Israel. Here is a picture of Jesus as the judge standing up for those who testify to him. He will return as judge before the overall mission to Israel is completed. Said another way, Jews must be evangelized until Jesus returns.

None of this opposition should surprise them. Disciples and servants are like their teachers and masters. They live together and suffer alike. They are not to seek this rejection (cf. 1 Tim. 3:7; 1 Pet. 2:12; 3:15–16), but they should expect it to occur.[16] Thus, if people have called their master "Beelzebul" (cf. Matt. 9:34), then "how much more" will those in the master's house be accused.

Jesus understands the intense opposition he is causing and is aware of the danger of the mission for him. He desires that the disciples be fully prepared emotionally for what they will face. Loyalty is expressed in a testimony that will require dependence for emotional strength and courage.

Nothing quite like this discourse appears in Mark or Luke, although some individual points similar to it appear in the Matthean, Markan, and Lukan versions of the Olivet discourse (the delivery up to synagogues and governors, delivery by family, and enduring to the end), as well as in the Lukan journey context (Luke 12:11–12). The image of a disciple being like the teacher appears in a completely different context in Luke 6:40, where Jesus notes the likeness between student and teacher. The differences and repetitions of these themes reinforce the point made above that Jesus' remarks extend beyond the short-term mission. In fact, the points are repeated later to drive home the idea that this extended perspective is present. Here is another so-called doublet that is better seen as conscious repetition.

14. See Keener, *Matthew,* 207.

15. These words need not be overly literalized. Peter will "deny" Jesus but then recover to indicate his loyalty. Peter has a failure of nerve, but Judas will deny Jesus with a true failure of heart, showing his real lack of spiritual condition.

16. Blomberg, *Matthew,* 177.

88. Knowing Whom to Confess and Whom to Fear

(Matt. 10:26–33; Luke 12:2–9, in a later context) (Aland §101; Orchard §126; Huck-Greeven §72)

The threat of persecution, beating, and death leads Jesus to reassure missionary laborers not to fear, because everything will be revealed and made known. Those who persecute will be held responsible by God. The disciples are simply to follow Jesus' direction to declare openly from rooftops, above the noise of the street, what Jesus tells them. The images here are of bold and public testimony. Their choice of whom to fear, either God or those who can kill them physically, determines their ability to carry out this call. So Jesus urges them to fear God because he can destroy the soul and cast the body into hell. Jesus' point is not to motivate with fear, but to make clear the choice between being safe in a world that cannot give life, although it can take life, and pleasing the one who will judge the loyalty of people's hearts.

God does care, as Jesus points out in the example of two sparrows that are worth one of the least valuable coins, an assarion ("penny"). This coin is only one-sixteenth of a denarius, so each one represents only forty-five minutes' worth of labor, as a denarius was a day's basic wage. God cares about them, because he knows when they fall. God also knows disciples intimately, knowing the number of hairs on each person's head. Thus, disciples need not fear, because they are far more valuable to God than the birds that he also watches over.

Jesus begins to conclude his discourse by promising that those who acknowledge him before people will be acknowledged by him before the Father in heaven. In making this remark, Jesus underscores yet again his authority to judge at the end, even though in the Matthean version the title Son of Man is not used (cf. Luke 12:8–9). To deny Jesus is to face denial before the Father.

Mark has no real parallel to these remarks. His use in 4:22 of the "nothing hidden" image comes in a context after the kingdom parables. Mark's point in using the image is that revelation serves to expose for judgment (see also Luke 8:17, where it refers to the "light" quality of the word of God as preached by Jesus). Luke 12:2–9 is conceptually quite parallel. It comes after a warning to avoid the hypocrisy of the Pharisees. The implication is not to seek traditional religious acceptance like the false piety that the Pharisees represent. Judgment will expose all someday, and God is the one to be feared. The Lukan version of the confess-deny contrast does use the Son of Man image to underscore Jesus' judging authority. This material appears to include themes that Jesus repeated, possibly to constantly reassure them about suffering.

89. Divisions within Households (Matt. 10:34–36; Luke 12:51–53, in a later context) (Aland §102; Orchard §127a; Huck-Greeven §73)

The rise of opposition and the warnings about persecution cause Jesus to issue another "mission" statement about what his coming means. It does not mean peace for everyone but conflict and division—what Jesus metaphorically calls a "sword." This division will penetrate into families: son against father, daughter against mother, and in-laws against each other, so that a person's opponent will come from within his or her own home. The language of the saying is from Mic. 7:6. This text pictured division in Israel before the judgment, but it was seen in Judaism as a pattern for what would happen in the end. Mishnah *Soṭah* 9.15 discusses the signs of the end at the Messiah's return and cites this text as part of the general moral breakdown that precedes his coming. The text in this reading sees disrespect between elders and children. Other texts make this note more generically (*Jubilees* 23.16, 19; *1 Enoch* 56.7). Second Timothy 3:2 is written to make a similar point. The implication is that the division is a result of someone in the family not heeding the way of God.

Luke 12:51–53 makes the same point in a distinct context in which Jesus also is discussing opposition that will lead him to experience a baptism of death that will be tied to a fire that purges. Luke does not refer to bringing a sword, but division, thus making explicit what Matthew presents metaphorically. He also speaks of houses divided before making allusion to Mic. 7:6. This is a separate use of the same image.

90. Taking Up the Cross and Finding Life (Matt. 10:37–39; Luke 14:25–27; 17:33, in later, distinct contexts) (Aland §103; Orchard §127b; Huck-Greeven §74)

Jesus follows with a culturally shocking statement that loyalty to him is more important than loyalty to parents or children. In Judaism, no human relationship was more significant than the one to family. As Josephus said in *Against Apion* 2.27 §206, "The law ordains also, that parents should be honored immediately after God himself, and delivers that son who does not requite them for the benefits he has received from them, but is deficient on any occasion, to be stoned." The only exception, according to Deut. 13:6, is when one is enticed to be unfaithful to God by someone in the family.[17]

17. In alluding to Levi's loyalty metaphorically, Deut. 33:9 affirms that loyalty to God is more important than loyalty to parents.

In addition, Jesus teaches that an unwillingness to "take up a cross," that is, to face the shame of rejection or even death, makes a person unworthy of him. The point is that if someone prefers popularity with his or her family to following Jesus, then that person never will embrace him and find life, because many in a person's family will reject Jesus. Thus, the one who finds life in this world by protecting it from the rejection and opposition to come will lose true life. On the other hand, the person who loses his or her life "for my [Jesus'] sake" will gain it. Here is a high claim, that loyalty to Jesus can result in life even when physical life is lost. In these remarks Jesus makes it clear how challenging and demanding knowing him will be for those who follow in his footsteps in a hostile world. He also uses a "reversal of fortune" theme in which what seems to be the case in this life is reversed in the next.

The parallel from Luke 14:25–27 involves a remark similar to the initial saying of this unit in a distinct context that comes in a pure discipleship unit of that Gospel. Discipleship cannot happen without Jesus having a place above the family and without a willingness to take up the cross and walk Jesus' course. The latter part of this unit has a parallel in Luke 17:33, where the context involves Jesus discussing elements of the tensions associated with the kingdom's consummate coming and the opposition associated with that coming time. A conceptual parallel appears in John 12:25, where Jesus teaches about loving one's life but losing it, and hating one's life but finding it. This theme seems to have been a repeated one in Jesus' teaching (also Matt. 16:25; Mark 8:35; Luke 9:24). Luke seems to suggest as much when he disperses the discipleship passages across the entire journey section (as just noted in Luke 9, 14, and 17).

91. Reward for Reception (Matt. 10:40–42; conceptual: Mark 9:41; Luke 10:16; John 13:20) (Aland §104; Orchard §128; Huck-Greeven §75a)

The representation of Jesus is so strong that to receive one of his representatives is to receive him and the one who sent him. That is precisely what an apostle is, a fully commissioned representative. The nontechnical use of the term "apostle" in the early church, even when it refers, beyond the Twelve, to missionaries planting churches, has that meaning (Rom. 16:7 [Andronicus and Junia]; 1 Cor. 9:5 [Paul and Barnabas]; cf. "ambassadors" in 2 Cor. 5:20 [includes Paul]).

Jesus discusses three groups of emissaries: prophets, righteous, and disciples. In effect, Jesus is saying that no matter how prominent (prophet) or how average (disciple) the representative is, there will be a reward for receiving them. God knows who will welcome his representatives with the hospitality of even something so simple as a cup of water (see Matt. 10:42). Jesus will bring division, but some will be responsive. On this upbeat note, the Matthean discourse ends.

Differing portions of these remarks have conceptual parallels in the other three Gospels. Mark 9:41 speaks of the reward that comes to the person who gives "you" a cup of water to drink "because you bear the name of Christ." It comes in a context in which Jesus is urging the Twelve to be supportive of others working in his name, a text similar to Luke 9:49–50. In addition, Luke's equivalent to this discourse in the mission charge of Luke 10:16 has the idea that the one who hears Jesus' messenger hears him, and the one who rejects Jesus' messenger rejects him and the one who sent him. John 13:20 makes a similar point with respect to acceptance in a context in which Jesus has washed his disciples' feet and prepares to announce his rejection. The image of the commissioned linkage between Jesus and his messengers appears to have been another frequent theme of Jesus' teaching.

92. Transition to Ministry (Matt. 11:1) (Aland §105; Orchard §129; Huck-Greeven §75b)

This Matthean note is how he concludes discourse material and transitions back to describing Jesus' ministry (cf. 7:28–29). Jesus completes his remarks to the Twelve and goes on to teach and preach in the cities. This short summary is like 9:35.

93. Jesus Answers John the Baptist (Matt. 11:2–6; Luke 7:18–23) (Aland §106; Orchard §130; Huck-Greeven §76)

This key text about John and Jesus is virtually identical in Matthew and Luke in the portions that do overlap. Matthew's version again is more concise, because he does not repeat John's question to Jesus. The reference to Jesus as possibly being "the one to come" looks back to Matt. 3:11 and Luke 3:16, where the one who is to come is mightier than John, a point that allows Jesus to make another allusion later in Luke 11:22. Jesus' style and his lack of a powerful political dimension appear to have raised questions in John's mind about Jesus being the Messiah. John's own arrest and confinement may have added to the uncertainty.[18] Some of the circumstances of suffering make this

---

18. Matt. 14:1–12 tells how John died. He probably was held at Machaerus, a fortress of Herod Antipas. It would have been east of the Dead Sea, thirteen miles southeast of Herodium (Josephus, *Ant.* 18.5.2 §§116–119, tells the Baptist's story as well; see chap. 3, unit 20 above).

time look unlike the anticipated messianic era (cf. John 6:15), so John asks if another is to come. The Greek (ἕτερον) is emphatic here. Should they expect another type of figure?

Contrary to what might be expected, Jesus does not directly affirm or deny who he is. Rather, he simply describes his activity to John. The list is in the same order in each Gospel: blind receive sight, lame walk, lepers are cleansed, deaf hear, dead are raised, and good news is preached to the poor. The language comes from the eschatological portions of Isaiah, where the prophet describes what will happen in the era of deliverance (Isa. 29:18–19; 35:5; 42:18; 26:19; 61:1). In effect, Jesus is answering positively by describing his activity as evidence that the expected era is present, as the language of Scripture shows. He closes the reply by noting that blessing comes to the one who is not "offended" at him. An allusion to Isa. 8:13–15 may be present, where God is a stumbling stone to those who do not trust him. Jesus may not quite match the anticipated style of the Messiah, but Jesus' work explains Jesus' messianic identity. Jesus' activity reveals the nature of the time and the person. John's perplexity also indicates how unprepared people were for the type of messianic activity that Jesus brought.

94. Jesus' Witness about John (Matt. 11:7–19; Luke 7:24–35)
(Aland §107; Orchard §131; Huck-Greeven §77)

So who was John? John's question prompts Jesus to talk to the crowds about the Baptist. They did not go out to see a weak man, who could be bent by the wind (on this image, see 1 Kings 14:15; 2 Kings 18:21). Nor did they go out to see a man finely dressed in silks, like those found in palaces.[19] What they saw in John was a prophet and even more than a prophet. John was a messenger of God, but one with a special task. Jesus then cites a combination of Mal. 3:1 and Exod. 23:20. John is a commissioned, end-time messenger. He is sent to guide the people as Yahweh's cloud had done in the wilderness. The way to follow God was revealed by him.

John represents the greatest person ever born in the old era. He is the culmination of that era, pointing the way to the new era that Jesus brings. Yet the difference between the two eras is so great that the least person in the new era is greater than John. How can the lowest participant in the kingdom be greater than an end-time prophet of the old era? The benefits of the new era, such as full provision of forgiveness, total acceptance as God's children, and the enablement of the indwelling Spirit, make participating in this era a far

19. The allusion here is to the finest clothes of "soft raiment" (RSV).

greater position. Jesus' point is not to put down John but to highlight how truly special the offer of kingdom hope really is.

The next saying has a disputed force. Two options exist for the idea of violence in the verse. When Jesus says that the kingdom of God from John's time until now suffers violence, is the point negative (many are fighting against it) or positive (spiritual warriors are storming their way in)?[20] If one takes the normal usage of the term βιάζομαι and the opposition mounting in the context, then a negative sense is likely.[21] The kingdom, since John announced it, is under attack, but that will not stop its effective presence.

What is happening is what the law and prophets up to John prophesied. Thus, Jesus' ministry is in continuity with the promise of the Hebrew Scriptures. If you understand, then you will see that John is Elijah. Luke 1:17 said it this way: John came in "the spirit and power of Elijah."[22] John did not perform miracles as Elijah did, so the reference is to his preaching and the warning that Israel must turn and prepare for God or else face judgment. Thus, Jesus calls on those with ears to hear. In other words, pay attention to this (cf. Matt. 13:9, 43; Luke 8:8; 14:35).

Following this, Jesus tells a parable whose meaning is debated. The parable's background is a children's game in which they play a tune and others dance to it. Does the comparison with the children playing the tune describe the contrasting styles of John and Jesus, neither of which this generation is following? Or does this generation describe those who play the tune and complain that John and Jesus do not follow their choice of either dirge or celebratory music?[23] The introduction of the parable compares "this generation" to those playing and calling to their mates. This seems to favor the idea that the generation is complaining that John and Jesus do not meet their expectations and follow their ways. The complaints are that John was too ascetic and strange. He has "a demon." Jesus, on the opposite side, is not separatistic, nor is he pious enough. He is "a glutton and a drunkard, a friend of tax collectors and sinners." These messengers of God will not follow the people's tune, so Jesus accuses the generation of being like a bunch of complaining brats. He concludes by noting that "wisdom is justified by her deeds." In other words,

20. Compare Blomberg, *Matthew*, 187–88 (negative), with Keener, *Matthew*, 217–18 (positive). The problem with deciding is that the Lukan parallel, which is in a distinct context in 16:16, looks to be positive in thrust, while the Matthean context for this saying contains reference to opposition, making this text look negative.

21. Both the warnings about persecution in Matt. 10 and the following parable show that the note about opposition is high. The kingdom's announcement has activated a fierce battle.

22. On Elijah in Judaism, see Darrell L. Bock, "Elijah," *DJG*, 203–6.

23. Again, Blomberg, *Matthew*, 189–190 (John and Jesus), and Keener, *Matthew*, 218 (this generation), go different ways. Regardless of which view is taken, the point is that the people in general are going in one direction, and John and Jesus in another.

the wisdom of God's way will show itself to be right, although it seems different from what was anticipated.

Luke 7:24–35 is substantially parallel to this text. The remarks about John follow after the question from John's disciples about whether Jesus is the coming one, as in Matthew. Up through the remark about John being the greatest born of women, Jesus' teaching appears as in Matthew. Luke's remark about the kingdom being preached "since John, with everyone strongly urged to enter it" appears not here but in 16:16 and is a positive statement about the shift of eras. Thus, it appears in a separate context and probably is a distinct saying, given its distinct tone. Its use appears to have led Luke to omit the more negative reference that Matthew uses. Luke also lacks any Elijah allusion here, although he already had something similar in 1:17. Luke adds a narrative parenthetical note that God was justified by the people and tax collectors responding to John's baptism, while the Pharisees and lawyers rejected God's will by not receiving his baptism. This sets up the parable about the brats, making a slightly more specific reference in Luke to the leadership as the specific people of the generation being rebuked. It would seem that because the leaders' opinion leads the way, Luke singles them out. Luke also adds a note about John not eating bread or drinking wine, which makes a slightly closer contrasting parallelism to what is said next about Jesus eating and drinking. Luke's closing remark also is slightly different: wisdom "is justified by her children." This is a more personified form of Matthew's "is justified by her deeds." Yet both the parable and the closing remark follow Matthew's order, suggesting that a genuine parallel is present. This juxtaposition of agreement and slight interpretive variation in what is surely a parallel is common in the Gospel tradition. This unit is one of the better and clearer examples of this tendency.

95. Woes for Galilean Cities (Matt. 11:20–24; Luke 10:12–15, in a context of the disciples' mission) (Aland §108; Orchard §132; Huck-Greeven §78)

The lack of response in Galilee leads Jesus to rebuke the cities. Matthew specifically notes that the cities where Jesus' miracles were performed are singled out for their failure to respond with repentance. The rebuke is especially severe, taking the form of woes, like the judgment of the Old Testament prophets against both the nations and Israel (Isa. 13–23; Jer. 2–11; 46–51; Ezek. 16; 25–32; Amos 1:3–3:8). In addition, Jesus adds insult by arguing that some of the most sinful of the pagan cities, such as Tyre, Sidon, and Sodom, would have responded by repenting with sackcloth and ashes had they had the benefit of seeing what these cities had seen (cf. Esth. 4:3; Jon. 3:6–9). Here is a Jesus who teaches accountability for responding to his teaching and warns of a great judgment for rejecting him. Those ancient pagan cities of sin will have it better in the judgment than will Chorazin, Bethsaida, and Capernaum. Jesus' headquarters, Capernaum, is even compared in arrogance to the Babylonian king who aspired to be like God (Isa. 14:12–14). In effect, to refuse God's chosen messenger is to claim to know more than God does about his ways. So this city will be brought down to Hades, and Sodom will do better in the judgment.

The Lukan version comes in the midst of the discussion of the mission of the seventy(-two).[24] Luke mentions the same three Galilean cities, but his version is more concise because he attaches the remarks about judgment being more tolerable for Sodom to the introduction of this unit. Luke has these sayings following instructions about what to do if the disciples are not accepted in a given locale. Luke's point also focuses on the accountability that emerges when one rejects these messengers' word about the kingdom. In its Lukan form, heeding the messengers' announcement of the kingdom is as key as heeding Jesus.

96. Jesus' Thanksgiving to the Father (Matt. 11:25–27; Luke 10:21–22, in a context of the disciples' mission) (Aland §109; Orchard §133; Huck-Greeven §79)

Despite the difficulty, Jesus rejoices over those whom God has given to him. In a prayer that comes close to a praise psalm in style (cf. Dan. 2:19–23; Rom. 11:33–36), Jesus thanks the sovereign God of heaven and earth, who has hidden these truths from the wise and the understanding while revealing them to babes. The contrast is not between the smart and the ignorant, but between those who think they can wisely negotiate their way through life and those who, like babes, appreciate their need for someone to guide them. This approach Jesus attributes to God's gracious will. There is a plan that God is directing, even as people respond (Matt. 11:20–24, 28–30).

The focus of that plan is that blessing and access to knowledge of God reside in Jesus. The Father has delivered all things to Jesus. Knowledge of the Son is the Father's prerogative, just as knowledge of the Father is the Son's prerogative and belongs to anyone to whom the Son chooses to give it. Thus, this note of thanksgiving also shows how intimately bound together the Father and Son are. To deal with one, a person must deal with the other. This statement has them so closely bound that it recalls such statements in the Gospel of John and asserts their united role in the divine work.

The Lukan parallel in 10:21–22 also comes in the context of the disciples' mission, as the previous parallel of Luke 10:12–15 did with Matt. 11:20–24.

24. The textual problems in Luke 10:1, 17 make the number sent out in this mission uncertain. See discussion in unit 161 below.

Luke's parallel is almost an exact verbal match with Matthew. Where Matthew uses the more intense Greek verb ἐπιγινώσκω, "to fully know," Luke has the simpler γινώσκω. Luke personalizes the knowledge that the Son gives of the Father by indicating that the Son reveals "who" the Father is, an emphasis on the disclosure of God's character. The basic point is the same, and the remark is a parallel.

97. Come to Me (Matt. 11:28–30) (Aland §110; Orchard §134; Huck-Greeven §80)

Jewish background helps with this remark about taking up Jesus' yoke.[25] The picture of life as hard is stated in Sir. 40:1, where a heavy yoke is the inheritance that comes to Adam's children because of his sin. In Sir. 51:26, wisdom from the law is seen as a yoke that a person should take on in order to be instructed. Wisdom also makes an invitation to come to her to eat of her sweet fruit, which is better than honeycomb (Sir. 24:19–20). Thus, Jesus' imagery has parallels to the wisdom and the law of Judaism, but it is to him instead of the law that people should come. The association of Jesus with law or wisdom was not unusual in the church (1 Cor. 1:24; Rom. 10:5–13). In addition, his burden is light, not heavy, because he bears it with us (contrast the scribes and Pharisees in Matt. 23:4). What Jesus offers is rest, not because labor will stop (Matt. 10 showed that there is much labor to do), but because in humility and in leaving one's care truly up to God by trusting him, the disciple's burdens are lessened. Jesus' example of meekness and dependence instructs the disciple and lightens the burden. The proximity of this saying to the previous one suggests that a dependent walk is what lightens the load. The result is rest for the soul because Jesus gives a yoke that is easy to wear, creating a light burden. Thus, despite all the hardship and opposition that Jesus has noted, these remarks about God's plan end on a positive note before Matthew returns to detail more miracles by Jesus.

98. Plucking Grain on the Sabbath (Matt. 12:1–8; Mark 2:23–28, in an earlier context; Luke 6:1–5, in an earlier context [see unit 38 above]) (Aland §111; Orchard §135; Huck-Greeven §81)

This passage was treated in detail when it was discussed earlier. The one point to note here is that it begins a chapter in Matthew in which confrontation is dominating. After two controversial Sabbath miracles (12:1–14), Mat-

25. H. D. Betz, "Take My Yoke upon You [Matt 11:29]," *Journal of Biblical Literature* 86 (1967): 10–24.

thew offers a summary (12:15–21) and then reports the charge that Jesus heals by the power of Beelzebul, which causes Jesus to warn about blasphemy of the Spirit (12:22–32) and discuss knowing a tree by its fruit (12:33–36). Jesus also issues a warning in the face of this rejection. No sign will be given to this generation but that of Jonah. The sign appears to be a combination of three days and nights in the earth's belly and a message of repentance (12:37–42). The refusal to respond is compared to a demon being exorcised from a person and then returning with seven others because nothing was done after the exorcism to prevent future possession (12:43–45). Finally, a visit from his family elicits from Jesus the remark that whoever does the will of his Father is a member of his family (12:46–50). Thus, in all of this the primary issues are confrontation, rejection, and the need for response. This initial Sabbath controversy leads off the sequence, whereas in Mark and Luke it had been the fourth of five consecutive controversies. What all the Synoptics share is the recognition that these two Sabbath controversies were the last straw that led to a heightening of opposition.

99. Healing the Withered Hand on the Sabbath

(Matt. 12:9–14; Mark 3:1–6, in an earlier context; Luke 6:6–11, in an earlier context [see unit 39 above]) (Aland §112; Orchard §136a; Huck-Greeven §82)

This passage was treated in detail earlier. The "labor" of simply declaring the man healed causes the Pharisees to plot to destroy him. The account is told less pointedly in Matthew than in Mark and Luke, as Matthew lacks the challenging question of whether it is right to do good or harm on the Sabbath, that is, to save life or kill it. Rather, Matthew adds the illustration of saving a sheep from the pit on the Sabbath, which leads to the legal judgment that it is lawful to do good on the Sabbath, a point that Mark and Luke do not make for their likely more Gentile audience.

100. Summary: Jesus Heals the Multitudes by the Sea

(Matt. 12:15–21; Mark 3:7–12; Luke 6:17–19 [see unit 40 above]) (Aland §113; Orchard §§136b–37; Huck-Greeven §84)

Matthew now rejoins the story at the place where both Mark and Luke are preparing to go through kingdom parables. The actual summary was discussed earlier. Matthew is the most concise. He speaks of multitudes being healed as Jesus continues to ask that they not "make him known."

Mark and Luke are close to each other. Mark speaks of people coming from Galilee, Judea, Jerusalem, Idumea, beyond the Jordan, as well as from Tyre and Sidon. They were responding to all that he did. Jesus both healed the multitudes and exorcised demons, who were naming him as the "Son of God." Jesus ordered them not to "make him known." Luke notes the crowds from Judea and Jerusalem and from Tyre and Sidon, these last two areas being Gentile. The crowds come for healing and exorcism from unclean spirits. The crowds sought to touch him because "power came forth from him," and he healed them all.

Matthew uniquely concludes his summary with a fulfillment citation from Isaiah. He cites 42:1–4 from the Isaianic Servant Songs.[26] It is the longest Old Testament citation in the Gospel. The reference is to God's Servant, who is chosen by God for a task. The language is very close conceptually to the language of the heavenly voice at the baptism, because to be chosen is to be the object of God's special favor. God is "well pleased" with his beloved. The Servant possesses the Spirit of God. This remark seems close to the remark of Luke in his summary that Jesus possessed power. But Matthew does not stop here. Jesus' withdrawal shows that Jesus will not fight the rejection with fire but with a continuing offer to restore God's way. So the Servant will proclaim justice to the Gentiles, a significant remark in the context of Matthew's Gospel and his Jewish concerns. He will go about the task, neither retaliating nor harming, until the job is done. Not many will respond to him, but that will not prevent success. He will be gentle, neither damaging a bruised plant nor putting out a flickering candle. Entrusting himself to God, Jesus will see justice come to victory. His name will be hope for the Gentiles.

101. The Sinful Woman Anoints Jesus at the Pharisee's Table

(Luke 7:36–50; similar but distinct event, Matt. 26:6–13; Mark 14:3–9; John 12:1–8) (Aland §114; Orchard §95; Huck-Greeven §96)

This anointing account is unique to Luke, although a similar event in the last week of Jesus' ministry is recorded in Matthew, Mark, and John. In Matthew and Mark, the event occurs in the house of a leper, where a Pharisee would not be present; in John, it occurs at the home of Mary, Martha, and Lazarus. In Matthew and Mark, nothing is said about the woman's status; in John, it is a righteous woman, Mary, who anoints Jesus. Thus, Luke's event reflects two major differences. The Lukan event reinforces Jesus' willingness

26. See J. H. Neyrey, "The Thematic Use of Isaiah 42,1–4 in Matthew 12," *Biblica* 63 (1982): 457–73. The song is a "one in the many" text that refers to Israel but also points to a representative figure. *Targum Isaiah* 42.1 reads a messianic element in this passage. After all, the Messiah represents the best of Israel and performs God's task ideally for Israel.

to associate with sinners (Luke 5:27–32; 7:31–35) as well as his right to forgive sins (Luke 5:17–26).

Jesus has had tension with the Pharisees, but that does not preclude him from associating with them. He accepts an invitation to dine with a Pharisee named Simon (vv. 39–40). Apparently, it was an open meal that allowed interested observers to sit on the fringes and listen to the conversation. The problem arose when a sinful woman came up to the place where Jesus was eating and began to anoint his feet with expensive perfume.[27] Although it is not identified, the perfume, if nard, which was common for the region, would have cost three hundred denarii per pound, or a year's average wage (cf. Mark 14:3–5; John 12:3–5). Such anointing often was practiced at civic feasts or important occasions (Exod. 30:25–30; Josephus, *Ant.* 3.8.6 §205; 19.9.1 §358). The woman surely knew that she was breaking convention and showed great nerve in carrying out her act of homage. She is weeping throughout the act and even lets down her hair to wipe Jesus' feet, likewise an act that was culturally unacceptable, although what she sought to communicate required deep humility.

The Pharisee instantly forms an opinion about the event. It does not involve the woman but Jesus. His view is that pious people do not get close to sinners. So his judgment is that Jesus cannot be a prophet, because he allows her to touch him. In Greek the objection in 7:39 is expressed as a class two, contrary-to-fact, condition, so the point is that this action and Jesus' lack of objection proves in the mind of the Pharisee that Jesus is not a prophet.

The account turns ironic. While the Pharisee is thinking that his guest is not a prophet, Jesus is about to tell a parable that shows that he prophetically knows exactly what the Pharisee is thinking! The parable is of two debtors, one who has a debt of fifty denarii (two-and-a-half months' wage), and another who owes five hundred denarii (almost two years' wage). Neither could pay, but both had their debt forgiven. Jesus asks Simon which of the two would love the creditor more. Simon rightly answers, "The one, I suppose, to whom he forgave more." Jesus notes that this is the correct answer. Jesus' point is that he must associate with sinners because upon being forgiven, they appreciate forgiveness. He also is arguing that this woman has experienced such forgiveness and that her actions show her appreciation of being forgiven. In contrast, those who think themselves forgiven little have only a little devotion. Great forgiveness leads to a great opportunity for great love.

To drive the point home, Jesus recounts the woman's gracious actions in contrast to the lack of such actions by his host.[28] Jesus' key initial conclusion

27. The unnamed woman is not Mary Magdalene; that Mary is introduced in 8:1–3 as if she is a new narrative figure.

28. Such actions may have been expected of a host; see L. Goppelt, "ὕδωρ," *TDNT,* 8:323–24 and n. 63, 328 nn. 93–95.

is that "her sins, which are many, are forgiven, hence she loved much; but the one who is forgiven little loves little." Jesus' associations are motivated by the knowledge that communicating the hope of forgiveness can create deep love in people. Thus, his view contrasts sharply with his host, who wants the pious to distance themselves from sinners. To drive the confirmation of forgiveness home to the woman and affirm her act as an act of love in response to forgiveness, Jesus tells her that she is forgiven. This upsets the others at the table, who ask, "Who is this, who even forgives sins?" This question about Jesus' identity is like one that will be raised later in Luke 8:25 about who can calm the seas. It also recalls the dispute over sin in Luke 5:21, where the note was made that only God can forgive sins. Jesus does not back off. He reaffirms her faith, which is displayed so vividly in her action. It has saved her. So she can go in peace. The entire scene not only explains Jesus' mission but also shows the authority he possesses to interpret the scene as he does. He has the right to give her such assuring words. Simon had questioned whether Jesus was a prophet. However, Jesus' response to the woman not only set an example about how the righteous should relate to sinners, but also raised a question about whether Jesus was far more than a prophet.

102. The Ministering Women (Luke 8:1–3) (Aland §115; Orchard §96; Huck-Greeven §97)

This uniquely Lukan text continues his affirmation of women's involvement with Jesus' ministry (cf. Luke 1:5–39; 2:36–38; 7:11–17, 36–50; 10:38–42; 13:10–17; 15:8–10; 18:1–8—all uniquely Lukan texts involving women). It stands in contrast to some Jewish views, such as that seen in *t. Berakot* 7.18, where a rabbi remarks that he is glad that he is not a pagan, woman, or unlearned. Luke notes three women who give monetary support to Jesus' work. This is not unprecedented; Josephus (*Ant.* 17.2.4 §§41–44) notes the example of wealthy women supporting religious figures.

The three women are very different. Mary Magdalene was rescued through an exorcism. She is not the same woman as the one in 7:36–50, but like her, has responded to Jesus' gracious work. Joanna is the wife of Herod's steward, and her presence shows that the message is climbing into the upper echelons of society, penetrating even the palace. We know nothing else about Susanna. Jesus' ministry produced gratitude expressed in the donation of resources. So Jesus' work was not limited to the poor. It was gender inclusive and socially broad in its outreach.

103. Family Seeks to Protect Jesus (Mark 3:19b–21) (Aland §116; Orchard §97; Huck-Greeven §98)

After noting the choosing of the Twelve (see unit 86 above), Mark turns his attention to the reaction to Jesus. Jesus returns home after naming the Twelve, and the crowd was so great that they could not eat meals (literally, "eat bread"). The impression is that the ministry is keeping them too busy to even think about eating. Jesus is drawing much attention. However, everything is not positive. The family ("those near him") hear of it and desire to seize him. The explanation is cryptic: "For they were saying that he is beside himself." The question is, Who are the "they" who see Jesus this way? In 3:34–35, the crowd seems to be excluded from this reference, since those in the crowd who are responding to Jesus are seen as his true family. Jesus makes this remark about the crowd when the family arrives to try to see him. The leadership seems to be excluded, because their view is that Jesus works through Beelzebul. That reaction causes the family to question what Jesus is doing. They go to see him. The statement is so surprising that it demands to be seen as historically authentic. The church never would make up such a statement. What the incident reveals is that Jesus' messianic style was surprising, even alarming, to his family, just as it had been to John the Baptist and others. Even they did not understand how he would represent God's way. Mark uses the remark to set up his account of the Beelzebul charge. For Mark, the controversies of 2:1–3:6 have led to rejection. Initially, it was unclear how Jesus would bring God's way, especially given his ministry style and claims.

104. The Cast-Out-by-Beelzebul Charge (Matt. 12:22–30; Mark 3:22–27; Luke 11:14–15, 17–23, in a later context) (Aland §117; Orchard §138a; Huck-Greeven §99a)

This miracle account breaks the pattern of that form in that virtually the whole unit covers the reaction to a miracle. The reversal of the pattern indicates the text's importance as commentary on Jesus' miraculous ministry. A preliminary raising of the charge that Jesus heals by evil means in Matt. 9:34 prepares us for this account in Matt. 12. There, a healing of a mute demoniac had led to the charge that Jesus did his work by the "prince of demons." The sequence there also is evident here: Jesus heals, crowd reacts, and Pharisees charge. In Matt. 12, the healing causes the crowd to consider whether Jesus might be the Son of David, although the use of the Greek μήτι anticipates a negative reply, denoting severe doubt that this really is the case. The impression is that the crowd raises the messianic option but does not embrace it, as 11:16–19 also suggested.

The Pharisees have an even stronger explanation. Not only is Jesus not messianic, but he is also directed by Beelzebul, the prince of demons, who is identified in Jesus' response in 12:26 as Satan. This figure is present in Jewish materials in the *Testament of Solomon* 2.8–3.6 and 6.1–11. Both references to Beelzebul and prince of the demons are in an emphatic position in the Greek. The source responsible for Jesus' power is diabolical. The claim is that Jesus is a magician, a sorcerer.[29]

Jesus' reply tackles the absurdity of the claim, and he does so having known "their thoughts," a trait tied to prophetic figures in Judaism (*t. Pisha* [= *Pesahim*] 2.15). Jesus' refutation makes several points. The first is that these works cannot be Satan's, for if they were, then he would be reversing his own work and leaving his kingdom divided and exposed to defeat. Jesus' assumption is that by reversing damage done to creation, he shows that Satan is not trying to undo what he has wrought.

Second, Jesus raises a question about other exorcists. The point made in the question is disputed. Most argue that Jesus' point is that a condemnation of his exorcisms is a condemnation of Jewish exorcism in general. For if the works that Jesus does are of Satan, then what of similar works by other sons of Israel? If the Pharisees condemn their works, then they will judge the Pharisees one day. This sense is possible, but then the text is highly rhetorical, being a generalized endorsement of Jewish exorcism.[30] Another sense is more natural. Jesus is noting the work that his own disciples, as sons of Israel, have done (10:8, 25 [the disciples will be said to work in the name of Beelzebul!]). His point is that his works are not the only ones that they must judge. He has also empowered others. One day these others will be judges of the accusatory Pharisees. On this reading (i.e., that "your sons" refers to Jesus' own disciples), the retort is a warning of what will actually happen.

Third, Jesus makes a positive deduction. If he casts out demons by the Spirit of God (note the contrast to the diabolical spirit), then the kingdom of God (not that of Satan) is exercising its powerful presence. Jesus' point here has to be a reference to the current effective presence of God's rule as expressed in the evidence of Satan's being overcome. So the kingdom has come upon them.

The following illustration solidifies the claim for the presence of kingdom authority. A strong man's home cannot be plundered until its owner is bound. Then plundering will follow. Jesus portrays his healings as evidence that the

---

29. The historical impact of this charge was such as to leave traces into the second century. That powers such as these came through spiritual agents is well attested (*PGM* 1.88–89, 164–66, 181–85, 252–53; 2.52–54). See Keener, *Matthew*, 230; Darrell L. Bock, *Studying the Historical Jesus* (Grand Rapids: Baker, 2002), 61–63.

30. Blomberg, *Matthew*, 202.

strong man (Satan) has been overcome by a stronger man (himself) who now goes through Satan's house taking away the devil's work. The Pharisees' charge could not be more incorrect. Jesus does not cast out by Satan; he casts out Satan's work!

So anyone who does not side with Jesus is against him. The one who does not gather in support of him scatters. This final remark is a warning that sets up the next unit, on blasphemy by the Spirit.

The Markan version is more concise. It comes in reaction to the heightening of controversy that was noted in Mark 2:1–3:6. Also, it is triggered not by a healing by Jesus, but by the suggestion in 3:21 that he has lost his mind. Mark lays the charge of being possessed through Beelzebul at the feet of the "scribes who came down from Jerusalem." He too notes the accusation that Jesus casts out demons by the prince of demons. These specifics suggest that Jesus was being examined by experts from Judea. Jesus' reply is similar to the retort in Matthew, although it is described as replying in parables. Mark's point is that a divided kingdom cannot stand (versus being laid waste, in Matthew) and that a divided house shows that Satan is "coming to an end." Mark lacks a reference to miracles as evidence of the kingdom having come, moving instead directly to the image of the plundered house. With this note of triumph in overcoming the evil one, Mark's account ends. The miracles, for him, picture Jesus' superior authority and victory, as well as Satan's end. Mark says what Matthew says about the arrival of the kingdom, but in a way that highlights what has happened to the enemy.

Luke's version comes in a context that leads into a series of texts that show the nation not responding well to Jesus (Luke 11:24–26 [with its warning about not ignoring God's work]; 11:29–32 [no sign given to this generation but that like the preaching of Jonah]; 11:37–54 [the woes to Pharisees and scribes]). For Luke, this charge is but an initial example of the poor response. A healing brings the charge, although Luke does note that others had not made up their mind, waiting for a sign from heaven.[31] Jesus' retort goes in a line similar to that in Matthew: a divided kingdom is laid waste and a divided house falls. So how can Satan's kingdom stand? Then Jesus raises the issue of the other exorcists.[32] Next comes the citing of the miracles as evidence of the kingdom of God having come, because they are worked by "the finger of God" (not Matthew's "Spirit of God"). Thus, Luke's version alludes to the language of God's saving power in Exod. 8:19. The plundered-house image

31. The remark about the undecided is ironic because Jesus had given a host of signs in his miraculous work. What else do they want? Apparently, some type of specific cosmic sign is desired. Matthew will make the same point in a separate unit; see unit 106 below.

32. Matthew and Luke agree in another way here. Both state the "cast out by Satan" option and the "cast out by God" option in equally vivid class-one conditions in Greek, presenting each option as one to consider. But what is presented as rhetorically equal is distinguished by the surrounding logical evidence favoring a work of God.

follows, although Luke lacks the "binding" language of Matthew and Mark, speaking only of the strong man being overcome. But the imagery of impotency is intensified as Satan's armor is taken and the spoil of victory is divided. Jesus' remarks conclude with the note that anyone who is not with him is against him. Thus, Luke closely parallels Matthew in this unit, while still making unique points.

105. The Sin against the Holy Spirit (Matt. 12:31–37;
Mark 3:28–30; Luke 12:10, in a later context; conceptual: Matt. 7:16–20; Luke 6:43–45) (Aland §118; Orchard §§138b–39; Huck-Greeven §99b)

Jesus' claim to cast out demons in the power of God means that those observing him need to be warned. Matthew notes that every type of sin and blasphemy will be forgiven except one, blasphemy against the Holy Spirit. One can speak, in a moment of weakness, against the Son of Man and be forgiven, but blaspheming the Spirit—decisively rejecting what the Spirit says about Jesus—will not be forgiven, either in this age or in the one to come. To reject with a determined, hard heart the evidence of God's Spirit, who has empowered the work that Jesus is doing (Matt. 12:28), is to face the judgment of God. Do not be mistaken about who Jesus is or the source of his work. Jesus is not a soft-spoken teacher of religion saying "Consider my way as one of many choices to finding God." He boldly asserts that a person's eternal fate is wrapped up in the choice.

Matthew's account goes on to speak about how trees reveal their character by their fruit, whether good or bad. The narrative point seems to be that the judgment that one renders about Jesus points to the quality of one's heart. The danger is that the judgment that the Pharisees give will steer others. The Pharisees will be accountable. So he calls them snakes, as John the Baptist had (Matt. 3:7), and challenges them on how they think they can speak good when they are evil. The mouth speaks from what is in the heart, so that good treasure comes from a good heart and evil treasure from an evil heart. Every careless word will be assessed on judgment day, because people will be justified or condemned by their words. Jesus' warning is that an expressed decision that Jesus casts out by Satan's power is, no matter how carelessly expressed, a word of evil that will be judged.[33]

Mark is far more concise. After noting the plundering of the strong man's house by the stronger man, Jesus issues a warning. All sins and blasphemies

---

33. This imagery also appears in a completely different context in the Sermon on the Mount (Matt. 7:16–20) and the Sermon on the Plain (Luke 6:43–45). Matthew speaks of false prophets being revealed by their fruit; Luke refers to the character of people being seen through their actions and speech.

uttered by the "sons of men" will be forgiven, but whoever blasphemes against the Spirit "never has forgiveness" (literally, "has no forgiveness unto the age").[34] That person is guilty of an "eternal sin." Mark makes it clear what the sin is: saying that Jesus has "an unclean spirit." The settled idea that Jesus was possessed is an insult to God and a rejection of a unique, divinely commissioned agent—a blasphemy that cannot be forgiven.

Luke has his statement about blasphemy against the Holy Spirit in a context in which he is urging the crowds to fear the one who can cast the body into Gehenna. Those who acknowledge the Son of Man before people will be acknowledged by him at the judgment before God's angels. Those who deny him will be denied by him. Anyone who speaks a word against the Son of Man will be forgiven, but anyone who blasphemes the Spirit will not be forgiven. So they must be prepared to testify on Jesus' behalf before rulers and authorities. The Spirit will give them what to say. Luke's version shows how the Spirit is involved in testimony about who Jesus is. This adds a dimension to blasphemy against the Spirit that associates it not only with miracles (as in Matthew and Mark), but also with the oral testimony of those allied to the Son of Man.

106. The Sign of Jonah (Matt. 12:38–42; Mark 8:11–12, in a later context; Luke 11:16, 29–32; conceptual: Matt. 16:1–2a, 4) (Aland §119; Orchard §140; Huck-Greeven §100)

Matthew now shows that not every scribe and Pharisee thought that Jesus did his work through Beelzebul. They request a sign from Jesus. Matthew will repeat this request later in 16:1–2a, as well as Jesus' response in 16:4. The repetition serves to show that the interaction is changing nothing.

Jesus rebukes the request. He has given sufficient indication that God has been at work. They are an "evil and adulterous" generation, a description of major unfaithfulness and unresponsiveness (Hosea; Ezek. 16). He will repeat the charge in v. 45. Such a generation of unbelief asks for a sign in the face of so much extraordinary activity.

So only one sign, that of Jonah, is given. In Matthew, this is a complex figure. It includes a parallel to the three days and nights that Jonah spent in the belly of the great fish.[35] This is an allusion to the death and resurrection of Jesus, a surprise deliverance. They will not see the entire event itself, just as the Ninevites in the Book of Jonah did not. They will see the effect of the sign.

34. Note that Mark lacks the difficult statement in Matthew that sin against the Son of Man is forgivable.

35. It is a Semitic custom to count such days inclusively, which means any part of a day involved is counted as a day.

They may try to eliminate Jesus, but his presence will remain. So the Ninevites (Gentiles!) will arise at the judgment against this generation and condemn it. They responded with repentance to the message that Jonah gave. Jesus is greater than Jonah and so even more deserving of such a response. A second example drives home the point: Jesus notes that the Queen of Sheba (another Gentile!) also will stand at the judgment and condemn them. She came from the ends of the earth to hear Solomon's wisdom. This story made a deep impression on Jews (1 Kings 10:1–13; 2 Chron. 9:1–12; Josephus, *Ant.* 8.6.5–6 §§165–175). Jesus is greater than the great king. He deserves a hearing much more than Solomon does. So the image of the sign of Jonah includes both the picture of a surprising deliverance and its effect, the preaching and call of repentance that came with it. The sign is a message that comes with verification. But with the sign came an insult for the Jewish leaders' lack of faith: Gentiles are more sensitive and receptive than they are. Thus, Matt. 12 closes its interaction with the Jewish sects by giving a strong rebuke.

Mark 8:11–12 raises the issue of the Pharisees' request for a sign in a later context, just before Jesus is confessed as the Messiah by Peter. Here, Jesus declines entirely. This generation will get no sign. In context, this means that the request for a sign from heaven will be denied. No such sign is coming. God already has shown his support for this ministry publicly as far back as Mark 2:1–12, with the healing that demonstrated Jesus' authority to forgive sin.

Luke 11:16 also notes that some sought a sign, when the evangelist treats the Beelzebul charge (see unit 104 above). The rebuke of being an evil generation that gets no sign but that of Jonah comes later, in vv. 29–32. Luke makes no mention of three days and nights in the belly of the fish. Rather, he concentrates exclusively on the teaching of repentance that Jonah gave to Nineveh and of wisdom that the Queen of Sheba sought from Solomon. Luke also has the illustrations in reverse order: Solomon, then Nineveh. For Luke, the spoken word and evidence already given are enough. A similar point comes from Luke 16:19–31, in Abraham's words to the rich man: sending someone from the dead will not be convincing, and hearing Moses and the prophets should be sufficient. Jesus' ministry and teaching are sign enough. Response should follow.

107. The Return of the Evil Spirit (Matt. 12:43–45; Luke 11:24–26)
(Aland §120; Orchard §141; Huck-Greeven §101)

Matthew closes his remarks about opposition with a warning. Jesus compares the condition of those around him to a person who benefits from an exorcism but then does nothing about it. This person leaves the home empty, swept, and put in order but brings nothing into the house to replace the expelled demon. So the demon gathers seven others more evil than itself and returns to dwell there. The result is that the exorcism does no good and the new situation is worse than the initial one. Jesus concludes uniquely in Matthew, "So it will be with this evil generation." God had been at work in their midst. The demon was cast out and opportunity knocked. However, they had refused to accept or acknowledge that fact. The empty house had not been filled with God. So the risk is that a new situation worse than the original one will take hold. This rebuke is intended and should be read corporately. It is a statement about the generation as a group.

The Lukan parallel comes in the context of the Beelzebul charge in Luke 11:24–26. It is almost verbally identical to Matthew in the portions that it shares. It also has a role similar to Matthew's use, although it is more proximate to the Beelzebul dispute. Luke's version is more concise. He does not note that the house is empty, but only that it is swept and in order. The return of the demon with its seven evil partners leaves a worse situation. In both versions, the stress in the remarks is that a failure to respond to God's work leaves one in a position to get even worse. In Matthew, Jesus predicts that this will be the case. The nation is duly warned.

108. Jesus' True Family (Matt. 12:46–50; Mark 3:31–35; Luke 8:19–21, in a later context) (Aland §121; Orchard §142; Huck-Greeven §102)

In Matthew, the affirmation of a new kind of family for Jesus comes in the context of his family's desire to speak with him. Matthew does not give a reason for their request. It is implied that there is concern over the opposition and rising note of confrontation. The attempt to visit causes Jesus to motion to his disciples and declare that whoever does the "will of my Father in heaven is my brother, sister, and mother." The reference to God as Father is unique to Matthew. Jesus has a spiritual family that is more important than his earthly family. In the first century, this would be a shocking statement because the family constituted the most important of human relationships.

Mark 3:31–35 also has the remarks preceding the kingdom parables and following the Beelzebul dispute. Earlier in 3:21–22, he has noted the reason for the visit and the concern. The family is worried that Jesus "is beside himself," so they wish to speak with him. Looking around, he asks who his family is and replies that it is here in the group gathered around him. It is made up of "whoever does the will of God." Spiritual sensitivity to God has provided a new family in the face of their questions and challenges (see John 7:1–5).

Luke 8:19–21 makes this note just after the portion of kingdom parables that he presents. He notes that the crowd prevents Jesus' family from reaching him. When told of their desire to see him, Jesus simply replies that those who hear and do the will of God are his mother and brothers. The Lord's brother James eventually got the message (James 1:21–25; 2:14–26). Jesus' solidarity comes with those who walk with God.

Conclusion

This survey of Jesus' Galilean ministry has reached a point where each Synoptic will discuss the kingdom parables. The fundamental character of Jesus' ministry is evident: preached word supported by the evidence of miraculous deed. These deeds are to be neither focused on nor promoted as the main point of his ministry. Rather, they are a picture of the restoration he seeks to bring. Jesus has proclaimed fulfillment of promise and of law in his message. He is one with authority to forgive sin and to determine what is right on the Sabbath. He also seeks to reach out to the lost and those who know their need. He comes to challenge the ravages of sin and Satan on the earth. His ministry reaches out to those on the fringe of society. He calls the nation to repent and turn to him in turning back to God. His ethical call is that relating well to God involves extending love even to outsiders and enemies, as well as examining one's own walk with God, looking especially to attitudes on the inside. These claims are focused in a figure whom he refers to as "Son of Man" by way of self-description. He is God's commissioned representative for humanity. This authority represents the approach and arrival of God's rule, something he will discuss in even more detail as the ministry moves ahead.

The issues of authority that Jesus raises suggest that the way that the current leadership of Judaism interacts with God is inadequate. This view has raised a strong opposition to him. So Jesus calls a group of disciples to himself and has them engage in mission, knowing full well that they too will face opposition. He prepares them for it in his teaching and stresses that alliance with him will cost them, just as it will cost him.

In considering the authenticity of Jesus' ministry, critical studies often work one event at a time, operating unit by unit in detail. Such close examination of the details of the texts is appropriate and has its place, but often the effect of such study is "to divide and conquer." By cutting the ministry of Jesus up into microbits, the critic can lose a sense of the whole and by means of the separation make claims about the lack of credibility in the little portions that are left in isolation from one another.

In contrast, when one looks at Jesus' ministry as a whole and sees the interlacing and overlapping between the parts as the Synoptics present them, a credible story of the whole of his ministry emerges. His challenge of the leadership did give rise to intense opposition, an opposition that one could sense might become a formidable opponent and a threat to life. Anyone tied to Jesus would be associated with the cause and evaluated in a similar way to the teacher. After all, Jesus' challenge to the Jewish leadership and his direct call for repentance formed a severe critique of the leaders' own way of walking with God. Jesus presented a real threat to the leaders' own authority.

When the student works with this general portrait and the way that the major themes are woven into every level of the Synoptic tradition, a solid case emerges for the credibility of the Gospel portrait of Jesus' ministry and the reaction that his ministry produced. The general class of dispute texts is multiply attested, yet this type of passage comes with both similarities and distinctness in terms of both Jewish practice and later church practice, showing itself to be a set of transition events. If these disputes are real, then the portrait of the reaction to them is a natural consequence of such challenges, as are the words about opposition to the disciples. In other words, the character of Jesus' ministry as the Synoptics set it out makes cultural sense for the first century, once the reader sees that these disputes are rooted in history. Thus, the controversy accounts are important as historical sources and as the historical base from which to appreciate the confrontation that Jesus' ministry produced within Judaism.

Obviously, there are worldview issues wrapped up in how the miracles associated with some of these disputes are assessed. Yet the historical record, even of Jesus' opponents, shows that they did not doubt his powers, only their source. Thus, these ancient sources, both Christian and non-Christian, do not leave as an explanation the one that skeptical modern readers like to provide: the miracles are key and are manifestly inauthentic, merely reflecting a premodern embrace of the supernatural and the miraculous that history cannot affirm; they are simply a fabrication motivated by enthusiasm to exalt Jesus. My response would be that these ministry miracles, though controversial and significant, are supportive of a more central element in the tradition, namely, these controversies. The controversies and the issues they raised, not the miracles as such, were the bone of contention, because these disputes spotlighted the issue of whose way and authority spoke for the hope of Israel and of God. After all, it was not the miracles of Mark 1–3 that brought controversy, but the claims of forgiveness associated with one particular healing. It is these controversies that demand the careful attention of anyone who seeks to study and understand Jesus' ministry historically. The miracles, though important, only enhance the issues that these disputes reflect. Interestingly, even the Synoptic tradition moves in this direction as Jesus repeatedly is careful to make sure that the miracles do not get too much attention. This is not the early church creating legendary material to exalt Jesus, because the Synoptics' presentation of the miracles often downplays these events and their promotion. The Gospel evidence does not match the alleged crime! Once the miracles are given their proper place in the tradition, then the real issues of Jesus' ministry surface.

Jesus claimed to have authority. The miracles served to underscore that claim. The issue explains why the leadership later will raise the question directly to Jesus, "Where did you get the authority to say and do these things?" Put another way, "Who gave you the right to challenge us?!"

In other words, do God's rule and way come in the faith that Jesus advocated, with its focus in him as the representative of humankind ("Son of Man"), or was the hope rooted in the law and tradition, as the Jewish leadership argued? To gain further insight into this dispute and how the issue of opposition and rejection could be explained as a part of God's plan, the reader's attention must turn to how Jesus explained God's kingdom program. What moved his disciples to confess him as the Christ, the Son of God? That topic is the focus of the next chapter.

SEVEN

From Kingdom Teaching to Confession

How the Disciples Began to Understand Jesus
(Matt. 13:1–16:12; Mark 4:1–8:26; Luke 8:4–9:17)

At the same time, the theme of growing opposition goes hand in hand with the increasingly pressing question of Jesus' role and identity. The issue is raised by the lunatic at the synagogue of Capernaum, by the crowds amazed at his healing and teaching, and by Jesus' various claims to a special kingdom status and authority (forgiveness of sins, lord of the Sabbath, the bridegroom at the feast). Even more acutely, the question was raised by a number of unusual experiences of which apparently only the disciples were aware, like the stilling of the storm (Mark 4.35–41 par.), the feeding of the five thousand (Mark 6.34–44 par.; cf. 8.1–9 par.) and Jesus walking on the water (Mark 6.47–51). Whatever original incidents may underlie these stories, they certainly serve to illustrate the pressing need for an answer to the disciples' terrified question, "Who is this, that even the wind and the sea obey him?" (Mark 4.41 par.).[1]

Although one might ask questions about a detail or two in the above quotation, it does reflect clearly a rising question that the Synoptic narratives are bringing to prominence as Jesus' teaching and action continue to appear side by side.[2] The Gospels focus on how the disciples begin to appreciate who Jesus is and the challenges to faith that Jesus makes as a result. Miracle and kingdom teaching serve to point to a Jesus intimately tied to God's rule and promised hope. It is a Jesus who can be trusted even in the face of imposing opposition.

1. Markus Bockmuehl, *This Jesus: Martyr, Lord, Messiah* (Edinburgh: Clark, 1994), 84.
2. For example, one might question whether the feeding of the five thousand was a private miracle that only the disciples knew to be a miracle.

This chapter covers the movement from kingdom parables up to Peter's confession at Caesarea Philippi (Matt. 13:1–16:12; Mark 4:1–8:26; Luke 8:4–9:17). Matthew and Mark run fairly parallel for the entire sequence. Luke also is similar, lacking only the material found in Mark 6:45–8:26.

Jesus embarks on instruction that is focused on helping especially his disciples gain an appreciation of who he really is. Questions concerning Jesus' identity and activity challenge them to respond to him properly with complete trust. Such challenges dominate the section until Peter's significant confession. The topic of Jesus' authority continues to be prominent. This also explains why Jesus discusses the kingdom of God. His presence represents the arrival of promise as it is expressed in the renewed presence of God's power and authority for his people. The offer is before them to embrace God's way and promise, if they will only grasp it with patience. But Jesus is a realist. Many things stand in the way of the seed taking root and bearing fruit.

109. The Parable of the Sower (Matt. 13:1–9; Mark 4:1–9; Luke 8:4–8) (Aland §122; Orchard §§143–44; Huck-Greeven §103)

This parable begins major discourse sections in Matt. 13 and Mark 4. Matthew contains eight parables, while Mark has five. This is why each notes that Jesus said "many things" in parables (Matt. 13:3; Mark 4:2). Luke has only the parable of the sower in this context, along with one other brief parable that he shares with Mark, the parable of the lamp. He chooses to distribute a few other kingdom parables across his Gospel (Luke 13:18–21). It is likely that this teaching was typical of Jesus' traveling ministry and that Matthew and Mark have presented a sample here. The section is the third of five Matthean discourse units. While Matthew chose to give the summary after a long survey of Jesus' ministry, Mark preferred to present it relatively early on in the ministry. In this regard, Luke's position is like that of Mark.

All the Gospels place the discourse in a Sea of Galilee setting with Jesus out on a boat at the edge of the shore. Luke mentions this kind of setting for the second time (Luke 5:1–3). Jesus loved to use parables and to draw them from everyday life. His use of the agricultural background of Palestine influences many of these parables. These parables have more than one point, although they are not to be allegorized for every detail.[3]

3. See Craig Blomberg, *Interpreting the Parables* (Downers Grove, Ill.: InterVarsity, 1990). He argues rightly that more than one point often is at work. He suggests plausibly that a point per major character is a good approach. There are examples of teaching by parable in Judaism as well; see H. K. McArthur and R. M. Johnston, *They Also Taught in Parables* (Grand Rapids: Zondervan, 1990).

The parable of the sower is the first parable narrated, while its interpretation is saved for later. Its introductory position indicates that it is a basic parable about the kingdom. Many will be exposed to the kingdom and hear about it, but only some will internalize what they have heard and bear fruit for it. The message is especially appropriate in this context because Matthew has discussed opposition and rejection in some detail, while Mark 2:1–3:6 and Luke 5:17–6:11 covered this earlier, in their five controversies. The story itself is fairly common. A farmer is throwing seed by hand into a field that has a path running either through it or along its edge. Matthew speaks of groups of seed, while Mark and Luke speak in the singular, although a differing yield of the good seed in Mark 4:8 shows that a collective reference to a group is intended. Only Mark opens the account with a command to hear, while all the versions end the parable with Jesus' common expression "Let anyone with ears to hear listen."[4]

The three versions are very similar. The seed falls in four areas: on the path, on the rocky ground (rock in Luke), among the thorns, and in the good soil. The first seed was lost to the hungry birds. Luke adds that it was also trodden down. The second seed withered, without fruit. Matthew and Mark give a little more detail about how initially it had quickly sprung up. The seed among the thorns was choked, while the good seed did well. The latter yielded a hundredfold, sixtyfold, and thirtyfold according to Matthew, while Mark has the same variation in reverse order. Luke notes only a hundredfold yield. His version is the most compact of the three. This yield is exceptional, as most crops in Palestine averaged about a tenfold yield.[5] Thus, two elements of the story draw attention: the many obstacles to fruitfulness and the productiveness of the good seed. Jesus waits to explain the account until after the disciples ask him about his teaching in parables (Matthew, Mark) or what this parable meant (Luke).

110. Why Parables? (Matt. 13:10–15; Mark 4:10–12; Luke 8:9–10)
(Aland §123a; Orchard §145; Huck-Greeven §104)

Jesus' use of parables precipitates a question about that approach to teaching. Matthew is most explicit, noting that the question of why Jesus taught

4. The words "to hear" appear in only some manuscripts of Matthew.
5. Philip Barton Payne, "The Authenticity of the Parable of the Sower and Its Interpretation," in *Gospel Perspectives: Studies of History and Tradition in the Four Gospels*, vol. 1, ed. R. T. France and David Wenham (Sheffield: JSOT, 1980), 163–207, esp. 183–84. He also notes, among other things, the debate about whether sowing preceded plowing or vice versa in Palestine. The resolution of this question, which is debated, given the evidence for each, is irrelevant to this parable or its meaning. It is where the seed ends up that is key regardless of how it got there.

this way was raised. Mark and Luke present the query more indirectly. Luke limits the query to this parable, as he has presented only this one parable.

Matthew's reply notes that to the disciples it has been "allowed" or "given" (by God) to know the secrets of the kingdom of heaven, but to them (outsiders) it has not been given. Mark speaks of a unified, singular "secret" of the kingdom of God given to disciples, while "for those outside everything is in parables."

The differences between Matthew and Mark develop distinct points. Mark's reply suggests that outsiders do not "get it," as the following allusion to Isa. 6:9–10 confirms.[6] Jesus explains that this parabolic approach is used so that "they may see but not perceive, may hear but not understand, lest they turn and be forgiven." In compacting the citation (see Matthew's version below), Mark's account is harsher, suggesting a note of divine design. In other words, parables, with their inherent riddle quality, are a form of designed judgment. Mark will express this point again as a principle in 4:25: "To those who have, more will be given; and from those who have not [have not responded to revelation], even what they have will be taken away [they end up with nothing]." Matthew states the point as a matter of direct explanation: "This is why I speak in parables, because seeing they do not see, and hearing they do not hear, nor do they understand." However, the concept expressed in Mark 4:25 appears in Matthew (in expanded form) before this summary as the principle: "To those who have more will be given, and they will have an abundance; but from those who have not, even what they have will be taken away." Then, to emphasize the point and the issue of design as well as responsibility, Matthew cites Isa. 6:9–10, noting that outsiders ("them") fulfill this text. The Matthean citation is even more emphatic: "You will indeed hear, but never understand, and you will indeed see, but never perceive." The citation goes on to explain: "For this people's heart has grown dull, and their ears are heavy of hearing, and their eyes they have closed, lest they should perceive with their eyes, and hear with their ears, and understand with their heart, and turn for me to heal them."[7] Matthew's longer citation adds a note of human responsibility to the response. Their condition has prevented their response. In Matthew, the account explains the rejection just discussed in Matt. 11–12 and that a judgment has ensued.

Luke again is the most compact. He notes that to the disciples are given the secrets (cf. Matthew) of the kingdom of God, but for others they are in parables, "so that seeing they may not see, and hearing they may not understand." Thus, Luke compacts the citation as Mark did and highlights the fact of judg-

6. Mark notes that passage again later in 8:17b–18a.
7. Note the chiasm involving heart, ears, and eyes in the verse, which shows that it is the entire person that has failed to respond.

ment. He saves for later the principle about the one having receiving more (Luke 8:18b), just as Mark did.

The parables then are presented as a two-edged teaching: blessing and explanation for those who know Jesus, but a judgment preventing insight for those on the outside. Their topic is the kingdom, and their character is "mystery," a reference to the Jewish idea of *raz,* an idea introduced in Dan. 2:18 and even connected to kingdom in 2:44–45. It is a teaching that is a secret and requires revelation to be understood (Dan. 4:9). Thus, Jesus' parables treat the now-revealed elements about the nature of the direction of the kingdom. The focus of the mystery is on its divinely directed growth culminating in blessing and judgment.

111. The Blessing of Seeing These Things (Matt. 13:16–17;
Luke 10:23–24, in a later context) (Aland §123b; Orchard §146; Huck-Greeven §105)

Lest one read the mention of mystery as something entirely new and previously unknown, Jesus has this additional note in Matthew, one that Jesus makes in a distinct context later in Luke's Gospel (see Luke 10:23–24). The remark is a beatitude that declares blessing for those who do see and hear what the disciples are experiencing. He notes that they are honored to see and hear what the prophets and the righteous longed to see and hear. Thus, the kingdom realities offered to them are what the prophets and the righteous of the past had looked and hoped for. This note shows that what Jesus preaches, even though it gives new insight into the kingdom program, is part of what the saints of old had longed to experience. Thus, the parables reveal a note of continuity with the promises of old. The Lukan form of this affirmation comes when the larger mission to preach the kingdom reports its results. Luke makes the same point about continuity there.

112. Interpretation of the Parable of the Sower
(Matt. 13:18–23; Mark 4:13–20; Luke 8:11–15) (Aland §124; Orchard §147; Huck-Greeven §106)

All three Synoptics treat the interpretation of the parable of the sower next. Matthew turns to the interpretation by calling on the disciples to hear the parable. Here the exhortation to hear is a call to understand its meaning. In Mark, the interpretation comes with a rebuke, expressed as a rhetorical question, that a failure to understand this parable will make all the parables unintelligible. Luke simply launches into the interpretation.

The unit is rendered with some variation as each evangelist brings out the parable's force. Matthew describes the seed on the path as involving the person who hears the word of the kingdom but does not understand it. The evil one comes and snatches away what was sown in the heart. Mark speaks of Satan coming immediately after people hear and taking away the word that was sown in them. Luke names the devil and notes that his goal is to prevent belief and salvation. In Matthew, the "evil one" is seen to take advantage of a failure to understand, while Mark ("Satan") and Luke ("the devil") also stress the diabolical culprit, but with different names.

Matthew describes the rocky soil as hearing the word and receiving it with joy but having no root. Endurance remains for a while, but when trial and persecution come, the person falls away. Mark is like Matthew except that he adds that the trial and persecution are "on account of the word." It is the controversy surrounding the kingdom that is the subject. Luke speaks of people "believing for a while." Jesus is noting that some gather around him for a time. But superficial faith is not faith. It ends up not believing. The Old Testament shared such warnings about turning away (Jer. 3:13–14; Hos. 7:10–16; Amos 4:4–5:2). The disciples need to understand how diverse the responses will be, as well as the obstacles that prevent fruitfulness.

Next is what is sown among thorns. This one hears the word, but worldly cares and attachment to riches choke the word. Here there is no fruit. Mark adds that the desire for other things also distracts and chokes. Luke lays the blame on the cares, riches, and pleasures of life. He notes that this fruit does not mature. Riches are a theme that Luke's portrait of Jesus will dwell on (Luke 6:24; 12:16–21; 14:12; 16:1–13, 19–31; 18:23, 25; 19:1–10; 21:1).

Each of these three soils fails to bear fruit. None of them accomplishes what a farmer tries to do by sowing seed. Two of the soils initially engage the word, but Jesus does not intend any assurance by that imagery. Nor does the difference in the failures of the second and third seeds make any real difference in the long run, because neither seed produces fruit. The result is tragic in all three cases. Seed was sown, but fruit did not emerge. The way to fruitfulness is strewn with obstacles for the heart.

The good soil is different. This one, Matthew says, not only hears the word but also understands it. This seed bears fruit, but in different measures, depending on the response. Matthew's rendering had more than one seed falling into each type of soil, so that yields of one hundred, sixty, and thirty emerge. Mark speaks of the one who accepts the word and bears fruit, thirty-, sixty-, and a hundredfold. Mark, although he spoke of seed in the singular, treated the sowing as a class, and here he switches to the plural. Luke is the most descriptive. These hear the word and hold fast to it with an "honest" and "good" heart. The high priest Onias was described this way by Jews (2 Macc. 15:12). So the expression of having an honest and good heart speaks to their spiritual integrity. Luke uses two Greek synonyms for "good" here to highlight this quality within the person. The recipient also has patience, since fruit comes slowly over time. Luke does not speak of differing yields, focusing instead on the steadfastness that produces fruit. The interpretation shows that Jesus is not psychologizing about a single moment of the spiritual life here but is considering the life of response as a whole. Only with the passing of time does trial come. In the parable, only over time does a person get drawn away to pursue riches. Only as time moves on does fruit grow. Thus, kingdom preaching goes into the world and meets with varied responses. Getting to fruitfulness takes tenacity in embracing the word and patience in cultivating it. The other results fall tragically short.

113. Revelation as Light to Be Heeded (Mark 4:21–25; Luke 8:16–18)[8] (Aland §125; Orchard §104; Huck-Greeven §107)

Matthew moves on to treat another parable (the wheat and the darnel), but Mark and Luke note what the teaching about the kingdom and the word represents. Mark does this in two short parables, the lamp and the measure, while Luke has only the first. The word about the kingdom is like light. Light is not lit to be hidden under a bushel basket (Mark), vessel (Luke), or bed (both). In Mark, the point is stated as a question that expects a negative answer: "Is a lamp brought in to be put under a bushel basket, or under a bed?" Light is for use on a stand. Mark states this as a question that expects a positive answer: "Is it not to be put on a stand?" In the ancient world, the light for a stand was an oil-burning lamp. Luke adds the purpose of the lamp. Light is for those who enter to be able to see by the light. The assumption is that without it, one is left in the dark. Not only does light enable one to see, but also it exposes. It prevents things from being hidden; it brings secrets to light. Light brings accountability.

So Mark urges that anyone with ears to hear should listen. In other words, pay attention, because the standard used will be the standard applied. The parable of the measure shows how God reacts toward one's response to the word. The measure one gives to hearing will be the measure one receives. So measure in such a way as to receive the word. To give by receiving the word means that one will get even more. The one who has gets more, but the one who lacks response will lose even what he or she has. In other words, the latter person ends up with nothing. In context, the image is an exhortation to appreciate the word and be responsive. To lack a response is to have nothing, and the same is true of being fruitless. It means that there has been no true response.

8. Matthew uses some parallel imagery that is conceptually similar to parts of this unit in 5:15; 10:26; 7:2; 13:12, but none of these is a true parallel to this unit.

Luke is more compact but makes the same point. One should pay attention to the word of the kingdom and "grab hold" of it to fruitfulness. The one who has gets more, but from the one who has not, even what he or she thinks to be in possession of is taken away. Again, the result is that the one with nothing in terms of response also ends up with nothing.

So the parables do not merely describe; they urge their listeners by their character as revealing, exposing light to be sensitive to the guidance that this teaching provides. The wise listener, Jesus says, will pay attention. There are benefits to being responsive.

114. The Parable of the Seed Growing Secretly
(Mark 4:26–29) (Aland §126; Orchard §105; Huck-Greeven §108)

Mark's fourth parable explains how mysteriously spiritual seed produces fruit in the kingdom. It is like the way a crop springs up over time from the earth for a farmer who simply waits for it to come to harvest. The sower in this parable is anyone who shares the word, because he is unaware of exactly how things work. The stress is on the gradual progression of the growth as the harvest comes forth in steps (blade, ear, full grain). No mention is made of a farmer's labor; the seed just grows over time. Its growth is mysterious, taking place "on its own," as the Greek (αὐτομάτη) emphatically indicates. The harvest in this context is not the eschatological judgment, as it often is, but simply seed reaching its goal of bearing fruit. God is powerfully and mysteriously at work in the preached word of the kingdom.

115. The Parable of the Wheat and the Darnel
(Matt. 13:24–30) (Aland §127; Orchard §148; Huck-Greeven §109)

The second Matthean parable surfaces yet another mystery: the mixed character of things in the kingdom until the harvest comes at judgment. The mixture does not occur because of the work of the sower but because of the behind-the-scenes work of the "enemy," the devil. Thus, the seed sown to bear wheat coexists with other seed sown by another. No effort is made to sift it now, since that would be risky for the wheat.

This parable receives specific interpretation later in vv. 36–43. Nevertheless, it is evident already that the scope of the kingdom covers the world as a whole, because the judgment to come is comprehensive in magnitude. Thus, evil and good are allowed to coexist within the kingdom until God judges the whole of it. The imagery apparently refers not to weeds as we know them, because those are easily distinguished from grain, but to darnel, which is so much like wheat that it is hard to tell the difference for much of the growth cycle. Sometimes, a farmer feuding with a neighbor would spoil a crop this way. Thus, the conflict adds a tone of animosity to the imagery. The enemy seeks to corrupt the presence of the good seed that has taken hold. Those who bear fruit in the kingdom must live intertwined with the seed sown by the enemy until the judgment comes.

116. The Parable of the Mustard Seed (Matt. 13:31–32; Mark 4:30–32; Luke 13:18–19, in a later context) (Aland §128; Orchard §149; Huck-Greeven §110)

The next two parables share one feature. They describe something very small that eventually becomes something very large. The mustard seed, which is compared to the kingdom, takes root and ends up being a conspicuously large shrub. Matthew and Mark are in the same context, while Luke notes these two images in a pair of kingdom parables after the Sabbath healing of a woman. In that locale, they illustrate how the rule of God is breaking in on the world and overcoming Satan, so that each person should repent (Luke 13:1–21). Mark has only the first of the pair, perhaps seeing them as redundant.

A mustard seed was proverbial in Judaism for something very small. In *m. Niddah* 5.2 and *m. Ṭoharot* 8.8, it is the basis for a measure of how tiny a discharge may be to count for establishing uncleanness. According to *m. Kil'ayim* 2.9 and 3.2, it was not to be sown in a garden but was permitted for the field. The concern apparently was for the size of what the mustard seed would grow to become. In Matthew, the seed is sown in the field; in Mark, it is simply the ground; in Luke, it is a garden. However, the image is important not because of where the seed is sown, but because of what happens to it. Matthew and Mark make a point of the seed being "the smallest of all seeds."

In Mark, what the seed becomes is the "greatest of all shrubs." Such plants could grow to ten feet or so. The contrast with the initial seed is explicit. Matthew mentions it becoming the greatest of shrubs and a tree. Luke has just the image of a tree. The point is that it has branches in which birds can dwell. This is an image of protection and peace (Ezek. 17:23; Dan. 4:12, 21). The Ezekiel context is important because there the prophet refers to the "sprig" of the rebuilt Davidic house that becomes like a cedar of Lebanon in which the birds can dwell. That Ezekiel image anticipates a day when even the nations will be present, so the allusion may well anticipate Gentile presence. Thus, the kingdom starts out looking insignificant, but it will become a safe dwelling place.

It is sometimes discussed whether the image here is negative or positive, but in the kingdom parable context, the kingdom itself, when it refers to God's rule, is seen in a positive light. The Ezekiel background also suggests a positive image.

117. The Parable of the Leaven (Matt. 13:33; Luke 13:20–21, in a later context) (Aland §129; Orchard §150; Huck-Greeven §111)

This image makes a point similar to the previous one. Here a woman places leaven in three measures of flour, about fifty pounds' worth, enough to feed over one hundred people.[9] The amount of leaven required is so small that when placed in the flour, it can be described as being hidden. However, it leavens the entire loaf. Jesus' point here also contrasts the insignificant start with the significant finish. The kingdom, so seemingly insignificant at the start, one day will completely permeate the world into which it has entered.

Again, the positive or negative nature of the image is debated. However, the image appears to be positive, as leaven can bear this force (Lev. 7:13–14; 23:17), and the image is paired with the previous parable. Another key point is that the kingdom is present, starting with Jesus' seemingly insignificant ministry. In fact, the imagery is surprising in possessing this starting point because normally the kingdom was anticipated to arrive as large and dominating from the start. This "small to large" dimension is what makes the teaching a mystery, because it is different from what many in Judaism had anticipated about the kingdom.

118. Summary on Parabolic Teaching (Matt. 13:34–35; Mark 4:33–34) (Aland §130; Orchard §151; Huck-Greeven §112)

At this point, Mark completes his parabolic discourse with a summary. Matthew also has a summary here but continues on to narrate one interpretation and three more parables. Mark notes that Jesus taught many such parables, indicating that he has not shared all that Jesus taught in this manner. Jesus gave out the word "as they were able to hear it." One of two senses could fit here. He could be speaking of the ability of some in the crowd to pick up on what has been said. If this is the sense, then the earlier introduction seeing the parables exclusively as judgment for outsiders is softened (Mark 4:10–12). Those who think that this is too harsh a contrast see the verses only as a remark that Jesus taught them as long as they would listen. This second sense seems a little vacuous in force. These may not be the only two options. Mark may simply be saying that Jesus spoke parables and left them on their own to understand, in contrast to the access that insiders receive. Mark's point is that Jesus often addressed them in these parables even though these parables were hard to comprehend. Outsiders were left to fend for themselves completely, while the disciples had the benefit of private explanation.

9. The pairing of the parables is balanced. The seed would involve a man's labor, while the flour involves work that a woman would do.

Matthew's summary lacks the difficult "as they were able to hear it" phrase. He notes that Jesus addressed the crowd in parables and "said nothing without a parable." He then cites the fulfillment of Ps. 78:2, a verse that introduces the psalm as a disclosure of what had been hidden through parables. Jesus' teaching is like that in approach. This psalm of Asaph recalls God's mighty deeds but does so by highlighting a pattern of divine deliverance: the people's unfaithfulness met with God's continued mercy. Jesus' teaching takes on the same character. But one other feature of the parable may have made the citation appropriate. The psalm ends by affirming the establishment of the tribe of Judah and of David as the shepherd who guides his sheep with an upright heart and skillful hand. Here is where hope and victory lie.

119. Interpretation of the Parable of the Wheat and the Darnel (Matt. 13:36–43) (Aland §131; Orchard §152; Huck-Greeven §113)

Matthew now interprets the parable of the wheat and the darnel. This is a private explanation to the disciples in the house. The sower, Jesus notes, is the Son of Man, a reference to himself. Jesus is the planter of the kingdom's word. With him it has come in announcement. The field is the world. This is significant because Jesus' claim is that the kingdom is intended to have the world as its realm. The authority that Jesus has as Son of Man, as eschatological judge, extends over all humanity, whether they recognize it or not. In the world, where he is making this claim, emerge good and bad seed, children of the kingdom and children of the evil one, mixed together. The enemy sowing the evil seed is the devil. The harvest at the end is the close of the age, when judgment will be rendered. Angels will serve as reapers, making them the servants who want to know if they should pull up the darnel now. The angels are seen as God's servants and those who observe his plan working itself out. At the close of the age, the darnel is gathered and burned. The angels will gather together the evil ones and all causes of sin and cast them into the furnace, where there will be much intense suffering, which Jesus alludes to as weeping and gnashing of teeth. Even the children of the evil one are accountable to God and his Son of Man. Jesus' ministry and the kingdom he preached are ultimately about the authority he wields. In contrast, the righteous will remain, shining like the sun, an image of glorification.[10] They will reside in a kingdom purged of evil and sin. The kingdom, despite its current mix, will end up glorious one day. Jesus concludes

10. The imagery of seed in the end at a harvest and of shining have precedent in Judaism (Isa. 54:11–12; Wis. 3:7–8 [righteous souls like shining lights and sparks in the midst of stubble]; 4 Ezra [= 2 Esdras] 7:97 [righteous shining incorruptible]; 2 Baruch 70.2).

the explanation with his call to hear. The parables are ultimately a declaration of the anticipated victory of the kingdom, which will explain why it is so precious and worth any price.

120. The Parables of the Hidden Treasure and of the Pearl
(Matt. 13:44–46) (Aland §132; Orchard §§153–54; Huck-Greeven §114)

These two short parables make the same point in slightly different ways. They argue that the kingdom is so valuable that it is worth selling everything one owns to be sure of having it. Whether it is a treasure that a worker in a field stumbles upon and discovers or a visible, valuable pearl that a merchant works to buy, every effort is made to obtain the precious item. The one who stumbles on the treasure plans for its recovery by burying it before buying the field. In Judaism, the purchase of a field brought the buyer everything that was contained within it except that which could be removed as support property, such as a watchman's hut (*m. Baba Batra* 4.8–9). Jesus' story about the pearl belongs to background that had pearls worth, in terms of modern currency, tens of millions of dollars.[11] Simply put, Jesus says that entering the kingdom is worth giving up everything.

121. The Parable of the Net (Matt. 13:47–50) (Aland §133; Orchard §155; Huck-Greeven §115)

Jesus returns to the theme of the parable of the wheat and the darnel, but here he concentrates on the judgment at the end. He compares it to fishing and the sorting that follows the catch. In the Sea of Galilee, there were a couple dozen types of fish, but only some of them were good for eating. So after the catch, which hauls in every "race" of fish, the fishermen had to sort out the good from the useless fish. Jesus says that the kingdom is like the net that makes a mixed catch. Note again how the kingdom involves the whole world. It will consist of every race. Good fish are kept and placed into vessels, while the bad are thrown away. At the close of the age, angels will do the same, separating the evil from the righteous. Jesus stresses the fate of the judged, who are tossed into the furnace of fire, where people will weep and gnash their teeth (see 13:42). In other words, one should not fail to embrace the kingdom, because the cost of missing it is too high. In this way, this parable is a contrast to the previous one. The kingdom is worth everything, and no one can afford to miss it.

11. Craig Keener, *Matthew*, IVPNTCS 1 (Downers Grove, Ill.: InterVarsity, 1997), 246.

122. Kingdom Scribes and Treasures Old and New
(Matt. 13:51–52) (Aland 134; Orchard §156; Huck-Greeven §116)

Jesus concludes his kingdom parable discourse with a question and one final image. He asks the disciples if they have understood all that he said to them. They reply that they do. Subsequent events will show that no matter how much they do understand, they still have much more to learn. What they should see is that the kingdom begins to form with Jesus' sowing of the word, but that opposition will exist in its midst, just as there will be varied reactions to the message. Nevertheless, it still is the most precious thing, worthy of any price.

Jesus compares his disciples to scribes. Just as scribes were taught the law and traditions, so he has taught them with the "mysteries." These mysteries contain God's way and wisdom. What the law is to the scribes, the kingdom is for them, and they are learning about it. A look at the kingdom compares it to valuable treasure. Within it are old and new things. Jesus is claiming that his teaching is built on what God had already revealed to the nation, but the kingdom also contains new, complementary teaching. Some of what they see they could have anticipated. On other matters Jesus must instruct them. The association of the kingdom with a scribe who is trained to instruct suggests that these disciples will be teaching others these things. In one sense, the Gospels themselves are a product of this saying.

123. Jesus' True Kindred (Luke 8:19–21; Matt. 12:46–50, in an earlier
context; Mark 3:31–35, in an earlier context [see unit 108 above]) (Aland §135; Orchard §108; Huck-Greeven §117)

When Luke finishes his rendering of the parable of the sower and the image of Jesus' teaching as light, he tells of Jesus' family's attempt to see Jesus. This event appeared in Matthew and Mark just before the parable discourse. The account is more concise in Luke. Jesus is simply told that his mother and brothers are outside, wishing to see him. Jesus replies with the remark that his mother and brothers are those who hear the word and do it.

Luke's placement makes some key points. Luke's unique placement of this exchange lacks any hint of Jesus' family's concern over his teaching. It also means that Jesus is showing how his own commitment to God's leading means that a new wave of relationships is being formed that has priority over normal familial ties. Highest of all is an allegiance to God's will. That means that those who hear and do the word—here closely tied to responding to the kingdom message—are his family. The remark concludes a discourse section in Luke before he turns to a series of miracles. It also functions as an exhortation in the narrative flow: Do not think in the old ways about family. The word that Jesus teaches shines as light; respond to it by hearing and doing. Then you are a part of the family that God is building.

124. The Stilling of the Storm (Mark 4:35–41; Luke 8:22–25; Matt. 8:23–27, in an earlier context [see unit 77 above]) (Aland §136; Orchard §112; Huck-Greeven §118)

This event was treated for its details above. Here we note the contextual placement in Mark and Luke. The most prominent feature is that this miracle begins a sequence of four consecutive miracles, one of which is a paired set of miracles. The progression also is significant. It starts with nature, moves to an exorcism, then to disease, and finally to death. Thus, the threats in creation to humankind are treated in consecutive order, moving from outward to inward with respect to the spatial imagery involved. The account also is timed to correspond in Mark to the day of the parable teaching, thus placing word and deed side by side again. Luke only notes that it happened "one day." As in Matthew, the passages in Mark and Luke close with the fundamental christological question "Who is this, that even wind and water obey him?" No ordinary human is present.

125. The Gerasene Demoniac (Mark 5:1–20; Luke 8:26–39; Matt. 8:28–34, in an earlier context [see unit 78 above]) (Aland §137; Orchard §113; Huck-Greeven §119)

This is the second miracle in the Mark-Luke sequence. Its details were treated above. However, it is the only time in Luke that Jesus is explicitly in Gentile territory. This version, unlike Matthew, closes with the exchange between the recovered man and Jesus. Mark has Jesus order the man to tell the people at home what the Lord had done for him rather than follow him. He tells those in the Decapolis what Jesus had done. Luke has the command be that the man should go and tell what God has done. However, the man tells them what Jesus has done. One cannot explain God's work without mentioning Jesus.

126. Jairus's Daughter and the Woman with the Hemorrhage (Mark 5:21–43; Luke 8:40–56; Matt. 9:18–26, in an earlier context [see unit 82 above]) (Aland §138; Orchard §117; Huck-Greeven §120)

This event completes the four-miracle cycle in Mark and Luke. The details of this event were covered above. Mark reconnects for a while with Matthew after this event discussing the rejection at Nazareth (of the units between 127 and 141, only two do not match between Matthew and Mark). Thus, for Mark, these miracles, as impressive as they are, do not impress the crowds enough to lead to response. God's power is being ignored. Luke already has treated that event earlier, so he moves on to a treatment of the initial mission of the Twelve. For him, this sequence of events is part of what impressed the disciples and helped them to appreciate who Jesus was.

127. Jesus Is Rejected at Nazareth (Matt. 13:53–58; Mark 6:1–6a; Luke 4:16–30, in an earlier context [see unit 25 above]) (Aland §139; Orchard §157; Huck-Greeven §121)

The rejection at Nazareth is narrated concisely in both Matthew and Mark without any detail of what Jesus taught, unlike Luke's earlier, more detailed version. Matthew notes that the rejection took place after the parable discourse and after a return home that led Jesus into the synagogue. Mark uniquely notes that the disciples are with him and that the teaching takes place on the Sabbath. The crowd is amazed. They acknowledge two things: his wisdom (what Mark calls "all this") and his mighty works. But the one obstacle to responding is his ordinary pedigree. Mark notes, via the crowd's rhetorical question, that Mary is his mother; James, Joses, Judas, and Simon are his brothers; and he has sisters besides. They also inquire rhetorically whether he is a carpenter or not. The question is stated in Greek in a way that expects a positive reply. The implication is clear. How in the world can Jesus be anyone significant in God's work? So "they took offense at him."

Matthew is similar. Is this not the carpenter's son? This form of the question in Greek expects a positive reply. It brings in the relationship to Joseph more directly than Mark. The same relatives are noted. Matthew then adds the question "Where, then, did this man get all this?" The narrative comment that "they took offense at him" matches Mark. Their intimate knowledge of Jesus' ordinary past was too great to overcome.

Both accounts close with Jesus' retort that a prophet is without honor only in his own country and house, with Mark adding a reference to his kin, an allusion back to Mark 3:20–21, 31–35. Matthew then explains that Jesus did not do many mighty works there because of their unbelief. Mark states it more emphatically: he did no mighty work there except to lay hands on a few sick people. He also marveled at their unbelief. In the flow of Mark, this is in light of the comprehensive display of the four miracles just noted. The marvel is that they accept that mighty works are being done but cannot accept the claims that Jesus makes. For Mark, this illustrates the hardness of unbelief.

128. The Commissioning of the Twelve (Mark 6:6b–13;
Luke 9:1–6; Matt. 9:35; 10:1, 7–11, 14, in an earlier context [see units 85–86 above]) (Aland §142; Orchard §§121, 122, 124; Huck-Greeven §122)

Mark and Luke note the sending out of the Twelve before examining the report to Herod that led to speculation that John the Baptist had risen or that Jesus was some other prophet. The mission had increased the attention concerning Jesus. The instructions are similar to those noted in Matt. 10. In Mark, Jesus is teaching from village to village and begins to send out the Twelve in pairs. He extends his authority by giving these commissioned agents authority over unclean spirits. They are to take nothing with them as provision. Only a staff and sandals are mentioned as included.[12] When they enter a village, they are to stay in one house, but if they are rejected they are to shake the dust from their feet. This symbolic act indicates a separation from those who have rejected them and from the judgment they have made. It stands as testimony that the villagers have rejected the way of God. Mark says that the disciples' message was a call to repent. The imagery is like that of John the Baptist (Mark 1:4) and Jesus (Mark 1:15). With the preached word came the acts of compassion and power as they cast out demons and anointed the sick with oil while they healed.

Luke does not note the going out in pairs, but he does point to the authority they received over demons and disease. They were to preach the kingdom and to heal. In v. 6, Luke calls this same activity preaching the gospel and healing everywhere. So Luke links kingdom and gospel in this passage in a way that the other Gospels do not. Luke also mentions traveling light and staying at one house unless they are rejected, in which case they are to shake the dust from their feet. This mission is not to linger but to move quickly from one locale to another. Like Jesus in his own ministry, they preach and heal. The preached word is accompanied by authenticating acts of compassion.

129. Opinions about Jesus (Matt. 14:1–2; Mark 6:14–16; Luke 9:7–9)
(Aland §143; Orchard §158; Huck-Greeven §123)

The opinions circulating about Jesus reach Herod. In Matthew, the ruler seemingly has a sense of guilt as he hears the reports about Jesus' powerful

---

12. This verse is difficult, given the remark in Matt. 10:10 that they are not to take a staff or sandals. It may be that the difference has to do with an extra set of these supplies. The point, regardless, is that they should travel as light as possible. On this, see Darrell L. Bock, *Luke 1:1–9:50,* BECNT 3A (Grand Rapids: Baker, 1994), 815–16.

work. The same term for "miracles" is here as in Matt. 13:54, 58 (δυνάμεις). Attempting to account for Jesus' power, Herod concludes that Jesus is John the Baptist risen. Two things are interesting to note. First, what is meant here is that Jesus possesses a spirit like John or that John has passed on his authority (cf. 1 Kings 17:21–22; 2 Kings 4:34–36; Josephus, *War* 1.30.7 §§598–600 [on the "ghosts" of Alexander and Aristobulus]). The recognition of the linkage is an important point. Second, the reemergence has come in an intensified form, because John himself did not perform works of power. In effect, what Herod had sought to remove had now returned with even greater authority. The attempt to stop God's plan by execution had only intensified its presence, again perhaps revealing a sense of guilt. This may also foreshadow the effect of Jesus' removal, a new community that spreads over the world.

Mark's remarks are similar, except that he notes other options. Alongside the claim that the power of Jesus was from a risen John the Baptist, was the suggestion that it was Elijah or one of the prophets of old. Mark notes Herod's conclusion that it was John the Baptist risen, whom Herod had beheaded.

Luke describes Herod as being perplexed by the three alternatives that Mark also mentioned. In Luke, Herod does not resolve the question. The ruler simply notes that he beheaded John, but asks, "Who is this about whom I hear such things?" The text also notes that the ruler longs to see Jesus, something that will happen in Luke 23. The Lukan account highlights the deliberation about who Jesus is, a theme that has been at work since the stilling of the storm in Luke 8:22. The resolution comes in Luke 9:20 and Peter's confession.

130. The Death of John the Baptist (Matt. 14:3–12; Mark 6:17–29; conceptual: Luke 3:19–20) (Aland §144; Orchard §159; Huck-Greeven §124)

Both Matthew and Mark recount the death of the Baptist after Herod's concern about Jesus being John raised. In both accounts the details look back into earlier events and explain why Herod might feel guilty about what he had done to John. Luke had noted the arrest of John earlier but never gives the details of John's demise.

Both accounts tell us that the complaints of John about Herod's marriage to Herodias caused the arrest, as Luke 3:19 also noted. Herodias had divorced Antipas's half brother to marry Herod, an act that violated Lev. 18:16 and 20:21 on incest. John complained that it was not lawful for Herod to have his brother's wife. Josephus narrates the death of John the Baptist in the midst of a political explanation about John's death but treats it in a section in which Antipas is in conflict with Aretas, the Nabatean king whose daughter had been Herod's first wife (*Ant.* 18.5.1–3 §§109–125).[13] It seems likely that this conflict and Josephus's placement show that private as well as public issues motivated the death.

Mark has more nuance and detail than Matthew does. While Matthew's portrayal is decidedly negative, Mark notes the inner struggle of Antipas. Although Herodias held a grudge against John, Antipas feared him and regarded him as a righteous and holy man. Matthew attributes Herod's fear to the people's regard of John as a prophet. Mark alone cites the details of the fateful occasion: a banquet held for Herod's courtiers, officers, and the leading men of Galilee. Both, however, note that it was Herod's birthday celebration. When Herodias's daughter, probably Salome, dances at the party, Herod honors her with an oath that she may have whatever she wishes, Mark alone supplying the detail that Herod offered up to half his kingdom.[14] At her mother's prompting, she asks for John's head. Herod chose to save face, although he could have opted out, given the nature of the request (*m. Nedarim* 3.1; 9.4). Succumbing to the pressure, he executes John. Antipas, as Rome's political representative in the region, could execute John. In all likelihood, this event took place at the fortress of Machaerus. Only Matthew notes that John's disciples went and told Jesus what had taken place. Both evangelists note that John was given a decent burial by his followers.

131. The Return of the Apostles (Mark 6:30–31; Luke 9:10a)
(Aland §145; Orchard §160; Huck-Greeven §125a)

Mark notes the return of the Twelve in the midst of this disturbing review about what had happened earlier to John. Thus, Mark juxtaposes notes of John's rejection and Jesus' ministry. Jesus has them withdraw from the crowds, because they "had no leisure even to eat."

Luke simply reports that the disciples returned and told Jesus what they had done. Because Luke will give a fuller account of the larger mission in Luke 10 and its many successes, he only summarizes here.

13. This text was treated in chapter 3, unit 20 above. For the moral and political dimensions of John's death, see Harold Hoehner, *Herod Antipas,* SNTSMS 17 (Cambridge: Cambridge University Press, 1972), 147–71; Robert Webb, *John the Baptizer and Prophet: A Socio-Historical Study,* JSNTSup 62 (Sheffield: Sheffield Academic, 1991), 373–76; S. Sollertinsky, "The Death of John the Baptist," *Journal of Theological Studies* 1 (1900): 507–28.

14. For the debate over the identity of Herodias's daughter, see Hoehner, *Herod Antipas,* esp. 151–54, where Hoehner opts for and defends the view that Salome is the dancer.

132. The Five Thousand Are Fed (Matt. 14:13–21; Mark 6:32–44; Luke 9:10b–17; John 6:1–15) (Aland §146; Orchard §161; Huck-Greeven §125b)

It has been some time since Matthew has noted a specific miracle (12:22). Here Jesus shows his disciples what they will be capable of through him. Although it has not been as long between miracles for Mark and Luke, they also place this event very close to the mission of the Twelve (Mark 6:6b–13; Luke 9:1–6). So this miracle is not only an example of Jesus' compassion but also of how the disciples will be the ones through whom Jesus will work. The Synoptics do not date the event, but John 6:4 says that it happened near Passover.

In Matthew, despite Jesus' attempts to withdraw, the crowd presses around him. The scene leads Jesus to have compassion for the crowds, so he cures the sick. At the end of the day the disciples ask Jesus to dismiss the crowd so they can find something to eat, but he refuses, telling the disciples to feed them. A check of inventory shows that only five loaves and two fish are present, so the disciples express some doubt over the request, but less emphatically than in the Lukan and Johannine parallels. Nonetheless, Jesus persists and orders the crowd to sit in the grass. Giving thanks for the provision, Jesus gives the food to the disciples, who distribute it to the crowd. There was more than enough for five thousand men, excluding women and children, as twelve baskets of leftover food remained. The entire scene shows Jesus providing food for the crowd through his disciples. Jesus can supply the basic needs of the people; the disciples are the agents of that distribution. The whole miracle is a metaphor for how Jesus will work. One final point is the juxtaposition of two banquets in Matt. 14: Herod's, which ends in a death, and Jesus', which ends in provision. For Matthew, the contrast between life in the world and life in connection to Jesus is significant. The disciples will be the bearers of God's provision through Jesus.

The Markan account is like Matthew's except that it has more detail. He adds a note about Jesus' compassion in v. 34. The people were like sheep without a shepherd (cf. Ezek. 34:1–10; Matt. 9:36). He also notes that Jesus taught on this occasion and does not mention healing at all. Mark also details the disciples' pause at being told to provide something for the crowd; they inquire whether they should spend two hundred denarii (two hundred days' wages!) to feed them (so also John 6:7). Mark also describes the crowd as being grouped into units of fifty and one hundred.

Luke says that the apostles had withdrawn to Bethsaida. When the crowd gathered, Jesus taught about the kingdom of God and healed them. Like Mark, Luke notes that the disciples protested Jesus' desire to feed the people in remarks about needing to buy provisions, though with less detail than Mark. At this point, Luke notes that five thousand men are present. Seated in groups of fifty, they are fed and filled. All the accounts note how Jesus "blessed and broke" the bread, giving a sacred feel to this unusual event, as well as a typical Jewish feel, because the blessing was a typical part of any meal. Luke alone makes it clear that only the Twelve among the disciples participated as the intermediaries. The twelve baskets left over would be one for each.

The miracle itself recalls the provision Jesus had made when he called the disciples in Luke 5:1–11, not to mention what Elijah had done in 2 Kings 4:42–44. The imagery of being fed in the desert also recalls the manna imagery of Exod. 16 and Num. 11. Thus, the event evokes images of the beginning of the nation, the restoration of the nation, and the initial call of Jesus' group.[15] There is one difference: the provision of manna never had leftovers to be collected as this feeding does.

John 6:14 indicates that the people, seeing this sign, concluded that Jesus was the prophet to come, evoking a messianic hope, as John 6:15 shows. Mark explicitly presents the miracle as an answer to the shepherdlessness of the people. In all its versions, the miracle highlights how it reawakens hope by its connection to great acts of the past, with Luke making the tie most explicit by linking the event to teaching about the kingdom. This is the only miracle of Jesus' ministry present in all four Gospels. It is hard to know why. One plausible suggestion is that the picture of Jesus as a mediating provider of sustenance was a poignant picture.

133. Walking on the Water (Matt. 14:22–33; Mark 6:45–52; John 6:16–21) (Aland §147; Orchard §162; Huck-Greeven §126)

With this account comes a sequence of events in which Luke does not provide any parallels. This omission runs from Mark 6:45–8:26 and has been called Luke's "great omission." There is no entirely satisfactory explanation for it if Luke knew Mark, although many note that most of the section repeats miracles similar to material elsewhere in Mark.[16]

The walking on the water is used in diverse ways by Matthew and Mark. It is similar to the stilling of the storm (Matt. 8:23–27 and parallels). For Matthew, it leads to a deepened understanding; for Mark, it is an account that exposed the ignorance of the disciples and their need to understand what had been happening.

In Matthew, Jesus dismisses the crowd, sends the disciples on to the other side, and withdraws to pray. The disciples had been unable to cross the sea be-

---

15. Joel Green, *The Gospel of Luke*, NICNT (Grand Rapids: Eerdmans, 1997), 363–66. Green observes how the meal is distributed without any note of care to observe various practices of cleanliness, indicating the openness of the bestowal to all.

16. Bock, *Luke 1:1–9:50*, 950–51.

cause the wind and current had been against them. Alone, they had had a hard night. When Jesus came to them on the water, they were terrified and cried out in fear that they were seeing a "ghost." Jesus calmed them by announcing that it was he. In a detail unique to Matthew, Peter asks permission to walk to Jesus. He seems to have learned from the feeding of the five thousand that he can do unusual things in light of Jesus' presence. So Peter starts to come to Jesus, only to be frightened by the wind and begin to sink. When he cries out, Jesus reaches out and rescues him. Jesus challenges Peter, noting his lack of faith and asking why he had doubted. The distraction of the wind became greater than his focus on Jesus. When they return to the boat, the wind ceases. The event led to worship of Jesus and a confession that truly he is the Son of God. Thus, the event ends on a triumphant note while at the same time urging reflection on why Peter had needed a rescue.

In Mark, Jesus sends the disciples to Bethsaida and withdraws to pray. In what appears to have been a test of their faith and growth, Jesus comes toward them on the sea but appears to intend to pass them. How well will they do when left to trust in his care of them in the midst of his seeming absence? Upon seeing him, they cry out in fear, thinking that a ghost is threatening them. Jesus calms them with the announcement that it is he. The wind ceases as he enters the boat, astounding them. Here is where Mark differs from Matthew, because he highlights their lack of understanding of what had taken place. He notes that they had not understood the provision and care evidenced in the provision of the loaves, and their hearts were hardened. The seeming contrast between the two accounts appears harsh, but it may be that Mark is looking back at what they had failed to learn about what Jesus' presence meant for them from the immediately previous event. Thus, Mark connects the account to previous events, looking back in perspective. On the other hand, Matthew notes the christological understanding that the event had produced. They understood that his transcendence of the physical world implied something magnificent about his person (Matthew), but that understanding had not yet translated to an understanding of what Jesus' position meant for his care of them (Mark). For Mark, this is a major lesson about disciples that stands at the heart of his Gospel. The event is a test, because once Jesus gets into the boat, they arrive quickly on the shore.

134. Summary about Healings at Gennesaret (Matt. 14:34–36; Mark 6:53–56) (Aland §148; Orchard §163; Huck-Greeven §127)

Jesus and his entourage end up at Gennesaret, a fertile plain located southwest of Capernaum. Mark gives this summary in slightly more detail than

Matthew does, because he notes the excitement that Jesus' arrival generated. People ran through the neighborhood, bringing the sick to him, and wherever he went, people laid the sick at his feet in the marketplace. Matthew notes only that the sick were brought to him. Their belief in his power was such that they only needed to touch his garment, and they expected to be healed. That is exactly what took place. The almost "magical" feel to the text recalls how the woman with the hemorrhage approached Jesus (Matt. 9:20; Mark 5:27; Luke 8:44). Contact with him brought deliverance. Jesus' compassion is evident again.

135. Disputes over Traditions of the Elders and Defilement
(Matt. 15:1–20; Mark 7:1–23) (Aland §150; Orchard §167; Huck-Greeven §128)

Despite the beneficial presence of Jesus and his work, others were bothered by Jesus' lack of concern for certain practices. Again Mark has more detail than does Matthew. Pharisees and scribes had come from Jerusalem. They noted that some of Jesus' disciples ate with unwashed, "defiled" hands, which meant that they ate food in a ceremonially unclean state. The concern was not hygienic, but assumed an ideology of clean and unclean worship and living. Mark explains the practices that Matthew assumes his more Jewish audience to know. These concerns were supported by the traditions of the elders. They neither ate without washing the hands nor did they return from the marketplace without engaging in washings of purification. They also cleansed cups, pots, and vessels of bronze. Many of these practices are noted in detail in the Mishnah (*m. Yadayim* 1.1–2.4; *m. Toharot*).[17] The issue of ritual cleanliness appears in the Torah (Lev. 11–15; Num. 5:1–4; 19). However, the practices complained about here are not in the Scripture.

The complaint comes against the disciples for transgressing (Matthew) or not walking (Mark) according to the tradition of the elders, because they eat with defiled hands. However, what is implied is that Jesus has failed to guide them adequately in these matters. The reply, though the same in the two Gospels, comes in a different order.

Matthew begins with a rebuke in kind: "And why do you transgress the commandment of God for the sake of your tradition?" Then comes an illustration involving the highest human duty, the honoring of one's parents (Sir. 3:7–8, 12–15; Josephus, *Against Apion* 2.27 §206). The practice of declaring an item "given" to God meant that no one else could use it (*m. Nedarim* 1.2–

---

17. For details, see Emil Schürer, *The History of the Jewish People in the Age of Jesus Christ (175 B.C.–A.D. 135)*, vol. 2, ed. Geza Vermes, Fergus Millar, and Matthew Black, rev. ed. (Edinburgh: Clark, 1979), 475–78.

4; 3.2; 9.7).[18] So in this way people could protect their property and prevent themselves from allowing others access to it. Thus, Jesus accuses the leaders of using the law to selfish ends, in a context of claimed piety, while refusing to meet needs that their parents might have. He concludes that for the sake of their tradition, they have "made void" the word of God. The Greek term for "make void" is a technical legal term often used of annulling a contract. In effect, they have not kept their word before God by their actions by failing to love and honor their parents. So Matthew cites Isa. 29:13, where the prophet rebukes Israel for honoring God with the lips while the heart is far away. Such worship is empty, because they teach human doctrines, not those of God.

Mark begins with the Isaiah citation as introducing Jesus' reply and then states the violating principle: "You abandon the commandment of God and hold fast to human tradition." In fact, they reject God's command in order to keep the tradition. Then Mark relates the "Corban" (given to God) example, naming the practice that Matthew's Jewish audience did not need to have named. The practice releases the person from having to do anything for the parent. Mark adds to the rebuke as Jesus declares that they do many such things.

At this point, both accounts note a final teaching that Jesus made to the crowd. Nothing that goes into a person from outside defiles. It is the things that come out from a person that defile. Matthew's version highlights speech, mentioning what comes out of the mouth.

Jesus then teaches the disciples privately in order to explain his remarks. The response in Matthew comes as a result of the disciples telling Jesus that he had offended the Pharisees, a remark that probably was a courteous suggestion that he had gone too far. Jesus does not back off. He notes that every plant not planted by God would be rooted up. The image of a plant to depict a community is common in Judaism (Isa. 60:21; Jer. 45:4; *Jubilees* 1.16; 7.34; 21.24; *1 Enoch* 10.16; 84.6; 93.2; 1QS 8.5; 11.8; CD 1.7). God will not bless them, so leave them alone. They are like blind guides who lead one another into the pit. So Jesus tells his disciples that his antagonists' way is not the way of God. These unique Matthean details would be of concern to his audience, but not to Mark's.

Both accounts pick up the final explanation. Jesus rebukes the disciples in a rhetorical question that asks if they are still without understanding. What is eaten does not defile, because it passes through the body and out again. At this point, Mark adds a parenthetical note that presents the implications of Jesus' remark: the effect is that all foods are clean. It is clear that this was not understood at the time, because in Acts 10 Peter needs to have this explained to him. Nonetheless, Mark notes it in passing, while Matthew, perhaps out of sensitivity to his Jewish audience, lacks any such remark.

18. Many of the texts in this tractate discuss when vows are not binding, suggesting that there are ways to get out of frivolous or unwise vows.

Jesus concludes that it is what comes out of the person (Mark) or out of the mouth (Matthew) that defiles. Matthew lists seven relational items, while Mark has thirteen in his vice list, including a reference to an "evil eye," a category that many translations equate with envy but that may suggest an all-encompassing jealousy and evil (cf. Matt. 6:23). Both lists focus on the relational dimensions of sin, just as the earlier illustration of Jesus had done. Jesus' point stated positively is that the commandment of God and the true worship of him should lead to positive relationships and treatment of others. The opposite, the evil that emerges from within, is what defiles. Mark ends on that challenging note. Matthew states a contrastive principle to end his account: vices coming from within defile, while eating with unwashed hands does not. Clearly, Jesus and the leadership have different priorities and different sources of authority.

136. The Syrophoenician (Canaanite) Woman (Matt. 15:21–28; Mark 7:24–30) (Aland §151; Orchard §168; Huck-Greeven §129)

Jesus travels into predominantly Gentile territory, which Mark names as Tyre, while Matthew mentions Sidon as well. They were noted as notorious cities in Matt. 11:21–22. The treatment of a move into Gentile territory makes sense after the discussion on defilement and purity. Although Israel is the focus now, Gentiles will not be cut off from Jesus and his work.

Only Mark gives the motive for Jesus' excursion, while Matthew simply goes directly into the request for an exorcism. Jesus was seeking to withdraw and have some time alone with his disciples. For Mark, Jesus' public acclaim and attention is a problem because it prevents him from getting the needed time to instruct his disciples. Even the attempt to go outside the nation to gain rest will fail.

The request comes with more detail in Matthew. A Canaanite woman cries out to Jesus as "O Lord, Son of David" and asks for mercy for her severely demon-possessed daughter. Her address betrays some knowledge about Jesus and indicates that word about him had spread beyond Israel. Mark gives her nationality as Syrophoenician. He also notes that she fell at his feet, but he summarizes the request rather than having her address Jesus. In fact, the Markan version is more compact, while Matthew has Jesus remain silent at the initial request and the disciples plead on her behalf, in part to get rid of her persistent crying as she follows them. Jesus' initial reply is that he is called only to the lost sheep of Israel, repeating a note made in Matt. 10:5–6 (this perspective will change in Matt. 28:19). The woman repeats her request, asking for help. This explanatory detail, unique to Matthew, highlights the implications involved should Jesus respond to this woman, a Gentile.

At this point the accounts converge somewhat. In Matthew, Jesus notes that it is not fair to take the children's bread and throw it to the dogs. The dogs referred to here are not wild dogs, which Jews often compared to Gentiles, but house pets, because the diminutive form (κυνάριον) is used.[19] Jesus' point is that his power and teaching are aimed at Israel, although there is a hint of openness in the "pet" image.[20] In Mark, the opening is slightly more conspicuous. Jesus notes that the children must be fed first, because it is not right to take children's bread and throw it to the dogs. The same "pet" image is present, but Jesus does note that later some leftovers may come to the dogs. The point here is that the teaching of Jesus is a priority, and this teaching is for those he has gathered around him. The nationalistic element is less prominent in Mark, although it is implied. Neither version develops Jesus' hesitation to act for her, although they both leave a slight opening in his reply. The sense is that Jesus is drawing her out. She has been understanding and persistent up to this point in the Matthean version, so how will she respond to this seeming obstacle?

In a reversal of the normal pronouncement account where Jesus' remarks are central, the woman's response becomes key. She notes that these pets get the benefit of the crumbs from the master's (Matthew) or children's (Mark) table. The humility in the reply should not be missed. She does not challenge the priority that Jesus gave to the children. She simply wishes to be worthy of what might be left over. The response is similar to the returning prodigal son's desire to be received back as a mere servant in Luke 15:18–19. Jesus commends her response. In Matthew, it is an example of great faith, like that of the Gentile centurion in Matt. 8:10, so that Jesus pronounces her request granted. In Mark, the saying is commended, but surely it is the humble faith that is affirmed as her daughter is pronounced healed. The account closes by noting the instantaneous nature of the healing (Matthew) and the evidence that the daughter was well when the woman returned home (Mark). Jesus had done his work for a faithful Gentile and had done it from a distance. It is yet another miracle that mirrors the work of Elijah (1 Kings 17:8–24).

137. Jesus Heals Many Others/Deaf Mute (Matt. 15:29–31
["others"]; Mark 7:31–37 ["mute"]) (Aland §152; Orchard §169; Huck-Greeven §130)

On the edge of the Decapolis along the Sea of Galilee, Matthew and Mark pause for another summary of Jesus' healing. Matthew presents it strictly as a summary. Jesus is faced with the crowd bringing him the lame, the maimed,

19. C. E. B. Cranfield, *The Gospel according to Saint Mark,* Cambridge Greek Testament Commentary (Cambridge: Cambridge University Press, 1959), 248.
20. The remark is similar in perspective to Paul's more famous statement that the gospel is to the Jew first and also to the Greek (Rom. 1:16). See also John 4:22; Acts 3:25–26; 13:46; Rom. 15:8.

the blind, the mute, and many others. His healing them all leaves the crowd amazed as they see the lame walk, the maimed made whole, the blind see, and the mute speak. They recognize that God is working powerfully through Jesus, and they glorify God. The placement in Matthew is significant. The remark recalls Jesus' reply to John the Baptist in Matt. 11:5–6. These "deliverance" events are still in evidence. They even follow an excursion into Gentile territory and come despite rejection within Israel. Rejected or not, the plan will move ahead.

Mark focuses on one exemplary healing of a deaf mute. The condition described involves a man who was "deaf and had an impediment in his speech." The second part of this phrase uses a rarer Greek word and serves by the addition to present the condition as an intensified one. In telling about this healing, he gives much detail to Jesus' every move. The details, strange as they are to a modern reader, fit with ancient expectations of such a healing but with far less "bravado" than the normal ancient rendering of such detail.[21] So Jesus sticks his fingers in the man's ears, spits, and touches his tongue in an act that was seen as purifying because of the source. Then Jesus looks up to heaven to indicate the source of the healing and groans in Aramaic with a command that the man's ears and tongue be opened. The healing is described in part as "the bonds of his tongue were loosed." It is as if a prisoner were set free (Luke 4:16–18). In Mark, Jesus is very concerned that the miracles not become the center of his work. The drawing of crowds is something he has sought to avoid. So he commands the people not to say anything. The purpose is not to pretend that a miracle did not happen but to prevent the public relations problem of the healings' sensationalism producing overwhelming obstacles for Jesus' public ministry. Despite his wishes, the word is even more zealously distributed. The people are exceedingly astonished as they proclaim that closed ears are opened and bound tongues are set free. Jesus presents a ministry that pictures the reversal of impediments afflicting humanity. Thus, for Mark, the singular healing is a summary of the general character of Jesus' ministry. However, the crowd is drawn to his miraculous work more than to the delivering work those miracles illustrate.

138. The Feeding of the Four Thousand (Matt. 15:32–39; Mark 8:1–10) (Aland §153; Orchard §170; Huck-Greeven §131)

This miracle parallels the feeding of the five thousand (Matt. 14:13–21; Mark 6:32–44; Luke 9:10–17b; unit 132 above). It is one of several events that have been called doublets. The name suggests one event rendered in

---

21. Robert Gundry, *Mark: A Commentary on His Apology for the Cross* (Grand Rapids: Eerdmans, 1993), 383–84.

two versions. The term is unfortunate because it is not the best explanation for this kind of repetition. The tradition about Jesus is clear that he did far more than what is recorded. Thus, it is likely that certain classes of event took place more than once. The so-called doublet traditions fit here. They represent actions that Jesus did on more than one occasion and that one or more of the evangelists decided either to include or omit for their own reasons. Their inclusion makes an important point: the continuation of these kinds of actions in the face of ongoing opposition indicates that Jesus' ministry proceeds to offer blessing. The continued rejection of him in light of the repetition reveals how deep the hardness of heart was in refusing to embrace the stream of work that Jesus provided. These so-called doublets really are "mirror" miracles, since they reproduce earlier scenarios and yet indicate that little has changed. The multiple opportunities for response have made no difference.

This miracle comes after the crowd has spent three days with Jesus. They are hungry, but he does not wish to send them away to get food for fear of their lack of strength. Mark alone adds that some have come a long way. The text tells us that Jesus' compassion moves him to tell the disciples to act. The disciples, despite the earlier example of provision, do not think in terms of a sequel, so they ask where they can get enough bread to feed the crowd. Inventory shows only seven loaves and a few fish, although Mark only later notes the presence of the fish. As with the earlier miracle, the crowd is asked to sit and receive the food, which Jesus dispenses through his disciples after giving thanks. At this point Mark adds his note that the few fish were blessed and distributed. Everyone had their fill, with seven baskets left over. The number may suggest completeness. Four thousand men were fed, plus women and children. Jesus had provided for the people again. The disciples left and went to Magadan (Matthew) or Dalmanutha (Mark). Each name may be a variant for Magdala.[22] We have returned to the west coast of the Sea of Galilee.

139. The Pharisees Seek a Sign (Matt. 16:1–4; Mark 8:11–13; conceptual: Matt. 12:38–39; Luke 11:16; 12:54–56; 11:29) (Aland §154; Orchard §171; Huck-Greeven §132)

The continued proliferation of miracles has not convinced the leadership, which still presses Jesus for a sign from heaven. The specific request for some type of apocalyptic sign was a "test" and an attempt to dictate what should be provided as evidence that God really was at work, despite the variety of what already had been provided. A sign is "an outward compelling proof of divine

22. Ibid., 403.

authority" (see Exod. 4:8–9; Deut. 13:1; Isa. 7:10–17; 38:7).[23] Matthew alone notes that the test came from Sadducees as well as Pharisees, indicating both an alliance between the rivals and the inclusion now of the sect with the most sociopolitical power in the nation. Mark uniquely notes Jesus' emotion, as that evangelist often does. The debate, which Mark calls an "argument," causes Jesus to sigh deeply. The whole scene is rather tragic.

Matthew alone details Jesus' teaching that they can read the weather by observing how a red sky in the evening signals fair weather, while in the morning it portends rain. As good as they are with the physical world, they have no clue how to read the spiritual realities that Jesus brings, what he calls the "signs of the times." Luke 12:54–56 has a similar argument in another context.

Then Jesus rebukes them in each version. In Mark, it opens with a question of why this generation seeks a sign. Jesus simply states that no sign will be given and then departs. In Matthew, there is a statement that only an evil and adulterous generation would ask for a sign (probably meaning that it asks for a specific sign) but that only the sign of Jonah will be given, an allusion to Matt. 12:38–39 (see also Luke 11:29). Thus, Matthew has an intensified form of the rebuke, an intensity that parallels 12:38–39. Despite his work, Jesus' repetition of miracles and teaching does not lead to response. The evangelists are showing how stubborn and blinding the sin of rejection can be.

140. The Leaven of the Pharisees (Matt. 16:5–12; Mark 8:14–21; conceptual: Luke 12:1) (Aland §155; Orchard §172; Huck-Greeven §133)

As Jesus' entourage crosses the sea yet again, Matthew and Mark note how the disciples have not brought enough bread. Matthew states this absolutely ("had forgotten to bring any bread"), while Mark notes in addition that they had "only one loaf," having "forgotten to bring bread." Jesus has other issues on his mind, so he warns them to take heed of a different kind of leaven. In Matthew, it is the leaven of the Pharisees and Sadducees, a combination that is to be expected, given the "testing" they did of Jesus in 16:1. The Sadducees hold major political reins, and their approach to compromise at the expense of religious commitment may be in view. In Mark, it is the leaven of the Pharisees and of Herod. This also is not surprising, as the mention of Herod raises the issue of moral corruption, which alludes back both to the discussion of de-

---

23. Cranfield, *Mark*, 257–58. Cranfield argues that it is something "unbelief demands but Jesus resolutely refuses to give." The miracles never were signs in the sense of attempts to wipe out the need for faith. This is why the Synoptics prefer the term of "powers" (δυνάμεις) for these acts. John prefers the word "sign" (σημεῖον) because for him the miracles are a disclosure of who Jesus is and the power to which he has access.

filement in Mark 7:1–23 and to the review of the Baptist's death in 6:17–29. The Pharisees certainly are mentioned because they have directed the reaction against Jesus. It is their skepticism and cynicism that the disciples are told to avoid.

Unfortunately, the disciples' initial reaction has them so focused on physical bread that they do not appreciate the thrust of Jesus' remarks. They are left to look quite obtuse. The point is that they are so consumed with the mundane issues of life that more central spiritual questions do not even edge naturally into their thinking. So Jesus rebukes them. In a sense, the disciples are no better than the Pharisees except for the fact that they are seeking to be responsive to Jesus. In Matthew, it comes as one of his several "you of little faith" rebukes (Matt. 6:30; 8:26; 14:31; 17:20). To the rebuke is added a query: do they not yet perceive what is going on? A review then follows of his previous provisions for them of physical bread in the feedings of the five thousand and the four thousand as a reminder that they should understand (14:15–17; 15:33). In Mark, Jesus asks them if they do not yet understand and whether their hearts are hardened. Jesus then walks them through the fact that he has provided bread for them in the past. The questions are expressed in the challenging language of the prophets: having eyes that do not see and ears that do not hear (see Jer. 5:21; Ezek. 12:2; Isa. 6:9–10). The point is that to worry about such an item makes no sense in light of what Jesus has done, but even more important is to recognize that this mundane matter (earthly bread) is not even his topic—spiritual reality is. So in Mark, Jesus closes by urging them, "Do you not yet understand?"

Matthew is more direct. Jesus asks, "How is it that you do not perceive that I did not speak about bread?" He then repeats the warning about the leaven of the Pharisees and Sadducees. Then the unit ends with a narrative comment, that the topic was not real bread but the teaching of these groups.[24] Jesus' ministry is about who speaks for God. The warning is not to be deflected from Jesus' teaching because of the sociopolitical position that these groups occupy within Judaism. Their teaching, spreading like leaven, ultimately undermines the way to God. The disciples still need to develop their sensitivity to spiritual issues.

141. A Blind Man Is Healed at Bethsaida (Mark 8:22–26)
(Aland §156; Orchard §173; Huck-Greeven §134)

Mark notes yet another healing of a blind man. The image may be significant, coming as it does before Peter's confession. Jesus' healing not only pro-

---

24. Craig Blomberg, *Matthew*, New American Commentary (Nashville: Broadman), 249, notes that an Aramaic wordplay underlies the saying; the words for "teaching" and "yeast" are almost identical (*ʾamira* and *ḥamirʾa*).

vides sight, but also is a picture of his work to make the will of God steadily clearer. This is the only miracle that comes gradually, in a two-step progression. Does this mirror the two-step development of the understanding of the disciples in Mark? First, Jesus is the Messiah, and then their understanding comes into better focus when they appreciate his suffering as the Messiah. Beyond the miracles and power are the sacrifice and the service of how deliverance will be provided for in Jesus' work. This is where Mark is headed as a narrative. For the disciples in Mark, life comes gradually into focus. The scene also is unusual because this miracle is unique to Mark, one of the few events in the Gospel tradition that we know only from Mark. Jesus heals in private again, as he did with the deaf-mute man of Mark 7.[25] In fact, much about this miracle parallels that one, even down to noting the detailed acts of the healing itself, which include the private nature of the healing, spitting into the eyes, and the laying on of hands. The gradual character of the miracle is evident from Jesus' initial request about what the man sees. He replies that he sees people, but they look like trees. A second laying on of hands leads to clear sight for the man, who is then sent home. He is not told to be silent, but he is told to go home without returning to the village. The reversal of his condition will be self-evident. Jesus is not interested in the self-promotion of his ministry. His acts should speak for themselves.

Conclusion

Jesus' ministry is part of a program revealing the powerful release of the fruitful promise of God. It is the message of God's rule being reasserted in the world. There are many obstacles to its taking hold, but in the end a judgment will sort out where response has taken place. In the face of that announcement, Jesus continues his powerful work. Some of it, like his teaching, is taking on a private note, being given only to the disciples. A separation is developing, which Jesus does not prevent. His many miracles show his comprehensive authority, but those who reject him continue to press him on their own terms, asking for specific kinds of signs. Jesus refuses to give such signs, in light of what he is doing. In addition, he is challenging the way in which issues like cleanliness are seen, by raising the issue of cleanliness of the heart to prominence over ritual concerns. This inner dimension was introduced in the Sermon on the Mount. It is a primary critique of Jesus against the leadership. In seeking God's will and way, Jesus' critics major in the minors and ignore the more relational dimensions of God's will. In the context of this swirling, rising conflict, evidenced already in the execution of John the Baptist, Jesus will ask his disciples who people confess him to be and who they as his

---

25. For the case against a doublet here, see Cranfield, *Mark,* 263.

followers see him to be. The difference is revealing and significant, leading Jesus to intensify his instruction of his followers while continuing to challenge those who reject him. In particular, it is his approaching suffering that they must comprehend. It is the result of the incipient but rising opposition. The disciples will share the same path. If there is one aspect of Jesus' work that re-quires time to be appreciated, it is that whatever glory he possesses must be entered into through the way of intense suffering. To know Jesus is to face a world that does not know him.

EIGHT

Confession and Prediction

*The New Reality—Part 1 (Matt. 16:13–18:35;
Mark 8:27–9:50; Luke 9:18–50)*

If, then, Jesus believed himself to be Israel's messiah, the focal point of its long history, the one through whom Israel's God would at last deal with its exile and sin and bring about its longed for redemption, he also seems to have believed that this messianic task would be accomplished through his own suffering and death. This, I must stress, is not a particularly odd thing to be thought by a first-century Jew with a strong sense of God's presence and purpose and a clear gift for charismatic leadership. In short, we have every reason to suppose that Jesus did in fact locate his own vocation within precisely this complex of biblical and traditional reflection. The visions of Zechariah, so dark and opaque to the twentieth century, seem to have been luminous to him, to have shaped his vocation and choice of action. Daniel's vision of vindication of "one like the son of man," the symbolic representative of Israel, seems to have provided him with inspiration and cryptic vocabulary. And the poems about the "servant" in Isaiah 40–55 gave particular focus to his sense of call and direction.[1]

We come to a major turning point in Jesus' ministry in all three Synoptics: Peter's confession of Jesus as the Messiah at Caesarea Philippi. After this confession, which Jesus accepts but asks for silence about, Jesus begins to instruct them about his suffering and what this rejection will demand of them. It is a new reality about what following God will entail. It is a proclamation of coming victory, but not coming down the path that the disciples had expected. In Mark, this story is part of the basic two-step progression in his narrative. The confession of Jesus as the Messiah leads to further instruction about the nature

---

1. N. T. Wright, in *The Meaning of Jesus: Two Visions*, by Marcus J. Borg and N. T. Wright (San Francisco: HarperSanFrancisco, 1999), 97.

of his messianic office. Luke uses this material to set up further instruction to come in the Jerusalem journey section that follows. Matthew mostly parallels Mark, with a few additional points in his discourse in Matt. 18.

This chapter covers the confession and the material immediately after it. This involves Matt. 16:13–18:35, Mark 8:27–9:50, and Luke 9:18–50. The section shows why Jesus wanted to silence the disciples. They had much to learn about what God would be doing through him. He corrects them often in this section. It also shows Jesus working to form a new community around him that would live by standards different from those of the world.

142. Peter's Confession (Matt. 16:13–20; Mark 8:27–30; Luke 9:18–21) (Aland §158; Orchard §174; Huck-Greeven §135)

In the old city of Paneas, located in Dan, some twenty-five miles north of the Sea of Galilee, Jesus has this significant exchange with the disciples. The city had been renamed Caesarea Philippi by Philip the Tetrarch, after himself and Caesar. It was renowned for its paganism. Matthew is the most detailed, while Mark and Luke are brief. Luke notes that the discussion took place after Jesus was praying, adding a serious tone to the setting.

Jesus begins by asking who people say that he is. Three answers are given: John the Baptist, Elijah, or one of the prophets. Matthew alone mentions Jeremiah in the third option. The threefold reply matches the speculations noted in Mark 6:14–16 and Luke 9:7–9. Jeremiah seems to be noted as a prime example of a prophet who challenged the nation to repent. The people recognize Jesus as sent by God and as his spokesman, but as we will see, the understanding is inadequate.

The simple accounts of Mark and Luke cover only Peter's confession and Jesus' charge to them not to say anything about it to anyone. When Jesus asks them, "Who do you [plural] say that I am?" Peter speaks up and confesses Jesus as the Christ (Mark: "You are the Christ"; Luke: "The Christ of God"). Jesus is more than a prophet; he is the promised anointed one sent from God. Here is the core confession about Jesus' identity. It is an identity that he will have to teach them about, so that they understand what it does and does not mean. So he tells them not to say anything to anyone. Although neither Mark nor Luke has Jesus accept the confession outright, as he does in Matthew, the very fact that he instructs them to silence indicates that Jesus accepts the confession, but that it will take time and instruction to appreciate all that it means.

Matthew's version includes a longer form of the confession and a full reply from Jesus before the command to tell no one that Jesus is the Christ.

Everything about Matthew's version is more explicit. Peter replies, "You are the Christ, the Son of the living God." The reply harks back to Matt. 14:33 and suggests that Peter has a sense that Jesus is especially empowered by the living, active God. However, it does not mean all that the term comes to mean in the early church in terms of Trinitarian detail.[2] Peter sees Jesus as the specially enabled promised one, the royal Son. Jesus can develop who he is, working up from this category. Of course, for Matthew and for his readers who know the whole of the story, the greater implications of the term are appreciated.

So Jesus issues an accepting and affirming beatitude for the one who makes the confession. It is significant to note that Peter in answering spoke not only for himself but also for the whole group. Nonetheless, it is Peter, as representative confessor, who is affirmed. Jesus tells him that his understanding is sourced in a work of God; the Father in heaven has revealed this. Then, making a wordplay on Peter's name, Jesus calls him a "rock" for being the type of person who makes this solid confession on which Jesus will build his church. Jesus is building a new community. "Church" is simply a term for an assembly, but it often refers to a specific community that is being built. Here is the first time that this term appears in Matthew, as well in the sequence of events depicted in the New Testament. Mark, Luke, and John never use the term. The image pictures Jesus starting a new building, a new work. The gates of Hades—the authority of death and the forces of the underworld—will not prevail against it (cf. Isa. 38:10). In the community formed around this confession, there is victory provided by accepting the revelation of God. In fact, this community will have the "keys" of the kingdom of heaven (cf. Isa. 22:22; John 20:23; contrast Luke 11:52). Entrance into the rule of God and into the life and victory it contains is bound up in the authority of the message coming from this new community. They will have the right "to bind and loose." Jesus is describing a community engaged in a struggle against other forces residing below, but the note throughout is of eventual victory. This community, with its message of promise, will be binding and loosing what God already has bound and loosed. The mysteries of both divine and human involvement and their interaction are intertwined in this promise. Jesus' remarks surely led to the later church imagery of the apostles as the foundation of the church (Eph. 2:20; Rev. 21:14). With this affirmation of Peter's confession and the note of authority that comes through the recognition of Jesus, the confessed one issues his instructions that they should not tell anyone that he is the Christ. More instruction is needed first, and it follows immediately.

2. Craig Blomberg, *Matthew*, New American Commentary 22 (Nashville: Broadman, 1992), 251.

143. Jesus Foretells His Passion (Matt. 16:21–23; Mark 8:31–33; Luke 9:22) (Aland §159; Orchard §§175–76; Huck-Greeven §136)

Jesus now issues his first prediction of his suffering. Many question the historical authenticity of these sayings, but there is good evidence that they are authentic. First, the pattern of response to Jesus up to now shows that a formidable opposition exists. Second, there was the precedent of the slaying of John the Baptist, to whom Jesus felt connected. Third, the prediction itself, with its "after three days" (Mark), includes a potentially misunderstood imprecision that argues against a saying created after the fact.[3]

Luke's version is the most compact, possibly because he will have a total of six such sayings in his Gospel. Jesus notes that the "Son of Man" will suffer many things, be rejected by the elders, chief priests, and scribes, be killed, and on the third day be raised. Here is the suffering Son of Man saying, in effect, "The one who will judge will also face judgment."

Mark and Matthew place the prediction in a context in which Jesus "began" to teach (Mark) or show (Matthew) them such things. Thus, they introduce it as a new theme in Jesus' instruction. The wording of the teaching is quite close to that in Luke, although Matthew speaks not of the Son of Man but of Jesus more explicitly, matching the explicitness of Peter's confession. Matthew also adds the note that Jesus must go to Jerusalem to face what comes. Two features are significant. First is the use in all three Synoptics of the term for divine design, "it is necessary" (δεῖ). What Jesus will face is a part of the divine will for him. Second is the reference in Mark and Luke to being rejected (ἀποδοκιμασθῆναι). This wording appears to be influenced by Ps. 118:22, showing the scriptural and revelational roots associated with the plan. The rejection is focused in the leadership.

Mark and Matthew also note Peter's reaction, whereby he attempts to move outside his role as disciple to the Christ and instruct the master. Peter rebukes the idea that the Christ will be rejected. Matthew notes the reply in detail: "God have mercy on you, Lord! This will never happen to you." For Peter, the Messiah is a glorious, powerful figure, not one whom the nation rejects. Here is the very reason that the disciples sorely needed instruction. They did not understand God's plan.

Jesus' response is even more emphatic: "Get behind me, Satan!" The cosmic conflict that Matthew noted in Jesus' response to Peter's confession surfaces here. Peter is thinking that suffering will not come. In doing so, he is thinking like Satan and like humanity, as both Mark and Matthew point out. Such thinking is not of God. As Matthew alone notes, Peter's thinking is an

---

3. The expression surely intends inclusive reckoning, but it was subject to being misunderstood so that other "three day" phrases, such as "on the third day," arose to remove the ambiguity.

obstacle to Jesus and to the way he must go. The "rock" has become a hurdle, a "stumbling stone" of offense. The disciples need to understand that Jesus will suffer. The new reality is that the way of glory is down the road of suffering. The disciples never could quite absorb this message until it took place. The hope of glory was too great to see the necessity of suffering until it came and forced its reality upon them.

144. If Any Would Follow Me (Matt. 16:24–28; Mark 8:34–9:1; Luke 9:23–27) (Aland §160; Orchard §177; Huck-Greeven §137)

The rejection that Jesus anticipates is not limited to him. He warns that those who would follow him must prepare for suffering. Mark and Luke note that Jesus said this to others besides the disciples, while Matthew focuses on the disciples as the audience. There is one exhortation followed by a series of three elaborations. The exhortation is that if any would follow (Mark) or come after (Matthew, Luke) Jesus, then those disciples must deny themselves, take up their cross (daily [Luke]), and follow him. The shift of verb tenses is important: two Greek aorist imperatives followed by a present. Self-denial and taking up the cross are fundamental commitments, while following is a continual activity. Luke notes that the commitment to bear the cross is made each day. The image calls for one to accept rejection, using the picture of the shame that came with carrying the cross to one's death. It is subjecting oneself to "the howling, hostile mob."[4] One is subject to insult and ridicule before the world for thinking, acting, and living differently.

So one is faced with a choice. To seek to save one's life by pursuing the world's acceptance results in the loss of real life; to give one's life for Jesus' sake (and for the gospel's [Mark]) will result in saving (finding [Matthew]) that life (Matt. 10:38–39; Luke 14:27). This is the great chasm between the world's perspective, seen in human thought, and Jesus, who reflects the thought of God. Self-preservation may result in self-destruction.

Two rhetorical questions follow in Matthew and Mark, while Luke has only the first. Turned into statements, Jesus' point is that there is no profit in gaining the whole world only to lose one's soul (self [Luke]). There is nothing one can give in exchange for one's life. One's real, eternal life is too high a price to pay for temporary earthly acceptance.

Jesus places the perspective of the future, with its judgment, over the entire set of remarks. He declares that the one who is ashamed of him and his words will face being shamed by the Son of Man when Jesus comes in the glory of his Father. Mark specifies that this rebuke is directed to "this adulterous and

4. Joachim Jeremias, *New Testament Theology*, vol. 1, trans. J. Bowden (London: SCM, 1971), 242.

sinful" generation (cf. Hos. 2:2). The warning may well be more generic than a reference to one specific time frame. It may refer to an ethical class of people across time who are characterized by wickedness. The allusion to the Son of Man and glory refers to the final judgment. Matthew makes this point even more explicitly, because instead of speaking about coming shame, he declares that the judgment will repay every person for what he or she has done (cf. Ps. 62:12; Prov. 24:12; Rom. 2:6; 2 Cor. 11:15; Rev. 22:12). A commitment to Jesus is worth everything because of who he is.

The unit closes with a prediction that some will not taste death until they see the kingdom. Matthew notes that it is the "Son of man coming in his kingdom," while Mark says only that "the kingdom of God has come with power." Luke, the most concise, speaks of seeing "the kingdom." The meaning of the verse has been much debated. Is Jesus speaking of the return in the lifetime of the disciples or of the aftermath of resurrection? It appears more likely that the remarks anticipate the transfiguration, with its glimpse of the future glory of Jesus.[5] This kind of "patterned" event, where a short-term event patterns one coming later, is common in Jesus' teaching, as the Olivet discourse will show. Only the reality of Jesus' future glory and authority foreshadowed in transfiguration makes sense of this exhortation to self-sacrifice. That sacrifice will be exchanged for glory later.

145. The Transfiguration (Matt. 17:1–9; Mark 9:2–10; Luke 9:28–36)
(Aland §161; Orchard §178; Huck-Greeven §138)

About one week later, the great glimpse into glory came for a select group of disciples—Peter, James, and John.[6] The locale of the event is uncertain. Mt. Hermon (9,200 ft.) and Mt. Meron (about 4,000 ft.) are the most likely candidates because the traditional site of Mt. Tabor (1,900 ft.) is not all that high and was inhabited by a fortress at this time, making it an unlikely spot for such a private experience. As is common in Luke, the scene takes place in the context of prayer.

Jesus is transformed before them into a dazzling, bright form wearing glistening white garments, a description indicative of glory (see Dan. 7:9; 12:3; 2 Baruch 51.3, 5, 10, 12; 1 Enoch 38.4; 62.15–16; 104.2; Rev. 3:5; 4:4; 7:9). With him were Moses and Elijah (Mark has them in the reverse order), who probably represent the law and the eschaton, because Elijah was anticipated as the prophet of the end (Mal. 4:5; Sir. 48:10). The three are engaged in discussion. Only Luke indicates the topic: Jesus' "exodus," which he was to accomplish in Jerusalem. Glory and suffering both are central to who Jesus is.

5. Robert Gundry, *Mark: A Commentary on His Apology for the Cross* (Grand Rapids: Eerdmans, 1993), 440, 457.

6. Matthew and Mark give the timing as six days later, while Luke speaks of about eight days.

Luke also uniquely notes that Peter and the others slept and then woke up to the scene. Peter's response is to suggest that the disciples build three booths as a way of honoring the three and prolonging the experience. Both Mark and Luke observe that Peter did not know what to say. Typically, Mark notes the emotion of the disciples: fear had motivated Peter's remark. Luke points out the fear when the cloud, a sign of God's Shekinah presence, descends around them (see Exod. 13:21–22; 14:19–20; 33:9–10; Num. 9:15–23; Lev. 16:2; Isa. 6:4–5; 2 Macc. 2:8). The imagery of the entire scene recalls the giving of the law in Exodus, especially 24:16. A new era and reality appear with Jesus and the glory that his presence represents.

So a voice speaks from the cloud, repeating what had been uttered more privately at Jesus' baptism. Mark's report is the shortest: "This is my beloved Son; listen to him." The language of Ps. 2:7 and of Deut. 18:15 is present. The addition of the note about listening underscores that the disciples still had much to learn. Matthew's version adds "in whom I am well pleased" in the middle. This means that the first two-thirds of the saying matches the baptismal remark. The new element is the call to listen. Luke has an explanatory "my Chosen" for the middle portion of the saying. This title highlights the fact that Jesus is part of a plan that God is working out. It is God's sovereign pleasure to choose to use the Son. The need to heed Jesus also is present. Peter had wanted to honor Moses, Elijah, and Jesus as equals. The voice, in contrast, singles out the Son.

According to Matthew, the voice causes the disciples to fall down in fear, but Jesus tells them to rise and not to fear. As his disciples, they have access to God's presence. Then they were alone with Jesus. The glimpse of glory was over. Matthew and Mark note how Jesus instructed them to say nothing about this event until the Son of Man is raised.[7] Mark notes that they kept the matter to themselves. Luke does not discuss the command but mentions that they were silent in those days about what they had seen. Again the silence is requested because they still have much to learn before they can appreciate what it is that they have seen. Their testimony surfaces in 2 Pet. 1:16–18.

146. About Elijah (Matt. 17:10–13; Mark 9:11–13) (Aland §162; Orchard §179; Huck-Greeven §139)

Elijah's presence raises the question about why Elijah must come first. No doubt the query results because Jesus has come announcing the eschaton, yet Elijah seems not yet to have appeared. How can this be? The roots of the Eli-

---

7. For a defense of the event's historicity, see C. E. B. Cranfield, *The Gospel according to Saint Mark,* Cambridge Greek Testament Commentary (Cambridge: Cambridge University Press, 1959), 292–96.

jah expectation appear in Mal. 4:5 and Sir. 48:10. Jesus accepts the premise that Elijah does come. Elijah will come before the end. However, in Mark, Jesus adds an additional observation through a question: "How is it written of the Son of Man, that he should suffer many things and be treated with contempt?" Jesus in Mark does not discuss glory without noting the presence of suffering as a part of the plan laid out in Scripture. No texts are specified, but the images of the righteous sufferer and the Servant probably are in view. Then Jesus complicates the imagery by noting that Elijah already has come.[8] Is it possible that people missed Elijah's presence? If so, then the premise would be wrong that the eschaton is preached without Elijah having come. The problem is that people did to this Elijah what they pleased. Matthew adds that they did not know him. The allusion is to John the Baptist, the prophet who preached eschatological hope and restoration to the nation in preparation for the arrival of God's deliverance. Matthew alone closes the unit by saying that the Son of Man will suffer in a similar way and that the disciples understood that Jesus had described John the Baptist. In Matthew, the disciples are beginning to listen and to understand what God has been doing, because they are listening to Jesus, as the heavenly voice had urged.

147. Jesus Heals a Demon-possessed Boy (Matt. 17:14–21; Mark 9:14–29; Luke 9:37–43a) (Aland §163; Orchard §180; Huck-Greeven §140)

In contrast to the glorious moment on the mountain stands the disciples' dilemma below. "Down there" things are not as marvelous as those on the mountain. This event is told in far more detail by Mark. He opens by noting an ongoing argument between the scribes, the crowd, and the disciples. Luke places the encounter on the next day. A man approaches Jesus about his son. Luke alone says that the boy is an only child (as also in 7:12 and 8:42). The condition is serious. Matthew describes it as the shakes (possibly epilepsy), which seize him and throw him into the fire or into water. Mark describes it as the product of a mute spirit that throws him down and makes him stiff as he foams at the mouth and grinds his teeth. Luke's description parallels Mark's. The sad point is that the healing efforts of those who did not go up the mountain have failed.

Jesus' rebuke extends to all as a faithless (all Synoptics) and perverse (Matthew and Luke) generation. Jesus asks how long he must put up with them and then asks for the boy to be brought to him. The issue seems to be that the

8. Here is yet another example of a "pattern" text like the allusion to glory in the prediction of the transfiguration. Elijah is both to come, as Jesus just noted, and already has come. John the Baptist patterns what Elijah will do.

disciples assumed a kind of automatic healing would take place. Mark 9:29 suggests that they had lacked a faith dependence expressed through prayer.

At this point Mark has detail that Matthew and Luke lack. The spirit throws the boy into another attack when he approaches Jesus. Jesus inquires as to how long the condition has existed. The reply is "since childhood." The demon has been well established, and the condition is long-term. The father notes how the spirit often has sought to destroy the boy by sending him into the water. He asks for Jesus' help: "If you can do anything, have pity on us and help us." Jesus replies, "If you can! All things are possible for the one who believes." Jesus' point is that God can work unusual things through the presence of faith. This explains why Jesus had labeled this generation as faithless. The father's conflict is confessed: "I believe; help my unbelief." He knows Jesus' capability but struggles to respond to that capability. The account is told to plead for such total trust. By now the crowd is approaching, so Jesus acts. He commands the spirit to come out of the boy, never to return. The spirit responds with another attack that leaves the boy limp like a corpse on the ground. However, the spirit is expelled from the boy. The exorcism is complete when Jesus lifts the boy up. Matthew and Luke are parallel here in summarizing only that the spirit came out of him and that the boy was healed after the rebuke. Luke closes with the crowd's reaction of astonishment at the majesty of God.

Matthew and Mark continue with the disciples' reflection over what just happened, especially as they ask about their own failure to exorcise the demon. Matthew focuses on the lack of faith and remarks that faith as small as a mustard seed will lead to mountains being moved and the impossible being done (note Matt. 13:31–32, 36; 15:12). Moving mountains was proverbial in Judaism for accomplishing the difficult (Isa. 41:15; 54:10; Hab. 3:10; Zech. 4:7; *b. Berakot* 63[b]). Luke 17:6 will use this image in a later, distinct context. However, for Matthew in this context, Jesus' point was that although they had been given authority to accomplish these things, they still needed to believe that God would work through them and not just assume it. Mark focuses on prayer. This was a particularly difficult case that could be solved only by prayer.[9] God must be approached and invoked. Nothing routine or formulaic will work. Nothing can replace dependence on God. Nor can one take the divine presence for granted.

---

9. There is a textual problem here in both Matthew and Mark: the mention of fasting along with prayer. This reference does not look original in either case because it is harder to explain why a scribe would remove an original reference to fasting than to explain that it may have been added to the passage to give a full round of pious acts to move God to act. However, it should be noted that the textual evidence for including a reference to fasting is stronger for Mark 9:29 than for Matt. 17:21. If Mark did refer to fasting, then the likelihood is enhanced that it was added to Matthew later to make them similar.

148. Jesus Predicts His Suffering Again (Matt. 17:22–23;
Mark 9:30–32; Luke 9:43b–45) (Aland §164; Orchard §181; Huck-
Greeven §141)

The disciples find themselves again in Galilee (Matthew and Mark), and Jesus issues another prediction of his suffering. Mark notes that Jesus attempted to keep the journey a secret as he was engaged in instructing his disciples. Luke's version is the most concise after uniquely noting how the crowds were marveling about all that Jesus did. Jesus urges the disciples to let "these words sink into your ears" and then speaks of the Son of Man being delivered over into human hands. Matthew and Mark expand on the same detail: the Son of Man will be delivered over into human hands, and they will kill him, and then he will be raised. Matthew has the resurrection on the third day, while Mark has it after three days (counting inclusively), a difference that also appeared in the first prediction (Matt. 16:21; Mark 8:31).

Mark and Luke note the reaction by saying that the disciples did not understand the saying and were afraid to ask about it. Luke adds that the understanding was concealed from them so that they could not perceive it. What seems to be in view is a failure to appreciate and apprehend the magnitude and synthesis of what was said and how it fit into God's program rather than a complete lack of comprehension. In their view, the Messiah was to be a glorious, eternal figure, not a crushed, dying one. Matthew notes that the remarks left them "greatly distressed." This detail does suggest that they understood the meaning of what Jesus said. It would take more instruction and the events themselves to permit them to really understand what God was doing. The Gospels are exceedingly honest about how slow the disciples were to grasp what God was doing. It is not the kind of detail one would invent about the eventual leaders of the new movement. As such, the case for its historical credibility is strong.

149. Payment of the Temple Tax (Matt. 17:24–27) (Aland §165;
Orchard §182; Huck-Greeven §142)

When the disciples came to Capernaum again, they entered a major tax collection locale. This raised the question of the two-drachma (or half-shekel) tax required for the temple's upkeep by Exod. 30:13–16 (cf. Exod. 38:25–26; Josephus, *Ant.* 18.9.1 §§312–313; this became a state tax for Rome after the temple's destruction in A.D. 70 [*War* 7.6.6 §§216–218]). The question came from the collectors whether "the teacher" paid the tax. It is asked in a way that anticipates payment, yet the fact that the question was raised at all suggests some uncertainty about the answer, perhaps because of the way Jesus handled other issues. Peter answers the query affirmatively, but that is not the end of the matter.

Jesus meets Peter and asks him whether kings collect their taxes from their own children or from others. When Peter replies that it is from others, Jesus observes that the kings' children are free from tax. Jesus' point is that those connected to him would normally be free from having to pay taxes to another. Jesus' community is distinct from empire citizenship (and, by implication, over it, since they are related to the ultimate King). However, another principle is that one should not cause offense (see 1 Cor. 9:15–23; 10:29–33). So for that reason, Jesus tells Peter to go and catch a fish, in which he will find the shekel that can pay the tax for both of them. The text notes that although the allegiance to political authority is not absolute, a disciple should be a good citizen (cf. Rom. 13:1–7). It also stresses how Jesus will help care for the responsibilities he asks of others.[10]

150. On Greatness (Matt. 18:1–5; Mark 9:33–37; Luke 9:46–48)
(Aland §166; Orchard §183; Huck-Greeven §143)

These verses begin fresh sections in both Matthew and Mark. In Matthew, they begin the fourth of the five major discourses in his Gospel (Matt. 18:1–35). The discourse covers key relationships among believers, presenting attitudes essential to community well-being. In Mark, there is a series of teachings linked together in catchword form (Mark 9:33–50) as the flow of thought moves freely from one idea to another. In contrast, Luke briefly notes two incidents, the dispute over greatness and then the discussion of the outsider exorcist. Otherwise, Luke has other elements of the catchword teaching about community in separate contexts, reflecting the floating and repetitive nature of this teaching's proverbial character.

The dispute about greatness receives a specific setting only in Mark. They are in Capernaum and are in the house when Jesus asks what they were discussing along the way. There is a note of embarrassment because they had been disputing with one another about who was the greatest. The Greek word here (διαλέγομαι) is different from the first reference to discussion and often refers to a lecture or dialogue that ends up in a dispute.[11] Luke simply summarizes that they were arguing about who among them was the greatest. Matthew has the disciples raise a theoretical question: "Who is the greatest in the

---

10. This kind of directed-discovery-of-provision story was familiar in the culture. See Craig Keener, *Matthew*, IVPNTCS 1 (Downers Grove, Ill.: InterVarsity, 1997), 283; W. Horbury, "The Temple Tax," in *Jesus and the Politics of His Day*, ed. E. Bammel and C. F. D. Moule (Cambridge: Cambridge University Press, 1984), 265–84.

11. BAGD, 185; BDAG, 232.

kingdom of heaven?" He gives no hint of the dispute. The issue of rank was important in their hierarchical culture of honor. Jesus had just separated out three of them for a momentous experience (the transfiguration), so the issue might have been a natural one to surface. But Jesus will reject all such attempts to engage in this kind of ranking and comparison. Although the disciples are equal in access to blessing, some will be given more leadership responsibility. They should not misconstrue the call to a key role as a call to be ranked over others.

Luke notes that Jesus perceived their thoughts, and this is what motivated him to call a child as an exemplar. Mark has Jesus eventually take the child up into his arms, suggesting a very small child. The act was significant because children in this culture had next to no status at all. Often they were regarded at best as neither seen nor heard, an attitude that the disciples take in Luke 18:15.

Matthew's account makes two points from the singling out of the child, while Mark and Luke make only one. First, Jesus points out the need to turn, an allusion to repentance, and become like children. Without such humility, entry into the kingdom will not take place. The issue is not only children's inherent humility, but also their inherent dependence. Their lack of independence is the point. Greatness usually is measured by one's independent achievements, but Jesus is changing the standard by explaining how the disciple should depend on God. Such dependent humility commends one for the kingdom. This is the point that Matthew makes alone.

One's attitude toward others also is important. To receive such a child in the name of Jesus is the same as receiving him. All people are important, even those whom society suggests are not. Jesus' equating a child with himself lifts the child's importance to the highest degree. Such an exhortation relativizes ranking by showing the importance of every person. Mark and Luke go on to develop the point. The one who receives Jesus receives the one who sent Jesus. It is an acceptance that welcomes God through his messenger or those who are tied to him. Jesus takes the basic image of accepting anyone and now shifts the attention to how he is received, an important consideration, given the opposition he has faced. Luke drives home the key application with a final point: "The one who is least among you all is the one who is great." The child illustration now is a metaphor for how they should see each other. Greatness is not a matter of rank; it is matter of simply being present.[12] The entire exchange explains why Jesus spent so much time with the marginalized and "insignificants" of the world. To this extent, humility is implied in the discussion, because humility is against rank.

12. On how this reverses the normal cultural expectations, see Joel Green, *The Gospel of Luke*, NICNT (Grand Rapids: Eerdmans, 1997), 391–92.

151. The Outsider Exorcist (Mark 9:38–41; Luke 9:49–50; conceptual: Matt. 10:42) (Aland §167; Orchard §184; Huck-Greeven §144)

Mark and Luke show that the issue of potential rivalry and rank still needed treatment, because since Peter's confession, both Mark 9 and Luke 9 have noted numerous missteps by the disciples. Peter misread the transfiguration. They failed to exorcise the demon. They argued over rank. They tried to stop an exorcist who was not in their inner circle. This series of corrections shows how much the disciples needed to listen even though they had a healthy appreciation of who Jesus was.

The disciples tell Jesus about an exorcist casting out demons in Jesus' name. Apparently, the man was doing it with success. However, the disciples forbade the effort because the man was not following Jesus as the disciples were. This kind of group control might have made logical sense, but again Jesus challenges the response. Luke gives the briefest version. The one who is not against them is for them. Leave a nonopponent alone. Mark's account is more detailed. Jesus first makes the point that one who does a mighty work in Jesus' name will not be able soon after to speak evil of him. The possible presence of God's work should not be halted, for it may lead to recognition of him. Then Mark follows with the note that the one who is not against them is for them. A final reason is added in terms of a picture of hospitality. Anyone handing a disciple something as simple as a cup of water because he or she bears the name of Christ will not lose the reward. Given the climate of rejection, acceptance and response is not to be muzzled and will be appreciated by God. Those who are opening up to God are rewarded by him for their kindness. Matthew 10:42 has an image similar to this last idea in discussing the mission of the Twelve. It also appears in a context in which opposition is also being noted.

152. Warnings on Temptations (Matt. 18:6–9; Mark 9:42–50; conceptual: Luke 17:1–2; 14:34–35) (Aland §168; Orchard §185; Huck-Greeven §145)

Besides rivalry and rank, the other obstacle that can undercut a community is a lack of holiness. So Jesus warns those who would cause disciples to fall away. This is what the Greek says is to "cause stumbling" (σκανδαλίζω).[13] The culprit would be better off with the cruelest of deaths, a drowning in the sea with a donkey's heavy millstone around his or her neck. Jesus alludes in the millstone to the practice in which grain was ground in huge quantities. A

---

13. BAGD, 752, and BDAG, 926, are clear in noting that the issue is causing a severe lapse, a falling away.

donkey with a millstone yoked to its neck walked in circles around a receptacle in which the grain was crushed by the stone rolling over the grain.[14] In Matthew, Jesus then issues a woe for the world and for the one who causes such sin even though it inevitably will occur.

Matthew and Mark then turn to a series of illustrations designed to highlight the need to take responsibility for not being the cause of sin. The triad of hand, foot, and eye is used. If they cause one to sin, then it is better to mutilate them, cut them off, or pluck them out so that they do not cause one to sin again. Such separation from the cause of sin is better than to end up in the fire that is hell.[15] The use of mutilation imagery is significant because in this culture it was prohibited (Deut. 14:1; 1 Kings 18:28; Zech. 13:6). Jesus is being rhetorical here, saying that we should go to every length to avoid allowing our members to lead us into sin. Avoiding sin requires ruthless diligence. Such a rejection of sin is also, contextually, another sign of dependent humility that seeks to follow God in holiness.

Mark alone closes with a final image of fire that tests like salt. The connection is not obvious but seems to be that just as salt is sprinkled indiscriminately and is spread wide, so also the fire of judgment will cover all. The point is that our accountability requires the diligence that Jesus is asking for in avoiding being a cause of sin. Then the image shifts abruptly to salt alone. Salt is good only when it acts like salt and retains its quality. It cannot season if it loses its saltiness. So Jesus exhorts them one final time to have (i.e., be) salt and be at peace with each other. Here, salt is a metaphor for a kind of preserving role. In the larger context, Jesus is saying that rivalry and destructive leading into sin are to be avoided. Disciples should be a source of peace within the community.[16]

153. The Parable of the Lost Sheep (Matt. 18:10–14; conceptual: Luke 15:3–7) (Aland §169; Orchard §187; Huck-Greeven §147)

On the surface, this parable looks similar to Luke 15:3–7, but contextually it uses the lost sheep image in a distinct way, pointing to a separate use of similar imagery. In Luke, the text refers to finding a lost sinner, but in Matt. 18, it refers to regaining a lost or straying disciple. The issue up to this point in

14. Luke 17:1–2 has a similar image in a distinct context.

15. The association of judgment and unquenchable fire is rooted in Isa. 66:24. The picture of the worm alludes to the filth that accompanied the burning garbage of the Valley of Hinnom, a place also known as Gehenna, from which hell derives its imagery. Mark 9:47 alludes directly to the language of Isaiah.

16. The conceptual parallels to this image in Matt. 5:13 and Luke 14:34–35 reflect distinct uses of the image. Their point is more negative and serves as a warning that salt gone saltless is thrown out.

18:1–9 has been about believers who are led into sin or fall into sin, as well as believers taking responsibility for sin. So when the text now turns to an exhortation not to despise "any of these little ones," the setting has not changed. Even believers who fall into sin should be pursued and recovered. Jesus explains that "their" angels always see God's face. There is discussion about what this remark means. Is it an allusion to an individual guardian angel for each person?[17] Or is it a reference to the angelic oversight of the corporate church in general, as one sees in Rev. 2–3 (see also Heb. 1:14)? The text is so brief as not to be clear. Regardless of this detail, Jesus' point is that believers should not despise those who are important enough to God that even the angels keep watch over them. If they are important to heaven, then they should be important to us.[18]

So Jesus turns to an illustration. If a shepherd has a hundred sheep and one of them wanders away, does he not leave the ninety-nine and look for the one? The interrogative in Greek expects a positive reply. Of course that is what a shepherd does! When the sheep is found, he rejoices over it more than over the ninety-nine that did not stray. The implication is clear that one should seek to restore the straying disciple. Jesus has used shepherd imagery earlier, in Matt. 9:36. God is the great shepherd of his people in Ezek. 34. Jesus ends the unit with a note that God's will is that none of these little ones should perish. The passage suggests that the pursuit of stray disciples is one of the means that God uses to bring them back, an interesting juxtaposition of God's will and the disciple's call.

154. On Reproving a Fellow Disciple (Matt. 18:15–18; conceptual: Luke 17:3) (Aland §170; Orchard §188; Huck-Greeven §148a)

Pursuing a straying disciple raises the question of how one engages in the process of dealing with a disciple in sin. Jesus outlines a full process. The goal is to pursue the matter as privately as possible until one has no choice but to involve a wider circle. Initially, the one sinned against is to go to the offender and speak directly about the fault. The issue should remain private between the two of them. If the offender listens, then a brother or a sister has been

17. The idea of a guardian angel was suggested to Judaism by Ps. 91:11 and does show up in a later rabbinic text, *b. Šabbat* 119[b]. The more collective idea is found in Dan. 10:10–14. Texts at Qumran appear not to make a distinction (1QSa 2.9–10). The point of comparison to children means that the point is not about children having guardian angels, but that God uses the angelic realm to protect believers.

18. Matt. 18:11 reads, "For the Son of Man came to save the lost." The text is not in the better, older manuscripts of Matthew and makes Matthew parallel to Luke, that is, about lost sinners, in contrast to the Matthean near context. It seems to be an addition by a later scribe to make Luke and Matthew agree, ignoring the distinct contexts.

gained, and there has been no unnecessary public embarrassment, an important point in this culture of honor and shame.[19] The next step, if the private
discussion fails, is to take one or two others, so that witnesses are present. The
ethical backdrop to this text appears to involve both Lev. 19:17–18 and Deut.
19:15. Once again the point is to limit public exposure during the process. If
there is still a refusal to acknowledge fault, then the matter is taken to the
church, although no detail is given as to how this is to proceed. This appears
to involve a situation where the facts are not in dispute; there is no suggestion
that some type of adjudication is necessary. If the church as a community
challenges the offender and he or she still does not listen, then that person is
to be treated as an outsider, "like a Gentile or tax collector." The picture is one
of exclusion from fellowship. The hope is that the isolation and corporate rebuke might be important enough to the offender to gain a response. Perhaps
the closest analogy in our culture is the way in which sanctions by nations
might "persuade" another nation to respond in order to prevent being isolated. Second Corinthians 2:5–11 discusses an apparently successful resolution of such a situation, while Gal. 6:1 shows how Paul advised that such sit-
uations be handled. Second Thessalonians 3:14–15 treats an unresponsive
situation. The accountability in this situation and the potential for a positive
response assume that the community and its rebuke mean something to the
person being challenged.

Jesus finishes by noting that what is bound and loosed on earth through
this discipline already will have been bound and loosed in heaven. In this way,
Jesus indicates divine sanction and support for the action of a unified church
in discipline against a believer who unquestionably has sinned and who has
refused to respond positively. The goal of the entire exercise is not to shame
or rebuke but to restore. The community is to check the destructiveness of sin
and show that one is accountable to God and his people. Holiness means
being serious about dealing with sin.

155. Two or Three Gathered in My Name (Matt. 18:19–20)
(Aland §171; Orchard §189; Huck-Greeven §148b)

It is in the context of church discipline and the authority to exercise it that
Jesus' next remark comes. If two or three agree on earth to ask about anything,
it will be done for them. The remark appears to be contextually determined;
the Greek term πρᾶγμα ("thing") often has a judicial connotation.[20] Thus,
Jesus is affirming the unanimity of the church in acting to deal with the erring

19. A similar process may have existed at Qumran (1QS 5.25–6.1).
20. Blomberg, *Matthew*, 281; BAGD, 697 §5; but BDAG, 859 §3, moves the term out of
its legal connotation, though it notes that force in §4.

disciple. That we have not left the topic of how to deal with sin is indicated by the following passage, which also treats the same question, so that this unit is sandwiched contextually by this one topic. It is the centrality of forgiveness and the readiness to offer it that serves to balance the prospective harshness of discipline and that prevents the holding of grudges that destroy community.

156. On Reconciliation (Matt. 18:21–22; conceptual: Luke 17:4)
(Aland §172; Orchard §190; Huck-Greeven §149)

This unit and the next conclude the discourse on community in Matt. 18. Given the need for discipline and maintaining standards of righteousness, how does a community prevent itself from becoming oppressive in its exercise of accountability? The answer is that the community is to be generous about forgiveness. The question Peter raises, when he asks how often he should forgive, is how generous the community should be. Should he forgive up to seven times? Peter's question appears to show an awareness of teaching like that in later Jewish texts that specify a limit of up to three times (ʾAbot de Rabbi Nathan 40a; b. Yoma 86ᵇ, 87ᵃ). Set against this standard, Peter is being generous to ask about forgiving seven times. The question, however, also has within it the premise that one should keep count of how often forgiveness is given and prevent its being abused.

Jesus' reply is significant. He notes that one should forgive without counting. The number used in the verse (ἑβδομηκοντάκις ἑπτά) can be read as either seventy-seven or seventy times seven.[21] If it is the latter, then it reverses the image of revenge noted in Gen. 4:24. Regardless, Jesus' point is that the number is so high that counting is excluded. Forgiveness is to be readily available in the new community.

157. The Parable of the Unforgiving Servant (Matt. 18:23–35)
(Aland §173; Orchard §191; Huck-Greeven §150)

How important was the offer of forgiveness to Jesus? He illustrates it with a vivid parable that draws upon the imagery of debt, with which sin often was associated in the ancient world. The parable comes in three scenes. The first involves a servant who has run up an impossible debt of ten thousand talents. The value of a talent is variously estimated from sixty to ten thousand denarii. But Jesus is selecting the highest number possible; a talent was the most valuable coin, and ten thousand was the largest single number for which Greek

21. BAGD, 213; BDAG, 269.

had an individual word. The number is huge, consisting of as much as 275,000 years of labor for an average worker![22] It is a debt that no one person would ever be able to repay. In the imagery of the parable, where the servant is the person and God is the king, the point is how human sin constitutes an unrepayable debt, if strict accounting is made. The debt is so large that the king plans to sell the servant and his family. But the servant appeals from his knees to the king, "Lord, have patience with me, and I will pay you everything." Of course, he never would raise that money, but the king, out of compassion, forgave the debt. The picture is of God's forgiveness given freely.

Scene two involves the servant with his own debtor. This debt is infinitesimal compared to the debt just forgiven. It is one hundred denarii, or one hundred days' average working wage. It pictures the relatively small debt of our sins against one another versus the ones we have before God. When the servant demands payment and the debtor cannot pay, the servant seizes him by the throat as a threat. The debtor falls to his knees with the appeal, "Have patience with me, and I will repay you," an expression that parallels his own earlier appeal. The servant rejects the appeal and jails his debtor.

Scene three opens with the distress of other observers who tell the king what took place. The king summons the servant and reminds him of the debt cancellation that he had experienced. The slave should have had mercy on his fellow servant in the same way. The remark is expressed with a Greek interrogative that indicates that this should have been the response. So in anger the king delivers the servant to the jailers until he has repaid his debt. However, it is a debt that he never would be able to repay on his own. Jesus warns that a similar judgment from the Father awaits those who do not forgive their brothers and sisters from the heart.

The standard of judgment that the servant had applied was applied to himself. His failure to forgive left him without forgiveness. Jesus' point is that God's grace is not a matter of justice or strict accounting fairness but of grace. As grace, it should teach us to be gracious in our own relationships. We should forgive others as the Father forgives us. Only someone who appreciates the forgiveness that God has given is in a position to forgive in a similar manner. The fact that the discourse ends with two units stressing forgiveness in a context in which accountability for sin also is prominent shows how Jesus wants community relationships to be governed by an incarnate expression of grace. This is the only way a community can survive a strict sense of mutual accountability.

Conclusion

The confession of Jesus as the Messiah has led to his warning about his coming suffering. Victory comes in, through, and after suffering. In the con-

22. Keener, *Matthew*, 292.

text of such rejection, one must be prepared to suffer. But victory is assured, as the glimpse of the glorified Jesus at the transfiguration shows. Dependence also is needed. Ministry will not be a matter of mere routine but must be accompanied by prayer, as the disciples' failure to exorcise a demon showed. In fact, these disciples have much to learn, such as the simplicity of childlike dependence and an appreciation that God will work through many servants, not an elite clique. So Jesus highlights the importance of community. Sin will come into the community and should be handled, but woe to the one through whom it comes. Reproof is necessary, but in a way that minimizes shame and seeks to restore. In fact, what is to be most readily available is forgiveness for the one who seeks it. If God's forgiveness should teach disciples anything, it is that they in turn should be quick to forgive.

This section shows Jesus instructing his disciples about how to face the world in the context of rejection and how to do it together. Having received their allegiance, Jesus prepares them for what it will cost them and require of them. So Jesus turns his face toward Jerusalem and a journey of divine fate that awaits him, preparing his disciples more and more for the new reality that awaits them. To understand and face what is ahead, they must, as the divine voice said to the disciples at the transfiguration, "listen to him."

NINE

Toward Jerusalem

The New Reality—Part 2 (Luke 9:51–18:14)

The eschatological theory is, therefore, undoubtedly right in the assertion that Jesus went up to Jerusalem to die and not merely on a teaching mission. But the going up and dying are not to be conceived as an attempt to precipitate the final catastrophe and force the Kingdom to come. They are rather to be regarded as the first and decisive battle in the campaign of the Kingdom of the Messiah against the whole kingdom of evil. In that battle Jesus will fight in the front rank and, if need be, alone. He is a leader who leads. And his utterances in this closing phase of his earthly ministry are marked by the precision and peremptoriness that belongs to operation orders in a military campaign.[1]

The emphasis on Jesus' rejection is supported by the way Luke frames the travel narrative with an inclusio of rejection. In 9.51–56 a Samaritan village "did not welcome Jesus because he was heading for Jerusalem." Likewise, the section culminates in Jesus' lament and prophecy of Jerusalem's destruction, which is coming "because you did not recognize the time of God's coming to you" (19.41–44).

In contrast to the Galilean section, which primarily emphasizes Jesus' miracles, the travel narrative emphasizes his sayings and teachings. Jesus is pictured in interaction with three audiences that Luke keeps fairly distinct: the disciples, the crowds and the religious leadership.[2]

If we step inside the formal pattern, we discover that to a considerable degree (an impressive degree when the traditional nature of the material is recognized),

---

1. T. W. Manson, *The Teaching of Jesus: Studies of Its Form and Content* (Cambridge: Cambridge University Press, 1955), 209.
2. Scott Cunningham, *"Through Many Tribulations": The Theology of Persecution in Luke-Acts,"* JSNTSup 142 (Sheffield: Sheffield Academic, 1997), 93.

248

the content of the sayings addressed to each group is appropriate to the nature and stance of each group. To the disciples, Jesus speaks what is essentially a positive catechesis concerning his identity, their mission, the nature of service and authority within the community, confessing Christ in persecution, the nature of the end-time, etc. To the crowds, Jesus speaks words of warning, threat, and calls to repentance. Against the Pharisees and Lawyers, Jesus uses the language of attack and condemnation, tells parables in which the element of rejection is dominant and parables in defense of His mission against their attacks.[3]

This long chapter covers a substantial portion of what has been called Luke's central section, the "travel narrative" (Luke 9:51–19:44). This large portion of substantially unique Lukan material makes up the major section of his Gospel. In it also is the bulk of the parables unique to Luke, as well as teaching found in other contexts in the other Synoptics. This chapter covers the journey narrative up to the point where Mark and Matthew rejoin it at Luke 18:15.

In the journey, Jesus heads for Jerusalem to meet his death, not in a direct chronological route but in a journey of divine fate.[4] The entire time he is instructing his disciples, challenging the crowds, inviting them to follow, and confronting the leadership. He is preparing the disciples for what lies ahead and the ministry they will undertake after he is gone. Jesus is giving the crowds more opportunity to respond. He is showing that the way of the current leadership is not the way of God. In this section we get the clearest glimpse of his teaching during the time when many forces are converging against him. This rising conflict sets up climactic events in Jerusalem, and Jesus can see the handwriting on the wall.

158. To Jerusalem (Luke 9:51) (Aland §174; Orchard §192; Huck-Greeven §151a)

Jesus "set his face" to go to Jerusalem. The idiom used here points to the determined completion of a task (cf. Gen. 31:21; Isa. 50:7; Jer. 21:10; 44:12). This brief remark opens the Lukan travel narrative. Luke notes that it came as the "days drew near for him to be received up." These narrative notes underscore how Jesus' career was following a path set by God. These were events to be fulfilled (Luke 1:1). Jerusalem always will be the goal (Luke 9:53; 13:22, 33–35; 17:11; 18:31; 19:11, 28, 41). Luke leaves the Markan and Matthean story line at this point, because they have Jesus leaving Galilee for Judea

---

3. Luke T. Johnson, *The Literary Function of Possessions in Luke-Acts,* SBL Dissertation Series 39 (Missoula, Mont.: Scholars, 1977), 108–9.

4. For a detailed overview of this section's makeup, see Darrell L. Bock, *Luke 9:51–24:53,* BECNT 3B (Grand Rapids: Baker, 1996), 957–64.

(Matt. 19:1–2; Mark 10:1). Luke collects an array of Jesus' teachings characteristic of his ministry in Galilee and Judea and organizes it around the theme
of a divinely directed journey.

159. Jesus Is Rejected by Samaritans (Luke 9:52–56) (Aland §175; Orchard §202; Huck-Greeven §151b)

The journey begins with a mission into Samaria. This region was dis-
liked by Israelites because Samaritans were a mixed race. They were composed of descendants of the ten tribes of northern Israel, which largely had
intermarried with Gentiles after Israel fell to Assyria in 722 B.C. They were
seen as a nation that had compromised its faith (2 Kings 17:30–31; Ezra
4:2). They also established their own cult center at Mt. Gerizim. Many
Judean Jews preferred to travel around Samaria rather than be "defiled" by
going through it.

This scene carries two potential points of significance. First, Jesus is expanding his outreach beyond "pure" Israel, although northern Israelites ethnically were a part of original Israel. Even ethnically mixed Jews were candidates for reform.[5] Second, the disciples probably started with the hope that
things in this region would be different from what they had been in Galilee.

But just as the Galilean ministry began with a note of rejection in Nazareth,
so also this outreach meets with rejection, because "his face was set toward Jerusalem." The people's refusal to receive him met with an instinctive reaction from
the disciples. James and John ask if they should bring fire down from heaven
against the people as Elijah had done (2 Kings 1:10, 12, 14). The disciples still
are thinking exclusively of a kingdom of power and authority. They want to exercise the right of judgment and flex their muscles. But Jesus refuses. The text
notes that he rebuked them but gives no detail. Once again the disciples must
watch, learn, and listen. Their mission moves on, but the need for instruction
continues. Their mission is one of outreach, not of carrying out final judgment.
Disciples gather now. Separation of wheat and chaff comes later.

160. On Following Jesus (Luke 9:57–62; Matt. 8:18–22 [see unit 76 above]) (Aland §176; Orchard §203; Huck-Greeven §152)

The details of this unit were treated earlier. What is important to note
about the context is that Luke presents these challenges about serious commit-

---

5. This is the only example in Luke-Acts in which ministry to the Samaritans has a negative
result or provides an exclusively negative example (cf. Luke 10:33; 17:16; Acts 1:8; 8:1–14, 25;
9:31; 15:3).

ment in discipleship after the note of rejection in Samaria. Association with the kingdom will not mean immediate power and authority over others but service to them and suffering. It is also important that the remarks are made to prospective disciples, not to the inner circle. Any who desire association with Jesus should reflect on his remarks. Luke will keep this theme prominent throughout the journey section by mentioning it again in 14:25–35 and 18:18–30.

Luke has three incidents. The first two are paralleled in Matt. 8:18–22. These are the remarks about the Son of Man having no place to lay his head and the denial of the request to bury one's father. The third, unique incident involves a man who wishes to tell his family farewell before joining Jesus. It elicits a response that the desire to look back makes a potential disciple unfit for the kingdom. To be a disciple worthy of the kingdom means that the old attachments are severed so that one does not long for the old life. The remark about looking back is proverbial. Hesiod (*Works and Days* 442–43) speaks approvingly of "one who will attend his work and drive a straight furrow and is past the age of gaping after his fellows, but will keep his mind on his work." Discipleship requires single-minded dedication and constant commitment with no looking back.

161. Commissioning the Seventy-two (Luke 10:1–16; conceptual: Matt. 9:37–38; 10:7–16; 11:20–24; 10:40; Mark 6:8–11 [see units 86 and 95 above]) (Aland §§177–79; Orchard §§204–5; Huck-Greeven §153)

This text expands the earlier Lukan commission involving the Twelve. Many of the instructions tied to that mission and its description in the Synoptic parallels are repeated here, although only Luke notes the expanded mission. The number sent out is part of a complex text-critical problem that places the number either at seventy or seventy-two, depending on which Greek text reading is accepted as original.[6] They went out with the Twelve, so that the actual number in mission is more than these seventy (or so) newly commissioned representatives. More important than how many are sent is what they are told to do.

As Matt. 9:37–38 noted, the harvest is seen as full. The need is for more laborers. Jesus urges them to pray to the Lord of the harvest for an expansion in the number of workers. It will be dangerous because they will be like lambs

6. For details about this problem, see Bock, *Luke 9:51–24:53*, 1014–16. The problem appears in v. 1 and is duplicated in v. 17. Good arguments exist for each option. The number seventy-two is slightly better attested and may be a slightly harder reading, making it the more likely reading.

among wolves. The instruction about traveling light and moving quickly also is repeated—taking neither bag nor sandals and not stopping to be greeted on the road. They are to stay in the home into which they are received, eat what is set before them, and heal and preach. Their message is "The kingdom of God has come near to you." If they are not welcomed, they are to wipe the dust from their feet and repeat the message that the kingdom has come near. The implication of the rejection is that Sodom will have a more tolerable judgment than the rejecting town. The mission carries both great opportunity and great risk for the towns where the message is preached.

The real danger of rejection is highlighted by the woes on Chorazin, Bethsaida, and Capernaum that follow. Luke has juxtaposed two units here that Matthew has separated by a chapter. The woes are almost verbally identical in the two accounts, suggesting that Luke has brought the units into a tighter relationship. Jesus repeats a common theme: if the events that these towns were seeing had been done in the old era, very sinful places such as Tyre and Sidon would have repented. Rejection of Jesus' obvious work represents real hardness of heart that God will judge. So Tyre and Sidon will have a more tolerable judgment, while Capernaum will be brought down to Hades. Luke's arrangement means that these woes contribute to the tone that the Samaritan mission also raised. Rejection of Jesus takes place, but its ultimate cost is to those who do not respond.

Nonetheless, not everything is negative, even though the stress does remain on the note of rejection. In Luke 10:16, Jesus also notes that the one who hears them also hears Jesus, just as the one who rejects them rejects both Jesus and the one sending Jesus. The doubling of the remark about rejection reveals where the emphasis is. The emphasis also explains why Jesus had stressed in Luke 9:57–62 what discipleship would require. The mission is neither triumphalistic nor a call to health-and-wealth prosperity. Jesus knows the difficulty that the disciples will face. His own earlier ministry had made that evident, as had the work of John the Baptist.

162. The Return of the Seventy-Two (Luke 10:17–20) (Aland §180; Orchard §206; Huck-Greeven §154)

To the disciples, the mission was a wonderful success. What they were most impressed about was their power over the demons; they affirm that "even the demons are subject to us in your name!" The disciples are thrilled to have such power and authority.

Jesus responds in two ways. First, he notes how he saw Satan fall like lightning from heaven. The imagery is from Isa. 14:12, the picture of a king fallen in his arrogance. Here the image indicates Satan's demise, because this activity represents his defeat. The cosmic battle with Satan is on. The work of the disciples points to Jesus' victory. In Judaism, the Messiah's coming would mean the defeat of evil (*1 Enoch* 55.4; *Jubilees* 23.29; *Testament of Simeon* 6.6; *Testament of Judah* 25.3; *Testament of Moses* 10.1).[7] The disciples' ministry, an extension of messianic power and expression of God's work in reversing the elements of the fall, is a significant event. Their power represents a successful invasion against Satan. They are capable of expressions of great authority in overcoming Satan's presence (cf. Acts 28:3–6). The imagery of trampling over snakes has roots in the Old Testament (Deut. 8:15; for the snake imagery in a destructive sense, see Sir. 21:2; 39:30; conceptually, it might recall Gen. 3:15 and the curse, but the vocabulary does not match the LXX). All of this power is impressive. The disciples are thrilled.

Nonetheless, this note of power and victory is not what Jesus wishes them to embrace. Their rejoicing should not focus on the fact that the spirits are subject to them, but that their names are written in the book of life. The greatest blessing is the everlasting relationship they have with God. The book of life is yet another rich image (Exod. 32:32; Ps. 69:28; Isa. 4:3; *1 Enoch* 47.3; 104.1; 108.7; *Jubilees* 5.13–14; 23.32; 30.19–23; 1QM 12.2). The blessing of disciples is their permanent inclusion in the divine census.

163. Jesus' Thanksgiving to the Father, and the Blessed Disciples (Luke 10:21–24; conceptual: Matt. 11:25–27; 13:16–17 [see units 96 and 111 above]) (Aland §181; Orchard §§207–8; Huck-Greeven §§155–56)

The disciples' success launches Jesus into a prayer of thanksgiving for the structure of God's plan. In Matthew, this prayer comes in the context of discussing Jesus' relationship to John the Baptist, as well as treatment of the theme of Israel's rejection of John and him in Galilee. Luke's placement comes in the context of mission alongside the disciples' sense of success. The mission divides people. Rejection is the other half of the mission's equation. There is both reaction against the mission and acceptance of it. The division is between those who feel that they are so self-sustaining that they do not need God ("the wise") and those who sense their dependent place in the creation ("the infants"). Paul uses a similar theme (1 Cor. 1:26–31).

Luke adds a note that Jesus' rejoicing took place "in the Spirit." In form-critical terms, the prayer is a thanksgiving psalm. God is thanked for his choice of hiding these blessings from the wise and revealing them to "infants." The image of the disciple as a simple, dependent child reappears (Luke 9:46–

---

7. For this imagery of the demons, see *Testament of Solomon* 20.16–17.

48). The Son carries out the plan received from the Father. The beneficiaries are those to whom the Son chooses to reveal it. In the midst of the seeming chaos of rejection and acceptance, there is the outworking of an unfolding divine design.

The prayer leads to Jesus' beatitude, offered to the disciples privately. It strikes a major note of continuity about the plan and current events. What they are seeing, though it seems surprising, is what had been longed for by the great ones of old. The disciples are blessed to see what they are seeing. Their experience is what prophets and kings longed to see and hear but did not. The clear implication is that these events, planned as they are, represent the realization of prophetic promise. Luke again strikes the reassuring note of fulfillment that he raised in Luke 1:1–4. What Jesus brings is what God had long promised.

164. The Lawyer's Question and the Good Samaritan
(Luke 10:25–37; conceptual: Matt. 22:34–40; Mark 12:28–34) (Aland §§182–83; Orchard §§209–10; Huck-Greeven §§157–58)

This unit begins a sequence of three Lukan passages that examine various kinds of relationships. This one looks at how one relates to God and others, with the focus being on others. The next unit looks at how one relates to Jesus in the context of a life full of responsibilities (Luke 10:38–42). The final unit, which includes the disciples' prayer, looks at how one approaches God (Luke 11:1–13).

This lawyer's exchange with Jesus comes in two stages. Both scenes are important and belong together.[8] First, as a test, a lawyer asks Jesus what he must do to inherit eternal life. How can he know that he will participate in the resurrection to come? Jesus turns the question around and asks the lawyer for his opinion about what the law teaches. The lawyer does go to the law and juxtaposes Deut. 6:5 from the Shema and Lev. 19:18. Practicing first-century Jews recited the Shema twice a day (*m. Berakot* 1.1–2). Faithful Jews still recite it today. The combination of texts teaches that one should love God totally and one's neighbor as oneself. We do not possess texts in Judaism that juxtapose

8. This observation is important in light of attempts to equate this event and tradition with the exchange in Matt. 22 and Mark 12, which take place in the last week in Jerusalem. This Lukan text appears to be a separate event from that parallel, because this initial exchange sets up the discussion about who is one's neighbor, leading directly into the parable of the good Samaritan. Matthew and Mark lack the parable. If this were one event, and if, as seems likely, Luke knew either Matthew or Mark, then it is hard to explain its placement here. Luke does note several controversies in the last week. Thus, it seems slightly more likely that we have a distinct event in Luke. However, its presence here caused the absence in Luke 20 of a similar controversy in the last week.

these two texts, but the idea that love for one's neighbor was a central point of the law was not new.[9] *Testament of Benjamin* 3.3 speaks of fearing God and loving one's neighbor. In fact, the Ten Commandments are structured in such a way that love for God is followed by a proper treatment of others. Jesus commends the reply as a wonderful summary of the devotion central to possessing life. The New Testament often affirms an ethic where love for God translates into love for one's neighbor or fellow believer (Rom. 13:9; Gal. 5:14; James 2:8; John 13:34–35; 15:9–12; 1 Pet. 2:17).

The lawyer knows his obligation but also wishes to know if the commitment to others is restricted only to some. This limitation would allow him to claim that he had followed the command, leading to self-justification. In fact, with a narrative note, Luke observes that the question about who is one's neighbor was asked in order to allow the lawyer to justify himself. In his view, some obligation existed for those who were neighbors; however, some people could be ignored as "non-neighbors." This type of distinction is what Jesus challenges in the parable of the good Samaritan.

The parable involves the seventeen-mile road from Jerusalem to Jericho, which was notorious for its danger. A man of unidentified race falls among the robbers, is beaten, and is left for dead. A priest and a Levite pass him by, offering no aid. In fact, they use the other side of the road to go by. In contrast, a Samaritan stops out of compassion and takes care of the man. At a literary level, the account slows down here and gives very detailed attention to highlight the Samaritan's action. Every act of kindness is noted: he dresses the victim's wounds, comforts him by anointing the wounds with oil, places him on his animal, takes him to an inn, cares for him, and even leaves money to pay for his stay until he returns. Jesus asks who acted as a neighbor to the wounded man.

The narrative takes a twist at two points. First, Jesus took a question about who is a neighbor and turns it around to tell a story about being a neighbor. The issue is not thinking about who someone else is, but what kind of person I am. In effect, Jesus cuts the premise of classes of people out from the question. Second, he makes a hated Samaritan the example. The statement is that neighbors can come in surprising packages and places. It is likely that the lawyer would have thought of a Samaritan as a non-neighbor. So Jesus has challenged the premise in a second way by making the exemplary neighbor a person whom the questioner would have rejected as a neighbor! In fact, when the lawyer has to answer Jesus' query, he cannot bring himself to say that the Samaritan was the neighbor. Rather, he says that it was "the one who showed mercy on him." The implicit indictment is that the priest and the Levite, who know the law, should

9. Bock, *Luke 9:51–24:53,* 1025–26, 1035–36. Akiba and Hillel, two of the great rabbis of the first and second centuries, are said to have regarded love for one's neighbor as representative of the entire Torah (*Sipra* 200 on Lev. 19:18 [Akiba]; *b. Šabbat* 31[a] [Hillel]).

have stopped and helped. However, the religiously ignorant Samaritan practiced the law better than the clerics did. When Jesus says to the scribe, "Go and do likewise," he is saying, "Do not worry about who is the neighbor; just be one." Love does not figure how to get out of loving; it just loves. In contrast to one who wanted to know what was the minimum to do, Jesus describes a neighbor as one doing whatever is needed to help.

The parable illustrates a fundamental human value of Jesus: all people count and are worthy of respect and care. Although Jesus did go first to Israel, his ministry is such that the worth of every person is affirmed. This is like the "no distinction" between races that shows up in the preaching of Acts 10. It means neither that people are absolved of responsibility for their actions nor that salvation is a privilege of birth. Rather, as Jesus challenged this lawyer, God calls people to be prepared to love every type of person.

165. Mary and Martha (Luke 10:38–42) (Aland §184; Orchard §211; Huck-Greeven §159)

This unit reveals the tensions that often fill life's choices as two siblings respond to Jesus in different ways. Jesus is eating at the home of Martha and Mary. Martha is busy preparing the meal, while Mary is parked at Jesus' feet. The image already is culturally unusual in that the teacher is spending time exclusively with women. The image of Mary seated like a disciple at Jesus' feet also is unusual.

Martha is busy preparing the meal, which would be the more normal activity for a woman in that culture. Luke notes that she was "distracted with much serving." So she asks the Lord to intervene: "Lord, do you not care that my sister has left me to serve alone?" The question is asked with a Greek interrogative that anticipates a positive response. She expects Jesus to act on her behalf. But Jesus declines to intervene. His reply is full of compassion for Martha's anxiety, as seen in Jesus' use of the emotional double vocative of direct address ("Martha, Martha"). This will not be the last time that Jesus refuses a request to intervene (Luke 12:13). The teacher notes that Martha is troubled by many things, so much so that she has become embittered at the different choice her sister has made. As a result, Martha has a poor attitude. In contrast, Mary has made a different choice, and a good one. She sits at Jesus' feet. It is important to note that Jesus does not rebuke Martha for her choice, but for her attitude about her sister's choice. Mary has made a good choice for her own needs. The Greek text at the end of this passage is uncertain as to the better reading. Does it read "One thing is necessary"? Or is the reading "Few things are needed, or one"? Fortunately, the point is essentially the same. Mary's choice to sit at Jesus' feet and learn from him is to be commended, even in the face of daily chores. Mary's choice should be fully affirmed. Martha should not direct her sister and in the process undercut her relationship with her. Relationship to Jesus is worth the time.

166. Teaching the Disciples' Prayer (Luke 11:1–4; conceptual: Matt. 6:9–13 [see unit 55 above]) (Aland §185; Orchard §212; Huck-Greeven §160)

This version of the disciples' prayer is shorter than the one that appears in the Sermon on the Mount. It also comes in a distinct context in which the disciples ask Jesus to teach them to pray as John the Baptist taught his disciples.[10] The details of the prayer were covered in the treatment of the Matthean placement. Luke's version is more compact but also is less figuratively expressed and liturgically influenced, lacking some of the lyrical balance of Matthew's version. Thus, forgiving debts is simply forgiving sins. Luke lacks reference to the Father being in heaven, omits the petition for God's will to be done on earth as it is in heaven, and has no request for deliverance from evil. The prayer expresses the fundamental dependence that a disciple should have on God. It recognizes the intimacy of relationship with God ("Father") and the uniqueness of his person ("Hallowed [or, set apart] be your name"). It looks to the full expression of God's rule ("Your kingdom come"). It expresses an awareness that God provides ("Give us each day our daily bread"). It recognizes a need for forgiveness with an awareness that the disciple also is forgiving ("Forgive us our sins, as we forgive everyone who is indebted to us"). It makes a request to be protected in how God leads ("Lead us not into temptation"). The disciple knows that well-being in life depends on God and prays accordingly so that the heart is directed toward the Father. The prayer expresses dependence on him.

167. The Parable of the Friend with Nerve at Midnight (Luke 11:5–8) (Aland §186; Orchard §213; Huck-Greeven §161)

In continuing to discuss prayer, Jesus sets out a parable that highlights how God should be approached. The example is significant because it is easy to think either that God is too great and preoccupied to be bothered by prayer or that he need not be troubled by requests because he already knows our needs.

10. The differences again raise the tricky and complex question about whether one tradition is here or two distinct events. A set prayer is not unusual in Judaism, so repetition in a distinct event is not improbable. In Luke, Jesus gives the prayer to his disciples, while in Matthew, he presents it to a larger audience.

There is some debate surrounding the parable about whether the two characters represented in it point to God as the example or to someone who makes
a request of God. Does God respond because his honor is at stake? On this
reading, the potential for shame is the issue, because in the first century being
a poor host was a matter of shame. This reading, however, seems to contradict
what Jesus will say about God's graciousness in Luke 11:11–13, a divine attribute that Jesus regards as a given. It is better to see the comparison in the
parable as residing in the gall of the petitioner to ask his neighbor for help,
even at midnight. It looks at the boldness and the nerve that come in the effort
to make the request. The petitioner possesses a focused intensity, as the disciples should have in prayer. The disciple goes to great lengths to make petitions
known to God. Thus, the example emerges from a willingness to go next door
and ask the friend for help at midnight. There was a "shamelessness" (ἀναί-
δεια) to the asking that reflects how the disciple should pray.[11] Here, Jesus exhorts the believer to pursue an engaging relationship with God and not be de-
terred by God's greatness.

168. Encouragement to Pray (Luke 11:9–13; conceptual:
Matt. 7:7–11 [see unit 63 above]) (Aland §187; Orchard §214;
Huck-Greeven §162)

This unit completes Jesus' private teaching on prayer extending back to
Luke 11:1. The unit was treated in detail in the earlier discussion of Matt. 7.
The wording of the Lukan version is a very close match except that the illustrations differ and come in a distinct order: fish-serpent, egg-scorpion (Luke)
versus bread-stone, fish-serpent (Matthew). The point is the same: ask of
God, and he will give what you need, not what is destructive to you. One
other difference is that Matthew speaks of "good things" being given by God,
while Luke mentions the Holy Spirit. Thus, this private teaching appears to
focus on asking about requests for wisdom. The promise is that God will supply such wisdom.

The entire Lukan section emphasizes the need for dependent prayer. Nevertheless, there can be boldness and a faith that God will give what is needed,
especially a provision of the Spirit to enable the believer to live righteously and
boldly in the world. Jesus can mention the Spirit this early in his ministry because the Spirit is the major figure to be provided by the Messiah, as John the
Baptist indicated (Luke 3:15–17). As such, this is not an exclusively postres-

---

11. On this Greek term, see BAGD, 54; BDAG, 63. The term is not so much about persistence, as is often claimed, but rather about "nerve" and "boldness." If Jesus were not giving
permission, it almost would be impudence.

urrection perspective, though the promise does look especially to something made available in the postresurrection setting (Acts 2).

169. The Beelzebul Controversy (Luke 11:14–23; Matt. 12:22–30; Mark 3:22–27 [see unit 104 above]) (Aland §188; Orchard §215; Huck-Greeven §163)

This unit was treated in detail earlier. It summarizes the reaction of the crowds to Jesus. Some attributed his clear exercise of power to Beelzebul, while others wanted to see a heavenly sign, a specific miracle to indicate the end of Satan's kingdom and the presence of God's. In this text comes one of Jesus' most fundamental remarks about the kingdom and its presence. It follows a refutation of the idea that Satan is responsible for Jesus' power, because that would mean that Satan is reversing his own work. Such a reversal would indicate that Satan's house is divided. That conclusion makes no sense. Jesus' acts are not of the destructive character that Satan would perform. In Luke, the key kingdom remark is "If it is by the finger of God that I cast out demons, then the kingdom of God has come upon you." The work of the "finger of God" looks back to the image of God's power like that unleashed in the exodus (Exod. 8:19). Matthew 12:28 refers to work by the Spirit, giving the agent rather than a metaphor. This basic declaration in Luke says that the kingdom is about the cosmic conflict that God has with the forces of evil. Part of the kingdom's work is overcoming Satan's presence and reversing the evil one's labors. The victory is pictured in Jesus' miracles and ministry of power. This note of emerging triumph is reinforced by the parable that follows. Jesus is the stronger one who overtakes the house of the strong man (Satan), dividing the spoil. Victory belongs to Jesus. It comes even now in the glimpse of the reversal of evil that permeates Jesus' work. The rest of Jesus' teaching indicates that what is beginning now will be completed one day (Olivet discourse). Matthew and Mark render the parallel as a "binding" of the strong man, a work that shows that Satan is confined by Jesus' presence. God is invading this world through Jesus to reassert his sovereign presence. Jesus' miracles picture that victory.

170. The Return of the Evil Spirit (Luke 11:24–26; Matt. 12:43–45 [see unit 107 above]) (Aland §189; Orchard §216; Huck-Greeven §164)

Luke appears to have arranged this unit topically to underscore Jesus' declaration of victory over Satan. The details of the unit were treated above. When a person has the opportunity of experiencing God's work, he or she must respond to benefit from his work. In the Lukan context, with the opportunity to experience God's work comes a responsibility. The disciple must understand that the exercise of God's grace, even in an act so dramatic as exorcism, does no good if there is no subsequent response to that grace. So Jesus describes an exorcism that has left the person with an empty house. When nothing has gone into the house in place of the evil spirit, the spirit returns to fill the void and makes matters even worse than before. It brings seven companions to fill the vacuum. Implicit is a warning not to take God's present powerful work through Jesus for granted. Respond. Neutrality is not an option. Either God or the forces of evil will fill the void. Thus, a choice to respond to God's work and embrace it is crucial. Although the text issues a warning, it also issues an implicit exhortation lest the warning apply. The next unit reinforces that connection.

171. True Blessedness (Luke 11:27–28) (Aland §190; Orchard §217; Huck-Greeven §165)

The discussion of conflict and the warning make a woman in the crowd nervous. So she utters a beatitude for Jesus' mother: blessed is the womb that bore him and the breasts that nurtured him. Jesus' response is just as direct. Blessed are those who hear God's word and keep it. If his birth is a reason for blessing, then even more so is responding to him. Jesus would prefer that she dwell not on the blessedness of his birth but on the reason for his coming. Jesus likes to make this point about being responsive to God's word (Luke 8:21; Matt. 7:24 = Luke 6:47).

172. The Sign of Jonah (Luke 11:29–32; Matt. 12:38–42; Mark 8:11–12 [see unit 106 above]) (Aland §191; Orchard §218; Huck-Greeven §166)

This passage was treated above, but the Lukan setting needs attention. Luke makes the point that Jesus rebuked this wicked generation at a time when the crowds were increasing. In other words, Luke highlights the fact that the popularity that Jesus seemed to possess revolved more around curiosity and superficial enjoyment of his work than substance. Jesus rebukes this evil generation for seeking a sign, which in context appears to refer to a heavenly sign and looks back to Luke 11:16. Jesus responds by noting that the only sign he will offer is that of Jonah and Solomon. It is a sign of the divine word. This is what the Son of Man brings. Just as the Queen of Sheba responded to the wisdom of Solomon, and the Ninevites to Jonah's preaching, so now God is asking them to respond to the words of Jesus, who is greater than both. As a result, the people of those responsive generations will rise up against the current generation and condemn it, because they received God's teaching, while this generation has not. The remark not only underscores the issue of Jesus' teaching reflecting God's will, but also introduces one Gentile woman and a set of Gentiles as judges over a predominantly Jewish crowd. This point only adds to Jesus' challenge and rebuke. The Lukan emphasis is on the sign entailed in Jesus' message and action, while Matthew's version also notes Jonah's three days and nights in the belly of the great fish, adding a point about God's supportive miraculous work.

173. On Light (Luke 11:33; conceptual: Matt. 5:15; Mark 4:21; Luke 8:16–18 [see units 45 and 113 above]) (Aland §192; Orchard §219; Huck-Greeven §167a)

The issue of response is raised again in the brief metaphor of the light. It repeats an image already noted, even in Luke (Luke 1:78–79; 8:16–17). The repetition serves to indicate the importance of the idea. The repetition also shows that some teaching is not context specific or limited, but appears in multiple settings and contexts. The image involves the purpose of lighting a lamp. Its function is not to be hid in the cellar or under a bushel basket, but to be placed on the stand. Then those entering a room may benefit from the light. The theme is Jesus' word, which as a word from God is light. Light is intended to be seen and followed as a guide in a previously dark place. Thus, throughout this section of Luke 11:14–36, the point is the need to heed the inbreaking of God's rule as reflected in the presence of his revelatory guidance.

174. The Sound Eye and the Lit Body (Luke 11:34–36; Matt. 6:22–23, in an earlier context [see unit 58 above]) (Aland §193; Orchard §220; Huck-Greeven §167b)

This exhortation reuses the image of the body as light in a context in which the eye is of good quality. This imagery was treated in detail in the earlier unit. One Lukan note is that the image ends on a positive note in contrast to the Matthean use, where the closing remark is on the darkness that comes from an unsound eye and body. The Lukan exhortation is to take care that the light in us is not darkness, but rather to let our bodies be full of light, like a lamp. The disciple is to pay careful attention and be self-accountable for his or her spiritual well-being.

175. Rebuke of the Pharisees and the Lawyers (Luke 11:37–54;
conceptual: Matt. 23:25–26, 6–7, 27–28, 4, 29–32, 34–36, 13; 15:1–9;
Mark 7:1–9) (Aland §194; Orchard §221; Huck-Greeven §168)

The sharpest confrontation in the whole of Luke's Gospel comes in a scene in which a Pharisee invites Jesus to eat with him. The discourse is caused by the Pharisee's reaction to Jesus' omission of the ceremonial washing before the meal (see *m. Yadayim* 1–2). Matthew 15 and Mark 7 noted this lack in Jesus' disciples, but here it is Jesus himself whose behavior is questioned. Also in contrast to those parallels, Jesus addresses what is lacking in his contemporaries, while in Matthew and Mark the issue is to define what truly defiles.

Jesus' rebuke is extensive. First there is a general complaint followed by three woes against the Pharisees and three against the lawyers. Often with the woe comes the recommendation for a corrective action.

The general complaint is that the corruption of the Pharisees is internal, although they keep clean the "outside" of the cup and dish. The allusion to dish cleanliness appears to raise the issue of secondary cleanliness, since utensils were washed to prevent uncleanness from being transferred from a fly to the dish (Lev. 11:31–38; 15:12). The concern here was not for hygiene but for ceremonial uncleanness (*t. Demai* 2.11–12; *t. Berakot* 5.26).[12] Jesus' mention of cups and dishes gets at the whole area of uncleanness, not just at hand washing. For Jesus, what is inside is what counts. With this emphasis, Luke 11 and Matt. 23 make the same point as Matt. 15 and Mark 7.[13] Wickedness and extortion are of greater concern to Jesus than hand washing. The solution is "to give for alms those things that are within." Then cleanliness results. This figurative expression appears to argue that attention should be given to the inner person like an offering made to the needy. It takes the same kind of conscious sacrifice to produce cleanliness.

Three woes follow. The first deals with tithing down to the smallest herbs (see *m. Demai* 2.1; *m. Maᶜaśer Šeni*) while neglecting the justice and love of God. The latter should be done alongside the former. The second deals with pride, as seen in taking the best seats in the synagogue and having special greetings in the marketplaces. Special greetings for such dignitaries appear in the later Jewish text *y. Berakot* 4b. The Jews also warned of such dangers (*Testament of Moses* 7.4). The final woe to the Pharisees accuses them of being like hidden uncleanness because they are like unseen graves that people walk over without realizing it (see Lev. 21:1–4; Num. 19:16). In other words, these leaders were the opposite of the paragons of purity that they thought themselves to be. They not only were failing to lead others to cleanliness, but also were contributing to their defilement.

12. H. Maccoby, "The Washing of Cups," *Journal for the Study of the New Testament* 14 (1982): 3–15.

13. Matt. 23 probably is not the same event as Luke 11. Not only is there a distinct setting, but also there is virtually no overlap in vocabulary, and the order of the woes is quite dissimilar.

These remarks were so strong that a lawyer speaks up in the Pharisees' defense by noting that such a rebuke would apply to the lawyers as well. Apparently, this lawyer thought that this might give Jesus pause, but it did not. Three woes to the lawyers follow.

The charges against the lawyers are just as severe. First, they load down people with burdens and do nothing to help people bear them. Second, they build the tombs of the prophets whom their fathers killed. Jesus is sarcastic here. What they did to honor the prophets, Jesus takes as an act confirming their support of their ancestors' slaying the prophets. Thus, the charge is that they ignore and dishonor the prophets just as much as the murder of them did. It is a form of consenting to the deed. In fact, Jesus, speaking for divine wisdom, predicts that nothing different will follow from God's sending a new round of prophets and commissioned messengers known as apostles. These divine agents will receive the same persecution and rejection from them.[14] So Jesus warns that the blood of all the prophets stretching back from Abel, the first martyr, to Zechariah, the last, will be required of this generation.[15] The final woe is the most devastating for those who prided themselves in accurately dispensing knowledge about God and his will. They have taken away the key of knowledge. They themselves fail to enter, and they block entrance for others. They have accomplished the exact opposite of what they had devoted their ministry to doing.

The reaction to this rebuke is predictable. The leaders now press him to say something that might allow them to get him. The text is very explicit that they were "lying in wait" for him "to catch" him. The terms here (ἐνεδρεύω and θηρεύω) refer to pending attack and hunting for something.[16] Their commitment was to stop him. This confrontation reveals how different Jesus and the leadership were when it came to emphases about religious practices. The woes also show that Jesus' way was a direct challenge to the pious way of life that the Pharisees sought for Israel.

176. The Leaven of the Pharisees (Luke 12:1; Matt. 16:5–6, in an earlier context; Mark 8:14–15, in an earlier context [see unit 140 above]) (Aland §195; Orchard §222; Huck-Greeven §169a)

Jesus issues a warning to his disciples in this context of confrontation and alongside his growing popularity with the crowds. They should watch out to avoid the leaven of the Pharisees, that is, their hypocrisy. This hypocrisy ap-

14. Acts details the initial realization of this prediction.

15. It is not entirely clear whom Jesus alludes to here, but Zechariah the prophet is possible if later tradition is accepted. See S. H. Blank, "The Death of Zechariah in Rabbinic Tradition," *Hebrew Union College Annual* 12–13 (1937–38): 327–46.

16. BAGD, 264, 360; BDAG, 334, 455.

pears to have involved what was just condemned: claiming to be of help to people only to end up leading them astray. The Lukan locale for this unit also is revealing. Not only does it follow immediately after Jesus has launched his most direct attack against the Pharisees' practices, but also it comes amid the noting of how large the crowds were becoming. Hypocrisy normally surfaces when a person seeks approval of others. The large crowds represented a danger that the disciples would court popularity and engage in hypocrisy rather than do what is right and challenge the multitudes where needed in the same way that Jesus had just rightly challenged the leadership. This warning that these leaders did not reflect the right way is something "he began" to say to them here. Thus, this remark was but the first of many like it in tone and emphasis. Jesus continues to distinguish between himself and the leadership.

177. Exhortation to Fearless Confession (Luke 12:2–9; conceptual: Matt. 10:26–33 [see unit 88 above]) (Aland §196; Orchard §223; Huck-Greeven §169b)

Jesus had called the crowds to consider how they were responding. He had rebuked the leadership and warned the disciples not to be hypocritical. So Jesus turns to consider some basic spiritual attitudes, especially fearing God (12:2–12). Disciples should consider whom they are most accountable to as they labor. Jesus begins by noting that nothing is hidden that will not be revealed. What is said in the dark and in private will be revealed in the light and proclaimed from the housetops. The point of this imagery is slightly different from that in Matt. 10, where what Jesus says to them in the dark or whispers will be revealed. In mission the disciples are to be sure to reveal what has been taught. The Matthean context of mission leads to teaching about carrying out that mission responsibly with boldness. The Lukan context focuses on having an awareness that one ultimately is accountable to the sovereign, omniscient God. What takes place in the dark, God will expose one day.

So Jesus warns the disciples that they should fear God, not people. People only can kill the body, but God has the power to cast anyone into Gehenna. It is God's response that should concern them. They also should know that God is concerned for them.[17] Even a group of five sparrows, worth next to nothing at two assaria, is not forgotten before him. An assarion is among the least valuable coins (one-sixteenth of a denarius, or the wage for forty-five minutes' labor; only a lepton, mentioned in the widow's gift at the temple, is smaller). Given that even the hairs on one's head are all numbered, God

17. Matthew speaks of the "Father" throughout this section.

knows what is happening. They should not be fearful about what will take place, even in a context of rejection, for a person is more valuable than a sparrow. Thus, in the midst of accountability to God, Jesus emphasizes that God is aware of what standing up for him will mean for the disciple. The tension between accountability to God and the disciple's value to God is a key component of the disciple's faith and self-understanding. Disciples are to be responsible to a God who cares about them.

The key choice involves identifying with the Son of Man before a hostile world. Those who acknowledge Jesus will be acknowledged by the Son of Man before God's angels; those who deny Jesus will be denied before those angels. Fearing God means acknowledging that Jesus is sent from God. On the surface, the reference to the Son of Man looks as if it could be a reference to a distinct figure of judgment, someone other than Jesus. But it is not. The title is Jesus' indirect way of referring to himself.[18] It resembles the way in which a famous British prime minister, Lady Margaret Thatcher, described herself in her own rhetoric when she would say that "'the Lady' is not for turning." What the text reveals is the authoritative judgment role that Jesus sees for himself one day. It also declares that fearing God means responding to Jesus as an expression of that fear.

178. The Sin against the Holy Spirit (Luke 12:10; conceptual: Matt. 12:31–32; Mark 3:28–30 [see unit 105 above]) (Aland §197; Orchard §224; Huck-Greeven §169c)

Jesus tightens the identification between fearing God and responding to him. To embrace Jesus means responding to the Spirit. Luke's form of this remark is more concise than its parallels. A word against the Son of Man can be forgiven, but blasphemy against the Holy Spirit will not be forgiven. Jesus' point is that this blasphemy is the most serious offense against God's work. It is slander in rejecting the Spirit's testimony, which has come through both word and deed during Jesus' ministry (Luke 4:16–19; 11:20). The contrast is that a word against Jesus can be forgiven, but God will not ignore a settled conviction that rejects the Spirit's testimony for him. Everything that Jesus is saying about himself in this portion of the journey highlights that he is more than a religious teacher of ethics. There is more to Jesus than his ideas about God. There is something about who Jesus is that people must embrace. So Jesus stresses the imperative of responding in personal terms to him and accepting the true witness of God's Spirit about this.

18. The parallel in Matt. 10:31–32 simply uses the first person, "I."

179. The Assistance of the Holy Spirit (Luke 12:11–12; conceptual: Matt. 10:19–20; Mark 13:11; Luke 21:14–15 [see unit 87 above]) (Aland §198; Orchard §225; Huck-Greeven §169d)

Opposition to Jesus will be real and intimidating. Disciples will be brought before synagogues, rulers, and authorities. Rejection must be faced. Still, the disciple should not be anxious about how to reply. The Spirit, who testifies to Jesus, also will witness through the disciple in that very hour, teaching him or her what to say.

This remark has multiple parallels. It shows up in the discourse on mission in Matt. 10 and is reaffirmed in the Olivet discourse in Mark 13:11 and Luke 21:14–15, where Jesus again raises the issue of persecution for those who embrace him. Jesus continues to prepare disciples for what they will face in light of the reaction that Jesus brings. Discipleship means that many in the world will not appreciate one's identification with Jesus. They will act to stop the disciples' testimony of that identification. Yet the Spirit will give enablement to those who seek to acknowledge him. In responding to the Spirit, the disciple shows fear for God, which Jesus will acknowledge one day as Son of Man.

180. Warning against Greed (Luke 12:13–15) (Aland §199; Orchard §226; Huck-Greeven §170a)

Jesus' attention turns to another topic that Luke loves to discuss: possessions. Actually, this unit and the next go together. Luke often sets up a parable with a kind of prediscussion that explains why Jesus addressed the topic. Here, a man comes out of the crowd and asks Jesus to perform a mediating function often sought from a rabbi. He wants Jesus to intercede on his behalf and force his brother to divide their inheritance with him. Jesus refuses to intercede, just as he did with Martha in Luke 10:38–42. The refusal is joined to Jesus' query about who appointed him to be a judge over the man. The reply apparently urges the man to settle his own affairs. But with it comes a warning that something more destructive may be going on. Jesus feared that the issue of possessions would become a barrier between the man and his brother. So he warns the crowd to watch out and beware of covetousness because one's life does not consist in one's belongings. Jesus says to "be on guard with respect to covetousness." The issue is more than merely money; it is a materialism that defines and destroys relationships. For covetousness is desiring what one does not have and that another possesses. Thus, it has not only a material dimension, but also inherently a relational dimension that damages our contacts with others.

181. The Parable of the Rich Fool (Luke 12:16–21) (Aland §200; Orchard §227; Huck-Greeven §170b)

Jesus follows the warning with an illustrative parable. The example is very close to a saying in Sir. 11:18–19. It reads, "One becomes rich through diligence and self-denial, and the reward allotted to him is this: when he says, 'I have found rest, and now I shall feast on my goods!' he does not know how long it will be until he leaves them to others and dies" (NRSV). Jesus takes the imagery one step further by criticizing a life built around possessions alone and presents an instant judgment. A landowner has the good fortune of a bumper crop, so he must plan what to do with the great harvest. What follows is a plan that shows how much personal possession he took of what God had provided for him. Eight times in the space of a few verses the man uses a first-person pronoun or adjective. It is *his* plan and *his* harvest. He will keep it for himself. The problem in the parable is not having the harvest, because that was a gift. Nor was it a problem that he planned; he had to do that. The problem was hoarding it all as "my grain and my goods." He was going to use it for himself (contrast Luke 16:9). God labels his approach as that of a fool. God would make his soul accountable that very day. The goods, stored away as his, are now left behind. God says to him, "The things you have prepared, whose will they be?" One thing is for sure: they do not belong to the man anymore. They have not done him—or anyone else—any good. The concluding point is "So it is with those who lay up treasure for themselves but are not rich toward God." The person who uses what God enables him or her to receive only for self-consumption is a fool before God. That is the danger that covetousness breeds.

182. Do Not Be Anxious (Luke 12:22–32; Matt. 6:25–34 [see unit 60 above]) (Aland §201; Orchard §228; Huck-Greeven §171a)

The flip side of not hoarding possessions and caring only for oneself involves how a person will watch out for life's necessities. So this unit takes up that question. In this context, the point of this imagery, which also appeared in Matt. 6, brings in the additional dimension that God will care for his own, namely, for the disciple who relies on God and not on possessions for security. God can be trusted for these basic needs.

The details of this passage were treated earlier. The Lukan differences involve more references to God, whereas Matthew speaks of the "Father." Only Luke 12:30 and 32 mention the Father. Luke speaks specifically of ravens at first, while Matthew has the generic category of birds. Luke notes the generic category at the end of his example. These ravens, which actually describe a host of Palestinian crows, are unclean creatures (Lev. 11:15; Deut. 14:14). If God cares even for them, surely he will care for disciples. Luke drives home the point about not being anxious by noting that because one cannot add to the length of life by worrying, worry is useless. Finally, Luke ends on the note that the disciple should seek the kingdom, and these other things will be added. The flock need not fear, because God's pleasure is to give them the kingdom. Possessing the kingdom is the only thing that matters. Luke 12 as a whole teaches "Fear God and nothing else. Seek God and no one else."

183. Treasures in Heaven (Luke 12:33–34; Matt. 6:19–21 [see unit 57 above]) (Aland §202; Orchard §229; Huck-Greeven §171b)

This unit gives an application for disciples to show that they are trusting God and not being covetous. One should sell his or her possessions and give alms. Alms already were mentioned by Jesus in the Sermon on the Mount in Matt. 6:1–4. The point there was not to draw attention to one's generosity. Shortly after that discussion, Matt. 6:19–21 appears, a text conceptually parallel to this text in Luke. There, the remarks begin to raise the theme of God and possessions. In Luke, the proverbial remark closes off the discussion. It is the kind of proverbial remark that can appear in a variety of settings.

Generosity sees needs and meets them. There is no sense of "my possessions." Rather, there is a readiness to use resources to serve others. In Luke 19:1–10 Zacchaeus is an example of the wealthy person whose attitude is right. The result of such giving is the storing up of treasure in purses that do not wear out. The allusion is to a merchant's money bag (cf. Luke 10:4).[19] A thief cannot steal nor can a moth destroy such heavenly treasure. The image of the moth shows that what is in view is material possessions and not just money, because the moth destroys nice clothes. Jesus' remarks are directed at the heart to show where the disciple's own attitude stands. The question that this exhortation raises is where one's heart resides. Jesus says that the pursuit of serving people generously places one in pursuit of heavenly treasure. What a person really values determines his or her pursuits. So where the person's treasure is, there also is the heart. Jesus encourages disciples to seek the treasure that lasts, a treasure that comes from relating to others with generous service.

19. BAGD, 130; BDAG, 163.

184. Faithfulness in the Midst of Watchfulness

(Luke 12:35–48; conceptual: Matt. 24:42–51; Mark 13:33–37) (Aland §203; Orchard §§229–32; Huck-Greeven §§172–73)

How does the disciple walk faithfully? One of the reasons that Luke is writing is to reassure Theophilus. This text suggests that Jesus will be away for a time long enough that people may begin to doubt that he will return any time soon. They may become unconcerned about their accountability to him. So Jesus issues a series of exhortations and tells a parable to reinforce the need to remain faithful, even if the absence seems prolonged.

Disciples are to have their loins girded (i.e., be ready to act) and keep their lights burning, like a servant waiting for the return of the master from a wedding feast. Such celebrations could go on for days, so that the time for a return is unclear (Tob. 11:18). Being a disciple involves keeping watch like a servant ready to greet and serve the master upon his return.

Jesus' beatitude is for those disciples who are ready when the Lord returns. In a reversal of the normal pattern, the master promises to gird himself and serve at the table when he returns. There is the reward of rest and fellowship upon the return, even if it comes in the deep watches of the night. The meaning of the second and third watches (literally, "guard") depends on whether a three-watch (Jewish) or four-watch (Roman) time structure is in view, a point that is not clear from Lukan usage, since this is the only Lukan text in which φυλακή is used with this sense. Either way, these watches would be located in the middle of the night. The point is to be ready always, even at those hours when most are not alert and when return is least expected. Do not be careless like a person who leaves a house unprotected. A person who has been warned as to the exact time when a thief might come will be ready only at that time. But the disciple does not know when the Son of Man comes, so he or she always must be ready.

The remarks cause Peter to raise his own questions about the audience. Is this teaching for these disciples or for everyone? There is ambiguity in Peter's question and in Jesus' remarks. Is the "us" a reference to the Twelve or to all disciples? Is "all" a reference to all disciples or to all people? Jesus' answer bypasses the question, just as he did with the lawyer when he told the parable of the good Samaritan. Rather, Jesus calls for faithfulness and discusses the various consequences of the possible responses. A faithful person will have nothing to worry about. Jesus is more concerned with each person's response than with discussing the scope of who is covered by the parable.

The blessed and wise servant is the one "whom, when the master comes, he finds so doing," that is, responding faithfully to what the master has asked. In the parable, this involves caring for the household and making sure that the servants are fed. In contrast to the faithful one stands the wicked servant, who concludes that the master is gone for some time, abuses the servants, and squanders the master's resources on personal partying. This servant does the exact opposite of what the master commanded. The master returns unexpectedly, and the assessment follows. The master will "dismember" this servant, who then will be placed among the "unfaithful" (ἀπίστων). The images are harsh. The servant literally is "cut into pieces" (διχοτομήσει).[20] The picture is of a severe judgment. In the Matthean version, this slave is to be "cut in pieces" and placed with the "hypocrites," where people will weep and gnash their teeth, a Matthean image for judgment and rejection by God.

The subsequent development of the parable in Luke 12:47–48 lacks any parallel with the similitude in Matt. 24:45–51. Luke's account gives two more pictures: one servant who knows the master's will but does not make ready or act accordingly and one who fails out of ignorance. The one with knowledge is severely beaten, while the ignorant servant receives a lighter beating. The key to the parable at a literary level is to contrast the three punishments given: cut in pieces, severe beating, light beating. Three grades of punishment are involved: one that excludes, one that disciplines severely, and one that disciplines less harshly. Thus, the parable teaches types of unfaithfulness: one that contradicts the master, showing complete disdain for his instruction (exclusion); one that fails to obey the master even though knowing his instruction (severe discipline); and one that disobeys the master in ignorance (light discipline). Jesus' point is to be faithful because all are accountable to him for their relationship to him.[21] So Jesus says, "From everyone to whom much is given, much will be required; and from the one to whom much has been entrusted, even more will be demanded." The more a person knows, the more is required, with the standard of accountability being raised according to the increase in one's knowledge. The point is that faithfulness obviates any need to be concerned about a harsh assessment of accountability. So be faithful.

185. Mission: To Bring Division (Luke 12:49–53; conceptual: Matt. 10:34–36; Mark 10:38 [see unit 89 above]) (Aland §204; Orchard §233; Huck-Greeven §174a)

Jesus issues a mission statement that is almost shocking, especially given the way people tend to characterize his ministry today. A similar statement ap-

---

20. BAGD, 200; BDAG, 253.

21. This is another "odd man out" parable in which a figure who appears to be "in" at the start of the parable ends up being excluded. These parables appear to treat those who claim a relationship to Jesus, even do ministry in his name, but fail to have a genuine trust relationship with him, which shows up in their complete lack of response to him. Their presence in the group is one of appearance, not substance. The wicked servant has this role in this parable.

peared at the end of the mission discourse in Matt. 10. In Luke, it appears in the flow of Jesus' ministry, where opposition is a growing reality for him and his disciples.

Jesus' mission is to bring a fire upon the earth. The image is of judgment, a division of humanity. The association of water with judgment is frequent in the Old Testament (Ps. 18:4; Isa. 8:7–8; 30:27–28). It is related to John's prediction that the stronger one to come will baptize with the Spirit and with fire. Part of that baptism entails the judgment that the promised one executes (Luke 3:15–17). In a sense, Jesus wished that this fire already had come. However, it must be preceded by a baptism that he has to experience. This allusion to his death refers to the fate he must meet when he finally gets to Jerusalem, the goal of his journey. He even uses the heavily emotional term συνέχω to describe that he is under duress until it is done.[22] All his emotional energy is directed at accomplishing what God has sent him to do. The experiencing of that baptism is a key component in what must be done.

Jesus is clear that his coming does not mean peace but division. His coming means divided households because of the variety of responses that people make to his presence. Households will split down the middle, some members opposing others. Luke lacks the Matthean younger-to-older progression. The reversal of the image involving an array of familial relationships indicates the variety of possible permutations and makes the comparison more intense than its Old Testament roots. The imagery is from Mic. 7:6 (on this image in Judaism, see *Jubilees* 23.16, 19; *m. Soṭah* 9.15; *4 Ezra* [= 2 Esdras] 6:24). Jesus' teaching does offer an opportunity to join with him. The different choices among family members produce the division. This sorting out of the "heart" is part of what his coming involves (Luke 2:35).

186. Interpreting the Times (Luke 12:54–56; conceptual: Matt. 16:2–3 [see unit 139 above]) (Aland §205; Orchard §234; Huck-Greeven §174b)

Jesus continues to challenge the crowds. He contrasts their perceptiveness about the weather with their blindness about spiritual things. They can sense a storm coming if a cloud shows up in the west, because they know it means moisture approaching from the sea. They also can know that a heat wave will come when the wind blows from the south because that wind comes from the desert. But they are hypocrites when it comes to spiritual things because they cannot interpret the present times based on all the activity that they see springing forth from Jesus' work.

Matthew has a similar remark, using different weather examples, in a context in which the Pharisees and Sadducees ask for a sign. In Matthew, Jesus speaks of not being able to interpret the signs of the times. In both Gospels,

---

22. BAGD, 789 §5; BDAG, 970–71 §5.

there is something tragic and lamentable about this inability to comprehend and appreciate what Jesus is doing. In Luke, the rebuke begins a series of texts in which the issue is either culpability for the lack of response or a warning that time is running short.

187. Agreement with One's Accuser (Luke 12:57–59; conceptual: Matt. 5:25–26 [see unit 47 above]) (Aland §206; Orchard §235; Huck-Greeven §175)

The image of the dispute before the magistrate appeared in the Sermon on the Mount to make the point that it is better to settle anger with a brother or sister than to end up before the magistrate having to pay a debt. Luke's use of the image comes in a separate context and differs in force. Here the point is settling debts with God. Jesus challenges the crowd to determine for themselves what is correct. It is better to settle decisively with an accuser than to face the alternative, which is to end up before a magistrate who can put them in prison, punish them for their debt, and make them pay down to the last coin (a lepton).[23] The image assumes a financial, civil suit, because a πράκτωρ is a financial officer in charge of administrating debt.[24] The remark has two assumptions. First, it assumes that there is guilt on the part of the audience for which they are culpable before the judge. Second, it compares sin to debt, as is often the case (Matt. 18:23–25; Luke 7:41–43; 11:2–3). Sin, if it is not settled with God, will be punished. There is one dimension of the illustration that differs from the point. If there is judgment, there is no prospect for release. The point of making payment is that one will be held fully responsible for the debt, not that release from judgment is possible once one gets there. The application here is personal, not a corporate challenge to Israel. The context, both before and after, is of individual response. The corporate warning to Israel comes in the vineyard image of Luke 13:6–9.

188. A Question about Sin and the Parable of the Unfruitful Fig Tree in the Vineyard (Luke 13:1–9) (Aland §207; Orchard §§236–37; Huck-Greeven §176)

The topic of sin and debt leads the crowd to ask some questions of its own. Two incidents are raised. In the first, Pilate, who could be ruthless in his en-

---

23. The Greek infinitive ἀπηλλάχθαι ("to settle") is in the perfect tense, indicating that a fixed settlement is the goal. A lepton is an ancient coin worth about 1/128 of a denarius, about six minutes' basic wage for the average worker (see BAGD, 472 §2; BDAG, 592 §2).
24. BAGD, 697; BDAG, 859.

forcement of law and order, had slain some Galileans as they had brought sacrifices.[25] In the second, a tower at Siloam had fallen, killing eighteen. Both instances resulted in premature death, even though one was caused by political events and the other was a random event. For both events, the question was the same: were those killed worse sinners than others? In both cases Jesus' reply also is the same: "No; but unless you repent you will all likewise perish."

The effect of Jesus' reply is that he refuses to engage in comparison and places the responsibility to set things right with every sinner. In fact, the reply argues that everyone is culpable and needs to repent. Furthermore, it makes the point that the timing of death is not the major concern. Rather, everyone should come to grips with death's inevitability and what death represents—the presence of sin. Repentance will not prevent death, but it can alter its consequences. This is the major point. So each person had better be assured that repentance has taken place, or else real, eternal punishment will consume that person. In that case, how a person dies or how soon will be irrelevant.

Once again Jesus has taken a question and turned it around to a different angle. He did this with the lawyer in telling about the good Samaritan. He did it in replying to Martha about Mary. He did it to the man who asked Jesus to settle his inheritance dispute. In each case, the burden of the remark was to alter the perspective of the ones who had raised the question and had assumed themselves to be in the right or in the better position.

Jesus closes this series of texts on culpability by telling a "national" parable about Israel.[26] Israel is compared to an unfruitful fig tree in a vineyard. For three years it had failed to produce fruit, which meant that the tree was six years old, because normally it took three years for a tree to gain sufficient maturity to bear fruit. The master now wants to cut the worthless tree down because it only takes up space and uses the ground's resources for no purpose. The vinedresser appeals for one more year. If the tree bears fruit, then all is well. If not, then it can be cut down. The Greek here is important. The possibility of its bearing fruit is expressed as a class three condition, while the likelihood of its not bearing fruit is in a class one condition. The point is that the probability of the tree's not bearing fruit is presented more vividly as the more likely result. Nevertheless, the request is made. Jesus' point is that the nation's record involves a consistent failure to bring forth what God desired. The time allowed before God performs judgment is running out. Jesus' presence is their only chance. God is long-suffering, but they have to respond. So this series of texts, extending back to Luke 12:54, challenges the crowd to respond to Jesus and warns them that consequences follow for failure to do so. In the Lukan

---

25. Although Josephus narrates many events of this type, this particular incident does not appear in his histories. See *Ant.* 13.13.5 §372; 17.9.3 §§213–218; 18.3.1–2 §§55–62; 18.4.1–2 §§85–89.

26. On vineyard imagery and Israel, see Isa. 5:1–7; Mic. 7:1.

sequence of the journey, the question becomes how the crowd will respond. The events to follow answer the question.

189. Sabbath Healing of a Crippled Woman (Luke 13:10–17)
(Aland §208; Orchard §238; Huck-Greeven §177)

Luke introduces a miracle that is similar to earlier acts in Jesus' ministry. The repetition is important, because Luke has just told a parable that gives the nation one more chance. The question is whether this additional opportunity will change anything about the response. The miracle is the first indication that nothing will change. A woman has suffered for eighteen years from a spirit-induced condition of being bent over. The combination of evil spirit and malady is not unexpected in Judaism (1QapGen 20.16–29). Jesus initiates the healing and declares her healed. His "Sabbath labor" consists of his announcement and the laying on of hands. Her ability to straighten up indicates her immediate healing.

The reaction of the synagogue leader is to complain because "there are six days on which it is necessary to work." The healing should occur on one of those days. Jesus responds by calling the leader a hypocrite, noting that if an animal such as an ox or donkey were in distress on the Sabbath, one would rescue it or lead it to water. The Mishnah discusses such rules about feeding, handling, and rescuing animals on the Sabbath (*m. Šabbat* 5; 15.2; *m. 'Erubin* 2.1–4). So on a day set aside to honor God, it is especially appropriate that a daughter of Abraham be freed from Satan's binding power. Jesus' remarks divide the crowd from the leaders and their followers, as the opponents are shamed and the crowds are delighted at the "wonderful things" that Jesus was doing. The leadership had learned nothing from God's activity or Jesus' teaching. They are not taking advantage of their additional chance.

190. The Parable of the Mustard Seed (Luke 13:18–19;
Matt. 13:31–32; Mark 4:30–32, in an earlier context [see unit 116 above]) (Aland §209; Orchard §239; Huck-Greeven §178a)

Jesus' use of parables and his teaching on the kingdom were characteristic of his ministry, so it is no surprise that Luke notes some kingdom miracles here that Mark 4 and Matt. 13 treated in one locale. Luke's earlier kingdom parable, the seed on various soils, appeared in Luke 8:1–15. The mustard seed is one of those parables that was covered in detail earlier. A small seed grows into a tree large enough for birds to find shelter. The imagery probably has roots in Ezek. 17:22–24. The parable primarily stresses the contrast between the kingdom's insignificant start and its massive and protective finish. Do not be deceived. The kingdom may look unimportant at its start, but it will become so large and powerful that it will be a place of shelter. The placement in Luke reaffirms the plan even in the midst of the continuing opposition. Even amid this violent opposition, the kingdom *will* grow to maturity.

191. The Parable of the Leaven (Luke 13:20–21; Matt. 13:33, in an earlier context [see unit 117 above]) (Aland §210; Orchard §240; Huck-Greeven §178b)

The leaven image makes a point similar to that of the mustard seed. What begins as insignificant becomes a comprehensive presence. The woman works with about fifty pounds of flour. She places only a bit of leaven in it. However, eventually that leaven permeates the entire mass. This penetration is inevitable. Telling such a parable at this time reassures those around Jesus that even though it might appear impossible that such a small start could signal the arrival of God's grand kingdom, it is the way God has designed his plan. As such, these parables are a note of hope as well. The kingdom will show its comprehensive presence one day.

192. Exclusion from the Kingdom (Luke 13:22–30; conceptual: Matt. 7:13–14, 22–23; 8:11–12; 19:30) (Aland §211; Orchard §241; Huck-Greeven §179)

Luke notes the journey motif again (cf. 9:51). Jesus' many warnings provoke a question from the crowd: "Will the saved be few?" Jesus compares entry into salvation to striving to walk through a narrow door that many will seek to enter and fail to do so. It takes a concentrated effort to enter. It takes listening and responding in coming to know him. He warns the crowd that many will stand outside the shut door asking to come in, but it will be too late. Their request to open the door is refused, as Jesus explains to them, "I do not know where you are from." Entry is not automatic. The rejected will claim to have had table fellowship with Jesus and to have seen him teach. But again the overture is refused. The Lord repeats that he does not know them, tells them to depart, and calls them workers of unrighteousness. It will be a sad day, with weeping and gnashing of teeth. The image is of rejection. The patriarchs and the prophets will be there in the kingdom, but "you" are all cast out. The teaching is a warning to the Jewish crowd that has not responded to him. People will come from every direction and sit at the table, so the last are first and the first last. The remark is the reverse of much Jewish expectation (1QSa 2.11–22; *1 Enoch* 62.14; *2 Enoch* 45.2; *2 Baruch* 30.4; *m. ʾAbot* 3.17). Once again Jesus turns the question around. The question for those in the nation is not "Will the saved be few?" but "Will it include you?" The contrast of the text shows Jesus' continual warning to those in Israel. Many people from every part of the earth will fill the kingdom, but the tragedy will be the many of the nation who missed the call despite being first in line for blessing. Abrahamic descent does not mean salvation (Luke 3:8; Rom. 9:4–6).

Various themes present here are scattered throughout Matthew in distinct contexts. Jesus' remark about not knowing some is made to people who claimed to minister in Jesus' name (Matt. 7:21–23). When Jesus commends the centurion, it is one example of the many from other nations who will be at the table while "heirs of the kingdom" are cast out (Matt. 8:5–13). The remark on the first/last reversal shows its proverbial quality by its application to the rich being last, while those who had nothing and sacrificed their possessions for Jesus are first (Matt. 19:30).

193. A Warning to Herod (Luke 13:31–33) (Aland §212; Orchard §242; Huck-Greeven §180)

Some Pharisees express concern that Herod wants to kill Jesus. They advise Jesus to leave. It is debated whether the warning is sincere or not. The text does not say. When they tell Jesus, he refuses to leave. Jesus will cast out demons and heal for a short time, and then he will complete his task. The time frame is figuratively expressed as three days. Nothing will deflect Jesus from his mission, because a prophet must perish in Jerusalem. Jesus understands where his ministry will take him. He will complete his path of suffering. In effect, Luke notes again that Jesus has set his face to go to Jerusalem.

194. The Lament over Jerusalem (Luke 13:34–35; conceptual: Matt. 23:37–39) (Aland §213; Orchard §243; Huck-Greeven §181)

Jesus' suffering, while painful for him, will have even sadder consequences for the nation. Jesus speaks to Israel using the first person for God. He addresses the nation through its capital in an emotional double vocative ("Jerusalem, Jerusalem"). The city's history, as Deuteronomy warned and the prophets have shown, is to kill and stone the messengers sent to it (Deut. 28–32; Hosea; Ezek. 16). Numerous times God wished to protect Jerusalem by gathering the city under his wings, but it was not willing. God as a protective bird is a common Jewish figure (Deut. 32:11; Ps. 17:8; Isa. 31:5; *2 Baruch* 41.3–4). Jesus applies the figure here to show God's desire to care tenderly for Israel, if they will come.

So Israel is in peril. Their house stands forsaken (cf. Jer. 12:7; 22:5). The judgment warned about in Luke 13:6–9 is taking place. They will not see the Lord in promised blessing until they as a nation acknowledge, "Blessed is the one who comes in the name of the Lord." This passage is from Ps. 118:26. They are to recognize and welcome the one whom God has sent. Until then, judgment is Israel's fate. The possibility of a future day for Israel that does not involve judgment is left open, if they will respond.

In a later denunciation in Jerusalem, Jesus utters nearly identical words (Matt. 23:37–39). There, the denunciation concludes the woes against the Pharisees. Israel's leadership has led the nation astray.

195. The Healing of the Man with Dropsy (Luke 14:1–6)
(Aland §214; Orchard §244; Huck-Greeven §182)

Jesus has warned Israel of rejection. He has continued to minister to Israel. Now that he has declared judgment on the nation, will he continue that ministry? The answer surfaces in yet another meal scene in Luke 14:1–24. Jesus again is at the house of a synagogue ruler who is a Pharisee. It is the Sabbath. A man with a case of dropsy is before him. In all likelihood, he is there to test Jesus, because the text says that they (probably the Pharisees) were "watching" him. This phrase refers to an almost leering eye. Jesus does not hesitate to reach out. He asks if it is lawful to heal on the Sabbath or not. Their silence allows him to proceed. Once again he heals, mirroring earlier Sabbath healings (Luke 6:6–11; 13:10–17; Matt. 12:9–14; Mark 3:1–6). Once more Jesus illustrates the healing with an example of a son or ox falling into a well and being rescued on the Sabbath. At Qumran, a distinction would be made. A person could be rescued; an animal could not be (CD 11.13–17). The illustration likewise meets with silence. Luke suggests that they were unable to reply. Tragically, the leadership has learned nothing from past events.

196. Teaching on Humility (Luke 14:7–14) (Aland §215;
Orchard §§245–46; Huck-Greeven §183)

The failure of the leaders to entrap Jesus was not their only problem. They also continued to face his rebuke of their spiritual choices. Jesus challenged their pride with a parable that came in reaction to seeking the seats of honor. He urges them not to take the seat of honor lest a more eminent person be given that seat by the host. It is better first to go to the last seat and then be asked by the host to sit in a higher position. Genuine honor is to receive honor from others. In sum, it is better for others to recognize you than for you to bring honor to yourself. Those who exalt themselves are humbled, but the humble are exalted. Luke has noted such reversal before (1:52–53; 6:21, 25; 10:15; 18:14).

Not only does Jesus challenge pride, but also he makes a note about to whom one should show hospitality (and thus, culturally, acceptance). Do not invite friends and relatives, who can return the favor of the hospitality. Rather, invite the marginalized: the poor, crippled, lame, and blind. The list recalls Luke 6:20 and parallels 7:22 conceptually. It also anticipates 14:21. The blessing comes in the fact that there is no reciprocal relationship. The hosting is purely an act of kindness that God will honor in the resurrection (2 Macc. 7:1–19, 30–38 treats the resurrection for those who follow the law). The point is that God honors those who are kind in giving to others. By doing so, they model the kind of sacrificial and unconditional love that God shows to people.

197. The Parable of the Great Supper (Luke 14:15–24;
Matt. 22:1–14, in a later context) (Aland §216; Orchard §247; Huck-Greeven §184)

Jesus' warnings made some listeners nervous. So one of those at the table offered a note of encouragement. He raised the issue of the approaching blessing for those who will eat bread in the kingdom. In all likelihood, he was saying that it will be great when blessing one day comes to all those present. The image is the fellowship at the banquet table of God in the end (see Isa. 25:6; Ps. 22:26). Jesus responds with yet another parable about a banquet. He challenges the optimistic assumption of the remark. The custom for a banquet was to send out invitations and get an initial commitment to come before sending a servant out on the day to inform the guests that it is time to come (Esth. 6:14; Philo, *On the Creation* 25 §78). In each of three cases (field buyer, oxen buyer, groom) there is a cancellation when the party is announced. Two excuses are economic (bought a field or oxen). In one case it is a new marriage. Other things have become more important. But the party is not postponed. The point is important. The promise of God is not postponed. It comes now with Jesus. Blessing will find its patrons elsewhere. The owner is angry but decides to invite others. So the poor, maimed, blind, and lame are invited (see 14:13). They come; yet room remains. So the servant is sent even to the hedges and highways to extend invitations so that the house will be full. This pictures the expansion of blessing outside the bounds of the fringe of Israel. The story concludes with the note that none of those originally invited will share in the meal. So the decision made now not to respond will prevent one from having a future place at the table.

The parable reinforces the note of judgment and exclusion that comes from failing to respond to Jesus' invitation to share in the blessing. It has been an important theme in Luke 13–14. In effect, the one seeking to encourage should not assume that the places at the banquet table are reserved for those present at this party. Blessing is not a right but a gift, and it is received by responding to God's invitation when he offers it. Jesus warns again that an opportunity is being lost.

198. Conditions of Discipleship (Luke 14:25–33; conceptual: Matt. 10:37–38 [see unit 90 above]) (Aland §217; Orchard §§248–49; Huck-Greeven §185a)

Jesus speaks to the crowds and makes it clear to all what discipleship requires. It demands a total commitment, even in the face of opposition like that being raised against Jesus. He is honestly setting forth the demands of what it means to walk after him. The topic is not addressed in terms of what the "minimum" is, but in terms of the priority that discipleship is. Nothing else comes first, neither fields, oxen, nor marriage, as 14:15–24 showed. It requires "hating" father, mother, wife, children, brothers, sisters, and even one's own life. Here "hate" is a rhetorical term. It means that a person's loyalty to following Jesus has priority over family or acceptance by them. In a context of opposition and rejection, it means that a person will not even be drawn to Jesus if he or she wishes to have family acceptance. Those who come to Jesus should understand that family may well reject a person's choice for Jesus. So those who "love" family will not opt to respond to Jesus. Discipleship means "bearing a cross," accepting the suffering and rejection that Jesus faces (see Luke 9:23–24). Without such a total commitment, discipleship is not possible. The teaching using family and cross appeared earlier, in Matt. 10:37–38, in a context in which mission and opposition were treated.

Two examples follow. They make slightly different points. The first example involves a man who plans to build a watchtower that protects a vineyard or a home. However, he does not assess the cost. So he starts it but does not finish. The result is that others mock his lack of foresight and preparation. The effort was a waste. Discipleship takes preparation for going the distance, including realizing what one is getting into by responding to Jesus. The second example involves one king assessing going to war against a king who has more troops. It is better to seek peace than pursue a war that cannot be won. Here the point is that it is better to settle with God, who is more powerful, than to go to war against him. So opting for discipleship is better than the alternative.

The unit closes with an application: "So whoever does not renounce all possessions cannot be my disciple." Discipleship, to be accomplished, requires everything, even a renunciation of possessions. To follow Jesus and learn from him means that nothing else has more "pull" on the follower. Luke 14:26 made a similar point but with a different kind of earthly attachment (family and self). A person's greatest possession becomes following Christ.

Jesus presents responding to him as a package, rather than in stages. He wants prospective followers to know what is involved in following him before they enter in. It is clear that Jesus is teaching the crowds here who do not yet embrace him. He wants them to appreciate what a decision for him will involve. Knowing the call of God as one enters it makes for better responsiveness when times get tough and the world's rejection comes.

199. The Parable of Salt (Luke 14:34–35; conceptual: Matt. 5:13; Mark 9:49–50 [see units 44 and 152 above]) (Aland §218; Orchard §250; Huck-Greeven §185b)

An illustration closes the teaching on discipleship. The picture is of salt. The image here is like that in Matt. 5:13. Salt was used as a catalyst for burning fuel, as a preservative, and as fertilizer. In the Lukan context, with its reference to land and the dunghill, the use looks to its role as fertilizer or preservative. However, once salt loses its saltiness, it becomes useless and is cast out. Jesus warns that the one who has ears should hear. Jesus' teaching is something to respond to profitably while one has the opportunity to be useful. Failure to hear and be useful brings the risk of being cast aside. In this context, it is the call to discipleship that needs attention. To those in the nation, the warning is to respond or to be cast aside. The use of this imagery in Matt. 5:13 is close to its use here, while Mark 9:49–50 is discussing people being "salted" by being at peace with each other. There, salt refers to a particular valuable quality, being a peacemaker.

200. The Parable of the Lost Sheep (Luke 15:1–7; conceptual: Matt. 18:12–14 [see unit 153 above]) (Aland §219; Orchard §251; Huck-Greeven §186a)

The Pharisees and the scribes continue to murmur about Jesus' relationships (see Luke 5:27–32; 7:36–50). They do not like that Jesus eats with sinners. Jesus presents a set of parables that highlight why he seeks sinners.[27] The first picture is of a shepherd of modest means who loses one sheep out of a hundred. Modest flocks had about two hundred sheep (Gen. 32:14; *t. Baba Qamma* 6.20 treats three hundred as a large flock). Since his responsibility is to care for the sheep, the shepherd leaves the ninety-nine to seek out the lost animal. His recovery of the one sheep brings intense joy. He places it on his shoulders, calls his friends and neighbors together, and asks them to share in the celebration and joy of having found the sheep (cf. Isa. 40:11; 49:22). Jesus' application is that there is more joy over one sinner who repents than over ninety-nine righteous who need no repentance. In other words, God is pleased with the righteous, but he is even more pleased to recover one who is lost. So Jesus' priority is to pursue the lost.

201. The Parable of the Lost Coin (Luke 15:8–10) (Aland §220; Orchard §252; Huck-Greeven §186b)

The second illustration is like the first. The picture involves silver coins, probably drachmas; each was equal to a denarius in value. It was not much money; a single coin was an average day's wage for a worker. Jesus pictures a woman who looks for such a modest coin. His example is introduced by a Greek interrogative expecting a positive reply. She will look for the coin. Jesus notes her diligent search. Her joy at finding the coin is passed on to her neighbors. This is like the angelic joy over one sinner who repents.

202. The Parable of the Prodigal Son (Luke 15:11–32) (Aland §221; Orchard §253; Huck-Greeven §187)

Jesus' third parable about why he associates with sinners is much more detailed. This passage is known as the parable of the prodigal son, but really it is about the compassionate father, because his reaction to events is key to all that happens from start to finish. It begins with a son requesting his inheritance prematurely. This is something that Jewish wisdom said a father should not do. Sirach 33:20 reads, "To son or wife, to brother or friend, do not give power over yourself, as long as you live; and do not give your property to another, in case you change your mind and must ask for it." If Jewish law is in view, then the elder son would have two-thirds and the younger son one-third (Deut. 21:17). The request is somewhat of an insult because it suggests that the son wishes to have nothing to do with his family. The fa-

---

27. The context in Matt. 18 is very different. There, the image illustrates pursuing the recovery of a lost brother or sister among disciples.

ther kindly grants the request. The detail pictures how God often lets us go our own way.

The younger son travels to a far country and squanders his resources irresponsibly on "loose living." His situation becomes worse when famine arises, leaving him in great need. He ends up tending swine, which in this Jewish context is a disgraceful job because it left him tending unclean animals. What is worse is that they were eating better than he was.

It dawns on the son that his father's servants have it better than he does. So he decides to return. Humbly, he will ask only to be treated like a slave. Though it is debated, this depicts the son's repentance. He admits his failure and longs to return. His willingness to assume a nonfamilial status shows that he understands that he is owed nothing and that he has made himself an outcast by his choices.

As he returns, the father spots him and, against the custom, runs out to greet him, "hanging on his neck" and greeting him with a kiss.[28] It is the father's compassion that motivates the father's reaction throughout the parable. The son launches into his apology and confession, but the father will have none of it. Instead, he instructs that a robe, ring, and shoes be brought. In addition, a grand celebration, complete with a fatted calf, is planned. The father's explanation is, "My son was dead, and is alive again; he was lost, and is found." The son is welcomed back into the home as if nothing had happened. The event pictures God's compassionate grace and acceptance of the sinner who returns.

The elder brother discovers the new reality when he returns from the field. He hears the celebration. A servant explains to him the partying, and the elder brother becomes angry. In a beautiful literary use of space, the elder brother is now outside, while the younger brother is inside with the father, who now ventures out to talk with his discontented son. The son's complaint is typical of sibling rivalry. What is happening, the elder argues, is not fair. It ignores his years of faithful service and obedience. Never has the father granted him a celebration, even with a kid, much less a fatted calf. But it has been done now for "this son of yours." The kinship with his brother is no longer in play for the elder, who apparently simply wants to regard him as dead. The father explains that nothing about the elder's status has changed in the midst of the exercise of the father's compassion for his brother. Note how the father points to the sibling relationship in the reply. The response was fitting because what had been lost now was found. The father argues that the son should be accepted back because it was the reversal of a "death." The parable ends in an open-ended manner, with the elder brother and the audience left to consider

28. In this honor-and-shame culture, the father was under no obligation to welcome the son. In fact, it would be expected that the son apologize before the father would respond. Even then, the father need not act.

what to do next (or what should be done). Jesus' point is that sinners should be pursued like lost sheep or coins. They should be welcomed back upon return, not shunned, since their return represents a recovery from death that deserves celebration. To simply cast aside sinners, as the grumbling leadership is doing, is not right. Rather, sinners should be sought out. They also should be waited upon, so that if they return, they are embraced.

203. The Parable of the Unjust Steward (Luke 16:1–9)
(Aland §222; Orchard §254a; Huck-Greeven §188a)

Jesus' attention now turns to stewardship. He tells a story about a dishonest steward. Scholars debate the nature of his "unrighteousness." Does Jesus argue that the steward was unrighteous not only when he worked for his master but also when he lowered the bill of the master's debtors on collecting the bills a final time? This is the traditional view of this parable.[29] Or is the point that he was unrighteous, but when he was told that he would be let go, he reacted wisely but still honestly by removing his commission? The result was that those old clients would be pleased with him and become understanding toward him when he lost his position. He also did not cheat his master. This is a more recent view.[30] Either of these readings might be correct, although the commission view has the advantage of making Jesus' point not turn on an unethical act. Even more likely, however, is that the reduction of the debt, whatever its motive, involved the steward reclaiming honor for the owner while showing himself to be a competent steward in a society where honor and shame meant much.[31] Though the move cost the owner in the short run, the goodwill that the reduction brought would bode well for both the owner's and the steward's relationships in the future. Either way, the parable's point is the same. The steward looked ahead and thought through the impact of his actions.

So Jesus' story involves a steward who squandered his master's goods and faces being released. When he does the books the final time, the steward, contemplating his release and not wanting to dig or beg, reduces the clients' bills by 20 to 50 percent. The parable ends with the master commending the "unrighteous" steward for his shrewdness. The point made from the parable is that those in the world are more shrewd with their own generation than God's children are. The implication

---

29. Dennis Ireland, *Stewardship and the Kingdom of God: An Historical, Exegetical, and Contextual Study of the Parable of the Unjust Steward in Luke 16:1–13,* Novum Testamentum Supplement 70 (Leiden: Brill, 1992).

30. Bock, *Luke 9:51–24:53,* 1337–40.

31. For this view, see David Landry and Ben May, "Honor Restored: New Light on the Parable of the Prudent Steward (Luke 16:1–8a)," *Journal of Biblical Literature* 119, no. 2 (2000): 287–309.

is that God's children should be more intentional about how they pursue life. In particular, they should use "unrighteous mammon" (that is, possessions, not just money) in a way that makes friends. They should be generous, like the unjust steward was in his dilemma. This sort of kindness will allow "them" to receive those who practice it into eternal habitations. The "them" alludes to the angels, as a picture of heaven's acceptance. Jesus' point is that possessions are not to be hoarded for the self but used for the benefit of others.

204. On Faithfulness in What Is Least (Luke 16:10–12)
(Aland §223; Orchard §254b; Huck-Greeven §188b)

This unit is the first of two that deal with implications from Jesus' parable of the unjust steward. Jesus' point is that how one handles little things shows how he or she will handle larger things. If possessions are not handled well, with their potential to produce unrighteousness, then how will one handle true riches? Why would someone entrust another with larger commitments if small ones are handled poorly? If a person cannot handle another's matters well, why would that person ever be given something of his or her own? Jesus is discussing the handing out of unspecified responsibility in the eschaton (cf. 1 Cor. 6:2; 2 Cor. 5:10). This appears to be one of the areas where the issue of heavenly rewards applies. The disciple's current life is a stewardship in preparation for that life. Roles then are determined by practice now.

205. On Serving Two Masters (Luke 16:13; conceptual: Matt. 6:24)
(Aland §224; Orchard §255; Huck-Greeven §188c)

In effect, each person has a choice about what will guide his or her life. Ultimately, a person gives greater devotion either to God or to possessions. Two masters cannot share the allegiance of one person. Either possessions or God will gain the loyalty when a choice is required. People should give priority to God and be generous with resources, as the parable has suggested. Jesus made a similar point in the Sermon on the Mount.

206. The Pharisees Reproved (Luke 16:14–15) (Aland §225;
Orchard §256; Huck-Greeven §189)

Jesus' teaching on possessions met with skepticism from the Pharisees. They scoffed at him (literally, "turned their noses up at him"). Luke explains with a narrative note that they were lovers of money. Scribes had this reputation among the Jews, and even Jewish teaching warned of this danger (*1 Enoch* 102.9–10; *Testament of Moses* 7.3; *t. Menaḥot* 13.22). Aware of their attitude, Jesus challenges the leadership's approach and notes that they justify their action before people, but God knows their hearts. Jesus adds the warning that what people exalt is an abomination in God's sight. An abomination is something God detests.[32] Jesus is challenging the Pharisees' pride, since it places them above criticism and causes them to value things that God does not. Jesus' challenge to repent is falling on deaf ears. The rebuke has a prophetic tone (cf. Hos. 6:6; Mic. 6:6–8). Regardless of the Pharisees' popularity or current power, the assessment that counts is the one from God.

207. On Jesus' Kingdom Preaching and Ethical Standards
(Luke 16:16–18; conceptual: Matt. 11:12–13; 5:18, 32 [see units 94, 46, and 49 above]) (Aland §§226–27; Orchard §§257–59; Huck-Greeven §190)

In the midst of Jesus' challenge to the leadership, a question might arise whether Jesus was being "loose" and "unfaithful" to the law. This unit affirms that what Jesus is doing is in line with God's plan and represents the completion of what the law was. It presents a standard twofold division of the divine plan. The law and the prophets extend until John. His ministry marks the transition into the new era, in which the good news of the kingdom is preached. A similar sense emerges from the portrait of John and Jesus in Luke 1 and from 7:28.

The next portion of the passage is difficult. The meaning hinges on the interpretation of the Greek verb βιάζεται. Is it saying, in the middle voice, that people "enter" the kingdom "forcibly themselves" or, in the passive voice, that they "are brought in violently"? If this is the sense, then the point is the conflict and opposition that have accompanied the kingdom's announcement. This is the sense of the verb in Matt. 11:12–13. Or rather, does the verb carry a nuance of "insistence," so that the idea is that people are "urged insistently" to come in?[33] The point here would be a comment about the preaching. Although either the "conflict" or the "insistence" sense is possible, a reference to preaching is the more contextually natural. Any of the meanings makes the point that the message of the kingdom is a key to Jesus' ministry and is part of the current dimension of God's plan.

None of what Jesus brings represents a change in the law's role in terms of promise. Nor does it mean that Jesus' ethical call is less than what the law expects. So the hyperbole is that it is easier for heaven and earth to pass away

32. BAGD, 137; BDAG, 172.
33. For details of this discussion, see Bock, *Luke 9:51–24:53*, 1351–54.

than for one point of the law to become void. The "point" figuratively refers to the small strokes used in the Hebrew alphabet. Thus, whatever kingdom preaching represents, it does not mean that the law has been neglected. So the kingdom preaching as a part of the plan correlates with the law's validity, although how this works is not specified. Jesus' coming does not undercut the law with respect to promise or righteousness. He completes the promise that the law anticipates and calls for a righteousness that the law strove to produce.

An example of this commitment is the seemingly arbitrary reference to divorce. Jesus' example shows that his coming and teaching do not alter the ethical demands involved in a commitment such as marriage. Rather, such demands may be heightened. Thus, the divorce remark illustrates the point about the law. Jesus' point is that divorce (with its assumed remarriage) produces adultery, as does marrying a divorced woman. The point is about the integrity of one's vows. A marriage vow is a commitment before God, which an earthly divorce does not alter. The remark appears also in Matt. 19:9 and Mark 10:11–12. Matthew has the much-discussed exception clause for πορ-νεία (sexual immorality). Luke lacks any such qualification in the remarks. Luke's brief citing of a general principle is not designed to be a detailed treatise on marriage and divorce. The example is about having integrity, especially in a vow involving marriage. Nothing about Jesus' preaching of the kingdom is "loose" morally, as the example shows.

208. The Parable of the Rich Man and Lazarus (Luke 16:19–31)
(Aland §228; Orchard §260; Huck-Greeven §191)

Another example of honoring the law and of having a relational integrity comes in the parable of the rich man and Lazarus. It is debated whether this is a parable, because one of its characters is named. Some think that it describes a real event. However, its introduction of "a certain rich man" is like the start of a parable, both from Jesus and from the rabbis (cf. Luke 10:30; 14:16; 15:11; 16:1; 19:12; possibly 20:9).[34] In addition, the dialogue between heaven and the underworld shows the story's literary quality, which reflects Jewish apocalyptic literature (*4 Ezra* [= 2 Esdras] 7:85, 93; *2 Baruch* 51.5–6).[35] The points in the parable made about afterlife in the underworld, however, still have merit. It is a place of intense suffering and a place from which there is no escape once judgment comes.

34. Craig Blomberg, *Interpreting the Parables* (Downers Grove, Ill.: InterVarsity, 1990), 205.
35. Some texts on the afterlife in Judaism are 2 Macc. 6:23; *1 Enoch* 22; 39; 102.4–5; *Psalms of Solomon* 14.6, 9–10; 15.10.

The basic story also underscores fundamental ethical values in Jesus' teaching. A rich man is contrasted with a poor man named Lazarus. The rich man lives lavishly, eating well each day, wearing fine garments, and living in a home fronted by an ornate gate. He lacks nothing. In contrast, the poor man bears all the marks of deep poverty. He is immobilized at the rich man's gate, possibly crippled. His inability to move makes him prey for dogs. They lick his sores, and such contact renders him unclean. Later Jewish tradition describes a life that is no life as one who depends on food from another, one who is ruled by his wife, and one whose body is full of sores (*b. Beṣah* 32^b). Lazarus has no life.

With death, everything is reversed. The rich man finds himself being tormented in Hades, while Lazarus dwells in comfort at Abraham's bosom. Yet some things have not changed. The rich man still views Lazarus as "beneath" him. The rich man implores Abraham to send Lazarus to relieve his suffering with a drop of water. The fact that the man knows Lazarus's name is an important point because it shows that the rich man knew that Lazarus was outside his house and knew who this impoverished sufferer was. Abraham refuses, noting that things now are reversed from the way they were in life. There is an implication that the rich man had done nothing to relieve Lazarus's condition even though he had the capability to do so. So now the measure by which the rich man had measured was being returned to him. In addition, Abraham notes that a great chasm exists between the place of blessing that Lazarus now is in and the rich man's new residence. No passage from one area to the other is possible. In other words, the rich man has experienced a permanent judgment.

So the rich man pleads for his family. He asks that Lazarus be sent from the dead to warn his family. How this would be done is not explained. The goal would be to inform them of their risk of meeting the rich man's fate—to tell them to repent. Abraham's next reply is the parable's oft-ignored point. He says that they "have Moses and the prophets." If they listen to them, then they will know what to do. So let the man's relatives listen to them. That repentance is the issue here is made clear in the remarks in v. 30. The rich man had lived wrongly by his lack of generosity. The passage then reaffirms what Jesus teaches about compassion to those in need, a point that is a proper reflection of the law. The law and the prophets repeatedly call for compassion toward the needy (Deut. 14:28–29; Isa. 3:14–15; Amos 2:6–8; Mic. 6:10–11). The parable also underscores a theme that Luke has raised consistently about the risks of wealth (Luke 1:50–53; 6:20–26; 12:15–21; 18:18–30). The parable affirms the ethical dimensions of the law. Jesus is no lawbreaker, as the previous passage also argued.

The rich man does not give up. He pleads that if someone speaks from the dead, then they will repent. There is irony in this note. What Abraham refuses within the story—a speaking to the living from beyond—is precisely what the parable gives in literary terms through these remarks. Abraham refuses with another touch of irony, noting, "If they do not hear Moses and the prophets, they will not be convinced if someone should rise from the dead." The note again is that what the law pointed toward is what Jesus represents. In addition, the failure to listen to God's revelation already given in the law means that they will not listen to the revelation to which it points, even when that revelation appears in a powerful sign. Jesus' ministry shows that this is true.

209. Warnings against Offenses (Luke 17:1–3a; conceptual: Matt. 18:6–7; Mark 9:42 [see unit 152 above]) (Aland §229; Orchard §261; Huck-Greeven §§192–93a)

This passage appeared in the discourse on community in Matthew. In Luke, it is part of a series of remarks that relate to issues of faith and relationship in Luke 17:1–10.

The first saying is a warning not to be the cause of stumbling. Here, stumbling probably refers to being a source of defection or some type of serious sin. The term here, σκάνδαλον, is used of evildoers, arrogance, and idolatry (LXX: Josh. 23:13; Judg. 2:3; 1 Kingdoms 18:21; Ps. 105:36; 140:9). Such stumbling is sure to come; Jesus understands the effect of the pressure of persecution on the faithful. Nevertheless, those who encourage such a departure would be better off suffering a cruel execution: being cast into the sea with a millstone around the neck. The severity of the rhetorical remark emphasizes Jesus' view of the crime. The passage stresses the corporate responsibility that community members have to care for each other and serves as a warning not to contribute to a believer's defection.

The final command, to take heed, is a transition remark that could underscore either this remark about woe or the one to come on forgiveness. The warning tone and the note of personal responsibility fit slightly more naturally here.

210. On Forgiveness (Luke 17:3b–4; conceptual: Matt. 18:15 [see unit 154 above]) (Aland §230; Orchard §262; Huck-Greeven §193)

Another element in relating is how to treat someone who turns from sin. Spiritual accountability means that confrontation and rebuke are a part of corporate relationship (see Matt. 18:15–18; Luke 6:37; Gal. 6:1; 1 Thess. 5:14–15; 2 Thess. 3:14–15; Titus 3:10). This passage describes actions between believers where the participants are involved in the act in question, since the sin is presented as "against you" in 17:4. Repentance leads to forgiveness. But how many times must we forgive? As often as forgiveness is requested, it should be given. Jesus says that as often as seven times a day, forgiveness should be given (cf. Luke 11:4; 6:37–38). The stress falls on the importance of an environment in which one can be restored from sin when there is recognition of wrong. Elements of Judaism also shared such a view of community (*Testament of Gad* 6.3–7, where requested forgiveness is granted, and vengeance is left to God if the request is insincere). Such restoration is important in preventing a spiritual accountability that produces an oppressive environment.

211. On Faith (Luke 17:5–6; conceptual: Matt. 17:19–21; Mark 9:28–29 [see unit 147 above]) (Aland §231; Orchard §263; Huck-Greeven §194)

The next issue in spiritually relating to others is faith. The apostles ask Jesus to increase their faith. Jesus replies by noting that faith's presence is more important than its quantity. He notes that faith, even if it is as small as a mustard seed, can do extraordinary things. The mustard seed tradition-ally was seen as the smallest of seeds in the region (see Matt. 13:31–32), so the point is that even a tiny bit of faith can accomplish a lot. The picture is of an extensively rooted sycamine tree that seemingly is anchored solidly in the ground. This black mulberry tree was so well nourished that it could live up to six hundred years. Yet a person with a tiny bit of faith could say to such a tree, "Be rooted up and planted in the sea," and it would obey. The rhetorical remark argues that even a small amount of faith can produce the seemingly impossible. The implication is to draw on the faith that one al-ready has. Do not worry about increasing faith's quantity; simply apply what faith you have.

212. The Parable of the Dutiful Servant (Luke 17:7–10) (Aland §232; Orchard §264; Huck-Greeven §195)

Jesus' final parable about relating properly involves a servant's faithfulness and humility. He compares the disciple to a servant who works all day in the field and then has to return to fix his master's meal. Jesus notes that the servant will not eat until his master has been served. Jesus' point emerges in a question that in Greek expects a positive reply. Jesus goes on to note that the master will not thank the servant for performing his duty. So also disciples, when they do what God has commanded, should say that they are merely "unworthy" servants. They have only done their duty. The key term is ἀχρεῖος.[36] The servants are "unworthy"

---

36. BAGD, 128, and BDAG, 160, discuss the force of the term "unworthy."

not in terms of their personal worth but in terms of their independent status and function, so that they cannot demand God's favor as their due. Their "worth" receives definition by reference to their faithful relationship to God.

213. The Cleansing of the Ten Lepers (Luke 17:11–19)
(Aland §233; Orchard §265; Huck-Greeven §196)

In Luke, Jesus is still traveling (Luke 9:51–53; 10:38; 13:22, 33; 14:25; 18:35; 19:1, 11, 28, 41). He is now moving east and west between Samaria and Galilee in the northeastern part of Israel. He encounters ten lepers, who call to him to show them mercy. It is a request for healing. Jesus tells them, as he did another leper earlier, to go and show themselves to the priest (cf. Lev. 13:19; 14:1–11; Luke 5:12–16; Matt. 8:1–4; Mark 1:40–45). Implicit in the remark is that they will be healed by the time they arrive. By heading for the priest, they will show their response. As they turn to go, they are cleansed. After the healing, only one of them turns back to praise God. He falls before Jesus to give thanks. This one appreciated how God was working through Jesus and sought to give him appropriate honor. The narrative points out that this one was a Samaritan.

Jesus responds by noting that although ten had been cleansed, the other nine are not to be seen. Only "this foreigner" returned to give appropriate praise to God. Jesus affirms the inward response of this one that led him to return thanks. Honoring God and thanking him for his gracious work cannot take place without acknowledging the role of Jesus in the process. So he commends the Samaritan and tells him to go, because his faith has made him well. The narrative also underscores again that many outside of Israel are more spiritually sensitive than those within Israel.

214. The Kingdom in the Midst (Luke 17:20–21) (Aland §234;
Orchard §266; Huck-Greeven §197)

This unit is the first portion of a longer unit treating issues of expectations about God's plan. Luke 17:20–21 involves an exchange with the Pharisees, while 17:22–37 reproduces a follow-up discussion involving only the disciples. Discussions and queries with the Pharisees often surface controversies or responses from Jesus, especially in Luke (5:21, 30; 6:2, 7; 18:18; in texts only in Luke: 7:39; 11:38, 45; 13:31; 14:15; 15:2; 16:14). This discussion is triggered by a query about when God's kingdom would be coming. In Judaism, the expectation was that the kingdom would be powerful and victorious over enemies (*Psalms of Solomon* 17–18). It would come with "cosmic" signs to signal its arrival (*1 Enoch* 91; 93; *2 Baruch* 53–74). Apparently, the issue of signs was raised with the suggestion that whatever Jesus was doing lacked this "cosmic" dimension. The issue had been raised earlier in Luke 11:29 (= Matt. 12:38). In that passage, Jesus noted that his teaching was the sign. The request for a sign ignored all the indications of God's work through Jesus that his ministry already had given. The request and its implicit doubt also stand in contrast to the sign that the Samaritan had just recognized, reinforcing Jesus' observation that foreigners were more sensitive to what God was doing than those in Israel.

Jesus responds by noting that the kingdom is not coming now with such kinds of specific signs. Nor will there be a need to point to its coming as being "over there" or "over here." The need to hunt for it and point it out is gone because the kingdom is "in their midst." This is one of Jesus' most important kingdom sayings. It declares that the kingdom is currently manifested in his presence. The key phrase is ἐντὸς ὑμῶν. It means either "in your midst" (before you) or "in your grasp." In this context of addressing Pharisees, the one meaning that it does not have is "within you." This romanticized meaning (popularized in the nineteenth century) independent of Jesus is one thing that Jesus is not affirming. Luke's journey section has been underscoring the tight link between Jesus, his authority, and the presence of promise. The kingdom and its promise of deliverance come with him (Luke 4:16–30; 6:20; 7:22, 28; 9:1–6; 10:17–24; 11:20; 16:16). The verb in the present tense, "is" (ἐστιν), is in an emphatic position in this verse, trailing as it does at the end of the verse. The search for the kingdom need not continue. All that is left is to respond. The following remarks to the disciples note that the kingdom, when it comes in consummation as the day of the Son of Man, comes in full visibility as well. This present-yet-future tension is fundamental to Jesus' picture of the kingdom. As the kingdom parables revealed, the kingdom starts out small in his present ministry, yet one day to come it will be a comprehensive presence on the earth. So the issue is not hunting for it as if it needs to turn up. The opportunity to embrace God's promised rule comes with Jesus. One need only respond to him.

215. The Days of the Son of Man (Luke 17:22–37; conceptual: Matt. 24:23, 26–27, 37–39, 17–18, 40–41, 28; Mark 13:19–23, 14–16) (Aland §235; Orchard §267; Huck-Greeven §198)

Luke, unlike Matthew and Mark, divides his eschatological discussions. What Matt. 24–25 and Mark 13 present within the Olivet discourse, Luke divides into Luke 17 and 21.[37] What is interesting is that the portions of Luke

37. Eschatological material in Luke 12:39–46 also has some conceptual overlap with Matt. 24:43–44, 45–51.

17 that overlap with Matt. 24 do not follow the order of the Matthean material (see the sequence presented above in unit 215's listing of Matthean parallels). In addition, some of what appears in Luke 17 is unique (vv. 22, 28–29,
32, 34, 37a). These differences raise the likelihood that what Luke has here is
part of a distinct discourse that he knew about through a distinct source.[38] The
one other editorial choice that Luke made beyond the use of this distinct
speech was not to repeat what he mentioned here in his eschatological discourse in Luke 21. The effect of this choice is that the Luke 17 discourse assures the disciples that a vindicating judgment by the Son of Man will come
one day, but that suffering will precede it. Thus, the text urges one to cling
faithfully to Christ until this vindication comes, a theme that also extends
through Luke 18:1–8.

Jesus begins by noting that the nature of the period to come is such that the
disciples will long to see the days of the Son of Man but will not. In other words,
they will long for God's vindicating judgment but will not experience it. The
assumption is that the period will be one of suffering and persecution from
which they will desire relief. During this time, people will be urging them to
look here and there for those days, but they are not to follow such people. The
reason is that the day of the Son of Man will be like the way lightning flashes
across the sky. The meaning of this remark is debated. Is the point that the day
will be obvious, like lightning flashing across a dark sky? Or is the idea that it
will appear suddenly like lightning? Or is it both? The contextual note of people
not needing to go where others have directed them to find the kingdom would
seem to favor the idea of its obvious visibility. When the day comes, it will be
obvious to all. The following examples of Noah and Lot suggest its surprising
coming in the midst of everyday life. Directions to find it will not be needed.
Lightning often was seen as a phenomenon that reflected God's presence and
power (Exod. 19:16; Ps. 97:2–4; Ezek. 1:4, 13; 2 Baruch 53.8–9).

What precedes all of this is the suffering that the Son of Man must face. He
will be rejected by this generation. Luke uses his common word δεῖ here to indicate the idea of divine necessity. At some unspecified point after this rejection, the judgment to come will take place as it did in the days of Noah and
Lot. It is here that Jesus highlights the judgment's suddenness. Life was proceeding in a normal way with eating, drinking, marriage, planting, buying, selling, and building. Then the judgment fell, as a flood (Noah) or as fire and sul-
phur (Lot) from heaven. This is how the day of the Son of Man will come. It
will be a time of judgment falling suddenly into the world's affairs.

It will be a period of intense suffering. There will not be time to gather possessions, so Jesus tells the disciples that anyone on a housetop had better not
try to return inside to gather his or her goods, nor should anyone in the field
turn back to gather goods. One should leave and not look back. The example

---

38. On this point, see Bock, *Luke 9:51–24:53*, 1420–24.

of what not to do is Lot's wife. She longed for the old life and looked back. The days of the Son of Man involve a judgment that will not spare those present who seek to preserve their world and life, so fleeing is advised. If anyone seeks to preserve life by staying identified with the world, it will be lost. To lose one's life, perhaps in suffering, ironically means that real life will be preserved when judgment comes.

The next image of the discourse emphasizes the separation that judgment brings. Two illustrations are present.[39] The images are of two people in a bed being separated and of two women at a mill being separated. The idea of a separating judgment is fundamental to Jesus' eschatology of the kingdom (cf. Matt. 13:24–30, 37–43, 47–49; Mark 4:26–29). A disputed question concerns whether those taken are removed for judgment or are taken for salvation. Two elements suggest that those removed are saved, while those left are judged. First, in the Noah and Lot examples, the departing or fleeing are the saved. Second, in 17:37, it appears that the "vultures" hover over those left behind, who are dead. The imagery causes the disciples to ask where this will occur. Jesus deflects the question, simply noting that where the body is, the "vultures" gather. The Greek term used here often means "eagles," but since the image is of birds gathered over the dead, vultures are meant. The gruesome image points to the judged dead.

Jesus' point in this discourse is not to give either a precise chronology or a locale, but to affirm that the vindicating judgment will come one day after his suffering is complete. When that day comes, it will not need announcement, nor will one need to search for it. The only thing to do will be to get out of the way of the judgment, which itself will separate those judged from those delivered. The Son of Man's authority is total, as his day will show. Again it is important to respond properly to him, just as it is important for disciples like Theophilus to be assured that the Son of Man will vindicate those allied to Jesus.[40]

216. The Parable of the Unjust Judge (Luke 18:1–8) (Aland §236; Orchard §268; Huck-Greeven §199)

The times to come will be hard. Just as Jesus will suffer as Son of Man, so also the saints will be persecuted for their commitment to him. They will long for vindication, but they will have to wait for it. So Jesus exhorts them to pray

39. A third illustration is not as well supported textually as being an original part of Luke.
40. The issue of the timing of these events, so much a part of current theological discussion, is not so much addressed in this text, which simply seeks to affirm the coming judgment. For various views of eschatology that have to work with texts like this, including interaction between those views, see Darrell L. Bock, ed., *Three Views on the Millennium and Beyond* (Grand Rapids: Zondervan, 1999). Attempts to sort out the timing of events described here must discuss how the Epistles and Revelation handle these themes and must correlate all the texts.

always and not lose heart. Contextually, Jesus is speaking of not losing heart about the hope of vindication. He compares such prayer to the persistence of a widow nagging a judge. Her constant request was for him to vindicate her against her adversary, a remark that shows the eschatological vindication theme. The judge, who is no respecter of persons, will vindicate her so as not to be "beaten black and blue" by her continual coming.[41]

It is this image that Jesus compares to God's response. To make the point, Jesus uses a rhetorical question about God vindicating his elect who cry out to him day and night. The vindication will come. Will God delay over them? No, that vindication will come speedily.[42] But apparently it will delay long enough that there is a question whether people will wait faithfully for that vindication. So Jesus concludes the unit by asking, "Nevertheless, when the Son of Man comes, will he find faith on earth?"

The parable affirms the speedy vindication of disciples, while also noting that the indefiniteness of the delay is long enough to cause the possibility that some will not endure with abiding faith. It is this very ambiguity that produced discussion about the "delay" of Christ's return in the early church. Nevertheless, the parable reinforces the previous unit's discussion of the day of the Son of Man and urges disciples to "hang in there" until he returns. One day the vindication certainly will come.

217. The Pharisee and the Publican (Luke 18:9–14) (Aland §237; Orchard §269; Huck-Greeven §200)

In many ways, the parable of the Pharisee and publican (tax collector) summarizes Jesus' attitude about the leadership and those to whom he directed his ministry. Luke explicitly notes that the account was told against "those who trusted in themselves that they were righteous and despised others." What Jesus' ministry challenged was a self-righteousness that led into contempt for others. God rejects the proud and exalts the humble (James 4:6, 10; 1 Pet. 5:5).

The scene in the temple has a Pharisee addressing God in praise. However, the Pharisee's praise psalm is distorted. His thanksgiving is not for God's grace but for his own righteousness: "I thank you, God, that I am not like other

---

41. The phrase meaning to be "beaten down" or "worn out" normally refers to being beaten up (BAGD, 848; BDAG, 1043). Here, it is used in a figurative way to describe how the judge felt after the ongoing requests.

42. It is discussed whether this is a reference to final vindication or includes an allusion to God's vindication through limiting the effect of persecution. It certainly includes a reference ultimately to final vindication, because the next verse refers to the state of things when the Son of Man returns. Luke 18:7 may be the most difficult verse in Luke. For a discussion, see Bock, *Luke 9:51–24:53*, 1451–54.

people: . . . I fast twice a week. I give tithes of all I get." In other words, "I praise you, God, that I am so good and wonderful. I am better than the extortionists, unjust, adulterers, and even people like this tax collector next to me." The petitioner is thankful not for anything God has done but for what he does. As with the rich fool in 12:17–19, what dominates the Pharisee's speech is the first-person pronoun. In turn, his pride alienates him from others.

In contrast, the tax collector humbly stands at a distance and does not lift up his eyes to the holy God. There is a rich literary use of space in the contrast between the tax collector and the Pharisee. The tax collector beats his breast and appeals to God to be merciful to him, a sinner. Here is humility, faith, and dependence. So Jesus notes that this man's prayer was heard, as he, rather than the "other," went home justified. Self-exaltation results in being humbled by God, whereas humility expressed in a cry to God for mercy leads to God exalting the humble. It is this very openness to transformation on the part of sinners that caused Jesus to minister to them and seek them out (Luke 15). The parable warns that pride before God for accomplishments is a danger to the disciple's walk. Such pride also subtly moves to destroy relationships with others.

Conclusion

This long section on the Jerusalem journey actually continues in Luke through 19:44. However, at this point, the account rejoins Mark 10:1 and Matt. 19:1. Luke has used mostly material unique to himself in this section to summarize Jesus' ministry as Jesus sought to prepare the disciples for his death and departure. The disciples did not truly appreciate this teaching's full function until his resurrection, since they did not fully comprehend Jesus' announcements of his coming suffering until then. Nonetheless, Jesus was facing increasingly hostile opposition, as this section documents. This opposition came despite numerous warnings by Jesus of the risk involved in rejecting him. It came despite his pleas to read the signs of the times that he worked. It continued even after he warned that there was not much time left to respond before the nation would be at severe risk for their consistent denial of him. Even the repetition of miracles continued to yield a negative response. Jesus' challenges and warnings caused hostility to rise.

Jesus warned his disciples that this opposition would spill over against them, so they needed to be prepared. Discipleship, as a result, would be hard. Attachment to public acceptance or to possessions also could be an obstacle to following Jesus. Jesus warns them to watch what excessive attachment to possessions can do to destroy relationship with God and others. Nevertheless, God will be with his disciples, even if they have to suffer. They can trust God for provision of the kingdom and all that they need to live as disciples. The Spirit will tell them what to say when they are persecuted now, and the Son of Man one day will bring a vindicating judgment on behalf of his followers. In the meantime, disciples are to press on faithfully with the ethical standards that Jesus called them to embrace. They should live with integrity, rejoicing that they have a place in the book of life. After all, they were experiencing what prophets and kings had longed to see. Jesus was bringing what God had promised long ago. So the exhortation was to be dependent on God, pray to him, and be faithful to him. In addition, love one's neighbor and seek the lost.

This was how Jesus drew near to Jerusalem. Jesus prepared his disciples for what they would face in his absence, all the while assuring them that his approaching suffering would be followed by glory and vindication. He challenged Israel to reconsider their walk with God and rejection of him, for the stakes were high. Drawing nearer to Jerusalem meant that Jesus was entering into the completion of his mission for humanity, while helping his disciples face ministry in the midst of his approaching departure.

TEN

Continuing toward Jerusalem

Ministry in Judea and Final Lessons (Matt. 19:1–21:9; Mark 10:1–11:10; Luke 18:15–19:44)

The thrust of Jesus' esoteric teaching [his private teaching] was to structure the present and the future in a way which we may represent to ourselves as thesis, antithesis, synthesis. Thesis was Jesus' self-understanding as messianic builder of the house of God. Antithesis was the ordeal that would supervene upon his mission and appear to frustrate it: The shepherd would be stricken, the flock scattered (Mark 14:27 par.). Synthesis was the day of the Son of man, the coming of the reign of God, the shepherd's return to head the flock (Mark 14:28 par.), the building of the new temple. Now, elements of this scheme coincided with numerous public actions and teaching of Jesus. Nevertheless, his esoteric teaching transvalued the whole of his public performance, revealing it as integral to the drama of the end time. The great theme of apocalyptic—the victory over evil and especially over the adversaries and oppressors of Israel—was now made to incorporate a historical moment: God's final controversy with Israel in the face-to-face encounter between people and prophet. This moment included the proclamation that divided believers and unbelievers, the persecution of Jesus and his followers, the national disaster epitomized in the fall of the temple. Restoration was reserved for the messianic remnant self-assembled by faith.

Some may suppose that to define the aims of Jesus in terms of so grandiose a vision of things is to do theology, not history. But the history of Israel in general, and above all in the centuries preceding and following Jesus, was not the prosaic affair evoked by a facile division between theology and history. All the issues and actors were immersed in religious schemes and visions. As we shall presently see, they were the hinges on which Israel's history turned.[1]

1. Ben Meyer, *The Aims of Jesus* (London: SCM, 1979), 221–22.

This quotation argues that Jesus' original message is rooted solidly in both the history and the theology of Israel. It is why separating history and theology even in the Gospels is so hard to do. In fact, such a separation risks missing an important dimension of the accounts about Jesus. My study is arguing that the consideration of Jesus' life as a synthetic whole is an important dimension of the study of Jesus, *both* historical and theological. Here we see both the similarities and differences in each Synoptic's conception of Jesus even though they share so many themes, teachings, and events. We focus on the Synoptics here because of their well-known extensive overlap. How John's Gospel fits into this portrait is another dimension to be raised later.

Jesus' historical and theological message produced both a new following and intense opposition. His unique wedding of history and theology produced both followers and challengers. As Jesus drew near to Jerusalem, the final act in his call to restore Israel took place. His preparation for the deliverance of humanity entered its crucial, decisive stages. This chapter covers Matt. 19:1–21:9, Mark 10:1–11:10, and Luke 18:15–19:44.[2] It is the final stage of Jesus' approach to Jerusalem, as portrayed in Luke. It extends through Jesus' entry into the city, culminating in his weeping for the city that will reject him. As a result of this rejection, Jesus warns them that tragic consequences will follow. The themes in this chapter are very similar to those on discipleship revealed in the earlier parts of Luke's long journey section. As Jesus draws close to his death, the major exhortations are to commitment, intense faithfulness, and responsive stewardship before God. Jesus will model what is required in the face of opposition.

218. To Judea (Matt. 19:1–2; Mark 10:1) (Aland §251; Orchard §192; Huck-Greeven §201a)

Jesus has just taught on community accountability and forgiveness in Matt. 18 and in Mark 9:42–50 with a focus on the need for fidelity and unity. Those Gospels now interject a summary that indicates a shift in the locale of Jesus' work. Interestingly, Matthew speaks of large crowds following Jesus and that he healed there. Mark points to large crowds as well but adds a note about Jesus' custom of teaching. The next six events in Mark 10:2–45 focus on Jesus' teaching. Matthew 19:3–20:28 also contains a sequence of seven consecutive teaching units. Thus, though the region has changed, the fundamental patterns of ministry activity have not. One suspects that Jesus took the same basic message to these various locales.

2. It is likely that events in John 7:1–10:21 fit in the time frame that moves within the Jerusalem journey but before the events noted here in Matthew, Mark, and Luke. See Aland §§238–50.

219. On Divorce and Kingdom Eunuchs (Matt. 19:3–12; Mark 10:2–12; conceptual: Luke 16:18) (Aland §252; Orchard §§274–75; Huck-Greeven §201b)

This unit is famous today because of its role in the debate about divorce. However, its role in the Gospels was not as an isolated unit on that theme but as an event that represented a test of Jesus and his sensitivity to issues related to the law. Both Matthew and Mark underscore the fact that the question about the legality of divorce was asked as a challenge to Jesus. Thus, the account is a controversy story.

The Jewish background to divorce and the debate about it was noted earlier.[3] Judaism had a range of beliefs on the matter, running from divorce for immorality only to divorce for "burnt toast." Jesus' reply that even the granting of the divorce decree represented a concession to sin reversed the emphasis raised by the Pharisees' question. Jesus sought to shift the issue from what will allow one to get out of a marriage to an emphasis on staying in it.

Matthew and Mark take up Jesus' reply in a different order. Mark begins with Jesus asking about Moses and what he commanded. The reply refers to the certificate of divorce from Deut. 24:1–4. Then Jesus notes that this provision was "for your hardness of heart." He contrasts that provision with the creation design for marriage as stated in Gen. 1:27 and 2:24. God created humanity as male and female, with marriage as the joining of man and woman into a one-flesh relationship. The conclusion Jesus makes is that a married couple no longer consists of two persons, but one. What God has brought together, no human being should divide. Here is the most important point: marriage is designed to be permanent. Matthew discusses the same elements in a reverse order. He starts with the creation and then discusses the certificate. His stress also is that divorce was the exception and that it was not a premise in the original design.

At this point, a famous difference between Matthew and Mark emerges, a difference that was previewed in the earlier Matthean handling of this topic in Matt. 5:32. Matthew notes that Jesus said, "Whoever divorces his wife, except for immorality [πορνεία], and marries another, commits adultery."[4] Mark has "Whoever divorces his wife and marries another, commits adultery against her; and if she divorces her husband and marries another, she commits adultery." Thus, Matthew has an exception clause that Mark lacks. Mark also stresses how the one initiating the divorce is the cause of the adultery and

---

3. See unit 49 above.
4. On this term, see Craig Blomberg, *Matthew,* New American Commentary 22 (Nashville: Broadman, 1992), 292; B. Malina, "Does *Porneia* Mean Fornication?" *Novum Testamentum* 14 (1972): 10–17; J. Jensen, "Does *Porneia* Mean Fornication? A Critique of Bruce Malina," *Novum Testamentum* 20 (1978): 161–84.

notes the balance of gender in making the point. The gender balance in Mark possibly emerges out of sensitivity to his Hellenistic audience, for whom the possibility of divorce coming from either party was real. Both accounts suggest that an almost assumed element in the divorce is a movement toward opening up the option of remarrying. In other words, part of the purpose of divorce is to undo the original ties and put one into a position to marry another. The actual remarriage triggers the adultery. The stress in all of this is the sacred nature of the original bond, which is not to be broken.

The one contested point is the function and scope of the exception clause.[5] It is sometimes suggested that Matthew is responsible for the interpretive addition for the sake of showing his Jewish audience that Jesus did not violate the law (see Matt. 5:17), because only his Gospel versions, here and in Matt. 5, mention it.[6] However, another explanation also can be offered without nullifying the point that Matthew's remark addresses Jewish-Christian concerns. Mark has chosen to stress what Jesus was trying to highlight: the design of marriage was that it would be lifelong. In light of the misplaced emphasis in the original query, this was the correction in emphasis that Jesus sought to bring to the testing question. To introduce the exception might somewhat cloud this emphasis. In other words, although Jesus did qualify his answer, divorce still represented a departure from the ideal. Mark stays with the ideal alone. On the other hand, Matthew brought the full reply, qualification and all. He did so without any elaboration, just noting it. In a Jewish context, its import would be appreciated as a reference to the potential damaging effect of fundamental infidelity in the marriage. This additional qualification would need no explanation, given that the thrust of Jesus' reply shows that divorce for any whim clearly is being excluded. It also would show that the law, in this case, was not being altered. Matthew's point is still that Jesus' emphasis would not be on how a person can get out of a marriage but on how marriage was designed to be permanent.

Matthew has one more element that Mark lacks. It is the follow-up discussion with the disciples, who raise the point that perhaps it is better not to marry if the standards are so high and the dangerous impact of divorce is so great. It is important not to exaggerate this text's setting. The disciples' reaction is not because Jesus set a "no exception" standard but because adultery was so common, a result of the many divorces taking place for reasons beyond

5. For a survey of the various views surrounding this topic and text and a good bibliography for the textual issues involved, see Robert Stein, "Divorce," *DJG*, 192–99. In addition to those that Stein mentions are W. House, ed., *Divorce and Remarriage* (Downers Grove, Ill.: Inter-Varsity, 1990); W. A. Heth and G. J. Wenham, *Jesus and Divorce* (Nashville: Nelson, 1985); Craig Keener, *". . . And Marries Another": Divorce and Remarriage in the Teaching of the New Testament* (Peabody, Mass.: Hendrickson, 1991); Pat E. Harrell, *Divorce and Remarriage in the Early Church* (Austin: Sweet, 1967).

6. So Stein, "Divorce," 196.

those that Jesus had mentioned.[7] The disciples' reaction shows an awareness that meeting this standard of permanence, with only a rare exception, is difficult for sinful people. So they conclude that it is better not to risk marriage. Jesus' affirming reply accepts the premise but notes that this is not a law. Such a lifestyle is only for those who can accept it. Some can make the choice not to marry and be "eunuchs for the kingdom," just as there are eunuchs by birth and those who are made eunuchs. The figurative remark would be startling, given the Jewish attitude about eunuchs (Deut. 23:1). But to remain single is a choice, not an obligation. So Jesus says, "Those who are able to receive this, let them receive it." The motive is neither a fear of marriage nor that marriage is sinful, but the desire to serve the kingdom with a singleness of focus. It is an attitude that Paul also will reflect in 1 Cor. 7:25–35. The point of this unit contextually is that it highlights the disciple's fidelity. Matthew's account adds a call to serve God with a singleness of dedication, if marriage is not consciously pursued for the sake of the kingdom.

220. Jesus Blesses the Children (Matt. 19:13–15; Mark 10:13–16; Luke 18:15–17) (Aland §253; Orchard §276; Huck-Greeven §202)

The next event shows how far Jesus would go to include people, repeating a point made earlier in Matt. 18:1–6. In ancient culture, children largely were regarded as insignificant.[8] So when the crowds sought to have Jesus touch them, probably expressing a desire that he bless and pray for them, the disciples sought to block the children's approach. The allusion is to a form of laying on of hands (Gen. 48:14–15; Matt. 19:15). Only Luke uses the term βρέφος to refer to the children. The scene looks at small children from babies to early childhood.

Jesus urges that the children be allowed to come to him. The kingdom belongs to such. The picture is that the "child" and the seemingly insignificant not only are allowed in but also are encouraged to come. Matthew simply notes that Jesus laid hands on them. Mark does this as well, but he precedes the note with Jesus remarking, "Whoever does not receive the kingdom of God like a child will not enter it." Luke has only this kingdom saying, leaving the implication that Jesus said this as he was blessing the children. Again the

---

7. An important argument against a "no exceptions" view is that Paul, who knew Jesus' teaching, feels free to consider the additional issue of desertion by an unbeliever as another category in which divorce was permitted (1 Cor. 7:12–16). Had the sense of Jesus' instruction been that divorce never was allowed, would Paul have responded to this additional option this way? Thus, it appears that Jesus did originally raise a real exception here.

8. Ernest Best, "Mark 10:13–16: The Child as Model Recipient," in *Biblical Studies: Essays in Honor of William Barclay,* ed. J. R. MacKay and J. F. Miller (Philadelphia: Westminster, 1976), 119–34.

call is to dependent faithfulness and a simplicity of devotion like that which a child has for a parent.[9]

221. The Rich Young Man (Matt. 19:16–22; Mark 10:17–22; Luke 18:18–23) (Aland §254; Orchard §277; Huck-Greeven §203a)

The rich young man's question is very similar in emphasis to the lawyer's question in Luke 10:25–28, although this appears to be a distinct event. There are some differences between the versions of the young man's interview of Jesus.[10] For example, only Matthew's account says that the man is young, while all three say that he is rich. Only Luke says that he is a ruler. Young probably means that he is less than forty years old. Thus, the title "rich young ruler," often used for this episode, also is a composite of the versions.

Matthew's version of the exchange is more complex than Mark's and Luke's. In Mark and Luke, the man, after addressing Jesus as a good teacher, asks what he must do to inherit eternal life. Inheriting life is a common Jewish expression (Ps. 37:9, 11, 18 speak of inheriting the land but also of an abiding heritage; Dan. 12:2; 1QS 4.7; CD 3.20; 4Q181 1.4; 2 Macc. 7:9; 4 Macc. 15:3; *1 Enoch* 37.4; 40.9; 58.3; *Psalms of Solomon* 3.12). As the later discussion with the disciples shows, this topic is about being saved. Jesus rebukes the address of him as good and then cites some of the commandments as his answer. The portion cited emphasizes the relational part of the commandments, what has been called the second table of the ten: do not kill, commit adultery, steal, bear false witness, defraud (Mark), and honor your father and mother.[11]

Matthew's version has a few differences. In Matthew, the man calls Jesus simply "teacher" in the address. It may be that Matthew felt that Jesus' refusal to accept the "good" accolade might be misunderstood somehow as suggesting unrighteousness in Jesus. Instead, the idea of "good" ends up in the body of the question, so that Matthew has "What good must I do to inherit eternal life?" This certainly is the thrust of his question, which Matthew appears to summarize, given the Jewish expectation that it is the righteous who are saved. Both Mark and Luke note that he asks, "What must I do?" In these two Gospels, Jesus deflects the question to remark that only one is good, so why ask about what is good? The remark shifts the attention from the man's goodness to God's. The shift is important, for the attention properly belongs on relating

---

9. Although historically this text often is invoked in discussions about infant baptism, it has nothing to say about that specific question. The point it does make is that spiritual issues are of relevance even to the young. God does care about them.

10. For a good discussion and analysis of these differences, see D. A. Carson, "Redaction Criticism: On the Legitimacy and Illegitimacy of a Literary Tool," in *Scripture and Truth,* ed. D. A. Carson and John Woodbridge (Grand Rapids: Zondervan, 1983), 131–37.

11. Luke mentions killing after adultery.

to God and his goodness, not pursuing goodness in the abstract as personal merit. In all three Gospels, Jesus then urges the keeping of the commandments to gain life, though Matthew has a kind of give-and-take exchange including some questions that the other Gospels lack. In Matthew, the man asks about which commandments. It is hard to know why the man made the distinction about commandments. Was he raising the issue of some laws being more weighty (more important) than others, as in the rabbis' debates? Or was he looking for some reduced list to obey, so that he could pick and choose? Jesus' reply mentions killing, adultery, stealing, false witness, and honoring father and mother, as well as noting (uniquely in Matthew), "You shall love your neighbor as yourself." In Mark and Luke, a more compressed exchange simply notes the commandments that were named.

The theology of the exchange is significant. The man asks about eternal life, but Jesus, in assessing the discussion later, will discuss the kingdom. The disciples, in reacting, will speak of being saved. It is clear that the Gospels are clustering these ideas together as associated with each other. The kingdom does touch on issues of eternal life and being saved. Ultimately, those who share in the kingdom are experiencing eternal life as part of the saved. Jesus' reply makes it clear that the standard for entry into heaven is righteousness and responsiveness to God. Although the second table is cited, it reflects Jesus' belief that devotion to God was best seen and expressed by how much respect one gives to others. The spirit of Jesus' reply is found in Deut. 30:15–20. As Jesus' other teaching has shown, the person who appreciates the standard of these demands approaches God in terms of his mercy and relates to others accordingly. In fact, Jesus' teaching in Luke 18:9–14 contrasts the self-righteousness of a Pharisee with the humble plea of a tax collector, showing the difference. Part of the gospel that Jesus and the early church develop is that God gives the source of the enablement that will permit one to live righteously (John 14–16; Luke 24:49; Rom. 6–8).

The man's reply indicates that he is confident that all this is within his reach; he notes that he has done all of these things from his youth. Mark notes that Jesus' next reply was filled with love as he challenged him with the one thing that would show that his priority was not God. The challenge will show him to be lacking with respect to the first table of the commandments. Jesus tells the man that he lacks one thing (Mark and Luke). Matthew speaks of what he must do to be "perfect," recalling the language of the Sermon on the Mount (Matt. 5:48). Here is the righteousness that God requires of this man: to go, sell what he has, and give to the poor, knowing the promise that treasure in heaven will follow the act. In this way, he will be prepared to follow Jesus, which is the way to life. It is important to note that the man's question about eternal life is not fully answered until this point of the exchange. So Jesus makes following him the final component. Jesus' remark presses the man's devotion to possessions versus his responsiveness to God's call. It exposes the fact that the man could not keep the law by his own strength. If the man really saw Jesus to be a good teacher representing God, then he should be responsive and recognize his own shortcomings and need to change his way of responding to God. Proverbs 8:1–11 is similar in emphasis. Jesus offers full heavenly reward, so the seeming sacrifice is balanced by the counteroffer. The remark tests the man's heart.

The man departs, sad (Luke), sorrowful (Mark and Matthew), and with a fallen countenance (Mark). His riches demanded his allegiance. They counted for more than the hope of reward from God.

222. Commenting on the Rich Man Incident—On the Riches and the Rewards of Response (Matt. 19:23–30; Mark 10:23–31; Luke 18:24–30) (Aland §255; Orchard §278; Huck-Greeven §203b)

The exchange with the rich man brings commentary from Jesus. He notes how difficult it is for the rich to enter the kingdom. In Mark, the observation is emphasized with a second remark that entry into the kingdom is hard in general. It is so difficult that it is easier for a camel to pass through the eye of a needle than for a rich person to enter God's kingdom. Jesus' remark is rhetorical. It is impossible for a rich person to get in through self-effort. Someone else must intervene.

The remark astonishes (Matthew and Mark) the disciples. They wonder, "Who, then, can be saved?" The reply surfaces because of an underlying assumption that the rich are the blessed (Prov. 10:22). If they are excluded, then who could be saved? Jesus' reply is the key to the unit. What is impossible with humans is possible with God. Salvation takes place because God is at work. Anyone, even the rich, may enter the kingdom when God has worked on the heart and made the provision.

At this point Peter looks for reassurance. He notes that the disciples have left everything and followed him. In effect, Peter is observing that what Jesus had asked of the rich young man, all the disciples had done. So what was their status? Indeed, in the Matthean version, Peter closes with "What, then, will we have?"

Once again Matthew here has more detail. He alone notes that in the "new world" to come, when the Son of Man sits on his throne, they will sit on twelve thrones, ruling the tribes of Israel. Jesus has been reconstituting the rule of the nation as a part of the kingdom. The Twelve will have a major role in that rule in a way that will be obvious at the consummation. This detail is an important component of Jesus' kingdom teaching, since it shows how focused on Israel Jesus is even when he considers the completion of eschatological hope. Israel always is a part of the divine plan. The Twelve have a major role in the nation's governance even at the end.

All the versions note the next portion of the reply. Jesus acknowledges the sacrifice of having left houses or family or possessions for the calling of God. That calling is variously summarized as "for my name's sake" (Matthew), "for my sake and for the gospel" (Mark), and "for the sake of the kingdom of God" (Luke). The different expressions point to the same fundamental motive. To ally oneself with Jesus is to join in the kingdom program and share in the gospel. Thus, in a sense, the teaching to the disciples is the theological capstone to the exchange with the rich young man. Jesus' initial answer to that man about keeping the commandments was but the beginning of a much fuller reply that the entire passage brings. That reply makes it clear that eternal life and the kingdom are inseparably bound up with Jesus. What that man had failed to do in responding to Jesus had left him outside, looking in at the kingdom. In contrast, the disciples had done what was called for, making them full beneficiaries.

What would they receive? Matthew notes that it is a hundredfold return in addition to inheriting eternal life, taking us right back to the young man's question. He also notes the "reversal" of the first being last and the last first in the end. Mark also speaks of a hundredfold benefit, but specifies it in terms of brothers, sisters, mothers, children, and lands, but with persecutions now. This is not a "health and wealth" return, but a new kind of community that is better than merely receiving material possessions. In the age to come, it also means eternal life. He also notes the reversal of first to last and last to first. Luke speaks of receiving manifold more in this time, and in the age to come eternal life. Thus, Jesus reassures the disciples that they have done what has been asked for. They are being richly rewarded for it both now and into the future.

223. The Parable of the Laborers in the Vineyard
(Matt. 20:1–16) (Aland §256; Orchard §278; Huck-Greeven §204)

This parable about grace reinforces the discussion about the rich young man. It is unique to Matthew. A landowner goes to the marketplace early in the morning and hires workers for the vineyard for that day. A vineyard often is used as a figure for working the field of Israel for fruit (Isa. 5:1–7). This hiring practice was a common one; labor was procured as needed on a daily basis in the marketplace. Workers were paid the standard basic wage, a denarius for the day, and this is what the owner agrees to pay these workers. The owner then repeats the hiring ritual four times, each time at a later hour as the day wears on, and each time sending the workers to labor in the vineyard. He simply promises to pay these workers "whatever is right."

At day's end, the owner has his steward gather them all and pay them, proceeding from the last to the first. When the last hired receive a denarius, the first are certain that they will get more. However, they receive the same, previously agreed upon denarius. They grumble about this to the owner. They had worked longer and harder. Fairness says that they should get more, especially because they had worked in the scorching heat all day. The owner reminds them that they had agreed to work for one denarius. The owner had delivered to them what was promised. It is his choice what to pay the others. He asks, "Is your eye evil because I am kind?" In other words, have their hearts turned to evil jealousy and bitterness because another also has received grace? So the first are last and the last first.

Here the point of the final saying is that all beneficiaries are equal, regardless of when they entered into blessing. Thus, the proverbial saying has a meaning distinct from that in Matt. 19:30, where it described distinction, a reversal of fortune. In Matt. 20:16, the proverb describes equality as a function of God's choice to be gracious. God's kindness should not be a cause of complaint. To share in salvation is to share in the same benefit, regardless of whether one comes in early (first) or late (last). The parable seems to apply individually to the listeners, but there is also a sense in which it would be true in principle of Jews and Gentiles in terms of salvation history. Though the Jews were the first to be invited, those invited later would get the same benefits.

224. Another Prediction of the Passion (Matt. 20:17–19; Mark 10:32–34; Luke 18:31–34) (Aland §262; Orchard §280; Huck-Greeven §205)[12]

Luke has a clear journey-to-Jerusalem motif that dominates the central section of his Gospel. Matthew and Mark also note a similar idea in association with this prediction of the passion. This is the third such prediction in Matthew (16:21; 17:22–23) and in Mark (8:31; 9:31). It is Luke's sixth announcement or allusion to Jesus' death (9:22, 44–45; 12:49–50; 13:32–33; 17:25).

Mark's introduction is the most detailed. The crowds and disciples are in the process of going up to Jerusalem. The note is somber. The group is amazed and afraid. It seems that Mark makes a distinction triggered by the use of a contrastive δέ. So the crowds are amazed, following Jesus and unaware that a tension point approaches. However, in contrast, the disciples fear because the drawing near to Jerusalem surely suggests that the real drama is just ahead. They sense that a key point is being reached, although, as will become

12. Aland places several events from John 10:22–11:57 between the vineyard parable and this prediction.

clear, they really do not understand what is going to happen. It is at this point that Jesus tells the Twelve that they are going up to Jerusalem, where the Son of Man will fulfill his task. Matthew and Luke simply have Jesus taking the Twelve aside and making the announcement.

Of the predictions, Mark's also is the most detailed. The Son of Man will be delivered to the chief priests and scribes, who will condemn him to death and deliver him up to the Gentiles to be mocked, spit upon, scourged, and killed. After three days he will rise. Matthew does not mention spitting or killing. Luke lacks the detail about the chief priests and scribes condemning him to death. Rather, Luke emphasizes the fulfillment of Scripture more directly by noting that "everything that is written of the Son of Man by the prophets will be accomplished." Luke also speaks in general of Jesus being "treated shamefully" as a part of his suffering. Only Luke goes on to mention that the disciples did not understand these things because this saying was hidden from them, and they did not grasp it. Luke probably does not mean that these remarks were unintelligible, because what is said is not hard to grasp conceptually. What they did not grasp was how these things could happen to a person in Jesus' supposed role as God's promised agent of deliverance. Suffering and death were hard to consider for a figure called to bring their deliverance. If he were removed, how could physical salvation happen? Their expected victorious Messiah would be placed in the hands of Gentiles and slain! It was the opposite of what they expected. How his death could mean hope and victory, they could not yet comprehend. Only the events themselves would provide that understanding. Note the honesty of the Gospels here.

These predictions are so detailed that some question their authenticity and whether they go back to Jesus. However, this should not be questioned. First, the rising opposition to Jesus and what his opponents' political solution to the controversy might involve leads to the real likelihood that Jesus could meet a political death at the hands of the Romans. The fate of John the Baptist showed what could befall a controversial figure. In addition, the way Rome tended to handle those perceived as a political threat meant that Jesus could anticipate how his claims might be received with hostility and result in death. Second, the details in this text do not match the order of their fulfillment in Mark 15:15–20, suggesting no attempt at correlation or creation of details. Third, allusions to Isa. 1:6 and Ps. 22 come from well-known texts about suffering that could well serve as a frame for Jesus' remarks.[13]

13. C. E. B. Cranfield, *The Gospel according to St Mark,* Cambridge Greek Testament Commentary (Cambridge: Cambridge University Press, 1959), 334–35. On the passion predictions as a group, see Hans Bayer, *Jesus' Predictions of Vindication and Resurrection: The Provenance, Meaning and Correlation of the Synoptic Predictions,* WUNT 2.20 (Tübingen: Mohr, 1986).

225. The Request for Precedence by the Sons of Zebedee
(Matt. 20:20–28; Mark 10:35–45; conceptual: Luke 22:24–27)
(Aland §263; Orchard §281; Huck-Greeven §206)

The disciples' lack of sensitivity is even more pronounced than simply not understanding what the future holds. In the midst of Jesus' remarks about his coming suffering, they are jockeying for positions of prominence in the glory that they all anticipate is about to come. Jesus will address this desire for personal status.

Details between the Gospels differ slightly here. Matthew notes that the mother of the sons of Zebedee came with her sons. She kneels before Jesus in a sign of respect for the "ruling" figure and asks that her two sons may be placed on his left and right "in your kingdom." It may be that her sons had put her up to this request, because culturally, elderly women often could ask sensitive questions that others could not.[14] Mark has the two sons engage Jesus with a request to do "whatever we ask of you." When Jesus asks what that is, they request to sit on his left and right "in your glory." The expectation is that Jesus will come into great power. This family wants to be sure that they have a prime role and ministry in that rule.

Jesus' response comes in two steps. First, he notes the suffering that seems to be missing from their expectation. Then he talks about how authority in the kingdom is turned upside down from the world's expectations by how it is exercised. Jesus' rule will call for a different type of leader.

Jesus asks if they can drink the cup he is about to drink, a clear allusion to suffering, given its use in the Old Testament (Ps. 75:8; Isa. 51:17; in other Jewish writings, *Martyrdom and Ascension of Isaiah* 5.13). Mark adds a question about whether they can be baptized with the baptism he will face, another metaphor of suffering (Gen. 6–8; Isa. 30:27–28; Jon. 2:2–6; Ps. 18:4–5; 2 Sam. 22:5–6). They reply that they are able. How much this really did sink in is hard to know. The remark may be like Peter's later claim that he will stand up for Jesus despite Jesus' prediction of disciple abandonment. The disciples' response perhaps came without much serious reflection on their part as to what really is being anticipated for them. Nevertheless, Jesus responds by noting that they will drink his cup of suffering. Mark adds that they will share in his baptism as well. Their visions of power will be washed away by another kind of experience for which they must be prepared. To follow Jesus means following him in this step as well. However, Jesus refuses their request for position. The right to sit at his right and left is not his to give, but rather is "for those for whom it has been prepared by my Father" (so Matthew). Mark speaks only of those for whom it was prepared, but the

---

14. Craig Keener, *Matthew*, IVPNTCS 1 (Downers Grove, Ill.: InterVarsity, 1997), 308. He cites as examples Luke 18:2–5; 2 Sam. 14:1–21; 20:16–22; 1 Kings 1:11–16; 2:17.

implication of God's choice is clear. Jesus' rule still takes place in the context of the Father's sovereignty.

The ten become angry at the two sons' request. So Jesus addresses all of them and redefines ruling. He contrasts the way Gentiles rule with what they should do. Gentiles exercise power over people. Luke adds the note that Gentile kings are addressed with respect and revered in a special position as "benefactors." That is not how to lead—"not so with you." Greatness, leadership, and rule are to be defined by service and by ministry. Jesus uses the words διάκονος and δοῦλος. They are words for the labor of bond servants. Rather than asking what the masses can do for the leader, the leader seeks to do whatever possible to serve the people. The only power that leaders who follow Christ should seek is that which gives of itself to the people they are called to serve. The footwashing scene in John 13 epitomizes this teaching.

The example in this is the Son of Man. Jesus' example is that he came "not to be served but to serve, and to give his life a ransom for many." These remarks could not yet be fully appreciated by the disciples. In context, it is a metaphor for Jesus' giving his full self on behalf of others. That is likely how it was appreciated at the time Jesus said it. In light of his death, it would mean that in this giving he paid the ultimate price to perform that service. In doing so, he became the example for all (see Phil. 2:5–11). The remark is rich in Old Testament roots appealing to Isa. 43 and 53.[15]

226. Healing of the Blind at Jericho (Matt. 20:29–34; Mark 10:46–52; Luke 18:35–43) (Aland §264; Orchard §282; Huck-Greeven §207)

This account resembles an earlier miracle in Matt. 9:27–31, but its setting is placed in all three accounts as taking place near Jericho. Jesus and his disciples are now about fifteen miles from Jerusalem. Matthew has Jesus leaving Jericho, while Luke has him entering. Mark has both an arrival and a departure before telling the story. Luke may be engaged in literary compression here as a part of his larger journey motif, reducing Mark's complex construction to one element, or ἐν τῷ ἐγγίζειν may simply indicate being in the vicinity of

15. Although the authenticity of this key saying often is questioned, it also makes good sense in the context of Jesus' ministry. It goes back to him. See Otto Betz, "Jesus and Isaiah 53," in *Jesus and the Suffering Servant: Isaiah 53 and Christian Origins,* ed. William H. Bellinger and William R. Farmer (Harrisburg, Pa.: Trinity Press International, 1998), 83–87. Betz argues for the influence of Isa. 43:3–4, 23–24, as standing behind the remark, as well as Isa. 53:10, though cautioning that the ransom idea is influenced more by Isa. 43 than by Isa. 53. For the case supporting the input from Isa. 53, see Rikki Watts, "Jesus' Death, Isaiah 53, and Mark 10:45: A Crux Revisited," in ibid., 125–51.

Jericho, without a directional emphasis.[16] The other contrast between the accounts is that Matthew describes two blind people being healed, while Mark
and Luke mention only one. The blind often did move about together. It appears that Mark and Luke have simplified the account by mentioning only
one.

The other fundamental elements of the account are similar. It is to Jesus as
Son of David that they cry out. The request is for Jesus to extend mercy. The
significance of this association of Son of David (Solomon) with healing was
treated in unit 83 above. The crowd rebukes the effort, calling for silence, but
the cry continues "all the more." Jesus stops to respond to the request. Mark
renders it directly, while Matthew and Luke summarize. The direct address
by Jesus brings an additional note of the crowd's reaction, telling the suppli-
cant, "Take heart; rise, he is calling you." Mark alone also notes how the man
sprang up in response. In all the versions, Jesus asks them "What do you want
me to do?" The request is for sight, with Matthew's "Let our eyes be opened,"
and Mark and Luke's "Let me receive my sight."[17]

In Matthew, Jesus touches the eyes of the pair. They are immediately
healed and follow him. In Mark, the blind person is told to go on his way,
while Luke has Jesus issue a command to receive sight. Then in both Mark
and Luke, the man is told that his faith has made him well. His sight returns
immediately, and the man follows Jesus. Luke closes with the note that the
man was glorifying God as the crowd gave praise. This is Luke's typical celebratory note about God's activity, like the hymnic material in Luke's infancy
account.

The miracle is a significant contrast to the seeming blindness of the disciples and especially of the rich young man, who did not perceive what Jesus
was about. Here, the blind see clearly that Jesus is about deliverance. Luke will
add a second example of insight when he alone turns to mention Zacchaeus.

227. Zacchaeus (Luke 19:1–10) (Aland §265; Orchard §283; Huck-Greeven §208)

Luke notes that insight comes not only for the blind, but also for the rejected, reinforcing Jesus' commitment to those on the fringe. Jesus' encounter

16. Craig Blomberg, *The Historical Reliability of the Gospels* (Downers Grove, Ill.: InterVarsity, 1987), 128–30; S. E. Porter, "'In the Vicinity of Jericho': Luke 18:35 in the Light of Its
Synoptic Parallels," *Bulletin for Biblical Research* 2 (1992): 91–104. Jesus' encounter with Zacchaeus in Jericho follows in Luke 19:1–10, so that Luke tells a cluster of Jericho events, but it
is not certain that that event had to follow this one in sequence.

17. Luke alters the blind man's address of Jesus in Mark as "Rabboni" to "Lord," its Gentile
equivalent.

with Zacchaeus, a rich chief tax collector, makes the point. Here is one rich person who gets into the kingdom and through whom God works the impossible (cf. Luke 18:25–27).

As Jesus travels through Jericho, he draws such a big crowd that Zacchaeus, short in stature, cannot see him. So he runs and climbs a tree to see Jesus. The teacher stops and addresses Zacchaeus, declaring that he must stay with him this very day. When Zacchaeus descends joyfully and welcomes Jesus, the crowd murmurs. The complaint is that Jesus would be the guest of a sinner. The complaint recalls Luke 5:27–32; 7:36–50; 15:1–2; 18:9–14.

Zacchaeus's response shows his heart. In all likelihood, the present tense of the verbs δίδωμι and ἀποδίδωμι indicates a present resolve to give in response to Jesus' grace. It is as if he understands the crowd's complaint. He offers to give half of his goods to the poor and to repay fourfold anyone he defrauded. Built into the remark is a confession of wrongdoing for fraud. Thus the remark evidences a repentant heart. Legal restitution required adding 20 percent (Lev. 5:16; Num. 5:7), but a maximum doubling of that fine was the penalty for rustling (Exod. 22:1; 2 Sam. 12:6). Zacchaeus takes the harsher penalty, fitting the harsh contemporary penalties.[18] Jesus fully affirms the response, announcing that this very day salvation has come to Zacchaeus's house. Zacchaeus did not have to give away everything, as the rich young man was asked to do, because God saw that his heart was in the right place, being generous and unselfish. Jesus also identifies Zacchaeus as a "son of Abraham," a remark parallel to what was said about a restored woman in Luke 13:16.[19] Zacchaeus is an example of the mission of the Son of Man. Jesus' task is to seek and save the lost. A lost sheep is recovered. The cynicism of the crowd stands challenged by the outreach.

228. The Parable of the Pounds (Luke 19:11–27; conceptual in a later context: Matt. 25:14–30; more briefly, Mark 13:34) (Aland §266; Orchard §284; Huck-Greeven §209)

Luke presents a parable that is similar to one that Matthew has in the Olivet discourse, although there are enough differences in detail that the two parables can be considered variations on the same theme.[20] It is another parable on

18. Darrell L. Bock, *Luke 9:51–24:53*, BECNT 3B (Grand Rapids: Baker, 1996), 1520.
19. The remark reflects Luke's narrative gender balance.
20. For these parables the setting differs (Jericho, Jerusalem), the audience differs (public, disciples), the complexity of the details differs (Luke has citizens who refuse the kingship), the main figure differs (nobleman, businessperson), the number of slaves differs (ten, three), the monetary unit differs (mina, talent), and the reward differs (different amount to each, same amount). This appears to be a teaching that Jesus presented with some variation.

stewardship. However, it also is told because as Jesus neared Jerusalem, "they supposed that the kingdom would appear immediately." So Jesus' point is that he will be away for a while; the key to the parable is a nobleman who goes away to a far country to receive a kingdom. The kingdom's appearing is a way to refer to its final, decisive presence, although its reception comes in the far country. Jesus' arrival in Jerusalem will not bring that moment. He faces something else there. However, what he faces will send him to a place where the kingdom will be acquired.

The background to the parable is the history of the Herodian family and the selection of Archelaus. He was not popular with the Jews, so they sent a delegation of fifty to Augustus to ask that he not be made king (Josephus, *Ant.* 17.8.1 §188; 17.9.3 §222; 17.11.4 §317; *War* 2.6.1 §80; 2.6.3 §93). As a result, the Romans made him only an ethnarch. Jesus compares that situation to Israel's refusal to accept him. The Jewish people had a way of refusing leaders appointed for them. However, beyond those who refuse him outright are those who are interested in him. Much of the parable deals with those who have made an effort to connect to him.

The basic parable involves the nobleman calling ten servants and giving them ten minas (one each). A mina was one hundred drachmas or denarii, and it represented one hundred days' basic wage. Their responsibility was to trade the minas and make money. In contrast to the servants given the minas, the citizens, hating him, sent emissaries to ask that he not be made king. The nobleman returns after an unspecified time and gathers his servants together. At this point the parable is compressed, and Jesus tells what happened with only three of the ten servants. It is here that the contrast between the two faithful servants and one unfaithful servant surfaces. The first earned ten minas with the one. The second earned five. Both are commended and given authority over ten and five cities, respectively. Their faithfulness has led to commendation and an expansion of responsibility.

The key figure is the third, unfaithful servant, who earns nothing with his one mina. He simply hid the money away and claims that he feared the nobleman as a severe man, who takes up what he did not lay down and reaps what he did not sow. In other words, he neither respects nor trusts the nobleman, viewing him as dishonest and only to be feared. The third servant is rebuked. If that is how the servant viewed the nobleman, then why did he not at least put the money in the bank, where interest would be gained? The one mina then is transferred to the one who had made ten. This move shocks the crowd. They note that this servant already has ten minas.

Jesus' reply is the key lesson of the parable. He says, "I tell you, to all those who have, more will be given; but from those who have not, even what they have will be taken away." In other words, the third slave, by disrespecting the nobleman and doing nothing in response to him, showed his heart. That servant ends up with nothing at all. Not every servant with a seeming connection to Jesus will end up blessed, because some will not have embraced him and will end up with nothing. This slave is one of many "odd man out" figures in Jesus' parables (Matt. 13:29–30, 41, 49–50; 18:32–34; 22:11–13; 25:41; Luke 12:46).[21] The parable is told to urge faithfulness even in Jesus' coming absence. The parable closes with a note of how the citizens, "these enemies of mine who did not want me to reign," are slain. They picture those in Israel who never even pretended to draw near to Jesus. They are judged. As Luke 23 will show, this alludes to the national judgment of Israel in A.D. 70, which itself is a picture of ultimate judgment that the presence of the consummated kingdom will bring with Jesus' return. As Jesus prepares to enter Jerusalem and face the opposition, he warns those following him of their need for patient faithfulness. It is a major theme in Luke's Gospel, which a troubled Theophilus needed to hear.

229. Entry into Jerusalem (Matt. 21:1–9; Mark 11:1–10; Luke 19:28–40; John 12:12–19) (Aland §269; Orchard §288; Huck-Greeven §210a)[22]

Jesus' entry into Jerusalem culminates the journey and sets up the decisive confrontation between Jesus and the Jewish leadership. The entry comes in the context of the pilgrims' arrival in preparation for the feasts associated with Passover and Unleavened Bread.

The disciples reach Bethphage and the Mount of Olives, east of Jerusalem. Luke also mentions Bethany. Jesus sends two disciples into the village to obtain an animal on which Jesus will ride into Jerusalem. Matthew alone discusses two animals, a donkey and a colt, just as he alone mentioned two blind men earlier in Jericho. This detail makes the passage recall Zech. 9:9 more clearly. John 12:16 notes that the connection to this prophetic text was not appreciated until after Jesus' death. Mark and Luke note that the animal is previously unridden. When the two disciples go to get the animal and are asked what they are doing, they are merely to say that "the Lord has need of it." Matthew and Mark note the promise to return the animal. This represents an appeal to the custom of *angaria,* the temporary procurement of resources on behalf of a leader, either ruler or rabbi.[23] The sense of each of the versions

21. Another view sees this parable as only treating the issue of rewards for the third servant. It is a possible understanding of this text. However, against it is the imagery that leaves the "wicked" servant with absolutely nothing (see vv. 22, 26). Another factor against it is that the parallel in Matthew refers to the third servant's fate as involving weeping and the gnashing of teeth, a figure that denotes rejection in judgment.

22. Aland places events from John 12:1–11 before this event.

23. J. D. M. Derrett, "Law in the New Testament: The Palm Sunday Colt," *Novum Testamentum* 13 (1971): 243–49. See Num. 16:15 and 1 Sam. 8:16.

is that Jesus is directing events despite the appearance that events are spinning out of his control. The account is full of irony for those who can see what God is really doing.

At this point Matthew cites Zech. 9:9. This allows the reader to see the fulfillment. Zechariah announces the coming of Israel's king to Zion, riding on a donkey and the foal of the donkey. Matthew's account explains what the events represent. Mark and Luke leave the imagery of the event to make the point. While Matthew notes that the disciples did as directed, Mark and Luke detail the disciples procuring the animal in a way that shows the events taking place just as Jesus predicted.

Now that the ride is available, garments are placed on the beast, and Jesus sits down. Denoting the arrival of an important person, the crowd places garments before him as a makeshift carpet. The description recalls 1 Kings 1:33, when David endorsed Solomon as successor. It also is like an entrance made by King Jehu in 2 Kings 9:13 (cf. Josephus, *Ant.* 9.6.2 §111). Matthew and Mark add a description of palm branches placed in with the garments. The actions are celebratory and show respect for Jesus. Luke's omission may be motivated by the fact that this was a Jewish practice, often associated with the Feast of Tabernacles (*m. Sukkah* 3.1, 8–9, 12). Matthew and Mark note how the crowds cried out, while Luke specifies those crying out as the disciples. Luke also specifies that the praise was motivated by all the mighty works they had seen. They recognize that Jesus has been God's powerful agent, an allusion back to the dispute over the source of Jesus' work in Luke 11:14–23.

The praise coming up from the crowd is summarized in various ways. Matthew notes praise given to "the Son of David." Then there is a citation of Ps. 118:26, a welcoming beatitude to the "one who comes in the name of the Lord." Psalm 118 is one of the Hallel psalms. It often was used to greet pilgrims at the Feast of Tabernacles (*m. Sukkah* 3.9, 11; 4.5, 8). The celebratory summary concludes with praise offered to the highest heaven. Mark mentions the hosannas and then the citation of Ps. 118:26. He adds another note: "Blessed is the kingdom of our father David that is coming." He also concludes with a note of praise to the highest heaven. Luke translates all of the Jewish expressions into terms intelligible to Gentiles. So the allusion to the psalm reads, "Blessed is the king who comes in the name of the Lord." The praise of heaven is explained as "Peace in heaven, and glory in the highest." For Matthew and Mark, the climactic moment of the entry is the praise in hope of the Messiah's arrival and the kingdom's approach. Jesus comes to Jerusalem as the promised Son of David, the king of the promised kingdom.

Luke alone notes the leadership's alarm. If Jesus is the promised one, then there are implications about what his teaching and his rebuke of them mean. So the Pharisees go to Jesus and tell him to rebuke his disciples. But no rebuke comes. Rather, there is the note that if the disciples did not speak, creation would. In fact, this is a rebuke of the leadership, because it says that creation is more sensitive to what is taking place than they are. They are dumber than rocks! Such a rhetorical appeal to creation is an Old Testament figure of speech (Gen. 4:10; Hab. 2:11). Jesus enters the city as Son of David, but the leadership will hear nothing of it.

230. Jesus Weeps for Jerusalem (Luke 19:41–44) (Aland §270; Orchard §289; Huck-Greeven §§210b–11)

Luke alone notes Jesus' mood as he enters the city. The tragedy of the crowd's refusal to accept him moves him to tears. The city and the nation it represents are missing the moment that could make for peace. The account sees the nation speaking in the lack of response of its leaders. The account's assumption of the nation's rejection also suggests that the crowd's praise of Jesus during his entry may have not been heartfelt but rather a joining in with his disciples, who really had meant it. So Jesus addresses them as a prophet and predicts their suffering the consequences of covenant unfaithfulness. They are missing the "time of your visitation." Jerusalem overrun was the penalty for such unfaithfulness when Babylon came (Ps. 137:9; Jer. 6:6–21; 8:8–22; Isa. 29:1–4; Nah. 3:10).[24] Jesus foresees the repetition of the pattern of such judgment as he uses the common Old Testament phrase "days are coming" (1 Sam. 2:31; 2 Kings 20:17; Jer. 7:32–34; 31:38; Isa. 39:6; Zech. 14:1). He predicts a siege of the city. Surrounded, the people will be utterly defeated and crushed. They and their children will be dashed to the ground. No stone will be left on another. The city will be rubble. Josephus described Titus's victory over Jerusalem in A.D. 70 in ways that cohere with this picture of Jerusalem's demise (*War* 5.10.4 §466; 5.12.1 §508; 7.1.1 §§1–4; 7.8.7 §§375–377). Nothing about this prediction brings rejoicing to Jesus. Israel's rejection is pure tragedy. Here is what is at stake for Israel when Jesus comes: peace or judgment. The choice is a picture of the choice that Jesus' ministry leaves for everyone.

Conclusion

The king has entered his city. The choice is before the nation. Jesus arrives in Jerusalem, still performing miracles and calling for faithfulness. The

---

24. On the language of such a prediction fitting Old Testament expectation and thus having a strong claim to authenticity, see C. H. Dodd, "The Fall of Jerusalem and the 'Abomination of Desolation,'" *Journal of Roman Studies* 37 (1947): 47–54. The rhetorical commonality of the imagery is seen as well at Qumran in 1QpHab 9.5–7 and in the Old Testament in Ezek. 4:1–2 and Isa. 3:26.

fateful final visit has come. Jesus' final week of ministry is crucial to understanding his work. It is a week filled with controversy before his arrest. In that confrontation the major issues of his life and ministry come to the fore. This is why these events occupy such a significant amount of space in each Gospel.

ELEVEN

The Passion Week

*Controversy, Prediction of Judgment and Return, Trial,
Death, and Resurrection (Matt. 21:10–28:20;
Mark 11:11–16:8; Luke 19:45–24:53)*

When one takes a look at the path which Jesus took on his way from Galilee to Jerusalem as recorded by the first three gospels one quickly notices that his path was marked by confrontations of increasing severity with representatives of all the important Jewish factions of the time. Although Jesus' disciples followed him without condition, placing all of their hopes in him, and although the poor and downtrodden were constantly surrounding him, his call to repentance and his message of the kingdom of God in parables, his discussions and his messianic symbolic actions (i.e., table fellowship with the poor and outcast and the miracles of healing) became an increasingly intolerable provocation for not a few of the Pharisees, Zealots and rich Jews. The most powerful of Jesus' enemies, however, emerged from the faction which wielded the most influence in Jerusalem, that of the chief priests and the Sadducean nobility. They controlled and administered the temple affairs, and it was precisely this group which Jesus had provoked exceedingly through the demonstrative act of the cleansing of the temple during his last days of ministry.[1]

The final week of Jesus' life is crucial to understanding what his ministry involves.[2] The controversies summarize well the decisive conflict, as

1. Peter Stuhlmacher, "Jesus of Nazareth—The Christ of Our Faith," in *Crisis in Christology: Essays in Quest of Resolution,* ed. William R. Farmer (Livonia, Mich.: Dove Booksellers, 1995), 292–93.
2. An important critical study of the events of this week is Raymond Brown, *The Death of the Messiah,* 2 vols., ABRL (New York: Doubleday, 1994). He surveys and evaluates virtually every debated point in this material through Jesus' burial. These volumes therefore are a good resource to consult for how criticism has handled these events. Brown's study is expressive of where many moderate New Testament critics are: to the right of the Jesus Seminar but not as conservative as most evangelicals.

do the issues of authority that the temple cleansing raises. The leadership becomes convinced that Jesus must be stopped. It is this decisive confrontation that Jesus foresaw as he approached Jerusalem. He had prepared the disciples for what would come, although they did not seem to appreciate what he had told them. It is in the midst of these controversies and Jesus' teaching about what they would bring that some of the most important elements of Jesus' message emerge. This chapter covers those events in slightly more detail than is found in the previous chapters in order to highlight their significance. Also, how John's Gospel fits into the Synoptic sequence is noted more often, although the details of his presentation await the discussion of his Gospel. It is a sign of how important this material is that Mark's Gospel spends so much of its account on these scenes. In fact, many have described Mark's Gospel as containing the "passion with a long prologue." This perhaps makes the point too strongly, but it is the case that, for all the Gospels, everything comes together in these final events.

231. The Cleansing of the Temple and the Cursing of the Fig Tree (Mark 11:11–17; Matt. 21:10–19; Luke 19:45–46; conceptual: John 2:13–17) (Aland §§271–73; Orchard §§291–93; Huck-Greeven §§212–14a)

These two events belong together in the narration. Matthew and Luke narrate one visit to the temple, which leads to the cursing of the fig tree in Matthew. Luke omits the cursing altogether, probably because this issue was conceptually covered in Luke 13:6–9 and because a judgment against Israel was just declared in Luke 19:41–44. Mark has a visit to the temple, a cursing, and then the passing of evening, followed the next day by a return to note the tree's condition and cleanse the temple. Matthew has collapsed the events, which Mark details.[3] Luke has simplified the whole sequence by leaving out the fig tree incident. The effect of Matthew's move is to place these events closer to each other and to make the key temple cleansing as the initial confrontation

---

3. Craig Blomberg, *The Historical Reliability of the Gospels* (Downers Grove, Ill.: InterVarsity, 1987), 136; Robert Gundry, *Mark: A Commentary on His Apology for the Cross* (Grand Rapids: Eerdmans, 1993), 679. The issue of whether John 2 narrates the same event, which John has moved forward to overview Jesus' ministry, or describes a separate incident is difficult to determine. If it is one event, it is far more likely that John has moved it forward than that all the Synoptics have moved it back, especially because the temple is such a key issue at the trial. The fact that the temple is an issue makes it likely that the temple confrontation is a fresh event. However, the probability of two events being present can also be made; see Darrell Bock, *Luke 9:51–24:53*, BECNT 3B (Grand Rapids: Baker, 1996), 1576–77.

more prominent by having it begin the sequence of events. Luke retains that prominence as well.

After the triumphal entry, Mark notes that Jesus went into the temple and looked around. Given the late hour, he departed and went out to Bethany with the Twelve. What he saw in the temple area was something that apparently was a recent innovation.[4] Money changers are operating in the temple courts in the court of the Gentiles to provide pure sacrifices and exchange money for the temple tax, which was to be paid in shekels. The practice was created for convenience. The law commanded pure sacrifices and a temple tax paid in native currency. Setting up this convenience in the temple courts is what Jesus finds most objectionable. This innovation will become a catalyst for Jesus' reaction.[5] The practice of money changing itself is treated in the Mishnah (*m. Šeqalim* 1.3; 3.1; *m. Berakot* 9.5 shows an awareness of the problem of commercialism and treats the sanctity of the temple; see also Josephus, *Ant.* 12.3.4 §145; 15.11.5 §417, where foreigners are excluded). The problem with the money changers was not a matter of economic exploitation, despite popular readings of this scene that paint the issue this way.[6] Rather, Jesus' action in the temple was fundamentally a prophetic one to point the nation in a fresh direction and announce the arrival of a key figure in God's program.

So a second key element of background is that there was an important expectation that the Messiah would share in a renewed temple worship.[7] This view may have been motivated by Zech. 14:21: "And there shall no longer be traders in the house of the LORD of hosts on that day." The idea of the hope of the eschaton was that the Messiah was needed because he would bring a righteousness to the people as well as deliverance (Isa. 9–11). A premise of that scenario was that Israel needed to reform its ways. The mood is like Jer. 19, where the prophet smashes the pot to predict judgment. It is an acted parable in a similar mood.

4. For the details of the timing of this innovation as fitting into this period, see V. Eppstein, "The Historicity of the Gospel Account of the Cleansing of the Temple," *Zeitschrift für die Neutestamentliche Wissenschaft* 55 (1964): 42–58.

5. For a discussion of this event and its historical background, see C. A. Evans, "Jesus' Action in the Temple: Cleansing or Portent of Destruction?" *Catholic Biblical Quarterly* 51 (1989): 237–70.

6. Craig Keener, *A Commentary on the Gospel of Matthew* (Grand Rapids: Eerdmans, 1999), 495–501.

7. See especially the juxtaposition in *Shemoneh Esreh*, benediction 14; other examples and discussions of God's coming to the temple in the end are Josephus, *Ant.* 18.4.1 §§85–87; *War* 6.5.2 §§283–285; Tob. 14:5; 2 Macc. 2:7; *1 Enoch* 24–25; 89–90; *Jubilees* 1.15–17; CD 3.19–4.1, where a future sacrifice associated with eternal life is in view; 1QM 12.12–18 and 19.4–8, where the nations come defeated into the city as Israel rejoices in worship; 11QTempleᵃ 29.8–10.

According to Mark, Jesus, on the way to the temple, apparently on the next day, was hungry.[8] He saw a fig tree in leaf. In the early spring, the only thing on a fig tree is the early formation of buds. It was not yet the season for any figs, which normally fell in early budding in June, with harvest coming a few months later. In a surprising move, Jesus issues a curse on the tree.[9] The act is an indication that certain things in this week will be symbolic, because the curse is a symbolic declaration of the power of Jesus' word and the importance of faith (see Mark 11:20–26; Matt. 21:20–22). That word acts against a symbol of the nation, a fig tree, picturing a judgment to come in the confrontation that lies ahead (see Mic. 7:1–6; Jer. 8:13). Mark 11:20 notes that the next day, the disciples saw the fig tree withered. This event in Matthew follows the temple cleansing, and the description of the withering is collapsed into a simple note that it withered immediately.

The temple cleansing comes just after the crowd's excited acclaim for Jesus at his entry. It is a volatile combination of events. Matthew notes how some in the crowd asked who this one was, indicating that some did not know who was causing the stir. The reply was that it was "Jesus the prophet from Nazareth of Galilee." This description fits the public perception of Jesus noted in Matt. 16:14. Jesus acts against the money changers and those who sold pigeons for sacrifices. His goal does not seem to have been to stop sacrifices, but to complain about how the temple was being transformed into a place of corruption. He cites Isa. 56:7 and Jer. 7:11, making his act a prophetic complaint, as well as an act of messianic, eschatological cleansing. Mark's citation is the fullest: "Is it not written, 'My house shall be called a house of prayer for all the nations'? But you have made it a den of robbers." Only Mark mentions the temple as being for the nations, while Matthew and Luke merely juxtapose the reference to a house of prayer with the issue of robbers. It is the picture of encroaching commerce as a sign of a heart moving away from worship that Jesus challenges here. In other words, the tables of the money changers represented a worship that was efficient in providing access but did not come with the requisite preparation of the heart. This is what made the temple the home of "robbers." It was proper worship in part that was being robbed. The appeal to Isa. 56, with its eschatological hope for the spread of worship among the nations, shows Jesus' eschatological vision, which he bore as a messianic claimant as he entered the city. The appeal to the rebuke of Jer. 7, which is

8. Mark sandwiches the account to show the relationship between the temple scene and the state of the nation as pictured by the fig tree. Matthew simply presents the two scenes in sequence.

9. This is one of only two miracles that result in any destruction. The healing of the demoniacs whereby the pigs drowned in the sea was the other such incident. However, this is the only miracle in which Jesus is directly responsible for the destruction. For a defense of its authenticity, see C. E. B. Cranfield, *The Gospel according to Saint Mark,* Cambridge Greek Testament Commentary (Cambridge: Cambridge University Press, 1959), 356–57.

one of the Hebrew Scripture's most scathing sermons, shows that the temple situation is but symptomatic of a larger national problem. Such a critique of the temple would not have been unique to Jesus; the Qumran community also saw the temple as corrupt (1QpHab 9.4–5; CD 5.6–7). What added fuel to the fire was the additional and unique physical nature of the protest. The "table turning" carried a potentially explosive vividness that the leadership could not ignore. The last thing the leadership needed was a popular "prophetic" figure to challenge them. Nor did they want the crowds to engage in messianic hope. No wonder the leadership was so concerned about Jesus' presence.

In contrast to all of this was Jesus' activity for the blind and the lame, which only Matthew notes. Jesus is healing them. Given that some would have excluded these groups from the temple (LXX 2 Kingdoms 5:8; *m. Ḥagigah* 1.1), Jesus' work with them was significant. The crowds are crying out, "Hosanna to the Son of David!" The contrast is stark. The temple establishment, although working in conjunction with practices that the law prescribes, is dealing with the temple crowds in a commercial context, while Jesus is ministering deliverance to those in need. The leaders are nervous and go to Jesus to complain of these exclamations of praise. Jesus responds, "Out of the mouth of babes and sucklings you [God] have brought perfect praise" (Matt. 21:16). The language alludes to Ps. 8:2 and accepts the crowd's exclamations as appropriate. The exchange resembles Luke 19:39–40, when Jesus entered the city. Matthew's point is that the leaders are nervous, while some in the crowd sense the messianic moment. So Matthew narrates the cursing of the fig tree after moving through this rising tension within the nation and the leadership's rejection of what is taking place. It is easy to see why the pressure was building toward some kind of resolution.

232. The Leadership Decides against Jesus (Mark 11:18–19; Luke 19:47–48) (Aland §274; Orchard §294; Huck-Greeven §214b)

The cleansing of the temple (Mark) and the additional factor of Jesus' teaching in the temple (Luke) cause the leadership of the chief priests and scribes to commit themselves to destroying Jesus. This joins them to a commitment made much earlier by the Pharisees and Herodians in Mark 3:6. The major Jewish groups, including the most politically powerful elements, now were united in seeking to stop Jesus. Now, both theologically motivated and politically motivated opponents have joined together to stop Jesus. Ironically, he had brought the leaders of the nation together, but in rejection, not acceptance, of his message. The honesty of the text here speaks for the account's authenticity.

Both Gospels focus on the effect of Jesus' drawing power on the leadership. Mark expresses it as their fear of Jesus because the crowd (ὁ ὄχλος) was astonished at his teaching. The threat is that the leaders' way will come under challenge and scrutiny. Luke expresses it as their impotence to act against Jesus in the face of his popularity. The leadership thought that they could do nothing because the people (ὁ λαός) hung on his words. Normally, the people are a positive referent in Luke, but in the passion material they will turn on Jesus in 23:13.[10] Jesus' teaching had caught the populace's attention, leading to their openness, but eventually the leadership would get them to join in rejecting Jesus. Still, things were finely balanced, so the leadership would have to act carefully so as not to incite the people.

233. The Explanation of the Fig Tree (Matt. 21:20–22; Mark 11:20–26) (Aland §275; Orchard §295; Huck-Greeven §215)

The fig tree incident brought a response from Jesus' disciples. Matthew describes it as a marveling by all of them. They ask how this could have happened. In Mark, it brings a response from Peter, who remembered what Jesus had said the day before. He points out to Jesus that the tree "you cursed has withered."

Jesus' response leads to a declaration of the importance of faith. This is a theme that Luke already raised in 17:5–6, but in this distinct setting a specific promise may emerge. Matthew has Jesus note that a faith that does not doubt will lead to deeds even more amazing than withering a fig tree. One can say to "this" (τούτῳ) mountain, "Be cast into the sea," and it will be done. The remark possibly is about Jerusalem, given the context. The city represented by the fig tree also can be seen as Mt. Zion. It will suffer a judgment. If the "this" is not so important to the reading, then the remark is more generic. Faith will allow the disciple to do the seemingly impossible, a meaning more like Luke 17. Whatever you ask for in prayer you will receive, if you have faith. This teaching recalls another theme of Luke raised in 11:9–13. Effective prayer involves trust in God's ability to provide and in his goodness to do what is right.

Mark has an opening exhortation that Matthew lacks: "Have faith in God." Mark repeats the word about "this" mountain. He also calls for an absence of doubt in prayer but expresses it as the idea that one should believe that what one says will come to pass. The mood here is like James 1:5–8 in asking for wisdom.[11] So when the disciple prays for something, he or she should believe that it has been received, and it will be given. A believer can rest in God's goodness. This prayer will be answered. Mark has one more unique

---

10. One can trace the sequence in Luke 20:1–6, 19, 26, 45; 22:2, 23:2, 35; 24:19–20.

11. In John's Gospel, this theme appears to surface in the context of asking "in my name" or of "abiding in him" or in the context of the guidance of the Spirit; see John 14:13–14; 15:7; 16:23.

note. Prayer should include a readiness to forgive others, because this frees the Father's forgiveness. Matthew already had made this point about forgiveness in 6:14–15. So the fig tree becomes an occasion for Jesus to underscore that faith, especially as it is expressed in the context of dependent and believing prayer and in a setting of forgiveness, can accomplish great things. In other words, God will be responsive to the petitioner who has paid attention to how he or she relates to others. In 1 Pet. 3:7, a similar point is made to husbands in regard to efficacious prayer and considerate treatment of wives.

234. By Whose Authority? (Matt. 21:23–27; Mark 11:27–33; Luke 20:1–8) (Aland §276; Orchard §296; Huck-Greeven §216)

This section begins a series of climactic controversies, much like Mark 2:1–3:6 began that Gospel. Six controversies follow in tight succession. Matthew adds two parables to the sequence that the other Gospels lack. They come before and after the parable of the wicked tenants. This addition makes for another Matthean triad, as is his custom (see Matt. 8–9). Matthew and Mark add a discussion in the sequence on the great commandment, which gives a contrasting look at someone who is on the right track in responding to Jesus and the law in a proper way. Ultimately, the controversial question that the leadership raises in the first of the controversies lingers through the sequence: Who gave Jesus such authority? Underneath the narrative, an equally important question lingers: In whose authority will the reader trust, that of the leadership or that of Jesus?

The initial controversy is very similar in each Gospel. The leadership asks Jesus about the source of his authority for doing "these things" (ταῦτα). So the dispute is about more than the temple cleansing, although that certainly brought the issue to the fore. Chief priests and elders are noted by all the Synoptics, and only in Matthew are scribes not mentioned. The issue of the source of Jesus' authority has been a point of contention since he claimed to forgive the paralytic's sins in Mark 2 and parallels. It was in dispute in his miraculous work in Luke 11:14–20 and parallels. The temple cleansing has made the issue of special importance because now he has acted upon the central symbol of Jewish worship. Of course, the hidden premise in the leadership's question is that Jesus has acted without their sanction.

Jesus replies with a question of his own. He asks about the origin of John's baptism. Is it "from heaven or of human origin?" It is an important retort because John worked "independently" as well. The dilemma of the reply was real. Both options are posed in class three Greek conditions as equal options. If they acknowledged a heavenly source, then Jesus' response will be to ask why they did not respond ("believe"). On the other hand, if they say that John was acting only as a mortal being, then the crowd will be skeptical of them, because the multitude regarded John as a true prophet. Luke states this dilemma most emphatically: "They will stone us." The leadership will be revealed as false themselves. They have not recognized a true prophet. Exodus 17:4 and Num. 14:10 are cases where the people wrongly threatened to stone Moses. There, they were rejecting his claim to be a true prophet and saw him as a false one who should be stoned (cf. Deut. 13:1–5). The leaders feel the threat of the weight of popular opinion and sense being rejected by them as a result, but they do not want to admit any opening to Jesus. They contemplate their answer not in terms of truth but in terms of how it will play. Their trap has sprung back on them. The narrative power of the account resides in that very sense of reversal.

They pretend not to be able to know the answer. In "taking a pass" on the reply, they cede the ground, so that Jesus refuses to answer their question. There really is nothing that Jesus needs to say. In a sense, his question answered theirs, because if one saw God's call behind John the Baptist, then they could understand the source of Jesus' call as well. Given what God has done through Jesus, how can they question Jesus' authority? Nonetheless, the rest of the controversy narrative will provide another answer to the question about authority. How does Jesus fare in these disputes versus the leadership? Who seems to understand the way of God in these final controversies? The question of authority rests in these two options: either the leadership or Jesus expresses the way to know God. The consistent presentation of Jesus' upper hand in these controversies provides another ground for the answer to the choice posed by the leaders' question. Jesus' responses and work show that he has divinely bestowed authority.

235. The Parable of the Two Sons (Matt. 21:28–32) (Aland §277; Orchard §297; Huck-Greeven §217)

Matthew begins a sequence of three parables. Matthew's placement of this parable of the two sons makes it a commentary on the previous scene. Two sons picture the possible responses to Jesus and his message. The first is asked to work in the vineyard but initially refuses; the second is asked and initially agrees. The first son repents and goes to work in the vineyard, while the second son changes his mind and does not. Jesus asks a simple question: "Which of the two did the will of his father?" The leaders reply correctly that the first son did what his father asked.

Jesus applies the parable. The tax collectors and the harlots go into the kingdom before the leaders. The explanation follows: "For John came to you in the way of righteousness, but you did not believe him, but the tax collectors and the harlots believed him; and even when you saw it, you did not afterward repent and believe him." Jesus comes back to the issue of John the Baptist as a way to challenge the leadership about their lack of response to God's appointed messengers. The remarks are shocking at several levels. First is Jesus' open acceptance of the response of these "sinful" types. Second, the remark shows how strongly Jesus did connect his mission to that of John. In this sense, it provides a Matthean answer to the previous controversy about the source of Jesus' authority. Like John's, it is from God. Third, there is Jesus' declaration of multiple opportunities for the leadership to respond. When sinners turned, they did not turn after them. So Jesus argues that they are hypocrites without directly calling them that. They are like a son who says he will go into the vineyard and work for the Lord but does not. In contrast stand the tax collectors and harlots, who initially refuse but eventually turn. Jesus' remarks have an earlier conceptual parallel in Luke 7:29–30. Themes raised here also appear elsewhere in Matthew (3:2; 7:21; 12:50; 23:3). Finally, the idea that tax collectors and harlots would have a greater role in the kingdom than the leadership is a frightening reversal of expectation and full of challenge to them.

236. The Parable of the Wicked Tenants (Matt. 21:33–46; Mark 12:1–12; Luke 20:9–19) (Aland §278; Orchard §298; Huck-Greeven §218)

This parable is one of the most important that Jesus tells, because it overviews the history of the leaders' response to Jesus.[12] Here is a case of a parable with clear allegorical features, since virtually every step in the story has a correspondence in Israel's history. The leaders are the tenants who are at work in the vineyard, which itself pictures Israel in promise as a field of potential blessing to be tended (see Isa. 5:1–7; Ezek. 17:6 [of the king]; Hos. 9:10). The parable's imagery is more complicated than Isaiah's picture, for Jesus notes custodians of the field. Mark 12:12 and Luke 20:19 make it clear that the leaders as those custodians are the main target of Jesus' criticism. Matthew and Mark describe the vineyard and the protection given to it in great detail (cf. Ps. 80:12–14; 2 Chron. 26:10; Isa. 1:8). By contrast, Luke keeps the account simple. The detail of the building of the vineyard shows God's lavish provision for the nation. All the conditions for fruitfulness existed. Uniquely, Luke notes that the owner went away "for a long time." God has had a long history of involvement with the nation, even though he appears to have been away.

12. A careful, detailed study of this parable is Klyne Snodgrass, *The Parable of the Wicked Tenants: An Inquiry into Parable Interpretation*, WUNT 27 (Tübingen: Mohr, 1983).

At various times the owner sends servants to collect the fruit from the vines. But they are poorly treated. There is variation in the details of the accounts. Matthew has them beaten, killed, and stoned, while a second group meets a similar fate. Mark has an escalating reaction. The first servant is beaten and sent away empty-handed. The second is wounded on the head and sent away in shame. The third is killed. Many others are sent, some beaten and some killed. Luke has the first beaten. The second also is beaten and treated in shame. Both leave empty-handed. A third is wounded and cast out. In each case the details serve to indicate the rejection of the prophets (cf. Jer. 7:21–26; 25:4).[13] The repetition of the action shows God's patience and the tenants' hostility to his will.

Next he decides to send his son. Mark and Luke describe him as the "beloved" son, possibly tightening an allusion back to Jesus' title at the baptism. Here Jesus shows his own self-understanding as involving a unique relationship to God.

Logic would dictate respect for someone in the owner's family, but sin is cruel and blind. The tenants decide to kill the son in hopes of inheriting the land. It often was the case that land left without an heir went to those who worked it.[14] However, such a benefit would not come to those discovered to have murdered the rightful heir! There is something illogical about the way these tenants think and act. So the son is slain. Matthew and Luke have him cast out of the vineyard and killed, while Mark has the reverse order.

Jesus asks what the owner will do. In each Gospel, he answers the question. Mark and Luke have it most compactly: "He will come and destroy the [Mark]/those [Luke] tenants, and give the vineyard to others." Matthew elaborates: "He will put those wretches to a miserable death, and let out the vineyard to others who will give him the fruits in their seasons." The current leaders are judged and exchanged by God for other leaders. The new set of leaders includes Jews, as surely the reference looks at its base to the Twelve. It also implies that leadership eventually will come from other sources, a hint that perhaps other nations might be represented in the work that God will do. However, for the current leaders of God's people, there is only the prospect of judgment. Only Luke notes the reaction of the crowd. It is a nervous exclamation: "God forbid!"[15]

Jesus then cites Scripture from Ps. 118:22–23, a psalm already noted in Luke 13:35 and in the triumphal entry as an eschatological psalm of hope to

13. W. F. Arndt, *The Gospel according to St. Luke* (St. Louis: Concordia, 1956), 404, notes these variations in the versions and speaks of an *ad sensum* rendering. Jesus told the account with wave after wave of rejected messengers. For a defense of fundamental authenticity, see Cranfield, *Mark*, 365–68.

14. Joachim Jeremias, *The Parables of Jesus*, rev. ed., trans. S. H. Hooke, New Testament Library (Philadelphia: Westminster, 1963), 75 n. 99.

15. The "they said" (εἶπαν, *eipan*) of Luke 20:16 looks back to v. 9.

first-century Jews. But now the tables of that psalm's meaning are turned on the leadership. In its original setting, the psalm would have depicted the Gentiles' rejection of the king of Israel in battle, a king who now returns victorious and is welcomed by the nation. But now, tragically, it is the leaders of Israel who are the rejectors.[16] Nonetheless, the king, the stone, will be lifted up to be a capstone, despite their rejection, and it will all be a marvelous work of God. The note about God's work is only in Matthew and Mark.

Matthew has an additional point here. Jesus says, "The kingdom of God will be taken away from you and given to a nation producing fruits of it." This does appear to suggest the possibility of Gentile inclusion because of the use of the term ἔθνος (nation) in that verse.

Matthew and Luke then include a conceptual allusion, tied by midrashic link to the idea of the "stone." It involves the image of the destruction of pots: either they fall on the stone or the stone falls on them. The remark is a proverb whose point is that whichever way the stone and the pots meet, it is bad for the pots! It is like *Esther Rabbah* 7.10, which reads "If a stone falls on the pot, alas for the pot; if the pot falls on the stone, alas for the pot." The background for this image appears to be Dan. 2:44–45. The shattering is complete, a breaking to bits.

The parable is too much to bear. The chief priests (Matthew and Luke), Pharisees (Matthew), and scribes (Luke) understand that Jesus told the parable against them and want to arrest him.[17] Their fear of the crowd prevents them from doing so. Matthew says that the crowd's view was that Jesus was a prophet, not a surprising deduction in light of so condemnatory a parable. The confrontation is becoming stronger and more heated.

237. The Parable of the Great Supper (Matt. 22:1–14; conceptual: Luke 14:15–24 [see unit 197 above]) (Aland §279; Orchard §299; Huck-Greeven §219)

In this context, Matthew gives the final parable in his triad. The picture is of a marriage feast, which often is a figure for eschatological blessing, as was noted in the earlier treatment of Luke 14. The custom is of inviting friends, who accept and then are told at a later date when the party is ready. The key player here is not an owner but a king. An invitation to the marriage feast now is extended by the servants, who announce that the feast is ready. However,

16. A similar tragic note of rejection and reversal takes place in Acts 4:25–26 and its use of Ps. 2:1.
17. It is often suggested that Luke is less harsh against the Pharisees, so he has omitted them here. Mark simply refers to "they," which appears to go back to 11:27 and its reference to chief priests, scribes, and elders.

the invited will not come, an insult contrary to the expected response (cf. Sir. 13:9–10; *Ruth Rabbah* proem 7). A second gracious extension of the invitation is met with derision, the pursuit of other matters, and the slaying of the messengers. This final act would be considered as a severe insult to the king and worthy of a harsh response (see Josephus, *War* 2.17.10 §§450–456; *Ant.* 9.13.2 §§264–266). The king responds in anger and sends his troops to slay the insolent murderers and destroy their city. An allusion to the approaching covenant judgment of Jerusalem is in view here. It is Matthew's equivalent of Luke 19:41–44.

The remaining servants are sent out to invite others. Those originally invited were not worthy, so the servants are sent out to gather "as many as you find." Both good and bad now come, so that the wedding feast goes ahead despite the absence of the original invitees.

The Matthean version of the parable has a unique section next. The king comes in to look at the guests. One man is not appropriately dressed in the wedding garments expected for the occasion. He has either refused the wedding garments provided for him, or he is wearing soiled, inappropriate garments.[18] The man is asked how he got in without an appropriate garment and is left speechless. The man is cast out. There follows detail that breaks the symbolism of the parable to make the point of application: he is cast into outer darkness, where there is weeping and gnashing of teeth. This figure is consistently used in Matthew of those who are decisively rejected (8:12; 13:42; 24:51; 25:30). "For many are called, but few are chosen." This is another example of the "odd man out" in a parable. It represents the person who professes a relationship to Christ, gets close to him, but never really knows him. The prime example in Jesus' ministry of such a figure is Judas, who, like the figure in the parable, will be addressed with the description of "friend" at the betrayal (Matt. 22:12; 26:50). Thus, Jesus issues a warning here to the leadership and to any close to him who might betray him. It was a warning that went unheeded by many.

238. On Paying Tribute to Caesar (Matt. 22:15–22; Mark 12:13–17; Luke 20:20–26) (Aland §280; Orchard §300; Huck-Greeven §220)

The next controversy involves both the Pharisees and the Herodians according to Matthew and Mark, as they seek to trap Jesus. Luke speaks only of spies who pretended to be sincere in order to use what he said so that they could deliver him to the authority and jurisdiction of the governor. The issue is the poll tax paid to Rome, which Jews hated because it reminded them of their subservience to Rome (Josephus, *Ant.* 18.1.1 §1–10 notes how Judas the

18. Keener, *Gospel of Matthew*, 325.

Galilean tried to raise a resistance movement against it). The Herodians had made peace with the tax because they supported the ruler whom the Romans had appointed for the nation. The idea was that either way Jesus responded to the question would lead to someone being unhappy with him. If Jesus urged that the tax be paid, then Jews hoping for a nationalistic messiah would be disillusioned with him; if he rejected payment of the tax, then they could go to Pilate and present Jesus as an insurrectionist. After some flattery about how Jesus truthfully teaches the way of God and does not bend to public opinion, they ask, "Is it lawful to pay taxes to Caesar, or not?"

Jesus is aware of their motive. Matthew describes it as malice. Mark presents it as hypocrisy. Luke characterizes their action as craftiness. In Matthew and Mark, Jesus questions their testing of him. Matthew adds a note of Jesus calling them hypocrites directly. He asks them for a coin and points out through a rhetorical question that Caesar's image is on it. In producing the coin, Jesus' opponents show that they already operate with the currency, nullifying any complaint of principle. They produce a denarius, a coin about the size of a dime, with Caesar's likeness on it. It would have carried an inscription of Tiberius as "God and High Priest" and "Son of the divine Augustus."

Jesus replies that they should "render unto Caesar the things that are Caesar's and to God the things that are God's." Jesus turned their either/or question into a both/and, thus escaping the trap. They should pay the tax *and* honor God. What is a part of Roman government, they should respect, but they also should honor God. The implication is that just as a coin is stamped with Caesar's image, so our life is stamped with God's imprint and we owe him proper allegiance as well. After all, humanity is made in God's image. What is taught here is not a "separation of church and state," but the recognition of existing spheres of given relationship and responsibility. Both God and the state need to be properly honored. An implied critique that God is not being honored is present. The answer amazed them. In Matthew, they leave, while in Luke, they are silenced.

239. Question about Resurrection (Matt. 22:23–33; Mark 12:18–27; Luke 20:27–40) (Aland §281; Orchard §301; Huck-Greeven §221)

The Sadducees take a turn at trying to catch Jesus in a theological controversy. Their topic is resurrection, a doctrine they did not believe (cf. Josephus, *Ant.* 18.1.4 §16; *War* 2.8.14 §§164–165). They try to show the absurdity of the doctrine by appealing to the example of levirate marriage (Deut. 25:5; *m. Yebamot* [this tractate on levirate marriage has sixteen chapters]; Josephus, *Ant.* 4.8.23 §§254–256). This practice required that a brother of one who died without producing any children had to marry the widow of the deceased brother. In the example that the Sadducees bring to Jesus, a woman marries and suffers through her husband's death while childless, forcing a levirate marriage. The sequence then is repeated six times, involving seven husbands altogether. The question is "When she dies, whose wife will she be in the resurrection?" The question's premise is designed to induce shock at the prospect of a woman facing seven husbands!

Jesus replies in various ways. In Matthew and Mark, he rebukes them for not knowing either the Scriptures or the power of God. Luke launches right into the substance of the reply by noting that although people of this age marry and are given in marriage, that is not so for those considered "worthy to attain to that age and to the resurrection from the dead." All the accounts observe that in the resurrection "they neither marry nor are given in marriage." Luke alone adds that they cannot die anymore, while all note that they are like angels. Luke goes on to identify the righteous as the children of God because they are children of the resurrection.

Most Jews believed that angels did not eat, drink, or propagate, although in some traditions evil angels are seen to have done so inappropriately long ago (*1 Enoch* 15.6–7; 51.4; 104.4–6; but *Testament of Abraham* 4, 5–7 has an angel [Michael] eat at God's command; 1QH 3.21–23 [= col. 11]; but note *1 Enoch* 6–9; also 2 Pet. 2 and possibly Gen. 6:1–4). The Jews even compared the righteous to angels (*1 Enoch* 39.5; 104.4–6; *2 Baruch* 51.10–11). So Jesus would not be covering new ground here. The challenge and irony for the Sadducees from Jesus' reply is that they did not believe in angels (Acts 23:8)!

For the resurrection, Jesus turns to a text from the Torah because that is the portion of Scripture that the Sadducees accepted. He notes Exod. 3:6, which speaks of the God of Abraham, Isaac, and Jacob. Matthew and Mark cite the verse using a present tense: "I am the God of. . . ." This description of God was common in Judaism to focus on God as the God of promise (see Acts 3:13). The point is not so much a result of the verb tense as it is a theological point. God has made a commitment to the patriarchs as the God of promise. To fulfill that commitment to them, they must be alive to receive what he promises. All of this presupposes resurrection and the capability of God's power to bring it to pass. So the closing remark in Matthew and Mark is that he is "not the God of the dead, but of the living." Mark emphatically adds, "You are quite wrong." In Luke, Jesus goes on to note that all live to God, to highlight the accountability that leads into judgment. In Luke, some scribes are delighted enough to commend Jesus' reply. Luke also notes that no further questions came forward. In Matthew, the crowd is left astonished at Jesus' teaching. Once again Jesus comes out looking as if he knows what he is talking about in contrast to the leadership.

240. The Great Commandment (Matt. 22:34–40; Mark 12:28–34; conceptual: Luke 10:25–28) (Aland §282; Orchard §302; Huck-Greeven §222)

One final question appears in Matthew and Mark. It comes from a scribe. Matthew has the question raised as a test, while Mark notes that it was asked because Jesus had answered the previous question well. The question concerns which commandment is first. This often was discussed in Judaism (*Genesis Rabbah* 24.7; *m. Ḥagigah* 1.8; *Mekilta* 6).

In Mark, Jesus begins his reply with Deut. 6:4, the Shema, a portion of Scripture recited daily by Jews, about the oneness of God. Matthew, with Mark, picks up next with Deut. 6:5 about loving God fully with one's entire person—expressed as heart, soul, and mind in Matthew; and as heart, soul, mind, and strength in Mark. Matthew alone calls this the "great and first commandment." To this, Jesus adds a second commandment from Lev. 19:18: "You shall love your neighbor as yourself." Matthew closes the scene with the note that all the law and the prophets depend on these. Mark transitions to an additional exchange with "There is no other commandment greater than these."

In Mark, the scribe responds by commending Jesus' reply that God is one, and that one should love him fully as well as love one's neighbor. The scribe goes on to add that to do so is "much more than all whole burnt offerings and sacrifices." This response delights Jesus, who responds to the "discreet" (νουνεχῶς) reply, "You are not far from the kingdom of God." The scribe had recognized one of the central points in Jesus' teaching. Properly relating to God translates into properly relating to others. This is more important than any ritual. The rule of God presses for people to live righteously with one another.

241. The Question about David's Son (Matt. 22:41–46; Mark 12:35–37a; Luke 20:41–44) (Aland §283; Orchard §303; Huck-Greeven §223)

The final controversy in the passion week sequence is the climactic one, and here Jesus initiates the discussion. Matthew specifies the audience as the Pharisees, while Mark and Luke place the event in a less specific context of Jesus' teaching. Matthew details a series of Jesus' questions: "What do you think of the Christ? Whose son is he?" They answer that he is the Son of David. There is good reason for this answer (2 Sam. 7:12–14; Ps. 89:29–37; Isa. 9:2–7; 11:1–9; Jer. 23:5–6; Ezek. 34:23–24; 37:24; *Psalms of Solomon*

17.21–25; 4QFlor 1.11–13). The early church also will make this point (Rom. 1:3; 2 Tim. 2:8).

This leads to the key exchange of the scene. Luke notes a passage that comes from David in the psalms. Mark notes that David was inspired by the Spirit when he declared what is recorded in Ps. 110:1. Matthew is the most explicit, not only noting the inspiration of the Spirit but also that David called the Christ "Lord." All the accounts then cite Ps. 110:1, one of the most important texts for Christology in the New Testament (Acts 2:34–35; 1 Cor. 15:25–28; Eph. 1:20; Heb. 1:13; 5:6, 10; 7:17, 21; in the early church, Justin Martyr, *First Apology* 45): "The Lord said to my Lord, 'Sit at my right hand until I put your enemies under your feet.'" Jesus asks, if David calls him Lord, then how is he David's son? Matthew alone notes that they neither answered him nor asked him any more questions. Once again Jesus emerges as superior to his opponents.

Jesus' query poses a dilemma about the Messiah's identity and person. Why is the Messiah known as David's son when David himself calls him Lord? Just as important, why would a father in a patriarchal society give his son such honor? The question works especially well in the Greek, where the term for "Lord" is repeated in the psalm quotation's opening line (κύριος/κυρίῳ). In the Hebrew of Ps. 110:1, Yahweh and Adonai are clearly distinguished. However, in the first century, the divine name, Yahweh, was not pronounced and Adonai, the term for "Lord," was substituted, so the point, contained in the play of words using the concept of Lord, would be made in the oral rendering of the psalm, whether in Hebrew or in Aramaic. However, the point of the query is not the presence of the title "Lord" as much as it is David's use of this title of respect for one who comes after him, a reversal of the normal line of respect in a patriarchal society. Why would David call his son "my Lord"? Why share a title that also is used of God? The query shares certain assumptions about Ps. 110, namely, that the psalm is from David and that it addresses, in some form, the Messiah.[19] These points Jesus accepts, and so does his audience. This style of query involves a seeming contradiction that is to be resolved through reflection. Jesus' point is not to deny that the Christ is David's son but to argue that the key name for him is "Lord." This question provides yet another answer to the query of the leadership earlier about Jesus' authority and its origin (see unit 234 above). If he is the Messiah, then the authority he possesses is one that David acknowledged to belong to the Messiah as Lord. This ruler is the one to whom God gave the right to sit at his right hand, a picture of shar-

---

19. For a discussion of the hermeneutics of this psalm, see H. W. Bateman IV, "Psalm 110:1 and the New Testament," *Bibliotheca Sacra* 149 (1992): 438–53. Bock, *Luke 9:51–24:53*, 1635–40, defends its authenticity.

ing rule on a throne and a metaphor for the sharing of his authority (Matt. 20:21; Eph. 1:20; Heb. 1:13) One of the elements of the Synoptic narrative is to pose this question here theoretically and then develop in the rest of the story how the "right hand" scene will play out. Luke-Acts develops all that this means theologically in Acts 2:30–36. So the answer to Jesus' question comes in what happens later in the week when he is examined by the leadership (see unit 271 below) and then in the preaching of the church in Acts.

242. Woe to the Scribes and Pharisees (Matt. 23:1–36; Mark 12:37b–40; Luke 20:45–47; conceptual in earlier contexts: Luke 11:46, 52; 6:39; 11:42, 39–41, 44, 47–48, 49–51, 43 [see unit 175 above]) (Aland §284; Orchard §304; Huck-Greeven §224)

In Matthew, the hostility between Jesus and the leadership is portrayed in its most intense form.[20] This is only natural in a Gospel in which Jewish issues are so prominent. A variation of these woes and complaints in Matt. 23 appears in a different setting and in a far different order in Luke 11. This is not surprising. Like remarks made about a political opponent during the length of a campaign, it is likely that such remarks took place repeatedly in Jesus' ministry. The presence of Jesus seriously challenging the leadership on a variety of matters is multiply attested in the tradition. Here we see the strongest of those challenges. It is a natural result of things coming to a head. Mark and Luke have far shorter versions of this exchange. Luke probably regarded Luke 11 as the equivalent of this. In contrast, Matthew will not record the account of the widow's mite, which Mark and Luke have, possibly because it would break up the theme of judgment introduced here. So Matt. 23 opens a set of remarks comprising a long section of Matthew treating judgment, as the Olivet discourse and several parables about that judgment follow in Matt. 24–25. Israel and judgment form the issue in Matt. 23, while the nations are brought into the mix in Matt. 24–25.

The audience for these remarks is not those who are rebuked, but the crowds (23:1). Thus, there is a warning here not to be like the leadership. It also represents Jesus contending for his different way of approaching God. Matthew takes the condemnation and makes a pastoral plea to his readers not to repeat the spiritual errors of the past.

Jesus begins by noting the prominence of the Pharisees and the scribes, who sit in "Moses' seat." In later Judaism this expression was used for those who sat and taught the law (*t. Sanhedrin* 7.8; 8.1 discusses such ranking; 1QS

---

20. Steve Mason, "Pharisaic Dominance before 70 CE and the Gospel's Hypocrisy Charge," *Harvard Theological Review* 83 (1990): 363–81.

2.19–23).[21] Deuteronomy 17:10 speaks of obeying what the priests and judges say about legal questions. It formed a type of precedent for this kind of instruction. Jesus goes on to urge that the people follow what these leaders teach but avoid the way these leaders practice it in life. Two points are key. First, Jesus was communicating an awareness that to the extent that the teaching was reflective of God's way, it should be followed. The remarks are better seen in this light than as ironic in force. An examination of Jesus' critiques of and controversies with the leadership shows that his major complaint was the way they added to the law, applied it without compassion, and were hypocritical about how they worked with the law. Jesus did not engage in a wholesale rejection of what the law taught or even what the leadership claimed to teach about following the law. Second, Jesus hated religious practice that was hypocritical, insensitive to others, and directed at gaining self-praise. The fundamental complaint is that they set burdens for others but did not lift a finger to deal with those burdens themselves. They also are guilty of serving to draw attention to their piety. So they make their phylacteries broad and tassels long, and they love to sit in seats of honor at feasts and receive special greetings in the marketplace (cf. *t. Moʿed Qatan* 2.17), and to be called rabbi. Phylacteries were prayer boxes that contained copies of Exod. 13:3–16; Deut. 6:4–9; 11:13–21. They were worn on either the head or the arm, a practice based on Deut. 6:8 and 11:18. The tassels were the fringes on prayer shawls (Num. 15:38–40; Deut. 22:12), which a petitioner fingered while praying, often to keep track of the number of requests.[22]

In contrast, Jesus says that the title "rabbi" is not to be used. God is their only teacher, and all are kin equally. Nor should a disciple call another father or master, for there is one Father, who is in heaven, and one master, the Christ. Here is another remark underscoring the idea of the Christ as Lord. The unity of the work of the Father and his commissioned, anointed agent also is highlighted here. These remarks are in Jesus' typical rhetorical style. His point is to be careful not to unduly elevate personal status into a special category that separates someone from his or her status as under God as well. So it is the servant and the service that are to be exalted, as is humility. That virtue God will exalt. Thus, Jesus' remarks are aimed against the hypocrisy and pride of the leadership. Rabbinic teaching also spoke against these (*m. Soṭah* 3.4; *ʾAbot de Rabbi Nathan* 37a; 45).

At this point Jesus introduces specific woes. These are severe rebukes, arguing that in fact these leaders accomplish the very opposite of what they set out to do. First, they shut down access to the kingdom of heaven for people.

21. K. G. C. Newport, "A Note on the 'Seat of Moses' (Matthew 23:2)," *Andrews University Seminary Studies* 28 (1990): 53–58.

22. J. H. Tigay, "On the Term Phylacteries (Matt 23:5)," *Harvard Theological Review* 72 (1979): 45–53.

They fail to enter the kingdom, and the effect of their teaching is that others are prevented entry as well. There is hardly a more stinging charge that Jesus could make against people claiming to lead others into the truth.

Second, they go to great lengths, traversing land and sea, to make a follower of a Gentile, a proselyte, but when they are done, that person is twice as much a child of hell as they are![23] This rhetorical remark says that their fruit is the exact opposite of what they claim to bear.

Third, they are in the habit of making burdens but failing to keep them by an escape through special provisions. So oaths are binding only when one has appealed to the sacred elements of the temple, its gold or temple gifts. An oath mentioning only the temple is not binding. Jesus speaks against such distinctions. The background appears to be making a oath on the basis of something that could serve as a lien against the oath. In effect, Jesus says that oaths are oaths (cf. Matt. 5:34). To swear by the temple, altar, or heaven is to make a binding oath. The disciple's word and integrity, not a person's possessions, should stand behind an oath. The allowance of exceptions by how the oath is uttered is hypocrisy. This is why Jesus rebukes them as blind guides when he addresses them.

Fourth, they are hypocrites when it comes to relationships. They tithe down to the finest grain or herb (see Lev. 27:30; *m. Demai* 2.1; *m. Maʿaserot* 4.5; *m. ʿUqsin* 3.6; *m. Šebiʿit* 9.1; *ʾAbot de Rabbi Nathan* 41a), but they neglect law, justice, mercy, and faith (see Mic. 6:6; Hos. 6:6). While all these are important, things such as justice and mercy outweigh tithing herbs and grain. Jesus indicts them as blind guides, straining out the gnat and swallowing the camel, which indicates that what they have neglected is particularly important. Because a camel was an unclean animal (Lev. 11:4), the remark is particularly stinging to Jewish sensibilities. The roots of the remark reflect a wordplay in Aramaic (camel = *gamla;* gnat = *galma*).[24] Their action is like manicuring one leaf on a tree and ignoring the care of the rest of the forest.

Fifth, they also are hypocrites when it comes to personal appearance. There is a superficial piety and appearance of cleanliness, but inside there is the filth of extortion and self-indulgence. The real cleaning that makes for a clean cup works from the inside out, because then the whole person is genuinely clean. This remark parallels debates within Judaism (*m. Berakot* 8.2). Their hypocrisy makes them like an unclean grave. Surely the image is designed to shock. On the outside, they look like the perfectly clean whitewashed stone of a tomb, but on the inside, they are full of dead bones and uncleanness. They look righteous to the observer, but really they are full of

23. On Jewish evangelism among Gentiles in this period, see Scot McKnight, *A Light among the Gentiles: Jewish Missionary Activity in the Second Temple Period* (Minneapolis: Fortress, 1991).

24. R. H. Stein, *The Method and Message of Jesus' Teaching* (Philadelphia: Westminster, 1978), 13.

hypocrisy and iniquity. Jesus' critique is the honest challenge of one Jew against the hypocritical practice of another Jew, in good prophetic tradition. Though some have seen these woes as anti-Semitic, it must be recalled that the Old Testament tradition has numerous examples of such direct challenges of Israel's religious practice.

Finally, they honor the tombs of the prophets, claiming that they would not have rejected them, but what their care really shows is how they support and walk in the footsteps of those who killed the prophets. Jesus charges the Pharisees with being the descendants of those murderers. The premise is that in failing to heed the prophets, they have shown their contempt for their message. So he urges them sarcastically to fill up and complete the work of their fathers. They will not escape being sentenced to hell. The language parallels that of John the Baptist in Matt. 3:7.

The confirmation of who they are and how poorly they are responding will come in how they treat those whom God is sending now. Some of these messengers they will beat; others they will persecute or kill. Their debt will be the blood-guiltiness of the righteous from Abel to Zechariah.[25] For these new messengers are nothing other than the descendants of those righteous people of old and heirs of the message they presented. In rejecting the new messengers, the Pharisees also reject the forebears of these messengers.

So Jesus predicts a complete judgment against the leadership. His indictment is another claim to authority, like the temple cleansing. It is like a judge pronouncing a national sentence over the leadership. It represents how he bears the right to call the nation to reform. The setting is particularly appropriate. It leaves beyond any doubt that Jesus is forcing a choice of who will direct the nation and, more importantly, represent both the people of God and the way to God.

Mark and Luke take a distinct direction here. Neither has the long indictment. Luke already has given something similar in Luke 11. Mark notes that the crowd enjoyed Jesus' responses to the controversies that culminated with his citation of Ps. 110:1. Then he taught them to constantly beware of the scribes. They like to wear long robes and receive greetings in the marketplace, but they devour widows' homes and make a public show of prayer. They will be condemned for this hypocritical life. It may be that Mark knows about the longer indictment, since this remark shows elements of what Matthew gives in detail. If so, Mark seems to have omitted those remarks because the details were not as relevant to his audience.

---

25. On Abel as a martyr, see Pseudo-Philo, *Biblical Antiquities* 16.2; *Jubilees* 4.1–3; *1 Enoch* 22.6–7. The Zechariah alluded to here is not clear, but it could be the prophet. See S. H. Blank, "The Death of Zechariah in Rabbinic Literature," *Hebrew Union College Annual* 12–13 (1937–38): 327–46; Craig Blomberg, *Matthew,* New American Commentary 22 (Nashville: Broadman, 1992), 349. See also *Lives of the Prophets* 23.1.

Luke's short rebuke of the leadership is similar to Mark's. However, he notes that Jesus spoke to the disciples in front of the people. The rebuke is verbally identical to Mark except that Luke uses a different verb for watching out (Mark: βλέπετε; Luke: προσέχετε). The terms are synonymous, but Mark never uses the verb that Luke has. Luke has it in 12:1; 17:3; 21:34.

243. Jesus' Lament over Jerusalem (Matt. 23:37–39; conceptual: Luke 13:34–35 [see unit 194 above]) (Aland §285; Orchard §305; Huck-Greeven §225)

Jesus' lament over Jerusalem shows that his indictment is no cause for joy. The remarks here are virtually parallel to those in Luke 13:34–35. The double vocative cry for Jerusalem shows the emotion of the declaration (cf. 2 Sam. 18:33; 19:4). The perspective is prophetic. The image of the frustrated hen expresses God's desire to gather and protect his chicks under his wing (see Exod. 19:4; Deut. 32:10–11; Ps. 36:7; 63:7; 91:4; Ruth 2:12; Isa. 31:5; *1 Enoch* 39.7; *2 Baruch* 41.4). But the nation would have none of it. So the result is the declaration of a house forsaken. The language is from Jer. 22:5, an exilic-like judgment (also Jer. 8:21–22; 9:1, 10). Jesus then declares that they will not see him again until they welcome him, in the language of Ps. 118:26, as one who is to be blessed because he comes in the name of the Lord. The remark holds out hope that the judgment coming upon the nation now will not be the final word. Hope for Israel comes from the nature of Old Testament promise as well.

244. The Widow's Mite (Mark 12:41–44; Luke 21:1–4) (Aland §286; Orchard §306; Huck-Greeven §226)

Mark and Luke move from the controversies to an assessment of real worship. While the rich are putting many large sums into the treasury, a poor widow drops two lepta into the collection. The location is either the thirteen trumpet-shaped receptacles in the temple forecourt by the court of women or the rooms by the court where such receptacles also were placed. Lepta were small copper coins, each worth next to nothing, less than one one-hundredth of a denarius, or one one-hundredth of an average worker's daily wage—that is, about six minutes' work! So on the surface, the woman's gift would hardly be significant.

Jesus assesses things differently. Mark notes that he made the remarks to his disciples. They will need to discern between how things look and how God sees them. The widow's gift was the more significant because she gave of her very life, in contrast to others who gave from their abundance. Significant gifts come from what we otherwise would use for ourselves. Thus, the widow's sincere and costly devotion stands in contrast to the routine gifts of others from their surplus. Her giving also implies a trust of God. She can give to him out of her very life, knowing that God will care for her.

245. Prediction of the Temple's Destruction (Matt. 24:1–2; Mark 13:1–2; Luke 21:5–6) (Aland §287; Orchard §307; Huck-Greeven §227a)

The Olivet discourse is one of the more complex elements of the Jesus tradition. The opening question looks at the destruction of the temple, part of the covenant judgment for unfaithfulness. Such predictions about the temple or Jerusalem were not unprecedented within parts of Judaism that regarded Israel as currently unfaithful and thus at risk (*Testament of Levi* 15.1; *Testament of Moses* 6.8–9; 1QpHab 9.6–7; Josephus, *War* 6.5.3 §301). However, there also is discussion of a return of the Son of Man with great authority, which invokes the era of a final, decisive judgment. The fact that one discourse would discuss both of these events, now seemingly separated in time, as subsequent events seem to indicate, has led to a variety of opinions about this discourse.[26] In fact, one of the goals of the discourse, at least as it appears in Matthew and Mark, is to show that much activity intervenes between events associated with the temple's destruction and the return.

Another key feature of the speech is that it works with eschatological "pattern."[27] This approach to describing prophetic events is common in the Old Testament. The example of the Day of the Lord is instructive. The "Day" in the prophets often referred to a short-term judgment in such a way that it pictures what the final, decisive judgment will be like. Thus, the temple destruction pictures a period of intense disruption that is like the end.[28] One event is the pattern for the other or mirrors the other. So it appears that the

26. For overviews of these discussions, the details of which exceed the space available here, see Cranfield, *Mark*, 387–91; D. A. Carson, "Matthew," in *The Expositor's Bible Commentary*, vol. 8, ed. Frank E. Gaebelein (Grand Rapids: Zondervan, 1984), 488–95; Bock, *Luke 9:51–24:53*, 1650–58. Cranfield notes two themes in tension that are key to the speech: (1) one cannot know the exact time of the end, and yet (2) there are signs for which a disciple should watch as a way to know and be encouraged that God is still at work and is drawing near.

27. The term "typology" also is applied to such readings of the text. "Typology" is used to mean so many different things in popular discussion that preference is given here to "pattern."

28. Henry W. Frost, *Matthew Twenty-Four and the Revelation* (New York: Oxford University Press, 1924), 15–19.

destruction of the temple, which we now know came in A.D. 70, also pictures
the type of period that characterizes the end. This kind of "pattern" reading
also had precedent in Judaism (*Jubilees* 23.11–32). Some argue that Jesus
predicted the end within a generation and that the temple's destruction essentially was that event, while others argue that Jesus simply was wrong in his
prediction about the timing of the establishment of the kingdom.[29] The
problem with both of these suggestions is that they seem to underestimate
the language of the unprecedented extent of the tribulation in the Matthean
and Markan versions, as well as the promise of a universal mission that must
precede the end that Jesus describes. There is no sense in the early churches
that when destruction came in A.D. 70, they viewed that event as the end.
What is evident is that the early church saw this judgment on Israel as an act
of God, but something less than the final act. That view seems to reflect the
inherent typology of this speech. Against the idea that Jesus was wrong about
expecting the end within a generation are the factors of universal mission and
the very indefiniteness that Jesus expresses about the exact end time. These
factors show that he could speak of the end's potential nearness, which he refused to specify, without desiring to commit himself to a definite time frame.
It seems clear that Jesus anticipated some of these interim events, such as the
mission, taking some time.

The discourse was triggered by the disciples' comments on the splendor of
the temple, widely regarded as one of the great buildings of the ancient world
(Josephus, *War* 5.5.1–6 §§184–227; Tacitus, *History* 5.8). The temple was
central to the Herodian family's massive rebuilding program (Josephus, *Ant.*
15.9.1–7 §§380–425; *War* 1.21.1 §401). Mark summarizes these comments
as mentioning "wonderful stones" and "wonderful buildings." Jesus then predicted that days were coming when the temple would be destroyed, left in a
condition in which one stone was not left on top of another. Jesus already had
noted the coming destructive siege of the city (Luke 19:41–44), so his predicting the temple's destruction only completes that scenario.

29. Postmillennialism prefers to look to A.D. 70, while many critics argue that Jesus was
wrong. Of course, many critics argue that the speech is substantially a work of the early church
and does not reflect Jesus' teaching. This view goes back to Timothée Colani in 1864, who saw
the discourse as a product of Jewish Christianity in what became known as the "little Apoca-
lypse." For these critics, discussions about what Jesus taught cannot be determined from this
speech. However, the ambiguities in the speech argue against it being a church creation. It
would seem that the allusions to the end and a better effort to distinguish events would be a
part of a speech originating from the later church. For a view that defends A.D. 70 as Jesus' exclusive point of focus while arguing for the authenticity of the remarks, see Scot McKnight, *A
New Vision for Israel: The Teaching of Jesus in National Context* (Grand Rapids: Eerdmans,
1999), 120–55; and R. T. France (*Commentary on Mark,* NICNT [Grand Rapids: Eerdmans,
2002], 501–2, 530–33, 535–36), who sees A.D. 70 in the text until Mark 13:32. For a view
arguing that A.D. 70 does not exhaust the imagery, see Craig Evans, *Mark 8:27–16:20,* WBC
34B (Nashville: Nelson, 2001), 328–29.

246. Signs before the End (Matt. 24:3–8; Mark 13:3–8; Luke 21:7–11)
(Aland §288; Orchard §308; Huck-Greeven §§227b–28)

Each Gospel words the question that triggers the discourse differently. Mark has, "Tell us, when will these things be, and what will be the sign when these things are about to be completed?" The question focuses solely on the fate of the temple and its city.

Matthew has, "Tell us, when will these things be, and what will be the sign of your coming and of the completion of the age?" This form of the question injects more explicitly an anticipated role for Jesus in the events of the end. It has two questions, with the second question having two parts. It is the first part of the second question that is unique to Matthew. There is a tension in that question that must be noted. The reference to Jesus' coming is not really a question about the Lord's return, because these disciples did not yet appreciate or anticipate his resurrection. Without an expectation of resurrection, they would not be raising a question to discuss a return. Rather, the disciples sense a purging of the city for righteousness and probably tied it to the judgment that Jesus had predicted for Jerusalem. Without yet appreciating the prospect of Jesus' departure, they anticipate that the judgment of the city is part of the messianic purging and judgment that belong to his exercise of messianic power. Their sense was right, but not quite in the way they currently anticipated. Only subsequently did it become clear to the disciples that the events foretold in Jesus' answer are part of Jesus' later return.

Luke's questions are, "Teacher, when, therefore, will these things be, and what will be the sign when this is about to take place?" Luke, like Mark, has the question focus on the city.

All versions of the question speak in the plural: "these things." So the question is asking about the destruction of the temple as well as any events with which its destruction connects. It is this dimension of the question that opens the discourse up to the future.

Jesus goes on to indicate several events that precede "the end" (Matt. 24:6: Mark 13:7; Luke 21:9). Luke even adds the note that the end will not be "at once," despite these things Jesus initially names. Thus, these events are signs that a divine plan is unfolding, without their being the indication of the end.

What does Jesus name in this category? First, he warns his disciples not to be led astray by those claiming to be the Christ. In all likelihood, the idea of coming "in my name" involves a false claim to be him. Luke adds that they will claim that the "end is at hand." These claims should not be heeded. However, Jesus notes that many will be drawn to these claimants. In fact,

Palestine did have several messianic-like movements in the first century that attracted many followers.[30] Jesus also notes that wars and rumors of wars will surface, but the disciples are not to be alarmed. These events "must take place," but it is not yet the end. Jesus goes on to explain that nations and kingdoms will rise against each other. Thus, he predicts a period of international chaos. Also present will be earthquakes and famines. Luke adds pestilences, terrors, and great signs from heaven. It will be a disturbing period of both political and natural disaster. Mark and Matthew add the note here that all of this is but "the beginning of the birth pangs," pointing to the start of what will be a long and painful period. Thus, the initial list of features before the end foresees a period of chaos. Mark and Matthew see it as a start of the march to the end. From here on in the discourse, Luke will have the most temporal notes.

247. Persecutions (Matt. 24:9–14; Mark 13:9–13; Luke 21:12–19)
(Aland §289; Orchard §309; Huck-Greeven §229)

Luke begins the next unit with "but before all of this." In other words, before the chaotic and disastrous events just noted, which are "not yet the end," comes another series of events. Matthew and Mark refer to these initial events as the "beginning of the birth pangs." The imagery of birth pangs is a common Jewish metaphor for events tied to the start of the end (*1 Enoch* 62.4; *4 Ezra* [= 2 Esdras] 4:42; *Targum Psalms* 18.14). So Luke at this point winds time back toward the disciples from the beginning of the end, or what Matthew and Mark call birth pangs. However, Matthew and Mark simply launch into the description without any time frame. This means that Luke is being more precise in noting the time line than are the other Gospel writers. All of them discuss the same phenomenon: persecution of disciples. So Jesus foresees an intense period of persecution that comes before the start of the end.

Mark raises the somber note by warning the disciples to watch out for themselves. He then, like Luke, describes them being handed over to synagogues and governors for Jesus' sake to bear testimony. Matthew simply describes the fact that they (= the world) will deliver Jesus' followers over to tribulation and put them to death, for the nations will hate them for Jesus' name's sake. There will be betrayal, many who fall away, false prophets, and increased wickedness. This last expression is literally "lawlessness being fulfilled." Peo-

---

30. For a discussion of these groups, see Richard A. Horsley and John S. Hanson, *Bandits, Prophets, and Messiahs: Popular Movements of the Time of Jesus* (San Francisco: HarperSanFrancisco, 1985); R. A. Horsley, "Popular Messianic Movements around the Time of Christ," *Catholic Biblical Quarterly* 46 (1984): 471–95. Actually, the bulk of these movements came a few decades after Jesus' time.

ple's love will grow cold. Matthew's exhortation is to endure to the end and be saved. Despite all of this persecution, "this gospel of the kingdom will be preached throughout the whole world, as a testimony to all nations; and then the end will come." So for Matthew, there is much persecution but also world-wide mission that precedes the end.[31]

Mark and Luke, as they relate the handing over to synagogues and governors, urge the disciples not to be anxious about what to reply. Mark, apart from Luke, also notes that the gospel will go out to the entire world. Jesus promises the presence and enablement of the Spirit for them to be able to give a reply at these examinations. Matthew also notes this promise slightly later in his version. Jesus also predicts in Matthew and Mark that family members will hand over disciples for death. Luke adds a note that friends along with family will hand over disciples. Luke also says that some will be put to death. So an intense period of persecution both precedes the beginning of the end and comes before the end. Mark and Matthew stress a "precede the end" timing, while Luke notes that it appears before the beginning of the end. Thus, until Jesus returns, persecution will be a part of the picture. Some fulfillment of these words appears in the Book of Acts. Luke moves to the end of this portion of the exhortation by declaring that not a hair on the head of a disciple will be harmed, despite his prediction that some will die. Jesus here is stressing that those who destroy the body cannot touch the real person. Both Mark and Luke close this unit with a note that those who endure to the end will be saved. Luke expresses this in terms designed to encourage Theophilus: "By your endurance you will gain your lives." In other words, they should cling to Jesus to the end, despite the persecution. As Jesus noted in Luke 8:13, such persecution could hinder fruitfulness. Difficult times are ahead for the disciples.

248. The Desolation (Matt. 24:15–22; Mark 13:14–20; Luke 21:20–24)
(Aland §290; Orchard §310; Huck-Greeven §230)

It is this unit that displays the biggest difference between the accounts. Matthew's account is very specific. It describes "the desolating sacrilege spoken of by the prophet Daniel, standing in the holy place." The allusion is to Dan. 9:27 and foresees an act of desecration in the holy place of the temple, like that which Antiochus Epiphanes performed (1 Macc. 1:54; 4:38; 6:7) in 167 B.C. These texts form the backdrop for the description of a "man of lawlessness" in the Epistles (2 Thess. 2:3–4). Mark describes the same event with the phrase "when you see the desolating sacrilege set up where it ought not be." This event shows Jerusalem at risk. Those present should flee to the

31. Blomberg, *Matthew*, 356–57, notes how all of the descriptions of this section describe events that took place both before and after A.D. 70.

mountains, while those on the housetops and in the fields should not seek to gather their possessions. Those who are pregnant or who have little children will suffer. Jesus indicates the uncertainty of when this event comes, because he tells them to pray that it not come in winter. Matthew adds a note that the disciple should hope that it does not come on a Sabbath day, for on those days the city gates were left shut. He summarizes by describing the period as one of unprecedented "tribulation," unlike anything before or after. Matthew calls this great period of suffering the "great tribulation." Jesus' allusion to Dan. 9:27 puts us in the climactic period of Daniel's seventieth week after the covenant with Israel is broken. This is what the Christian premillennial tradition has called the "great tribulation" period.[32] The remarks in Matthew and Mark close by noting that had not the suffering of this period been cut short, no human being would have survived—another text that gives the impression of a worldwide period of persecution. The days will be shortened for the sake of the elect. Even though Israel was in view in the initial question about the temple's destruction, the world is brought into the answer with these points about the extent of the suffering. These descriptions appear to discuss the end and its unique period of tribulation. Matthew and Mark cover the issue of the final return, although Mark's way of doing so is a little more ambiguous than Matthew's.[33]

Luke takes a different but related direction. He focuses on the event that establishes the pattern of the end that Matthew and Mark cover. Three major clues point to this distinction. First, Luke does not discuss the desolation of sacrilege, but speaks of "*its* desolation." This is a reference to Jerusalem's desolation, a description that is broader than a sacrilege at the temple, although for the temple to be desecrated, the city would have to be sacked as well. Luke is consistently concerned with the nation's culpability for its rejection of Jesus, and the near-term Jerusalem judgment underscores this point (also Luke 19:41–44). An implication of this perspective is that when the nation experiences this judgment, this will be another confirmation that the message of Jesus was true. Second, and just as significant,

32. The eschatology represented in the speech and the full eschatological systems derived from it and other apocalyptic texts are debated among Christians. For the three major views among evangelicals, see Darrell L. Bock, ed., *Three Views on the Millennium and Beyond* (Grand Rapids: Zondervan, 1999). For options related to Matt. 24, see Keener, *Gospel of Matthew*, 348–49.

33. Blomberg, *Matthew*, 359, is right to note that these descriptions of the unique intensity of the tribulation are against a reference to A.D. 70. Less certain is whether the great tribulation is the period from A.D. 70 until the return. The allusions to Daniel suggest that a more specific time period is in view, probably Daniel's seventieth week and the descriptions of the intense persecution in Rev. 4–19, which themselves may have "pattern" bases in the Roman persecutions of the first century but really are references to the events before Jesus' return. It is the "pattern" elements in this imagery that make specific identification difficult and debatable. However, in the end, the imagery looks at the time before the return.

Luke lacks the description of the unique level of tribulation in the period surrounding the sacking of the city. Finally, Luke has a unique reference to people falling by the edge of the sword and being taken captive into all the nations. It closes with the thought that "Jerusalem will be trodden down by the Gentiles until the times of the Gentiles are fulfilled." So Luke foresees Jerusalem overrun for a period with an exile following that extends until the period of the Gentiles is complete. The implication in this naming a following period involving the Gentiles is that a period for Israel follows still after the Gentile period—why else point out the approaching period's Gentile focus?

My contention, then, is that Luke highlights the destruction of Jerusalem as a "pattern" type of the end. Thus, he omits all discussion of the unique level of suffering because he, at this point of the speech, is still looking at what later became clear was the short-term realization of the promise: the temple's destruction. He is not yet discussing the ultimate realization of the end. Those times of the near term also will require those in Judea to flee to the mountains, those in Jerusalem to leave it, and those in the country not to enter the city. A Christian fleeing of the city did take place when Jerusalem was overrun in A.D. 70 (Eusebius, *Eccl. Hist.* 3.5.3). This judgment of Jerusalem is "days of vengeance" to fulfill all that is written. This appears to allude to Jesus' prediction in Luke 19:41–44. It also patterns judgment at the end, which is what Matthew and Mark treat.

249. False Christs and False Prophets (Matt. 24:23–28;
Mark 13:21–23; conceptual in an earlier context: Luke 17:23–24 [see unit 215 above]) (Aland §291; Orchard §311; Huck-Greeven §231)

Part of what is associated with the end is a series of signs and messianic claims that can lead even the elect astray. According to Matthew and Mark, it will be a period of false Christs and prophets. But Jesus tells them that he has warned them about this. Luke lacks any reference to this remark, having covered a similar idea already in Luke 17:23–24. Here is yet a fourth clue of Luke's unique emphasis in this speech.

Matthew alone goes on to note that as lightning shines out from east to west, so will be the Son of Man's coming. It will be obvious; it will not need someone to point it out. Matthew goes on to note that where the body is, the eagles (vultures) gather (on eagles/vultures, see unit 215). In other words, it will be a time of judgment and death. Luke has a similar remark at 17:37b. The thrust of this unit is for disciples to be on the watch. With the end will come possibilities for being deceived if the disciple does not heed Jesus' warnings.

250. The Coming of the Son of Man (Matt. 24:29–31; Mark 13:24–27; Luke 21:25–28) (Aland §292; Orchard §312; Huck-Greeven §232)

All the accounts converge here with the description of the Son of Man's return. It is sometimes argued that this apocalyptic language is merely heavily symbolic, expressing that God will do "earthshaking" and "creation-altering" things at the end, usually seen as a description of Jerusalem's fall in A.D. 70. Against this view is the seeming connection in the early church of the return being the obverse of the ascension, as Acts 1:9–11 expresses. Thus, the promise, as made clear after the resurrection, is that Jesus will return just as he departed. The ascension is a guarantee of a return. The hermeneutical significance of this connection is that the figure of Jesus going to the side of God pictures a return of a similar character. Also supporting this not strictly metaphorical reading are the cosmic signs tied to Jesus' crucifixion, which show creation reacting to key events in ways that illustrate how apocalyptic language was described and understood. Like the judgment at the cross, so creation will respond at the final judgment. So this language has elements of literalism, even within a powerful metaphor that these events will shake the creation.

Matthew and Mark foresee days "after" the tribulation. Here, even the creation will react. An example of this might be the kind of cosmic testimony that the creation gave at Jesus' crucifixion, when the skies became terrifyingly dark. Prophetic and apocalyptic literature are full of such themes (Isa. 13:9–10; 24:18–20; 34:4; Ezek. 32:7–8; Joel 2:10, 30–31; 3:15; Hag. 2:6, 21; *1 Enoch* 80; *Testament of Moses* 10.5; *2 Baruch* 70; 72.2). The cosmic reaction and the signaling of the important events lead to a few unique remarks in Luke. He speaks of the people of the nations being distressed at the roaring of the sea and waves, with people fainting from fear at what is coming for the world. The language foresees something far more than a regional conflict involving only Rome and Israel. It is the heavens shaking that leads to mention of the Son of Man's coming.

As Matthew notes, it is the cosmic display that announces the "sign of the Son of Man in heaven." It will be a time of mourning for the tribes of the earth, for it is a time of judgment for many. Here Matthew alone alludes to Zech. 12:10. All the Gospels describe the sign as seeing the Son of Man coming on the clouds with power and glory. Mark speaks of great power, while Matthew and Luke describe great glory. The allusion is to Dan. 7:13. Thus, the image is of a human figure given judgment authority from God on behalf of his people. The image of riding the clouds is reserved for God or as a description of pagan gods in the Old Testament, outside of this text in Daniel (Exod. 14:20; 34:5; Num. 10:34; Ps. 104:3; Isa. 19:1). So the image shows how intimately the function of the Son of Man is tied to divine authority even though the description is of a human. It is this combination from Dan. 7 that made it a title that Jesus could develop as a self-description. Here is the first text where the Son of Man expression is explicitly tied to an Old Testament text. The Son of Man became a powerful figure of judgment in later Judaism (*1 Enoch* 37–71; *4 Ezra* [= 2 Esdras] 13; *b. Sanhedrin* 38[b], 98[a]). The return means that God's judgment and his vindication of the righteous come with the sent one, who comes from heaven. Matthew and Mark note that with the return, the angels will join in to gather God's elect from the ends of creation. Gathering was a common image for eschatological deliverance (Isa. 11:12; 27:12–13; 43:5; 49:5; 56:8; 60:1–9; Zech. 2:6; *1 Enoch* 62.13–14; *Psalms of Solomon* 8.28; 11.2–5; 17.26; *4 Ezra* [= 2 Esdras] 13:39–40). Luke speaks a word of encouragement: "When these things begin to take place, look up and raise your head, because your redemption is drawing near." In other words, the start of these events, even hard things like the persecution mentioned earlier, is a guarantee that God's plan is in the process of realization.

251. The Parable of the Fig Tree (Matt. 24:32–36; Mark 13:28–32; Luke 21:29–33) (Aland §293; Orchard §313; Huck-Greeven §§233–34)

Jesus turns to the fig tree again for a lesson. Here the exhortation is that when disciples see its branches tender (Matthew and Mark) or coming to leaf (Luke), then they can see for themselves (Luke) and know (all three) that summer is near. So when they see "these things taking place," they can know that "he [the Son of Man] is near" (Matthew and Mark) or that "the kingdom of God is near" (Luke). Luke's alteration shows how closely associated the culmination of the kingdom is with the presence of the Son of Man.

The next verse is one of the most discussed in the Gospels. Jesus says in Matthew and Mark, "Truly I say to you, this generation will not pass away until [Matthew]/before [Mark] all these things take place." Luke has, "Truly I say to you, this generation will not pass away until all has taken place." The key point turns on the meaning of "this generation." The initial impression that many gain from the text is that all these events are predicted to happen by the end of "this generation," so the Son of Man's return is predicted to occur within the disciples' lifetime. However, this reading undercuts two points that the speech already makes, making it an unlikely reading. First, the Synoptics describe the Son of Man's appearing as obvious, like lightning, evident in the cosmic signs that accompany his coming. So this event is not included in the "leaf" remark of the parable, which is pointing to what indicates the approach of the end, not its presence or conclusion. This means that "all these things" refers to those events described before the coming of the cosmic signs.[34] They are "all the events" that make up the leaf before the fruit. Thus, Jesus predicts the signs pointing to the end taking place within a generation, but he is not including the end itself in that assessment. In other words, the picture tied to the destruction of Jerusalem is a sign itself that the end will come. In addition, it means that the end is imminent in the sense that it is the next thing on the divine calendar. In another sense, it means that the end is as good as fulfilled, since the sign of the end has come. The fulfillment of one part is the guarantee that the rest will be fulfilled.

Jesus' next remarks serve to underscore the certainty of what he tells them. Heaven and earth will pass away, but this teaching will not pass away. Rhetorically, Jesus says that this teaching is more secure than creation, which itself is very secure. In other words, these things *will* happen. In Matthew and Mark, Jesus concludes by noting that the exact timing of the Son of Man's arrival is not known. Matthew and Mark note that the angels and the Son do not know, but the Father does.[35] The point is that the exact time is unknown. It is hidden in the Father's will.

252. Take Heed and Watch (Mark 13:33–37; Luke 21:34–36; conceptual: Luke 12:40 [see unit 184 above]) (Aland §§294–95; Orchard §320; Huck-Greeven §§236, 242a)

This section of the discourse ends with a final exhortation to keep watch in both Mark and Luke, although they have slightly different emphases. Matthew's

34. See Carson, "Matthew," 506–7; Cranfield, *Mark*, 407–8. A few other readings might be meant here but are perhaps slightly less likely, given their subtlety. "This generation" may be ethical, either positively or negatively, as opposed to temporal in force. Then Jesus' point would include the idea that this evil or good generation will not pass away until all of these things have taken place. Read this way, the remark underscores either the certainty of judgment coming on the wicked or the certainty of redemption for the righteous. Another option is to reverse the emphasis of the reading adopted above. Jesus is now referring to the sequence of end events, having just mentioned that he is near or the kingdom is near. Thus, Jesus' point is that when these final events, starting with the heavenly signs, do come, their completion will take less than a generation. The three readings noted here, the one in the text and the two in the notes, are the same three options presented in my commentary (Bock, *Luke 9:51–24:53*, 1688–92). However, the last reading mentioned in this note is slightly preferred in the commentary, whereas I now lean toward the reading given above in the text. Any of these options could be what Jesus means, given the difficulty of the verse. The difficulty with the view taken in the text above is that it makes A.D. 70 the dominant point of the "abomination" reference, which fits better with Luke than with Matthew or Mark. The explanation making this view cohere is that the signs of A.D. 70 are like the signs of the end, so the "pattern" event can picture the short-term or long-term event, depending on the emphasis. However, the ambiguity in the reference makes it difficult to be certain of the precise sense.

35. There is a textual problem in Matt. 24:36 about whether the Son is mentioned or not. However, the inclusion of the Son, a reading that matches Mark, is supported by the better manuscripts and is likely original. In fact, had a corrector to Codex Sinaiticus not attested the omission, it is unlikely that there would be any dispute. Interestingly, Mark has no textual dispute here despite the issue it raises about the Son's lack of knowledge.

version goes on to describe some other details of what the end will be like, as well as five more parables about the end (householder and thief, good and evil servants, ten virgins, talents, and sheep and goats). The nonparabolic material in Matt. 24 and variations of the householder and thief and good and evil servant parables have shown up already in Luke 17, so Luke does not have them here.

Mark closes his version of the discourse with an exhortation to take heed and watch, because the disciples do not know when the time of the end will come. The disciples are like stewards who have been told by the master, who is leaving home, to do their individual work until he returns. The doorkeeper is to keep watch for the master's unknown time of return. So the disciples are to watch, because they do not know when the master will return home. Will it be in the evening, at midnight, when the cock crows, or in the morning? The times mirror the four Roman watches during the night, times when people would be less likely to be prepared for an arrival. The one thing that should not happen is that they be found asleep when the master returns. So the exhortation to watch ends the Markan discourse and places a key emphasis on that theme in his account.

Luke ends his version with a more concrete description of what watching means. It fits in with his Gospel's consistently ethical and practical thrust. The disciples are to take heed not to get weighed down with dissipation, drunkenness, and the cares of life. These warnings go back to Luke 8:14 and recall the parable in 12:41–48. The danger is that "that day" will come upon them like a snare, entrapping them. The implication is that if they do not watch and live carefully, then the judgment will catch them in an embarrassing state. That day is something that all people on earth will experience. The key premise is that the coming is a day of judgment and accountability. Being ready and living well in the interim is what is required. So they are to watch at all times and pray that they can have the strength to escape the suffering that may well come in the interim. The hope is that when the Son comes in judgment, they will stand before him, having lived in a way that prepared them for that day.

253. Be Ready, for the Day Comes Suddenly (Matt. 24:37–44;
conceptual: Luke 17:26–36; 12:39–40 [see units 215 and 184 above]) (Aland §296; Orchard §§314–15; Huck-Greeven §§235–37)

Jesus compares his coming to the days of Noah. Back then, judgment sprang suddenly on humanity. People were engaged in everyday life: eating, drinking, marrying, being given in marriage. Then the flood came and swept them all away. The Son of Man's coming will be like that sudden appearance. The images of two men in the field and of two women grinding at the mill with, in both cases, one taken and the other left depicts the separation that takes place in the judgment.[36] Some are saved; others are judged. So the disciple is to keep a constant lookout, because the time is not known. It is like keeping vigilant watch over a house to prevent a thief from breaking in during the night. The image is another common metaphor (Joel 2:9; 1 Thess. 5:2, 4; 2 Pet. 3:10; Rev. 3:3; 16:15). Be ready, because the Son of Man comes at an unexpected hour. The next parable, that of the good and wicked servants, illustrates what keeping watch means. It is being faithful until the Son of Man comes.

254. The Parable of the Good and Wicked Servants

(Matt. 24:45–51; conceptual: Luke 12:41–46 [see unit 184 above])
(Aland §297; Orchard §316; Huck-Greeven §238)

In Matthew, Jesus asks what a faithful and wise steward is like. This short parable is like Luke 12:41–46, pointing to a steward who is told to care for the other servants. The faithful steward is blessed because, when the master comes, he finds the steward doing what he asked of him. This is the one who is rewarded by being set over the master's possessions. The reward assumes a period when more responsibility can be exercised.

In contrast, the wicked servant revels in the master's delay and physically abuses the other servants and engages in self-indulgent practices. The master then returns on a day that the steward does not expect and at an hour that he does not know. When the master returns, he will "cut him [the servant] to bits" and place him with the hypocrites, where there will be weeping and gnashing of teeth. The imagery is of total exclusion.[37] Here is yet another "odd man out." Thus, Jesus warns that complete unfaithfulness will be exposed in the judgment to come. Some who seemingly are associated with Jesus will be excluded from blessing. Thus, the basic exhortation of the parable is to be faithful until he returns.

255. The Parable of the Ten Virgins (Matt. 25:1–13) (Aland §298; Orchard §317; Huck-Greeven §239)

This parable also stresses preparedness, as well as warning that such preparedness is each person's responsibility. The background to the parable is the

---

36. Debate exists, as with Luke 17, whether a person is taken away in judgment, swept away by the flood, or whether those taken away are delivered, like Noah, who was taken away in the ark. It is hard to be certain, although the imagery of Luke 17 favors a leaving behind for judgment where the birds gather over the dead, while those taken away are delivered like Noah. Regardless, more fundamental is the image of the separation of the saved and the judged.

37. Otto Betz, "The Dichotomized Servant and the End of Judas Iscariot," *Revue de Qumran* 5 (1964): 46–47.

first-century custom of escorting the bride to the groom's home when he comes for her. This often happened in the evening and was part of a grand celebration. The light was provided by torches or sticks soaked in oil. It was an important part of the ceremony that was not to be ruined. Such processions were important enough that rabbis would suspend lectures to acknowledge them, and ritual obligations would be superseded (*ʾAbot de Rabbi Nathan* 4a; 8; 22b; *t. Berakot* 2.10).[38]

These ten virgins, then, were the escort for the new couple, much like the bridesmaids and groomsmen of today. Their job was considered to be highly important in Jesus' culture of honor and shame. The virgins would not know exactly when the groom would show up, since it followed the completion of final delivery of the bridal presents. So announcements of the approach were given, although the groom could appear hours later.

The parable foresees a situation where five virgins have enough oil for the journey but five others do not. The issue is not that the escorts fell asleep, because all ten did that. The problem is that after the delay, which is what the sleep points to, some were prepared and others were not. When the arrival of the groom is announced, the five whose lamps are dying out ask the others for oil. It is unlikely that the oil itself symbolizes anything beyond the imagery it contributes to the parable. The point is the contrast between those who were ready for the groom's coming and those who were not. The request for oil by the unprepared virgins is wisely refused by the others because of the risk that all ten would run out. Then everyone would be in the dark, ruining the procession. The five responsible escorts do not want to be the cause of that cultural catastrophe. So they tell the five who need oil to go and get their own. Therein lies the parable's point: each disciple must be responsible for his or her own preparedness.

The groom comes while the negligent five are away getting more oil. The prepared party goes to the feast, where the door was shut, leaving the unprepared outside. At this point, the parable diverges from cultural practice, but it is not unusual for Jesus' parables to have a surprising twist to drive home his point. Unlike at the normal wedding, where the door would remain open, here the door is shut. When the request comes from the latecomers to open the door, it is refused. The reply is "I do not know you." This is like Matt. 7:23 and Luke 13:25. Thus, it is too late to enter, because they were not ready to come when the groom appeared. Jesus closes with the main point: "Watch, therefore, for you know neither the day nor the hour." The issue here is that those who miss the day of the Son of Man's arrival cannot recover from being unprepared for his return. Repentance is not possible after his coming.

38. Keener, *Gospel of Matthew*, 356–58.

256. The Parable of the Talents (Matt. 25:14–30; conceptual: Luke 19:11–27 [see unit 228 above]) (Aland §299; Orchard §318; Huck-Greeven §240)

This parable, though similar to Luke 19:11–27, probably is a distinct account that treats the same theme. The setting is different from Luke 19, as are several details of the imagery (talents versus minas, different distribution to each servant versus the same distribution, three servants versus ten).

The parable's story line is simple. A master is headed on a journey and assigns each of three servants a responsibility over some financial resources. The differing levels of five talents, two talents, and one talent reflect the variations in responsibility that people have in serving God. A talent is variously estimated in value as being worth between ten thousand and sixty thousand denarii. So this is a significant amount of money. At the least, for the third servant, a talent at ten thousand denarii is about thirty years' wage at a minimum-wage level. That one talent could be, on the higher value estimate, a lifetime of basic wages. The other, larger amounts for the other servants certainly are lifetime wages.

The servants take two approaches. Those with the five and two talents go to work and earn five and two more talents, respectively. The one with one talent does nothing but hide his money in the ground. When the master returns, the results are made public.

When the five- and two-talent servants come forward with their profit, the master praises them and gives them the promise of being set over much and experiencing the joy of their master. Apparently, there is responsibility in the future in which they share a role as a reward for their faithfulness.

The third servant is handled differently. He comes forth and explains how he saw the master as a harsh man, reaping where he did not sow, and gathering where he did not winnow.[39] This is why he hid the talent and is returning it intact. The idea of keeping money safe this way was common (*m. Baba Meṣiʿa* 3.11). Not only did the servant do nothing in response to the master's directions, but also he viewed the master in very unflattering terms.

The rebuke is clear. This is a "wicked and indolent" slave.[40] If the servant meant what he said, then he should have put the money in the bank to earn interest. The master takes the one talent and gives it to the servant with ten talents. The third servant now has nothing.

39. For the term "harsh," see σκληρός, BAGD, 756; BDAG, 930. This refers to a cruel person.

40. The term ὀκνηρός refers to laziness. See Prov. 6:6, 9; BAGD, 563; BDAG, 702. The rebuke takes the earlier mention of harshness and uses a term that rhymes with it, making a wordplay and adding a note of derision (see previous note). The earlier mention of fear in 25:25 had become an excuse to disobey. There was no trust of the master here.

Two principles conclude the parable to explain its significance. First, to the one who has, an abundance will be given. This point is represented in the first two servants. It is interesting that both get the same level of benefit: double what they earn. Their benefit is measured in terms of the gifts they had been given. Second, from the one who does not have, even what he has is taken away. In other words, the one who appeared to have something actually had nothing; and what he had the opportunity to have, he also lost. This is the third servant. The inherent warning is to make use of what God gives you. Be faithful.

The result for the third servant is that he is judged to be a worthless servant. He is cast out into outer darkness, where there is weeping and gnashing of teeth. Here is another "odd man out" parable, where one seemingly related to the master ends up on the outside. The lack of faith in the third servant left him exposed in the judgment. Jesus' warning is not to be like that servant.

257. The Sheep and Goats (Matt. 25:31–46) (Aland §300; Orchard §319; Huck-Greeven §241)

It is hard to know whether this final portion of the Matthean discourse is a parable or merely possesses metaphorical categories in describing the righteous and the wicked as sheep and goats. Such imagery has good precedent (Ezek. 34:17). Regardless, the point of the text is clear. Jesus declares how humanity will be separated "when the Son of Man comes in his glory, and all the angels with him." The scene is like Zech. 14:5 except for the additional feature of the Son of Man. What comes with the Son of Man will be a rule that executes a decisive judgment. It will involve the separation of the nations, so its scope is to deal with all of humanity. People will be divided into two groups: sheep in a place of honor on the right, and goats in a place of rejection on the left. The reasons for blessing and judgment later in the passage show that although all nations are in view, the judgment deals with individual responses. Interestingly, the Son of Man has the role of final judge, something normally reserved for God but which some in Judaism also came to place in the hands of a designated representative (*1 Enoch* 9.4; 60.2 compared with *1 Enoch* 49–54; *Testament of Abraham* 13 [rec. A]; 11 [rec. B]).[41] So Jesus' teaching draws

---

41. In the background is imagery that recalls the work of the great shepherd, who normally is seen to be God (Ps. 23:1–4; 74:1–2; Isa. 40:11; Ezek. 34:11–17; Sir. 18:13; *1 Enoch* 89.18; Pseudo-Philo, *Biblical Antiquities* 28.5; 30.5). However, in Ezek. 34:23–24, there is contemplation of the closely interconnected role between God as shepherd and the "David" he will designate to serve with him. As is common in Jesus' teaching, the background to the imagery combines several roles.

on background ideas that Jews were already beginning to entertain about a great end-time judgment figure.

The sheep on the right are given the blessing of entering into "the kingdom prepared for you from the foundation of the world." This pictures the promised, fully consummated kingdom, which ultimately will be a place of eternal blessing and fellowship with God. The reason for their acceptance is made clear. The sheep had responded to Jesus in need, whether he was hungry, thirsty, a stranger, naked, sick, or in prison. They had fed him, given him drink, welcomed him, clothed him, visited him, and come to him in prison. When the king is asked when they did this, the reply comes that when it was done for one of the least of his brothers and sisters, it was done to him. This pictures blessing coming as a result of a willingness to identify with Christ and respond compassionately to his representatives.

This parable is often misread as a general reference to the poor of humanity so that the connection of Jesus to those cared for is removed from its context. That misreads the way that "the least" and "brothers" are used in Matthew when people are in view and familial siblings are not meant (least [10:42; 18:6, 10, 14]; brothers [5:22–24, 47; 7:3–5; 12:48–50; 18:15; 21, 35; 23:8; 28:10]). In fact, Matt. 10:42 is probably the closest in sense to what is meant here.[42] Jesus is affirming a theme that has run through the entire discourse. The judgment by the Son of Man is a vindication of those who have aligned themselves to him. Their allegiance will be rewarded.

The judgment proceeds with the rejection of the goats on the left. They are told to depart from the king and are cursed, sent to the eternal fire originally prepared for the devil and his angels. They had failed to respond with compassion to the king when he was hungry, thirsty, a stranger, naked, sick, or in prison. When the rejected ask when they failed to minister to him, the king replies, "Truly I say to you, as you did it not to one of the least of these, you did it not to me." The result is eternal punishment.[43] It stands in contrast to the fate of the righteous, who have eternal life. Thus, the Son of Man and allegiance to him and his people are seen as the basis for the judgment, an authority that he possesses and will exercise in the final judgment at his coming. On this decisive note, the Matthean version of the Olivet discourse ends.

The structure of Jesus' description of the end is fairly simple. The Son of Man returns. The saints are vindicated, received, and rewarded with more service. The unrighteous are judged. Jesus gives no further details. However, the

42. Blomberg, *Matthew*, 377–78.
43. This text, although it is in a highly pictorial context, argues against any form of annihilationism as the result of the judgment. The judgment for rejecting God is consistently represented in this text as lasting for eternity.

rest of the New Testament, along with what the Old Testament already has declared, fills in the rest of the details of what the end is like.[44]

258. The Ministry of Jesus in Jerusalem (Luke 21:37–38)
(Aland §301; Orchard §321; Huck-Greeven §242b)

Luke alone has a summary note after the discourse. Jesus taught in the temple during the day and lodged in the evening outside the city on the Mount of Olives. Each morning a crowd gathered at the temple to hear him. Surely, his ability to draw people also made the leadership nervous. So the final movement to his arrest follows the series of controversies of the last week and a promise of judgment for the nation, raising the issue of whose authority came from God. In addition, there was the increasing threat that his popularity raised for the leadership.[45]

259. The Desire to Kill Jesus (Matt. 26:1–5; Mark 14:1–2;
Luke 22:1–2) (Aland §305; Orchard §325; Huck-Greeven §243)

The final stage of Jesus' ministry begins with the leadership caught in a dilemma. They want to stop Jesus, but his popularity is a major obstacle because they are nervous about how the crowds will react to any move against him. All the Synoptics note this tension and date the time of the reflection. In Mark, it is two days before the Passover and the Feast of Unleavened Bread. Luke notes only that the celebration of Unleavened Bread is drawing near, a feast that is called the Passover. It is not unusual to refer to these two feasts as one event, because one followed directly after the other (Josephus, *Ant.* 3.10.5 §249; 14.2.1 §21; 17.9.3 §213). Passover fell on Nisan 14–15, while Unleav-

---

44. The details about the end are debated among Christians because of the different ways this synthesis gets performed at a hermeneutical, theological level. For a summary of the issues of method informing this debate, see Bock, ed., *Three Views on the Millennium and Beyond*, esp. 278–309. The views revolve around three basic sets of biblical material and how they are read: (1) how Revelation is read (significantly futurist or not; is the millennium a description of a specific period of time, or is it a figurative expression for the future?); (2) how the epistolary material, especially 1 Thess. 4:13–18, is viewed (is the taking up of the saints to meet Jesus in the air the next thing on God's calendar or not?); (3) how the promises to Israel from the Old Testament are read (do those promises still include national Israel, ethnic Israel but not the nation Israel, or are these promises now only for the church?). The answers to these other questions, all falling outside the issues raised by Jesus' teaching, determine an interpreter's approach to eschatology at a systematic theological level.

45. At this point, the Aland synopsis places the disputes covered in John 12:20–50. It notes how Jesus continued to discuss his departure, and many did not believe it.

ened Bread was on Nisan 15–21 (Exod. 12). Both commemorated different aspects of the nation's deliverance from evil: the passing over of the firstborn in the last plague and the people's leaving Egypt in haste (Exod. 12:1–28; 23:15; 34:18; Num. 9:1–14; Deut. 16:1–8). Large crowds could be expected because many pilgrims traveled to Jerusalem to celebrate the feast.

Matthew presents Jesus making remarks to his disciples following directly from the Olivet discourse. It is the fourth passion prediction in Matthew (16:21; 17:22–23; 20:17–19). So what Mark and Luke summarize as a narrative note, Matthew shows to be a remark of the Lord. Jesus says, "You know that after two days the Passover is coming, and the Son of Man will be delivered up to be crucified." Matthew reinforces the sense that Jesus knows exactly what is coming and when.

All the Synoptics also note the leadership's desire to stop Jesus. Matthew again has more detail. The chief priests and elders gather in the palace of Caiaphas, the high priest.[46] They take counsel to figure out how to arrest Jesus by stealth and kill him, a remark that Mark shares. Luke is more compact, simply noting that they were seeking how to put him to death. Matthew and Mark also note their fear of the people. They want to kill Jesus apart from the festal crowds in order to obviate a reaction among the people.[47] As Luke summarizes it, they "feared the crowd," so they would have to be careful.

260. The Anointing at Bethany (Matt. 26:6–13; Mark 14:3–9; John 12:1–8) (Aland §306; Orchard §326; Huck-Greeven §244)

A meal at the home of Simon the leper in Bethany (Matthew and Mark) becomes another signature event. Luke lacks it, in all likelihood because he already has recorded a similar, yet distinct event in Luke 7:36–50. John notes that the timing actually is a little earlier than its Synoptic placement, six days prior to Passover. The reason for the juxtaposition becomes clear when all the Synoptics render the betrayal by Judas next. It may be that Matthew and Mark move the scene closer to the time of Judas's actual betrayal, which grew from this event. The contrast between the devoted woman and the defecting disciple is shocking.

46. John 11:47–53 details the leadership's discussion where Caiaphas speaks to the concern about the threat of Roman reaction that Jesus might provoke because he represents independent leadership. John notes that Caiaphas spoke prophetically without being aware of it when he argued that it is better for one man to die than for the whole nation to perish. They decide that Jesus should be stopped.

47. This portion of the verse often is translated "not during the feast," but ἑορτή can be rendered as "festival crowd" (John 2:23; 7:11), and Luke 22:6 suggests that if the circumstances were right, as developed later, they would get him when they could; see Cranfield, *Mark*, 414.

The woman, who John says is named Mary, takes some very costly nard (Mark and John; Matthew and Mark refer to the more generic term for perfume, "myrrh" [μύρον]).[48] She anoints Jesus. It is very expensive; Mark 14:5 puts its cost at three hundred denarii, or a year's wages for a common worker. She anoints his head (Matthew and Mark) and feet (John). It is a full anointing.

The act leaves the disciples displeased. John 12:4–5 has Judas express the displeasure in terms of the three hundred denarii cost and the need to serve the poor, a remark that John takes as disingenuous because Judas pilfered from the group's money box. The Synoptics see the reaction as one that other disciples share, because they too sense the wastefulness of the action and that the perfume could have been sold, with the proceeds helping the poor. Mark adds that they rebuked her.

Jesus steps in and asks why they trouble the woman. She has "worked a good work" for Jesus, a Jewish idiom for declaring the presence of a great work. Matthew, Mark, and John interpret the act as preparation for the day of burial, an anticipation of what is to come. The poor can be and should be ministered to in the future. That is the point of Jesus' remark about "always" having "the poor with you." However, time is running out to show honor to Jesus (see Mark 2:18–22; Matt. 9:14–17; Luke 5:33–38—the idea of the groom departing). So the act will be remembered wherever the gospel is preached in the world. Her good act will be memorialized as a praiseworthy act of respect. The recording of the event in the passion tradition did just that.

261. Judas's Betrayal (Matt. 26:14–16; Mark 14:10–11; Luke 22:3–6)
(Aland §307; Orchard §327; Huck-Greeven §245)

Judas stands in contrast to the woman who anoints Jesus. Luke specifically attributes his act to Satan entering into him, a reference not so much to possession as to direction. The disciple goes to the chief priests and offers "to deliver" (Matthew) Jesus. Again Matthew has in dialogue what Mark and Luke summarize as an offer to "betray him." Matthew notes that the price was thirty pieces of silver. These pieces were probably shekels, the temple currency. Judas later will toss the money into the temple (Matt. 27:3–10). If these were shekels, then the reward for serving up Jesus was 120 denarii, as a shekel equaled four denarii.[49] From that point on, Judas sought "an opportunity."

48. On myrrh, see BAGD, 529–30; BDAG, 661. Matthew used a related term (σμύρνα, which is myrrh plus some aromatic spices [BAGD, 758; BDAG, 933]) in 2:11, so there are "bookend" anointings in Matthew. In the distinct anointing by the sinful woman in Luke 7, myrrh (μύρον) is also used.

49. Blomberg, *Matthew*, 386. This would be about 120 days of an average worker's wage.

The hope was to seize Jesus in the absence of the crowd (Luke). Everything was now in place to get Jesus.

262. Preparation for the Passover (Matt. 26:17–20; Mark 14:12–17; Luke 22:7–14) (Aland §308; Orchard §328; Huck-Greeven §§246–47a)

The Synoptics all present Jesus' final meal with his disciples as a Passover meal.[50] The beginning of the feast is referred to as the start of Unleavened Bread in all the Synoptics because the two feasts were combined in popular idiom. As was typical of feast pilgrims, Jesus and the disciples needed a place to eat this meal. So the disciples (Matthew and Mark) ask where the Passover is going to be prepared. Luke says that Peter and John were given the assignment to prepare the meal and make the arrangements. Jesus' insight is emphasized as he describes a man carrying a jar of water meeting the two to show them the upper room that will hold the meal. Mark and Luke note that this man will walk them into the correct house. Matthew, as has been his custom elsewhere, collapses the scene and moves directly to the conversation with the owner and omits reference to the scene involving the man with a jar. In Mark and Luke, the question to the owner is, "Where is the [Luke]/my [Mark] guest room, where I am to eat the Passover with my disciples?" Jesus' authority is presented a little more strongly in Mark as he calls the room his. Matthew has "My time is at hand; I will keep the Passover at your house with my disciples." Jesus is portrayed as very much aware and in control of events. Mark 14:15 suggests that the arrangements had already been made with the owner. In Mark and Luke, the account goes on to note that the disciples "found it as he had told them." This underscores a note of fulfillment about what Jesus said. In Matthew, the emphasis is on the disciples' obedience. They did "as Jesus had directed them." At evening, which would be around 6 P.M., at sundown, they gathered together at the table in the upper room. This table likely would have been in the shape of a U, not a

50. This question has been debated, mainly because John portrays Jesus as being slain on Passover (John 13:1; 19:14, 31). For a discussion of the issues, see Joachim Jeremias, *The Eucharistic Words of Jesus,* trans. N. Perrin, 2d ed., New Testament Library (New York: Scribner, 1966); I. Howard Marshall, *Last Supper and Lord's Supper* (Grand Rapids: Eerdmans, 1980); and Bock, *Luke 9:51–24:53,* 1951–60. If the references in John to meals is associated with the Passover week rather than the meal itself, then a problem does not exist; see Carson, "Matthew," 531–32. This is the most likely explanation. Another option is that the events are so close to the Passover season that the association was made by John in a more symbolic way (so Cranfield, *Mark,* 420–22; Evans, *Mark 8:27–16:20,* 370–72). If this is a Passover meal, then its relationship to the Passover seder becomes significant. However, even if this is not a Passover meal, its proximity to that key festival still makes these connections likely. For this, see G. J. Bahr, "The Seder of Passover and the Eucharistic Words," *Novum Testamentum* 12 (1970): 181–202.

long, straight table. The last meal Jesus would have together with his disciples before his suffering commemorates the releasing of the nation into freedom and deliverance at the exodus. Jesus will take the symbolism of this meal and expand it to commemorate another release to freedom and deliverance.

263. Jesus Foretells His Betrayal (Matt. 26:21–25; Mark 14:18–21; Luke 22:21–23, in a slightly later context; John 13:21–30) (Aland §310; Orchard §330; Huck-Greeven §247b)[51]

Matthew and Mark set up a stark contrast in noting Jesus' awareness of betrayal before the meal is described. Luke saves the announcement of betrayal until he covers the events of the meal, but his account otherwise is very parallel to this one. The juxtaposition of betrayal with the meal is particularly powerful and vivid. In the midst of corporately celebrating one of the great days of Israel's history looms the gathering dark cloud of Jesus meeting his call to suffer. The trigger for that event comes from a defector from within the circle of Jesus' most intimate followers. When Jesus announced that he knew what had been done and who had done it, imagine how the betrayer must have felt to have been discovered. The event suggests that this is what it is like for judgment to come and one's actions to be exposed.

Jesus simply announces that one of those eating with him will betray him. This brings sorrow to all the disciples. Each begins to question, "Is it I?" Jesus' reply is that it is one of those dipping his hand in the dish with him. Mark notes that it is one of the Twelve. Then Jesus issues a woe, which reads in Matthew and Mark, "For the Son of Man goes as it is written of him, but woe to that one by whom the Son of Man is betrayed! It would have been better for that one not to have been born."[52] In Luke, the woe brings questions among them as to who would do this, but Matthew has a poignant and revealing exchange between Jesus and Judas. Like the others, Judas asks, "Is it I, Master?" Jesus' cryptic reply is, "You have said so." In the chaos of the moment and all the questions coming to Jesus about who the betrayer is, the force of Jesus' response would have been lost on the others until the betrayer's identity became clear. At a literary level, however, Jesus' acknowledgment to Judas sets up an equally cryptic reply in Matt. 26:64 at the trial when a question raised by the Jewish leadership about whether Jesus is the Christ, the Son of God, gets a similar "You have said so" affirmation. Matthew makes the link between the two events explicit and transparent. Judas's betrayal enabled Jesus' trial and conviction.

51. Aland places the footwashing scene of John 13:1–20 before this event. Luke notes the remark about betrayal slightly later in his sequence, narrating the supper first.
52. Luke's version of this woe is simply more condensed, "For the Son of Man goes as it has been determined; but woe to that one by whom he is betrayed!"

264. The Last Supper (Matt. 26:26–29; Mark 14:22–25; Luke 22:15–20)
(Aland §311; Orchard §§329, 331; Huck-Greeven §248)

The major feature of the supper, besides the discourse material that surrounds it, is the way Jesus gave new symbolism to the elements. The very fact
that Jesus would resignify these elements and fill them with fresh meaning is
revealing about his self-understanding. The very act means that a new era
filled with new relationships has come. The meal is another way to underscore
that the old era is passing away and that Jesus brings a fulfillment of promise
even as he turns to face his death. This supper takes a look back at the exodus
with its protective sacrifice (Exod. 12) and points forward to another death
that will deliver. In the exodus, many firstborn died; here, it will be a uniquely
firstborn who provides life. There, the presence of blood of sacrificial lambs
meant that judgment passed over the firstborn of those faithful Israelites who
waited for God to act; here, it will be the shedding of the blood of only one,
who will open up the way to a new era. So this meal looks forward. This Last
Supper will become the Lord's Supper and look back at the turning point that
Jesus' death was for divine history. In the sacrifice of this one, the lamb was
provided for others.

In other words, the symbolism of this meal is rich with significance. Its
message is informed not only by Jesus' words but also by the pattern of meaning that the original Passover provided.[53] Jesus need not say much for the symbolism to be present because the background is so clear. It is explicitly expressed later in 1 Cor. 5:7. This lack of direct reference to Passover in the meal
scene itself may explain the variations in the wording at the meal, even though
the Passover backdrop is present. What the variations represent are different
ways of making explicit what was implicit in the setting. The point is important because much interpretive energy has been spent trying to figure out what
wording at the meal was original and what has been added, even though the
differences do not alter the basic imagery. This exercise, though historically
valuable and important to pursue, risks obscuring a more obvious unity between the versions.[54] Jesus' death points to the inauguration of the promised

53. Although this point is based on the association of this meal with the Passover, the point
probably remains even if this was not a Passover meal. The Passover is so close that the associations are natural, much as the timing and mood of the Christmas season linger both before
and after the actual day.

54. This point has recently been made by William R. Farmer, "Reflections on Isaiah 53 and
Christian Origins," in *Jesus and the Suffering Servant: Isaiah 53 and Christian Origins,* ed. William H. Bellinger and William R. Farmer (Harrisburg, Pa.: Trinity Press International, 1998),
273–75, although we question his attempt to make so much of the issue of Gospel priority in
making the point. To the extent that an interconnected tradition makes these points about the
event, whether explicitly or implicitly, the order of the Gospels becomes less relevant, because
the basic symbolism of the event is there in all these elements in all versions.

covenant through his death. In that death come the provision and the opportunity for forgiveness.

Luke has the longest version, with two cups and one offer of bread. If this was a Passover meal, then what we see here is an excerpt of a meal that would have had four courses in it. This means that a repetition of cups is not surprising. It is likely that we see in Luke's first cup a reference to the first cup of the Passover meal.[55] The Lukan account begins with Jesus expressing his intense desire to share this meal before he suffers.[56] Jesus then notes that he will not celebrate this meal again until it is fulfilled in the kingdom. Jesus is anticipating a day, made possible by his suffering, when the Passover will be celebrated in a context of complete fulfillment. This cannot be a reference to the Lord's Supper of the church, because even that looks forward to another day when the Lord returns (1 Cor. 11:26). Jesus appears to be looking to the time of the celebratory banquet table fellowship when all that the Passover represents, along with its tie to his approaching suffering, is realized. So he offers an initial cup as a signal of the symbolism that points to that future day.

Next, he takes bread. At this point, the parallels from Matthew and Mark enter into the sequence. Jesus takes the bread and turns it into a symbol of his death. "Take, eat, this is my body." Luke alone adds, ". . . which is given for you. Do this in remembrance of me."[57] Luke's version does nothing but make explicit what the symbolic connection to Passover already communicated. Even the association of the meal as a repetitive memorial is implied in the setting, because this was a meal celebrated annually. Granted, the celebration of the Lord's Supper quickly broke with its Jewish roots, but that was because Jesus had transformed the meal into a new celebration that led to its being celebrated more than once a year. The meal became a recognition of Jesus' death and resurrection, a fact that his followers could commemorate on any given worship day.

Then comes the cup, a second cup for Luke. Mark's version is the shortest. "This is my blood of the covenant, which is poured out for many." The sym-

55. For the possible relationship to the Passover sequence, see Bock, *Luke 9:51–24:53,* 1721–28. The basis of the four cups is lines from Exod. 6:6–7a. See *m. Pesaḥim* 10.6–7. Again, even if this is not the Passover meal proper, it is being given these associations by its proximity to that feast.

56. The emotion is indicated by the use of a Semitic idiom, retained in the Greek, whereby the emotion is stated twice: literally, "with desire I have desired" to eat this Passover.

57. There is some debate whether Luke 22:19b–20 is textually original to Luke. The effect of its inclusion is the unique cup-bread-cup sequence. The reading should be regarded as original because not only is it well attested, but also it is a good example of the "harder reading" principle. What copyist would add a complication like this? It is far easier to explain its omission to remove a problem. A claim that it was added to fit 1 Corinthians, which was written earlier, ignores the fact that the addition makes the text more complicated by creating the reference to two cups. For discussion, see Bock, *Luke 9:51–24:53,* 1721–22; about the debate on original wording, see 1717.

bolism here is informed by Exod. 24:8. The initiation of a newly cut covenant looks to Jer. 31:31, a point that Luke's version makes explicit. The idea of an offering "for many" is a conceptual allusion to Isa. 53:11–12 (Mark 10:45).[58] What is key is how personalized the reference is: "*my* blood of the covenant." It is his suffering that will accrue to the establishment of the covenant with its new realities and promises.

Matthew's version adds to the saying at the end that the blood is poured out for many "for the forgiveness of sins." Again, what is implicit in the association with Exod. 24 and Isa. 53 is made explicit here. What is more, one of the explicit elements of the promised new covenant is the benefit of the forgiveness of sins. So all that these additional words do is make explicit what the allusions in Mark already suggest. Matthew is making the exact theological goal of the sacrifice clear.

Luke's version reads, "This cup that is poured out for you is the new covenant in my blood."[59] Luke's account highlights the new relationship created by Jesus within which is implied the forgiveness of sins, to which Matthew and Mark refer, using forgiveness and "beneficiary" language, respectively. Luke thus shows how kingdom hope and covenant promise are merged in the suffering of the Son of Man, a suffering that has been predicted numerous times in Luke by appeal to the Son of Man. Jesus' death, which was his calling in ministry, opens up the way for the rest of the career of the Son of Man, a career that itself is crucial to the progress of kingdom hope and covenant promise.

Here, Matthew and Mark place Jesus' promise of not drinking of the fruit of the vine until that day when he drinks it new in the Father's (Matthew) or God's (Mark) kingdom. Jesus is pulling all the strands of his career together. What his death means has been predicted as something to happen to the Son of Man. In the imagery comes allusion to the Servant. In the context of these Jerusalem events, Jesus has been presented as the Messiah, the Son of David. Now he speaks solemnly of what he will face and do in connection with a meal that was the foundation of the establishment of the nation. By his work, Jesus is reestablishing the way to God. He is reforming the nation, laying the basis of forgiveness that is fundamental to that reform. In doing so, he opens up the way for all of humanity as well. In the allusion to the new covenant in Luke, the goal of the renewal of a previously broken relationship becomes explicit.

The one plan resides in the work of one person, Jesus. What is fascinating about these words at the table is that there are no titles for Jesus in this section. He speaks strictly in the first person. All the veiling that accompanied many parts of

---

58. See the careful discussion in Rikki Watts, *Isaiah's New Exodus in Mark*, WUNT 2.88 (Tübingen: Mohr, 1997), 349–65.

59. Interestingly, Paul's version of the wording in 1 Cor. 11:23–25 is closest to Luke's.

his ministry is gone. This is another indication of how crucial a turning point this event is for his career, as well as for our understanding of his mission. This is why the message about Jesus and forgiveness stood at the core of early church teaching, as the speeches in Acts show. Jesus' death provided the gateway to new life.

265. Jesus Foretells His Betrayal (Luke 22:21–23; Matt. 26:21–25, in a slightly earlier context; Mark 14:18–21, in a slightly earlier context [see unit 263 above]) (Aland §312; Orchard §333; Huck-Greeven §249)

Luke saves the announcement of the betrayal for here, an event that Matthew and Mark noted earlier, before the words of the meal. The details of the event were treated above. The Lukan account closes with the disciples questioning each other about which of them would do this. However, one point should not be missed. Luke's remarks about the plan for the suffering Son of Man follow his personal declaration about what Jesus' death will mean. This allows a reinforcement of the point that in speaking about himself and his death, Jesus is tracing the career of the Son of Man, who is about to suffer before entering into unprecedented public glory. In contrast, Matthew and Mark set up the remarks at the final supper by the same means but place the discussion earlier in the sequence. It is another example of different literary choices achieving the same point in diverse ways.

266. The New Way of Greatness (Luke 22:24–30; conceptual in an earlier context: Matt. 20:24–28; 19:28; Mark 10:41–45 [see units 225 and 222 above]) (Aland §313; Orchard §334; Huck-Greeven §250)

The irony in Luke continues when a dispute arises among the disciples as to which one of them is the greatest. It is amazing how self-concerned the disciples are at this point. The description is so unflattering to the disciples that the evidence speaks for the event's authenticity. The remarks show that the disciples still do not grasp Jesus' teaching about the kingdom or the suffering to come. Rank is still the preeminent concern. Luke will proceed through this dispute and trace several other remarks by Jesus through v. 38 so that this event in his Gospel has the mood of both a Greek symposium, where wisdom is dispensed, and a farewell discourse, where final instructions are made.

The dispute leads Jesus into a response like that in the earlier parallels in Matthew and Mark. The counterexample is how Gentile leaders use authority as an exercise of rank and power. Their goal is to assert lordship and be hailed as benefactor. In this they are not unlike the Jewish leadership, as Luke has shown in 14:7 and 20:46. Benefaction came from the wealthy as a way of "serving" the city and yet maintaining one's rank and prestige in the society.[60] The system allowed elevation only of those who had wealth. The cultural practice served to perpetuate the position of wealthy people.

Jesus explains that greatness for them will not be defined by a standard set in the world. Greatness will not involve rank, as greatness comes to the one who becomes like the youngest. Greatness does not come through the use of power, because the leader is to be the servant. Jesus points to the reversal of values in his own ministry. Although the world defines the leader as the one who sits at the table to be served, Jesus has ministered to them as one who serves. That is the example to be followed.

Yet that call to serve does not come without honor and reward from God to the Twelve for standing by Jesus in his trials. Even in their confusion and failure, Jesus shows his faithfulness to them, because they have been faithful in staying with him. So he is assigning them a kingdom, just as he has received a kingdom from God. These are not two distinct kingdoms, but rather a share of the same right to participate in the rule of God that Jesus brings. The reward will be a place at Jesus' table in the kingdom to come, a place of abiding fellowship and life. They also will receive authority to judge the twelve tribes of Israel. In effect, Jesus is transferring leadership in light of his departure, much like a farewell discourse.[61] The apostles, who have remained with him, will now be the point people for God's message and hope. Enabled with his authority, they are freed to serve. Jesus' promise for them to rule the tribes is for these chosen only. It shows how Jesus is reconstructing the nation around a faithful, responsive group that he has chosen to help him. The leadership has forfeited their claim to represent God and his message. That task now will be taken up by the faithful among the Twelve.[62]

267. Peter's Denial Predicted (Matt. 26:30–35; Mark 14:26–31; Luke 22:31–34; John 13:36–38) (Aland §315; Orchard §336; Huck-Greeven §§251, 253)[63]

Nevertheless, the disciples still have much to learn. Peter, as a representative of them, overestimates his own strength and ability to withstand trial.

60. Joel Green, *The Gospel of Luke*, NICNT (Grand Rapids: Eerdmans, 1997), 767–68.
61. Ibid., 770.
62. One of the burdens of Acts 1 is to note the replacement of Judas for the twelfth spot. Everything about that selection—the gathering and waiting in Jerusalem in obedience, the mood of prayer, the Spirit-guided remarks of Peter, and the dependence on God as seen through the choice by lot—shows that Luke portrays that event positively. It brings completion to the group mentioned here.
63. Aland places Jesus' issuing of a new commandment in John 13:31–35 before this event.

Matthew and Mark note how the meal ended with a hymn. If this was a Passover meal, then this probably refers to the traditional Hallel psalms that offered praise to God and expressed hope for the coming of the great day of deliverance. These would have included Ps. 115–18, especially Ps. 118.[64] Luke presents the prediction of Peter's denial as an extension of the meal. John's Gospel has a similar setting, placing it before the Paraclete section of the upper room discourse (John 13:36–38). The worship connected to hymns is part of the celebration attached to the meal. So the difference in timing is a superficial one. The difference between geographical detail and the linkage reflects a long, multifaceted event.

In Matthew and Mark, Jesus predicts abandonment by the rest of the disciples. Only Judas flat out betrayed him, but the rest of the disciples will be too scared to stand by him. Jesus predicts, "You will all fall away; for it is written, 'I will strike the shepherd, and the sheep will be scattered.' But after I am raised up, I will go before you to Galilee." Matthew notes uniquely that the falling away will happen that very night. The citation is from Zech. 13:7. What are commands in Zechariah are recorded as first-person acts here. God is the actor, who has determined that the shepherd will be struck, leaving the sheep vulnerable for a brief moment. In that moment the sheep will scatter. The image in Zechariah appears to be of a moment when the leader is struck, but a remnant is preserved. The death does not prevent the reforming of the nation. This is perhaps the significance of Matthew alone mentioning the sheep "of the flock" being scattered.[65] Although there is a death and much rejection, a flock of the faithful remains, though temporarily exposed. After the resurrection they will be directed again from Galilee.

Luke does not record resurrection appearances in Galilee, so he lacks these remarks. Instead, he opens with a note that Satan has demanded to have Simon and sift the disciple like wheat, a figure for testing. But Jesus has interceded for him that his faith might not fail. Thus, when Peter has turned again, implying a coming temporary failure, he is to strengthen his brothers and sisters.

Peter is confident that he will not fail Jesus, even if all the others will.[66] What is a promise not to fall away in Matthew and Mark is stated most emphatically in Luke: "I am ready to go with you to prison and death." John's Gospel is similar to Luke, with Peter promising to follow Jesus and lay down his life for him. At least it is becoming clear to Peter what Jesus is saying about

64. See *t. Ketubbot* 5.5; *t. Pesaḥim* 10.8; some lists of the Hallel include Ps. 113–14 as well, as *Pesiqta Rabbati* 2 (5a) alludes to Ps. 113:1, but this is a late text. The importance of Ps. 118 is clear from the *Midrash Psalms* 118 §22. See Jeremias, *Eucharistic Words*, 256–62.

65. Carson, "Matthew," 540–41. On the background to Zechariah, see Ralph L. Smith, *Micah–Malachi*, WBC 32 (Waco: Word, 1984), 284.

66. Vincent Taylor, *The Gospel according to St. Mark*, 2d ed. (New York: Macmillan, 1966), 550, attributes these Markan details to Peter himself.

coming rejection. His heart is in the right place. He wishes to stand with Jesus, a far different choice than Judas already has made.[67] But he fails to appreciate how powerful are the forces lined up against him if he relies on his own self-assessed strength.

So Jesus predicts Peter's failure. Again Matthew and Mark stand close together. Jesus predicts that this very night, before the cock crows for the morning, Peter will deny Jesus three times.[68] Mark alone speaks of the cock crowing twice, while Matthew speaks only of a denial in the evening before the cock crows. Luke's prediction is of denials before the cock crows "this day." John speaks, like Matthew, of the sequence of a threefold denial and then the cock crowing. Before sunrise, Peter will succumb. Luke and John end with Jesus' prediction being the final word, while Matthew and Mark note a second promise of fidelity by Peter. Mark, noting emotion as he often does, makes the point that Peter was vehement. Even if he must die, Peter claims that there is no way that he will deny Jesus. Both versions use the emphatic οὐ μή to affirm the certainty that denial will not come. But Peter was not alone. Taking the lead from the prominent disciple, they all said the same. Jesus knows what is coming far more clearly than do the disciples. In fact, he knows them better than they know themselves. Such independent overconfidence left them vulnerable.

268. The Two Swords (Luke 22:35–38) (Aland §316; Orchard §337; Huck-Greeven §252)

The approach of Jesus' death brings a change in the way the disciples will conduct their mission. In the two missions of Luke 9 and 10, the disciples had to roam Israel and trust the towns they visited to furnish their provisions. So Jesus asks them to recall if they lacked anything. They respond that they lacked nothing then. Now they will have to travel with provisions. They are to take a purse and a knapsack. The one without a sword will need to purchase one. The openness to reception has changed into the environment of rejection, for Scripture is in the process of being realized in Jesus, a point the text makes emphatically by introducing and concluding the citation with remarks about fulfillment. To describe his fate, Jesus cites Isa. 53:12: "And he was reckoned with the transgressors." The cross will show how skewed things have become. The one who proclaimed the hope of Israel will be executed as if he

---

67. Note also the difference after their respective actions (Matt. 26:75 versus 27:5). Peter learned from his failure and turned.

68. For the debate over the timing of the cock crowing, see Keener, *Gospel of Matthew,* 370–71, note on 26:34. Jesus' prediction is of a denial during that evening.

were seeking to undermine the nation. Just as the teacher is rejected, so it will be for the followers.

Peter takes Jesus' remarks as a sign that they must fight, a belief that will show itself when Peter wields a sword at Jesus' arrest (John 18:10; the Synoptics note only that one of them used a sword). He notes that they already have two swords, again indicating his seeming willingness to go down fighting in the face of what surely will be superior numbers of opponents. The misunderstanding is so great that Jesus chooses instead to end the conversation and allow events to run their course. Jesus' teaching in Luke ends on this note that the disciples still have much to learn. Subsequent events will teach them.

269. Gethsemane (Matt. 26:36–46; Mark 14:32–42; Luke 22:39–46)
(Aland §330; Orchard §345; Huck-Greeven §254)[69]

Matthew and Mark already noted that the entourage had made it to the Mount of Olives. Luke notes that they journeyed here, while Matthew and Mark note the locale as Gethsemane, a place that John 18:1 calls simply a garden in the Kidron Valley. Luke's account of this scene is the most concise, while Matthew and Mark again are very similar. This situation is common in the passion material.

The Lukan version stays focused on the issue of temptation approaching for the disciples and on Jesus' request to the Father. He tells the disciples before he prays that they should pray not to enter into temptation, a point that Matthew and Mark save for later. Then he withdraws from them about a stone's throw to pray. Jesus asks if the cup of suffering and judgment that is coming might be removed from him. Yet what Jesus really desires is to do God's will and not follow his own desire to be extracted from this situation. In the request to follow God and in contrast with the disciples' ignoring their need to avoid temptation comes the scene's example lesson. Jesus is submitting to the Father's will even though it means intense suffering for him. Everything about the scene shows Jesus coming to grips with the reality of his approaching sacrifice.

The next portion of Luke is disputed textually. It describes angelic support for Jesus and the intensity of his praying. It reads "And there appeared to him an angel from heaven, strengthening him. And being in agony he prayed more earnestly; and his sweat became like great drops of blood falling down upon the ground." It is hard to be sure whether these verses are original to Luke, although a case for their authenticity can be made. The external evidence is finely balanced, with $\mathfrak{P}^{75}$ and B omitting the verses and ℵ and D including

---

69. Aland places the upper room discourse of John 14–16 and Jesus' final prayer of John 17 before this event.

them. Justin Martyr knows of the reading (*Trypho* 103.8). Some suggest that a copyist removed the verses because they suggest Jesus' need for help. It is harder to explain how this text would have been added in the second century, when there was contention over the nature of Jesus' person. If original, then the very human portrait of Jesus' preparation to face his suffering through intense prayer is enhanced.

On his return, Jesus finds the disciples sleeping, leading him to ask them why they sleep. Once again he repeats his exhortation that they should pray that they might not enter into temptation. They need to appreciate the spiritual struggle that lies just ahead. What he had just done, they should be doing. What Jesus will face involves so intense a spiritual struggle that prayer and divine strengthening are what is required. Disciples will fail if they are not diligent in turning to God in the face of such rejection. That is precisely what does happen when Jesus is arrested.

Matthew and Mark add many details to the scene and intensify its themes. First, Jesus takes with him Peter, and James and John, the sons of Zebedee. Narrative notes indicate that Jesus became distressed (Mark), sorrowful (Matthew), and deeply troubled (both). Then Jesus tells them that he is sorrowful even to the point of death.[70] Jesus asks them to watch. As Jesus goes to pray, Mark notes in a narrative summary that Jesus asks if it is possible that this hour might pass from him.

The prayer as uttered in Matthew and Mark contains small differences.[71] The emotion of the request recalls Ps. 116:1–4. Matthew's version reads, "My Father, if it is possible, let this cup pass from me; nevertheless, not as I will, but as you will." The reference to the cup refers to suffering (Matt. 20:22–23; 26:27). Background may also include allusions to the cup of wrath that Jesus will drink (Ps. 60:3; 75:8; Isa. 29:9–10; 51:17, 21–23; Jer. 25:15–29). Mark's account reads, "Abba, Father, all things are possible for you; remove this cup from me; yet not what I will, but what you will." Thus, although Jesus' request is more directly stated in Mark, the thrust of the accounts is the same: what Jesus wants most, even in the face of his desire not to suffer, is to do God's will. In the end, the prayer affirms Jesus' desire to submit to God.

On his return, Jesus finds Peter's group sleeping. Jesus rebukes them through Peter for not being able to watch for one hour. He issues the exhortation to pray not to enter into temptation and notes that the spirit is willing, but the flesh is weak. This battle can be fought only with spiritual focus and

70. Matthew uses a more intense word form for "sorrow" in v. 38 than in v. 37, strengthening the note. Hebrews 5:7 alludes to the event and says that God answered Jesus' prayer to be delivered from his depth of despair here through the resurrection.

71. It is sometimes questioned how the content of this prayer could be known, given that the disciples were a distance away and asleep for much of the time. Blomberg, *Matthew*, 395, suggests either that Jesus recounted the prayer for them in his resurrection appearances or that the three taken with Jesus were close enough and awake long enough to hear it when spoken.

concentration. The remarks surely are seen to anticipate Peter's upcoming denials and the disciples' fleeing at Jesus' arrest.

Jesus then departs to pray again. Mark says only that Jesus repeated the same words, while Matthew notes Jesus' acceptance of the divine will with his prayer, "My Father, if this cannot pass unless I drink it, your will be done." Once again on Jesus' return, the disciples are dozing and unresponsive. When a third round yields the same result, prefiguring the denials with a current set of failures, Jesus notes that they are taking their rest, but that the hour has come (Mark) or drawn near (Matthew).[72] He goes on to say, "The Son of Man is betrayed into the hands of sinners. Rise, let us be going; see, the one who betrays me is at hand." Jesus is very aware that he must face his suffering. He faces it voluntarily in submission to God. God has answered his prayer. God's will must be done so that the kingdom can come.

270. Jesus Arrested (Matt. 26:47–56; Mark 14:43–52; Luke 22:47–53; John 18:2–12) (Aland §331; Orchard §346; Huck-Greeven §255)

Jesus' arrest is told with the most detail in Matthew. Luke again is the most concise. John 18:2–12 also adds important details but lacks any mention of the betraying kiss. This perhaps is because it already was so well known in the tradition. John's version places Jesus at the center of the scene, ready to face his arrest, causing his captors to fall back in respect. They step back also perhaps because of uncertainty as to his response at the initial sight of him. In John, Jesus appeals for all the others to be released. When the disciples wish to fight, John has Jesus address Peter and tell him that he will drink the cup that the Father has given to him. This is John's way of showing that Jesus will face the call that God has given to him and will do so majestically.

In each account, Judas approaches Jesus after the time of prayer. With Judas is the leadership.[73] Chief priests are mentioned in every account, while the elders are noted by all the Synoptics. Mark alone names the scribes. John mentions soldiers and officers from the chief priests and Pharisees. Later, John speaks of the officers of the Jews.

Matthew and Mark note that they came with swords and clubs, just in case a battle erupted. John describes lanterns, torches, and weapons. The presence of swords, which probably are short daggers, suggests a mix of people of vari-

---

72. Given the significance of the term "draw near" in regard to the nearness of the kingdom, this parallel is interesting (cf. Matt. 3:2; 4:17; Mark 1:15). It shows that the term means that something has come very close, right up to the edge of happening. Some even use the metaphor "beginning to dawn" to summarize the image.

73. Luke at the start refers to the "crowd" but later in v. 52 mentions chief priests, officers of the temple, and elders.

ous backgrounds who joined with those who brought clubs. The entourage possibly consisted of auxiliary troops (mostly mercenaries) and Jews. The auxiliary forces could have been added as support that the leadership would have requested. However, the text seems to indicate that the bulk of those arresting Jesus were assembled by the leadership, making the arresting party primarily Jewish. The presence of such an assembled crowd of makeshift troops might explain why Judas had to identify Jesus with a kiss.[74] The arrest is well planned. John 18:12 mentions a cohort of soldiers. Luke also saves a similar detail for later in the account when Jesus responds to the arrest, referring to the officers of the temple guard (Luke 22:52). Another detail emerges from Matthew and Mark. Because it was very dark and not everyone would recognize Jesus, Judas indicated that he would give a sign. The one he kisses is the one to arrest.

In Matthew, Judas greets Jesus and kisses him, leading Jesus to remark literally and elliptically, "Friend, [do that] for which you are here." This either is a command to go ahead and do what they have come for, or it is a statement that Jesus knows why they are here, so they should go ahead. The leaders seize Jesus as they follow through on the plan. Mark has the same detail except that he lacks Jesus' elliptical remark to Judas. Luke has a poignant exchange as Jesus asks, "Judas, would you betray the Son of Man with a kiss?" Thus, in Luke, Jesus' knowledge about what is taking place is explicit, and so is the placement of responsibility on Judas, setting up the description of his end in Acts 1. In addition, the note of betrayal is heightened because an act of respect and intimacy has become hypocritically twisted into a sign of treachery and defection.

At this point the accounts have a mix and match of detail. In Luke, there is a question about whether Jesus' followers should strike back with the sword, as the discussion described in Luke 22:35–38 is fresh in their minds. Matthew and Mark move directly into the action, and all the Synoptics depict one of them striking the slave of the high priest on the ear. Luke specifies the right ear, while John gives the slave's name as Malchus. Jesus stops the assault. Luke simply has Jesus tell them, "No more of this!" Then Jesus graciously heals the slave, illustrating his principle of loving your enemy (see Luke 6:27–36). Only Luke notes this detail. Matthew has a much more detailed response. They are to put their swords back in place, because "all who take the sword will perish by the sword." Jesus then notes that he could call down through the Father

74. On the ethnic makeup of various militia groups in the Roman world in Judea, see Doran Mendels, *The Rise and Fall of Jewish Nationalism: Jewish and Christian Ethnicity in Ancient Palestine* (Grand Rapids: Eerdmans, 1992), 333–49. Priestly forces would have been composed of the citizenry, as they did not possess a standing army. Any Roman forces or support troops from Herod, if present, would have been mercenaries of mixed origin. But it is not certain that Rome or Herod supplied any troops yet, as the narratives seem to suggest that their involvement came later.

twelve legions of angels (up to seventy-two thousand angels!), if he wished. However, to intervene in this way would prevent the Scripture from being ful-filled and the divine plan from being accomplished. The prayer at Gethse-mane had taken hold. Jesus will do God's will. Mark lacks any rebuke. Next, Jesus moves to address his captors with a point that all the Synoptics record. They have come to arrest him with clubs as if he were a dangerous figure. The key term here is λῃστής, which often refers to a revolutionary or insurrection-ist, not merely a robber.[75] He notes that when he was in the temple teaching daily, they made no effort to seize him. This private arrest, away from the mul-titudes, points to hypocrisy and cowardice, as the authorities make their move out of sight of the crowds.

Luke concludes the scene with Jesus noting that this is their hour and that of the power of darkness. The cosmic battle has entered a key and bleak stage. Matthew and Mark record Jesus' indication that all this has taken place for the fulfilling of Scripture. Matthew speaks explicitly of the writings "of the proph-ets." Then these two Gospels note how the disciples flee. Mark alone tells of a young man wearing nothing but a linen cloth, who was seized but then tore away from their grasp and ran away naked. No one had the courage to stand with Jesus, and this escape makes that point graphically. In different ways, all the Gospels set a somber mood as Jesus is arrested and left by himself to face examination. Alone, yet armed with the knowledge that he is doing God's will, Jesus will still be very much in control of the apparent chaos taking place around him.

271. Jesus Examined before the Council and Peter's Denials
(Matt. 26:57–75; Mark 14:53–72; Luke 22:54–71; John 18:13–28)
(Aland §§332–33; Orchard §§347–55a; Huck-Greeven §256)

The presentation of Peter's denials and the Jewish leadership's examination of Jesus differs within the Synoptics. Luke chooses to present the denials first and then gives his summary of the examination. Matthew and Mark present the denials after their presentation of the examination. John intermixes the denials with the trial movement, while alone noting a brief stop at Annas's home before Jesus is sent on to Caiaphas (John 18:13, 24). The choices of how to sequence the denials are narrative ones.

In addition, the summary that Luke presents of Jesus' examination lacks any mention of the temple charge and takes place early in the day. The ac-counts in Matthew and Mark have an evening setting. Luke simplifies the pre-

75. BAGD, 473 §2; BDAG, 594 §2; C. F. D. Moule, *The Gospel according to Mark,* Cam-bridge Bible Commentary (Cambridge: Cambridge University Press, 1965), 119.

sentation by focusing on the charge that became the basis for taking Jesus to Pilate. As for the event's timing, either Luke has disclosed the manner in which the long evening examination ended, showing that it extended into the morning, or he is summarizing a final review of the testimony that took place once all the council had gathered.

It is sometimes questioned how there could be sources for this examination scene when no disciples were present.[76] However, candidates abound. Prominent Jews with connections to the council included Joseph of Arimathea and Nicodemus, not to mention Saul, who became Paul the apostle. In addition, the controversy that Jesus' death provoked in Jerusalem lasted for years. It involved Annas and his family, who controlled the high priesthood, for decades (John 18:13; Luke 3:2). It lasted at least into the 60s, as far as the death of James, the brother of Jesus, who was slain by Annas the younger (Josephus, *Ant.* 20.9.1 §§197–203). These later events have the feel of a family vendetta by the relatives of Caiaphas, Annas's son-in-law and high priest at Jesus' trial (Matt. 26:57). The debate caused by such a public feud between the high priestly family and the Jewish Christians surely would have included news about why the leadership had handed Jesus over to Pilate. It would be in the leadership's interest for the reasons to become known.

Technically, the scene is not a trial. It is more of a charge-gathering phase, much like our grand jury process. The Jewish leadership did not possess the legal authority to execute Jesus.[77] They could only recommend a course of action. This restriction is why they eventually brought Jesus to Pilate. It also was a sound move politically. A Roman execution would make the foreign rulers responsible for Jesus' death, thus mollifying those who objected to it. This would limit any public impression about the leadership's ultimate culpability.

The absence of an official trial is important for two reasons. First, it is often said that the leadership violated their own legal rules in at least three ways by having a capital trial during a religious festival, at night, and without defense witnesses.[78] However, if this was more like a grand jury recommendation than an official trial, no such violations took place. Second, the goal was not to bring a religious indictment, because that would be of little legal interest to

---

76. E. P. Sanders, *Jesus and Judaism* (Philadelphia: Fortress, 1985), 298.

77. This has been a disputed point because some have argued that events such as the deaths of Stephen and James show that such authority did exist. But these other executions have the feel of mob justice (the stoning of Stephen) or the violation of authority (Annas's execution of James, which Josephus notes was complained about as an abuse of authority). The relevant texts are Josephus, *War* 2.8.1 §117 and *Ant.* 20.9.1 §201; John 18:31 and 19:10. See Darrell L. Bock, *Blasphemy and Exaltation in Judaism and the Final Examination of Jesus,* WUNT 2.106 (Tübingen: Mohr, 1998), 7–15, 189–95.

78. These procedures are described in *m. Sanhedrin* 4.1; 11.2. The rules regarding blasphemy are in *m. Sanhedrin* 7.5. The prohibition of examination on a feast day is in *m. Besah* 5.2. Exceptions were allowed in particularly important cases, as *m. Sanhedrin* 11.3 (11.4 in some translations) indicates.

the Romans (e.g., Acts 25:18–20). The goal was to bring a political allegation that would cause the Romans to act in their own self-interest. This explains the examination's starting point being Jesus' remarks about the temple in Matthew and Mark. Actions against the temple had both political and religious overtones, including the potential for charges of blasphemy to undercut Jesus' Jewish support. This sacred locale, as an extremely sensitive religious site, was a potential flash point for trouble. If Jesus could be shown to have designs on damaging this site, he would be a threat to law and order, something on which Pilate was charged to keep tight rein. This also explains the interest in a messianic claim. If Jesus claimed to be a competing king, Caesar would not be pleased.

While Jesus is being brought to the leadership for examination, Peter is trailing behind to see what happens. John's Gospel mentions one other disciple present, whom the high priest knew (John 18:16). This disciple gains access into the residence for them. Peter finds himself in the courtyard of the high priest, sitting at the fire (Mark, Luke, John) with the guards (Matthew, Mark, John). At this point, Luke narrates the denials. Over an interval of more than an hour, Peter denies Jesus three times before the cock crows, just as Jesus had predicted. He responds to the remarks of a servant girl and two others in succession. The final denial comes when Peter's Galilean roots are exposed because of his accent. With the third denial, "the Lord turned and looked at Peter," as the disciple was likely in a central courtyard area that could be seen from within the house. Luke's account recalls Jesus' prediction and records Peter's weeping bitterly as he departs. Events may seem to be out of control, but Jesus is quite aware of what is taking place.

It is also here that Luke records the mocking of Jesus as the soldiers hold him. The soldiers beat him, blindfold him, and taunt him to prophesy. Luke speaks of the soldiers "reviling" him, using a word that also can be translated as "blaspheming" him.

Matthew and Mark begin their fuller treatment of the examination scene by noting that the whole council was present. This is a reference either to the Sanhedrin or to some other high council of the major Jewish leadership. The examination begins with the note that they sought testimony by which they might put Jesus to death. Matthew adds that they sought false testimony, while Mark will mention false witnesses later as he notes that their testimony did not agree. The main effort focused on Jesus' remarks that he could destroy the temple and in three days rebuild it. At the time, the temple was in the midst of a multiyear expansion and was a topic of national pride, as the disciples' remarks before the Olivet discourse show. Jesus did say something like this, according to John 2:19, but it was not of the earthly temple that he spoke. Mark's version suggests that difference in the contrast between the temple made with hands and the temple not made with hands. The point of the effort was to prove that Jesus was fomenting religious-political tension by challenging the temple's existence, which also implied a rejection of its current authority structure. Significantly, Matthew and Mark make it clear that this unsubstantiated charge fell through. The leadership knew that they would have to bring a solid case before the Romans.

The high priest now intervenes. He asks if Jesus has any reply to these charges, but Jesus remains silent. Luke's account appears to reenter here, as he has ignored the temple charge. The high priest now begins to consider the question of whether Jesus is the Christ. Some have claimed that this transition is abrupt and shows the scene to be artificially constructed. However, the transition is natural. The idea that the Messiah at the end would reform and rebuild a previously divinely disciplined Jerusalem was embedded in Judaism.[79] For example, benediction 14 of the national prayer known as the *Shemoneh Esreh* reads, "And to Jerusalem, your city, return with mercy and dwell in its midst as you have spoken; and build it soon in our days to be an everlasting building; and raise up quickly in its midst the throne of David. Blessed are you, Lord, who builds Jerusalem." The request shows the close connection between the anticipated restoration of Jerusalem to full glory and the presence of Messiah. Similar in tone is *Psalms of Solomon* 17.30, which reads, "And he will purge Jerusalem holy as it was even from the beginning." It was on beliefs such as these that the high priest drew to ask about Jesus' messianic claims. The transition to a question about the Messiah makes sense, especially in light of Jesus' recent temple action.

So the high priest asks Jesus if he is the Christ, the Son of the Blessed One. Matthew adds that the priest ties the question to the invoking of an oath under the "living God." Mark's "Son of the Blessed" is a respectful way to say what Matthew notes is "Son of God" (on "Blessed One," see *1 Enoch* 77.2; *m. Berakot* 7.3).[80] Obviously, the priest does not use the title in the Christian sense, but rather is asking if Jesus is the Messiah, Son of God (see 2 Sam. 7:14). If he can get a royal claim from Jesus, they can go to Pilate. Luke simplifies the question to being about the Christ.

Mark has Jesus reply positively, "I am." Matthew has a more indirect answer: "You have said so." However, Matthew's earlier use of that response in 26:25 shows that this too is a positive reply. It denotes agreement but with a note of hesitation that the affirmation needs some type of qualifying,

---

79. Otto Betz has defended the credibility of this transition in a key summary of the trial scene in "Probleme des Prozesses Jesu," *Aufstieg und Niedergang der römischen Welt*, 2.25.1 (Berlin: de Gruyter, 1982), 565–647.

80. The expression shows up in an old Jewish prayer known as the *Kaddish*. This prayer may date to the second century A.D., although the earliest evidence for it is in fourth-century documents. See *Sipre Deuteronomy* §306, where it is connected to Rabbi Jose b. Ḥalafta (ca. A.D. 150). On the issue of the date of this prayer, see John Meier, *A Marginal Jew: Rethinking the Historical Jesus*, 2 vols., ABRL (New York: Doubleday, 1994), 2:361–62 n. 36. The expression is the respectful language of worship.

which Jesus' additional remarks will give. Luke's initial response also looks back to a previous incident, the query in Luke 20:1–8 about the source of Jesus' authority. Jesus says, "If I tell you, you will not believe; and if I ask you, you will not answer." This alludes back to that earlier controversy in which the issue of the source of Jesus' authority was raised. The reply's point is twofold. First, this question already has been pursued. Second, a reply from Jesus is of no use at this point.

Now, Jesus makes the key statement. Matthew and Mark report Jesus saying, "You will see the Son of Man seated at the right hand of Power, and coming with the clouds of heaven."[81] Matthew adds a note of timing that they will see this "hereafter." Luke only raises the issue of the seating at the right hand of God, with Jesus saying, "But from now on the Son of Man will be seated at the right hand of the power of God."

Two Old Testament allusions are key. First is a reference to Ps. 110:1. This is a text on the royal authority of God's vice-regent, a text ultimately related to the Messiah's authority. In effect, Jesus replies positively with this allusion. But the claim goes beyond what they ask. Jesus is claiming that there is coming a vindication whereby he will demonstrate his sharing of God's authority. He is claiming the right to go directly into God's presence in heaven. The guarantee that this is what Jesus is claiming comes in the second allusion, to riding the clouds, from Dan. 7:13. This text describes the vindicating judgment authority of a figure who shares end-time judicial power received from God. Jesus applies this role to himself. In other words, Jesus ironically claims that rather than the council being his judge, he is the judge of the final judgment. The authority that Jesus possesses, he has received from God directly, like the Son of Man image of Daniel. Implicit here is a claim to be able to go directly into God's presence and work at his side, a claim that he is really their judge.

Aspects of this claim have possible precedents in Judaism. The Son of Man figure of *1 Enoch* 37–71 was said to possess such authority in the final judgment. In the context of that book, this figure is said to be the raised Enoch (70.1–71.14). So the idea of a human being receiving such authority is not unprecedented. A second example comes from *Exagoge to Ezekiel* 68–85, where Moses' power during the exodus is portrayed in a dream as if the Ancient of Days of Dan. 7 had invited him to sit on his throne (Dan. 7:9) to exercise great authority. This text is an exposition of Exod. 7:1, where God tells Moses that he will be "god" to Pharaoh. Such an exalted description might be possible to consider for a great saint whom God exalted to heaven or for the

---

81. The use of the term "Power" is another respectful circumlocution referring to God in terms of his authority. It is like speaking of the "Almighty." See *1 Enoch* 62.7 and *Targum Job* 5.8. The expression is especially common in describing God's acts during the period of Moses, when the nation was being delivered. See Bock, *Blasphemy and Exaltation,* 217–19; for details on this entire scene and a defense of its authenticity, see 184–237.

venerable leader who directed the exodus, but for this Galilean teacher to claim such authority was too much for the leadership to bear. For them, it was blasphemy.

The claim that Jesus makes would have evoked strong images to a Jewish mind. The idea of being seated at God's right hand and returning on the clouds, though metaphorical in descriptive force, would be quite offensive in its imagery. It would be worse, in the leadership's view, than claiming the right to be able to walk into the Holy of Holies in the temple and live there! The sequence of sitting at the right hand and then riding the clouds would make it clear that Jesus was claiming an authority directly from heaven.[82] Jesus' remark was totally offensive to the leaders, who did not believe that he had such authority. Luke follows up with a final question. Is Jesus claiming to be the "Son of God"? Jesus responds with another qualified affirmation, "You say that I am."

So the high priest, in Matthew and Mark, tears his garments in response to the remark about the Son of Man seated at the right hand of God. Garment rending was a sign that blasphemy has been uttered or a shameful act has taken place (Num. 14:6; 2 Sam. 1:11; 1 Macc. 2:14; *b. Sanhedrin* 60ª). He asks what need they have of further witnesses, noting the blasphemy and that Jesus has testified with his own lips. The irony of the scene is twofold. First, Jesus is the one who gives the testimony that leads to his death. The evidence that the leadership could not get by false testimony, Jesus supplies. Second, although they think that they are conducting a trial to censure Jesus' claim of authority, Jesus is claiming that in reality they are the people on trial, and he will be their judge. In the midst of the trial in all the accounts, Jesus affirms that he is the Christ, the Son of God, and makes claims to possess the judgment authority of the Son of Man.

Matthew and Mark conclude with a council judgment that Jesus deserves death. They will take Jesus to the authority of Rome. At this point, Mark narrates the mocking of Jesus involving the council and the guards. Matthew also notes the "prophesy" game as he relates how they taunt Jesus to name who struck him.

After the trial, Matthew and Mark present Peter's denials. The first charge, from a servant girl, connects Peter with "Jesus the Galilean" (Matthew) or "the Nazarene, Jesus" (Mark). The second charge comes in Matthew after Peter has moved out to the porch. The charge comes from another servant girl. Mark simply speaks of "the servant girl" and does not record any movement. Matthew alone notes that this second denial came with an oath. The third charge comes from bystanders who comment on his accent (Matthew)

---

82. As noted above in the discussion of clouds imagery and the Son of Man in the Olivet discourse, only God or pagan gods are said to ride the clouds (Exod. 14:20; 34:5; Num. 10:34; Ps. 104:3; Isa. 19:1).

or his ethnicity as a Galilean (Mark). John includes a relative of the slave in-jured at Jesus' arrest as precipitating the third denial. This third denial is the most emphatic, because it comes with Peter putting a curse on himself and swearing. At this point, the cock crows. Mark notes that it is a second crowing, so the prediction corresponds with the cock crowing twice, as Jesus predicted in Mark 14:30. In both accounts this leads Peter to remember Jesus' predic-tion and leave weeping. Despite the best of intentions, Peter has failed. Temp-tation has overcome him. Jesus now faces his death and the power of Rome alone.

We have noted that the leadership viewed Jesus' remarks as blasphe-mous. It is also important to put these remarks in a more complete reli-gious-political context. In all likelihood, the Jews saw Jesus as subject to the death penalty as a false prophet who also was bringing the nation into danger with his challenge of the leadership (John 11:50). The back-ground here is Deut. 13:1–5. This is not very far from the charges about sorcery found in the Jewish materials about Jesus.[83] Similar to this is a view that shows up in the Temple Scroll at Qumran (11QTemple[a] 64.7–9), which reads, "If a man slanders his [God's] people and delivers his peo-ple up to a foreign nation and does evil to his people, you shall hang him on a tree [Deut. 21:22–23], and he shall die. According to the mouth of two witnesses and the mouth of three witnesses he shall be put to death, and they shall hang him on a tree." In other words, if someone's teaching is such that it puts the nation at risk before foreigners, then that person should be executed.[84]

For the leadership, Jesus' claim to be their judge and to intimately share God's authority had not only offensive religious overtones in terms of God's uniqueness, but also political overtones in terms of their own authority. A dis-ruptive religious dispute within Judaism was an invitation to the Romans to assume even tighter control of Israel. There was ample precedent for this in the high priestly dispute that had led to Rome's entry into Israel in 63 B.C.[85] Tension like this also is what brought about Rome's eventual involvement that led to the city's destruction in A.D. 70. The leadership knew their history. In their view, to act against Jesus was to protect not only their religion and power base but also the nation. Although they were offended by the blas-phemy they saw in Jesus' remarks, they had obtained an affirmative reply to their question about Jesus being the Messiah. That charge enabled them to present Jesus to Pilate as a self-proclaimed king. The leadership now had enough to take to Pilate.

83. See Darrell L. Bock, *Studying the Historical Jesus* (Grand Rapids: Baker, 2002), chap. 1.
84. Otto Betz, "Jesus and the Temple Scroll," in *Jesus and the Dead Sea Scrolls,* ed. James A. Charlesworth, ABRL (New York: Doubleday, 1992), 80–89.
85. See chapter 3 of Bock, *Studying.*

272. Jesus Delivered to Pilate (Matt. 27:1–2; Mark 15:1; Luke 23:1) (Aland §334; Orchard §355b; Huck-Greeven §257a)

Matthew and Mark note a morning consultation involving the chief priests, elders, scribes (Mark), and council (Mark). They lead Jesus to Pilate, prefect of Judea. Pilate's task was to keep the peace, collect taxes, and make sure that no threat to Caesar arose in the region. Luke refers simply to the whole company bringing Jesus before Pilate for examination. They are either at the fortress of Antonia or the palace of the king, which would have been made available to Pilate for the feast. Pilate was responsible for the high priest's appointment annually. During his rule, he appointed Caiaphas ten times to the post.

273. The Death of Judas (Matt. 27:3–10) (Aland §335; Orchard §356; Huck-Greeven §258)

Judas now experiences some level of regret for his action in betraying Jesus even though it is now too late to reverse the consequences of his defection. Matthew does not use the standard verb for "repent" (μετανοέω) here, but μεταμέλομαι. The use of the less common term probably indicates only a sense of regret or a change of mind.[86] Matthew is interested in contrasting Judas's response to Jesus' plight and Peter's reaction. In avoiding the standard term for "repent" and describing a suicide that has shown Judas despairing and responsible for guilt, Matthew reveals how isolated Judas's action had left him.

Judas tries to return to the chief priests and elders the thirty pieces of silver he received for his betrayal. There is recognition of wrong, as he declares, "I have sinned in betraying innocent blood." Thus, even Jesus' betrayer declares Jesus' innocence before he experiences his decisive trial. This should have ended matters, but of course it did not. The leaders' response is to ignore Judas and tell him that he needs to see to the righting of the wrong himself. The narrative's impression is that they wish to rid themselves of any responsibility for Judas and these actions. The leadership has used the disciple. They are done with him. In no sense does the leadership fill the role of being ministers in how they react to Judas.

Judas despairs. He throws the money down in the temple, possibly in the treasury, and the chief priests collect the money and note that they cannot use blood money in the treasury. There is excruciating irony here. Also, here, the leadership confesses to the nature of the actions against Jesus. They do noth-

---

86. For both terms, see BAGD, 511–12; BDAG, 539–40; MM, 403–4.

ing to stop the injustice, but they will honor their purity laws, as if treating the money by rules of the law while ignoring their responsibility in the action against Jesus honors the law they seek to uphold. The account is as much about the leadership as about Judas. With the proceeds from sin, they buy a field in which to bury strangers. As Blomberg says, "Unclean money buys an unclean place for unclean people!"[87] Matthew might add that unclean people have made the purchase as well. A seemingly kind gesture really is rooted in an unjust act. Matthew shares the nickname that the field carries to the day of his writing, "Field of Blood." That is likely what Christians called it. The entire account is heavy with irony.

Matthew closes his description by citing Scripture. In all likelihood, there are composite contexts to which appeal is made. The thirty pieces of silver recalls Zech. 11:12–13. The context is one of rejection, where the prophet depicts the unfaithfulness of shepherds and takes thirty silver pieces for his trouble. It can even refer to the "treasury" if one engages in a revocalized wordplay with the term for "potter" in the passage, a common practice in Jewish exposition. Matthew, however, points to Jeremiah as the source. It is unclear exactly to which text he alludes. Two candidates often are mentioned. Jeremiah 32:6–14 describes the purchase of a field for seventeen pieces of silver. It is a field that one day will be used even though Israel was besieged by Babylon at the time. The act is one of hope that this is not the end of the story for the land. Against this choice is the thoroughly negative tone in the passage. Another option is Jer. 18–19, where the prophet of doom speaks of the "blood of the innocent" (19:4) filling the place as evidence of unfaithfulness, and of covenant justice being done in judgment on the nation as a result. The reference to the potter's field may envelop the image of the broken pot of this Jer. 18–19 text. The leadership's refusal to act justly will meet with God's justice. This tone fits the notes of conflict and hostility that have been a part of Matthew's account from the start.

274. The Examination before Pilate (Matt. 27:11–14;
Mark 15:2–5; Luke 23:2–5; John 18:29–38) (Aland §336; Orchard §357; Huck-Greeven §259)

The initial examination by Pilate is introduced by Luke with a list of three charges: (1) Jesus is perverting the customs of the nation; (2) Jesus forbids Jews to pay the tax to Caesar; and (3) Jesus claims to be a king. Thus, Jesus presents a threefold threat to Roman authority and law and order, to which Pilate must respond. The charges are significant, as the second and third

87. Blomberg, *Matthew*, 408.

touch directly on Pilate's responsibilities as the governor for Rome. The first charge fits with what Jewish sources came to say about Jesus (i.e., he misled the people).[88] It also appears first as a type of comprehensive charge, summarizing the whole complaint. Except for how it relates to the next two charges, it would not be of concern to Pilate. The prefect would care about a violation of Israel's customs only if it disturbed the public peace. So the key charges follow. The second charge is patently false to anyone who followed Luke's account (20:20–26). Jesus had told them to render to Caesar the things of Caesar. The third charge is true, but not in the way the leadership frames it to Pilate. The submission of charges to Pilate leaves him with no choice but to examine Jesus.

In all the accounts, Pilate asks Jesus if he is the king of the Jews. In fact, Matthew and Mark start here directly. Jesus replies with the cryptic "You are saying." As we have seen already, this form of reply is a qualified affirmative. It means, "Yes, but not quite in the sense you are saying it." The leadership launches into further accusations. To them he makes no reply. When Pilate raises the issue of their many charges, Jesus remains silent. Pilate is amazed at Jesus' silence. In Matthew and Mark, he seems to be a little at a loss as to what to do.

Luke has more detail. Pilate expresses the first of his three declarations of Jesus' innocence in Luke 23 (vv. 4, 14–15, 22). But the leadership is insistent, saying, "He stirs up the people, teaching throughout all Judea, from Galilee to this place." This harks back to the initial charge. The raising of the note of law and order highlights Pilate's primary responsibility, besides collecting taxes for Rome. They are telling him that he must do his job. Pilate already had had trouble with the Jews early in his tenure (Josephus, *War* 2.9.2–4 §§169–177; *Ant.* 18.3.1 §§55–59; Philo, *Embassy to Gaius* 38 §§301–302). He would not want to give Caesar cause to watch over him again. The mention of Galilee will cause Pilate to share responsibility and seek the counsel of Herod Antipas.[89]

John's Gospel has the Jews accuse Jesus of evildoing, but they complain that they cannot handle the situation by themselves according to the law as Pilate initially desires. In other words, they cannot put Jesus to death. Only Rome can do that (18:31). It is in this context that Jesus explains that his kingship is not of this world and that his calling is to bear witness to the truth. Pilate asks, "What is truth?" and then tells the leaders that he sees no crime in the man, probably dismissing Jesus as not significant enough to take up his time.

---

88. See Bock, *Studying*, chap. 1.

89. This scene may be significant for dating the year in Jesus' life. The cooperation between Pilate and Herod Antipas may suggest that Sejanus, the powerful anti-Semitic "foreign secretary" in Rome who may have made Pilate bold in offending the Jews, now has died. If so, this points to a date of A.D. 33.

All the accounts show Pilate trying to get a grasp on the events and the reason for the inquiry. He has a Jewish leadership that wants to remove a man who seems not to be of any real legal threat to Rome, although apparently the man has a significant following. Luke explains that Pilate sought a second opinion.

275. The Examination before Herod (Luke 23:6–12) (Aland §337; Orchard §358; Huck-Greeven §260)

Luke's description of the examination by Herod is far less flattering to this ruler. Herod seems more interested in entertainment than justice, perhaps because he was aware of Jesus and already had decided that Jesus was no real threat to his rule. The reason Herod gets to see Jesus is that this ruler is responsible for Galileans. The act shows Pilate's honoring of his role. Herod wishes only to see Jesus perform some sign. At the examination, Jesus makes no reply even though Herod questions him at some length. Again, the leadership is there, pressing the case, "vehemently accusing him."

Herod's attitude surfaces in the fun that he and his soldiers have on the occasion. They treat Jesus with contempt and mock him, dressing him in "bright" clothes. It is debated whether white or bright purple royal attire is meant; the text is not clear. What is evident is that Herod is having fun at Jesus' expense and seeks to shame him, perhaps to teach him a lesson. Herod has no serious regard for the teacher and sends Jesus back to Pilate with a verdict of innocent (23:15). Luke notes how Pilate's act of acknowledging respect for Herod made them friends from that day on, whereas before they had been enemies. Still, the basic issue remains unresolved despite the clear views of the political leaders that Jesus is not worthy of death. Justice would suggest his release, but justice is not at work here.

276. Pilate Declares Jesus Innocent (Luke 23:13–16) (Aland §338; Orchard §359; Huck-Greeven §261a)

One of the emphasized themes in the Lukan portion of the trial sequence is Jesus' innocence. This is defined in 23:15 as his having done "nothing deserving of death." Pilate makes the declaration to the chief priests, rulers, and people when Jesus returns from the examination by Herod.[90] Luke's ref-

90. A general outline of the normal Roman procedure for the entire sequence is traced here by A. N. Sherwin-White, *Roman Society and Roman Law in the New Testament* (Oxford: Clarendon, 1963), 24–27. The steps are noting the arrest, charges, *cognito* (examination), verdict, support for the verdict (in Herod's judgment), acquittal, and judicial warning.

erence to "the people" is significant, for normally in Luke, this group is open, if not favorable, to Jesus. In effect, the nation is gathered to make a judgment. They become the audience when the choice comes between Barabbas and Jesus.

Pilate refers explicitly to the charge of "perverting the people," the first and summary charge made in 23:2. Pilate declares that neither he nor Herod found Jesus guilty of these charges, a double declaration of innocence. So Pilate proposes something natural, an olive branch, of sorts, out of the dilemma: Jesus should be chastised and released. The chastisement would have been a scourging to discourage Jesus from causing any more trouble.

Jesus' innocence should have brought the end of examination and the Galilean's freedom. However, other forces are at work, so that what normally would happen does not take place. Part of Luke's goal in his version of the account is to underscore how many times Jesus' innocence was declared. Even so, he was not released. As Jesus had noted in 22:53, it is "your hour, and the power of darkness."

277. Jesus or Barabbas? (Matt. 27:15–23; Mark 15:6–14; Luke 23:17–23; John 18:39–40) (Aland §339; Orchard §360; Huck-Greeven §261b)[91]

At this point, Matthew, Mark, and John all note the custom of releasing one prisoner of the people's choice at feast time.[92] Matthew and Mark describe the custom, while John has Pilate note that the custom is a Jewish one that the Roman leader applied as a favor on the Passover. In Mark 15:8, the crowd initiates the movement toward performing the custom. This custom is unattested outside of biblical materials, but this is not surprising, since we know next to nothing about Pilate's procedures outside of the biblical texts. The custom can be defended as historical because there is rich precedent for Greco-Roman clemency at festival time.[93] Another objection is that Jesus is portrayed as innocent, so how could he be offered for release? However, the key is that Jesus is innocent of a capital charge. Pilate is planning to scourge him for disturbing the peace. Pilate is trying to work out a solution that is politically palatable and in line with his sense of justice.

91. After this event Aland has John 19:1–15, where Jesus is presented to the crowd after they choose Barabbas for release.

92. A text-critical problem is tied to Luke 23:17, where the custom also is mentioned. The manuscript evidence supporting the original presence of the verse in Luke is not strong (it is lacking in $\mathfrak{P}^{75}$ and B), so Luke may not have explicitly mentioned the custom.

93. See Bock, *Luke 9:51–24:53*, 1833, and especially John Nolland, *Luke 18:35–24:53*, WBC 35C (Dallas: Word, 1993), 1130. See examples of similar acts in Josephus, *Ant.* 20.9.3 §§208–210; 20.9.5 §215.

The crowd's option besides Jesus is a "notorious" (Matthew) prisoner, Barabbas. Mark describes him as an insurrectionist (στασιαστής) who had caused chaos in the streets.[94] Luke makes the same point slightly later in his version. John calls him a λῃστής, which can be a robber or a revolutionary.[95] Pilate is trying to stack the deck in favor of Jesus.

In fact, all the Synoptics try to lessen Pilate's responsibility in different ways. Matthew and Mark both note that Pilate perceived that envy is what motivated the leaders' animosity toward Jesus. Matthew also adds a premonition that Pilate's wife had through a dream that urges her to advise him, "Have nothing to do with that righteous man, for I have suffered much over him today in a dream." Matthew previously showed how dreams were prominent in the protection of Jesus (Matt. 1–2). Here, divine signs ultimately will be ignored. Luke simply portrays Pilate as doing all he can to get Jesus released. However, by the time of Acts 4:24–26, Pilate is seen as part of the conspiracy against Jesus that fulfills Ps. 2:1–2.

In line with the custom of clemency for one, Pilate presents the choice of Barabbas or Jesus, the one called "Christ" (Matthew) or "King of the Jews" (Mark, John). The question highlights the royal claim that is at issue surrounding Jesus. Matthew and Mark lay at the leadership's feet the major responsibility for inciting the crowd. It is the chief priests and elders (Matthew only) who lead the crowd to ask for Barabbas and call for Jesus' crucifixion. Luke keeps the blame broad at this point. In Luke, the crowd repeatedly asks for Barabbas, even when Pilate comes back to them a third time asking, "Why, what evil has he done?" This question is in all the Synoptic accounts. Luke adds, "I have found in him no crime deserving death; I will therefore chastise him and release him." Where the accounts in Matthew and Mark have the crowd directly shouting all the more for Jesus to be crucified, Luke summarizes indirectly, noting how they all demanded with loud cries that he should be crucified. In resignation, Pilate bows to the public pressure, as Luke concludes simply, "And their voices prevailed."

The substitution of an innocent Jesus for a guilty Barabbas is a metaphor for the entire experience of the cross. Although none of the Gospels make anything of it, the name Barabbas means "son of the father" in Aramaic. Those who know the language and are sensitive to religious symbolism understand that one son had been exchanged for another. One condemned to die had been set free so that an innocent could die in his place. Here is a classic example of narrative teaching not by explicit statement, but by portrayal.

94. On this Greek term, see BAGD, 764; BDAG, 940.
95. BAGD, 473; BDAG, 594.

278. Pilate Delivers Jesus to Be Crucified (Matt. 27:24–26; Mark 15:15; Luke 23:24–25) (Aland §341; Orchard §362; Huck-Greeven §261c)

Mark attributes Pilate's decision to release Barabbas and execute Jesus as his "wishing to satisfy the crowd." Luke notes that Pilate "gave sentence that their demand be granted" and delivered Jesus "up to their will." Matthew adds an emotive note to the detail. Pilate saw that "he was gaining nothing, but rather that a riot was beginning." The choice was either yielding to the will of the crowd or defending his sense of justice and having to handle a major public disturbance. He clearly did not like the choice. In all the Gospels, Pilate is caught in the vortex of forces moving in a direction that he does not have the will to stop. Nevertheless, the portrayal, though showing Pilate's absence of malice, still indicates that he did not defend justice honorably at the end. Instead, he washed his hands before the crowd. Trying to shirk his responsibility, he declared, "I am innocent of this man's blood; see to it yourselves" (Matt. 27:24). This dismissal of responsibility recalls 27:4, where the Jewish leadership did the same to Judas.

However, the crowd accepts the responsibility: "His blood be on us and on our children!" The remark is highly controversial, as some argue that it indicates Matthew's anti-Semitism. However, in that culture, it is perfectly natural (2 Sam. 3:28–29; 21:6, 14).[96] The crowd views itself as defending God and his honor against one who has made a false claim (cf. Deut. 13:1–5). The people think that they are doing the right thing, so they feel no hesitation for taking responsibility for the act. In a context in which many have refused to be directly responsible, Matthew tries to indicate that someone did take responsibility. If they were right to act, then no risk would ensue. If they were wrong, then the responsibility is tremendous. It is this choice that Matthew seeks to bring forward. The decision about Jesus is no minor detail in life. The decision turns on determining whether Jesus represents God and his way or not. After all, the choice was posed in Matthew as deciding for or against Jesus as "the Christ." The crowd votes negatively here. The people reject the one sent for them (cf. Isa. 53:3).

So Jesus is scourged and released to face crucifixion. The scourging was cruel and painful, involving whipping until the flesh was torn by the metal or bone tips on the end of the whip. In conjunction with crucifixion, the whipping was designed to speed the loss of blood that led to death. It was so frightful that it horrified a later emperor, Domitian (Suetonius, *Domitian* 11).[97] Barabbas goes free. Jesus is beaten until his flesh is torn and is sent to a cross. Justice, both divinely directed and humanly driven, has taken a strange yet significant turn.

96. Blomberg, *Matthew,* 413. There is an allusion back to Matt. 23:29–36.
97. For other ancient descriptions of whipping by the Romans, see Josephus, *War* 2.14.9 §§306–308; 6.5.3 §§302–304; Philo, *Against Flaccus* 10 §75. For a thorough examination of crucifixion and how the ancients viewed it, see Martin Hengel, *Crucifixion in the Ancient World and the Folly of the Message of the Cross,* trans. J. Bowden (Philadelphia: Fortress, 1977).

279. Jesus Mocked by the Soldiers (Matt. 27:27–31a;
Mark 15:16–20a; John 19:2–3, in a slightly earlier context)
(Aland §342; Orchard §363; Huck-Greeven §262)

In the period between the decision to execute Jesus and the actual procession, Pilate's soldiers take Jesus into the palace and gather the whole cohort of anywhere from two hundred to six hundred soldiers.[98] This fulfills Matt. 20:19, where the prediction was that Jesus would be given over into Gentile hands and mocked. Such action is not unprecedented in the culture (Philo, *Against Flaccus* 6 §§36–39; Dio Cassius, *Roman History* 15.20–21; Plutarch, *Pompey* 24). The mocking involved dressing Jesus up in a robe of scarlet (Matthew) or purple (Mark and John), making him a crown of thorns, and placing a reed (Matthew) in his hands for a scepter. The robe symbolized royalty along with the other elements, although it probably was a scarlet military cloak. They greet him with "Hail, King of the Jews!" This recalls Pilate's remarks in 27:11. Matthew and Mark add the note of bowing before him. They strike him on the head with a reed. John mentions striking with the hands. Matthew and Mark also note that they spit on him as well. Mark uses verbs in the imperfect tense to give a sense of ongoing action to the descriptions. When their fun was over, they stripped Jesus of the robe and dressed him in his own clothes. In a Roman context, the guilty party would go to the cross naked, but clothing Jesus appears to be a concession to Jewish sensitivities about nakedness. The symbolism of this mocking should not be missed. These soldiers would not have been Romans but Gentiles from the region. Most outside of Israel also do not take Jesus seriously either. The nations are also a part of the movement that executed Jesus.

280. The Road to Golgotha (Matt. 27:31b–32; Mark 15:20b–21;
Luke 23:26–32; John 19:17a) (Aland §343; Orchard §364;
Huck-Greeven §263)

With no sleep overnight and suffering from his recent scourging, Jesus is led away to bear his cross to the hill that will be his place of death. Simon of Cyrene (= modern Tripoli) is pressed into service to help him carry the cross. Mark's description of him as the father of Alexander and Rufus suggests that the family is known to some familiar with the passion tradition. Luke says that Simon followed behind Jesus. John's Gospel never mentions Simon.

Luke alone narrates that a great crowd of people followed the procession, including a group of women who were lamenting what was taking place.

98. For a defense of the historicity of the scene, see Gundry, *Mark*, 941.

Jesus turns to them and tells them not to weep for him but for themselves and their children. He warns in prophetic style of coming days when barrenness and childlessness will be a blessing. The remarks surely allude to the national judgment to come. People will prefer to experience a national disaster such as being buried alive by an avalanche versus what they will face. An enigmatic expression follows: "For if they do this when the wood is green, what will happen when it is dry?" The language is that of judgment from Hos. 10:8. In other words, if this is the divine fate of one who is full of life like a healthy tree (Jesus), what fate will befall dead wood (the unresponsive nation)? His death impacts their future. Rejection of Jesus is not a matter to be dismissed lightly.

Luke notes that two other criminals accompanied Jesus to the cross. This point is picked up in Luke 23:39–43.

281. The Crucifixion (Matt. 27:33–37; Mark 15:22–26; Luke 23:33–34; John 19:17b–27) (Aland §344; Orchard §365a; Huck-Greeven §264a)

The crucifixion is told with great detail in each Synoptic. They all share discussion of the dividing of Jesus' clothes, the mocking, the cosmic signs, his death, the centurion's confession, and the watching women. Luke in particular has several points of divergence of detail, either by omission, inclusion, or partial overlap.[99]

Jesus is brought to Golgotha, whose Aramaic name means "place of a skull." The common name of the locale today is Calvary, which comes from the Latin word for "skull." All the Gospels name the locale, although Luke merely gives the name "skull." Matthew and Mark explain Golgotha's meaning. Crucifixion involved death by asphyxiation, the victim becoming too weak to lift his body to breathe, if the loss of blood from the scourging did not kill first. It carried a reputation as the worst form of death.[100] It was considered so terrible that Roman citizens could not be executed this way. Only two crimes received this sentence: treason and avoiding due process in a capital crime. Jesus is dying a rebel's death. The cross stood about seven feet high and, since the crossbar was either at the top or just below on the vertical pole, looked like a T or a †. He would have been held on the beam by rope or by nails, though the latter was less frequent. That Jesus' hands were nailed to the cross is indicated by John

99. For a list of twenty-three such differences extending to Luke 23:49, see Bock, *Luke 9:51–24:53,* 1837–39. The likelihood is that Luke had access to additional sources for his details.

100. Hengel, *Crucifixion;* J. Schneider, *TDNT,* 7:572–84; Raymond E. Brown, *The Death of the Messiah,* ABRL (New York: Doubleday, 1994), 945–47.

20:25 and Luke 24:40, when Jesus shows his hands at a resurrection appearance (cf. Col. 2:14). His feet may have been tied to the cross, although the later scene in Luke 24, in which the disciples are asked to view Jesus' hands and feet, could suggest nail marks. Rope burns might also be an option there. The crossbeam, which is what was carried, was raised up by forked poles and dropped into place on the already set upright pole. A tablet specifying the crime was hung around the accused or nailed to the beam. Jesus found himself placed between two criminals (Matt. 27:38; Mark 15:27; Luke 23:33; John 19:18).

An effort to offer Jesus wine mixed with gall (Matthew) or myrrh (Mark) is refused, although Matthew notes that an initial taste brought the refusal. Gall may be a way to allude to Ps. 69:21, but the process is described in Prov. 31:6. Seen in this context as an act of mercy and compassion, it is refused. Jesus will bear the fullness of his suffering.

Luke 23:34 is another textually disputed passage.[101] Jesus urges that those executing him be forgiven because they do not know what they are doing. Jesus again is interceding for those who hate him, following the example he urged in Luke 6:27–36. Stephen follows this model in Acts 7. That parallel is a major reason for accepting this text as Lukan. Luke often makes parallels between Jesus and his followers in Acts. The other Gospels carry no similar parallel. Its precedent helps us to understand Stephen's act. Jesus is interceding for his enemies because they have made an erroneous judgment about him.[102] This should not be their last chance. More chances to respond were graciously given as the disciples preached to them often in Acts about the opportunity to receive forgiveness. There is no vindictiveness in Jesus, only hope for a reversal.

Matthew and Mark fall into the Lukan sequence here to narrate the casting of lots, probably marked pebbles, for garments. This act recalls Ps. 22:18, which John's Gospel cites. The image of the psalm is part of the mocking of a righteous sufferer. Jesus dies in shame, unclothed, as those around him entertain themselves with his last possession.[103]

All the accounts, though at different points, mention the inscription that Pilate left, an important detail because it gives the sense of what Jesus was cru-

101. The text is absent from Papyrus 75 and Codices Vaticanus and Bezae but present in Codex Sinaiticus and the Byzantine text. It is hard to explain its addition by a copyist, as there is no parallel motivating its insertion, and the possibility of its being misunderstood as providing for his executioners' forgiveness might explain why it would be excluded by a copyist. Each Lukan unit of the crucifixion has an event-saying pattern that is broken if the text is omitted. All of this slightly leans for inclusion, despite the strength of the manuscript evidence for exclusion.

102. This is how Luke uses the concept of ignorance: Luke 13:34; 19:42; Acts 2:37–38; 3:17–19; 13:38; 17:30.

103. *Jubilees* 3.30–31 and 7.20 indicate the possibility of a loincloth remaining on the executed. John's Gospel may also suggest that the lots were cast for the outer garments.

cified for as the point of dispute.[104] John 19:19 notes that it was attached to the cross, while Matt. 27:37 places it over Jesus' head. There is some variation in what is recorded as the inscription. All mention "King of the Jews," a perfectly adequate ancient expression of kingship, although it has been challenged by some ("King of the Jews": Matt. 2:2; Josephus, *War* 1.14.4 §282; *Ant.* 15.10.5 §373; 15.11.4 §409; 16.9.3 §291; 16.10.2 §311).[105] That title is all that Mark notes on the inscription. Matthew notes, "This is Jesus the King of the Jews." John notes that the inscription came in Hebrew, Latin, and Greek. His version reads, "Jesus of Nazareth, the King of the Jews." Luke describes the inscription at a slightly later point, after noting some mocking, as "This is the King of the Jews."[106] These variations are like what we observe in the words of the voice at Jesus' baptism and in Peter's confession at Caesarea Philippi. The gist is the same, despite the variation. This is how the ancients summarized such events. In John, the chief priests protest this wording, but Pilate defends it, saying that Jesus made the claim and so Pilate will let stand what he has written. In the end, it was Jesus' kingship over the nation that was at the center of his death. The political charge and all that it implied had been the decisive point of contention.

It is after this note about the furor over the inscription that John gives his version of the casting of lots for Jesus' clothes. John then notes some who saw the crucifixion: Jesus' mother; his mother's sister; Mary the wife of Clopas; and Mary Magdalene. In addition, the disciple whom Jesus loved is there. Jesus tells his mother and this disciple that they are now mother and son. The text notes that this disciple (probably John) cared for her from this point on. As Jesus is dying, he is still thinking of the care of others.

282. Jesus Is Mocked during the Crucifixion (Matt. 27:38–43; Mark 15:27–32a; Luke 23:35–38) (Aland §345; Orchard §§365b–66; Huck-Greeven §264b)

As Jesus hung on the cross between the two thieves, people walking by mocked him. Luke mentions those standing by the side and watching all of this. Matthew and Mark speak of those passing by and "slandering" Jesus, using the term βλασφημέω. The one accused of blasphemy is now being blasphemed. They were "wagging their heads," an allusion to the mocking

---

104. This inscription stands behind the "INRI" often seen in paintings of the scene. It is an abbreviation for the Latin meaning "Jesus of Nazareth, King of the Jews" (*Iesus Nazarenus Rex Iudaeorum*), a wording that parallels John's Gospel. On the possible original wording, see G. M. Lee, "The Inscription on the Cross," *Palestine Exploration Quarterly* 100 (1968): 144.

105. For a defense of the expression, see Gundry, *Mark*, 959.

106. Matthew and Mark have the opposite order: inscription, then mocking.

of the righteous sufferer of Ps. 22:7 and possibly Lam. 2:15. The taunt involves Jesus' claim that he would destroy the temple and rebuild it in three days. The irony of the story is that he is fulfilling the very thing they taunt him for not doing. They urge him to save himself and come down from the cross. Matthew introduces this portion of the taunt, "If you are the Son of God," recalling the language of the devil's temptation in Matt. 4:3. There is irony here because there is and will be a "saving" of Jesus that God will bring about, which should prove the premise of their taunt. The passersby on the road near the crucifixion were not alone in taunting him. The chief priests (Matthew and Mark), rulers (Luke), scribes (Matthew and Mark), and elders (Matthew) also chime in. According to Matthew and Mark, their taunt is "He saved others; he cannot save himself." It continues with a chiding of him as "King of Israel" and a call to come down from the cross now so that they may believe. Mark refers to Jesus as "the Christ, the King of Israel" in this taunt. Matthew alone has "He trusts in God; let God deliver him now, if he desires him; for he said, 'I am the Son of God.'" As is often the case, the notes of hostility are strongest in Matthew's account. These final taunts allude to Ps. 22:8–9. Jesus is the "righteous sufferer," whom God eventually will vindicate. Jesus' ignoring the taunts is seen as an extension of his love and stands in contrast to the "fun" that those around him are cruelly engaged in. All of this sets up the irony of the mockers' claims that they will believe if Jesus comes down from the cross. Their claim proves empty when resurrection does take place. The irony recognizes that they should respond if Jesus ends up alive, but the real resurrection produces a different response for most. A hard heart does not see what a mocking heart affirms.

Luke's version of the taunt is the same in thrust with a slight variation in wording, as he collapses what is said by the rulers into one saying, "He saved others; let him save himself, if he is the Christ of God, his Chosen One." The reference to the "Chosen One" looks back to the Lukan transfiguration scene (9:35), when Jesus foreshadowed his glory. This serves as a reminder that Jesus *is* who they ignorantly deride him to be. Luke alone adds the soldiers to the mix. They now offer Jesus vinegar and chide him, "If you are the King of the Jews, save yourself!" It is here that Luke mentions the inscription hung above him, which said "This is the King of the Jews." In their report of the mocking, all the accounts make it clear that it is the religious-political claim to be king that was the point of contention with those who rejected Jesus.

Another key narrative feature of the crucifixion accounts also is emerging. There are numerous characters and responses to Jesus. Some weep, some watch, some mock, and some soon will confess him. In the scene of the cross is a microcosm of how the world reacts to Jesus.

283. The Two Thieves (Matt. 27:44; Mark 15:32b; Luke 23:39–43)
(Aland §346; Orchard §367; Huck-Greeven §264c)

In this scene, the differences between the version of Matthew and Mark and that of Luke are most prominent. Matthew and Mark note how the rebels (Matthew) crucified next to Jesus also revile him. Even the truly guilty make fun of him.

Luke's account portrays a debate between the two. Luke gives more detail about the scene and seems aware, assuming that he knew either Matthew or Mark, of a change of heart that one of the criminals had in the midst of the hours spent on the cross. One criminal derides Jesus, saying in the spirit of the earlier mockings, "Are you not the Christ? Save yourself and us!" However, the other criminal objects, "Do you not fear God, since you are under the same sentence of condemnation? And we indeed justly; for we are receiving the due reward of our deeds; but this man has done nothing wrong." This criminal adds to the earlier words of Pilate and Herod declaring Jesus' innocence in Luke 23. One who shares the same penalty is well aware of the difference between them. The responsive criminal goes on to ask Jesus to remember him when he comes into his kingdom. The words show amazing insight from another outsider, another key Lukan theme. He foresees, despite Jesus' seeming demise, that there will be a vindication of Jesus and that authority will belong to the king in a future kingdom. Jesus' response is just as surprising. Rather than expressing the realization of reward and acceptance in the unknown future, Jesus replies, "Today you will be with me in paradise." Jesus' authority is not limited to the unknown future, but expresses itself now, even beyond death. In other words, death and the cross ultimately are powerless to stop him. Although the kingdom is yet to come, in a sense it already has come.

284. The Death of Jesus (Matt. 27:45–54; Mark 15:33–39;
Luke 23:44–48; John 19:28–30) (Aland §347; Orchard §§368–70a; Huck-Greeven §265a)

All the accounts now turn to describe the last moments of the cross by giving a temporal note. At the sixth hour (midday), it became dark. Amos 8:9 describes this phenomenon in association with judgment. It was a testimony of creation that lasted for three hours until the ninth hour, which would be the normal time for the daily afternoon sacrifice. Luke describes the tearing in two of the temple curtain. The symbolism of this is often discussed. The most common reading is that it symbolized the end of sacrifices, a point that may emerge from reflection on this event like that which we see in the Book of Hebrews, but another idea may be more important to Luke.[107] It is that the division between God and humankind has come down and access to God has been opened up. Not only does the previous scene with the confessing criminal indicate this issue of access, but also Stephen's remarks in Acts 7 are critical of the idea that the temple can contain God. In a symbolic way, Jesus and the acts of creation around him are testifying to God's work though him in opening up access to God. The image is not so much that the door is open for humankind to go in as that God is now venturing out to seek the lost.

According to Matthew and Mark, at the ninth hour Jesus cried out in a loud voice, using a line from Ps. 22:1, "My God, my God, why have you forsaken me?" Matthew, in citing the cry, notes the Hebrew version of the sacred text, while Mark gives the Aramaic version of Jewish everyday discourse. Both Gospels translate the verse. Despair and a sense of abandonment are expressed here from a psalm whose contents have been alluded to throughout the description of the events. Jesus is suffering despite being innocent and righteous. It is something God has permitted, even directed. The note of despair is tempered by knowledge of the entire psalm, evoked by the scene as a whole, which eventually resolves itself in a note of trust in God. Jesus is acknowledging the real pain his suffering represents. He suffers seemingly alone.

Those standing around think that Jesus is making a final, eschatological cry, an appeal to Elijah of the end to show up. Combined with the eerie feel of the dark sky, it is not surprising that they thought of the possibility of the approach of the end. For the Gospel writers, it was indeed an eschatological moment with consequences for deliverance, but not of the type the observers thought.

Some around the cross try to give Jesus yet another taste of vinegar, but others try to stop them so they can wait and see if Elijah will come. They want to wait to see if deliverance will come, and yet it is taking place right before their eyes. Thus, the remark is yet another note of irony in the account.

John's account notes that the offer of vinegar is received as Jesus utters, "It is finished," bows his head, and gives up his spirit. Luke has the final moment include one last declaration as well. It involves words of trust from Ps. 31:5, "Father, into your hands I commit my spirit!" Luke continues, "And having said this, he breathed his last." Matthew and Mark describe the death as accompanied by a loud, final cry. No content is given to it, as in John and Luke. Matthew says simply, "Jesus cried again with a loud voice and yielded up his spirit." Mark is even more concise, "And Jesus uttered a loud cry, and breathed his last." Jesus' faithful completion of his work of suffering is noted in slightly diverse ways, but the point is the same. Jesus went to the cross as the Father had asked.

107. The Pauline Epistles in Eph. 2:14–16 and Col. 2:14–15, as well as Heb. 4:16, may be parallel to the Lukan idea.

Another contrast between Matthew-Mark and Luke emerges here. Matthew and Mark describe the rending of the temple curtain here.[108] Thus, they place as the first implication of Jesus' death this effect on the holy place. Luke chooses to portray this in the midst of the event. The effect of Luke's choice of order is that the first thing after Jesus' death is the confession of the centurion, which sits as a final, climactic commentary on the entire scene.

Matthew also does something unique here. He adds to the apocalyptic feel of events by not only noting the tearing of the temple curtain but also describing an "opening up" of the entire earth. The earthquake is another testimony of the creation to what has taken place. Rocks are split; tombs are opened; the bodies of many dead saints are raised and appear to many. Whereas Luke alluded to creation speaking when the leaders sought to silence the disciples during Jesus' entry into Jerusalem, Matthew saves a reaction of creation until the key moment of Jesus' death. Three points are significant here. First, Matthew is depicting in graphic terms that the entire creation was impacted by Jesus' death. That impact reached down to the dead themselves. Jesus' death was about life and death. This is a strong way to portray this. The testimony is focused on the "holy city." It was a confirmation that Jesus is who he claimed to be and that his ministry stands vindicated before the nation. Second, the eeriness of the entire scene, combined with the cosmic darkness, makes the idea and association of appearances from the dead less strange. There is little that is "normal" about what has taken place. In the ancient world the idea of the earth split open would naturally lead to an understanding of spirits of the dead set free. Third, the release of people from the grave is a proleptic picture of the saving impact of Jesus' death. It is yet another ironic response to the mockers' taunts to Jesus to save himself and others. It anticipates the breaking into new life that Jesus' resurrection will signify. Jesus' death did mean release and new life for some.[109] What Luke depicted with a single believing thief, Matthew portrays graphically by noting a powerful divine cosmic sign. The accounts complement one another nicely.

The crucifixion scene closes in all the Synoptics with the confession of a centurion. In the Matthean version, the centurion responds as part of a larger entourage to the earthquake and the other events. Filled with "great fear," they confess, "Truly, this was the Son of God." In Mark, it is the centurion alone who is the point of focus. For him the response appears to be a reaction to the darkness and the way Jesus has reacted to everything. The confession is

108. The description of the curtain does not make it clear which curtain is meant. Is it the one that separated Jews from Gentiles at the court of the Gentiles? Or is it the curtain at the Holy of Holies? The text in none of the accounts is specific. In one sense, it does not really matter, because the point is that the symbol of nonentry has been removed. The way to the Sacred One is opened up.

109. Blomberg, *Matthew,* notes a conceptual connection to 1 Cor. 15:20–23, a picture of the first fruits of the new hope.

"Truly this man was the Son of God." In Luke, the reaction seems to be a response to the same factors that Mark has noted. The confession fits the Lukan emphasis on Jesus' innocence. The confession here is, "Certainly this man was δίκαιος." The Greek term can be translated either "righteous" or "innocent." Either rendering makes good sense here, for to say that Jesus was righteous is to affirm his innocence. The affirmation of Jesus' innocence would be a Gentile recognition of something that Pilate, Herod, and the believing thief already have noted in Luke 23:4, 14–15 (2x), 22, 41. In light of the emphasis of the chapter, a seventh confession of Jesus' innocence is likely the meaning here. In effect, Luke is saying that Jesus was indeed the Messiah and Son that he was convicted and sentenced to death for not being. Luke closes by noting that the crowd went home mourning and beating their breasts, having seen everything. Luke may well be noting that some, on seeing the scene as a whole, have assessed the events and now have real remorse for what has occurred.

285. Witnesses of the Crucifixion (Matt. 27:55–56; Mark 15:40–41; Luke 23:49) (Aland §348; Orchard §370b; Huck-Greeven §265b)[110]

Women are prominent at both the crucifixion and the resurrection. Each of the accounts has a list of women and other witnesses. Women would be more likely to be left alone at such a scene, since they would not be viewed as a danger. John's Gospel had a list earlier in the account (John 19:25), noting Jesus' mother; her sister; Mary the wife of Clopas; and Mary Magdalene (cf. Luke 8:2), along with the beloved disciple. Luke notes that all Jesus' acquaintances and the women who had followed him from Galilee stood at a distance and saw these things. Mark describes women looking on from afar. In his list are Mary Magdalene; Mary the mother of James the younger and Joses (cf. Mark 15:47; 16:1); Salome, who had ministered to Jesus since Galilee; and many others. Here we see how inclusive Jesus' following was in a culture that tended to relegate women to insignificant status. Matthew also points to female witnesses. These women had been with Jesus in Galilee. Matthew's list has Mary Magdalene; Mary the mother of James and Joseph; and the mother of the sons of Zebedee. The notes do give the impression that many did see the details of what took place when Jesus was crucified. The many potential witnesses may also explain some of the diversity of detail that these accounts possess, because each person might recall distinct details.

110. After this event, Aland presents the piercing of Jesus' side in John 19:31–37. John notes that the soldiers do not break Jesus' legs, because he already was dead. A piercing of Jesus' side confirms his death, as "blood and water" pour out. There is the note of an unnamed witness to this and then the citation of either Exod. 12:46 or Ps. 34:20 and Zech. 12:10 as fulfilled. Jesus appears again as a righteous sufferer.

286. Jesus' Burial (Matt. 27:57–61; Mark 15:42–47; Luke 23:50–56; John 19:38–42) (Aland §350; Orchard §§372–73a; Huck-Greeven §§266, 268a)

All the accounts describe Joseph of Arimathea's effort to procure Jesus' body for an honorable burial. Mark describes it as the "Day of Preparation," which is Friday before the Sabbath. Matthew says that Joseph was rich, while Mark and Luke note that he was a member of the council. John describes him as a secret disciple who had kept his belief quiet out of fear of the Jews. Matthew also calls him a disciple. Mark and Luke note that he was looking for the kingdom. So not every leader rejected Jesus.

Joseph asks Pilate for the body. Otherwise, Jesus would have been buried with the criminals. Normally, a controversial figure such as this would not be released for a separate burial, but Joseph's position as a member of the council that sought Jesus' death probably relieved any concern that Pilate might have had. Mark notes that Pilate inquired whether Jesus was dead yet. This detail indicates that Joseph approached the Roman ruler fairly close to the time Jesus had died. The centurion confirmed that he had died, something John's account of the piercing of Jesus' side also affirms. Pilate allows the request.

So Joseph takes the body and wraps it in a linen shroud. John's Gospel describes a careful and complete anointing of the body in acts that fulfill Jewish custom. He places Jesus in a new (Matthew, Luke, and John) tomb, hewn out of the rock (Synoptics). John gives its location as being in a garden. He rolls a great stone up to the entrance (Matthew, Mark). Matthew and Mark note how Mary Magdalene and the other Mary saw the location.[111] Matthew indicates that they sat opposite the sepulchre as this took place. Luke only describes them as "women who had come with him from Galilee." John's Gospel notes that it was the "Day of Preparation," suggesting a quick burial before the Sabbath rest came, while Luke has them return, preparing spices and ointments for a later anointing before resting on the Sabbath in accord with the commandment. It was Jewish women faithful to the law who had followed Jesus.

287. The Guard at the Tomb (Matt. 27:62–66) (Aland §351; Orchard §374; Huck-Greeven §267)

In the chief priests and Pharisees' view, one more action was needed to secure the site and end the controversy. They go to meet with Pilate and ask for the tomb to be made secure until three days have passed. They report to Pilate that Jesus said, "After three days I will rise again." So they want to prevent the disciples from

---

111. It is uncertain whether the traditional site for the burial often toured today is the actual site. It dates to the fourth century. However, the "feel" of that site is similar to what the burial location would have been like.

stealing the body and making false claims about a resurrection that could further the "fraud" and make it worse than it already was. Note how the remark corroborates the view that Jesus was seen as someone who promulgated a false teaching.

It is sometimes objected that this detail was added by Matthew later and is so clearly apologetic in motive that it must be a created event. Yet Matthew's Gospel is the one written in a setting closest to Palestine. It is rich in Jewish concerns. So it is only natural that this internecine element in the dispute appears only here. If the account were false, it would be obvious to those in the area who knew the story. So a fabricated event here is unlikely. It would be natural for such strong opponents to make sure nothing unusual happened. Plus, Pilate had granted the disciples a favor. He owed the leadership one to keep things even.

Pilate grants the request, so a guard is sent. In addition, the door to the tomb is sealed. It will be obvious if anyone tries to get in from the outside. There is no doubt that Jesus died on the cross and that he was buried with the location under guard. Matthew argues that the guards were present to prevent any effort to steal the body. There is no other good explanation for why guards would be present. Nor is it clear, given that no body was ever produced, why Matthew would make up this detail to prevent a "stolen body theory" from arising. It is highly unlikely that disciples would die for a dead, unrisen messiah whose body they knew they had taken, much less preach him as risen when they knew otherwise. The reason for creating such a polemical detail does not convince. Something else happened, as the Gospels are about to disclose.

288. The Women Come to the Tomb (Matt. 28:1–8; Mark 16:1–8; Luke 24:1–12; John 20:1–13) (Aland §352; Orchard §§375b–76; Huck-Greeven §268b)

All the Gospels indicate that the initial report of the empty tomb came from women. This is unusual for the culture and shows that this detail was not one constructed by the church, because a woman's testimony would not be respected in the culture.

Mark opens the account by naming the women who went to anoint Jesus' body: Mary Magdalene, Mary the mother of James, and Salome. Matthew refers to "Mary Magdalene and the other Mary." Luke refers back to the women who had watched Jesus' burial, saving the naming of the women until the end of the account: Mary Magdalene, Joanna, Mary the mother of James, and other women who went with them. John mentions only Mary Magdalene.

In Mark, the women are wondering how they will roll away the great stone at the tomb's door. On their arrival, the stone already had been rolled away. Seated on the right was a young man dressed in white, leaving the women amazed. Luke simply notes that the stone was rolled away when they arrived.

They found no body when they checked inside the tomb, but they did encounter two men standing by them in dazzling apparel. The women became afraid and bowed their faces to the ground. Matthew describes a great earthquake, which an angel of the Lord had caused as he rolled back the stone and sat upon it. So for a second time Matthew narrates a cosmic disturbance in relation to these final events. The angel, descending like lightning and wearing bright white raiment, caused the guards to fear and become "like dead men."

The announcement of what has happened comes next. In Matthew, the angel says, "Do not be afraid; for I know that you seek Jesus who was crucified. He is not here; for he has risen, as he said. Come, see the place where he lay." So the angel announces the resurrection and the fulfillment of the prediction that Jesus had made. In Mark, the angel declares, "Do not be amazed; you seek Jesus of Nazareth, who was crucified. He is risen, he is not here; see the place where they laid him." The fundamental declaration is of the resurrection. The differences between Matthew and Mark are slight; the emphasis is the same. Luke notes a declaration from the two men: "Why do you seek the living among the dead? He is not here, but has risen.[112] Remember how he told you, while he was still in Galilee, that the Son of Man must be delivered into the hands of sinners, and be crucified, and on the third day rise." Like Matthew, Luke discusses that Jesus had told them about this event, but in addition he supplies the remark (cf. Luke 9:22; 18:32–33).

In Mark and Matthew, the women are told to tell the disciples. Matthew gives the specific topic: Jesus has risen from the dead. They also are to tell them that he is going before them to Galilee. There they will see him. Matthew notes that this instruction comes from the angel, while Mark attributes it to Jesus' instruction.

Mark has an abrupt ending.[113] The women, astonished, depart and flee. The text reports that they said nothing to anyone, because they were afraid. This appears to have been a temporary silence, given the parallels.[114] What Mark is stress-

112. This sentence is textually disputed. Only Codex Bezae and the Old Latin omit the sentence. It is unusual for the Western text to have the shorter reading, so many view the short text as original. But the manuscript attestation of the longer text is too strong to ignore.

113. Mark 16:8 is the final verse of Mark in many of the older manuscripts (א, B) and several church fathers (Clement, Origin, Eusebius, Jerome). Longer endings of Mark are more traditional but probably are not a part of the original ending of the Gospel. One can discuss whether this longer ending is canonical or not, given its long history of association with the Gospel. However, given the text's absence among key church fathers, it would seem that the case for its canonical status is not strong. The appearance to the women is noted in the longer ending in Mark 16:9–11, but the entire longer ending has the feel of a complete review going back redundantly to the events of 16:1–8. This review looks like a later addition intended to deal with Mark's original, abrupt ending. The details of the ending seem to combine elements of all the other Gospels as well, adding to the impression of a later addition, especially if Mark's Gospel was the first written Gospel.

114. Cranfield, *Mark*, 469–70. Their initial instinct was to say nothing. Perhaps they sensed how unbelievable it all was.

ing is the awesome and overwhelming reaction to the resurrection. At first there is an almost paralyzing fear. In Mark, there is a theme about the presence of fear leading to an opportunity for faith (Mark 4:41; 5:15, 33, 36; 6:50; 10:32–34 [during a passion prediction]). It is this theme that his ending evokes, leading the reader to make a choice about the announcement of resurrection. There also is irony here. Throughout Mark, people were told not to say who Jesus is. Now that there is a chance to do so, fear threatens to prevent it. Those who read Mark know the rest of the story and realize that eventually faith did overcome that fear. This also fits Mark's emphasis on suffering and rejection, where fear might debilitate the disciple. The call is to overcome fear with belief and to rest in faith.

Matthew has the women depart with fear and great joy to tell the disciples. He notes an appearance by Jesus before they make it back (Matt. 28:9–10). Luke adds that the women remembered Jesus' words (spoken in Galilee) and then returned from the tomb and told all of this to the Eleven and the rest. He gives no report of an appearance by Jesus to the women. It may be that their report met with so much skepticism that recording an appearance was viewed as not needed.

It is at this point that Luke lists the women. He then notes that the reaction was skeptical; the apostles viewed the report as an "idle tale" (λῆρος).[115] In medical contexts, the term described the talk of a sick patient delirious from pain. Thus, the ancients were as skeptical as any modern might be about such a report. They did not believe the women. But Peter ran to the tomb, looked in, saw only grave cloths, and left wondering.[116] The term for "wonder" here (θαυμάζω) is not one that indicates full faith or understanding, but it does suggest, given that Peter went to investigate, that he was open to the women's declaration (cf. Luke 1:21, 63; 2:18, 33; 4:22; 8:25; 9:43; 11:14). His amazement-filled experience with Jesus told him not to close out the options quite yet.

John has Mary Magdalene run directly back to Peter and the other disciples to report that Jesus has been taken from the tomb and laid in an unknown place.[117] This causes Peter and the "other disciple" to run toward the tomb. The other dis-

115. See BAGD, 473; BDAG, 594.

116. Like Luke 24:6, here is another "Western non-interpolation." Luke 24:12 is omitted in D and the Itala. But numerous other manuscripts, including the important 𝔓⁵, favor inclusion.

117. It is not entirely clear how the reports of John and the Synoptics fit together, given the apparent lack of an angelic appearance to Mary in John before she reports to the disciples. For four options, see Bock, *Luke 9:51–24:53*, 1885–88. Two basic options exist with some variation. The first option is that Mary, upon seeing the tomb empty, ran back with an initial report, which report the women who saw the angels later returned to fill out. This assumes some telescoping by John. The alternative is another type of telescoping in which John explains first how Peter and the beloved disciple (traditionally seen as John the apostle) came to hear about the resurrection before he goes back to retell how Mary originally came to finally believe. In this last suboption, the story jumps back to tell of how Mary came to see Jesus or else it tells how eventually she came to believe after her initial testimony was rejected by so many that she needed confirmation that what she had seen was true. This last suboption is not noted in my Luke commentary.

ciple reaches the tomb first, with Peter following. The grave clothes, left neatly in place, lead the other disciple to faith. John's Gospel notes that they did not yet understand the Scripture, that "he must rise from the dead." The event itself led to his faith. Mary is left outside the tomb, weeping. Two angels appear to her and ask why she is weeping. She replies, "They have taken away my Lord, and I do not know where they have laid him." This is the same report that she gave to Peter and John. Mary's despair is calmed in the next scene, when she sees Jesus.[118]

289. Jesus Appears to the Women (Matt. 28:9–10; John 20:14–18)
(Aland §353; Orchard §§377, 389; Huck-Greeven §269)

At this point Matthew notes an appearance of Jesus to the women. When he appears to them, they take hold of his feet and worship him. Jesus then repeats the angelic instruction to be unafraid, go, and tell the disciples to go to Galilee, where they will see him.

Jesus' appearance to Mary appears to fit in somewhere here if John has not rearranged the order for literary reasons. As Mary weeps, she asks a man she thinks is the gardener if he has taken Jesus away, so she can recover the body. When he speaks her name, she recognizes Jesus' voice and cries out, "Rabboni!" She grabs him, but Jesus tells her not to hold on to him, for he is not yet ascended to the Father. Rather, she is to go to the others and tell them that he is ascending to "my Father and your Father, to my God and your God."[119]

118. If John is giving events in sequence (see the first option in the preceding note), then a question would be, How does Mary's skeptical report this late in the sequence match with an earlier angelic vision, even to the other women? Asking the question this way assumes that she ran away first before the angel appeared to the others, but she still likely would have heard their report to the others. It may be that the skeptical reception of the report by the disciples gave her some doubt and plunged her back to her original account. Only a subsequent appearance by Jesus ends her uncertainty.

119. It is this concluding remark to the scene that makes an interpreter consider that John has held off telling this account until he told how Peter and the other disciple heard about the resurrection. If so, then it is possible that Peter and John took off before they heard the entire report of the women. If so, then all they heard was Mary's initial impression that the body had been taken. The two disciples left before the angelic vision was reported and before she got to the point where Jesus appeared to her. Thus, in this scenario, John 20:18 is a report to the disciples as a whole, but made after Peter and John had headed for the tomb. On the other hand, if John is running in sequence, then this appearance became a direct confirmation to her of Jesus' resurrection and confirmed what the Synoptics indicated in the initial angelic appearance. Luke's resurrection accounts indicate that the angelic appearances by themselves were not taken as ultimately persuasive. Only when Jesus appeared to them were they persuaded. So the same happens here eventually with Mary. Granted, the last several footnotes attempt to harmonize the details in a sequence that none of the accounts gives. Nonetheless, the accounts as we have them clearly have chosen to give different sets of details. To make sense of the whole, some proposed combination needs to be given consideration.

John's section closes with her reporting to the disciples, "I have seen the Lord."

290. The Report of the Guard (Matt. 28:11–15) (Aland §354; Orchard §378; Huck-Greeven §270)

Matthew is the only Gospel to mention the guards. He narrates how some of them went into the city to report to the chief priests. Once again money comes into play. Having taken counsel with the elders, the guards are paid and told to say, "His disciples came by night and stole him away while we were asleep." The leadership, in turn, will protect the guards from Pilate, agreeing to "keep you out of trouble." This was necessary because such negligence would normally lead to discipline, if not execution.[120] So the money was taken, and the story told. Matthew notes that this is the story spread among the Jews even to the time of the Gospel's writing.

291. The Emmaus Road Appearance (Luke 24:13–35) (Aland §355; Orchard §380; Huck-Greeven §272)

Luke alone recounts an appearance to two otherwise unknown disciples as they journey from Jerusalem to Emmaus. We are not certain where Emmaus was. A traditional site, tied to a Maccabean battleground (1 Macc. 3:40, 57; 4:3), is some twenty miles away and thus too far, since Luke places the distance at seven miles. Two other locations are a Crusader fort site known as el-Qubeibeh and an Emmaus that Josephus mentions, also called Mozah, where Vespasian once stationed troops (*War* 7.6.6 §217; cf. *m. Sukkah* 4.5). The Crusader locale is unattested as existing in the first century, while the second locale would mean that Luke's figuring of the distance is a round trip. It may simply be that we do not know the locale. The vagueness of the detail speaks to its authenticity. Why create an appearance to unknown disciples going to a little-known place? The account was recalled because it took hold in the early church's memory.

The literary element of the account is playful as it unfolds. The reader in Luke knows more about what is happening than the participants in the event at the time. The account is rich in irony. Two disciples are traveling, discussing what had just taken place in Jerusalem, when Jesus draws near to them, although his identity is not evident. Jesus asks them about their conversation.

---

120. The text literally says that if the report reaches Pilate, it will be the leadership's role to "satisfy him."

Luke describes these disciples as being sad. Cleopas asks Jesus, "Are you the only visitor to Jerusalem who does not know these things that have happened there in these days?" Of course, Jesus is the one person who most knows what has taken place!

What follows is a short description of how Jesus' disciples viewed him. The remarks are a reply to Jesus' query, "What things?" The events surround Jesus of Nazareth, "a prophet mighty in deed and word before God and all the people, and how our chief priests and rulers delivered him up to be condemned to death and crucified him." These disciples had hoped that "he was the one to redeem Israel." Three days later, some women had left them amazed, by reporting that they did not find the body at the now-empty tomb. Rather, they had experienced a vision of angels, who declared Jesus to be alive. But when others went to check out the scene, they did not see him. The disciples, in telling the story, review Jesus' ministry of word and deed and summarize the hope for Israel that Jesus represented. They also discount to some degree the women's testimony. Belief will not come until some of the others see Jesus. The account shows the hesitation of the disciples to embrace the resurrection, as it is almost beyond belief.

Jesus rebukes them, calling them foolish and slow of heart "to believe all that the prophets have spoken. Was it not necessary that the Christ should suffer these things and enter into his glory?" Here Jesus summarizes the two elements so crucial to his last week of ministry: suffering followed by glory. These events are part of a "necessary" divine plan, a point that Luke has loved to stress throughout his Gospel (Luke 2:49; 4:43; 9:22; 13:16, 33; 17:25; 21:9; 22:37; 24:7, 44). Starting with Moses and all the prophets, Jesus next opened up the Scriptures and interpreted them for these disciples. Jesus showed them how the Scriptures were about what had taken place or, as Luke puts it, "what was said in all the scriptures concerning himself."

Still unaware of who it is that is with them, the disciples invite Jesus in for a meal and to stay the evening. While Jesus is blessing and breaking bread with them in table fellowship, the disciples' eyes are opened so that they recognize that it is Jesus in their midst. With that recognition, Jesus disappears. Their reflection indicates that their hearts "burned" within them as he shared the Scriptures earlier. So they get up to go and tell the group back in Jerusalem. When they arrive in Jerusalem and join the Eleven, they learn, "The Lord has risen indeed, and has appeared to Simon!" The story of the Emmaus disciples did not stand alone. Once again over a meal, these two disciples tell their account. Luke's Gospel leaves the impression that Jesus is appearing frequently enough to generate much excitement. What the Emmaus disciples thought would be the crowning proof of Jesus' resurrection already had been anticipated in the appearance to Peter. Now it was reinforced by another appearance to leave no room for doubt. The women's account had substance. Their "tale" had become the amazing truth.

292. Jesus Appears to His Disciples and Later to Thomas
(Luke 24:36–43; John 20:19–29) (Aland §§356–57; Orchard §§381a, 390–91; Huck-Greeven §273a)[121]

The multiple appearances continue in Luke while they are at the table. Jesus appears in the midst of the large group and greets them, "Peace to you."[122] These appearances are so extraordinary that they are still unsettling to the disciples, and so Jesus' presence and greeting leave the group startled and frightened. They think that it is a spirit. Jesus challenges them. Why are they troubled? Why do they question in their heart? The disciples still are finding Jesus' resurrection and his risen presence hard to embrace. He asks them to observe his hands and feet and to touch him, reminding them that spirits do not have such form. He shows them his hands and feet, apparently with the marks of his death still visible.[123] As they still have trouble believing it and are wondering, full of joy, he asks for food and eats some broiled fish. The series of actions shows that what was experienced was neither a hallucination nor merely the appearance of a spirit in some kind of vision. Jesus truly was alive and in their midst.

John appears to relate the same scene. The disciples are gathered together in a room with the doors shut, as they fear the Jews. Jesus greets them, "Peace be with you." He shows them his hands and side, and the disciples are glad to see "the Lord." Jesus "commissions" them as he says, "Peace be with you. As the Father has sent me, even so I send you." Jesus breathes on them and says, "Receive the Holy Spirit. If you forgive the sins of any, they are forgiven; if you retain the sins of any, they are retained." This event designates these disciples as bearers of the Spirit and holders of the message of forgiveness. It is John's equivalent to the day of Pentecost in Acts 2. What happens at Pentecost for all disciples present is previewed here for the select group of gathered disciples. Jesus can dispense the Spirit now that he is dead and raised, as the upper room discourse had promised.

---

121. After this event, Aland notes the appearance to Thomas, which only John 20:24–29 describes (§357). The other intervening units in Aland include portions of the various other shorter and longer endings for Mark (§§358 [Mark 16:14–18]; §§362–63 [alternate Mark 16:8 and the full longer ending of 16:9–20]), other units from John (§360 [John 21:1–14]), Paul's note on the resurrection from 1 Cor. 15:3–8 (§361), and a description of Matthew's closing verses as they are tied to the longer Markan ending (§359). Huck-Greeven do not give entries for uniquely Johannine texts.

122. This greeting is another "Western non-interpolation" in Luke 24, missing in D and the Itala, but it also is likely to be original.

123. This sentence on the display of hands and feet in v. 40 is another "Western non-interpolation." It is omitted in D, the Itala, some Syriac manuscripts, and Marcion. Again the wider attestation favors inclusion.

John goes on to note that Thomas was not present at this event. He doubts their report, saying that he will not believe until he sees and touches the imprint of the nails and Jesus' side, the latter an allusion to Jesus' being pierced there after his death. Eight days later, Jesus appears to Thomas and tells him to place his fingers in his side. Jesus exhorts him, "Do not be faithless, but believing." Not only does Jesus appear to him, but also he knows the complaint and doubt that Thomas had expressed earlier. Thomas responds with a climactic cry, "My Lord and my God!" He now is finally convinced. Jesus responds with a beatitude that also is an exhortation to faith: "Have you believed because you have seen me? Blessed are those who have not seen and yet believe." Even those not granted an appearance by the Lord can believe that he is raised and alive. John's Gospel concludes with a miraculous catch of fish involving Peter and the others that includes a meal. Then Jesus restores Peter in a threefold confession of Peter's love.

293. The Great Commission from Galilee (Matt. 28:16–20)
(Aland §364; Orchard §379; Huck-Greeven §271)

Matthew's Gospel concludes with a commission given in Galilee on a mountain to which Jesus had directed his disciples. In Matthew, the key appearance is outside Judea, in Galilee, while Luke focuses on the appearances in Jerusalem. The appearances are met with both worship and doubt. All the Gospels note how difficult it was for the disciples to accept that Jesus was raised. It was not an "automatic" response of faith. These ancients acted much like modern people in their hesitation.

Jesus' commission notes that he has been given all authority in heaven and on earth. The language is the language of heavenly rule and mediatorial authority. The kingdom is here; Messiah is at work. God is working through Jesus, just as Jesus had claimed in his ministry. The kingdom has arrived. So the call is to make disciples of all the nations. Now God will make his gracious claim on people from every nation. They will become his disciples, followers of God.

Making disciples involves three steps. Three participles in these verses give the elements of discipleship. First, the mission requires that disciples go and seek to bring the message to the nations. Second, making disciples involves baptizing those who respond in the name of the Father, Son, and Holy Spirit. This is the Father's plan, mediated through the Son, who sends the Spirit as a sign that the fulfillment has come. Baptism is a symbolic representation of washing, an identification of this cleansing work, which enables the Spirit to dwell in them (Rom. 6). Third, making disciples involves teaching them to obey all that Jesus commanded them. In Matthew, this response of obedience encompasses the discourses where instruction was given in great detail, stretching from the Sermon on the Mount to the Olivet discourse, as disciples look for his return. Discipleship means not only trusting in Jesus and identifying with him, as baptism pictures, but also the pursuit of obeying him. Matthew ends with a note of assurance as Jesus declares that he will be with them to the close of the age. The assurance of Jesus' resurrection is not only that one day we will be raised to life, but also that he always is ministering to us from the side of God.

294. Jesus' Last Words and Ascension (Luke 24:44–53)
(Aland §365; Orchard §§381b–82; Huck-Greeven §§273b–74)

The timing of this final scene in Luke is uncertain. On the one hand, it looks like it belongs to the meal and appearance of resurrection evening. On the other hand, its tie to an ascension in 24:50–53 makes it possible that it belongs with the event narrated in Acts 1:9–11, which took place forty days later. The reference to ascension both here and in Acts 1 means that Luke repeats the event, linking Luke and Acts together. Luke likes to discuss important events more than once, as he does for other events in Acts, such as Saul's conversion. The possibility may exist that Luke has compressed time here and given a brief look at a later event, linked with another look at the same event in Acts. The departure from Bethany need not contradict a departure from the Mount of Olives, since the town was located on the side of the mount. A later setting also explains the idea of returning and being continually at the temple, as 24:52–53 describes. At some point during the forty days, Jesus instructed the disciples not to leave Jerusalem (Acts 1:3–5). That this is later on in the forty-day period makes sense in light of the Galilean appearance in Matthew, which must be earlier in the period. Regardless of the exact timing, the event is significant because it anticipates a phase of ministry that will take place despite Jesus' resurrection and seeming departure.

The Lukan final commission reminds the disciples that Jesus had spoken to them about the fulfillment of "everything written about me in the law of Moses and the prophets and the psalms." This threefold division of the Hebrew Scripture has precedent in Judaism (prologue to Sirach; 4QMMT 10). Jesus' point is that his suffering was a part of the divine plan revealed in Scripture, as he had often taught them. These things "are necessary" (δεῖ). Then came a more complete explanation as Jesus opened the Scripture and explained to them the plan.

Luke uses three Greek infinitives to lay out the plan of what stood written. (1) The Christ is to suffer. Jesus' focus is his role as the anointed one. The juxtaposition of the Christ with suffering is something that Jesus had continuously discussed, but to Jewish ears it was a surprising message. The Messiah was to be a victorious, powerful, glorious figure, not a suffering one. The nation might suffer, but the Messiah did not suffer. Rather, the current popular view was that he would deliver the nation. Yet Jesus combined images of the representative of the nation, the suffering Servant, and the righteous sufferer with the messianic figure. This ruler would represent the nation not only in victory, but also in suffering. Before exaltation, there would be the disfigurement of the cross (cf. Isa. 52:13–15; 53:3, 5, 9–12). This always had been in the plan.

(2) On the third day the Christ is to rise. It is hard to know whether the detail of the third day is part of the emphasis here, since no text of Hebrew Scripture makes a clear claim for the third day. There is the analogy with Jonah, but that is about the only option. Far more likely is that what is highlighted here is the idea of resurrection itself and its implied glorification. Here the exaltation themes of texts cited in Acts, such as Ps. 110 and Ps. 16:8–10, as well as the exaltation of the Servant are probably the points of scriptural contact.

(3) Repentance and forgiveness of sins are to be preached in Christ's name to all the nations, beginning from Jerusalem. Here is the message of the commissioned followers. They preach a now-exalted Jesus who offers the benefits of the new era he brings. In one sense, this promise goes back to Gen. 12:1–3. God would bless the world through the work of Abraham's seed. Isaiah's vision of nations as well as Israel being blessed in the end also are in view. Romans 15:7–13 lists a series of such texts. The provision of forgiveness looks to the hope of the new covenant, as will the allusion to the Spirit in Luke 24:49. Repentance is the appropriate response to this message. This also is connected to what the sacred Scripture had taught. The prophets loved to highlight a "turning change of mind" as the way to respond to God's message. Jerusalem is the launching point. It is where the story in Acts begins. The authority of Jesus, a point under constant contention during his ministry, is the ground for the gracious offer of forgiveness and for the right to make the offer.

In sum, Jesus' ministry was about a plan that Scripture itself had outlined and that he and those following him were carrying out. To make sense of Jesus, one must look at what God's revelation says about the many roles of the promised anointed one. Here was more than a man. Here was one qualified to go into God's presence and bear his authority. As Jesus' ministry showed, that authority included the right to forgive sin, the right to judge, the right to assess what happens on the Sabbath, the right to give life, the power to control the creation, and the exercise of power over the forces of evil. In the Synoptics, Jesus does not often claim who he is with titles, but regularly shows who he is and how God is working uniquely through him. The one title he does use is "Son of Man," a description that wonderfully melds his humanity with divine authority. Jesus possessed divinely granted prerogatives as one invited into

God's very presence. Only one who himself possesses divinity can sit permanently at the side of God.

Jesus describes the disciples as "witnesses of these things" (Acts 1:8). They
had seen the realization of Scripture's promise in the events of his ministry,
especially in the suffering of the final week. These disciples who had walked
through it all with Jesus were uniquely qualified to tell his story.

Beyond qualifications, however, what was needed was enablement. Jesus
promises this enablement to them with his last words in Luke's Gospel, "And
behold, I send the promise of my Father upon you; but stay in the city, until
you are clothed with power from on high." Jesus was raised and exalted to the
Father's side (Luke 22:69) in part to send the Spirit as an enabler for the mission. In Luke 3:15–17, John the Baptist had indicated that the way to know
that the Christ had come would be when he baptizes with the Spirit and fire.
The Spirit's coming was a promise of the Father back when John preached it.
It is the promise of the Father when Jesus notes it here. But soon it will be a
reality. Then the disciples will be empowered to preach the message. Acts 2
and 10–11 show how important the Spirit's bestowal was as an enabling sign.
The Spirit indicates that salvation and eschatological family connection had
come to Jesus' followers. For Luke, this forgiveness, deliverance, enablement,
and family connection are the heart of the gospel.

So Jesus heads out to Bethany. He blesses them and departs into heaven.
And the disciples worshiped him and returned to Jerusalem full of joy. They
were continually in the temple, blessing God. Jesus came to the nation to be
a light of deliverance. He departed never having given up on his mission of
light, a revelation to the nations and glory for Israel (Luke 2:32). It is appropriate, then, that as the disciples awaited their enablement, they would give
thanks to the God of Israel in the temple. Through Israel's Christ, opportunity for blessing had spread to the world because of the authority Jesus bore
as the now vindicated and exalted one.

Conclusion

The life of Jesus in the Synoptics ends with a resurrection that left disciples
in awe (Mark). That resurrection produced two commissions to take the message of vindicated hope from the rejected but raised Messiah out to the world
(Matthew and Luke). The Gospels are not about a great religious teacher; they
are about a great, unique deliverer whose appearance represented the claim of
the dawn of a new era. They are not about one prophet among many; they are
about a human being claiming to have received unique authority to give forgiveness and new life from the very side of God. They focus on a figure about whom
many contended. The dispute throughout Jesus' life and ministry centered

around the message he brought of the emerging of God's power and presence, a presence and authority that were inseparable from Jesus himself. It was an offer of deliverance and fulfillment made to a nation exposed to the promise long ago. The offer demanded a response. It left few who met him with a neutral view about him. The issues that his ministry raised were so fundamental that his message was controversial. The controversy led to his death. However, his importance meant that death could not be the end to his story. Jesus' resurrection showed that he was about the hope of life, not the power of rejection and death. In resurrection, God had cast his vote in the dispute in favor of Jesus.

How, then, should one respond to this Jesus? The wise person should listen to him and build a house on the rock. Why listen to him? There are a multitude of reasons. Forgiveness is his to give as the Son of Man. Exorcism showed that the forces of evil could not defeat him and that God's kingdom had come. Healings pictured his power to deliver as Son of David. Sabbath controversies showed that God would work through him even on the day of rest, as he was Lord of the Sabbath. Even the creation bowed and testified to him, during his birth, life, and death, leading the disciples to ask what sort of man this is that even the winds and waves obey him. His associations showed that anyone could come to him to receive what God offered, because he was called to be the great physician. His compassion was such that he pursued the lost like a shepherd searching for stray sheep—and he urged his disciples to do the same. Now, he was raised, vindicated, and taken to his rightful place at God's right hand. From there he is ready to dispense divine enablement to those who turn to him before that great day when, as Son of Man, he will return to exercise total authority and render a final, decisive judgment.

Jesus' coming is not about an ethic; it is about a relational entrance into God's power and presence. Although Jesus did point out the way to God and urged disciples to have integrity and show love even to those who hated, that character was to be the product of a life resting in the divine hope and promise that Jesus brought. Jesus' ministry was about the new era that he inaugurated along with the opportunity for forgiveness and enablement that he represented and supplied. That ministry compelled a choice. Had the new era come? Was the unique anointed one present? If he was, then embracing him and his message becomes an imperative from God. Death's inability to hold Jesus and devour him showed the way to the answer. The Synoptics together are telling us that anyone with ears to hear and eyes to see should use them to find forgiveness in Jesus and enter into his promise. They also tell us that having responded, we should stay the course until he completes what he started, no matter how tough the world's rejection of him becomes.

There is still one other portrait of Jesus. It comes from the Gospel of John. It tells the story in a way that both overlaps with the Synoptics and gives fresh insight into Jesus. It tells Jesus' story from heaven down, the Word become flesh. It is to that unique perspective that we now turn.

Part 3

Jesus according to John

But, last of all, John, perceiving that the external facts [τὰ σωματικά] had been made plain in the gospel, being urged by his friends, and inspired by the Spirit, composed a spiritual gospel [πνευματικὸν ... εὐαγγέλιον].[1]

And the genealogy of our Savior according to the flesh John quite naturally omitted, because it had already been given by Matthew and Luke, and began with the doctrine of his divinity, which had, as it were, been reserved for him, as their superior, by the divine Spirit.[2]

These summaries from the earliest history of the church, written about A.D. 324, show that the Gospel of John has long been recognized as unique. Not only does the story open with a prologue framing his entire Gospel in terms of the "Word became flesh," but John also goes on to detail parts of Jesus' ministry in Perea that the other Gospels do not mention. He also details speeches in a long, flowing style not seen in the Synoptics. These speeches speak openly of the direct connection between the Father and the Son, reflecting a Christology of the highest order. John pays special attention to acts that Jesus performed on feast days and lists a series of seven signs that dominate the first twelve chapters. His presentation of the upper room discourse, highlighting the sending of the Spirit, also is unique to his Gospel. When it comes to "Jesus according to Scripture," John is both a supplement to and capstone on the biblical presentation of Jesus' life. In a very real sense, John fills out the portrait of Jesus and gives us the "rest of the story," sometimes noting that what he describes, the disciples themselves did not understand or appreciate until after Jesus' death and resurrection (John 2:22; 12:16; 20:9). They, like us, had to discover who God had revealed him to be. Those who study John see his emphasis on Jesus as the revealer of God and his way. In a very real sense, it is a two-sided revelation, for as Jesus revealed what God was doing,

1. Clement of Alexandria, as cited by Eusebius, *Eccl. Hist.* 6.14.7.
2. Eusebius, *Eccl. Hist.* 3.24.13.

so also God was revealing what Jesus was doing, as well as who he was. John's fundamental thesis is that to see Jesus at work is to see revealed what the Father is doing. In their inseparability is found the revelation of God. Thus, Jesus can be described in a very real sense as the "Word" of God, for Jesus is the one sent by God to declare in deed and word what God is doing and what he asks of us.

TWELVE

Introducing Jesus in John's Gospel

The Word Incarnate and the First Witnesses— John the Baptist and the Disciples (John 1)

John has another answer to the identity of the Word/Wisdom/Torah of God. He has become incarnate in the person of Jesus Christ. He, not the Law of Moses, is the key to the meaning of life. Neither was he the first of God's creation, but is part of God himself, eternal and uncreated. He is thus the true revelation of God, it is he who speaks God's words, and he is the source of life. Though he does not again use the title, all of the absolute claims which Jesus will make in the following chapters are but the filling out of the consequences of this truth: not the Torah nor wisdom, but Jesus is the eternal Logos of God.[1]

The prologue has prepared us to see nothing less than the coming of the divine light, the Son of God, revealing the glory of God, full of grace and truth. The Son comes on the scene in the context of the ministry of John the Baptist. Jesus' first followers come from among the Baptist's disciples, and then several others are gathered together. All of this is preparation for the revelation of the glory beginning in chapter 2.[2]

Each Gospel plays its introductory overture in its own way, but John starts out with a full symphonic blast as he speaks about the Word become flesh. Setting the tone for all that follows, this is a prologue that makes it clear to the reader from the very first note that what became flesh in Jesus was no less than

---

1. John W. Pryor, *John: Evangelist of the Covenant People: The Narrative and Themes of the Fourth Gospel* (Downers Grove, Ill.: InterVarsity, 1992), 8.
2. Rodney A. Whitacre, *John,* IVPNTCS 4 (Downers Grove, Ill.: InterVarsity, 1999), 63.

the Word of creation, who has resided with God from the beginning. Following that high and most heavenly note, John returns to the story on earth, beginning with a witness, John the Baptist, whose role it was to point to that now-incarnate light. His witness stuck, especially with some of his disciples, who were among the first to join in following Jesus. John 1 sets the tone for the Gospel with titles being bestowed on Jesus by those who chose to ally themselves to him. But the chapter will end where it began with notes pointing to heaven and the picture of angels ascending and descending on the Son of Man. For John, when Jesus ministers on earth, heaven is never very far away.

I will cover John much as I did Matthew, Mark, and Luke, working with the basic units of the Gospel. I follow John's order and use the Aland synopsis to number the units.[3] In spots the story will be connected to the Synoptic story already told, but the emphasis will be to let John tell the story in his own terms, in light of his distinct structure. It seems clear that John constructed his Gospel to be read in this way, telling his readers things that the other Gospels did not cover. To indicate that the units are Johannine, the letter *J* precedes each number in the unit. As we survey John, I will be sensitive to how his story both parallels, differs from, and enhances what Matthew, Mark, and Luke have presented.

J1. The Prologue: The Word Became Flesh (John 1:1–18)
(Aland §1)

Whereas Mark starts with John the Baptist's ministry, Matthew with Jesus' birth, and Luke with John the Baptist's birth, John goes all the way back *before* the creation to introduce the saga of the preincarnate Word. Before anything that was created was there, the Word existed with God (John 1:1a–b). The theme of the Word has rich background that is important to John's choice of this term, because it compares and contrasts well with four themes of the Old Testament and Judaism: the creative Word of God, Wisdom, Torah, and the *memra* of the Jewish targums.[4] John's concept of the Word incarnate is unique and represents a significant development from this Jewish backdrop, but his audience did possess some understanding of the imagery that John used, to appreciate both the nature of the claim and the comparison.

The creative Word of God is seen in such Old Testament texts as Isa. 55:11, where the Word comes from above and yields fruit like a sown seed.

3. The numbering of Huck-Greeven and Orchard is abandoned in this treatment because they concerned themselves only with Matthew, Mark, and Luke.

4. Raymond E. Brown, *The Gospel according to John I–XII,* AB 29 (Garden City, N.Y.: Doubleday, 1966), 519–24.

The Word was present at the creation, the means by which things came into being (Gen. 1; Ps. 33:6). The Word is like a lamp that guides a person's way on a path (Ps. 119:105). God's word contains the authority of judgment (Ps. 147:15, 18). So the Word is God's "effective speech," a revelation of who he is and what he does, along with being the mediating means by which his purpose is performed. As the spoken word reveals the thoughts of the mind in tangible ways, so the Word expresses and reveals God in both word and act.

The parallels with Wisdom as seen in the Old Testament and Judaism also are numerous. Wisdom too is said to have been present at the creation (Prov. 8:22–31), although this personification of God's will is presented as both created and as feminine (Prov. 9:1–6).[5] Thus, John's remarks go beyond the portrait and associations of Wisdom, in that the Word had no beginning and is personal in nature (John 1:1, 14) and not merely an expression of an attribute of God in personification. Her commandments are a light (Prov. 6:23). Sirach has numerous references to Wisdom. Wisdom has been with the Lord forever, created before creation (1:1; 24:9). She is equated with the law and is rejected by the foolish (15:1–10; 24:23). She had a role in creation and possesses a glory (24:1–3). She has "tabernacled" with Israel (24:8, 10). The Book of Wisdom of Solomon continues in a similar vein. Wisdom was the fashioner of all things, working at the creation (7:22; 9:9). She is the breath of the power of God, an emanation of his glory, a reflection of his light, and a mirror of his working, ordering all things (7:25–29). The word of wisdom has made all things (9:1–2). Note how in this text word and wisdom are in parallelism. To mention one is to suggest the other. Thus, attempts to argue that the background is the Word of God but not Wisdom are hard to support, given the linkage in Jewish thought. One idea invokes the other. Wisdom also carries a word of judgment (18:15), carrying out God's will when Israel was saved from Pharaoh.

Associations that Jews came to make with Torah, probably because of its links to Wisdom, also might fit into this background. Later Jewish texts saw the Torah as present at the creation. *Genesis Rabbah* 1.2 taught, "There is no beginning but Torah." In the Babylonian Talmud, *Pesaḥim* 54ᵃ, the note is made that seven things were created before creation: among them were Torah, repentance, the temple, and the name of the Messiah. The text cited in this rabbinic discussion is Prov. 8:22. To invoke the Word and Wisdom would mean to invoke the potential presence of Torah. Proverbs 6:23 presents Torah as light. Luke and Matthew have already shown the Messiah as light, the bringer of God's righteous deliverance (Luke 1:78–79; Matt. 4:12–16). John's remarks will serve to underscore that one greater than the Torah is present (John

---

5. The Arians made much of this connection in the fourth century, but in doing so ignored the distinction and heightening that John's Gospel introduced in its portrait of the Word being with God and being God, even in the beginning.

1:17–18). Thus, in this case, if these themes existed in the Judaism of Jesus' time, the background that John works with is contrastive in nature and somewhat polemical.

Finally, there is the *memra* ("Word") of the Aramaic targums, the earliest translations of the Hebrew Testament. This term also appears in some key targums in the Torah. The *memra* is the presence of God among his people, giving them support (*Targum Onqelos* on Exod. 3:12). When the people were said to meet God in the targumic renderings of Exod. 19:17, it was the *memra* that they encountered. In other words, the *memra* served as the manifestation of God's presence in God's undertakings and relating to humanity, a role similar to what John says about Jesus in 1:18.

Appreciating this background helps us to comprehend the fullness of what John is doing and proclaiming in his prologue. All that Judaism had associated with creation, God's word and law, including the presence of divine wisdom in powerful fullness, is now explained as residing in the "Word become flesh," so that grace and truth have come decisively in Jesus Christ (John 1:1–5, 14–18). Not only is Jesus the Word incarnate, but also in him are the wisdom, law, and expressed word of God. He is the "revelator" of God, the one who shows in his life and person who and what God really is and the one who knows his plan. In fact, the Word can be equated with God while being described as distinct from him.[6] Thus, this background provides the setting for the grand declarations of the prologue. The prologue itself details the portrait.

The prologue divides into four basic units: cosmology-creation (vv. 1–5); John the Baptist, witness to the light (vv. 6–9); the response to the light (vv. 10–13); and the new era, which reveals God (vv. 14–18). The prologue is interesting because five terms appear that do not reappear in the Gospel itself: (1) Word as a reference to Jesus, (2) tabernacle, (3) grace, (4) fullness, and (5) explain. Yet sixteen terms of the prologue do reappear and carry much of the weight of the Gospel's message: (1) life, (2) light, (3) darkness, (4) send, (5) John the Baptist, (6) believe, (7) witness, (8) truth, (9) world, (10) know, (11) born of God, (12) glory, (13) only begotten, (14) Father, (15) Moses, and (16) see.[7]

The opening verse of the Gospel makes three major points. The first covers existence. The Word existed in the beginning, an explicit allusion to Gen. 1:1. In other words, before the creation, the Word was there. He was distinct from the creation. Second, he was with God. This treats his relationship. He is both distinct from the Father and was with him. In 1:14, 18, John again will make a distinction and refer to the Father and the "only begotten God" or "the only

---

6. It is a text like this that led the church to affirm the divinity of Jesus and move toward the detailed articulation of the doctrine of the Trinity.

7. Andreas J. Köstenberger, *Encountering John: The Gospel in Historical, Literary, and Theological Perspective*, Encountering Biblical Studies (Grand Rapids: Baker, 1999), 48–49.

begotten from God." In fact, nowhere in the prologue is Jesus called "the Son," using the noun υἱός.[8] That title is saved for the body of the Gospel, after Jesus' relationship to God is established by the prologue. Third, there is predication of the Word as God. The Greek construction here is the most concise way grammatically to call the Word "God" and yet make some distinction.[9] John opens his Gospel affirming the highest Christology possible, the absolute divinity and equality with God of the sent one (John 1:9). John tells Jesus' story very much from heaven down.

After affirming the Word's presence with God, John goes on to remark about the Word's role in creation, something that Gen. 1 also notes by observing how creation came into being through God's declaration. Paul also makes this note in his great hymn about Jesus in Col. 1:15–20. Nothing that came into being did so outside of him.

The role of the phrase at the end of John 1:3 is disputed. One option is to render "which came into being" as emphatically closing the final point of 1:3. So, "Without him came into being not one thing which came into being." The other option is to connect it with the beginning of 1:4, as did most of the earliest readers of John's Gospel.[10] Then the reading is "That which came into being in him was life." The reference is then not to creation but to an even more significant relationship "in him" that brought life and was the light of humankind, what Brown calls eternal life.[11] In other words, the Word's role in creation is but a precursor to his ultimate creative work. This second option seems to do a better job of making this first portion of the prologue cohere. The theme of gospel or Jesus as life and light is one to which John will repeatedly return (life: 3:15–16; 5:24–29; 6:27, 48; 8:12; 10:10; 11:25; 14:6; 17:2–3; 20:31; light: 1:7–9; 3:19–21; 8:12; 9:5; 12:35–36, 46). But the message is not all good, because although light came into the creation, the creation did not embrace it (1:10–11). At least, this is one way to understand John 1:5b. Another rendering of οὐ κατέλαβεν would be that the darkness did not "overtake" it. With this sense, the term is a combative image; light and darkness battle each other, and light wins (cf. John 12:35). This reading may have the advantage not only of suggesting the battle and the rejection by the world but

---

8. This remark assumes that "only begotten God" is the correct reading in the textual problem in 1:18. The better and earlier manuscripts (Papyri 66 and 75; Codices Sinaiticus, Vaticanus, and Ephraemi) have this reading, which also is the harder reading.

9. Daniel Wallace, *Greek Grammar beyond the Basics: An Exegetical Syntax of the New Testament* (Grand Rapids: Zondervan, 1996), 267–69. Thus, translations that have "and the Word was divine" are incorrectly indefinite and unclear. Greek has an adjective to make that affirmation. A good alternative rendering is, "What God was, the Word was" (NEB).

10. Brown, *John I–XII*, 6.

11. C. K. Barrett, *The Gospel according to John: An Introduction with Commentary and Notes on the Greek Text* (London: SPCK, 1955), 130–31, opts for the first reading but fails to note that the point is not about creation but about eternal life, as the following verse about John witnessing to the light makes clear.

also of affirming John's belief that the light was victorious in the battle. It is hard to be sure which reading most comprehensively expresses John's intent, but the idea of the light possessing victory fits in with later themes of how the cross glorifies and exalts the Son.

John the Baptist is introduced as a witness to Jesus, something that John 1:19–40 will detail. John's job was to witness to the light, so that through his testimony to "the coming one" people might believe in Jesus.

In contrast, Jesus was the true light, which, coming into the world, does enlighten all humanity. John is stressing here how Jesus' coming was an opportunity for everyone to experience the life that resides in the Word. He came into the world, having made the world, but the tragedy is that the world did not know him. Here is another indication, this time more explicit than in 1:5, that the world would not embrace his message. In fact, even "his own," a reference to Israel, did not receive him. These words would be a shock, since Israel thought of itself as a "distinct" people, a holy nation set apart to be different from the world. But here, because of its refusal to embrace the sent Word, which is light, Israel is joined to the world in opposition to God. However, life and adoption did come to some. Those who received the light were given the authority to become children of God. Here, then, is the gospel in a nutshell for John: those who believe in the person of Jesus, who is the sent light from God, are recipients of life and filial connection to God. The gospel for John is about unending, restored relationship with God that is not a matter of genealogy, biology, or merit, but of response. This is why it is neither a birth involving "bloods" nor "the will of the flesh" nor the "will of man." This birth entails being "born of God" (John 3:1–16). This is why life was "in him."[12]

So John announces a new era in God's plan, a time when the Word departed from heaven, became flesh, and came down to "tabernacle" (ἐσκήνω-σεν) with humanity on earth. Here the imagery recalls the language of Sinai and the formation of Israel as a nation, in which God "pitched his tent" with his people and went before them (Exod. 24:16; 25:7–8; 29:46; 40:35; Zech. 2:10 [MT 2:14]). Just like then, when the Shekinah glory walked before the people, so now John, among others, beheld the glory of the Word become flesh. It was glory befitting one "only begotten" from God. The idea of one being "only begotten" is crucial to the prologue. It stresses Jesus' unique and close relationship to the Father as the manifestation of the Father's presence. Thus, the idea is not that Jesus was born; 1:1 has already ruled out that point. Rather, it is that the relationship that exists between Father and Word-become-flesh operates uniquely at a level involving nothing but deity. The

12. This concept is yet another variation on Paul's concept of the blessings that come from being in Christ. For both writers, it is the relational dimension of life provided by Jesus that is at the heart of the good news.

"only begotten" is a being who is uniquely connected to God. The explicit absence of the idea of Son here is important. It is his closeness to the Father that is highlighted in the expression. In his person, then, is embodied a fullness of grace and truth, an idea reaffirmed in 1:17.

John the Baptist testified to this one. Here John alludes to a scene already made famous in the Synoptics (Matt. 3:11; Mark 1:7–8; Luke 3:16). John testifies to one coming after him who ranks before him. The explanation given is that this one to come really was before him. The evangelist John means this in a full sense; his prologue places the one to come with the Father in the beginning. However, an element of the meaning is not beyond the Baptist's understanding in his lifetime, because Judaism believed that the Messiah's name and existence were in the heart of God from before the beginning.[13] Still, this kind of Johannine reflection on what Jesus' life and ministry meant is typical of his Gospel.

Those who share in the life that the coming one gives receive a share of his fullness. The meaning of the next phrase ("grace upon grace") is debated. Is it grace in place of grace (substitution of one grace for another) or grace placed upon grace (an accumulation of grace)? The substitution idea may have in mind a movement from one era of grace to another, from law to grace and truth. A problem with this view is that "grace" is specifically said to come with Jesus after Moses, so that the law, though seen positively, is not equated with what comes later, nor is grace seen to come in stages in differing levels. An attempt to soften this criticism is the positive statement of 4:24, that salvation is of the Jews, yet this is not a reference to the law but to the promise in the law pointing to the Messiah. Thus, the accumulation idea seems to be a better reading and speaks of a procession of acts of grace coming one after the other in an unending string. When Jesus brought life, he brought grace piled upon grace.

The last two verses of the prologue represent the most direct claims with regard to the program of God and encase a challenge to Judaism. Here Jesus Christ is presented as a revelatory advance on Moses, the father of Jewish law. The law was through Moses, but grace and truth came through Jesus. John does not mean this as a negative way to describe Moses. In John 5, he will make it clear that Moses pointed to the hope that Jesus represents (John 5:39–47). Moses is left behind in the contrast because Moses was a step on the way to the hope that Jesus brings and reveals. But why should Jesus supersede and replace Moses? It is because of the more intimate quality of his relationship to God and contact with God. Here is one sent from above, one who has seen God, the only begotten, whose unique place is in the bosom of the Father (the Book of Hebrews makes similar kinds of arguments about Jesus' superi-

13. See, earlier in this section, the discussion on background to John's prologue and b. Pesahim 54ª.

ority to the greats of Judaism). The Word's oneness with God and his identity with him is the answer. That one is able to explain (literally, "to exegete") and reveal what God is about. The end of the prologue concludes where it started. Jesus is the Word and is uniquely qualified to reveal and explain God as Word because he has been with God from before the beginning and has his residence in the bosom of the Father. It is this view of Jesus that stands behind all the Johannine language that declares Jesus to be the Son, the one sent from the Father, and the one who ascends and descends. Each of these images underscores his close connection to and unique relationship with the Father. For John, in the beginning was the Word, and the Word was sent to take on flesh and reveal the Father, his way and will. In sum, the Word was God now come in the flesh.

J2. The Witness of John the Baptist (John 1:19–34)
(Aland §§13, 16, 18)

The witness of John the Baptist is where John's story of Jesus' actual ministry begins. It is a very focused summary. John does not treat John the Baptist's message as Luke does, nor his baptismal work as all the Synoptics do. He is interested in the Baptist solely for his testimony to Jesus (John 1:7). For John's Gospel, John is less John the Baptist and more John the Testifier.

What precipitates the testimony is the sending of priests and Levites, experts in issues of Jewish purity, to ask John about his ministry. The "Jews" send this delegation of inquiry. In John's Gospel, "Jews" often is not a reference to all Jews but to the Jewish leadership that ends up being hostile to Jesus or that challenges his practices (2:18; 5:10, 16, 18; 6:41; 7:1, 11; 8:52; 10:31; 11:8; 18:14; 19:7, 12). John refuses to identify himself as the Christ, as Elijah returned to announce the end, or as the prophet, probably a reference to the prophet like Moses (see Deut. 18:15). John is less interested in explaining who he is than what he does. So he presents himself as one who is "a voice crying in the wilderness, 'make straight the way of the Lord.'" The allusion to Isa. 40:3 is similar to the Synoptics except that here John gives the testimony directly, while there the narratives supply the connection (Matt. 3:3; Mark 1:3; Luke 3:4). John sees himself preparing the nation for the eschatological way of the Lord.

John's refusal to identify himself with Elijah has raised questions with interpreters because Luke 1:17, Matt. 17:12, Mark 9:13, and the Synoptics' use of Mal. 3:1 all make a connection between John and Elijah. Two observations might resolve the difference. First, perhaps John is denying that he is the ascended Elijah returning to earth as Jewish expectation held (2 Kings 2:11; *1 Enoch* 90.31; 89.52; Sir. 48:10). In other words, although he might function like Elijah (i.e., in the spirit of Elijah), he is not the same person. Second, John might not fully appreciate the "prophetic" role that he has even though he is not Elijah returned from heaven. Jesus suggests in Matt. 17:12 that to see John as Elijah is something one needs to be able to accept, suggesting that John's role might be slightly different from the expectation or a fresh twist on it.

John's denials raised a second query. If John is not the Christ or Elijah, why does he baptize? How can he explain his ministry? The suggestion in his reply that a stronger one comes after him is that the baptism is merely preparatory for the main ministry that follows his. As a "washing," it pictures the cleansing that really is yet to come. John repeats and elaborates on this idea in 1:33, where he notes that a baptism of the Spirit, not of water, is coming. These remarks also parallel the Synoptics, including the reference to John's sense of humility in the face of the greatness of the coming one. As was noted in unit 19 above, John's unworthiness to untie the thong of a sandal is an admission that he is not worthy of a task that was considered below Jewish slaves (*b. Ketubbot* 96ᵃ).[14] John the evangelist specifies that this testimony took place in Bethany of the Transjordan region.[15]

After the Gospel surveys how John defined himself and his baptism, it turns to discuss John's testimony to Jesus' identity. The Baptist makes two points here: (1) Jesus is the Lamb of God, who takes away the sins of the world, and (2) Jesus will baptize with the Spirit, showing that he is God's Chosen One or Son.[16] The association of Jesus with Spirit baptism has been made to show how one can identify the presence of the Christ in the Synoptics (esp. Luke 3:15–16). The core of John's witness stems from the sign given at the baptism: the one on whom the Spirit descends and remains. This is the

14. Whitacre, *John,* 66–67. This talmudic passage is a later text, but it is a second witness to this teaching, suggesting its ancient roots.

15. On the locale of Bethany, see D. A. Carson, *The Gospel according to John,* Pillar New Testament Commentary (Grand Rapids: Eerdmans, 1991), 147, also n. 1. He equates it with the region of Batanea (= Bashan in the Old Testament) and argues that alternate spelling, frequent in Hebrew and Aramaic, explains the reference to Bethany.

16. The issue of which title is named in 1:34 is part of a textual problem that is quite difficult to decide. In favor of "the Son" of God stands the bulk of the best manuscript evidence (Papyri 66 and 75; Codices Sinaiticus [corrected], Alexandrinus, Vaticanus, and Ephraemi). It also is the easier reading because it is easy to see a scribe changing "Chosen One" to the more familiar "Son," especially in light of John's use of the Son title. In contrast, some good manuscripts do read "the Chosen One" of God (Papyrus 5 [probably], Codex Sinaiticus [original], and some of the Old Latin). Papyrus 5 has a break at this point, but has room only for a reading of "Chosen One." Interestingly, both "Son" and the idea of "Chosen One" are present in the voice citation at the baptism of the Synoptics, because the idea that God is pleased with his "beloved" is a way of expressing his choice of Jesus (cf. Luke 9:35). The difference does not greatly alter the meaning except as to which aspect (sonship or chosenness) is being highlighted. In either case, it is the authority to baptize with the Spirit that is proof that the promise has come and that the greater one to come has this role.

one who ranks before John because he was before John, in the sense already noted above in treating John 1:15. This is the reason that John gives for his own work of baptizing: "that he [Christ] might be revealed to Israel." Again we see how focused John the evangelist's treatment is. He does not bring to bear any other element on his discussion of the Baptist but his role as testifier, and that includes the way the baptism is summarized. For this Gospel, John merely points to Jesus.

More interesting and controversial is John's testimony that Jesus is "the Lamb of God who takes away the sin of the world." What exactly does this affirm, and how can it be attributed to John when he seemed to be uncertain of the potency of Jesus' ministry in the Synoptics (as is seen in his question to Jesus in Matt. 11:3 and Luke 7:20)? The proposed options for this expression are so numerous as to be intimidating.[17] In essence, they break down into allusions to one of three concepts. Is it to suffering for sin (whether Passover imagery, the lamb led to slaughter of Isa. 53, of daily sacrifices, the scapegoat, the sacrifice of Gen. 22, or of a guilt or sin offering)? Is it explicitly only to the Servant of Isa. 53? Or is it to the triumphant Lamb of apocalyptic hope (*Testament of Joseph* 19.8–9; *Testament of Benjamin* 3; conceptually, *1 Enoch* 90.9–12, 38; also Rev. 5:6, 12; 7:17; 13:8; 17:14; 19:7, 9; 21:22–23; 22:1–3)?[18] Are the new covenant backdrop of the promise of the Spirit and the idea of a shepherd at work here, so that Jesus is *the* Lamb, who leads the sheep? Note how John's confession of Jesus as the Lamb in 1:36 leads to the confession of Jesus as Christ in 1:41. The problem is that no clear, specific background from among the sacrificial images decisively commends itself. Many argue that it is the idea of lamb in general in all its facets that is alluded to and not any particular specific background. Another problem is that the more sacrificial imagery apparently did not "stick" with the disciples who came from John the Baptist; the Synoptics make clear that they struggled to appreciate Jesus' suffering and that the Baptist had uncertainty about Jesus later on because of Jesus' more "humble" ministry style. An interpreter could argue that the Baptist spoke better than he knew, like Caiaphas does later, but the problem with this view is that it is John as testifier that is highlighted here.

17. See Leon Morris, *The Gospel according to John*, rev. ed., NICNT (Grand Rapids: Eerdmans, 1995), 126–30; Carson, *John*, 149–50. Morris and Carson note nine and ten options, respectively. See also Brown, *John I–XII*, 58–63; George R. Beasley-Murray, *John*, WBC 36 (Dallas: Word, 1987), 24–25. Earlier treatments include E. W. Burrows, "Did John the Baptist Call Jesus 'Lamb of God'?" *Expository Times* 85 (1973–74): 245–49; C. K. Barrett, "The Lamb of God," *New Testament Studies* 1 (1954–55): 210–18. One of the problems treated is that John uses *amnos* here and in 1:36 (only other New Testament uses: Acts 8:32; 1 Pet. 1:19) versus *arnion* in the Revelation texts. However, this rare use of this term argues against the usage being a creative Johannine one.

18. Whether the *Testament* references are pre-Christian is disputed, but there is reason for thinking that is likely. See J. C. O'Neill, "The Lamb of God in the *Testaments of the Twelve Patriarchs*," *Journal for the Study of the New Testament* 7 (1979): 2–30.

What seems clear from the entire portrait of John the Baptist in both the Synoptics and John is that Jesus for him was a powerful figure who would bring victory and judgment. This would seem to lend weight to the victorious dimension of the portrait. What also might suggest a more apocalyptic, prophetic background is the juxtaposition in this passage of forgiveness of sins and the coming of the Spirit, a combination that one sees in the new covenant eschatological hope of Jer. 31 and Ezek. 34–36. The fact that the removal of sin is expressed in the collective ("the sins of the world") also could suggest this background. John pointed to Jesus as the Chosen One, the long-awaited one who would bring the Spirit of the promised new age and the forgiveness that such a provision implied. It is here that the lamb image could be applied to Jesus by John and have its roots in the Old Testament picture of sacrifice. It was not because John the Baptist anticipated Jesus' sacrifice, but that his ministry would provide forgiveness like a sacrifice for God's people. It is as Leader-Lamb that Jesus takes away the sin of the world, a point also supported by the fact that the verb αἴρω usually means "to remove" or "to take away," not "to bear" as in an atoning death. The fact that the connotation of the term can take up additional meaning pointing to sacrifice in light of the whole of Jesus' story is part of the Johannine escalation that could have made the remark attractive to John, who loves double entendre.

Thus, the Johannine witness of the Baptist highlights Jesus as the one who takes away sin and brings the Spirit, themes that Luke also treated in connection with Jesus' coming (Luke 1:76–79; 3:15–17). It is against this backdrop that the first disciples of Jesus appear in John's Gospel.

J3. The First Disciples: Andrew, an Unnamed Disciple, Simon Peter, Philip, and Nathanael (John 1:35–51)
(Aland §21)

John now turns to discuss how some became exposed to Jesus. The catalyst was the Baptist's testimony, reaffirmed from 1:29, that Jesus is the Lamb of God (v. 36). Two of John's disciples, Andrew and an unidentified disciple, heard the remarks and followed Jesus. It seems likely that the unidentified disciple is John, apparently the one whom the Gospel refers to as the "beloved" disciple, although the point is inferred and not clearly proved. Many point to the detail in the account as indicative of deriving from a witness.[19]

Sometimes an effort is made to pit this account against the "call" of Peter and others in Mark 1:16–20 and parallels, arguing that the two accounts can-

19. Morris, *John*, 136; Carson, *John*, 154. For another view, see Beasley-Murray, *John*, 26–27.

not be reconciled. But John's passage involving Peter is not really a call text. It simply recounts how Andrew and Peter initially encountered Jesus. As such, this event may well come before the "call" of the Synoptics.

Their initial meeting with Jesus causes the teacher to ask what they seek. Respectfully calling Jesus rabbi, a title meaning "great one" and often applied to a teacher, they ask Jesus where he is "staying." The verb used here, μένω, will become theologically significant later in John. Here, it is a generic use of the term. They wish to know where he is residing, so that they may be with him. The implication seems to be that they wish to be students of his teaching. Jesus accepts the request by telling them that they may come and see. It was toward the end of the day, the tenth hour (about 4 P.M.). Jesus does receive those who seek to know him better.

Andrew goes on to tell his brother Simon about Jesus. To Simon he articulates their hope that Jesus is the Messiah, the Christ (1:41). In the line of the narrative, this expectation is the result of John's testimony that Jesus brings a powerful forgiveness and the promise of the Spirit, for the key figure of the eschatological age of deliverance and righteousness in the Jewish view was the Messiah. Upon meeting Simon, Jesus takes charge, giving him a new name, Cephas, which means "rock" ("Peter" is the masculine variation of the Greek word for "rock" [*petra/petros*], while Cephas is the equivalent in Aramaic). The exchange serves to underscore how a person who becomes engaged with Jesus takes on a fresh identity in him. The scene emphasizes the impact of Jesus and his insight as the one who is the anticipated Messiah.

The second scene has Jesus take the initiative, unlike the first scene, in which potential disciples initiate the exchange. John continues to present a sequence of days as someone goes into Galilee. The Greek text is not clear whether Jesus, Andrew, or Peter is meant; it simply says "he." If Andrew or Peter is meant, then everyone in the chapter has a witness that leads another to consider Jesus. The problem with this suggestion is that neither Andrew nor Peter is elsewhere in this scene. Thus, it is more likely that Jesus is meant and initiates the event.

Jesus issues an invitation to Philip to follow him, a call to discipleship. Philip is yet another witness besides Peter and John the Baptist who goes on to speak of what has been found in Jesus (see 1:41 above), namely, the one of whom Moses and the prophets wrote. What had been a "blank" to be filled in was realized now in the person of Jesus of Nazareth, son of Joseph. Philip makes this claim to Nathanael. The claim evokes a touch of sincere skepticism. Nathanael's honest question is whether anything good could come out of Nazareth. No messianic expectation involved such a location, and the locale also was apparently the object of regional derision. Philip's response is not defensive. He simply invites Nathanael to take a look.

Jesus greets his arrival with a declaration that indicates that he knows Nathanael's attitude. Here is a man in whom there is no guile, that is, no deception.[20] He was honest in his questions, but open in taking a look. When Nathanael asks how Jesus knew him, Jesus replies that he saw him under the fig tree before Philip called him. The issue is not, as many have speculated, what Nathanael was thinking about under the tree or even any possible symbolism of the tree, but that Jesus had an awareness of his whereabouts that was beyond normal human understanding.[21] Nathanael responds immediately with a confession of Jesus as both "Son of God" and "King of Israel," expressions that were synonymous in Judaism. Jesus was the promised one, as Philip had proclaimed to him.

Jesus then challenges his inquirer, "Do you believe because I saw you under the fig tree? You will see greater things than these." As part of the literary narrative, the remark serves to prepare the reader for a series of seven signs that Jesus will perform in John 2–12 to underscore and develop the confessions of this chapter.

Of all the signs, however, the key thing to be seen by many will be heaven opened up and angels ascending and descending on the Son of Man. Jesus' remark is to "you all," a plural that indicates that others besides Nathanael will see these things. Jesus' point is that what is to be seen is an "open connection" between heaven and earth as the Son of Man ministers in their midst. Jesus as the Son of Man is the "ladder" between heaven and earth, sent with divine endorsement. The allusion to the language of Gen. 28:12 recalls how God had come down to support Jacob. So also it would be with the divine support of the Son of Man. This title was encountered in the Synoptics as Jesus' favorite way to describe himself. The Son of Man is a human figure who has received divine authority. John uses the term thirteen times in association with remarks about the cross (3:14; 8:28), revelation (6:27, 53), and an end-time figure (5:27; 9:35–39). What will emerge from this account is that the Messiah is only the beginning point as the way to describe Jesus.

Conclusion

The introduction to John's Gospel is about confessing who Jesus is. The prologue has highlighted him as a preexistent figure who became flesh. Jesus reveals God because he was with God and is God. He also is light, the revealer of who God is and what God is doing. John the Baptist was the first witness, seeing the divine confirmation in the descent of the Spirit upon Jesus, an act that allowed the Baptist to appreciate that Jesus was the victorious Lamb of

---

20. There is no reference to Nathanael as a "true" Israelite. The term ἀληθῶς is adverbial, as in all other Johannine uses (4:42; 6:14; 7:26, 40; 8:31; 17:8).

21. For a discussion of the options, see Brown, *John I–XII,* 83, who rightly calls all such ideas "pure speculation."

God, who would bring forgiveness and a baptism with the Spirit. So some of John's disciples took the initiative and followed Jesus. They followed him in the hope that they had found the Messiah, the King of Israel. Just as with Luke, this narrative starts with a messianic base as the actual story of ministry begins. But John the evangelist suggests that greater things than this will be seen and realized by the one with eyes open, like Nathanael, to see. It is John the evangelist's invitation to read on for the rest of the story. Heaven has opened up, and angels are prepared to show divine support for the human endued with divine authority. Good things can come out of Nazareth because the real origin is from above.

THIRTEEN

The Book of Signs

Before the Hour (John 2–12)

One of the themes of Part II (chs. ii–iv) is the replacement of Jewish institutions and religious views; and Part III (chs. v–x) is dominated by Jesus' actions and discourses on the occasion of the Jewish feasts, often again by way of replacing the motif of the feasts. Jesus is the real temple; the Spirit he gives will replace the necessity of worshipping at Jerusalem; his doctrine and his flesh and blood will give life in a way that the manna associated with the exodus from Egypt did not; at Tabernacles, not the rain-making ceremony but Jesus himself supplies living water; not the illumination in the temple court but Jesus himself is the real light; on the feast of Dedication, not the temple altar but Jesus himself is consecrated by God. In view of this consistent theme of replacement, it seems obvious that in introducing Cana as the first in a series of signs to follow, the evangelist intends to call attention to the replacement of the water prescribed in Jewish purification by the choicest of wines. The replacement is a sign of who Jesus really is, namely, the one sent by the Father who is now the only way to the Father. All previous religious institutions, customs and feasts lose meaning in his presence.[1]

The Gospel of John breaks neatly after John 1 into two major parts: (1) the book of signs before the hour (John 2–12); (2) the book of glory: the hour of the great sign comes (John 13–20).[2] John 13:1 refers to the hour coming, an indication of the key transition in John. An epilogue in John 21 concludes the Gospel.

1. Raymond E. Brown, *The Gospel according to John I–XII,* AB 29 (Garden City, N.Y.; Doubleday, 1966), 104.
2. My outline of John proceeds slightly differently than Brown's. Brown starts the book of signs in John 1:19, with part 1 comprising John 1:19–51. So in the citation above, he refers to parts 2 and 3 of the signs section. I regard 1:19–51 as part of the introduction of John and Jesus and not part of the book of signs. The signs begin with Cana, as 2:11 notes. One of the difficulties in outlining this portion of John's Gospel, however, is that he also is in the middle of tracing a

My treatment of the rest of John appears in this chapter and the next, concentrating on the major movements within these two sections of signs and glory.

As the citation notes, John narratively argues that Jesus represents and surpasses the realization of Jewish institutions and imagery. However, the idea is not so much that Jesus replaces these older symbols as that he represents their completion and realization. What they could do only as a rite, Jesus did in reality. Thus, just as the Book of Hebrews argues for Jesus' spiritual superiority over Judaism, John narrates a series of signs that reveal the salvation plan of the Father and the unique superiority of the sent Son. The dominant pattern of this section is that of a sign event followed by a discourse, although the opening sign of Cana is a sign event alone. In this way, John is like Acts, which also tends to have some significant event followed immediately by a discourse giving the event's significance.

J4. The First Sign: The Water to Wine at a Wedding in Cana (John 2:1–12) (Aland §§22–23)

Weddings were not simply significant personal events in the ancient world; they also carried important symbolism. The notes of love, joy, and celebration associated with weddings or wine were a picture of the love, joy, and celebration of the messianic times (Isa. 54:4–8; 62:4–5; Jer. 31:12–13; Hos. 2:14–23; 14:7; Amos 9:13–14). Celebration associated with wine also characterized Jewish imagery on this end-time theme (*2 Baruch* 29.5; *1 Enoch* 10.19). Such symbolism also shows up elsewhere in Jesus' teaching (Matt. 22:1–4; 25:1–13), like the somewhat parallel imagery of the banquet (Luke 14:15–24; 22:16–18; Matt. 8:11). So when John calls this miracle a sign in 2:11, it pushes John's reader to see Jesus in these terms. The better wine comes later, after the earlier wine. The good wine comes now. All of this suggests that Jesus pictures the arrival of a new age, in which the full celebration can begin. The imagery is very much like Luke 5:33–39, Matt. 9:14–17, and Mark 2:18–22, especially the remark there about new wine going into new wineskins.

---

linked series of (probably) seven days, starting from John 1:19. So the first sign in John 2 is linked to what has gone before in 1:19–51. The days proceed as follows: day one (1:19–28); day two (1:29); day three and, probably, yet another day (four) with Jesus (1:35–42); day five (1:43–51); day six, an unrecorded travel day; then day seven, called by John "the third day" (counting inclusively—so days five, six, and seven—as was normal in the Jewish reckoning, from Jesus' meeting with Nathanael [1:43–51] in 2:1 (see D. A. Carson, *The Gospel according to John*, Pillar New Testament Commentary [Grand Rapids: Eerdmans, 1991], 167–68). If this reckoning of days is correct, then the Cana miracle takes place on the seventh day and mirrors a work of new creation.

Culturally, what triggers this miracle is that the hosts of the wedding party, a celebration that usually lasted up to a week (Tob. 11:18 [LXX 11:19]), had run out of wine. In a culture that honored hospitality, this would be seen as a social disaster. Mary[3] tries to get Jesus to help. It is not clear that she expects a miracle, because Jesus had yet to enter into extensive ministry and John calls this Jesus' first sign.[4] However, her request does show that she expected Jesus to have the resourcefulness to help the situation.

Jesus' reply raises a key theme to the surface. After an abrupt, but not impolite, rebuke to his mother, Jesus notes that his hour has not yet come.[5] The hour is a key theme pointing to the key time of his death (7:30; 8:20; 12:23, 27; 13:1; 17:1). In other words, the time was not right for him to show himself, nor could his mother have a role in the timing of his revealing himself. Nonetheless, Mary sensed that he would help and told the servants to obey him.

The imagery of the Jewish rites of purification are raised up for attention when mention is made of six stone jars, which preserved water for purification and protected it from uncleanliness (Lev. 11:29–38; *m. Beṣah* 2.3). A measure is about 8 gallons, so 2 or 3 measures (so the Greek) is 16 to 24 gallons for each jar, about 100 to 146 gallons total. This was a big wedding.

What happens next has been described differently. In the first view, Jesus asks that the jars be filled with water, which he directly turns into wine, a vast amount underscoring the wealth of provision in the messianic celebration. In the second view, after the jars are filled with water, Jesus asks the servants to draw water from another well, which is the normal source for water when it is said to be drawn out. It is this separate collection of water from the well, not that in the jars, that is turned into wine. The account is so concise that it is hard to be sure which scenario is intended, though the first description probably is the simpler view. Regardless of which scenario applies, this water is taken to the "steward of the feast," who functioned as a kind of master of ceremonies. By the time it gets to him, it had turned into wine.

The sign is only semipublic, for only the servants, Mary, and the disciples seem to know how this had taken place and who had done it. The work brought credit to the bridegroom, although he had nothing to do with it. Still, the steward tells the groom, "Everyone serves the good wine first, and when the guests have drunk

3. Jesus' mother is never actually identified by name in John's Gospel.

4. The ministry that John describes here took place probably in what today is known as Khirbet Qana, some nine miles north of Nazareth (Josephus, *Life* 16 §86; 41 §207). The location and Mary's action to engage Jesus may suggest that the wedding involves some of her relatives, although we cannot be sure. Joseph has no role in any of the Johannine accounts, except in his status as human father (John 1:45; 6:42).

5. "What have you to do with me?" is a common idiom that can have hostile (Judg. 11:12; 2 Chron. 35:21) or neutral (2 Kings 3:13; Hos. 14:8) force. His address to her as "woman" is not hostile, as John 19:26 shows. It has more the force of "ma'am."

freely, then the poor wine; but you have kept the good wine until now."⁶ Jesus had reversed the potential situation of shame for the groom and had brought him honor in the process. This also pictures how divine deliverance through Jesus' work takes place. The beneficiaries do nothing to earn the benefit.

The result is the first of Jesus' signs. The phrase "first sign" could mean a primary sign, as the symbolism here is foundational. In other words, the point is more than a mere numbering of the sign. Jesus also is said to have manifested his glory, a reference to his power even over the creation. The disciples are said to have believed in him. The journey of their growing, deepening faith and understanding of Jesus has taken another step here. It is the first of many steps in their faith.

No discourse accompanies this event, unlike other sequences in this first section. In one sense, perhaps, the explanatory element that replaces the discourse is the following scene of the cleansing of the temple, which alludes to the great sign that God will perform for Jesus and to which all Jesus' signs point, including this first one at Cana.

A final verse notes that they returned to Capernaum to stay there for a few days. The next scene picks up at some unspecified point after this stay.

J5. The Cleansing of the Temple and an Allusion to Resurrection, the Great Sign (John 2:13–25) (Aland §§24–26)

This event is well known in part because of the difference in chronology from its Synoptic counterpart. What John has early in his Gospel, all the other Gospels place in the last week of Jesus' career. Many simply argue that there was only one cleansing, almost ruling on the matter before considering the option of two cleansings.⁷ The accounts' differences do merit consider-

---

6. This is real wine, although in the ancient world such wine is said usually to have been diluted with two or three parts water, making it weaker than unadulterated wine (see Carson, *John,* 169; Leon Morris, *The Gospel according to John,* rev. ed., NICNT [Grand Rapids: Eerdmans, 1995], 157 n. 18). The remark about the dilution of wine comes from an editor's note in the Soncino edition of the Talmud on *Pesaḥim,* 561 n. 7. But *b. Pesaḥim* 109ᵃ notes that the rabbis held, "There is no rejoicing save with wine." That real wine is meant is clear from other texts that urge people not to get drunk with wine (e.g., Eph. 5:18). Carson says that its resultant alcoholic strength is less than that of an American beer. Estimates are that, undiluted, the wine had about 15 percent alcoholic content, compared with 12–13 percent for modern wines. The term for grape juice was another Greek word (τρύξ); see under οἶνος, BAGD, 562; BDAG, 701 §1.

7. For example, Brown, *John I–XII,* 117, writes, "That we cannot harmonize John and the Synoptics by positing two cleansings of the temple precincts seems obvious. Not only do the two traditions basically describe the same actions, but also it is not likely that such a serious affront to the Temple would be permitted twice." The first argument that Brown makes does not follow. Any temple cleansing would involve a certain overlap in detail. These accounts also possess important differences between them, such as the Scriptures appealed to and Jesus' remark about destroying this temple, which is only in John. As for the idea that this event could not happen twice, a first occurrence would have caught

ation that two cleansings are intended.[8] The sequence of three Passovers in John clearly leaves the impression that this is the first Passover visit of Jesus, suggesting a chronological frame for the event. Not only are there numerous differences of detail, including which Scripture was noted, but also the dispute at Jesus' trial about what the false witnesses say about the "destroy the temple" remarks suggests that a period longer than a week has passed since they were made (Mark 14:55–59).[9] It is plausible that this incident, if it took place twice, would not have caused such a great stir the first time, since Jesus was still unknown. It is also easy to see why a repeat of the offense would have met with more solid reaction, because now it was no longer a careless overstepping act of excessive enthusiasm.

On the other hand, there is the possibility that this event took place only once. If so, it is likely that what John did was move it forward as a type of foreshadowing capsule of Jesus' conflict with the leadership and their failure to appreciate his authority. In favor of this view might be the point that 2:23 alludes to numerous signs that Jesus had done in Jerusalem when none have yet been described in John. It is harder to imagine the Synoptists moving an earlier event later, since the temple cleansing sets off the series of controversies of the last week. Neither option is impossible, although two cleansings seem slightly more likely because the differences between the accounts outweigh the similarities, and each Gospel seems to give a specific setting to the cleansing each describes.

Regardless of how one takes the chronology, a look at the event shows how it raises the issue of Jesus' authority. Jesus is in Jerusalem observing the Passover, as was his custom (2:13; 11:55–56).[10] In the outer temple court (ἱερῷ) was a service provided for the convenience of worshipers. It involved selling oxen, sheep, doves, and pigeons for sacrifices, with doves or pigeons functioning as the sacrifices given by the poor (Lev. 5:7). The service meant that pilgrims traveling long distances did not need to travel with the sacrificial animals, which had to be kept spotless in order to qualify. In addition, money

---

everyone by surprise, while the second, at least two years later if John's Passover chronology is followed (6:4; 11:55), would have come after things had "settled down." If the precedent on blasphemy is any example, it is possible to warn someone and then hold them culpable a second time (*b. Šebuʿot* 36ᵃ; *b. Sanhedrin* 38ᵇ in an incident involving Rabbi Akiba; note also the repetition in Acts 3–5, where Peter and John are warned and released and then brought in again with a repeated offense). These counterarguments do not require a second cleansing, because it is possible that a literary relocation of a typical event has taken place (see the placement of Luke 4:16–30 versus Matt. 13:53–58). What they do suggest is that the decision is not as clear-cut as some make it.

8. Carson, *John,* 177–78; Morris, *John,* 166–69.

9. It is important to note how the Johannine backdrop does seem to inform that Markan trial scene, showing an important complementary overlap in the traditions.

10. Some think it possible that 5:1 also indicates a Passover feast.

changers provided the coins for the half-shekel temple tax because Roman denarii and Attic drachmas were disallowed currency (*m. Bekorot* 8.7 says that Tyrian coinage qualifies).[11] It may be, as our discussion in the Synoptics noted (unit 231 above), that this service recently had been moved into the temple court area.[12] The possibility of animals getting loose and profaning the temple was very real, given this locale.

So Jesus makes a whip, probably from branches, and drives out the money changers along with their animals, while turning over their tables. As he commands them to leave, he proclaims that they should not be transforming "my Father's house into an emporium" (i.e., house of trade). There is a probable allusion here to Zech. 14:20–21, which is a description of the messianic kingdom. There, the Hebrew word translated "Canaanite" also can be translated "merchant" or "trader." Thus, in the messianic era, no trade would be permitted in the temple. Jesus' act is seen in messianic terms as a purifying act to get the temple ready for the new era. It might be better to say, if one takes the early placement of this event as key, that the act was an eschatological purification whose exact force would not be initially clear to those who experienced it. They might have seen such a cleansing initially as a kind of prophetic challenge, which it was as well. In the context of Jesus' later ministry, its full force would become clear. However, in John, the possibility that Jesus is the Christ already has been noted in John 1, so the narrative sees it as a messianic act.

It was a belief of Judaism that the new era would come with a purity of worship, including a righteousness that the Messiah would bring about (Isa. 9–11; *Shemoneh Esreh,* benediction 14; 4QFlor 1.6–17). If the question was where did Jesus get the authority to do this (cf. v. 18), his reference to his Father's house is a clue to the answer.[13] The disciples connect the event at some unspecified point to Ps. 69:9, which describes the faithful heart of a righteous sufferer for God. Here the remembrance recognizes that it is out of a righteous zeal for God's house that Jesus acts.[14] The idea of that zeal consuming him may have a double force in this context. Not only does it impel his action now, but also that devotion and single-minded dedication

11. It is often said that the exchange was required because the foreign coins had images, but so did the permitted Tyrian coins (Morris, *John,* 170). The practice of providing animals is mentioned in *m. Šeqalim* 7.2, but without noting their location.

12. V. Eppstein, "The Historicity of the Gospel Account of the Cleansing of the Temple," *Zeitschrift für die neutestamentliche Wissenschaft und die Kunde der älteren Kirche* 55 (1964): 42–58. He argues that the move was made to give some merchants an advantage over others who sold their wares outside the temple courts in the Kidron Valley or on the slopes of Olivet.

13. In fact, in the Synoptic event, the cleansing produces a dispute about Jesus' authority shortly thereafter (Mark 11:27–33; Matt. 21:23–27; Luke 20:1–8).

14. Given that the significance of what Jesus said elsewhere in the scene is admitted to have been "remembered" later in the disciples' understanding (2:22), that same time frame may well apply here as well.

will lead to Jesus' death.[15] Jesus' concern is for a true, pure worship (John 4:24).

Needless to say, this aggressive deed raised the question of Jesus' authority to perform such a prophetic-messianic act. The Jewish request for a sign is a call to authenticate the right to act as a prophet or a purifying eschatological figure. The expectation is for some cosmic sign from heaven. Instead, Jesus points to what for John will be the great sign that glorifies the Father and the Son: his death and resurrection. He says, "Destroy this temple, and in three days I will raise it up." In a severe misunderstanding of a type that frequently takes place in this Gospel, the Jews, that is, the leadership, think that Jesus is discussing the actual temple building and some type of foreseen destruction (in judgment in light of Jesus' purification?). He will rebuild it in three days! It had taken forty-six years of construction to get the building to this point, and still it was not finished. Certainly, what took nearly five decades to build cannot be rebuilt in three days! John as narrator supplies the point of misunderstanding—Jesus was speaking of his body as the temple. The allusion, then, is to the great sign on which people in John's time and beyond should reflect—Jesus' death and resurrection. It is the great sign that authenticates his claim over the great institutions of Judaism, including the great temple. Students of John often argue that what Jesus is doing here is nullifying the role of the temple by pointing to himself as its replacement. Strictly speaking, this overdraws the point. Jesus has called for a purifying of the temple courts and presented his death and resurrection as the sign that points to his authority to make such a claim over the temple. Jesus' remarks do not serve to argue that he replaces the temple, but to argue that he has authority over its administration. John's point is that Jesus is greater than the temple and is qualified to rule over it. John 2:22 notes that when the resurrection came, the disciples recalled the utterance and believed both the Scripture and Jesus' word. John's remark makes it clear that they did not understand the point at the time of the saying. Another point that John loves to make is that Scripture and Jesus' teaching are one and match up with the events of his ministry. If one is to read Jesus' words and make sense of his work, they must do it "according to Scripture."

John goes on to note that a ministry of specific signs did follow in Jerusalem. In the narrative movement, this may well make the point that Jesus not only responded to the Jews' questions with a cryptic, initial reply that pointed to the final ultimate sign, but also did perform indicative signs to underscore his claims along the way while in Jerusalem.

Many believed when they saw these signs. However, John hints that faith grounded only in Jesus' signs was not really a faith that made for relationship

---

15. John's change of the psalm to a future tense is designed to highlight the prophetic connection that John sees in making Jesus to be one like David, the righteous sufferer of old.

with Jesus, because he did not entrust himself to these people.[16] There is a wordplay here as John uses the same verb for "entrust" in 2:24 that he used for "believe" in 2:23 (πιστεύω). Jesus knew all people and needed no one to explain people to him, because he knew human nature. In a Jewish context, this points to who Jesus is. The later rabbis taught that "what is in the heart of his neighbor" is one of the seven things hidden from people (*Mekilta* on Exod. 16:32 [tractate *Vayassa* 6, lines 60–64]; contrast Jer. 17:10).[17] So here, John again elevates the uniqueness of Jesus by pointing to his understanding, a point already made with Nathanael in John 1.

J6. What Do the Signs Show? Jesus and Nicodemus
(John 3:1–21) (Aland §27)

John's next account is of an evening visit by a leader of Judaism. Here, outside the tensions of a public confrontation, in the quiet of table talk, the two eras meet, one old and the other emerging. When Nicodemus is described as a Pharisee and a ruler of the Jews, he is being depicted as a representative of the "established" Jewish leadership. His appearing at night has been variously interpreted. Was it to meet in secret out of fear, or because of exhortations to study Torah also at night (Josh. 1:8; Ps. 1:1–2; 1QS 6.6–8 [including in the third watch]), or to symbolize Nicodemus's position as one residing in darkness?[18] Given the role of darkness in John (9:4; 11:10; 13:30), one suspects that something ominous stands in the scene's backdrop. There is also debate about the tone of Nicodemus's opening remarks that the signs indicate that Jesus is a teacher from God. Are the remarks ones (1) of faith, (2) of uncertainty as well as openness, or (3) of ironic skepticism? Given the portrayal of Nicodemus in John, it seems best to see them as an honest inquiry (the second choice). Nicodemus has not closed up the options yet and comes to find out more about Jesus. The tone here is different from the confrontational tone of other texts (7:15, 45–52; 8:48, 52). Regardless of these background questions, the narrative sets up the dialogue as a probe of what Jesus' signs actually mean. What, exactly, is he teaching and why?

Jesus' answer, in vv. 3, 5–8, is very direct. Each saying begins with the solemn "truly, truly" introduction to underscore the reply's gravity. A role in the

16. This kind of a distinction about the quality of faith in John is not a matter of grammatical construction (*pisteuō* + *eis* + accusative versus *pisteuō* + dative), but is a function of context (Carson, *John*, 183).

17. Among the other things said to be hidden are the day of death, the day of consolation, the depths of judgment, a person's reward, the time of the restoration of the kingdom to David, and the time when the guilty kingdom will be destroyed.

18. On the options, see Morris, *John*, 186–87; on evening study, see Birger Gerhardsson, *Memory and Manuscript*, Biblical Resource Series (Grand Rapids: Eerdmans, 1998), 236.

kingdom is possible only for the person who is born from above, born of water and Spirit.[19] The process is unseen and full of mystery, just as one can feel the wind but not see it. Jesus' explanation is built around the linguistic ambiguity of the Hebrew and Greek terms for "spirit," which in both languages also can mean "wind" or "breath." What is important to see in Jesus' reply is that new life is said to be the function of a divinely wrought birth, a birth that is inseparably connected to the work of God's Spirit. Here is John presenting his understanding of the gospel. The gospel is about the gift of unending, divinely enabled life, what will be called eternal life in v. 15.

Nicodemus responds with a literal understanding. He thinks that Jesus is referring to starting over in life. Jesus' words seem so odd to him that he depicts them in their seeming absurdity so as to underscore the difficulty. The elaboration that Jesus then gives only reaffirms the point. Jesus highlights in v. 6 that there is an earthly birth involving the flesh and one involving the spirit. When Jesus' elaboration brings Nicodemus's question of how this can be, Jesus rebukes him for not comprehending this idea even though he is a teacher of Israel. The lack of understanding that Nicodemus has is seen as representative of the nation's lack of apprehension. What Jesus is alluding to here are the numerous texts that associated a special work of the Spirit with the final age (Joel 2:28–32; Isa. 32:15; esp. Ezek. 36:25–26; also in some other Jewish texts: *Jubilees* 1.23–25, a slightly more ambiguous reference to the creating of a holy spirit for the righteous; 1QS 4.19–21). The idea of water and wind as symbols of the Spirit can be found in Isa. 44:3–5 and Ezek. 37:9–10. So Jesus, in effect, tells Nicodemus that what he is preaching is not new truth, but one embedded in God's promises of old. Jesus goes on to press the point by affirming in a representational first-person plural and with a solemn "truly, truly" affirmation that "we speak of what we know and bear witness to what we have seen." This may well allude back in part to the bestowal of the Spirit upon Jesus at his baptism as well as explain the roots of his work with signs. The allusion back to John's baptism may also explain the return to discuss John the Baptist after this scene in 3:19–36.

19. This is the only verse in John to mention the kingdom of God, a key concept of the Synoptics. Another interpretive problem is found in v. 5. What does it mean to be born of "water and spirit"? For the options, see Carson, *John,* 191–95, although I prefer to see an allusion to the Holy Spirit here in light of the appeal to Old Testament background (versus Carson's appeal to the sense "spirit"). Some see a contrast between (1) earthly birth and spiritual birth; others speak of (2) Christian baptism plus Spirit baptism; others argue for (3) John's baptism setting the stage for the coming of the Spirit; others argue for (4) a double reference to divine rebirth with the image of water being a way to speak of divine birth. Christian baptism is unlikely because Nicodemus would have no way to process what Jesus is telling him. A contrast with earthly birth, though possible, ignores that fact that both water and spirit share the same preposition. Either of the other two views (view 3 or 4) is possible, but given the tightness of the construction, it is more likely that the two elements are part of the same idea (view 4).

From here, Jesus turns to another contrast between the earthly (his ministry activity) and the heavenly (the sign to come). He speaks to "you all" as he notes what Nicodemus represents as a Jewish leader. Jesus suggests that the Jewish failure to understand what he already has said about the spiritual roots and goals of his ministry means that they will not be able to understand the more "heavenly" dimensions of his work, namely, that he will be lifted up as the Son of Man. Jesus speaks with authority, as one who has descended as the Son of Man, only to ascend one day. Just as the lifting up of the serpent by Moses led to healing for the people who looked to it with believing faith (Num. 21:4–9), so those who believe on the Son of Man in his exaltation will have eternal life. Jesus presents this truth as the Son of Man come from heaven. His origins highlight its authority as he again points, as he did in John 2:19, to the great sign of death and resurrection. Sometimes this text is objected to as pointing Nicodemus to something that he cannot yet understand. The claim is that this must be a text written by the early church. However, what is claimed is that Jesus is revealing in a prophetic way what is going to come to pass. He does so as the Son of Man, who has descended to reveal the Father and his way. Thus, inherent in the passage is the claim to authority, an authority that also knows what the call of God for the Son will be.

At this point, Jesus' teaching in all likelihood stops, and the evangelist summarizes what the previous discussion means, including Jesus' reference to being "lifted up" (John 8:28; 12:32, 34 [all Johannine uses point to this event]).[20] John's summary points to the divine giving up of the Son in death as evidence of God's love for the world. This love reflects God's desire to give eternal life to those who otherwise would perish. Jesus' mission as the Son is to save the world, not condemn it. Belief in him prevents condemnation and gives life. However, to fail to believe is to stand condemned for failing to believe in the spiritual renewal that the Son offers as light. John sees it as a choice for evil and its practices versus the choice to embrace righteousness. Those who refuse Jesus love the darkness because their deeds are evil, and those who are evil hate the light and refuse it so that their practice might not be exposed. In contrast, the one who does truth (cf. Gen. 47:29; Neh. 9:33) responds to the light. The result is that God is seen as having performed deeds for the benefit of the one coming to him. In other words, the spiritual renewal that Jesus discussed with Nicodemus comes by faith and yields a product, in contrast to the deeds of those who live in darkness. John's allusion to a practical righteousness emerging from faith recalls Jesus' emphasis on practical righteousness in Matt. 5–7. In all of this we see

20. In favor of vv. 11–15 being spoken by Jesus versus being the evangelist's comments is the use of the title Son of Man, which always is on Jesus' lips in the Gospels. Then, in favor of a shift to the evangelist at v. 16 are the way in which the cross is expressed as a past event and the reference to the "one and only Son" in vv. 16 and 18, which elsewhere is a phrase only John uses (1:14, 18; cf. 1 John 4:9). See Mary Steele, "Where Does the Speech Quotation End in John 3:1–21?" *Notes on Translation* 2, no. 2 (1988): 51–58.

that eternal life has to do not only with a life that lasts and that escapes condemnation, but also with a quality of life that the Spirit from above brings.

J7. Jesus and John the Baptist—The Bridegroom, the Christ, the One from Above Must Increase
(John 3:22–36) (Aland §§28–29)

The setting for the remarks of John the Baptist is a ministry that the Synoptics do not mention. Jesus and his disciples are baptizing in Judea after he leaves Jerusalem. The remark probably indicates that he left the city to minister in the region at large.[21] John 4:2 says that Jesus himself did not baptize, but that his disciples did. Such an act would express their identification with John's baptism and its role as a preparation for the eschaton. John was at Aenon near Salim doing the same thing. The exact location of Salim is unknown. Both proposed locales, one near Shechem and the other six miles south of Bethshan, are located in Samaria, which is part of the Roman province of Judea.

There arose a debate between John's disciples and a Jew over purification, possibly questioning John's relationship to more established practice, given that his baptism was unprecedented. The discussion led to the observation that people were flocking to the one "to whom you bore witness." John expresses approval of what is taking place, because his ministry is limited to what is given to him from heaven. His role is not to be the Christ, but to be sent before him (1:26–34). He compares his task to being the friend of the bridegroom who is in charge of the details of a wedding.[22] He gladly gives way to the groom when he appears. The idea is similar to remarks by Jesus in Mark 2:19 and parallels. The image of the people of God, whether Israel or the church, as bride is rich in Scripture (Isa. 62:4–5; Jer. 2:2, 3:20; Ezek. 16:8; 23:4; Hos. 2:16–20; 2 Cor. 11:2; Eph. 5:25–27; Rev. 21:2; 22:17). So Jesus is described as the faithful partner to God's people, who is wedded to them in love. John is thrilled to see the arrival of the promised one. So the Baptist's joy is full because the ministry and status of Jesus, referred to emphatically as "that

---

21. Some see here a relocation of this passage from an earlier locale, arguing that since Jesus already is in Judea when he is in Jerusalem, he cannot come "into" Judea (see Brown, *John I–XII,* 150–53). Others correctly argue that "the land of Judea" is a way to refer to the countryside (Carson, *John,* 209).

22. In Judaism, each family supplied a groomsman (1 Macc. 9:39), but the illustration is simplified here for the sake of the comparison, and the Talmud says that the custom was not followed in Galilee (Morris, *John,* 213 n. 110). The point would be the same regardless of how many groomsmen there were. Some refer to the role of the *shoshbin* here (*m. Sanhedrin* 3.5). See C. K. Barrett, *The Gospel according to John: An Introduction with Commentary and Notes on the Greek Text* (London: SPCK, 1955), 186; A. van Selms, "The Best Man and the Bride—from Sumer to St. John," *Journal for Near Eastern Studies* 9 (1950): 65–75.

one," must increase while John must decrease.[23] The point is underscored by the use of the Greek term δεῖ, which points to divine design.

The language shifts in 3:31 to a more generic reference to the "one from above" and "the Son," which suggests that now the evangelist is speaking.[24] It supplies the explanation for John's view. Jesus is "the one from above." The use here, in parallelism to "comes from heaven" later in the verse, shows that "from above" is meant. The remark also suggests that John 3:3 means the same thing. The point is that Jesus has come from heaven, while John is a prophet come from the earth. The one from heaven is "above all."[25] The remark looks to the comprehensive authority that the sent one possesses.

Jesus now is portrayed as giving witness to what he has seen and heard. Jesus speaks for God in heaven and reveals his way (John 1:11–12). John loves to say this again and again. However, that testimony is not received by the world. Anyone who does receive it sets a seal on the fact that God is true. The seal here is a technical term in Greek for giving approval on a legal document. This is because the heavenly witness utters God's words and has been given the Spirit without limit, or as John's Gospel says, "without measure."[26] In later Judaism, *Leviticus Rabbah* on Lev. 15:2 said of the prophets, "The Holy Spirit rested on the prophets by measure." So Jesus again is affirmed as being more than a prophet here. The groom is a heavenly sent Messiah-Son. Standing behind his enablement is the love of the Father for the Son (John 5:20; 10:17; 15:9; 17:23–24, 26). Also present is the Father's gift to the Son of putting "all things into his hands." This authority extends even to life, so that belief in the Son leads to eternal life. In contrast, disobeying the Son, failing to respond to his testimony, means that one will not see life because God's wrath remains or abides on that person.[27]

J8. Jesus and the Samaritan Woman—Worship in Spirit and Truth (John 4:1–42) (Aland §§30–31)

The setting of Jesus' discussion with the Samaritan woman follows a brief remark about his moving his ministry to Galilee. The note makes the point

23. Joy is an important theme in John (15:11; 16:24; 17:13; cf. 1 John 1:4; 2 John 12).

24. It is unlikely that Jesus is the speaker, because he is not present in this scene except as a topic for discussion.

25. There is some text-critical uncertainty about this phrase. If it is omitted, then the point is about Jesus as the one giving testimony (the remark about the one from heaven [v. 31] picks up the phrase in v. 32a): "The one coming from heaven testifies to what he has seen and heard." John likes repetition, so the fact that 31c repeats 31a (about Jesus coming from above) is not a surprise. Good witnesses omit the phrase "above all" (𝔓[75], ℵ, D), so it is hard to be sure which reading is original, although it is easier to explain the phrase being dropped by a copyist as repetitious than to see a copyist adding it. It is slightly more likely to be original.

26. For three options of the interpretive dispute here, see Morris, *John*, 218.

27. This is the one mention of God's wrath in John.

that Jesus moved his ministry because the Pharisees had heard of his having greater success than John. It also notes that Jesus himself did not baptize, but that his disciples did so for him.[28] This note appears to qualify what was said in John 3:22. The detail also surfaces a difference between the Synoptics and John: John's indication that Jesus did have a ministry outside of Galilee before pursuing the bulk of his work in the north. Mark 1:14 seems to suggest a move to Galilee after John's arrest and the implication of a call to disciples after this move. However, it is an impression versus a contradiction in fact that is present. Its cause may be simply that John chose to cover the earliest phrase of ministry, while Mark did not. It may be that Mark begins with what turned out to be the decisive calls of Jesus to his disciples, where they left their vocations to follow him.[29] Jesus had to pass through Samaria to go from the south to the north most directly. This was a common route, as Josephus shows, despite the animosity between Jews and Samaritans (*Ant.* 20.6.1 §118; *War* 2.12.3 §232; *Life* 52 §269).

The meeting with the Samaritan woman took place at Sychar in Samaria. This locale appears to have been near Shechem, possibly at the village of Askar, about one mile from Jacob's well and located on the shoulder of Mt. Ebal, opposite Mt. Gerizim. The well was one hundred or more feet deep.[30] Jesus is tired and finds himself there at the sixth hour, or noon.

What Jesus does next is surprising for two reasons. First, he speaks to a woman. Second, she is a Samaritan. The Mishnah indicates that Samaritan women were regarded as perpetually unclean. *Niddah* 4.1 argues that these women are menstruants from the cradle. If Jesus drank from a vessel handled by this woman, he would be regarded as unclean because many Jews would regard her as communicating ritual impurity to the vessel. In John 4:27, the disciples are surprised to see Jesus speaking with a woman, a practice also discouraged by the rabbis. Mishnah *'Abot* 1.5 argues that to speak much with a woman, even one's wife, was a waste of time and a diversion from the study of Torah. Such talk risked bringing evil on someone. Another text debates whether one should teach daughters the Torah (*m. Soṭah* 3.4; in fairness, the issue is debated, with some rabbis in favor of such instruction). John 4:9 points to the unusual nature of Jesus' initiative, explaining that "Jews have no dealings with Samaritans." This probably is a reference not to a total disassociation, but to avoiding the use of vessels from Samaritans.[31]

28. The imperfect tense in the Greek here may suggest only that Jesus did not regularly baptize (Morris, *John*, 223 n. 7).

29. See the suggestion of Carson, *John*, 215.

30. Ibid., 219.

31. David Daube, "Jesus and the Samaritan Woman: The meaning of συγχράομαι," *Journal of Biblical Literature* 69 (1950): 137–47. Some of the tone of discussion may be reflected in *m. Šebiʿit* 8.10, where rabbi Eliezar says, "He that eats the bread of Samaritans is like one that eats the bread of swine."

Jesus reverses the whole feel of the discussion. Rather than being worried about how unclean he is likely to get, he stresses what he could offer her if she realized who is speaking with her. If she knew the gift of God, which shortly will be described as "living water," and who is speaking to her, namely, one with the capability to give it, she would be asking him and would receive that gift of living water. Jesus' allusion here has Old Testament roots. The image of the eschaton involving a place where living water flows appears in Zech. 14:8 and Ezek. 47:9. More generic water imagery tied to the end appears in Isa. 12:3; 44:3; 49:10; and especially 55:1–7. An image of water that cleanses comes from Ezek. 36:25–27. The remark is ironic because many would have regarded Jesus as having become unclean if he had contact with the woman. The negative image of abandoning living water is in Jer. 2:13. John loves this imagery (3:5; 4:10–15; 7:38; esp. 6:63). So Jesus is speaking of a divine provision tied to the life-giving Spirit, which is a way that John refers to the gospel.

The woman misunderstands Jesus, thinking that he is speaking of well water and that he lacks a bucket to draw the water. So she asks, probably iron-ically, if Jesus is greater than Jacob, who provided a well that has served for so many years. Jesus replies by speaking of the water he gives, which will allow one never to thirst, as the imagery from Isa. 55 implies with its everlasting cov-enant. This water will leap up from within unto eternal life. The verb for "welling up" is used in the LXX of the Spirit falling on someone (Judg. [B] 14:6, 19; 15:14; 1 Kingdoms 10:2, 10 [= 1 Sam. 10:6, 10]; and esp. Isa. 35:6). The woman, still thinking of real water, asks for this water so that she will not have to make any more trips to the well.

Jesus turns from what he offers to reveal who he is. He asks her to go and find her husband. She replies that she has none. Jesus responds with her life history. She has had five husbands, and the one she has now is not her hus-band.[32] The woman, recognizing Jesus' insight, concludes that he is a prophet.[33] So naturally she then turns to ask him to address a nagging theo-logical question. It is not clear that she is deflecting the discussion from her-self, because it would be only natural to put such a question to an expert. The debate is whether one should worship at Mt. Zion, as the Jews did, or at Mt. Gerizim, as the Samaritans did. The Samaritans appealed to Gerizim as the first location mentioned in the sacred Torah where Abraham worshiped (Gen 12:6–7). Jesus replies that an hour is coming when the issue will be not where

32. There is no symbolism in this reference to five husbands, so correctly Brown, *John I–XII*, 171, who, although regarding it as possible, argues that John gives no indication of it.

33. Less clear is whether she sees Jesus as "the" prophet, the Samaritan Taheb (one to come), who was described as a revealer in the style of Moses, based on Deut. 18:15. This is possible but not certain. The lack of an article with "prophet" in the Greek does not necessarily speak against this possibility, but the text itself is not clear enough to suggest this more specific sense.

God is worshiped, but how. Although Jesus acknowledges that salvation is of the Jews, an hour approaches and now is when true worship of the Father will be in spirit and truth.[34] The reply hints at a new era and structure for worship, an era that has come. God seeks such worshipers, and such worship must (δεῖ) be given. This leads naturally into the question about the great figure of the promised new era, the Messiah. She asks about the Messiah, who will "show us all things." Jesus replies simply, "I who speak to you am he," returning the dialogue to the point about her needing to know who was speaking to her in John 4:10. John's point is that more than a prophet is here. The Messiah, the one who can give life from the ongoing supply of the Spirit, is here.

The sequence is theologically significant. The Messiah is the giver of the Spirit. The Spirit is given in a way that leads to eternal life. As living water, the Spirit works from within, creating worshipers of the Father who worship in spirit and truth. Rather than being concerned with external issues of location, God seeks people who can worship him anywhere from within. Jesus is the bearer of that gift. The text gives a summary of the gospel, which is about a promised new, unending quality of life in fellowship with God, grounded in his Spirit.

It is at this point that the disciples show up, amazed to see Jesus having this mixed-gender conversation. In engaging the woman, Jesus has crossed barriers of both race and gender. They will not be obstacles to his offer of the gift. The woman departs to the village and gives an uncertain witness to Jesus. She is clear that he knew all about her and asks, "Could this be the Christ?" The question is asked with the Greek interrogative μήτι, which expects a negative reply. She broaches the subject tentatively. The remarks cause those in the village to come out to see Jesus.

Their approach leads Jesus to address his disciples. Now the issue of mission is raised. The occasion is again a natural concern that Jesus turns into a spiritual lesson. The disciples want him to eat the bread they had purchased and brought. Jesus states that his food is that which they do not know. In context, this reflects the sharing of the living water that he just engaged in with the Samaritan woman. His lack of interest in eating the bread makes the disciples think that he already had received some food. This is the third case of Jesus being misunderstood by his remarks being read as dealing with physical reality (rebuilding of the temple in John 2; being reborn in John 3). Jesus repeats himself and notes that his food is to do the will of the one sending him and to accomplish his work (cf. Deut. 8:3; Luke 4:4; 8:19–21).[35] John loves

---

34. It is not clear whether Jesus intends to discuss a worship in genuine human spirit and truth or is alluding to the Holy Spirit and truth here. Perhaps Jesus' focus on the Spirit as the gift tied to water may place a slight advantage to a reference to the Spirit here. On the other hand, what the giving of the Spirit may do is produce a genuine worship from within the person. It is hard to be certain which is meant.

35. The reference to "*my* food" in v. 34 is emphatic by Greek word order.

to describe Jesus as the one sent and the Father as the sender (5:23–24, 30, 37; 6:38–39; 7:16, 18, 28; 8:16, 18, 26, 29; 9:4; 12:44–45, 49; 13:20; 14:24; 16:5). There is a unity of labor and spirit here. This means that the disciples need to appreciate that there are not four months to harvest, as is normally the case. Seed is sown and the fields already are white, ready to be harvested. In a text like Mark 4:26–29, the harvest looks into the future at the end, but here in John, it is "realized eschatology," just as the "hour now is" when the Father provides worshipers for himself regardless of location. The time has come to collect the harvest of those enabled to worship the Father in spirit and truth through the sent one and by the Spirit.

So Jesus speaks positively of the reaper (the disciples) receiving wages (reward) and gathering fruit that leads to eternal life, so that the sower (Jesus) and reaper (disciples) may rejoice together. That Jesus is the sower and the disciples are the reapers is clear from the "sent" language present in John 4:38. Jesus' note that others have labored so that they may reap may well suggest that the witnesses who sowed the word include John the Baptist and the message of Scripture, especially Moses for these Samaritans. In other words, from Moses to the Baptist, the message was prepared so that Jesus could sow the word that now yields fruit. The result was that many Samaritans did believe. Their witness joined the woman's as Jesus had revealed the way of the Father and the promise of the Spirit through Jesus to them. This is why they could confess Jesus as "Savior of the world," an expression with rich roots in the ancient world. For the ancients, a savior could be a person, such as Asclepius the healer or Hadrian the emperor, or a god, such as Zeus.[36] John's point is that the true Savior is not any one of those, but the one who delivers living water unto life, Jesus Christ.[37] Interestingly, it is the "foreign" Samaritans who make the point that Jesus' work is for the world.

J9. The Second Sign: The Healing of a Royal Official's Son (John 4:43–54) (Aland §§32, 85)

Another illustration of Jesus' power over life follows in the healing of the royal official's son. Two preliminary questions need treatment before we look at this second sign. They are the setting of this event and whether it is the same as the Synoptic healing involving the servant of a centurion in Matt. 8:5–13 and Luke 7:1–10.

Jesus stays in Samaria for a couple of days before departing for Galilee. John then remarks that "a prophet has no honor in his own country." This remark also shows up in Matt. 13:57 = Mark 6:4 = Luke 4:24, texts involving

36. Barrett, *John*, 204.
37. In the Old Testament, it is God who delivers (Ps. 24:5; Isa. 12:2; see Luke 1:47).

Jesus' rejection in Nazareth. What is puzzling is that Jesus seems welcomed by the Galileans in John 4:45, and there is no note of rejection yet in Galilee in John's Gospel. This has led some to posit that John portrays Judea as Jesus' home and as a place of rejection. However, this does not work either, because there really has not been any note of rejection in John's Gospel yet, only questions from the leadership (John 2:18). Moreover, John is clear that Galilee is Jesus' place of origin (1:45–46; 7:41, 52; 19:19). What seems to be going on is three things at once. First, John is contrasting Jesus' time in Samaria with his coming back to the land of the Jews, primarily Galilee, but not excluding necessarily Judea. Second, John's remark about rejection anticipates what is going to be taking place, not what has taken place. Thus, it is a reminder to the reader that Jesus will suffer rejection, just as John 1:11 declared. Third, although Jesus is welcomed here by the Galileans, it is in light of his miraculous work, something that John works to portray as superficial if that is all that draws one to Jesus.

A second question is whether this event equals the Synoptic healing from a distance involving a centurion. Many commentators take the text this way, pointing to the fact that this is a healing from a distance and that the situation involves a soldier figure from Capernaum.[38] But a case can be made for two distinct miracles.[39] There are numerous differences between the two accounts. (1) The soldier in the Synoptics is a Gentile centurion. In John he is a royal official of Herod's army, making him more likely a Jew. In John 4:48, he is compared with the miracle-seeking Jews. The term "royal official" (βασιλικός) refers to someone attached to the king (tetrarch) Herod Antipas (4 B.C.–A.D. 39), as Josephus's use of the word shows (*War* 1.1.5 §45; *Life* 72 §§400–402). (2) It is a slave (δοῦλος) who appears healed in Luke, while it is a son in John.[40] (3) In the Synoptics, Jesus heals in Capernaum, while in John, he is in Cana, near Capernaum. (4) Most importantly, in the Synoptics, the faith of the centurion is praised as being of the highest quality, while in John, there is a rebuke for seeking signs. (5) In the Synoptics, the centurion tells Jesus not to bother to come to his home, while in John, the official asks Jesus to come to the home. These details are enough to suggest distinct events.

As Jesus comes back to Cana, the scene of the wine miracle, an official in Capernaum is tending to a sick son. He goes to meet Jesus to beg the teacher to come and heal his son, who is at the point of death. Interestingly, John has not yet portrayed a healing, so this healer reputation for Jesus must have been circulating on the basis of things that John has not told. The request

38. So Barrett, *John*, 205; Brown, *John I–XII*, 192–93. Brown explains the differences between the accounts as differences between independent traditions.

39. So Morris, *John*, 288, although some of his contrasts seem overdrawn in light of ambiguities between Matthew and Luke.

40. Matthew has the ambiguous παῖς, which ordinarily refers to a servant but also could refer to a son.

brings a rebuke from Jesus: "Unless you [plural, making the official representative of others] see signs and wonders, you will not believe." John 2:23–24 had suggested this focus on miracles alone as already being a problem (cf. 6:26). Jesus' direct and challenging response resembles the way he treated the Syrophoenician woman in Mark 7:27 and his mother in John 2:4. Despite the challenge, the man asks Jesus to heal the boy. Jesus simply tells the official to return home, promising that the son lives. The man turns to go home, believing in Jesus' word. Here is the life-giving power of Jesus' word, effective even from a distance. The miracle illustrates the claim that Jesus is the Savior of the world (John 4:42). It also makes a claim on those who hear the claim.

The revelation of the miracle causes a growth in the official's faith. As he returns, the servants meet him to tell him that his son lives. When the official asks when the boy got better, the reply is at the "seventh hour" (1 P.M.). The official realizes that this was the very time of his conversation with Jesus and the moment when Jesus uttered the promised word of healing.[41] So the official and his whole house believe. The official had moved from faith in seeking a miracle to an appreciation for and trust of Jesus the person. The unit closes by noting that this was the second sign, tying this healing back to the opening of this section of John in 2:1–11. Jesus has shown how he brings the new era of the new wine. He brings the new birth. He brings the living water. All of it means that he is the Savior, the provider of life. John's Gospel has stayed focused on who Jesus is and what he does. To believe in him is to have access to life.

J10. The Third Sign: A Controversial Sabbath Healing in Jerusalem (John 5:1–18) (Aland §§140–41a)

This miracle raises the stakes in John. It presents a Sabbath healing that raises the first explicit note of controversy in John, although hints of the leadership's nervousness about Jesus were raised in John 2:18. The event itself is fairly straightforward, but it is the reaction and the aftermath that produce one of Jesus' most important discourses in John.

The setting of the healing is an unspecified feast. Much speculation exists on which feast is meant, with Tabernacles and Passover being the prime

---

41. An account of "healing from a distance" also appears in the Talmud (b. Berakot 34b). While in an upper room, Rabbi Ḥanina ben Dosa prays that God will show mercy to Rabbi Gamaliel's sick son. The outcome is made to rest on whether ben Dosa senses God's enablement as he prays. If the prayer flows smoothly, it is a sign that the person will be "accepted" (i.e., get well); if the prayer is difficult, then the person will be "carried away" (i.e., die). After the healing, the rabbi refuses to be called a prophet or the son of a prophet. Thus, although this account also involves healing from a distance, there is no effort to highlight the healer, putting the emphasis on God's choice as prayer is made.

candidates and Trumpets and Purim also suggested. There is too little information to decide. John notes the detail only to explain why Jesus is in Jerusalem. The location probably is in the general vicinity of what later became known as St. Anne's pool. The pool by the "Sheep Gate" was trapezoidal, measuring 165 to 220 feet wide by 315 feet long.[42] There were four colonnades plus one on the partition, making up the five porticos that John mentions. The location of the "sheep pool" was in Bethesda.[43] Associated with the site was a tradition of healing from being placed in the waters (v. 7).[44]

One sick man, who was an invalid of some sort, becomes the object of Jesus' attention. He had been incapacitated for thirty-eight years. When Jesus asks him if he wishes to be healed, he points out that he has no one to lift him so that he could be first into the special waters. Jesus has nothing to do with the waters and simply tells him to take up his pallet, which would have been made of straw, and walk. Instantly the man is healed, gets up, and walks. Muscles that would have been atrophied now worked.

However, there was a problem. It was the Sabbath. The Jews believed that "taking out anything from one domain to another" was prohibited on the Sabbath (*m. Šabbat* 7.2). The only exception would be to carry a paralytic (*m. Šabbat* 10.5 allows a person to be carried on a couch, but to carry a couch alone is not allowed). Technically, Jesus has not violated the Sabbath but has led another into doing so. Sabbath controversies also abound in the Synoptics (Mark 2:23–28; 3:1–6 par.; Luke 13:10–17; 14:1–6). There, Jesus claims to be Lord of the Sabbath. In John, he claims authority through his associative work with the Father.

The controversy flares up when the Jews tell the man that he is violating the Sabbath. The man explains that he is only following the orders of the man who healed him, a man whose identity he does not know. Later, Jesus encounters the man again and tells him to sin no more, after noting how he is healed. Jesus warns the man that something worse than his previous malady awaits him if there is no response. Jesus is alluding to judgment here. The man, hardly a paragon of faith, goes and informs the Jews that Jesus had healed him. John attributes the rise of official persecution against Jesus to his doing "such

---

42. Brown, *John I–XII*, 207.

43. A text-critical problem shows there was debate about how John presented the name. Options include Bethsaida, Be(th)zatha, and Bethesda. Texts at Qumran (3Q15 col. 11.1.12) suggest that Bethesda is correct. The name means "a house of pouring out," but John makes nothing of the name. The site is near the temple, on the eastern hill of Jerusalem.

44. This tradition receives elaboration in an early textual addition to the text that shows up in some English translations in vv. 3b–4. These verses were added to John; the manuscript evidence for the reading is late, and the variation of the additional clauses in the manuscript tradition argues for its inauthenticity (Carson, *John*, 242).

things" (ταῦτα is plural) on the Sabbath. Thus, we have but one representative act of many that offended the leadership.

Jesus' explanation of his action was even more offensive than the effort to heal on the Sabbath. Jesus said, "My Father is working still, and I also am working." Three points are important. First, Jesus calls God "my Father," denoting an intimacy of relationship unparalleled in Judaism. The claim revealed how Jesus saw himself as closely connected to God. Second, the Father continues to work on the Sabbath. This was a popular Jewish view, the idea being that life could not be sustained if God did not continue to labor on the day of rest. Philo explicitly claimed that God never ceased his creative activity, noting that after the sixth day of creation God caused things to come to rest but did not himself come to rest (*Allegorical Interpretation* 1.2–3 §§5–6). *Exodus Rabbah* 30.6 has four rabbis make the point that God need not rest, since the world and the creation are his home, so he can roam through it and be in his own courtyard. The third point is the one that causes offense, because Jesus claims to work as the Father does. Thus, because of the association they have and their joint work, Jesus claims to be able to work on the Sabbath as God does. In fact, the healing is evidence that God has healed and worked through Jesus. That is the point of Jesus' claim. John notes how the remark heightened the desire of the leadership to kill Jesus, because "he not only broke the sabbath but also called God his own Father, making himself equal with God." This functional co-laboring on the holy day of rest is what the Jews considered to be blasphemous. What other people were commanded to do, rest on the Sabbath, Jesus claimed he did not need to do. A close look shows how similar John's form of the Sabbath argument is to Jesus' Synoptic claim that he is Lord of the Sabbath. The Synoptics stress Jesus' position and authority; John stresses the relational foundation behind such a claim.

J11. The Discourse Defending the Sabbath Healing—"The Son Does Nothing of His Own Accord" (John 5:19–47)
(Aland §141b)

This discourse develops the issues raised by the Sabbath healing of the invalid. It is the Gospel's most focused discussion of the unity between the Father and the Son. The dominant feature is how the mission of the Father and Son are totally united. This affirmation is balanced by the Son's submission to the Father. The Son follows the Father and does only what the Father shows. One statistic indicates how unique this discourse is. The absolute use of the title "Son" appears thirteen times in this Gospel, but eight of those uses are in this discourse.[45] There is an uninterrupted communion but also an equality in the context of submission.[46]

The discourse itself comes in three parts: an articulation of the unity (vv. 19–24), the Son's bestowed authority over life and judgment (vv. 25–30), and the witnesses for Jesus (vv. 31–47). Embedded in this last subunit is a critique of those rejecting Jesus.

In discussing his unity with the Father, Jesus affirms his sonship as one that does nothing out of his own accord or initiative. Whatever the Father does, the Son does.[47] Thus, the two form an inseparable unit in their activity and exercise of authority. It is the functional unity that is highlighted here. However, that unity is grounded in a love relationship between the Father and the Son. This relationship leads the Father to show the Son all that the Father is doing. God is the actor, and the Son is the mediator. This frees up the Son to do even greater things in magnitude than the healing they have just observed. Those "greater things" are tied to the authority bestowed on the Son by the Father, an authority over life and judgment, as Jesus is about to describe.

What the Father does is raise the dead and give life. This is one of his unique and great powers. Such a view of God has rich Old Testament roots (Deut. 32:39; 1 Sam. 2:6; 2 Kings 5:7; Dan. 12:2). This idea also was argued in Judaism.[48] Jesus now argues that this unique authority also is in the hands of the Son. In fact, the Father has given all judgment into the Son's hands, just as the Father has willed that honor be shared equally between the Father and the Son. The two are so united that to fail to honor the Son is to fail to honor the Father. To believe that the Son shares this authority over life and embrace it is to have eternal life. It is to pass from death to life and no longer be subject to judgment.

45. Morris, *John,* 277. An absolute reference is one where "Son" appears without qualifying descriptions such as "of God" or "of Man."

46. Two quotations from Chrysostom, *Homilies on St. John* 38.4, nicely expound the balance. "What then means, 'Can do nothing of himself'? That he can do nothing in opposition to the Father, nothing alien from, nothing strange to Him, which is especially the assertion of One declaring an equality and entire agreement." Later, in reference to submission, he says, "You say that the expression does away with his power and his proper authority, and shows his might to be weak; but I say this proves his equality, his unvarying likeness (to the Father), and the fact that all is done as it were by one will and power and might."

47. It is sometimes suggested that John has adapted what originally was a parable of a son apprenticed to his father's trade, an image that fits the culture and a view going back to C. H. Dodd, *Historical Tradition in the Fourth Gospel* (Cambridge: Cambridge University Press, 1963), 386 n. 2. Although this is possible, there is no evidence for it from this text. Such a connection remains speculative.

48. See *b. Ta'anit* 2[b]: "rain, the womb, and the raising of the dead (Ezek. 37:13) are in God's hands"; *Shemoneh Esreh,* benediction 2: "Blessed art thou, O Lord, the shield of Abraham. Thou art mighty forever, O Lord; thou restorest life to the dead . . . quicken the dead. . . . Who can be compared to thee, O Lord, who kills and makes alive again? . . ." Only Elijah is sometimes placed in this role as a human.

All of this would be startling to Jewish ears, which venerated the uniqueness of God. Power over life was a matter of God's creative power. Jesus' claim is twofold. (1) He so shares in the authority of God, including authority over life, that the two work inseparably together. (2) However, none of this is a self-claim. It is an authority bestowed by the Father. Thus, to reject the claim is to reject what the Father has willed and set in place. This is why Jesus will highlight the role of witnesses later in the discourse. This is Jesus' explanation and challenge to his listeners.

Life is something that Jesus offers not just in the future but even now. He announces that an hour is coming and now is when the dead will hear the voice of the Son and will live. In this context, "hear" means to believe the Son and embrace the message of life that he brings. Here is a taste of John's "realized eschatology," in which the judgment of the end has broken into the present and is based on how one responds to the appointed judge, the Son. This is because the Father has granted to the Son that he have life in himself (authority over life) just as the Father has. This includes even the right to judge, because the Son is also the Son of Man. This is an allusion to the bestowed authority that the Ancient of Days gave to "one like a son of man" in Dan. 7:9–14.[49] The Son of Man will preside over a judgment to come in the future, which is set up by response now. Those who do good receive life, while those who do evil receive judgment. "Doing good" contextually begins with responding to God's revelation in the Son. As other chapters in John will show (John 7, 14–16), in response to faith Jesus will give the Spirit, who will enable God's children to walk in righteousness. In judging, the Son carries out the will of the Father and does not act on his own authority, judging truly. Here, Jesus affirms how united in will and perspective the Father and the Son of Man are.

Now Jesus turns to the issue of witnesses. He begins by noting that if he only bore witness to himself, that testimony would not be true. What is needed are witnesses beyond himself. That is precisely what he can offer. This list of witnesses makes the case for his claims. Jesus is claiming in vv. 31–47 that one fundamental witness stands behind all the witnesses that he will mention. That key witness is the Father, whose testimony is true (v. 32). His goal in pointing out such witnesses, especially one such as John the Baptist, is that his audience might be saved (v. 34).

---

49. The anarthrous construction "son of man" in the Greek of John 5:27 looks back to the image of "one like a son of man" in Daniel. Even though the reference is not to "the" Son of Man in John 5:27, clearly it is this image that is being appealed to here. The detail is important as one considers the historicity of these remarks. Son of Man is the most widely attributed name that Jesus used for himself, and it is the functional unity of authority that is the key to the imagery associated with this use as a title. The Synoptics also show this emphasis, although John develops the point more explicitly.

The first witness that Jesus points to is John the Baptist. This was a witness they rejoiced in for a while. He was "a kindled and shining lamp [ὁ λύχνος]." The image here is of a portable lamp of the ancient world, in contrast to a self-kindling light (φῶς) as Jesus is described in John 1:8 (also John 1:4; 8:12). In this way, John was like what Sir. 48:1 said of Elijah, whose words burned like a lamp.[50]

Now, Jesus' witness and teaching are greater than the work of John, who is merely a witness, because Jesus has greater works that the Father who sent him gave him to do. This is the second witness, the testimony of the Father through his works. When Jesus acts, God speaks. No one can do what Jesus does without the support of the Father. This may well allude to a whole series of things, including the authority over life already mentioned as well as the fact that John did no miracles. Jesus goes on to claim that he has the witness of the Father, someone his audience has never heard or seen and whose word does not abide in them. How can Jesus say such a strong thing? It is because they do not believe in the one whom the Father has sent.

This leads to the third witness, which is the Scripture. There is a fundamental difference in how Jesus and his audience view Scripture. The audience thinks that when they search the Scripture (and here we think primarily of Torah), it possesses eternal life.[51] Jesus reads Scripture and thinks of it revealing God's promise. The Scripture bears witness to Jesus. In addition, life is found through him, so in refusing to come to Jesus, they refuse to enter into life. They also refuse to believe the Scripture's witness.

Jesus picks up a side question next by noting that he does not seek human popularity and approval. He also addresses directly the problem of Jewish unbelief. Jesus knows that his rejecting audience does not love God, because he has come in his Father's name, as his work and these witnesses attest, and yet they do not receive the sent one. Even worse, if another comes in his own name (and thus not the Father's!), they will receive him. Jesus alludes here to following a series of leaders that are not commissioned by God. Jesus' rebuke continues in a question that actually is a rebuke. How can anyone believe who seeks glory from one another but does not seek the glory that comes from the only God? Of course, Jesus' point is that such an approach never will embrace God's way and messenger.

50. This image is common (Matt. 5:16; *b. Šabbat* 116[b]).

51. There is debate here whether "search" is indicative, referring to the practice of Jews reading the Scripture, or imperative, calling them to search the Scripture. In this context, where what they think Scripture contains is in view, the indicative should be read. Jewish thought often emphasized the life found in the law. According to *m. ᵓAbot* 2.7, Rabbi Hillel taught that if a man "has gained for himself the words of the Law, he has gained for himself life in the world to come." Baruch 4:1–2 reads "This is the book of the commandments of God, and the law endures forever; all they that hold it fast are appointed to life."

So they stand accused. However, it is not Jesus who accuses, but their very own hero, Moses, the one in whom they hope. Moses will make the accusations before the Father, because Jesus claims that Moses wrote of him. So to believe Moses is to believe in Jesus, "for he wrote of me."[52] Thus, the fourth witness is Moses. This may allude to Deut. 18:18 or it may refer to the whole of the promise. Failure to believe Moses leads to failure to believe Jesus and his teaching. If a person's hope does not appreciate what the one who is hoped for says, then how can the promised way to life be recognized when the hope comes? The discourse ends with this reflective question hanging in the air. It is a classic example of a literary open ending. The listener/reader is left to ponder the question, its truth, and to respond appropriately.

So Jesus explains that his Sabbath authority is a reflection of the fundamental unity of the Son's (and Son of Man's) work with the Father, including bestowed authority over life. All of this about Jesus' divine connection is supported by four witnesses: John the Baptist, the Father's working through Jesus, the Scripture, and Moses. All these point to the truth that one should believe in the unique sent one in order to have life.

J12. The Fourth Sign: The Feeding of the Five Thousand
(John 6:1–15) (Aland §146)

This is the one miracle that appears in all four Gospels (Matt. 14:13–21; Mark 6:32–44; Luke 9:10b–17). It is appropriate that it would surface, since it shows Jesus as the provider of that staple that sustains life, bread. This miracle is a nice supplement to the previous discourse of Jesus providing life, as well as setting up the bread of life discourse of John 6:22–51. There is a complex discussion concerning whether John's rendering of the event is independent of or dependent upon Mark. All in all, the case is good that John is aware of the tradition that shows up in the Synoptics, while having access to other details of the event. John's account is compressed compared to the other versions, although he does have several unique details.[53]

John has moved abruptly from Jerusalem in John 5 to Galilee in John 6, giving the locale as the other side of the Sea of Galilee, which by John's time also was called the Sea of Tiberias, named after a city created on its shores in

52. John 5:46 is a class two "if . . . then" conditional clause, so it means, "If you believed Moses [but you do not], then you would have believed in me."
53. Barrett, *John*, 226, argues for dependence, as does Carson, *John*, 267, while Morris, *John*, 300, notes what is unique to John's account: stress on signs drawing the crowd, detailing of Philip's role in expressing the difficulty of purchasing enough bread, Andrew's bringing a boy forward with some food, the time being near Passover, the bread as barley loaves, the reason for gathering the leftovers, the people's reaction, and the dismissal. Brown, *John I–XII*, 236–50, argues for some independence. Clearly, John had access to additional information.

A.D. 26. Josephus also uses this name for the sea (*War* 3.3.5 §57; 4.8.2 §456, where it is called a "sweet and fruitful" lake). Jesus' signs for the sick had drawn a great crowd to follow after him. The lake was located near a set of mountains, from which Jesus taught his disciples. John alone notes that it is Passover, the second such note in John's Gospel (John 2:23). This point is no accident. The Passover was the start of the nation's day of liberation and led in a real sense to their "life" as a nation, including provision of manna to sustain them through Moses' leadership. All of this backdrop will emerge later in John 6 in Jesus' discourse.

Jesus, seeing the multitudes and seeking to test Philip's faith and understanding, takes the initiative by asking how bread can be purchased to feed the people. That Philip is asked is not surprising, because he was the local boy from nearby Bethsaida (John 1:44). That Philip replies as he does also is not surprising, since Jesus did raise the issue of purchasing such bread. It was hardly to be expected that Philip would consider Jesus providing sustenance by his own direct means. What the sequence does, however, is set up the event as an act of instruction for the disciples about who Jesus is and what he is capable of doing. After all, the setting is one of his instructing the disciples. Philip knew that such a purchase would be a major task, costing two hundred denarii, the same figure that Mark 6:37 notes. Because one denarius was a day's wage (Matt. 20:2), this would represent two hundred days of work, or about thirty-three weeks of labor on a six-day work week. The text later says that there were five thousand men present (John 6:10), making a crowd of up to twenty thousand if one were to count women and children. Andrew shows up with meager provisions of five barley loaves (the bread of the poor) and two fish, which came from one of the young men present.[54] Philo (*Special Laws* 3.10 §57) says such bread is "for the use of irrational animals and of needy men." Such a supply hardly would do.

So Jesus has the crowd sit down. He takes the loaves, gives thanks, and distributes as much as the people want of both the bread and the fish.[55] Jesus has the disciples gather up the remainder, so nothing is lost. Just from the leftover bread, twelve full baskets remained. Many see here a symbolism of the twelve tribes of Israel, which is possible. The entire event invokes Jesus' supernaturally rooted ability to provide food and sustenance for life. The Old Testament had precedent for such an act in Elisha's provision for one

---

54. The term for "young man" (παιδάριον) here need not refer to a child; it is used of Joseph at seventeen (LXX Gen. 37:30), of Elijah's servant Gehazi (LXX 4 Kingdoms 4:12, 14, 25), and of a man of marriageable age (Tob. 3:6).

55. The blessing, if it followed Jewish patterns, would have blessed God for the food with expressions such as, "Blessed are you, O Lord God, King of the universe, who brings forth bread on the earth; and blessed are you . . . who gives us the fruit of the vine." The benediction is noted in Barrett, *John*, 230, who notes that nothing that Jesus does in terms of the blessing would be unusual in a Jewish setting.

hundred men (2 Kings 4:42–44). Even more, it is a miracle because of its proximity to Passover, which recalls the manna in the wilderness and evokes favorable and even surpassing comparisons with Moses. There also may be allusions to images of God's provision for any who are needy (Ps. 22:26), or Jewish images of messianic provision (Isa. 55:1–2; *1 Enoch* 62.14). This explains why John calls the work a sign and why the crowd concluded that Jesus perhaps was "the prophet who is to come into the world" (cf. Deut. 18:15–18).[56]

The crowd was correct to see Jesus as the coming one. The miracle made them think of Jesus as a leader-prophet like Moses, or maybe even as the king, the hoped-for ruling Messiah. However, the messianic overtones that the crowd seeks in making Jesus king gives him pause. They do not yet perceive the kind of kingship he intends to bring, an issue that John addresses more fully at Jesus' trial before Pilate (John 18:33–36). This is the same problem that Jesus has with the disciples after they confess his messiahship to him at Caesarea Philippi (Matt. 16:13–23). Jesus' feeding them did not involve a political goal, because his provision highlighted a more spiritual end. After this misunderstanding about kingship, Jesus withdraws to a mountain by himself.

J13. The Fifth Sign: Jesus Walks on the Water (John 6:16–21)
(Aland §147)

This miracle also appears in a similar context in Matthew and Mark and highlights Jesus' authority over forces tied to life and creation. Thus, in this section of John's Gospel, Jesus is giving signs of the extent of his authority. The account is told with extreme brevity in comparison to Matt. 14:22–32 and Mark 6:45–52.

The disciples are working their way back to Capernaum. As often happens on the lake, a strong wind arises, making their progress difficult, although they had made good progress because they were 25 to 30 stadia at sea. A stadion is about 600 feet. The lake is 109 stadia (12.5 miles) by 61 stadia (7 miles) at its longest and widest points. So they were about half way and anywhere from 2.75 to 3.5 miles across the lake. What they saw next frightened them: Jesus is walking on the water.[57] Jesus simply announces to them, "It is

---

56. There is a textual problem here, with the plural "signs" appearing in a few important witnesses ($\mathfrak{P}^{75}$, B); but the better manuscript distribution ($\aleph$, A, D, Byz) favors the singular.

57. Some note that the phrasing of the Greek could mean that Jesus was walking by the sea (i.e., along the shore). Although technically correct as a grammatically possible reading, contextually such a reading makes no sense. It explains neither why this event would be told nor the disciples' fear. John is portraying another sign.

I."[58] The next thing that John narrates is the disciples' joyous reception of Jesus into the boat and their safe arrival on land. Jesus not only had walked on the water, but also he had calmed the seas and brought them home safe. This image of authority and protection is precisely John's point, evoking images of texts such as Ps. 107:23–32, in which God has power over the seas and brings sailors home safe.[59] It is the display of this kind of authority that is the setting for the bread of life discourse, in which Jesus asserts his power over life and sustenance.

J14. The Discourse on the Bread of Life Come Down from Above (John 6:22–59) (Aland §§148–49)

The setting of the bread-of-life discourse involves the crowd's realization that Jesus had crossed somehow to the other side of the lake without journeying with his disciples. The search for Jesus included some from Tiberias who had come to meet him where he had multiplied the loaves and fish only to find that he no longer was there. They looked for him in Capernaum, which was his headquarters. When Jesus is found, they address him as a teacher ("Rabbi"). They ask him when he came, which really inquires more about the manner of his arrival than its timing, wanting him to reveal the route he took and its timing. He does not answer the question but instead turns attention back to the significance of the sign of the multiplication of the loaves and the inappropriate reason that the crowd has shown up.

Jesus accuses the crowd of being drawn to him because of the provision he makes, not to probe what his "signs" mean. So he proceeds to explain the importance of the feeding. The crowd should not journey and labor to find food that will perish. They should seek food that "abides to eternal life."[60] A similar remark about water is made in 4:14. This bread comes from the Son of Man. It is on this key figure that God has set his authenticating seal. This final remark probably explains the ultimate origin of the signs as rooted in the work of the Father through the Son.

58. It is unlikely that Jesus means anything more than an announcement of his presence by this saying. Nothing explicit points to the use of the divine name, "I AM." The elements of divine authority reside more prominently elsewhere in the scene.

59. Brown, *John I–XII*, 255, mentions the later *Midrash Mekilta* on Exodus, as it describes the nation passing through the sea, which taught that God made a way through the sea for himself when humans could not, suggesting an epiphany of divine power here. He cites B. Gärtner, *John 6 and the Jewish Passover*, Coniectanea neotestamentica 17 (Leer: Gleerup, 1959), 17, who notes a citation of Ps. 77:20 (v. 19 in English Bibles) in this *Mekilta* passage. I have been unable to locate this allusion.

60. Note the use of the verb μένω ("abide"), a verb that John works with in a different sense in John 15.

Jesus' remarks about labor and life cause the crowd to ask what works (plural) of God they must do. Jesus rejects the reference to works by redefining the work (singular) that a person must perform: "Believe in him whom he has sent" (cf. John 1:12; Rom. 3:28). The crowd responds by asking for a sign showing that Jesus is this important. The question seems odd at one level, given the signs Jesus already has done. However, the crowd seems to want Jesus to prove that he is one like or greater than Moses. There seems to have been in Judaism an expectation that the Messiah would renew the provision of manna or something like it. So *2 Baruch* 29.8 looks to the return of manna in the eschaton. *Sibylline Oracles* 3.49 looks to its restoration as well in the new age. *Ecclesiastes Rabbah* 1.9 also expects this of the "latter Redeemer."[61] The work of the loaves may have hinted at this, but now they want very specific proof. So they appeal to the example of Moses, even pointing to Exod. 16:4, 15, as well as ideas expressed in Ps. 78:24. Jesus needs to show that he is like Moses.

Jesus corrects them. Moses was not the source of the bread. Such a miracle is the work of God, whom Jesus provocatively calls "my Father." Manna was only a hint of the bread of God that now comes down from heaven and "gives life to the world." Jesus bridges Israel's past to the present by moving from a past tense in 6:32 to a present one in 6:33. The ascent-descent imagery recalls other such concepts in John 1:51 and 3:14–15. The crowd asks for this bread.

Jesus responds by identifying himself as this bread. This is the first of several "I am" statements in John (8:12 [the light of the world]; 10:7, 9 [the door]; 10:11, 14 [the good shepherd]; 11:25 [resurrection and the life]; 14:6 [the way, the truth, and the life]; 15:1, 5 [the vine]). The one who partakes of this bread neither hungers nor thirsts. The mention of no thirst recalls the discourse of John 4 and looks ahead to John 7. Not to lack for sustenance points to the provision's permanence. Old Testament and Jewish background is significant. Sirach 24:21 taught about wisdom through the law (see 24:23): "Those who eat of me will hunger for more, and those who drink of me will thirst for more." Thus, although a person never can get too much of wisdom, there is a sustenance that is superior in that it abides. This is the bread that Jesus offers and is. Eschatology drawn from Isa. 55:1–2 is the ultimate answer to seeking the knowledge of God.[62]

However, Jesus warns them that they have seen him (surely an allusion to his signs) and do not believe. But there are those who will respond. These are all those whom the Father will give to him. They will come to him. Those who come to him he will in no way cast out.[63] Jesus does not perform

---

61. Morris, *John,* 321 n. 88.

62. The comments of Carson, *John,* 289, that the background to this imagery is not wisdom as law but as eschatology is correct. This is because ultimately the hope of the last days allows one to walk in wisdom after God. The work of the Spirit in the person is ultimately in view in this hope.

63. This statement is emphatic, using a double negative οὐ μή.

his own will but that of the one who sent him. Their mission is united, as Jesus already has explained in John 5. Those whom the Father gives to him, he will not lose. The Father's will is that everyone who sees the Son and believes in him should have eternal life, and the Son will raise them up on the last day when judgment is given. It is significant that the right to raise to life is something that Jesus says is his, much like passages in the Synoptics that give this authority to the returning and glorious Son of Man, or passages in Acts that highlight Jesus as one appointed the judge of the living and the dead (Acts 10:40–42; 17:30–31). Just as in John 5, Jesus is affirming an indivisible union between his work and God's. They share a mission and calling, so much so that the mediation of the Son is to be appreciated as the will of the Father. The Father's sovereignty is highlighted here, but in a work that inevitably includes the Son.

This claim to be the bread that comes from above, with the intimate connection that it assumes, leads to Jewish murmuring—such murmuring was a part of the nation's grumbling in the wilderness (Exod. 16:2, 8–9; Num. 11:4–6). They choose to focus on Jesus' earthly relations, Mary and Joseph. How could Jesus possibly claim a heavenly origin?

Jesus does not answer the objection but continues to develop his theme. He repeats the point that he will raise up on the last day those whom the Father draws to him. Coming to Jesus is presented clearly as a work of the Father. The Father points out Jesus as the sent one. Thus, Jesus appeals to the Old Testament teaching that those blessed in the last days "will all be taught by God." Isaiah 54:13 (as well as Jer. 31:34) pointed out that God will teach his people from their heart. Jesus paraphrases Isaiah and sees in it how God eventually woos his people back to him. Such drawing from within will attract those who come to Jesus, and they come to him because they hear and learn from the Father.[64] Part of the reason that Jesus can make this claim is that he alone has seen the Father. He speaks as one who has a unique relationship with God that no one else has shared. The one who believes has eternal life. Jesus is the bread of life. However, he is not like the manna that came down in the wilderness, which the ancestors ate and yet still died; rather, he is bread coming down from above that one eats so that one will not die. Jesus concludes this part of the discourse in 6:51 with a summary. He is the living bread that comes down from heaven.[65] Then Jesus adds a new detail: the bread that he will give for the life of the world is his own flesh. In other words, to provide life for others, he will give his own life. The bread that sustains is the substitute

---

64. A variation and development of this idea will show up in the sheep who hear the shepherd's voice in John 10.
65. In the discourse up to this point, to eat is to believe. To eat is to seek in faith the sustenance that the bread of life provides.

who provides life through his death. This is why Jesus speaks of giving his flesh "for" (ὑπέρ) the world.[66]

As at other points in the discourse (vv. 25, 28, 30, 34, 41), the crowd's reaction causes Jesus to elaborate. In a sense, the discourse is not a speech but a dialogue. Now the Jews' objection is the offensive idea that Jesus could give his flesh to them to eat. As is often the case in John, Jesus' remarks are understood in a crassly literal sense (John 3:4; 4:11) when actually a spiritual reality is being depicted.

It is at this point of Jesus' teaching that a major debate over his meaning exists. Is Jesus speaking of the sacraments here and making an allusion to the celebration of the Lord's Table? That this is the major intention seems unlikely despite the very graphic "munching" that is represented in the Greek term used here for "eat" (τρώγω).[67] First, if this section is primarily about the supper, then it would contradict everything said earlier in the discourse about believing being the only work that God requires (6:29, 35, 36, 40). Second, there is little chance that the original Jewish audience could have appreciated an exclusive reference to the supper. However, it cannot be ruled out that the imagery Jesus uses here to express responding to him in faith could now be appreciated in terms that John's church now celebrated. The image may well suggest the supper to John's readers, but only as a picture of the communion and life that faith brings.[68] The major image is to receive Jesus (cf. John 1:12) and to do so from within as one's spiritual sustenance. This is the meaning of the bread of life considered as a spiritual image. Just as water baptism pictures the washing and the new life that come in the Spirit as the gift of grace, so the supper affirms the communion with the Son by faith that receives him as the bread of life.

Jesus affirms that life is possible only if one eats the flesh of the Son of Man and drinks his blood. The present tense of the Greek participles in 6:54 highlights the abiding, ongoing quality of the faith. This describes identifying with his death and offer of himself, which he has just alluded to as being part and parcel of who he is as the bread of life (v. 51). Those who receive what Jesus offers have eternal life; he will raise them to life in the last day (6:39, 40, 44). Truly, Jesus' flesh and blood are food and drink, leading those who partake into an abiding (lasting) relationship in him. This relationship of Jesus to those who share life through him is like the living relationship that Jesus has through the Father who sent him. In this way, Jesus completes his explanation that he is the bread that came down from heaven, bread unlike that which the

---

66. The preposition ὑπέρ expresses another key theme in John (10:11, 15; 11:50–52; 15:13; 17:19), that is, Jesus' substitutionary sacrifice for others. See Leon Morris, *The Apostolic Preaching of the Cross* (Grand Rapids: Eerdmans, 1965), 62–64.

67. Four of the six occurrences in the New Testament appear here (6:54, 56, 57, 58). See BAGD, 829; BDAG, 1019.

68. For such a reading, see Morris, *John*, 311–15; Carson, *John*, 296–98.

ancestors ate and yet still died. For those who partake of this bread will live "into the age" (i.e., forever). Once again, we see that the gospel in John is about the reception of life with the Father through the divinely sent Son. John closes the discourse by noting that it took place in a Capernaum synagogue.

J15. Reaction to the Discourse: The Offense and the Confession (John 6:60–71) (Aland §§157–58)

This is the final event in John's description of Jesus' Galilean ministry. It depicts the reaction to what has included one of his most exalted claims: to be the bread of life sent from God. Jesus is not merely teacher of Israel, nor is he merely a prophet. He is the source of life, inextricably knitted to the Father's mission of deliverance. The crowd, including some who have been disciples, give a mixed reaction to Jesus' grand claims, with many unable to receive them.

The passage opens with disciples recognizing the greatness of the claims and reacting against them. Where the crowd had heard the discourse in 6:24 and Jews were noted in 6:41, John now notes the response of disciples. As he is prone to do, John divides disciples into those who follow Jesus for a time and fall away, showing their lack of real connection to Jesus, and those who continue to attach themselves to him. This passage summarizes that difference and explains what caused the difference.

The disciples who walk away see Jesus' teaching as too hard to accept. The use of "listen" as accept was set up in 6:45. The saying was too harsh[69] to be believed. Jesus knew how some of the disciples were reacting, because he knew human nature (John 2:25). So he asks them if they take offense (literally, "trip over") what he has told them. If they think these claims are great, then what will happen if they should see the Son of Man ascending to where he was before? This verse in John is stated as an "if" premise without a "then." The idea is left open and needs filling in. What will be their reaction to such an "ascension"?[70] John leaves the result purposefully unstated. Will it cause them to be more offended? Or will it cause them to believe? That is precisely what remains to be seen. John leaves it as a rhetorical question carrying the implication that what Jesus does now is nothing compared to what is to come from the Son of Man in his glorification through death and resurrection.

Jesus returns to the issue of the Spirit, which gives life (cf. John 5:21; 1 Cor. 15:45; 2 Cor. 3:6). The remark may well stand in contrast to a view expressed in 6:42 about Jesus being Joseph's son. To understand Jesus, one should not

---

69. On this use of σκληρός, see Jude 15.

70. Here is another text that assumes Jesus' preexistence and states his relationship to heaven in absolute and unique terms. To ascend to heaven is to return to his real place of origin.

assess him in human terms, as they had done in 6:42, but rather appreciate the spiritual resources he offers. His words are a combination of Spirit and life. Jesus' remarks in John 3 and 4 to Nicodemus and the Samaritan woman set the stage for what Jesus teaches here (see 3:5–6, 8; 4:23–24). They stand in contrast to later Jewish texts such as *m. ʾAbot* 6.7 ("Great is the Law, for it gives life to them that practice it both in this world and in the world to come") and *Mekilta* on Exod. 15:26 ("The words of the Law which I have given to you are life for you"). What others saw embedded in the law, Jesus argues is found in him. Jesus recognizes that some disciples do not believe. John makes a narrative note explaining that Jesus knew who those were who did not believe, including one who would betray him. Belief is not something a person generates; rather, it is given by God. Those who come to Jesus, embracing and understanding who he is, do so because God has given them the understanding (see Matt. 16:16–17). So, some seeming disciples now fall away. They "go out." Their departure exposes the true condition of their hearts, a point made clear in how they are equated in this context with another who will betray, Judas.

The departure of many who cannot accept the claims of Jesus causes him to turn to the Twelve and ask them if they also wish to go away. The question is asked using the interrogative μή: "You will not leave also, will you?" This question expects a negative answer or is asked to express a kind of tentativeness about the topic. Its use here suggests that Jesus has a confidence that the Twelve will not be like those who have just departed. As is often the case, Peter speaks for the group, and he affirms their understanding of Jesus and their confession in three parts.[71] First, Jesus has "words of eternal life," a confession that accepts the premises of everything uttered in the earlier discourse on the bread (6:33, 35, 40, 47, 51, 54, 57–58).[72] Second, they have believed and come to know what is going on. The references to belief and knowing are given in the Greek perfect tense, a point that underscores that the Twelve stand and remain in this belief that they had embraced long ago. Third, it is as "holy one of God" that they accept Jesus. What they recognize about him is that he is set apart uniquely by God. This confession probably serves to embrace the idea that Jesus is "the one sent from above." The promised one is like no other and is greater than Moses, possessing the words of life. Thus, to call this confession messianic may say too little, although Peter does not yet fully appreciate all that he is confessing here. That deeper appreciation will come after the resurrection. This understanding explains why Peter sees no al-

71. Some like to suggest that this event is John's rendition of Peter's confession at Caesarea Philippi. It is better to say that it serves the same function as that event but is a distinct scene. For the difference, see Morris, *John,* 343–44 n. 161.

72. The way in which this scene summarizes all that has been said about life in John 6 shows that vv. 60–71 are connected to the whole of the discourse and not just vv. 25–51, as some argue in trying to make the case that vv. 52–59 are a later addition.

ternative but to embrace Jesus and his teaching. If they do not embrace him, "To whom shall we go?"

Peter's confession risks taking the credit for the decision. Jesus responds by noting that he chose them as the Twelve. Their role is his work. However, one ominous note remains. One of them "is a devil," that is, comes from and will act out of direction from the devil. John is clear that Judas, one of the Twelve, will betray Jesus. Built into the plan was dealing with the presence of sin and evil. The very betrayal that was motivated to stop Jesus will be the means by which he will bring life (6:51). Of course, the Twelve could not fully appreciate the meaning of this at the time, just as they did not apprehend the passion predictions in the Synoptics (Mark 9:32; Luke 9:45; 18:34). They will be able to reflect on such sayings with the aid of the yet-to-be-sent Spirit after the events that he described have come to pass.

Jesus' teaching in Galilee not only is creating a division among the Jews, but also now is even causing some disciples to walk away upon grasping all that Jesus claims. John is clear that there are classes of disciples, and some who attach themselves to Jesus are not really connected to him in a work performed by the Father. Those who come are drawn to Jesus because God has performed a work in their heart that causes them to embrace Jesus, as Peter does. In contrast, others are like Judas, their connection to Jesus being temporary and not from the heart.

J16. Jesus Goes from Galilee to Jersualem (John 7:1–13)
(Aland §§238–39)

Jesus continues to travel in Galilee, avoiding Judea because the Jewish leadership sought to kill him (cf. John 5:18). This unit explains how Jesus came into Judea. The move was associated with the celebration tied to the Feast of Tabernacles, the most popular of the Jewish feasts (Josephus, *Ant.* 8.4.1 §100, says that it was "especially sacred" and was regarded as "important by the Hebrews"). The feast celebrated the gathering of grapes and olives, as well as other produce (Exod. 23:16; Lev. 23:33–36, 39–43; Deut. 16:13–15; Zech. 14:16–19; *m. Maʿaserot* 3.7, produced material is tithed; *m. Bikkurim* 1.6, 10; *m. Šeqalim* 3.1). It also commemorated God's provision in the wilderness, so people lived in booths for a week. It fell about six months after Passover (John 6:4).[73]

Jesus' brothers, who will not come to faith until after the resurrection, still have advice for him. They believe that he is wrong to be tucked away in a cor-

---

73. Morris, *John*, 348–49, notes how John skips over six months of Jesus' work without mentioning anything. This shows how selective the Gospels are in recording only certain events.

ner in Galilee. A potentially great figure of God who wishes to be known openly and to the world must work in the most public and central of locales. That means going to Judea, where disciples there can see "the works." The idea is not that disciples in Judea have not seen Jesus' work, but that Galilee is not the place from which to launch a movement that claims to represent the hope of Israel. This is good advice from a worldly perspective. Jesus will challenge it by showing that he will not work in this way.[74]

Jesus replies that the specific time (ὁ καιρὸς ὁ ἐμός) when he will make his decisive display has not come, while their time (ὁ καιρὸς ὁ ὑμέτερος) is always here.[75] They can go to the feast whenever they wish, but Jesus must be directed to the time at which to show himself. This is because his brothers are not hated by the world, since they are a part of it. Jesus, however, exposes the evil of the world and so is hated. Thus, he must be careful about how he conducts his ministry. So his brothers should go to Jerusalem. Jesus will not go at this time, because his time is not yet fulfilled. As unusual as this discussion is, the text shows that Jesus is aware of the tension that he is causing and will be quite intentional when he shows up in Jerusalem.

So after his brothers go to the feast, Jesus goes, not openly (7:4), but in a more reserved way (7:10), probably unattached to any large caravan. He goes in a way that would not attract undue attention, "hidden." The situation in Jerusalem is tense; the leaders are looking for him and the crowd is discussing him. Two public views prevailed. Some saw Jesus as a "good man," but others believed that he was leading the people astray, a charge that remained a part of the official Jewish perspective, as Luke 23:2 and some Jewish rabbinic texts indicate.[76] All such discussion took place in hushed tones; no one spoke openly of him "for fear of the Jews." This is another reference to the leadership. The crowds seem to sense that they are watching out for him. John's Gospel is tracing the rising hostility and opposition to Jesus in this period, much as Luke 9–13 did.

J17. Jesus Teaches in the Temple to Mixed Reaction
(John 7:14–52) (Aland §§240–41)

Jesus' first developed instruction in Judea shows how controversial his ministry was. Jesus' ministry was grounded in major claims for his commission

74. Brown, *John I–XII*, 308, shows how conceptually parallel this advice is to one of the temptations (the temple display) of the Synoptics.
75. The Greek term καιρός points to a specific time and a specific calling for Jesus. This is not yet "the" time.
76. See chapter 1 of my *Studying the Historical Jesus* (Grand Rapids: Baker, 2002) and the discussion of Jesus as a sorcerer.

and work. Jesus' claim to teach what the one who sent him has revealed and his claims about being the messianic giver of the Spirit split the Jewish crowd. It also heightened the desire of the highest Jewish leaders, the chief priests (who would be Sadducees) and Pharisees, to stop Jesus. The unit has a clear structure that is repeated twice: Jesus teaches (vv. 15–24, 37–39), the audience reacts (vv. 25–31, 40–44), and the leaders seek to arrest Jesus (vv. 32–36, 45–52). Jesus' ministry and claims create tension because they force decisions. One cannot understand him and remain neutral toward him. This chapter outlines the nature of the debate that swirled around Jesus.

Jesus shows up in the middle of the feast to teach openly in the temple. When in the midst of the eight-day celebration is not specified, but it was not at the start or the finish. As was common for a rabbi, Jesus teaches in the temple. Although the public nature of his teaching was risky, he sensed that teaching in the midst of a feast with such rich symbolism was appropriate now. How Jesus drew on Tabernacles symbolism will become clear when Jesus associates water and Spirit in John 7:38–39. The teaching leaves the Jewish crowd amazed because Jesus was not formally trained as a man of rabbinic letters. This reaction to Jesus allows him to affirm once again that his teaching has its roots in the one who sent him. If someone really wants to determine whether Jesus speaks from God, that person can determine whether Jesus speaks from his own authority, distinct from God, or from God directly. Jesus claims that he does not seek his own glory (cf. John 4:34), but is true and speaks truly as he seeks to glorify God.[77] John's Gospel has consistently made the point that Jesus' message is attested to by the Father in part through the signs that Jesus works. This is a second claim to integrity. His works are true, as is his message.

Jesus challenges the Jewish audience in two steps. In contrast to his claim to have integrity, the Jewish crowd is not righteous, because they claim to follow Moses and yet seek to kill him when killing is outlawed. In fact, Jesus places his audience in a dilemma. Is he a true messenger from God to be heeded? Or is he a false prophet who should be executed (see Deut. 13:1–3)? The view of those seeking to stop Jesus would be that they were upholding the law. For them, Jesus possesses a demon and should be stopped (cf. Matt. 12:24; Mark 3:22; Luke 11:15). Such an act is not killing. The question and the situation turn entirely on the source of Jesus' authority. But Jesus has a second ground of appeal that such hostile reaction to him is inappropriate.

Jesus presses his point by looking at Jewish practice with respect to Sabbath law (see Exod. 31:15). He looks back to his Sabbath miracle detailed in John 5:1–18, which originally got him into so much trouble in Judea.[78] That mir-

---

77. Only God (John 3:33; 8:26) and Jesus (here) are said to be true in John's Gospel.

78. That Sabbath activity was a major point of contention between Jesus and the leadership is seen in the Synoptics as well. It was his Sabbath activity, including a miracle in Mark 2:23–3:6 and parallels, that got him into decisive trouble in the Synoptics.

acle had caused them to marvel, a point probably made with irony since it did not lead to faith. Their claim was that Moses' law had been violated. And yet if they think about circumcision, a rite that predates Moses and goes back to Abraham, then there is an act of labor that *is permitted* on the Sabbath because it, as an act of faithful relating to God, transcended any law about Sabbath labor. This was a fact that even the Jews knew and practiced. Even they hold that the command of Lev. 12:3 overrides any Sabbath restrictions (*m. Šabbat* 18.3: "All things required for circumcision do they perform on the sabbath"; *m. Šabbat* 19.1–2; *m. Nedarim* 3.11: "Rabbi Jose says, 'Great is circumcision since it overrides the stringent sabbath'"). If one can allow circumcision on the Sabbath, how can one complain that a person is restored to well-being on the Sabbath? So the crowd need not judge by outside appearances but by a right judgment that sees clearly into the heart of the matter.[79] Jesus' insight into such matters shows that he is on the right side of the argument.

Jesus' public teaching and the failure of the authorities to arrest him lead to the crowd's speculating that perhaps the leaders know that Jesus is the Christ, although the question is expressed tentatively, using an interrogative (μήποτε) that expects a negative reply. However, against this conclusion is their knowledge of Jesus' origin: the belief held by some Jews was that when the Christ appears, no one will know where he comes from. The idea of a hidden and suddenly revealed Christ took on various forms in Jewish hope. Some apocalyptic texts suggest that the Messiah is hidden from before the creation, only to be revealed when he acts (*1 Enoch* 48.6; *2 Baruch* 29.3; and the later *4 Ezra* [= 2 Esdras] 7:28; 13:51–52, possibly rooted in Dan. 9:25). Another Jewish view, noted by Justin Martyr, held simply that the Messiah would be born of flesh and blood, but that he would not be revealed until he acted to deliver Israel (*Trypho* 8.7). Thus, the question here seems to involve Jesus doing work in public before he actually delivers and without a "sudden" appearing.

Jesus responds by challenging whether they really know from where he has come. Regardless of his place of birth, Jesus really is sent. He has not come of his own accord. The one who has sent him they do not know, but Jesus does know him because Jesus comes from him, the one who sent him. This declaration of unity of mission recalls John 5 and splits the crowd. Some seek the opportunity to arrest him, but they cannot seize him yet because Jesus' "hour" had not yet come. The language suggests that a divine plan is at work. Others believed in him. They were convinced by his signs, asking the question, "Could anyone do more signs than he has done?" The question, asked with

79. Interestingly, a later talmudic text, *b. Yoma* 85[b], defending healing on the Sabbath to save a life, reads, "If circumcision, which attaches to one only of the 248 members of the human body, suspends the Sabbath, how much more shall [the saving of] the whole body suspend the Sabbath." Jesus' argument fits nicely with rabbinic logic.

the interrogative μή, expects a negative reply. Surely God had attested to Jesus through the scope of his work.

Jesus underscores his unique origin when he responds to initial efforts by the chief priests and Pharisees to arrest him. He tells them that he is with them only for a little while longer, and then he goes "to him who sent me; you will seek me and you will not find me; where I am you cannot come" (John 7:33a–34).[80] Not only is Jesus pointing to his resurrection-exaltation, but also he is reaffirming his roots, although the reference is so cryptic that the crowd does not get it. They think that Jesus is referring to a mission outside of Judea, into the Diaspora or to the Greeks. It is yet another case of someone misunderstanding Jesus by reading him literally, as Nicodemus had done in John 3. The point has the crowd stumped. At this point, the narrative takes a break for few days, resuming in "the last day" of the feast.[81]

These few verses are among the most important and most discussed in John. Their specific meaning and punctuation is disputed, although their ultimate sense is clear. Jesus presents himself as the one who permanently satisfies spiritual thirst by providing the gift of the Spirit, a theme that the Synoptics and Acts also highlight (Luke 3:15–17 par.; Acts 1:5; 2:14–41; 10:44–48; 11:15–18). In the background was the daily provision of water during the Feast of Tabernacles, whereby the priest would gather water from the pool of Siloam in a golden flagon and bring it, after a procession, to the temple amid sounds of trumpets and rejoicing. There the water was poured into a bowl beside the altar, where a tube would bring it to the altar's base (*m. Sukkah* 4.9).[82] This act thanked God for his provision of the past and expressed hope for his future provision. If the final day was the eighth day of the feast, then Jesus spoke of an unending provision on the day when the symbolism ended.

Two views exist.[83] (1) The "Eastern" (or traditional) reading argues that there is a full stop (= period) at the end of John 7:37 (as in the NIV: "Whoever believes in me, as the Scripture has said, streams of living water will flow from

---

80. The present tense in "I am" is interesting. It appears to highlight that in one sense where Jesus will go is also where he is now, residing with the one who sent him. It is another claim to an intense unity with God.

81. Whether this is the seventh or the eighth day of the feast is discussed. It is hard to be sure. Technically, the feast and its custom of invoking water and light went only to the seventh day (*m. Sukkah* 4.1). However, by the time of the Talmud, the rite seems to have gone to the eighth day (*b. Sukkah* 48[b]). On the other hand, the eighth day also was treated as a special day (Lev. 23:36; *m. Sukkah* 5.6). Josephus and other Jewish texts seem to reckon eight days for the feast (Josephus, *Ant.* 3.10.4 §245; 2 Macc. 10:6). See Morris, *John,* 373 n. 79. On the whole, the eighth day seems more likely.

82. This tractate suggests that the water rite did extend to the eighth day, although 4.1 speaks of the practice being done only to day seven. Perhaps in Jesus' day the practice would have only gone to day seven. If so, the symbolism already had come to an end.

83. Carson, *John,* 321–28, has a thorough discussion and opts for the Eastern, or traditional, view.

within him."). The result is that the "streams of living water" in 7:38 flow from within the belly of the believer (i.e., "from within him" refers back to "whoever believes in me"). This reading presents the smoothest syntax and fits normal Johannine style, in which a "whoever" clause often starts an idea, but it also results in the unusual idea that emphasizes abiding water in the believer (although it is assumed that the ultimate source is Jesus). (2) The "Western" (or christological) view holds that there is no full stop at the end of 7:37, so that a rough parallelism emerges: "Let anyone who is thirsty come to me, and let the one who believes in me drink. Just as the Scripture says, 'From within him will flow rivers of living water.'" This syntax is slightly more awkward, but it yields good sense in that Jesus is the provider of the water that quenches the thirst (so RSV margin and NEB). Regardless of the reading chosen, the scriptural background, paraphrased not cited, appears to be Isa. 58:11, although hints of the idea already are present in Isa. 55:1–2 (also noted are Prov. 4:23; 5:15; Isa. 44:3; Ezek. 47:1–12; Joel 3:18; Zech. 13:1; 14:8). The second view is slightly more likely theologically, although either reading is possible.

Either way, the point is that Jesus is the source of the living water that brings an abundance of refreshment, a claim similar to that in John 4:1–12. In 7:39, John explains Jesus' remarks as referring to the Spirit, a topic to which Jesus will return in John 14–16. Jesus gives this Spirit to those who believe in him, but that will happen only after Jesus is glorified, a reference to his approaching death, which is followed by his exaltation back to the one who sent him (7:33–34). Thus, Jesus associates God's provision of the Spirit with his mission. It is to him one must come for such a drink. The result is that either from the belly of the believer (Eastern view) or from Christ's belly (Western view) will well up rivers of living water that quench the thirst of the spiritually thirsty. Again John shows that as Jesus presents it, his mission is inextricably bound up with the plan of God. The claim forces a decision.

Once again, the crowd divides in its opinion. Some regard Jesus as "the" prophet, a herald of the new age (see Deut. 18:15). This estimation appears to see something less than a messianic figure, but it does not reject him outright. It is a compromise solution of sorts. Others opted for Jesus being the Christ. This yielded the objection of a third group, which argued that the Messiah could not come out of Galilee. This objection focused not on the place of Jesus' birth but on the locale of his upbringing and life. Ironically, the alternative they note is that the Messiah must be a son of David and come from Bethlehem (see Mic. 5:2). The crowd seems unaware that Jesus is a son of David and was born in Bethlehem, a fact that John seems to have fun with here for anyone who now knew the story of Jesus' birth as the Synoptics portray it in Matt. 2:1–12 and Luke 2:1–7. So Jesus' claims have split the crowd, and the desire to arrest him continued, although it did not happen here.

However, even those taking part in a potential arrest were uncomfortable. So they did not bring him in. Some of the potential arresting officers, when asked by the chief priests and Pharisees why they did not "arrest" him, reply, "No one ever spoke like this." The respect given Jesus unnerves the Pharisees, who ask if the officers now are being led astray. They ask the question carefully, using the interrogative μή to indicate that they expect a negative answer. The officers' wavering is troublesome. The leaders press their objection by noting that neither the authorities nor the Pharisees have believed in Jesus, stating this in the form of another question expecting a negative response. If the officers follow those in the know, they will drop any wavering. They do not want to be like the crowd, who do not know the law and who are accursed in their ignorance, which is the only reason one can explain their taking Jesus seriously. All of this reaction shows how emotional the issue has become.

Nicodemus, showing some nerve in the face of all of this pressure, raises the issue of fairness. Is it right to judge without a hearing and an examination of the evidence?[84] The remark gives the impression that he is at least open to Jesus, undercutting the question they had asked about the supposedly unanimous hostile attitude toward Jesus held by those who have knowledge of the law. It also raises a challenge about how the "knowledgeable" are conducting themselves in terms of justice, another ironic note in the account. This "neutral" suggestion from Nicodemus earns a sarcastic retort. They rhetorically accuse Nicodemus of being from Galilee and note that the Scripture teaches that no prophet emerges from Galilee. This final point actually may represent an overstatement of the Jewish view that shows how distorted things have become for Jesus' opponents. It ignores the fact that Jonah was from Galilee (2 Kings 14:25). It also runs counter to a tradition that shows up later in the Talmud (*b. Sukkah* 27[b]): "There was not a tribe from Israel from which there did not come prophets." In other words, prophets resided in every part of Israel.

John's discussion of Jesus in Judea shows that the movement toward rejection by the Jewish officials had grown to the point that the justice of the leaders' response might be questioned. In laying out this exchange, which covered sensitive issues such as Sabbath practice and the giving of the Spirit, the offensiveness of Jesus' claim to be so united to the Father becomes obvious. Some are giving him a hearing, but the powerful in Judea are reacting against him. Their minds already are made up.

[The Woman Caught in Adultery (John 7:53–8:11) (Aland §242)]

In all likelihood, this passage, though reflecting an event in Jesus' life, originally was not present at this location in John's Gospel. (This is why

---

84. Later Jewish sources knew of such standards and upheld them. *Exodus Rabbah* 21.3 reads, "Unless a mortal hears the pleas that a man can put forward, he is not able to give judgment."

the unit is bracketed and has not been assigned a unit number.) The evidence for this conclusion is both external (text-critical) and internal. Internally, little of the unit reflects John's style; the passage reads in spots, especially John 8:2, like something from the Synoptics, especially Luke.[85] Externally, the text does not appear in any important Eastern witnesses (ℵ, B, W, Θ)[86] or in the old Syriac or Coptic. Even some manuscripts that include it either leave a space after John 7:52 to communicate doubt about the placement or have asterisks or obeli to set it off for the same reason. No Greek writers on John comment on these verses in the first millennium, and the passage shows up in standard manuscripts ca. A.D. 900. Among those who omit it in treating John are Origen, Cyprian, and Chrysostom. Those who do include it are from the West: Ambrose, Augustine, Jerome, and in the Western witness of Codex Bezae. Some manuscripts have it in other locales, including after Luke 21:38, at the end of John, after John 7:36, or after 7:44.[87] This makes it unlikely that the text originally had this location in the Gospel.

On the other hand, most commentators believe that there is good evidence for this event being rooted in Jesus' life, because the tradition (or ones like it) gives evidence of being early. Eusebius records an event that Papias narrates about a woman accused of many sins before Jesus in the *Gospel of the Hebrews* (*Eccl. Hist.* 3.39.16). In *Apostolic Constitutions* 2.24 (= Syriac *Didascalia* 7), a third-century work, there is a similar story, which is used to caution the bishopric about being too severe with those who repent. Some suggest that one of the reasons the story was slow to gain acceptance is that it appears to be lenient on a topic about which the church in the third and fourth centuries was strict. I include the account here because of its later traditional location. However, I will not argue that it contextually belongs here in John.

Jesus' ministry in Jerusalem, with him staying at the Mount of Olives, is like Luke 21:37. This location in John might have been suggested because Jesus was ministering in Jerusalem, so that a tradition alluding to lodging habits suggested a setting during Jesus' work in the city. Jesus' teaching in the temple also reflects his pattern while in the city. During one such time, the Pharisees and scribes, who would be mostly Pharisees but not exclusively so, brought a woman to him who had been caught in the act of adultery. The demands of law and tradition make it clear that what had been witnessed was an intimate act of infidelity and not merely a compromising visit, for such was

85. The Greek for "dawn," "appear," and "sat down to teach them" reflect expressions in Luke-Acts but not in John. The verse looks like Luke 21:38. See Carson, *John*, 334.

86. That is, Codices Sinaiticus, Vaticanus, Washingtonensis, and Koridethi.

87. See Barrett, *John*, 490–91, for much of what follows; so also Morris, *John*, 778–79, who shows that the judgments summarized here are shared by conservatives.

required in order to bring this charge and seek a death sentence.[88] This detail is important for what Jesus does.

The teachers make the point to Jesus that the woman was caught in the act, and so the law requires that she be stoned to death. They are appealing to Deut. 22:23–24, if she is betrothed, and to Deut. 22:22 or Lev. 20:10, if she is married. Both the woman and her lover were culpable; adultery with a spouse or a betrothed was a serious crime. Of course, no man stands accused here, suggesting that the law is being applied selectively. Though Lev. 20:10 does not specify how death should occur, Ezek. 16:38–40 suggests stoning.[89]

The question to Jesus for his opinion is a trap. Either Jesus affirms the law of Moses and gets in trouble with Rome for advocating the death penalty for a crime when Jews were not allowed to exercise this right (John 18:31–32), or he denies the penalty and is seen to be denying Moses and the law. The attempted trap is similar to the approach of the question to Jesus about paying taxes to Caesar. John 8:6 exposes the action as a test, made so they might charge him. If Jesus rejects the death penalty, then the Jewish elders could be brought in to argue that he rejects the law. If he argues in favor of death, then Rome could be invoked.

Jesus bends down to write something on the ground. It is futile to speculate about what he wrote, although numerous suggestions exist.[90] We simply do not know. The text does not tell us. Jesus opts to challenge them by indicating that the one without sin should cast the first stone. The premise of the reply is that she is culpable, but only if those who bring the charge have done so with integrity and not as a trap. The appeal is to Deut. 13:9 or 17:7 (also Lev. 24:14). Those who begin the stoning must be the witnesses and must have had no part in the crime. Jesus probes against a double standard in this effort, exposing the hypocrisy of the test.[91] The appeal to those with clean hands

---

88. J. D. M. Derrett, "Law in the New Testament: The Story of the Woman Taken in Adultery," *New Testament Studies* 10 (1963–64): 1–26, has the details of this evidence. The key piece of evidence is late, *b. Baba Meṣiʿa* 91ᵃ, where it is said that the witnesses must have seen them "in the posture of adulterers." Deuteronomy 19:15 requires two such witnesses, excluding the husband. In other words, everything was done to prevent that penalty from being exercised out of revenge or as a setup. Susanna 36–40 also gives important evidence of the early practice of "catching someone in the act."

89. Mishnah *Sanhedrin* 7.4 distinguishes between stoning for a betrothed and strangling for a wife, but there is some question whether the distinction existed in the first century. See J. Blinzler, "Die Strafe für Ehebruch in Bibel und Halacha zur Auslegung von Joh. viii 5" (The Penalty for Adultery in the Bible and in Halakah as an Explanation of John 8:5), *New Testament Studies* 4 (1957–58): 32–47.

90. Options include writing the Roman sentence on the ground according to their practice, condemning them with Jer. 17:13, citing Exod. 23:1b about not accepting a malicious witness, or simply doodling in good Semitic custom to indicate that something was not right.

91. Jesus' point here, set culturally, is not that those who condemn her and cast a stone must be sinless, but that they must be without sin in this situation, starting with the witnesses who bring the charge. No trap could be present, which meant they should not have set her up to sin.

works, because after he writes something else on the ground, the gathered experts walk away, so that Jesus and the woman are left alone. The result is that no one is left to condemn her and carry out the sentence, so Jesus graciously lets the women go without condemning her to death. This is not strictly forgiveness, because no word about forgiveness is given, but Jesus' act is gracious in allowing her the opportunity to recover from her sin. In releasing her, he commands her to stop her sinful habit. Grace should lead to purity.

J18. The Dispute Deepens as Jesus Claims to Be the Light of the World, the Truth, and Abraham's Superior
(John 8:12–59) (Aland §§243–47)

Assuming that the scene involving the adulterous woman is not a part of John, Jesus' next discourse about light also is set in the temple (8:20) and also may well draw on Tabernacles imagery. During this feast (at least during the first night if not the entire feast), four candlesticks with bowls at the top were lit in the court of the women, where the treasury receptacles of 8:20 also were located (Mark 12:41–42; Luke 21:1–2; *m. Šeqalim* 2.1; 6.1, 5). Much reveling took place under these lights as the celebrants sang through the night (*m. Sukkah* 5.1–4). It was said that every courtyard in Jerusalem reflected this light. The light symbolized God's presence in the pillar of fire guiding the people in the desert (Exod. 13:21–22; 14:19–25; Ps. 27:1). Zechariah 14:5–8 mentions both flowing water and light.

In this context, Jesus declared himself to be the light, not just of Israel, but of the world. The image was widely used in Israel, not only for God's presence, but also for God's instruction in the law (Ps. 119:105; Wis. 18:3–4). Eschatological hope taught that the Lord will be light (Isa. 60:19–22) and that God's servant was to be light to the Gentiles (Isa. 49:6). So the image is rich with significance. The ethical dimension in contrast to darkness also shows up at Qumran (1QS 2.3; 3.7, 20–21). Jesus claims to be the presence, wisdom, and revelation of God for the world. Those who follow him by no means will walk in darkness but will possess the light that is life (cf. John 1:4).[92] Jesus is everything celebrated at Tabernacles and more.

The Pharisees challenge Jesus' testimony as invalid because it comes from himself. Jesus' reply is that even if he accepts their premise of a self-testimony, it still holds true because of his origins and destiny.[93] Jesus knows where he

---

92. The use of οὐ μή is emphatic and the genitive ζωῆς should be read as a comprehensive genitive, denoting light not only as the source of life but also as possessing life. Barrett, *John*, 277–78, notes how even the Gentile understanding of light as tied to divine knowledge could comprehend an aspect of Jesus' point. Still, the key backdrop is Jewish.

93. In *m. ʾAbot* 4.8, Rabbi Ishmael (second century) argues that no one should judge alone, because "none may judge alone save One."

came from and where he is going, while the Pharisees do not. The Pharisees are guilty of judging "by the flesh," that is, on the basis of false, surface, earthly standards (John 7:24). Jesus, however, does not judge anyone (stated with an emphatic Greek double negative) (cf. John 3:17; 12:47). He came to save. Any judgment that emerges through his coming arises from a failure to embrace the saving, illuminating opportunity that Jesus brings. He is not looking to pull down but to lift up. Even if he does judge, that judgment is true because Jesus does not judge on his own, but judges with the one who sent him (cf. John 3:17).[94] In this way, Jesus repeats the argument he made in John 5. He acts in response to and in dependence upon the Father. They work as one.

Seen in this light, Jesus tells the leaders that his testimony is supported by "your" law. Jesus is not separating himself from the law or making it apply only to the Pharisees here;[95] rather, he is highlighting that even that which serves as "your" standard upholds his claim because there are two witnesses, the Father and the sent one (cf. Deut. 17:6; 19:15). How the Father witnesses to Jesus and at how many levels, Jesus will affirm in 8:21–29.

The opponents ask Jesus where his father is. In John 7:27, they knew, so the remark probably is derisive, although it could be another example of the misunderstanding that John loves to note. They cannot imagine that Jesus speaks of God as his Father. They know he is from Galilee and feel that Jesus should acknowledge that origin. Their retort leads Jesus to affirm that they are ignorant both of him and of his Father. To know Jesus means to know the Father (cf. John 14:7; 16:3). It is no accident that the order goes this way. Jesus is inseparable from the Father in their mission. Jesus' role is what he stresses here as he speaks at the temple treasury. To know the Father, a person must see and embrace Jesus. Though speaking virtually across the street from the headquarters of the leaders, he challenges and presents his views in the most holy of Jewish locales. Yet no one arrests him, because his time ("hour") had not yet come (cf. John 2:4; 7:6, 30).

Jesus knows where he is headed. The leaders will not follow him there. They will seek Jesus, but will not share his exalted destiny, because where Jesus is going, they are not able to come. Rather, they will die in sin. In John 8:21, "sin" is singular, pointing to unbelief that prevents one from knowing God. Once again Jesus is misunderstood. They wonder, but with doubt, if Jesus will kill himself.[96] Jesus replies that he is from above, from heaven and the Father, while they are from below, a reference to their being merely creatures within the creation. This basic separation between Jesus being not of this world and

---

94. Jesus is contrasting his attitude and mission with the hostile reaction of his opponents. They are quick to judge and doubt him. Jesus comes in the hopes of saving.

95. Some critics argue that Jesus' distance from the law shows that this is a late text; they allege that Jesus did not separate himself from the law to this degree. This claim misses Jesus' perspective in underscoring how important the law was to his opponents.

96. The Greek of the question expects a negative reply and so is stated tentatively.

the opponents belonging to it explains why they are so unappreciative of him. The only way to escape dying in sins (now plural) is to believe in him who is sent from above. Literally, Jesus says "Unless you believe that I am." This description of himself does evoke the name of God given to Moses at the burning bush (Exod. 3:14; but also especially Isa. 41:4; 43:10, 13, 25; 46:5; 48:12; Deut. 32:39). However, it also begs for completion with a sense of "I am who I testify myself to be," namely, the one sent and working in indivisible union with the purpose of the Father.[97] The Isaianic passages speak of a God who acts for his people. The real debate about Jesus centers on his claim to authority in uncompromising association with God and his mission, something the Synoptics also affirm.

Jesus intensifies his claim by noting that he has much to say about them, things associated with judgment. These things he is saying to the world. They are things he has heard from the one who sent him (John 3:14, 17; 8:16, 18). What the one who sent him is saying through him is true. The Jews did not understand that this remark was about the Father, but Jesus does not stop here. He speaks next of the Son of Man being lifted up, a dual reference to Jesus being lifted up on the cross and being exalted. When that happens, they will know and have more evidence that Jesus is the sent one and the Son of Man. This means that he acts not on his own authority, but speaks what the Father taught him. Jesus does only what is pleasing to the Father. Once again Jesus' fundamental claim is to an unbroken communion with God, including the expression of God's will and way. These remarks lead many to believe in him.

However, this belief turns out to be superficial, short-lived belief that is not true faith, as the next exchange shows.[98] Disciples abide in Jesus' word (8:31). In other words, they continue holding to it. Here is introduced a theme that John 15 will develop in detail. In Greek, Jesus' words are expressed as a class three condition, leaving open whether it will happen or not. Faith trusts not just in one moment, but in an abiding way. Such clinging to the word leads to the truth, not a philosophical truth but spiritual truth. In turn, that truth leads to freedom. For John, Jesus is that truth. So truth is not an idea or a philosophy but a person sent from God to reveal the truth of God's ways. The mention of freedom implies that the Jews are in bondage, because they lack the truth. This implication the Jews deny, claiming that as descendants of Abraham they have never been in bondage to anyone. So how can Jesus sug-

97. This reads 8:25 as an affirmation and τὴν ἀρχήν as an adverbial accusative: "just what I told you at the beginning." For the options, see Brown, *John I–XII*, 347–48.

98. This verse has led to much discussion, including the claim that this remark is a gloss. This is not likely, as no evidence exists for this being a later reading. Others wish to distinguish between those mentioned in v. 30 and those in v. 31, but this also is an unlikely position, since no distinction is made. Rather, vv. 30–31 should be seen against the background of superficial faith, like John 2:23–24 and John 6:60–71.

gest that they will be made free? These remarks by Jesus' opponents forget the Jews' bondage under Egypt, Assyria, and Babylon, but it may be that they are claiming not to be currently in spiritual bondage to anyone. The claim is similar to one noted by Josephus, that the Jews denied serving the Romans and served only God (*War* 7.8.6 §323).[99]

Jesus makes it clear that the issue is spiritual bondage associated with sin, because the "one who does sin" is a slave to sin (conceptually like the imagery of Rom. 6:15–23). There is a contrast between a slave who does not remain in the house and a son who does. The illustration points to Jesus as the Son. Jesus makes people free, leading to genuine freedom. Jesus acknowledges his opponents' descent from Abraham but notes that their desire to kill him (a sin) results from their refusal to accept his word and that of the Father. This proves a lack of real descent from God (cf. Luke 3:8; Rom. 9:6–7). Jesus speaks of what he has seen from the Father, while their reaction against Jesus shows their roots in another father. With this move, Jesus potentially escalates the tension, turning the issue into a cosmic battle. There is no indication that the audience is different from that identified in John 8:31, which mentions some of (shallow) faith.

In response, the Jews insist that they are children of Abraham. Jesus challenges the remark by arguing that if they were, then they would respond like Abraham and believe God's testimony, but they seek to kill him for telling them the truth from God. So Jesus repeats the charge about their following their father. The implication leads to the retort that their paternity does not reside in fornication, a retort carrying a suggestion that Jesus' birth came in unusual circumstances that were the topic of rumors. In contrast, these Jews claim to have one father, even God. In claiming this, they are arguing that there is no defection in their religious practice. It is as if they are catching the drift and edge in Jesus' remarks, which will become explicit in v. 44.

Jesus responds with a Greek class two conditional statement: "If God were your Father [but he is not, as is indicated by your refusal to hear his voice through me], then you would love me [but, of course, you do not]." Again Jesus appeals to his being sent from God, not acting of his own accord but proceeding from him. In a real sense, Jesus' mission is not his, but God's. They do not understand Jesus' language (λαλιά) because they cannot bear to hear his word (λόγος; 8:43). They are spiritually incapable of appreciating what Jesus is saying. The challenge that Jesus' teaching represents is too hard to accept, so they do not even begin to reconfigure their thinking.

That incapacity has roots in their spiritual ancestry, in their father, who is the devil. Here, Jesus is as directly confrontational as anywhere in John. They are performing the devil's desires, which is why there is an imitating of his

---

99. In the Talmud, reflecting later Jewish teaching, it is argued that the Jews are "royal" children (*b. Sanhedrin* 128ª).

penchant to murder (8:40; 7:25), to lie, and to reject the truth.[100] That is why
when Jesus speaks the truth, they do not believe because they have embraced
the lies that are not from above. So they reject Jesus because he speaks the
truth.[101] In fact, Jesus asks, "Who can convict me of sin?" This claim is designed to underscore how Jesus reflects and lives authentically. Only someone
with a pure, clean conscience in communion with the truth could be like that.
On the other hand, if Jesus speaks the truth, then how can they not believe
him?[102] The one who is of God hears the utterances that come from God. The
leaders' failure to hear shows that they are not of God but of another pedigree.
Of course, what Jesus is claiming is that his words are God's.

The final section of this chapter leads to one of the greatest claims to be divine that Jesus makes anywhere in the scriptural material. The remark is provoked by the Jewish denial that Jesus speaks for God. Initially, their reaction
in v. 48 is that Jesus is unorthodox, like a Samaritan, and that he is possessed,
like the Beelzebul charge in the Synoptics (cf. 7:20; 8:52; 10:20; Mark 3:22;
Matt. 12:24; Luke 11:15). Though stated as a question, the query, using οὐ,
expects a positive reply. Jesus replies that, far from being possessed, he seeks
to honor his Father, while their remarks dishonor Jesus. Jesus does not seek
his own glory; there is another who seeks it. That one, God himself, will make
the judgment between them. Life, however, is a matter of keeping Jesus' word.
The one who does keep Jesus' word will definitely not see death. Jesus' statement is doubly emphatic, using οὐ μή and placing the Greek word for "death"
(θάνατος) at the front of the clause. The claim for authority over life is a claim
for heavenly authority. Jesus' claim that he can give life implies that Jesus also
will not die. It is this idea the Jews seize upon.

The Jews again misunderstand Jesus, arguing that the teacher must be possessed, because even Abraham and the prophets died. If these luminaries of the
past passed away, so would everyone else. They challenge him, "Surely, you
are not greater than Abraham and the prophets, who died?" They press him
further: "Who do you claim to be?" The confrontation has hit its high point.
The probe of Jesus' authority is direct.

Jesus claims not to glorify himself, because if he did so, it would mean
nothing. Rather, Jesus' Father glorifies him, the very one his opponents claim
as their father. Jesus implies that what allows him to live forever is the glorifying work of the Father. For John's Gospel, Jesus is glorified at the cross and
the exaltation-resurrection into vindicated life that comes from it. They have
not known God, but Jesus knows him. He cannot deny knowing the Father,
because that would make him a liar, like those who reject him. Jesus does two

---

100. In 8:44 there are numerous key shifts of tense from present to past and back to present.
What they are, the devil was and is.

101. The use of ὅτι in v. 45 is causal.

102. This is a class one condition, the premise being presented as true.

things: he knows God and keeps his word. This is what stands behind Jesus' message. In fact, Abraham rejoiced to see Jesus' day. He saw it and was glad.

The idea of Abraham's rejoicing has produced much discussion. Did he rejoice in Gen. 12 when his seed was said to be ready to bless the world? Or was it in Gen. 15 that he got a glimpse of the nation's future and of the Messiah?[103] Or was it in Gen. 25 that upon dying he entered into a glimpse of the future? If later Judaism is any guide, the Jews did think that Abraham was given a glimpse of what was to come. There is no way to know if any of these specific proposals are meant or if it was a general remark that argued that Abraham longed for this time of fulfillment (Heb. 11 expresses the latter idea). God's promises pointed to the outcome that Jesus' presence represented. That brought Abraham joy.

The Jews challenged this reply by questioning how Jesus could know what Abraham thought and saw, given that Jesus could not be more than fifty years old. Jesus does not back off. He replies, "Before Abraham was, I am." Jesus claims not only to predate Abraham, but also to share the divine name, "I AM" (Exod. 3:14). In sharing the divine name, Jesus is claiming to share in the divine person. Jesus existed before the patriarch. He is greater than Abraham. In fact, he is one with God. This left the audience with a choice: either Jesus had uttered words of outrageous blasphemy or he was who he claimed to be, the very revelator of God who is in equal union with God. Neutrality no longer was possible. What identified God identified him.

The Jews' conclusion was that this was blasphemy, so they took up stones to execute him, as required by Lev. 24:16. However, something prevented them from following through. Was it that they took up stones only to symbolize how they felt? Was it that they came to appreciate that if they acted, they would have exercised a right that only the Romans had, thus offending their political masters (cf. John 18:31)? The text says only that Jesus hid himself and left the temple. By the time they had picked up the stones, possibly stones being used to continue to rebuild the temple, he was gone. It was not yet the hour for "night" to come (13:30).

J19. The Sixth Sign: Healing of the Man Born Blind—Jesus, the Light of the World (John 9:1–41) (Aland §248)

Sometime after the Tabernacles scene, Jesus takes the initiative with a man blind from birth. There is no mention of the man's faith. Rather, the healing pictures Jesus' ability to bring someone from darkness to light. This kind of

---

103. Later Jewish texts taught that Abraham had a vision about the future at this point. Texts such as *Genesis Rabbah* 44 (28a) and *Mekilta* on Exod. 20:18 (78b) taught this.

miracle is unusual outside of Jesus' work. There is no healing of the blind in the Old Testament or from the disciples. Yet Jesus does it repeatedly.[104]

The disciples with Jesus see the man and ask whether the man or his parents are responsible for this situation. Such a view grew out of an understanding of the fall in Gen. 3, but to apply it to an individual was overly direct. A well-known later Jewish saying from the Talmud reads, "There is no death without sin, and there is no suffering without iniquity" (*b. Sanhedrin* 55ᵃ). Aspects of teaching in Job could suggest this idea as well. Other texts placed tragedy at the feet of parents, as in the case where the early death of a scholar is tied to a mother's engagement with idolatry during her pregnancy (*Ruth Rabbah* 6.4). Such stories also served to underscore the seriousness of the effects of sin. However, Jesus places the event at the feet of God's glory, since it was an opportunity for the works of God to be made evident. Those works, Jesus says, are something that Jesus and his disciples (note the "we" in v. 4) must do while the day of his ministry is present. When night comes, such work will cease, an allusion to his arrest and death. As long as Jesus is in the world, he is light for the world (cf. 8:12; 12:35–36). Thus, what he is about to do is a sign of the light that he brings to people of his own initiative.

Jesus works the miracle by taking some spittle and making a mud cake. Jesus only occasionally uses spittle with a miracle (Mark 7:33; 8:23). This probably is a triple violation of the Sabbath (9:14). A healer was only to heal if another's life was at risk (Luke 13:14). Also, one was not to knead on the Sabbath (*m. Šabbat* 7.2; 24.3). Most anointings also were prohibited (*m. Šabbat* 14.4 notes debate over the issue and exceptions). In the ancient world, spittle was believed to have magical powers, but Jews advised against its use; *t. Sanhedrin* 12.10 has a rabbinic saying that anyone who utters charms over a wound and spits has no place in the world to come.[105] There is nothing magical about what Jesus does here, although the symbolism could be the creative work of a fresh creation, using the dirt of the ground (cf. Gen. 2:7). There was debate in later Judaism over whether a person could anoint eyes on the Sabbath (*b. ʿAbodah Zarah* 28ᵇ). The healing is delayed as the man is told to take the mix and wash in the pool of Siloam, located in the southernmost sector of the city, near the Tyropoean valley. That pool is named "Sent," showing how symbolic everything about this passage is. If there is one theme that has dominated John, it is Jesus as the sent one. Jesus is sent to cleanse and bring light.

The reaction to the healing comes from those who have known the man only as a neighbor or a beggar. They recognize him as the begging blind

---

104. Morris, *John*, 422. He notes that seven different Synoptic texts record this type of healing. God does this (Exod. 4:11; Ps. 146:8). It was said that it would occur in the messianic era (Isa. 29:18; 35:5; 42:7).

105. Barrett, *John*, 296. In *m. Sanhedrin* 10.1, Rabbi Akiba says, "He that reads the heretical books, or that utters charms [or 'whispers'] over a wound" has no place in the world to come (Herbert Danby, trans., *The Mishnah* [Oxford: Oxford University Press, 1933], 397).

man.[106] Debate ensued, with some saying that it was the formerly blind man, and others disagreeing, thinking that it was someone like him. The miracle was that surprising. So the blind man confesses that he is the one and explains that Jesus healed him. He recounts the details, although he could not tell them where Jesus had gone.

Naturally enough, the crowd takes the man to the religious leaders with whom they had the most contact, the Pharisees. Narrating the details yet again, the man listens to them center on the fact that the healing took place on the Sabbath. Some of them conclude that Jesus cannot be from God, because he performed the healing on that day, while others ask how a sinner can perform such signs. Such a work could not take place unless God did the work through him. The healed man concludes that Jesus is a prophet. It is the first of several confessions he will make, each one being a step into greater understanding (9:27–28, 33, 35–38).

The argument by the blind man is not airtight, as both Testaments warn that works need testing (Deut. 13:1–5; Matt. 7:21–23; 2 Thess. 2:9). However, the healing of a man born blind is so rare that the burden certainly would be to show that this miracle is not from God. For the blind man, this experience with Jesus is decisive.

The healing did bother those Jews examining the healing, so they question the parents to be certain that the man is their son and was born blind. The parents dodge the hard question, affirming only that this is their son and that he was born blind. When it comes to the question of how he came to see, they pass the buck, noting that they do not know how he came to see but that the interrogators can go and ask the son. He is old enough to speak for himself. The reference to being of age probably is a way of stating that he is old enough to be responsible for his reply, making him at least thirteen.

The next verse is controversial because it attributes the hesitation to answer to a Jewish threat. The potential threat was that those who confessed Jesus as the Christ would be put out of the synagogue. Some scholars claim that this remark is anachronistic. They point out that in Acts, even in Jerusalem, believers seem to circulate openly. However, two factors must be kept in mind. First, there were different levels of exclusion, if later Jewish texts are any guide. There was a light punishment *(neziphah)*, a thirty-day isolation that could be extended to ninety days (known as both *nidduy* and *shammattah*), and finally the more severe ban *(ḥerem)*.[107] In addition, there is the reworking of benedic-

---

106. The question in v. 8 expects a positive answer, since it uses οὐχ.

107. For these categories, see Barrett, *John,* 299–300, who sees this remark as anachronistic, and the full discussion in Carson, *John,* 369–72, who correctly urges that such a conclusion is premature, given the inconclusive evidence. Texts here include *m. Taʿanit* 3.8; *m. Nedarim* 1.1; *m. ʿEduyyot* 5.6; *m. Middot* 2.2. See also the careful treatment in William Horbury, "The Benediction of the *Minim* and Early Jewish-Christian Controversy," *Journal of Theological Studies* 33 (1982): 19–61, who argues for the age of such actions against a variety of groups. Paul was excluded in Acts 13:50 but accepted elsewhere.

tion 12 of the *Shemoneh Esreh*, perhaps in A.D. 85–90. It is disputed whether it prays for the rejection of the Jewish Christians from the synagogue, where "the Nazarenes" are asked to be rooted out by God. However, there appear to be older roots for this tradition about those seen as heretics. This means that even if the rewritten benediction 12 is not about Christians exclusively, they cannot be excluded as possibly being in view. In fact, the text may well reflect an older tradition present for separating from perceived heretics. The second factor is the possibility that this was a local practice as opposed to a general one. We know that such responses varied during Paul's ministry. The disciples' initial freedom in Jerusalem after the crucifixion may well reflect the fact that the crucifixion made the leadership initially think that the threat was removed when Jesus was executed. Regardless of this debate, John 9 indicates that the threat of rejection led the parents to opt out of the key answer.

The leaders turn to the blind man and invoke an oath (see Josh. 7:19) to get him to speak the truth. They insist that God should be given the praise and that the blind man should know that the one who healed him and whom he confessed as a prophet is a sinner. The blind man cleverly responds that he cannot comment on whether Jesus is a sinner, but he can state that he is now a man who can see. When the retort comes as to how this was done, the blind man shoots back that he already has told them, but they do not listen. Then he toys with them, remarking that perhaps they want to hear the story again so that they can become disciples of Jesus. The examiners reply that they are disciples of Moses, not disciples of Jesus as the blind man is. Furthermore, the examiners know that God has spoken to Moses, but they do not know where Jesus is from. The blind man is amazed. How can they question where Jesus is from when he has opened the blind man's eyes? God does not listen to sinners. However, if someone is a worshiper of God and does God's will, then God hears that person. How else could someone heal one born blind? This never has been done before. The blind man concludes his logical argument by noting that if this man were not from God, he could do nothing. The experts reject the argument and respond angrily that this man was born in sin, so there is no way he can teach them about such matters. The passage drips with irony as a formerly blind man sees better than the religious leaders. The examination ends with the blind man being cast out.

Rejected, as Jesus had taught that disciples would be, the healed man is sought and found by Jesus. Jesus asks if the man believes in the Son of Man (see John 1:51; 3:13–14; 5:27; 6:27, 53, 62; 8:28). This probably is an allusion to the one with real authority to judge, a counter to the judgment he just received from the "experts." The healed man asks for Jesus' identity, so he can believe in him. The blind man speaks as one ready to follow Jesus' lead. Jesus' reply is ironic: "You have seen him." Jesus had given him sight, and the new ability allows him to know who the Son of Man is. In fact, Jesus says, "The one speaking with you is he." The restored man now sees clearly and confesses his faith, addressing Jesus with respect as Lord and bowing before him. It is uncertain whether this is full worship, but at the least it is intense respect and gratitude for how God had worked through him, something that had been confessed already and something that is a reaction to Jesus' identifying himself as the Son of Man with real authority to judge.[108]

Jesus explains his work by noting that for judgment he came into the world (contrast 3:17). Jesus' point here is that he naturally divides humanity. Those who do not see get to see, while those who see become blind. In this world Jesus reverses what seems to be, so that those who see actually cannot see, and those who do not see, can. The language here has Old Testament roots in Isa. 6:9–10. The Pharisees listening to this claim ask if they also are blind, sensing the implications of Jesus' remarks. Jesus' reply allows no room. If they really were blind, they might have reason to claim innocence; but they claim to see when actually they do not. So their guilt abides.[109] The scene ends with the formerly blind man seeing and affirmed, while those who reject Jesus as being sent from God are judged as abiding in guilt. The chapter nicely summarizes the entire book. The reappearance of this miracle later in discussions found in John 10:19–21 shows its lingering effect.

J20. Jesus, the Good Shepherd with a New Flock
(John 10:1–21) (Aland §§249–50)

In a sense, the chapter break here is unfortunate. This event really is a commentary on the conflict of John 9 (10:19–21). Jesus compares himself both to the gate of entrance into the sheep pen and to the good or ideal shepherd, who truly cares for the sheep. In describing himself this way, he contrasts himself both to thieves and to hired shepherds. Jesus' claim is that he genuinely cares for the sheep, in contrast to the Jewish leaders, who, when faced with the healing of the man born blind, tear into him because they (wrongfully) allege that the law was not being followed. Thus, the scene draws lessons from the previous event, placed during Tabernacles, as well as setting up the next scene at the Feast of Dedication, some three months later. It is possible that this event does fit in between the other two scenes.[110]

The background of the scene is sheepherding. Sheep could be gathered into a common pen, shared by many families who combined their flocks. This

---

108. Is this worship? Morris, *John*, 440, argues positively, while Carson, *John*, 377, is less certain. In favor of Morris's view is the consistent use of the verb προσκυνέω elsewhere in John (4:22–24; 12:20).

109. Note the use of the verb μένω here.

110. Carson, *John*, 379, makes the observation while arguing against any textual dislocation here.

seems the likely setting, more so than the individual pen of a single family and its courtyard. The references to sheep knowing the voice of their shepherd suggest the setting of the larger, mixed flocks. These enclosures had a gate and were surrounded by a wall or fence. The shepherd entered by the gate, while thieves, seeking not to be discovered and to harm the sheep, climbed over the walls.

The theological backdrop is the Old Testament image of the shepherd, especially the declaration of Israel's inadequate shepherds, who would be replaced by God and the messianic protector (Ezek. 34, esp. vv. 10–12, 23; also Isa. 56:9–12; Jer. 23:1–4; 25:32–38; Zech. 11). God as the good shepherd who guides, feeds, and protects is seen in Ps. 23 (cf. Ps. 80:1; Isa. 40:10–11). The Synoptics also employ this concept extensively (Matt. 9:36; 18:12–14; Mark 6:34; 14:27, using Zech. 13:7; Luke 15:1–7). Thus, Jesus argues that he is the shepherd who cares for and protects his sheep; they, in turn, recognize and follow him. In contrast, the leaders are like thieves and robbers, whose actions serve only to damage the sheep.

The solemn declaration opens with a "truly I say to you" statement that indicates the importance of what is about to be said (cf. John 1:51). Jesus first warns that the person who climbs over the wall is a thief or robber. The image is that the thief's goal is not to lead the sheep but to entrap and ensnare them. The one who enters by the door is the shepherd, who cares for the sheep. The gatekeeper, who guards the door, recognizes him and opens the pen to him. The shepherd calls the sheep, which hear him as he calls them by their names and leads them out. The note of intimate knowledge and guidance is the point here because he is a shepherd who goes before them and leads the way in front of him. The sheep follow him because they know his voice. The picture here is of recognition and obedience (see Num. 27:15–17). In fact, these sheep will not follow a stranger but will flee from him because they do not recognize that foreign voice.

At this point, John calls the teaching a παροιμία, a term used for the Hebrew *mashal,* a proverb or figure. The figurative nature of the story meant that the Pharisees (9:40) did not understand the point.

To underscore the image of the way, Jesus switches from the picture of himself as the shepherd to one of him as the door. He is the entryway to salvation and as such gives access to and from God's presence as expressed in the image of the pasture (Ps. 23; John 10:9). There is only one door through which to pass to get to the Father, and that is what God's shepherd represents. Again this stands in contrast to those who have come before him in Israel. Those "who came before" is not a reference to the prophets but to the leaders, like those who rejected the blind man's testimony in John 9, because the issue is the current choice that people have. The leaders pose as shepherds but really are thieves and robbers. The sheep who belong to the shepherd do not give heed to them. Whereas the thief comes to steal, kill, or destroy, the shepherd comes to give life and give it in fullness. Jesus' teaching highlights the division within the nation that is formed by his coming, since some come to him while the leadership rejects him.

So Jesus is the good, noble, or worthy shepherd. The term καλός is somewhat ambiguous but highlights the character and quality of the shepherd. Jesus is what a shepherd ought to be, the real shepherd. He shows his commitment to the sheep in willingly laying down his life for them. It is probably this portion of the "parable" that the audience did not yet understand. Both the Synoptics and John suggest that Jesus' death was hard for the audience to grasp, even though he was the promised one and predicted his death as noted in Scripture. In John, the preposition ὑπέρ when used of Jesus always points to his action for someone and has a sacrificial emphasis (John 6:51; 10:11, 15; 11:50–52; 17:19; 18:14). In contrast, the hireling, who is not a robber or thief, will desert the sheep and leave them exposed when the wolf comes, so that the sheep are scattered. He flees because he does not care for the sheep. In the Mishnah, it was taught that a hired shepherd must defend the sheep against a single wolf, but if more than one showed up, that was "an unavoidable accident" (*m. Baba Meṣiʿa* 7.9). The point here is that the owner of the sheep, the one with the established relationship with them, is fully committed to them. In the context of Jesus' work, whom the shepherd symbolizes, he seeks to establish the relationship with them, taking the initiative for their care. At the core of what Jesus does is his work as the good shepherd, who knows "his own" sheep, and they know him. The emphasis of τὰ ἐμά falls on the shepherd's possession of the sheep. That relationship is similar to the way the Father and Son know each other so that the Son lays down his life for the sheep.

Jesus goes on to mention other sheep not of this fold. This surely is an allusion to the Gentiles, who also are brought in by his death. They belong to another fold, but when his work is done, they also will be led by the shepherd because they also will heed his voice. So in the end there will be one flock led by one shepherd (cf. Eph. 2:11–22; Gal. 3:28).

The Father loves the Son because the Son does lay down his life only to take it up again. Here is one of the few places in the New Testament where Jesus is said to give life to himself or to raise himself up (see Mark 8:31; Luke 24:7; Acts 10:41; 17:3; 1 Thess. 4:14), because usually it is the Father who is said to raise him from the dead. Jesus does this willingly because he loves the Father and the sheep. He will obey the Father's charge and show his own care for the sheep.

The discourse divides the crowd into two groups, just as in 9:16. Some accuse him of being mad, that is, demon-possessed. In their view, Jesus' claims are too exclusive and exaggerated to be those of a sane person. No one, in their view, should listen to or accept such claims. In contrast, others are impressed by Jesus' work because it is neither the work of a deranged individual nor the work of a fraud or a falsely endowed person. Such utterances do not come from a demon-possessed person; even more, a demon cannot open the eyes of the blind. The question about the work of demons bringing sight is asked using μή. The question clearly expects a negative reply. The blind see only because God is at work.

The entire scene from John 9:1–10:21 virtually summarizes the gospel thus far and the point of the signs that Jesus gives. He, as the good shepherd, brings sight to the blind by the power of God. He will give life by giving up his own life. His sheep will recognize him and come. There is no one else who gives this access to the Father. The double use of "I am" statements about Jesus being the door and the shepherd underscores the point.

J21. Jesus Declares His Unity with the Father at the Feast of Dedication (John 10:22–42) (Aland §§257–58)

Jesus now finds himself in the temple area during the Feast of Dedication, known as Hanukkah. This feast celebrates the repurification of the temple after it had been desecrated by Antiochus Epiphanes in 167 B.C. After the three-year Maccabean War, the Jews regained control of the temple and purified it (1 Macc. 4:52–59). This eight-day feast was celebrated in late November to early December. So it was winter, and Jesus was on the eastern side of the temple at Solomon's colonnade. The Jews encircle him, indicating that they have a serious question. The statement in 10:24 is disputed. Does it mean "How long will you keep us in suspense?" Or is it saying "How long will you plague us?" Or is it "Why are you taking away our life?"[111] The idiom is "to lift up the soul," so that the idea seems to be to suspend their understanding. What they ask for is a plain statement about whether or not he is the Messiah, something that Jesus had done only with the Samaritan woman (4:26) and the blind man (9:35–38). Jesus' initial reply is that he already had answered the question. His actions and remarks served as replies. For John's Gospel, the signs are the reply. However, despite the clarity of what Jesus had done and said, they did not believe. The reason for their disbelief was that they were not among Jesus' sheep, an allusion back to Jesus' discussion in John 10. Jesus' sheep hear him, know him, and follow him. In return, Jesus gives them eternal life, and they will not perish. In fact, no one can, even by attempted violence, snatch them out of his hands.

The next remark in 10:29 also is debated, since it is rooted in a difficult textual problem. It means either "My Father who has given them to me is greater than all" ($\mathfrak{P}^{66}$) or "What my Father has given to me is greater than all" (the reading in B). Either way, Jesus' point is that God, who is greater than any opposing

---

111. On these three options, see Morris, *John*, 461.

force, will use that power to keep the sheep safe. Thus, no one can snatch them out of the Father's hand. Note the oneness of the Father and the Son. What in 10:28 cannot be snatched from Jesus' hands also cannot in 10:29 be snatched from the Father's hand. Thus, Jesus' conclusion is that he and the Father are one. The term for "one" is neuter, not masculine. Jesus is not saying that they are one in terms of person but that they work indivisibly together and in concert, as John 5 also had argued. What the Son does, the Father has willed and shared in. It is this intimacy of united action that the leaders object to as they take up stones as an expression of their view that Jesus has blasphemed. A stoning would be required for one who blasphemes (Lev. 24:16).

Jesus challenges their right to stone him by raising a specific question. He has performed many good (καλά) works from the Father, and so for which of these do they stone him?[112] The reply is that the works are not the source of their desire to stone him, but that he blasphemes by making himself God. Blasphemy was a religious crime of saying or doing something extremely dishonoring to God. To a monotheist, nothing could be more dishonoring than claiming to share God's role intimately.[113]

Jesus replies that the Jewish Scripture makes such associations when in Ps. 82:6 judges are described as gods. If God says this to and of human judges in his own revelation, then how can they complain about the one whom God has "consecrated" and sent into the world as Son? In other words, God's attestation supports Jesus' right to make the claim of sonship, to call God his Father, and to claim a oneness of mission with God. Jesus' claim, if it stood alone, without his ability to do the Father's works, would be disqualified. Without such works, he gives people no evidence for believing. However, the fact that Jesus can bring healing to the blind, for example, speaks for his claim. For even if they do not believe his words, the leaders must acknowledge the works that Jesus has performed. The result would be that they would come to know (aorist tense) and continue to understand (present tense) that the "Father is in me and I am in the Father." Now Jesus elaborates on John 10:30 and points out the union between Father and Son. The Jews still are not happy and seek to arrest Jesus, but he escapes. This exchange is Jesus' last public declaration to the Jews. It ends with him not only affirming his messiahship but also highlighting that sonship really is union with the Father. The question revealed an even greater claim in the answer than they had asked him to give. Jesus is not only Messiah; he is Son to the Father.

Jesus withdraws to Perea and the area where John the Baptist ministered. The evangelist does not say how long Jesus stayed there, but the Pereans' ex-

---

112. The Greek term noted here is the one used to describe Jesus as the "good" shepherd. Thus, the good shepherd has done good works from the Father.

113. Darrell L. Bock, *Blasphemy and Exaltation in Judaism and the Final Examination of Jesus,* WUNT 2.106 (Tübingen: Mohr, 1998), 30–112, discusses all the Jewish texts related to blasphemy in the Jewish tradition from the Old Testament through the Talmuds.

posure to Jesus left them with the clear impression that everything John had said as a witness to Jesus was true. John may not have performed miracles, but his word about the one to come could be embraced as coming from God. So, in Perea, many believed in Jesus.

This unit summarizes Jesus' claims for himself and the package that his work and word forms. The works testify to the reality of the Father's working through the sent one, the Son. The Son also is the shepherd. However, only the sheep that the Father gives to Jesus see this. They hear and follow the Son. In return, the Father and Son protect the sheep. No power can wrest the sheep from their hands.

J22. The Seventh Sign: Jesus Shows His Power over Life— The Raising of Lazarus and the Jewish Reaction
(John 11:1–54) (Aland §§259–60)

For John, the resuscitation of Lazarus is a catalyst to Jesus' death (John 11:53).[114] This sometimes is seen as a problem because the Synoptics say nothing of the event.[115] However, this is hypercriticism. The Synoptics themselves note numerous different points where official concern gets raised to a level at which something must be done to stop Jesus (e.g., Mark 3:6), although it is the temple cleansing that is the last straw. One probably should read John in a similar vein.

The account begins with Lazarus of Bethany being ill. His home is located about two miles east of Jerusalem, on the eastern side of the Mount of Olives (John 11:18 refers to fifteen stadia; cf. Mark 11:11; 14:3). John notes, in anticipation of the story in John 12, that Mary, Lazarus's sister, is the one who anointed Jesus' feet with her hair. Her sister is Martha, as Luke 10:38–42 also indicates. They send word to Jesus that "the one whom you love" is ill. Jesus does not come immediately, because he notes that the sickness will not result in death but will be an occasion whereby the Son of God may be glorified.

In fact, the text notes that Jesus stayed two days longer after getting word of Lazarus's condition, probably to indicate that he would work on the Father's timing and not by the urgency of a person's request. A review of the timing, which shows that Lazarus had been dead four days (John 11:39) when Jesus got to Martha and Mary, indicates that Lazarus already had died by the time Jesus got word asking for help, although he was told that Lazarus was

114. Lazarus's name is a variation on Eleazar and means "God helps," but John makes nothing of this.
115. For treatments of issues tied to historicity, including a critical evaluation of weak claims that interpret this event as one created from the story of the rich man and Lazarus in Luke 16:19–31, see Carson, *John*, 403–4; Morris, *John*, 473–76.

only ill. It thus appears that Lazarus died shortly after the messengers were dispatched. The four days appear to encompass a day's journey to reach Jesus, two days' wait, and then a day's journey back, although another scenario is possible.[116] It is significant that Jesus arrives after four days have passed since the death, because in Judaism there is seen to be no chance of resuscitation after four days. The rabbis held that the soul hovered over a body for three days in hopes of returning to the body. On the fourth day, there was no hope (*Leviticus Rabbah* 18.1; *Ecclesiastes Rabbah* 12.6; *m. Yebamot* 16.3 holds that a person is identifiable for only three days).[117] By the fourth day, the bulk of the mourning was done.

Jesus returns despite the risk of stoning. In fact, when Jesus proposes to go back to Judea, the disciples argue that he should not go, because it is too dangerous. He then mentions that the day has twelve hours and that one must walk while it is day. Jesus is noting that the time for his ministry is running out. He must act before it becomes night. As long as it is day, disciples will be safe because they will have light to see. So they will go and awaken Lazarus from his death sleep. The disciples misunderstand Jesus as speaking literally that Lazarus can wake up on his own. There is no need for a long trip to help him. So Jesus explains that Lazarus has died and that he must go, since it is an opportunity for them to see and believe that Jesus has power over life. This last idea is implied by what Jesus will do when he gets there and resuscitates Lazarus. Thomas, the Twin (the meaning of Didymus), anticipates another result, namely, that the opposition will overwhelm them all and they will die. He is ready to face such an end.

When they arrive, many Jews are consoling the family, as was common at such a time. Martha, always the activist, comes to meet Jesus. She notes that had Jesus been able to come, Lazarus would not have died, but that God will give whatever Jesus might ask. It is an initial statement of faith. Jesus replies that Lazarus will rise, which she understands to mean that he would be among the righteous in the resurrection of the last day. Jesus has far more than that to show about Lazarus and himself. For here the sign will indicate, as Jesus says, "I am the resurrection and the life. Those who believe in me, though they die, yet shall they live, and those who live and believe in me shall never die—forever." The statement about not dying is emphatic, using a double negative.

116. Carson, *John*, 407, gives an alternative scenario. It has Jesus too far away (in Galilee, not the Transjordan) to have been reached in a day by the messengers. On this scenario, Lazarus dies just before Jesus starts to return, about the time that Jesus notes his death in 11:11 (his "falling asleep"). Jesus' distant locale means a four-day journey back, assuming a pace of about forty to forty-five kilometers a day.

117. This remark includes the fact that a body was buried immediately upon death, as the haste to bury Jesus shows. The importance of such quick burials even overrode the command to rest on the Sabbath by allowing at least preparation of the body on the Sabbath (*m. Šabbat* 23.4–5). However, there is no indication that Lazarus died on the Sabbath.

This remark turns the coming miracle into a teaching about Jesus' authority to give unending life. So he asks Martha if she believes this. She responds with a threefold confession. While Jesus is greeted as Lord, he is confessed first as the Christ, then as the Son of God, and finally as the one who comes into the world. He is the promised sent one. Martha is about to learn all that this confession entails in terms of Jesus' authority and power.

At Jesus' request, Martha goes to get Mary. They journey to meet Jesus, who has stayed at the location where he met Martha. An entourage of Jews follows Mary, thinking that she is headed for the tomb to mourn. Mourners were common at a death, and Jewish texts describe even poor families as having two flute players and a wailing woman (*m. Ketubbot* 4.4). When Mary finally sees Jesus, she greets him much as Martha had, noting that if he had come earlier and been present, Lazarus would not have died. The scene draws a reaction from Jesus. Although many texts translate ἐτάραξεν as "troubled," the verb that precedes it actually means "angered" (ἐμβριμάομαι; cf. John 11:38; Matt. 9:30; Mark 1:43; 14:5 [all the Synoptic texts look at a harsh rebuke]).[118] The point is that the presence of death is something that angers Jesus. He already had said that he would work a miracle to deal with the tragic and frustrating situation (11:11). The idea that the anger is directed either at being urged to do something or at the crowd's disbelief appeals to themes not even raised by the text. Jesus does not feel pressured into performing the act of compassion; he was ready to heal when he departed to meet them. Nowhere up to this point does Jesus rebuke the crowd or the sisters for a lack of faith. In fact, his queries yield confessions, although they do not reflect a complete understanding. Moved by this scene, Jesus asks where Lazarus is buried. Jesus weeps as he nears the tomb, so that the Jews note Jesus' love for Lazarus. Jesus' tears reflect the apparent tragedy of the scene and the genuine intense emotion that death generates. However, others nearby take a more skeptical approach, noting that someone who is able to make the blind see should have been able to keep Lazarus from dying. The remark indicates a note of failure. In this group's view, nothing more can be done.

So Jesus, still angered by the scene, approaches the cave tomb and the stone that covers it. Jesus orders the covering stone removed, but Martha complains that after four days the stench will be intolerable. Jesus asks a question that expects a positive reply: Did he not tell her that if she believed, she would see God's glory? So the stone is removed. Jesus lifts his eyes to heaven (cf. John 17:1) and prays for a sign—the Father always hears him, but this request is made before the people so that they may believe that the Father has sent him. Jesus as the commissioned one is one of John's most basic themes (John 3:17; 7:28–29). So Jesus calls for Lazarus to come out, and the "dead" man, now

---

118. See BAGD, 254, 805; BDAG, 322, 990 §2 ("troubled" or "agitated"). Carson (*John*, 415–16) makes the point that ταράσσω is not about grief, empathy, or pain.

alive, emerges with feet and hands wrapped in the burial bandages and his face wrapped in a cloth. Some critics of the story object, asking how a bound man could walk, but there is no indication that he is wrapped in a way that prevents movement, albeit restricted. The normal process was to bind the ankles and tie the hands to the body.[119] Jesus commands that Lazarus be unbound. God has shown his glory and the power of his sent Son over life. Now comes the reaction.

As in other scenes in John, the miracle splits the crowd. Some believe in Jesus on the basis of "seeing what he did." His power over life was persuasive. Others go to the Pharisees to report on what Jesus was doing. The report spurs the leaders to action. The chief priests and the Pharisees convene a council. Some critics complain that John has erred here because the Pharisees were not members of the council, but again such skepticism about the account is overdrawn. The council was predominantly Sadducean, but the Pharisees' influence and the fact that scribes, most of whom were Pharisees, also comprised part of the membership mean that John's description is adequate.[120]

At the gathering, the leaders realize that the situation is politically volatile. If they do nothing and Jesus continues to perform signs and draw people to himself who believe, then his popularity and the kingdom hope that he generates might lead the Romans to come and destroy both the holy place and the nation. The reference to the "holy place" is literally to "the place" and can be a reference to Jerusalem, with the temple especially in view (*m. Bikkurim* 2.2; 2 Macc. 5:19). The irony was, of course, that the nation did act to remove Jesus and still, in A.D. 70, they lost both their holy place and their political role. By the time John's Gospel probably is written, this has taken place.

The high priest in that fateful year was Caiaphas. This "dating" of Caiaphas to a specific year is not, as some critics claim, an attempt to argue that the role of high priest was voted on annually, a view that would make John ignorant of how the high priest was selected. Rather, John is highlighting who the leader was at this key time.[121] Caiaphas and Pilate apparently had a solid arrangement that allowed the Jewish leader to remain in power, until Pilate was removed in A.D. 36.

Caiaphas is rather direct, almost boorish, matching the reputation that Sadducees have in some Jewish texts.[122] He tells them that they know nothing at all. They should understand that it is better for one man to die for the people than for a whole nation to perish. Caiaphas's point is that Jesus' death will benefit and protect the nation. Again irony is present, because his remarks are

119. Morris, *John*, 499.
120. Brown, *John I–XII*, 439.
121. For the grammar involved here, see BDF §186.2. Also note the repetition of the point in 11:51.
122. So Josephus on the Sadducees in *War* 2.8.14 §166: "Their conversation with those of their own party is as barbarous as if they were strangers to them."

seen by John as true but in a way Caiaphas never intended. In fact, John calls the remarks prophetic, emerging from Caiaphas's role as high priest. This kind of prophecy from a high priest, even an unrighteous one, is well known in Judaism (Josephus, *Ant.* 11.8.4 §327, relates that Jaddua foresaw Alexander the Great's sparing of Jerusalem; *Ant.* 13.10.7 §299 notes how the unrighteous Hyrcanus prophesied). Unconscious prophecy also was known in Judaism, if later texts are any guide (see [1] Pharaoh's daughter in Exod. 2:6, 9, according to *b. Soṭah* 12ᵇ; [2] Moses and the Israelites in Exod. 15:17, according to *b. Baba Batra* 119ᵇ; [3] *Midrash Psalms* 90 §4, which reports a rabbi remarking, "All prophets, who have prophesied, have not known what they have prophesied, only Moses and Isaiah have it known").

The remarks are significant in ways beyond what Caiaphas suggests, because although the high priest in speaking of the nation had only Israel in mind, John extends the remarks in 11:52 beyond the nation. Jesus' work will include the result of gathering "into one the children of God who are scattered abroad." This image recalls the work of the good shepherd who will gather the sheep of this flock and other sheep, in John 10:15–17. In the end, Jesus' death for others will unify the people of God.

For John, this meeting sealed Jesus' fate. In the Gospels, many such key meetings took place. Mark 3:6 has a fateful meeting early on, while all the Synoptics portray the temple cleansing as a decisive act. The point is not that any one meeting did it, but that once opposition arose, the movement to deal decisively with Jesus was underway. Certain events added to the desire and momentum to act decisively. The miracle with Lazarus was such a moment for the visible demonstration of Jesus' authority over life and was too threatening a sign to ignore, even more than giving sight to the blind.

Jesus withdrew at this point to the wilderness. Most scholars locate Ephraim where modern El-Tayibeh is, a locale noted in 2 Chron. 13:19 and in Josephus (*War* 4.9.9 §551). If so, Jesus is twelve miles northeast of Jerusalem.

J23. The Anointing at Bethany and Opposition near Passover Time (John 11:55–12:11) (Aland §§261, 267–68)

Jesus enters Jerusalem to celebrate a third Passover in John (see also 2:13; 6:4). When the text says that "many" went up to purify themselves, the estimates are that 85,000 to 125,000 pilgrims were added to a city population of 25,000.[123] Purification was required by Num. 9:10 (cf. 2 Chron. 30:17–18).

---

123. Brown, *John I–XII,* 445.

This was especially important for those who socialized or had contact with Gentiles (Josephus, *War* 1.11.6 §229).

Speculation was rampant. Would Jesus come? The question is stated in a way that emphatically rejects the likelihood that Jesus will show up. Everything about this setting is tense because the leadership had given orders to make known his whereabouts so that he could be arrested. But as John 12 will show, Jesus does not fear human power. He knows why he enters the city.

The next event John places at six days before Passover and in Bethany, where Lazarus lived. This is probably the preceding Saturday (and Friday night).[124] What follows is an anointing. This event is similar to Mark 14:3–9 and Matt. 26:6–13 and has some surface similarities to Luke 7:6–50. As in Luke, the woman anoints Jesus' feet, but that is about the only matching detail with Luke. The timing is different (in the earlier Galilean ministry versus near the end of Jesus' ministry). The host at the home is different (Pharisee versus Lazarus). The character of the woman is different (sinful woman versus Mary). The issues discussed at the meal are different (honor and complaining versus burial). The accounts in Matthew and Mark are much closer to John's report and probably refer to the same event, even though in those two Gospels Jesus' head rather than feet is anointed, and the event is placed after Jesus enters Jerusalem. It is clear that a large amount of perfume is used, and the comparison with the anointing of a body for burial suggests that the anointing may well not have been limited to one locale. The issue of timing may be nothing more than a different choice about where to place events tied to the end, especially given the fact that Matthew and Mark often work topically. It is quite possible that John's event matches Matthew and Mark and that the Synoptics' timing reflects Judas's act of betrayal growing out of this event.

Mary takes a liter of "pure" nard (about eleven fluid ounces) and anoints Jesus' head.[125] She uses enough that the house fills with its fragrance.[126] The complainers in Matthew and Mark are unnamed, but John is not so shy. Judas Iscariot, the one who would betray Jesus, speaks up. His complaint is that the money spent to purchase the nard, a year's working wage of three hundred denarii, could have been invested better for the poor. The narration explains that the issue was not that Judas cared about the poor, but that being keeper of the money box, he would steal coins. In other words, Judas was a hypocrite. Jesus responds by defending the woman, telling Judas to leave her alone. Jesus

---

124. For the chronology, see Carson, *John*, 427.

125. The term translated as "pure" is disputed in meaning, as πιστική probably derives from a term meaning "faithful." If so, the purity of the perfume makes it more expensive. Another option is that it is something like a trade name for a type of nard, a term that we no longer recognize. Other suggestions also exist, but they are less likely. See Morris, *John*, 511 n. 14.

126. A later Jewish text from *Ecclesiastes Rabbah* 7.1.1 says, "Good oil is diffused from the bed-chamber to the dining hall while a good name is diffused from one end of the world to the other." The proverbial image fits this scene well and speaks well of the one anointing Jesus.

seems to explain, in an apparently elliptical remark, that she has kept this perfume for this special act, which in turn prepares him for burial. The ominous
note of Jesus' approaching death is raised. Jesus notes that there always will be
time to care for the poor, but there is not much time left to honor him.[127]

The gathering of Jesus and Lazarus drew a crowd; the participants in the
unusual "resurrection" miracle became a reason for the crowd to gather. The
attention that Lazarus drew made the chief priests nervous, and they plotted
to remove Lazarus, the "evidence" who was causing many to be led away from
their influence and believe in Jesus. The final "sign" is a final reason to act.

J24. Jesus Enters Jerusalem at Passover (John 12:12–19)
(Aland §269)

This text is one of the few events present in all four Gospels (Matt. 21:1–
9; Mark 11:1–10; Luke 19:28–40). John places the entry in a context in
which the crowd has heard that Jesus is coming to Jerusalem. Unlike the Synoptics, John makes no effort to detail how Jesus procured the animal on which
he rides into town. Instead, he launches immediately into the celebration that
accompanied Jesus' entry. The crowd takes palm leaves, which grew in the
area, and begins waving them in praise. First Maccabees 13:51 describes another celebration using such leaves in Jersualem when Simon of Maccabees
celebrates his victory over the Syrians. The palm leaf had symbolic importance. Palms were used at the Feast of Tabernacles (Lev. 23:40) and during
other celebrations (1 Macc. 13:51 [of Simon Maccabaeus]; 2 Macc. 10:7 [at
the rededication of the temple]).[128] In earlier Jewish history, insurgent Jews
used the palm as a symbol on coins minted during their rebellion. The image
was associated with nationalistic hope. The people seem to be greeting Jesus
with nationalistic expectations.

The greeting underscores this point. The call of *Hosanna* is Aramaic and
means "Save, please." "Blessed is the one who comes in the name of the Lord"
comes from Ps. 118:26. It probably was a priestly greeting for a king leading
pilgrims into the temple after a victory (cf. Luke 13:35; 19:37). The identification of Jesus as "King of Israel" is parallel to the declaration in Luke 19:38
and conceptually similar to Mark 11:10, where the kingdom of David is
evoked. The "coming one" is a way to refer to Jesus in the Synoptics and in
John (Matt. 11:3; 23:39; John 1:27; 6:14; 11:27).

127. The remark about the poor here is not callous, but rather suggests that a ministry to
the poor always will be possible and is less important at this moment than worshiping God.
128. W. R. Farmer, "The Palm Branches of John 12,13," *Journal of Theological Studies,* n.s.,
3 (1952): 62–66.

Jesus rides a young donkey. John alone uses the diminutive term ὀνάριον to describe the animal, although later in the citation from Zech. 9:9 the term πῶλος is used (which also appears in the Synoptics) as well as the related ὄνος (which also appears in Matthew) when he describes two animals. This is not the horse of a victorious warrior. Although some interpreters question whether John highlights humility in describing Jesus' entry, it appears that the choice of an animal other than a horse indicates that a classic warrior is not present at this point.

The citation of Zech. 9:9 is a narrative comment by John. He notes that the significance of the passage was not appreciated until after Jesus was glorified. Nonetheless, the text serves as commentary of the event's point. The nation should not fear. This part of the citation is not from Zechariah, although it is like Isa. 40:9 and Zeph. 3:14.[129] The arrival of the king is a presentation and opportunity for Israel, addressed tenderly as "daughter of Zion." The Zechariah citation is important because of the context it evokes. Zechariah 9:10–11 makes the point that the nation will be at peace. The king will "proclaim peace to the nations. His rule will extend from sea to sea and from the River to the ends of the earth. As for you, because of the blood of my covenant with you, I will free your prisoners from the waterless pit." Thus, this king will bring peace, including to the nations, because the blood of covenant promise will be applied. The juxtaposition of the entry into Jerusalem with the anointing for burial may suggest that John is alluding to more than he cites. This is especially the case when the following text discusses how the Greeks are reacting.

As was noted, the citation of Zech. 9:9 is a comment by the evangelist, not a text used at the event. Barrett argues that this text means that the disciples did not appreciate the messianic import of the event even as the crowds raise a messianic note, showing a lack of historical accuracy.[130] This reading misses the point of the remark about the disciples lacking understanding until Jesus was glorified, which is about the event's tie to the scriptural citation, not the messianic association. John is honest in noting how some things about the events tied to Jesus were not fully appreciated until after his death.

Meanwhile, a second crowd, which had seen the sign involving Lazarus, also greets Jesus and adds its testimony. The image is of converging crowds acclaiming Jesus as they approach him from different angles. The whole scene troubles the Pharisees. They cannot accept such a high expectation for Jesus. Ironically, they declare to each other, "Look, you can do nothing. Behold, the whole world [κόσμος] has gone after him." The leadership is very worried about the effect Jesus is having. They are worried about the Jewish response

---

129. It is debated whether this is a fused citation because the wording does not match Zechariah exactly. More important is what the whole passage affirms.
130. Barrett, *John*, 349.

and equate it with the world, while John is thinking about a much larger world that Jesus will impact.

J25. The Son of Man to Be Lifted Up Issues an Explanation and a Warning (John 12:20–50) (Aland §§302–4)

The final event in the public ministry of Jesus reflects a turning point to come. Some Greeks, God-fearers who were in Jerusalem to worship at the feast, approach Philip to request the opportunity to see Jesus.[131] The scene shows that Jesus was gaining the attention of those outside of Israel. Although the passage does not say whether the request was honored, because the Greeks disappear from the scene after this, Jesus' reply in terms of his work to come shows that the inclusion of the world ultimately is in view in his work. The introduction serves to frame the discourse that follows.

Jesus takes the request as an indication that his "hour" had come. This "hour" is important in John. Up until now, it was approaching and still future (John 2:4; 4:21, 23; 7:30; 8:20). From now on, its immediacy is stressed (John 12:27; 13:1, 17:1). The glorification of the Son of Man, in terms of his death and his vindication, is present (on glorification, see John 1:14; 8:50, 54; 12:28; 13:31–32). The picture that Jesus uses to explain the glorification is of a "dead" seed being dropped into the soil and then springing to life with much fruit. Jesus refers to his death, a death that will only begin the new chapter of his mission. Jesus' ministry is described in terms of the fruit it bears, an image in contrast to a parable that Jesus told in the Synoptics in which a lack of fruit from stewards, signifying the Jewish leadership, led to judgment (Luke 13:6–9; Matt. 21:33–46; Mark 12:1–12; Luke 20:9–18).

The fruit that Jesus yields also is an opportunity for those willing to "hate" their attachment to this world. Those who love a worldly life will lose that life, but those who hate their life in this world, in terms of sharing the world's perspective and values, will keep life for eternity. This is similar to statements in Mark 8:34, Matt. 16:25, and Luke 9:24. Attachment to this world will only yield death, while association with what Jesus offers brings eternal life. Thus, the person who serves Jesus follows him. In this context, following must refer to rejection by the world and sharing in Jesus' death by identifying with what his death represents. The reward is that where Jesus is, the servant will also be. Thus, the Father will honor the one who serves Jesus. Here is the idea that with the life that the disciple gives up or loses, there comes adoption and re-

---

131. Philip appears to be chosen because he is one of the few disciples with a Greek name and comes from a locale, Bethsaida, just on the other side of the Decapolis, a predominantly Greek region. Philip in turn goes to Andrew for advice. Andrew is the only other disciple with a Greek name, although it is clear that both disciples were Jews.

ception into the family of God, as 12:36 also will affirm. Access to the Father is possible only through the glorified Son of Man. Heaven will be home to the Son and to those adopted into his family.

Nonetheless, the approaching death is troubling to Jesus. It represents genuine suffering. Will Jesus ask to be delivered from this hour? John does not relate the later scene at Gethsemene that the Synoptics present. The reflection that Jesus gives here is the equivalent of that scene. Jesus will not seek to escape the call, because this glorification is the very reason he has come. His glorification will allow the Father to glorify his own name. Jesus has come to honor God and perform his divine will. So Jesus affirms his commitment to do what God has called him to do.

At this point, the heavenly voice speaks, just as it had at the baptism and at the transfiguration in the Synoptics. It is the only utterance from heaven noted in John during Jesus' ministry. It comes in response to Jesus' call that God's name be glorified. The voice declares that God has glorified his name and will do so again. God thus affirms that Jesus' ministry to this point has glorified his name despite the "world's" rejection. Coming events will do the same. The work of Jesus and the will of God are one. Only Jesus understands the utterance, because to everyone else it sounds like thunder. In the Greek, the standing crowd is said only to have "heard and said it thundered." No grammatical object for the hearing appears; only their judgment surfaces about what was present. Some even suggest that an angel had spoken. When Jesus says that the voice came for the crowd's sake and not to benefit him, the point is that even though the crowd did not understand the utterance, they should have sensed in the creation's response of thunder that heaven confirmed what Jesus was affirming. Thus, the utterance stood as a heavenly endorsement.

With the glorification of God through the Son of Man affirmed, Jesus now speaks as one who bears such authority. The world's rejection means two things: the judgment of that rejecting world and the casting out of the "ruler of this world." Ironically enough, Jesus' removal and death mean renewed life for Jesus and those tied to him but judgment for those seeking and affirming his demise. It also means the removal of Satan. The "lifting up" of Jesus (cf. John 3:14) will allow Jesus to draw humanity to himself. Here is where the Greeks who triggered this discourse are addressed and included. Jesus' death means that those of any nation may come to him and find life. As John notes, in this way Jesus explained the significance of his death.

The crowd again is perplexed. If the "law," which here refers to Scripture, teaches that the Christ "will remain to the age," then how can he argue that the Son of Man will be lifted up? What kind of function and identity does this Son of Man have? These questions are not a request to identify the Son of Man but to explain his character in terms of the type of ministry he will have. They sense that Jesus is speaking about a death, so how can the exalted Son of

Man/Messiah have such a role? The texts that seem to be appealed to here are those that suggest the unending character of the Messiah's rule (2 Sam. 7:7–16; Ps. 72:17; 89:35–37; Isa. 9:7; Ezek. 37:25). In some strands of later Judaism, this was developed to affirm a highly exalted role for a figure called the Son of Man (*1 Enoch* 49.1; 62.14) or a messianic figure (*Psalms of Solomon* 17–18).[132] Jesus is introducing them to a new idea about the coming exalted figure that they have trouble grasping.

Once again, Jesus does not answer their question directly. Instead, he suggests "who" this Son of Man is by comparing that figure to the presence of light and noting the opportunity that still remains. This light remains for a little while longer. Consider his words and presence. Walk while the light still is present. Figuratively, Jesus is calling his audience to embrace the light and walk in the direction it illumines. The dangerous alternative is that darkness will overtake them and they will lose the ability to find the way. The contrast between light and darkness is a basic Johannine image (John 1:4–9; 3:19–21; 8:12). It also is a fundamental image in the Synoptics (Luke 1:78–79; Matt. 4:15–16). The call is to believe in the light while they have it, so that they may become "children of light." Those who believe inherit the position and identity of the one embraced. The point stands at the heart of the Johannine portrait of the gospel. Here is one of the last public words of Jesus in John's Gospel. It summarizes his ministry and issues in a choice that contains both a warning and an invitation. The invitation and warning will conclude the passage as well. Ultimately, being neutral about Jesus is impossible. His claims force a choice and demand a decision about him.

Having made his point, Jesus withdraws one last time and hides himself from the crowd until the hour truly arrives. John concludes this section of his Gospel with one final summary. Part of that summary is his own explanation, while the concluding portion is a final public word of Jesus. Given the remark that Jesus withdrew and hid himself, this summary may be an extract from what Jesus taught in this general period as opposed to belonging exactly in this time frame.

Jesus had performed a series of signs, some of them quite impressive, such as giving sight and raising the dead. Such demonstrations of divine power did not lead many to faith. John 12:38 explains that Jesus' rejection was a fulfillment of a divine plan revealed in Scripture.[133] John cites Isa. 53:1 and 6:10 in turn. The citation from Isa. 53:1 matches the LXX. It raises the question about who has believed the report surrounding the Servant and experienced the power (arm) of the Lord. The note of rejection is expressed in a rhetorical

132. Other strands in Judaism did foresee a time when the Messiah might perish (*4 Ezra* [= 2 Esdras] 7:28–29), but that is not the perspective of those who are speaking to Jesus here.

133. The use of ἵνα here has telic force. It signals that the unbelief is grounded in the goal of the plan revealed by God through Isaiah.

question. John 12:39 goes on to elaborate. This hesitation to accept the report was grounded in an inability to believe, as Isaiah stressed in his acceptance of his call. Like Isaiah, who also was given a ministry that met with rejection, Jesus ministered a divine call whose character was sketched before he came. John limits the citation to a discussion of the eyes and heart, for it was the signs in particular that were missed as Jesus worked. God has blinded eyes and hearts, lest they see, perceive, and be healed. God's sovereignty certainly is stressed here, but never in a way that removes responsibility for failing to see what God had done. Both the blindness and the power of darkness are staggering. Only a gracious exercise of divine power can reverse it.

John notes that Isaiah saw "his" glory and spoke of him. This reading of Isa. 6 may reflect Jewish targumic tradition, or a reading that also includes Isa. 6:3, or both. For where Isa. 6 says that Isaiah saw the Lord, the targums to Isa. 6:1 and 6:4 say that he saw his glory and his Shekinah, respectively. The difference may be a sign of respect for God and the idea that no one sees God directly (John 1:18a). So what one saw was his glory. John appears to go one step further than this Jewish view. Those who see God really see Jesus, who is the image of his glory and the revelator of the Father (John 1:18b). So John speaks of Isaiah seeing Jesus' glory, a glory that he understands to be reflective of the Father's glory because to see one is to see the other (John 12:45).[134] John closes his summary by noting that despite the rejection, he is explaining that some authorities did believe in Jesus, although the threat of excommunication kept them from speaking out because they loved the "glory" (praise) of people over giving "glory" (honor) to God. John has noted Nicodemus (John 3:1–3) and Joseph of Arimathea (John 19:38) in this category, although at the burial they seem to have found the strength to come forth.

Jesus' final public summary in John affirms again the inseparable connection between himself and God. To believe in Jesus is to believe in the one sending Jesus. The "sent one" is a key Johannine theme (John 1:18; 3:17; 4:34; 5:23–24, 30, 37; 6:38–39; 7:16, 18, 28, 33; 8:16, 18, 26, 29; 9:4; 13:20; 14:9). Jesus has come as light (12:46). Here the perfect tense stresses Jesus' lingering presence as light. Belief leads to escape from darkness (John 1:4–9). To fail to keep Jesus' words does not mean that he judges, because he came to save; it does mean that a judge remains, namely, his sayings, because they are from the Father. It is the Father's standard that one must measure oneself against, and that standard is inseparably tied to Jesus and responding to him. One's response to those words will be the basis of judgment on the last day. Jesus' point here is not that he does not judge, but that this judgment is not independent of God, whose will he reveals and teaches. Thus, Jesus does

---

134. Another less likely way to take the verse is to suggest that John is merely saying that when Isaiah saw God's glory, he was looking forward to seeing Christ's day. The verse is very much like John 8:58 in its force when taken as describing Jesus directly.

not speak on his own authority, but rather, Jesus speaks what the Father who sent him has commanded him to say. God's commandment is to believe unto eternal life. This remark may well explain how Jesus can be called God's Word in John 1. For God's Word resides in the one who is the Word and in the one sent to reveal the Word. Jesus merely speaks what God has spoken ("even as the Father spoke to me, so I am speaking"). Jesus' word yields life, just as the law was said to do in the past (Deut. 32:45–47). Jesus' word here is the contrast to the failure of the law, as expressed in John 5:39. He is the one who has the word of life (John 6:68; 10:10). Jesus' last public word is about the inseparability of the Father from the sent one and of the Father's word from that of Jesus.

Conclusion

The "book of signs" testifies to the work of the sent one of God. Divine power flows through Jesus' work. His power provides drink, heals, makes the lame to walk even on the Sabbath, feeds, allows him to walk on the sea, brings sight, and raises the dead. Divine revelation emerges from Jesus' teaching. He is the one who brings birth from above, living water that never will leave one thirsty, the bread of life that sustains, the source of the Spirit, the truth that sets one free, and the light that is the life of humanity; he is the shepherd of the sheep, the resurrection, and the life. For some, he was and is the ground of relationship with God. His work is inseparable from the Father. For others, his claims were extreme and impious, an indication that a blasphemer had come. Ignoring the divine signs, those who rejected him and had authority to do so pressed for his removal. What they saw as the removal of a heretic, Jesus saw as the suffering and vindication of the Son, a glorification in which the Father would lift up the Son to take up the sins of the world. The drama of that final confrontation and unique death lies ahead in John, in the remaining section of his Gospel. It is rightly called the "book of glory," for in the Father's glorification of the Son is the testimony to the glory of the Father as well as the provision of God to save people from every nation. This is what the sent one came to do: "Unless a grain of wheat falls into the ground and dies, it remains alone; but if it dies, it bears much fruit." As John 12:24 says, the book of glory is about the abundant fruitfulness of God that yields a rich harvest of new life to his glory.

FOURTEEN

The Book of Glory

The Farewell Discourse and the Johannine Passion Account—
The Hour Has Come (John 13–21)

There are notable differences between the Books ["Book of Signs" and "Book of Glory"]. First, during the public ministry, as described in the Book of Signs, Jesus' words and deeds were addressed to a wide audience, provoking a crisis of faith—some believed and some refused to believe. The Book of Glory, however, is addressed to the restricted audience of those who believed. Second, the signs of the first book anticipated what Jesus would do for men once he was glorified. The second book describes the glorification, i.e., "the hour" of passion, crucifixion, resurrection, and ascension wherein Jesus is lifted up to the Father to enjoy again the glory that he had with the Father before the world existed (xvii 5). These differences are apparent in the first verse of the Book of Glory, "Jesus was aware that the hour had come for him to pass from this world to the Father. Having loved his own who were in the world, he now showed his love for them to the very end" (xiii 1).[1]

It appears, then, that it was part of the evangelist's intention in these chapters [Farewell Discourses] to show how the life eternal, which has been set forth in sign and promise in the Book of Signs, is realized in the experience of the disciples (i.e. of all Christian believers), and to exhibit its true nature and character. It is described in various terms, but chiefly in terms of the mutual indwelling of Christ and His disciples, reproducing the archetypal mutual indwelling of Father and Son (xiv.10–11, 20, xv.4–5, xvii.20–23).[2]

1. Raymond E. Brown, *The Gospel according to John XIII–XXI,* AB 29A (Garden City, N.Y.: Doubleday, 1970), 541.
2. C. H. Dodd, *The Interpretation of the Fourth Gospel* (Cambridge: Cambridge University Press, 1953), 398.

The final section of John is composed of the farewell discourse (John 13–17), the passion (John 18–19), and the resurrection appearances (John 20–21). As we come to the final portion of John's Gospel, the focus turns in a twofold direction.

The first direction is the instruction and encouragement to the disciples, explaining why Jesus must depart. A key emphasis underlying the teaching is the union that Jesus will form with his own through the sending of the Paraclete. The sending of the Spirit will make disciples one with Jesus. The end of Luke has a similar emphasis (Luke 24:49), as does the assurance that Jesus gives at the end of Matthew that he will always be with them (Matt. 28:18–20). So also in John, Jesus' death clears the way through the forgiveness it provides for God to adopt the disciple and enable the believer with power through the indwelling Spirit. This provision stands at the core of the gospel as the Gospels see it. Also within the same provision is an exhortation to the disciples to show their unity with God by their abiding (or remaining) in Christ and by demonstrating love for each other. Here are the two major practical exhortations that Jesus gives: stay faithful even in the midst of a rejecting world, and love each other. All of this enablement is directed toward mission and witness to a needy world, evidenced in a service grounded in love.

The second direction of the unit is the telling of the passion and its aftermath. Perhaps no one gives the ethos of this final section better than C. H. Dodd. He says of the passion narrative, "It is as though the evangelist, having sufficiently set forth the meaning of the death and resurrection of Christ, turned to the reader and said, 'And now I will tell you what actually happened, and you will see that the facts themselves bear out my interpretation.'"[3] As intense as these final scenes are and as dramatic as Jesus' death was, the appearances to Thomas, Peter, and others made a lasting impact with their echoing calls to love and faithfulness, concluding the unit with the same themes that had opened this final section of the Gospel.

J26. Jesus Washes the Disciples' Feet (John 13:1–20) (Aland §309)

John introduces all the events of the last week in 13:1 by noting Jesus' knowledge that the time for him to return to the Father had come. In fact, the "hour" had come. What motivated him in these last moments of ministry was a love for "his own." The remark closes with a typical Johannine double entendre, as John notes that Jesus loved them "to the end/to the uttermost." The construction εἰς τέλος probably carries this double force. Thus, the frame of the last week is that it is the consummate expression of Jesus' love. God so

3. Ibid., 431–32.

loved the world that he gave his unique son (John 3:16), but Jesus so loved the world that he gave himself.

A second dimension of this last week is that it represented a cosmic battle. Satan was at work trying to stop Jesus. Behind Judas's act of betrayal stands Satan's initiative.[4] Jesus' ministry is so important that the personification of evil will do anything to try to stop it.

However, no cosmic opposition could stop what the Father had planned and the authority that the Father had given to the Son. Jesus acted knowing that the Father had given him all things and that he had come from God and was returning to him. It was in the context of this authority that Jesus' actions take on an additional poignancy when he moves to wash the disciples' feet. On the one hand, his rank explains why the washing has symbolic significance. It points to his service for them, especially in providing forgiveness of sins and the Spirit, themes of the upcoming discourse. He has the authority to cleanse them. On the other hand, his rank makes the washing all the more amazing because it is the one with all authority who takes on the task of a menial slave and humbly washes the feet of his disciples. In performing this act, Jesus is doing something that Hebrew slaves were instructed was too menial to perform for their Gentile masters.[5] When the time came for Jesus to wash Peter's feet, the disciple reacted in typical Petrine style, hesitating to let Jesus proceed by asking if he was going to do it.[6] Jesus explains that although Peter does not understand the importance of this act now, he "afterward" will understand, a remark very much like those made later in the discourse where the coming of the Spirit will bring understanding. Peter emphatically refuses to let Jesus wash his feet.[7] Jesus replies that if he does not permit Jesus to serve him in the way symbolized here, then Peter will have "no part" (i.e., no share) in him. The premise of Jesus' work and our sharing in it is that we receive the "washing" that he gives us. Any sense that we do not need his work is to exclude ourselves from its benefit. In this remark, we see that Jesus is portraying the cleansing that he has the authority to give. This washing is a precursor to what the provision of his death is, an act of service and love for his own, giving them a share in him.

4. There is a textual problem in John 13:2. Either Satan put it in his own heart to act through Judas (Ἰούδας) or Satan put it in Judas's heart to do the deed (Ἰούδα). The former reading is slightly more likely. The basic point is not altered either way.

5. Although in other settings it was permitted as an act of respect (*Mekilta* 1 on Exod. 21:2 [82a] cites Lev. 25:39 as the reason such an act should not be performed, though some texts instruct a wife to do this for her husband, or a son or daughter for their father).

6. A later Jewish text from the Jerusalem Talmud (*y. Peʾah* 1.15c.14) records an incident where the mother of Rabbi Ishmael took her son to rabbinic court for refusing to let her honor him by washing his feet. For the rabbi, the task was too demeaning, but for the mother, it was an honor. The scene is similar to the difference of opinion that surfaces between Peter and Jesus.

7. The text uses the emphatic οὐ μή here.

Peter's response is to swing to the other side of the pendulum. Now he asks to be completely washed—hands, head, and feet! Peter is well meaning, wanting all that Jesus can give, but still he does not appreciate what Jesus is doing. As a symbolic act, such a full bath was not required. So Jesus deepens the symbolism as he explains that the one having bathed does not need a full washing, as a washing has taken place that already makes them clean. Another textual problem impacts the verse and meaning here. Most manuscripts add a note "except for his feet" after the reference to no longer needing a washing after bathing, to make the point that only the feet are washed after the bath because the feet need repeated cleaning. This is the likely reading of the verse.[8] It makes the additional point that beyond the washing that makes the disciples clean, Jesus continues to "cleanse" the feet as he continues to serve the disciples after they are his by taking care of their subsequent need to have their "walk" cleansed. Thus, Jesus' service is not only for the initial moment of washing but also for the subsequent spiritual benefits that the disciples will receive. This makes a good preamble to the work of the Spirit.

However, not everyone is clean. Jesus notes that he is aware of what Judas has proposed to do. As is often the case in the Johannine passion material, John does not detail the human side of Judas's plot as the Synoptics had done. He simply reveals that Jesus knew of the act. In washing even the one who will betray him, Jesus symbolizes the readiness to cleanse but notes that for those who reject the offer, cleansing is not provided.

Beyond the symbolism of death and cleansing, Jesus now makes an additional point about the motivation of his act and its exemplary model. He asks the disciples if they know what he has done and then reminds them that he is their Lord and teacher, one who is ranked ahead of them. If Jesus, holding that superior rank, washes their feet, they as his students should do the same for each other. The act is an example of how they should treat one another. The word for "example" often points to a "pattern" of activity in its use (ὑπόδειγμα [Heb. 4:11; 8:5; 9:23; James 5:10; 2 Pet. 2:6]). The term is even thrown forward in the sentence for emphasis. He reminds them that the servant is not greater than the master, nor is the one sent greater than the sender. So if the Master-Sender does such things, so should the servants and sent ones. He then gives a blessing to those who do such things. The essence of the disciples' relationship to each other is to be grounded in the example of Jesus' humility, service, and love, where rank expresses itself in giving and serving.

Once again Jesus notes that the blessing is not for all of them. He has chosen them all, but Scripture (Ps. 41:9) has noted that one who shares in table

---

8. The text appears in Codices Vaticanus, Ephraemi, Regius, Cyprius, and Washingtonensis, Family 13, and the Old Latin. Variations on this addition include 𝔓⁶⁶ and 𝔓⁷⁵ as well as the Byzantine text. If the text lacks this addition, as in ℵ, then Jesus points only to the cleansing his ministry provides.

fellowship will "lift up his heel against me." Like the righteous sufferer of old, Jesus is betrayed by one who shares his friendship and table. Contempt, not love, motivates the act of that one. Jesus tells them that he reveals this so that when it happens, they may believe that "I am." This absolute use of "I am" indicates the fullness of Jesus' authority and his awareness. So he issues a commission that reminds them that whoever receives one sent by him receives him and the one who sent him. Once again Jesus links himself inseparably to the Father and includes the disciples in the link.

J27. Jesus Foretells His Betrayal (John 13:21–30; Matt. 26:21–25; Mark 14:18–21; Luke 22:21–23) (Aland §310)

The gravity of the hour that has come is heightened when Jesus, troubled in his spirit, announces that one of those gathered will betray him. Because this final meal involved only the Twelve, the list of candidates is quite limited (Matt. 26:20; Mark 14:17). It is important to remember that our familiarity with the later story makes the surprise of such an announcement and its initially vague character hard to appreciate. Jesus gives neither the timing of the betrayal nor any other specific detail of its being successful or not. What he announces is the fact of its attempt. Its juxtaposition to his discussion of departure and death does suggest a proximity to and connection between betrayal and death, as well as some "success" in the effort. However, none of the disciples is clued in as to what is taking place, so that much of what is said and the connections are lost on them, at least at this time. Their puzzlement is evident in their reaction, as they look at each other "uncertain of whom he spoke."

One cryptic note in the narrative is about the disciple "whom Jesus loved." This is the first of several such references in John's Gospel to this figure (19:26–27; 20:2; 21:7, 20). There is good reason to see this person being John, son of Zebedee, the disciple who stands behind this Gospel. First, the figure must be one of the Twelve and be closely associated with Peter, as the scene in John 21 suggests (also 13:24; 20:2). Second, Peter, James, and John are the key trio within the Twelve and are said to be close to Jesus. Third, James died young (Acts 12:2), while John 21 suggests that the beloved disciple will have a long life. Fourth, John is mentioned nowhere in the Gospel—a curious fact, given his prominence elsewhere. The description seems to have two purposes. It suggests a humility in being named the object of Jesus' gracious attention and affection, as well as underscoring the proximity of the one who testifies to Jesus (John 21:20–25).[9]

9. Leon Morris, *The Gospel according to John*, rev. ed., NICNT (Grand Rapids: Eerdmans, 1995), 5–8.

The scene presupposes a major meal because it was especially at major meals that one reclined as is described here. The usual configuration involved couches set in a U shape around a table, with the diners' heads toward the table and feet away from it. A diner would lean on one elbow and use the other arm to eat.[10] So this disciple is signaled by Peter, who appears to be seated at some distance from Jesus, especially given the suggestion earlier in John 13 that his feet were washed at some later point in the sequence of disciples. Peter asks the beloved disciple to inquire as to the identity of the betrayer. John makes the inquiry of Jesus, apparently in private, since vv. 27–30 indicate that the other disciples do not know of the identification. Jesus replies, also apparently in private, that it is the one to whom he gives the piece of bread that he has dipped into the dish.[11]

Such an act, uninterpreted, could be seen as a sign of honor, certainly of friendship, a "provision" from the guest of honor. In a sense, it also could be seen as a last opportunity for Judas to change his course. At this point, after he takes the morsel, the narration refers to Satan entering Judas, the only use of "Satan" in this Gospel. Certainly Judas, having heard Jesus' more cryptic remarks, realized that his plan was known, but the disciple did not back off. So Jesus tells Judas to act quickly on what he is going to do. Literally, Jesus tells him to act "as quickly as possible"; the final phrase of 13:27 is probably elative in force.[12] The text says that the remark was not clear to anyone at the table. Some thought that because Judas kept the money, Jesus was instructing either that supplies be bought for the rest of the week-long feast or that alms be given for the poor, as often took place on this holiday.[13] Ironically, Judas is not going out into the dark to celebrate but to betray his Lord. John highlights

10. The chief seats were "above" (to the left) and "below" (to the right) of the guest of honor (*b. Berakot* 46[b]). John appears to be in the third, or right-hand, position. See Brown, *John XIII–XXI*, 574, who cites F. Prat's article in *Recherches de science religieuse* 15 (1925): 512–22.

11. The issue of whether or not this meal is a Passover meal is debated (see Synoptic unit 262). It is tied to the question of the chronology between the Synoptics and John. If this is a Passover meal (the reclining perhaps is evidence of a formal meal), then we may be at the point where Jesus dips the bread into the bitter herbs, the *haroseth* sauce of dates, raisins, and sour wine. See C. K. Barrett, *The Gospel according to St. John: An Introduction with Commentary and Notes on the Greek Text* (London: SPCK, 1955), 373.

12. BDF §244.1.

13. Does the remark about no one knowing mean no one else but John, given that some thought that Jesus had given instructions about either purchases or alms? The disputed practice of working up to the last minute before the Passover is noted in *m. Pesaḥim* 4.5 and *m. Šabbat* 23.1. In the latter text, a person could buy necessities on a Sabbath before a Passover by paying in trust not cash. This is not the situation here, but it is similar because a week-long feast is in view. The practice of giving to the poor on Passover to help them celebrate the meal may be alluded to in ancient texts; *m. Pesaḥim* 9.11 may refer to inviting others in; cf. Josephus, *Ant.* 18.2.2 §§29–30. See Joachim Jeremias, *The Eucharistic Words of Jesus,* trans. N. Perrin, 2d ed., New Testament Library (London, SCM, 1966), 54.

the imagery of the night, but it implies a far more dire darkness into which events are headed (cf. Luke 22:53).[14]

J28. The Farewell Discourse Begins with a New Commandment and a Prediction of Peter's Denial
(John 13:31–38) (Aland §§314–15)

Although the location of the start of the upper room discourse is disputed, it is best to see the opening of it here. The genre of the discourse is often compared to the so-called farewell discourses of the Old Testament (Gen. 49; Deut. 32–33; Josh. 23–24; 1 Chron. 28–29) and intertestamental literature *(Testaments of the Twelve Patriarchs)*. In this type of scene, a great leader figure gives parting words to those being left behind. That is very much like what Jesus does here. He gives several key exhortations as he departs to the Father. These exhortations are to be reflected upon and embraced with special care. However, in one sense, this discourse is unique because Jesus does not die to depart permanently. Not only will he be raised, but also he one day will return. Thus, the farewell is not so final as in other examples of the genre.

The scene begins with Jesus highlighting the mutual glorification that comes to the Son of Man and to God as a result of what is about to occur. This inseparable identity between the Father and the Son is central to Johannine Christology. So, "The Son of man is glorified, and in him God is glorified; if God is glorified in him, God will also glorify him in himself, and glorify him at once." The glorification is so certain in what is coming that the Greek uses three aorist tenses followed by two future tenses, a construction that mixes "proleptic" realization (the future is so certain that it can be expressed as having happened) with future affirmation.[15] The key concept is the immediacy of the glorification, while the key phrase is the repeated "in him," which is exchangeable as a reference between God and the Son. The relationship between God and the Son is as close as a relationship can get.

Jesus tenderly addresses the Eleven as "little children," noting that he is with them only for a little while longer. They will want him to be present among them and will seek him, but they cannot go where he is going, something that he told his Jewish audience earlier. Given his departure, one command, a new one, is paramount:

14. A curious feature of John's account is the omission of any details of the Last Supper. It appears that for the most part, John decided to convey fresh details about the meal. Nonetheless, the reason for the omission is not transparent. Perhaps this detail was so well known and covered in such detail in the Synoptics, in the oral church tradition, or in worship that John felt there was nothing to add to what was known about the event.

15. I am reading the "if" clause at the start of 13:32 as the third aorist in the verse. A few key manuscripts ($\mathfrak{P}^{66}$, ℵ, B, D) omit this phrase, but I include it, regarding its omission as an example of an error of sight. If it is omitted, nothing changes about the force of the verse.

"Love one another. Just as I have loved you, you also should love one another. By this all people will know that you are my disciples, if you have love for one another."

In one sense, this command is not new. Love as a quality of the believer's life has been urged from the days of old under Moses (Lev. 19:18). The love for one's neighbor has been stressed as one of the two great commandments, alongside loving God (Mark 12:28–33). What is new here comes in two points. First, love is moved beyond an abstract exhortation stated as a principle by itself and is given a model that incarnates the standard of love required. They are to love *just as I have loved you.*" This example of serving, instructing, and encouraging, even unto death, brings a new dimension by mirroring the love required. Second, although Jesus had taught about loving one's neighbor and one's enemy (Luke 6:27–36), the love that is to exist in the community is to be unique in its intensity and serves as its own powerful witness and testimony to God (Gal. 6:10; 1 John 4:7–21 shows that the apostle never forgot this emphasis). In a sense, the great commissions of Matthew and Luke are impossible without the great incarnation of community love that is to mark the disciples as Jesus' disciples, modeling his very life and response to them. For Jesus to start the discourse here, as the initial point of what his departure requires, shows how important this instruction is to him.

Typically, the exhortation is lost on the disciples in light of Jesus' declaration about his departure. Peter wants to know Jesus' future address and asks where he is going. Jesus replies that Peter cannot come with him now to the place where he is going, but Peter will follow him later. Peter is insistent. Why can he not follow Jesus now? As well intentioned as Peter is, the disciple still does not appreciate how unique and necessary Jesus' pioneering death is. Peter argues that he is ready to lay down his life for Jesus now. Peter senses a battle is coming, maybe even to the death. He is willing to give his own life to fight to preserve Jesus' life. He will even draw a sword later, when Jesus is arrested. This whole scenario of Jesus dying is still being rejected, just as it was when Peter challenged Jesus' announcement of suffering at Caesarea Philippi. However, Jesus knows Peter better than he knows himself, just as he knows what is about to happen better than Peter does. Will Peter lay down his life for Jesus when the real trial comes? No, most certainly Peter will deny Jesus three times before the cock crows. In a way, the reply is not only a comment on Peter but also an affirmation that Jesus' suffering most certainly will take place. Even the most insistent of the disciples will leave Jesus to himself in suffering.

J29. Jesus, the One Who Shows the Father (John 14:1–14)
(Aland §317)

Jesus has just announced a betrayal and a denial as well as a departure. The whole set of confusing and emerging circumstances had the potential to be very disturbing. So Jesus exhorts the disciples not to allow their hearts "to be troubled." The verb ταράσσω already has been used three times of Jesus (John 11:33; 12:27; 13:21). The imperative here is in the present tense, which may add the nuance of "stop being troubled." What follows the exhortation is two references to belief that could be imperative ("Believe in God; believe also in me"), indicative ("You believe in God; you believe also in me"), or a mix ("You believe in God; believe also in me"). It is hard to be sure which sense is meant. Given that Jesus is in an exhorting mode and is reassuring a troubled, uncertain group of disciples, it is slightly more likely that imperatives are in view as he exhorts them on the right path. The point, regardless of which reading is taken, is that Jesus once again closely links belief in God with belief in him. To have faith in God should imply having faith in Jesus because of who Jesus is sent to be and what the sent one is doing.

The next few verses are difficult. The reference to μοναί is not a reference to "mansions," as older English translations suggest, but simply to "dwelling places." The term often referred to a lodging stop on a journey, but that cannot be the sense here because the entire passage has a feel of Jesus assuring the disciples about something that he is departing to do. More difficult is determining what the dwelling places refer to explicitly. It is often suggested that the reference describes the preparation of heaven to receive the disciples. Jesus' work clears the way for their unending life with God and permanent residence with him. John 14:6, with its reference to Jesus being the way, suggests such a force. However, another possibility is seeing a more figurative force for the reference to the Father's house, as John 2:19–22 and 8:35 suggest in referring to the house as a way of affirming spiritual relationship. If this is the sense, then Jesus is saying that his departure clears the way for relationship in him and in the Father. This also fits John 14:6, as well as 14:10. Jesus' coming to receive them to himself is the coming that takes place in the Spirit. This gift incorporates them into the family and household of God, like Paul's adoption imagery and "in Christ" metaphor. What follows in the discourse, including vv. 10–14, reassures the disciples about this coming provision. There is much to be said for this view, as John does emphasize the present reality of realization (4:21–24; 5:24; 7:38–39), and it fits contextually. If Jesus is referring instead to his coming at the end, then his point is that his death allows him to complete preparations for his return to bring them to heaven one day. Seen in this light, the remark reassures and then turns quickly back to the immediate present. Choosing between the two readings is hard. It is slightly more contextually unifying to see Jesus alluding to his preparing the way for relationship in the Spirit, although a double entendre is not beyond John, because the result of the Spirit's indwelling is ultimately a permanent relationship that one day will end up in heaven. As Paul argues, the Spirit is the down payment of more to come (Eph. 1:13–14).

Jesus assures them that they really do understand where he is going, even though the disciples are struggling to grasp it. Jesus' point here is that he goes back to the Father, where he can complete his calling.[16] Thomas responds that that the disciples know neither where Jesus is going nor the way there, so the disciple is asking quite literally that the teacher show them the way so that they can know. Jesus turns a seeming "geographical route" question into a spiritual affirmation. "I am the way, the truth, and the life; no one comes to the Father but by me." The road that Jesus travels is not about a location; it is about providing access to God for individuals. It is not so important to know the route that Jesus takes so that one can follow it. What is important is knowing that Jesus *is* the route to God. This is why he can describe himself as the truth and the life. These two descriptions elaborate on Jesus as the way. In calling himself the truth, Jesus reveals the way to God. He is the Word incarnate (John 1:4, 14; 3:15; 5:26; 11:25). To call himself the life is to give himself a role as the provider and sustainer of life that really is the prerogative of God. Once again the overlapping character of Jesus' work with God's attributes is affirmed. No text in Scripture is clearer than this one in stating that access to God is given only through Christ. No one comes to the Father except through Jesus.

The force of the next remark depends on another difficult textual problem (John 14:7). The "if" clause in Greek is either a class two condition, contrary to fact ("If you had known me [but you do not]") or a class one condition ("If you had known me [and you do]"). Variations of a class two condition show up in Codices Vaticanus and Ephraemi and the Majority text, possibly because Philip in the next verse seems not to get Jesus' point, exposing ignorance. If read this way, the verse is a rebuke, with the point being that Jesus' departure will change things. However, other key manuscripts argue for the class one condition ($\mathfrak{P}^{66}$, ℵ, D), a reading that keeps the mood of reassurance in the passage. The class one condition is more likely here. Jesus' point is that they have known him and thus the Father. They have the access that Jesus affirms. So this means that they can be assured that from now on they will know the Father and already have seen him. The mixture of tenses shows the future with such certainty that it is expressed as a done deal. From now on they "are knowing [present tense] him and have seen [perfect tense] him." To see God in the way Jesus describes here has a lasting effect, as the presence of the perfect tense in Greek underscores.

16. Some might regard this remark as proving that the issue is the locale that Jesus goes to in heaven, and thus a reference to the second coming, especially given Thomas's question. But three points bring pause to this conclusion. First, the disciples habitually misunderstand Jesus when asking him questions. Second, a text such as Acts 2:32–36 shows that a departure to God can lead immediately into a reference to the distribution of the Spirit as a sign of the new era's arrival. Third, the subsequent discussion in John 14 is about what Spirit enablement will provide.

Philip seeks assurance. He asks that the Father be revealed. That will satisfy them. Jesus has presented himself as God's revealer, so a nice display would settle matters. Perhaps Philip wishes to see God, as Isaiah did (Isa. 6). Once again Philip's expectation is mistakenly literal. Jesus rebukes Philip and the disciples as a whole (the "you" is plural) and points back to his entire ministry. How could they be disciples so long and not know Jesus better? The one who has witnessed Jesus' words and acts has seen the Father. Jesus' point is that his entire ministry has been a revelation of the Father's presence, will, and power, especially his power to restore and give life. So the question asking Jesus to show them the Father now has missed the point of what has taken place. Philip should know better. He should know that "I am in the Father and the Father is in me." Jesus rhetorically asks Philip if he knows this, to highlight what the disciple now should truly grasp. The relationship of mutuality expressed in each direction between the Father and Jesus shows their unity and equality (cf. John 10:30). Jesus is no mere commissioned agent bringing God's message. He is far more in his unity with the Father. Thus, when Jesus speaks, he does not speak on his own authority; rather, it is the Father who dwells in him speaking and working (see John 1:14–18). The Father and Jesus are inseparable, though not identical. So Philip and all the disciples (the "you" here is plural) should believe that Jesus and the Father share this mutuality in being and work. The evidence of their work should be proof of this (cf. John 5:36; 10:37–38), an allusion back to the many signs that John's Gospel narrated in the first part of the account.

What awaits the disciples as a result is an even more impressive period because Jesus goes to the Father. Those who believe in Jesus will do his works and even greater ones. What Jesus describes here is the preaching work that the disciples will do. They not only will announce the hope of life, but also will allow for it to be bestowed because Jesus has done his work and gone to the Father. What Jesus could only announce and show in the picture of signs, the disciples will be able to provide as divine agents as they go out and preach the message to a needy world, enabled by the one whom Jesus will send.[17] The effect of that preaching will have a far greater spread than it did in Jesus' time.

It is in this context that Jesus instructs them about prayer and a ministry carried out in full dependence on the name of the Son. Whatever is prayed for in the context of Jesus' name, not said as a mantra but as a request that rests in his will and for his glory, Jesus will do, so that the Father may be glorified in the Son. Once again, it is interesting to see that Jesus will be involved in mediating prayer and that the Son and the Father labor together in its answer.

17. As Morris, *John*, 574, rightly comments, "What Jesus means we may see in the narratives of Acts. There there are a few miracles of healing, but the emphasis is on the mighty works of conversion."

The issue in the answer is the glorification of the Father through the Son. Such prayer, given in harmony with the Son and his person, will be done.

This entire portion of the discourse highlights the access that disciples have to the Father through Jesus. They can see the Father and his works through that which Jesus has done. They will be able to see the Father in what Jesus will enable them to do. They can pray expectantly through the Son as they pray in unison with his desire to glorify God. All of this is possible because Jesus goes from their side to the side of the Father.

J30. The Promised Spirit, Love, and Obedience
(John 14:15–26) (Aland §318)

The unity between the Father and the Son not only enables access to God in prayer and the ability to accomplish great works, but also grants the provision of "another Paraclete" to aid in the relationship between the disciple and God. That relationship is grounded in love that expresses itself in obedience to Jesus. So this section of the discourse begins with a description of the love that a disciple should have for Jesus. That description is presented as a class three condition ("If you love me [and I am not saying if you do or do not, but merely presenting the condition]"). If love is present, then obedience is present, because the one who loves "will keep my commandments." Love here is not defined in terms of an emotion or feeling but as a relational bond that expresses itself concretely in loyalty and faithfulness, much as the Son's love is reflected toward the Father. This is an important theme for John (John 14:21, 23; 15:14; 1 John 5:3). Jesus' reference to "my commandments" looks at the whole of his teaching but especially to the call to love that he has just issued.

Jesus in turn will pray to the Father to provide "another Paraclete" in his stead. The term "Paraclete" is a transliterated term also used in Hebrew and Aramaic (John 15:26, 16:13). It often refers to an advocate, who comes to one's defense (*m. ʾAbot* 4.11: "The one who performs a precept gets for himself an advocate"; *Leviticus Rabbah* 6.1 on Lev. 5:1).[18] This force is close to what John 16:8–11 teaches except that in that passage there is not a defense attorney involved but a prosecutor. The Spirit is an advocate for God. Another dimension of the word group is its relationship to exhortation and encouragement, as related Greek words have this force (Acts 2:40; 1 Cor. 14:3). The word group also can refer to the offering of consolation (LXX Isa. 40:1; Matt. 5:4; Luke 2:25). The Paraclete is an encourager who speaks about

---

18. An important study of Johannine pneumatology is Gary Burge, *The Anointed Community: The Holy Spirit in the Johannine Tradition* (Grand Rapids: Eerdmans, 1987). When it comes to the Spirit as Paraclete, Burge discusses two roles: witness and advocate (pp. 208–16). As witness, the major function is to bring things to remembrance.

Christ and for him, exhorting and encouraging the disciples and offering believers consolation, much as Jesus is doing here. Thus, the Spirit can be called "another" Paraclete, of the same type that Jesus has been. The gift of that encourager will be given to remain with them "unto the age" (forever). This one is the "Spirit of truth," a Spirit that communicates the truth.[19] This Spirit the world does not receive because it neither sees nor knows him. In contrast, this gift from God dwells or abides with believers, being in them.[20]

Jesus' departure means the intensification of his union with disciples. Rather than leaving them desolate, he will come to them. They will not be orphans, but children richly provided for by God. Jesus comes to them in provision and relationship, showing that life is available. Jesus here seems to fuse the resurrection appearances with the benefits that grow out of resurrection. The coming that Jesus describes here is not his return but something that takes place in "yet a little while," when the world sees Jesus no more. In contrast, "You will see me; because I live, you will live also." In other words, the resurrection, which will be affirmed in appearances, will allow the Eleven to see Jesus and form the basis for establishing that Jesus lives, enabling him to give life to those who are his (cf. John 6:57). "In that day" when they see him, they will know the mutuality that exists between the Father, Jesus, and the believer. They will appreciate that "I am in my Father, and you in me, and I in you." John again closely combines the tie between Jesus and the Spirit here, because the sent Spirit dwells in the believer, but the believer is in Jesus as well. This concept is very close to the "in Christ" idea of Paul.

Jesus then affirms the benefits that emerge from the disciples' love for him. Expressed in a reverse order from 14:15, "The one who has my commandments and keeps them, that is the one who loves me." Love is expressed in terms of action. The one who loves receives the love of the Father and that of Jesus. To that one, Jesus will make himself known, manifesting himself to that one in the ways he has been describing. Judas (not Iscariot) presses Jesus for an explanation of how the teacher will manifest himself to them but not to the world. The answer is indirect, as is often the case with Jesus. The one who loves Jesus will keep his word, and the Father will love that one. The result is that both Jesus and the Father ("we") will come and make their dwelling place

19. The pronouns referring to the Spirit in v. 17 are neuter in grammatical gender. This agrees with the grammatical gender of the word πνεῦμα, which is neuter as well. Later, masculine pronouns are used (John 15:26; 16:7, 8, 13, 14). Those are constructions in which the Spirit, operating like a person, is rendered with that sense. See Brown, *John XIII–XXI*, 639.

20. The various Greek manuscripts raise two textual issues here. First, does the Spirit abide with them in the present or in the future? Second, is the Spirit in them in the present or in the future? The manuscript evidence favors the present on the first choice, while the context favors a future on the second choice because it is the harder reading (a tense shift from the earlier verbs). The change in tense expresses an enhancement of the presence of the Spirit that will come as a result of God sending him. The Spirit goes from being "with" them to being "in" them.

with that disciple. So the manifestation comes in the inseparable relationship that God establishes with the disciple. This stands in contrast to the one who does not love Jesus and keep his words. The implication is that no such benefit comes to the one who does not embrace Jesus. He reinforces the point with the reminder that what they hear does not come from Jesus but from the Father (John 14:10), which is precisely why Jesus' word should be embraced in faithful obedience. The offer of God's faithful love and provision demands faithful love in return. This act of divine love makes a distinction among those in the world. Those who receive Jesus and the word of life gain the benefits of God's indwelling presence.

Jesus makes the point that he has let them know what is coming while he is still with them. But what he says will be reinforced and brought to remembrance when the Father sends the Paraclete, the Holy Spirit, to them. This one will be a teacher and instructor to them of what Jesus has said and promised. To teach is one of the basic functions of the Spirit. Others are to testify (John 15:26) and to convict and guide (John 16:13–14). The remarks here recall Old Testament texts such as Ps. 25:5, 9. The teaching work of the Spirit is highlighted as well in 1 John 2:20, 27, and 2 John 9. One of the greatest reassurances that Jesus gives in this discourse is his teaching about the provision of the Spirit. This provision is a primary gift of life as far as Jesus is concerned, and is a key benefit that results from his departure.

J31. Peace, I Go to the Father (John 14:27–31) (Aland §319)

Jesus departs, but he does so after he has provided, even bequeathed, peace to the disciples.[21] This peace is not a feeling or even an absence of conflict, because Jesus has told them of rejection to come. Rather, it refers to the established relationship that disciples now have to God, much as Eph. 2:14–18 expresses except that there Paul highlights the additional point of peace with each other that also emerges from such a relationship. It is the Hebrew *shalom,* a characteristic of God's presence and rule (Num. 6:26; Isa. 9:6–7; 52:7). In the turmoil to come, they can rest assured in the peace they have with God. Such a peace is different from the transitory quality of the world's peace. So they need not be troubled or afraid.

Jesus reiterates his promise to come again after his departure. Then, using a class two (contrary-to-fact) conditional statement, Jesus says that if they had loved him (but they do not in the full sense he is speaking of), then they would have rejoiced, because they would have appreciated what Jesus' return to the Father means. They know the Father's greatness. The Father, Jesus

---

21. The verb translated "leave" (ἀφίημι) can be read as meaning "bequeath" (LXX Ps. 16:14; Eccles. 2:18).

says, is "greater than I." This statement has caused no small controversy in the history of interpretation. The Arians claimed that this text proved Jesus' inferiority to the Father. However, two other possible readings make that claim suspect. One reading argues that Jesus' point views his current work from the perspective of his current role as sent one confined to the earth. The sent one is always seen as "commissioned" and bearing the authority of the sender (*Genesis Rabbah* 78.1 on Gen. 32:27: "The sender is greater than the one sent"). This seems to be entailed in what Jesus is saying. The second reading goes beyond this to make the point in terms of what the return means. Jesus' going to the Father gives him proximate access to the divine sphere. It is a return to glory, where Jesus can continue to do the Father's work but in a more intimate, effective way, operating in glory, not in a mere incarnate state. The greatness of the Father is expressed in this "commissioned" way, especially in comparison to Jesus' role now. The relationship between Father and Son always is one of sender and sent, but it will be better for the disciples to have the benefit of Jesus being at the side of the heavenly Father—what other New Testament texts point to as his position at God's right hand (Acts 2:30–36).

Jesus announces all of these events beforehand, so when these events take place, they can believe. Jesus looks to reassure the disciples' faith and strengthen it. Thus, he indicates that the shocking events about to occur do not catch Jesus by surprise. It will be a time of great cosmic conflict, because "the ruler of this world is coming." Yet they can be assured that that one has no power over Jesus. Rather, Jesus goes to his death in obedience to the Father, demonstrating to the world his love for the Father, not to mention his love for humanity as he lays down his life for them (see John 3:16; 10:11).

Jesus then turns and tells the disciples that it is time to go. The remark gives the impression that the discourse has ended. The remark also has the feel of a rising to meet what lies ahead. John's style of writing certainly is capable of this double sense. Of course, the discourse does not end, since Jesus says far more in John 15–16. What has happened is either that the disciples have ended their meal and now journey through the city with the conversation continuing or that they have prepared to depart but the actual departure of so many takes a while to accomplish.[22]

As the first part of the discourse ends, Jesus has reassured his disciples that his departure is not a defeat. On the contrary, it will enhance the union that he has with them and allows the provision of the Spirit to guide them into a deeper appreciation of what Jesus taught and did. The explanation helps us understand why John sees the death and resurrection of Jesus as a glorification.

22. Morris, *John*, 586–87.

J32. Jesus the True Vine—Abide in Me (John 15:1–8)
(Aland §320)

For centuries, Israel had seen itself as the true vine of God (Ps. 80:8–16; Isa. 5:1–7; Jer. 2:21; Ezek. 15:1–8; 17:5–10; 19:10–14; Hos. 10:1). The vine was a symbol of the nation on some Maccabean coins. Given this history, certainly the one in the middle of God's promise who rules and represents the nation could be described as the vine. The Old Testament did not make such an association with the Messiah, preferring the image of the cedar tree (Ezek. 17:22–24). So what Jesus says here is a fresh twist on the vineyard imagery of the Scripture. He now is the true vine. What the nation has failed to be, he is.[23] Jeremiah 2:20–37 had issued such a warning about judging the national vine. This text is very similar in thrust to another "replacement" text with another image that Jesus uses as a developed metaphor, namely, Ezek. 34 and the image of shepherd (John 10). In both cases Jesus becomes what the nation was supposed to be, being supplied by God to fill the void. As "the vine," Jesus shows himself to be the key to fruitfulness before God. A person cannot bear fruit without being connected to the vine. In other words, no one can be fruitful outside of him (John 15:4).

Sovereign over the vine is the gardener, who is the Father, whom Jesus personalizes as "my" Father. He is the vinedresser. It is his plan and his design for fruitfulness that are in view.

Jesus now turns to the subject of the branches. There are two classes of branches: those that are dead, bearing no fruit, and those that bear fruit. Dead branches are removed (John 15:2, 6).[24] Fruitful branches are pruned so that more fruit is borne. The clear goal of being in the vine is to bear fruit, as everything that is done has that end in view. Even fruitful branches are worked over so that they may be even more fruitful, an allusion to the discipline of the believer's walk.

Jesus goes on to make it clear that the ability to bear fruit in the vine is because the disciples are "already made clean by the word that I have spoken to you."[25] Thus, Jesus' work makes their fruitfulness possible from start to finish. Jesus' cleansing work makes life in the vine possible. That cleansing work is revealed in his teaching. The remark alludes back in its imagery to John 13:10,

---

23. This declaration resembles the way Jesus alludes to Isa. 58:6 in Luke 4:16–19.

24. Some argue that the term αἴρει in John 15:2 means "lifted up." This is very unlikely given John 15:6, where the "nonabider," which is a sign of a dead branch, is cast out and burned. In addition, the majority of uses of this verb in John mean "to remove" (John 11:39, 48; 16:22; 17:15), although a few uses do mean "to lift up" (8:59; 5:8–12). The consistency of the imagery in the unit means that "remove" is the likely image here.

25. The picture of cleansing looks back to the earlier footwashing incident of John 13.

where Judas was excluded from those who were clean, perhaps picturing what it means to cease to have connection to the vine.

The passage now moves from image to exhortation. The syntax here is variously rendered. John 15:4 can carry one of three meanings: (1) conditional ("If you remain in me, I will remain in you"); (2) comparative ("Remain in me, as I remain in you"); or (3) mutual imperative ("Abide in me, as also I am to abide in you").[26] Either of the last two options is possible because both of them have the force of an imperative to remain in the vine. If a conditional were intended, there would be a clearer way to say it than the construction of John 15:4. The point, regardless of the more precise force chosen, is that fruitfulness is the product of abiding. That this is the point becomes explicit by what follows. "Just as the branch cannot bear fruit unless it remains in the vine, so neither can you unless you remain in me." Life cannot exist without staying connected to the vine. Now the exhortation moves outside the image here because branches cannot choose to remain in their vine. They are simply there, healthy or dead.

It is this move within the imagery that has made the passage difficult. Does the text assume that dead branches are believers disciplined, given that their position in the vine is affirmed and they are said to be cleansed? Or is the image that true branches abide, with abiding being a figure for having and experiencing life? Four points favor seeing abiding as equal to having life and nonabiding as lacking it. (1) Those who know the shepherd hear his voice and respond to his exhortation to follow (John 10). (2) The affirmation in John 15:6 means that nonabiders end up being taken out, placed in fire, and burned up. This is an image of final judgment.[27] The passage should be read from its conclusion back, to understand its ultimate force. (3) For John, bearing fruit is a sign of life (cf. John 8:39–41; 1 John 4:20). (4) In the passage's imagery, there are only two categories: those who bear fruit, and those who do not and are removed (John 15:2), with the consequences specified in John 15:6.

Positively, Jesus reaffirms the relationship that he is the vine and they are the branches. The one who abides bears much fruit. The reason for fruitfulness is simple: apart from Jesus as the vine, they can do nothing. Stated in a class three conditional form, which does not express itself for or against the possible option, the consequence for a nonabider is to be cast out like a branch, left to wither, gathered up, and placed in fire to be consumed (cf. Ezek. 15:4–6; 19:12; Matt. 3:10; 13:37–42; John 5:29). This is an image of rejection, not discipline, for discipline is described in John 15:2 as pruning for branches that have life and bear fruit. The image is not that believers have lost

---

26. Carson, *John*, 516.

27. The point of the fire as a judgment image is that this John 15 image is unlike 1 Cor. 3:11–15, where the fire purges but does not consume.

their salvation. Rather, it is a picture that having life means life and union with the vine, union sustained on both ends. Where there is no life, there is no union, even if there is an "attachment." The text seems to have in view some who "connect" to Jesus but do not receive him (John 6:66), a category that John has treated in the person of Judas and also treats in 1 John 2:18–19 of others who leave behind their association with Jesus (also 2 John 9).

Using another class three conditional statement, Jesus states the matter positively. Those who abide and have union with Christ respond to his word because his words abide in them. They can ask for what they desire (cf. John 14:13–14) because they are in union with him, and it will be done for them. Jesus is noting that obedience is a product of abiding, and so is answered prayer that is rooted in God's will. God is glorified in this relationship that unites him to disciples, leading to their fruitfulness. The presence of fruit is the proof that disciples are present.[28] In fact, such fruitfulness glorifies God (cf. Matt. 5:16).

J33. Union—Love, Obedience, and Abiding (John 15:9–17)
(Aland §321)

The root of the disciples' relationship to God is the example of the Father's love for Jesus and Jesus' love for them. The aorist tenses of the verbs chosen for "love" encompass the entire career of the relationship. Given such a solid foundation, the disciples are urged to abide in Jesus' love, to experience life, and to draw strength from and through it. Such abiding is expressed again in terms of obedience (cf. John 14:15, 21). Jesus already had set the example of love that is responsive in obedience (John 4:34; 6:38; 8:29, 55; 10:17–18; 12:27–28; 14:31). Such obedience produces a full joy for the disciple that comes from Jesus. That joy is rooted in a person doing that for which God has created him or her.

So Jesus reiterates his commandment to love (cf. John 13:34–35). Not only is one to love, but also to do so by the standard that Jesus has set in loving them (see Eph. 5:1–2). The example extends to Jesus' offer of his own life on their behalf. Jesus will die for his "friends." This intimacy of relationship is what Jesus affirms. Meaningful relationships have impact, forming an interpersonal connection so that one's allegiance drives one's responses. So Jesus

28. There is a textual problem in John 15:8. Should one read a future ("you will become" disciples; so ℵ, Byz), or an aorist subjunctive ("you are" disciples), a reading that has Alexandrian (𝔓⁶⁶, B) and Western (D) support? It is hard to be sure which verb is original, since the manuscript evidence is split, although the subjunctive is slightly more likely. The point, regardless, is that fruitfulness shows discipleship, being the outward evidence of union with Christ (John 15:5).

notes of the disciples, "You are my friends if you do what I command you."[29] Jesus is addressing a characteristic of what his friendship produces. It yields love from the one who has benefited from Jesus' love.

So disciples no longer are slaves. They are friends, intimates. Like Abraham (2 Chron. 20:7; Isa. 41:8) and Moses (Exod. 33:11), they are the recipients of revelation and instruction from God that has led them into deeper relationship with him. God has initiated everything about this friendship, leaving those brought close to him to respond in faithfulness as they draw on the example of the Father and his sent one. Jesus has made known to them what the Father has told him. So the disciples are not like slaves, because slaves do not know what their master is doing. The details of God's plan revealed in this discourse show the divine love for them, as Jesus makes known to them what God is about to do.

Jesus took the initiative. He chose them. More than that, he appointed them, or set them apart, for a task. They are called to go and bear fruit. This alludes to their mission to go and tell others about what God has done. So in this context, bearing fruit is telling others about God's work in Christ. Such fruit, planted and raised in bringing others to Christ, abides. Jesus truly has brought them in to do the Father's work. So whatever they ask "in my name," that is, pursuant to his will in this task, he will give (cf. John 14:13–14). At the root of this effort is the command to love one another. The outreach is rooted in the effectiveness of the community members' love for one another, just as the disciples' love is rooted in the love of the Father for Jesus and Jesus' love for the disciple. The extension of this love from disciple to disciple simply completes the cycle. To abide is to love. To love is to mirror the Father and the Son.

J34. The Hatred of the World (John 15:18–25) (Aland §322)

Jesus now turns to the opposition that disciples will face because of their union with him. Using a class one conditional statement, Jesus notes that if the world hates them (and it does), they should know that it hated him before it hated them. Jesus is making the point that the animus of the world is actually directed against him. Using a class two conditional statement, Jesus notes that their lack of belonging to the world is what fuels this hatred. "If you were of the world [but you are not], the world would love its own." However, it is because Jesus chose them out of the world that the world hates them. John 8:23 already had made the point that Jesus is not of this world, just as 15:16

---

29. The class three conditional form holds the possibility open as to whether this will take place in the presentation of the "if" clause.

pointed out Jesus' choice of the disciples. Here, Jesus' choice to take them out of the world has produced the world's opposition (cf. 1 John 4:5–6).

Jesus reminds the disciples that the slave is not greater than the master. So if people persecuted Jesus (and they did), they will persecute his disciples. The meaning of the second "if" statement in John 15:20 is less clear. There are two options: (1) "If they kept my word, they will keep yours [but they did not, so they will not]"; (2) "If they obeyed my word [and they do, at least some of them], they will obey yours [at least some of them]." The first option fits the negative tone that dominates the passage, but it runs against the force of the sentence's grammar. In favor of the second option is that this is not a contrary-to-fact condition, which it would need to be if the first option is correct. In other words, accepting the second option, Jesus argues that in the midst of this opposition, there will be some success, just as Jesus had in their case.

The real reason for the world's rejection of disciples is that it occurs on account of Jesus, because people do not know the one who sent Jesus. Once again it is the inseparable union between the Father and the sent one that Jesus affirms. In rejecting him, they reject God. But there is no excuse. They are guilty, especially now that God has revealed himself through the sent one. Jesus expresses it in yet another contrary-to-fact, class two conditional statement: "If I had not come and spoken to them [but I did], they would not have had sin."[30] Jesus refers to the sin of the clear rejection of God's way. This thought resembles several Synoptic texts in highlighting that the revelation tied to Jesus was an exceptional time (Matt. 11:20–24; Luke 11:31–32; also John 12:37). The presence and clarity of the revelation leaves them without excuse. This is another "without excuse" text in the New Testament, the other being Rom. 1:18–32, which looks to a condition before Jesus' coming. In sum, those who hate Jesus hate his Father also. They have rejected the one whom the Father has sent. To drive the point home, Jesus notes that had he not done the works among them that no one else had done (but he did), they would not have sin. However, the nature of the evidence of divine activity through Jesus is so great that no excuse for rejection exists (see John 1:18; 4:34; 14:9). To have seen these works and yet still hated is to reject both Jesus and his Father. In many ways, the remark of John 15:24 summarizes the book of signs in John's Gospel.

The hostile reaction is a fulfillment of something that was seen from the attitude of the unrighteous toward the righteous in the Old Testament: "They hated me without a cause." This remark is found in "their law" in both Ps. 35:19 and 69:4 (cf. Ps. 119:161; *Psalms of Solomon* 7.1). It affirms both the innocence of Jesus and the world's injustice and blindness that characterize its

---

30. The imperfect tense points to the class two condition, which appears here in mixed tenses (Brown, *John XIII–XXI*, 688). The perfect tense in "have had sin" indicates they are in a state of sin as a result of their rejection.

sin of rejection. In missing what "their law" taught, those who rejected Jesus have missed both the lessons of Jesus' work and of their Scripture. The hatred of the world makes no ethical sense, even though it is a powerfully real force and is no real surprise.

J35. The Paraclete as Witness (John 15:26–27) (Aland §323)

The disciples will not face this opposition alone. The Father, through Jesus, is going to send the Paraclete, the Spirit of truth. His job is to be a witness for Jesus. Jesus will elaborate on this witness in John 16:8–11. This Spirit proceeds in his coming from the Father, but Jesus shares in his distribution (see Acts 2:30–36).[31] That Spirit will share the witnessing with these disciples, who were with Jesus from the start of his ministry, thus enabling them to testify about him and for him. In fact, as the Synoptic texts on mission show, the disciples will work together to testify to Jesus as the Spirit will speak through them (Matt. 10:18–20; Luke 12:11–12; 21:12–15; Mark 13:9–11). The closing remark about being with Jesus from the beginning of his ministry shows that it is the Eleven who are in view here. The base of the church's testimony to Jesus rests on the foundation of these eyewitnesses to Jesus and his work (cf. Eph. 2:20).

J36. On Persecutions (John 16:1–4) (Aland §324)

Jesus now turns his attention to explain why he is telling them about both the persecution and the Spirit: he does not want them to "fall away." The term σκανδαλίζω means "to depart from the faith" in these Johannine texts (John 6:61) or at least be at severe risk (1 John 2:10), a usage that also shows up in the church fathers (*Didache* 16.5; "waverers," Hermas, *Vision* 4.1.3; *Mandate* 8.10). Jesus' revealing what will take place is an act of protection to strengthen the disciples' faith.

Persecution means that they will be kicked out of the synagogue (cf. John 9:22). In fact, some of them will be killed by those who think they are giving worshipful service (λατρεία) to God. The term for "service" is used rarely in the New Testament, but always elsewhere in a temple worship context (Rom. 9:4; 12:1; Heb. 9:1, 6). Paul also expresses the idea that persecution is moti-

---

31. There is no reference to the "eternal" generation of the Spirit from the Father (and the Son) in this verse. The "proceeding" is for the current mission and enablement of the disciples. For the theological dispute about "eternal" procession and whether it came from the Father alone (Eastern church) or from both Father and Son (Western church), see Carson, *John*, 528–29. This dispute eventually split the church in the Middle Ages.

vated by a jealousy for God (Acts 26:9–11). In later Judaism, elements of the "honor" of slaying the unrighteous are expressed, no doubt with memories of Israel's recovery under the Maccabees as 1 Maccabees records. These later texts include *Numbers Rabbah* 21.3 (191a) on Num. 25:13, which tells of Phinehas's work of faithfulness as the basis of an everlasting priesthood. The text then says, "It serves to teach you that if a man sheds the blood of the wicked, it is as though he had offered an offering." In *m. Sanhedrin* 9.6, various acts of blasphemy are reported to have led to execution: (1) idolators are slain by zealots (alluding to Num. 25:8, 11); (2) a priest who performs acts in uncleanliness is beaten to death; and (3) a nonpriest serving in the temple is slain by strangling or by "the hands of heaven."

However, the desire to serve God is not necessarily a correct motive. Jesus goes on to explain that they will persecute and kill "because they have not known the Father or me." There is something tragic about acting with a motive that really represents an act of self-deception. Again, Paul makes a similar point in Rom. 10:1–2. So Jesus tells his disciples these things ahead of time, so that when "their [the persecuters'] hour" comes, they might remember what he has told them. "Their hour" refers to a time when it seems that the opponents are winning but in fact God's plan is moving on through his followers. No element of the persecution should take them by surprise or lead them into despair. He did not say anything to them earlier, because he was still going to be with them. In a sense, there was less need to say anything then, because the attention of the leadership was focused on Jesus, not so much on his followers. With him leaving, they now will get the attention of the opponents. So the discourse is a time to prepare the disciples for the hard times that lie ahead.

J37. The Paraclete Who Convicts and Guides (John 16:5–15)
(Aland §325)

In the midst of persecution, it is important that the disciple know what resources he or she possesses. So Jesus comes back to the work of the Spirit. Jesus begins this transition back to discussing the Spirit by noting that no one is asking him about where Jesus is going. In fact, such questions had been asked earlier (John 13:36; 14:5). But it appears that they are less interested in getting an explanation for what God will do as in trying to understand why such a departure is necessary and how these things can be. Jesus, in effect, accuses them of not asking the right questions at the right time. That the disciples are focused on Jesus' departure is indicated by Jesus' additional remark that because of what Jesus has said, sorrow has filled their hearts. If they appreciated the benefits that emerge through Jesus' departure, sorrow would not be the response. It may well be that this difficulty in appreciating what Jesus is telling them is responsible for the cycling through of the same themes again and again.[32] Jesus is having to drive the basic points home even to the point of repetition because the disciples are too overwhelmed to process everything on the first hearing.

So Jesus' departure is to the disciples' benefit. His departure means that the Spirit is coming. If Jesus goes, then he can send the Spirit to them. What God sends in other texts, Jesus sends here (John 14:16, 26; but note 15:26, where Jesus sends and the Father and Son work in concert). The Spirit has a work to do with reference to the world (16:8–11) and with reference to the disciples (v. 13).

The Spirit's work in the world requires that the interpreter decide how ἐλέγξει is used. Does it mean "to convict" or "to expose"? In other words, is the Spirit's work to evoke a courtroom scene in which the Spirit acts much like a prosecutor?[33] Or is the scene less like a courtroom and more an act of "exposing and shaming" the world by what the Spirit reveals?[34] It is hard to choose between the options.[35] On the one hand, the term generally means "to expose" and does not carry an explicit legal force. On the other hand, the issues of justice and judgment suggest a "legal" context, which often is a part of judgment language. Regardless of which view is taken, the Spirit's role exposes and demonstrates to the world that it is out of step with what God has done in Jesus. So the world is culpable before God. If one is forced to choose the exact nuance, the legal-like setting of judgment points to a forensic type of exposure. The topics that bring exposure are sin, righteousness, and judgment.

Sin is exposed because of the world's failure to believe. Everything John has written has made the point that Jesus is the revelation of God, showing the way of access to God. To reject that testimony is to be guilty of sin. To read the ὅτι of this verse as indicating merely content ("concerning sin, that they do not believe in me") seems to understate what is present. If people reject Jesus' testimony, they do not need merely to have that fact exposed; they need to understand why rejection takes place. Thus, the ὅτι here is causal. Their sin is to fail to believe in Jesus, and for this reason judgment follows.

Righteousness is exposed because Jesus "goes to the Father, and you will see" Jesus no more. His exaltation is the way of righteousness and establishes that righteousness. It also is his vindication. The proof that Jesus is raised and

32. Such cycling has led to complex, scholarly theories about multiple sources or versions of this discourse being combined here by a later editor. The repetitions are seen as reflecting differing versions. However, it may well be that the disciples' difficulty with processing what Jesus is telling them has led to a genuine repetition within the discourse.

33. So Morris, *John*, 618–19.

34. So Carson, *John*, 536–37.

35. What is clear is that the term is not positive. It is not looking at converting; John 14:17 and 3:20 have shown that the world does not respond to the revelation.

active exposes the righteousness of God's way in Jesus. This convicting work against the world is accomplished in and through the testimony and the life that come through the disciples. This is why Jesus mentions that the disciples ("you") will see him no longer, rather than speaking about the world ("they") not seeing Jesus. His departure from them enables him to equip them with the Spirit.

Judgment is exposed because the ruler of the world (cf. John 12:31) stands judged. In the work of Jesus at the very moment when Satan seems to have crushed all hope, Satan's defeat is rendered and judgment against the evil one is sealed. Satan may remain active until the end, but his defeat is sure (see Rev. 12:5, 7–12). Christ's work destroys the devil's work.

There is much more that Jesus could say, but they cannot bear it now. To "bear" something is to face a burden (cf. John 19:17), although this is the only place where "words" must be borne. Their capacity to appreciate what Jesus says will be enhanced when the Spirit of truth comes to them. The Spirit will guide them into all the truth associated with Jesus' ministry, speaking as he will from the things he will hear and not by his own authority. In getting his information this way, the Spirit speaks as Jesus had (John 3:34–35; 5:19–20; 12:47–50; 14:10). The term for "guide," ὁδηγέω, has rich Old Testament roots. In the Psalter it is used of God leading the worshiper to understanding (Ps. 25:4–5; 143:10). So there will come a time when these witnesses to Jesus will understand what Jesus was all about because the Spirit will declare these things to them, including "things to come." The phrase "things to come" alludes to all that is to come, about which the Spirit will give enlightenment, as well as the connection of those things to what has already taken place. The passage is about the enablement that the Eleven receive, although those who understand their testimony through the Spirit also will come to possess this understanding. In a sense, this Gospel is a summary of such an understanding of Jesus.

The Spirit will glorify the Son. This will be his role. So the Spirit points to the Son, just as the Son had pointed to the Father. The Spirit takes what is true about Jesus and declares it to them. What the Spirit gives belongs to Jesus and came from the Father (John 17:10). So Jesus reveals that the mutual union between the Father and the Son extends to and through the Spirit, who in turn will become more actively present among Jesus' disciples.

J38. In a Little While—Sorrow to Joy (John 16:16–22)
(Aland §326)

Jesus again describes the intense shift of emotion that forthcoming events will bring. Enigmatically, he tells them that in a short time they will not see him anymore, and then in a short time after that they will see him again. Clearly, Jesus refers initially to his death, which is the foundation for all he is telling them in this discourse. More debated is what seeing him in a little while refers to. Three options are discussed: (1) Jesus' return, (2) the coming of the Spirit, and (3) postresurrection appearances. Against the return is the very absence of such a return "in a little while." In addition, there are no notes of judgment or vindication raised here, which are so prominent in judgment texts. More difficult is deciding between the other two options. Against the reference to the Spirit is that no "seeing" of Jesus takes place that balances the initial "no longer see" of the first part of the passage. What does fit the language is the idea of postresurrection appearances. This surely is what Jesus refers to that changes the grief of the disciples to joy. In saying that Jesus refers to his resurrection appearances, however, it should not be forgotten that this resurrection itself triggers a series of events that lead to the Spirit's coming, so that eventually the Spirit's coming is encompassed in what is said here. Seeing a raised Jesus proves God's vindication of him and his mission. From this event comes all that follows, both in the provision of the Spirit and his ultimate return. That is why resurrection triggers the shift from grief to joy.

The initial remark only puzzles the eleven disciples, who cannot fathom why Jesus keeps speaking of "in a little while." Messiahs, to them, do not die and depart, as Peter made clear in Mark 8:31–32; they fight and bring a glorious victory. So, as is often the case during Jesus' ministry, they do not understand him yet. So Jesus replies. A time is coming when disciples will weep and wail—a figure for a time of mourning (cf. Luke 7:32)—while the world rejoices. When Jesus dies, this will be their emotional state. However, their grief will become joy. The resurrection will trigger this reversal.[36] It is like the time when a woman is in distress while giving birth, only to rejoice when the child is born. This imagery of birth pangs is common in the Old Testament for the time of messianic salvation (Isa. 21:2–3; esp. 26:16–21, which shares much of the imagery of these verses; 66:7–14; Jer. 13:21; Hos. 13:13; Mic. 4:9–10). So they will have sorrow now in the events that are in the process of taking place. Everything will change when "I will see you again" (LXX Isa. 66:14, where John has changed the "you will see" to "I will see you again"). This language stresses Jesus' initiative in bringing the disciples back into view. When he dies, it will seem that he has lost sight of them forever. In fact, his

36. So George R. Beasley-Murray, *John,* WBC 36 (Waco: Word, 1987), 285, correctly explains, "It is the Easter resurrection that is in view. Consequent on that no man will have the power to rob the disciples of their joy, because Easter is not an isolated event but the beginning of the new creation (20:22), wherein disciples will know the presence of the Lord in a manner impossible in the days of his flesh. From that time on, therefore, life for them is existence in the shared fellowship of the Father, Son, and Holy Spirit (14:21, 23, 26)." The specifics of this emotional transition tied to Jesus' death and resurrection show that the eleven disciples are meant in this unit.

resurrection will show that they have been in his sight all along. This will lead to the disciples' joy. This joy will be permanent; no one can take it away. That is because this joy reflects the everlasting life that Jesus' resurrection represents. In resurrection, all things will become clear.

J39. Then You Will Ask in My Name (John 16:23–28)
(Aland §327)

Two benefits are among the final topics of Jesus' discourse: access to the Father, and understanding of Jesus' ministry and how it fits into God's plan. Access is treated first, and then their enhanced understanding.

Jesus takes the disciples forward to "that day," which usually in the New Testament is a reference to that day (or time) of significance when God's promise is being realized at the end of the ages (Mark 13:11, 17, 19; 14:25; Acts 2:18; 2 Tim. 1:12, 18; Heb. 8:10; 10:16 [= Jer. 31:32 or LXX 38:33]; Rev. 9:15). Jesus already has alluded to "that day" in discussing the resurrection (John 14:20). With resurrection, new spiritual realities and possibilities emerge. In that day they will not need to ask anything of Jesus. There is some question about how Jesus is using the term "ask" here. (1) Does he think of them asking a question, as they have been doing throughout this discourse and especially just recently in the context? Or (2) is he referring to their asking for something of spiritual benefit, looking forward in the context? The root of this question revolves around an attempt to argue that ἐρωτάω, the verb used in John 16:23, means "to ask a question," while αἰτέω means "to ask for something." But John's usage of the verb ἐρωτάω elsewhere is not consistent (to ask a question [John 1:19, 21; 16:5, 30]; to ask for something [John 4:31; 16:26]). So simply examining the term does not answer the question.

Three factors suggest that Jesus is looking back contextually in responding to their question (so view 1). First, the next remark begins with "truly, truly I say to you," which normally is used by John to add to what has been said, putting a new twist on things (John 1:51; 10:1). Second, the two uses of asking in this chapter up to this point are about asking for information (John 16:5, 19). Third, the summarizing use of the verb "to ask" in John 16:30 clearly has this force. So Jesus is noting that their lack of understanding and perplexity is about to be reversed by the resurrection. Then there will be no need to ask basic questions about what God has done through Jesus, why he has died, where he has gone, and what his ascension means.

However, beyond the change in their understanding comes an access to the Father that is made more direct through Jesus. Jesus assures them with his "truly, truly I say to you" statement that they can ask anything of the Father, and he will give it to them in Jesus' name. This is not a carte blanche promise that disciples can ask for whatever they want; rather, it is related to the mission tied to Jesus and to the honoring of his person, which is why Jesus' name is mentioned. Again it is not certain whether the disciple asks in Jesus' name, as John 15:16 promises and 14:14 teaches, or whether God gives the answer in Jesus' name, as 14:26 suggests about the sending of the Paraclete. It is hard to be sure which is meant because both ideas are present in John. Perhaps Johannine ambiguity is again present, which is why the Greek phrase shows up in the middle of the sentence. Regardless of which of the options is taken, the point is that these requests to God are taking place in a sphere in which the concern is to honor Jesus' name and reputation, in asking or in giving or in both. Again the Father and the Son are inseparable. A disciple asks the Father, but does so realizing the connection to the Son. Up to now there has been no prayer in Jesus' name, but then, after his resurrection to the Father's side, they can boldly approach God through him, as Heb. 10:19–22 says explicitly. This probably suggests that the asking is in Jesus' name, not the giving, because it is Jesus' new position that opens up this new door. Now they can ask and receive in the context of God's will. In receiving they will experience a fullness of joy tied to being united with God in life.

Jesus notes that he has spoken to them "in figures," in speech that is less than explicit and clear. But the hour is approaching in the events to come when he will speak plainly about the Father. In that day they will ask, and Jesus will not need to pray for them, because the Father loves them. That love is grounded in the shared regard that the Father and the disciples have for the one whom God sent. They have believed in the work of the Father in sending the Son from his side. So they have unique and direct access to the Father that also leads into a more sensitive understanding of the pursuit of God's will.

Finally, Jesus summarizes what they now have come to believe: "I came from the Father and have come into the world; again, I am leaving the world and going to the Father." Jesus is the sent one from God, whose home really is with God and in his presence. In returning there, he is accomplishing all that God sent him to do. In his departure come the benefits of what he has accomplished. Jesus' ministry of signs pointed the way to life and showed that he had authority over it. Jesus' departure means that he can give the eternal life and quality of relationship with God that he had promised.

J40. Tribulation to Come, but Also an Overcoming of the World (John 16:29–33) (Aland §328)

Jesus indicated that the disciples would understand him clearly when the Spirit comes, but the disciples believe that they have jumped the gun and understand now. In an ironic section, the disciples now claim that Jesus is speaking plainly and that they understand. Jesus knows differently. The disciples do offer, in the midst of their confidence, a confession. They understand that Jesus knows all things and that there is no need for anyone to question him. They believe that he is from God. The poignancy of the scene is that even though the disciples do not have all the insight that they claim to have, they are on the right track and in the right place, with still much more to learn. Their fundamental confession of Jesus differs from the world's assessment of Jesus and is fundamentally correct.

Nevertheless, if they really understood Jesus and that he knows all things, then they would have understood and embraced his teaching that a deeper understanding for disciples must await the Spirit's coming. They also would appreciate how Jesus' death is their gain.

The disciples' lack of understanding is underscored in Jesus' prediction. The weakness of their faith will be exposed in the hour that now has come. John now refers to the hour neither as near nor as coming but as having arrived, the perfect tense driving the point home ("has come" [John 12:23]). When Jesus' opponents come for him, the disciples will scatter and leave him alone in terms of human support. Jesus alludes to the language of Zech. 13:7 to make the point that his suffering will bring scattering (cf. Mark 14:27, 50). John's point is not so much spatial in force as it is emotional. The disciples will not stand behind him at the moment of his death. Nothing represents this defection more clearly than Peter's denials (John 18:15–18). Although some ran, others followed, and still others watched; none did so while understanding and supporting what took place. There was denial and grief in the moment when Jesus was glorified.

As alone as Jesus was at the human level, one other will stand with him, representing the inseparable union Jesus has taught about throughout this Gospel. Jesus says that the Father "is with me." Nothing will happen, no matter how terrible it seems, without the Father's knowledge, approval, and presence. So Jesus reassures these disciples and seeks to give them peace (cf. John 14:27) in the midst of the coming turmoil. The world will bequeath to them tribulation, like a woman in birth travail, as he noted in 16:21. However, they can be of good cheer because what is about to take place means that Jesus has overcome the world (cf. John 12:31; 1 Cor. 15:57; 1 John 2:13–14; 4:4; 5:4–5). Again the victory is expressed in a perfect tense (νενίκηκα). Once victory comes, it remains. Jesus' discourse closes on the note of triumph that also will conclude his earthly ministry.

This discourse has explained why Jesus' departure is necessary. He must return to the Father in order to provide for them in his absence. So his life paves the way for their life and will allow him to send the Spirit. The Spirit will guide them and will encourage them. Above all, the Spirit will instruct them and enable them to share the message with understanding. In going, Jesus will not be gone. He will be present in the one he sends. He also will bring with him the presence of, and union with, the Father. He will, in sum, bring life.

J41. Jesus' Prayer That the Disciples Be Consecrated and Be One, As the Father Is with the Son (John 17:1–26) (Aland §329)

Here, like the end of Deut. 32–33, a farewell discourse is followed by an address to God.[37] The prayer has three basic parts: (1) Jesus treats the relationship between himself and the Father (vv. 1–5); (2) Jesus addresses the relationships impacting the disciples whom he selected (vv. 6–19); and (3) Jesus speaks of the impact on the church and on disciples that emerges from the work of these disciples (vv. 20–26). It is discussed whether the prayer is (1) a "high priestly" prayer, (2) a prayer of "consecration" (see v. 19), or (3) simply some other kind of intercessory prayer. Some of these characterizations of the prayer depend on how the terms are seen. Jesus is making an intercessory prayer and acting much like a priest here, but there are no extensive sacrificial elements to what is being requested (vv. 5 and 19 only hint in this direction by being based in part on his work on the cross). Consecration is explicitly mentioned only in one verse. A far stronger case can be made for the themes of glorification and union. For these disciples and those who come after him, Jesus seeks a union with God whose quality is like that which the Father and the Son have. In keeping them and sustaining them in their mutual relationship, they will mirror and glorify God in precisely the way that the Son's work in this hour will. Just as the signs section showed how the Father and the sent one are inseparable, so this prayer asks for a strong union between the disciples and Jesus. In this sense, the prayer is the flip side and the divine side of Jesus' call to the disciples to abide, in John 15. He and the Father will work in concert to bring disciples into this relationship. Jesus is mediating for his disciples here. He prays as a priest intercedes on behalf of his people. However, he prays as far more than a priest.

Jesus makes his request after completing his discourse. He lifts his eyes to heaven (cf. Ps. 123:1; Mark 7:34; John 11:41) to address the Father, a name always present in Jesus' Johannine prayers, just as it is in the Lord's prayer (John 11:41; 12:27; Luke 11:2; Matt. 6:9). The hour has arrived (see John 12:23, 27–28; 13:31), so Jesus asks that God glorify the Son so that the Son may glorify him in return. Jesus' work and that of the Father are intertwined. When the Father honors the Son, the result is that the Son honors

---

37. This also occurs in other Jewish texts, as Carson notes, *John,* 550–51 (Gen. 49; *Jubilees* 22.7–23). This is one of three prayers in John, this one by far the longest (see John 11:41–42; 12:27–28).

the Father. In making the request, the Son's desire to be obedient to the Father in love is clear. Glorification of the Son refers not only to the work that Jesus will do on the cross in death but also to God's vindicating exaltation of the Son that will follow it. That vindication will testify to the cosmic importance of Jesus' death. In raising the Son, God testifies to and gives evidence for the plan that sent the Son to die. He reveals how great and significant the Son and his work are. This is but the realization of a plan worked out long ago. The glorification of the Son takes place now, just as the bestowal of the Son's authority over all people took place long ago in eternity past (see Dan. 7:9–14; Acts 10:42; 17:31).[38] The purpose of such authority was that eternal life might be given to all those whom God had given to the Son (cf. John 5:21–27). Thus, Jesus really is praying for the working out of the plan that God made long ago to save through the Son. God will keep his promise to the Son.

At the heart of the plan stands eternal life, defined not only for its endless duration but also for its abundant quality, since it represents a relationship ("know") with "the only true God, *and* Jesus Christ whom [God has] sent."[39] It is significant that the relationship with Jesus is expressed on an equal plane with the relationship to God. This shows how much is involved in the exaltation that the Father performs for the Son. They end up sharing the same stage. Some critics, arguing that it is odd for Jesus to refer to himself in the third person, suggest that John 17:3 is a Johannine parenthetical remark inserted into the prayer. However, it may simply reflect the solemn nature of the confession, much like Margaret Thatcher liked to call herself "the Lady" to highlight her unique position. The second-person verbs in the verse are hard to explain if John is inserting this remark as a parenthesis. John 17:3 is stated from the standpoint of the disciples about whom Jesus cares so much and for whom he is praying. He describes eternal life as it relates to them because it is for them, not him, that eternal life is given. Eternal life then becomes the relationship that a disciple has with both the Father and the Christ whom the Father sent, who also is God's son.

So Jesus did his work. He "glorified" the Father on earth. The aorist tense takes the work as a whole and summarizes it as a completed work. In speaking with such certainty before the work actually is done, Jesus highlights how he is participating in something that God has designed to take place as he has outlined. The Son has done the work that the Father gave him to do.[40] In the completion of that work, only one thing remains, that the Son be restored into God's own presence with the glory that the Son possessed before the

38. The giving of all sorts of things dominates this prayer (John 17:4, 6, 7, 8, 9, 11, 12, 14, 22, 24) (Morris, *John*, 636 n. 6).
39. Knowing God has Old Testament roots (Jer. 31:34; Deut. 30:20).
40. This helps to explain why Jesus utters, "It is finished," when he expires on the cross (John 19:30).

world was made. It is this verse that is so important, because it shows that Jesus is not elevated in glorification and ascension to new heights, but rather, he returns to the exalted position that he had even before the creation. It is also this verse that shows that God's plan is in view in John 17:2. The authority that Jesus has is authority that Jesus always had. The role that Jesus will receive after his death is an authority that he possessed before "the Word became flesh." What Paul said hymnically in Phil. 2:5–11, Jesus prays for here. Along with John 1:1, 8:58, and 16:28, John's Christology reaches its greatest height in this request. What Jesus prays for in glorification is the affirmation of the union that Father and Son always have had, as well as the completion of a work planned long ago.

From their long-standing relationship, Jesus turns to those whom the Father gave to him to effect their plan, to this key group of initial disciples. He is about to pass major responsibility on to them, so they can reach others. So Jesus prays for this special group of followers.

The basis of the prayer comes first. Many points move Jesus to pray. To begin with, the first part of Jesus' work is accomplished. He has manifested God's name—his character, power, and plan—to those whom God had given to him. Second, they have kept Jesus' word (note the singular). The verb for "kept" (τετήρηκαν) is in the perfect tense, and "word" is expressed in the singular because it represents a unit of teaching. This plan was kept in the past and the effects remain. The allusion is to a basic obedience to the fundamental message that Jesus is the sent one from God (17:3). Third, the result is that they recognize that everything that Jesus has been given is from the Father. The Father and Son work as one; Jesus has taught them the words (note the plural) that the Father gave (cf. John 7:16; 12:48–49). All these pieces of teaching led them to conclude that Jesus came from the Father. This teaching they received and know. This grounding in responsiveness to God leads Jesus to intercede for these various gifts of God's grace, especially their effective union with the Son. Fourth, Jesus' prayer is for them and not for the world, because the disciples are given to Jesus and belong to God in this special relationship that is eternal life. Jesus here affirms the special relationship he has to disciples. He regards it with a higher priority than the work he performs on behalf of the world, even though it is his work for the world that opens the door for access for his disciples. The emphasis shows that Jesus is after more than forgiving sins. He desires disciples to have a quality relationship with God. Only as those of the world step into relationship to him can they enter blessing and experience the blessings that he works to bring.

The unity of the work of the Father and Son is the next point of Jesus' emphasis before he prays for them. All that belongs to Jesus is the Father's; all that is the Father's belongs to Jesus. This reciprocal union (cf. John 5:19–30) now is expanded to include those who belong to Jesus because Jesus is glorified in them. Jesus' fifth point is that their belief honors Jesus and affirms the plan of God.

Finally, Jesus is departing, so they need prayer. Jesus will not be physically ministering in the world anymore, but these disciples remain to do his work as Jesus comes again to the Father. The change in circumstances brings the need for God's continuing work. So the Holy Father, the one and only God, who is set apart from the creation and over it, is to keep them. Is the request to keep them in his name or by his name (i.e., by his power that is at the heart of his person)? Either sense is grammatically possible. A good case can be made for both. In favor of "by your name" is the idea of John 17:6–8 that Jesus has manifested God's name in his ministry, which certainly has to do with a revelation of God and his power. This work brought the disciples to faith. In favor of "in your name" is the elaboration that follows, which leads to the request to "sanctify them in truth" in v. 17. The setting apart of the disciples also looks to their being entrusted into God's care, which must include the work of God's power but also entails his keeping them in union with him. In sum, it appears that the ambiguity is intentional. They will remain in union as God works in power for them. This is what Jesus asks for them as he faces the completion of his work for them. This "keeping in the name" involves a union that the disciples share with both the Father and the Son because Jesus has been given God's name.

The disciples will be united to each other in God, just like the union that the Son has with the Father. This is not a surface ecumenism, but a relationship that is rooted in allegiance to God, a connection that Jesus has given them all during his ministry with one exception, Judas Iscariot. What the Eleven were, Judas failed to be, because Jesus had guarded and protected them, while Judas had failed to embrace the Son. Only the "son of perdition" was lost, showing his real character and fulfilling Scripture. Judas was one destined for judgment (so perdition, as it is related to the noun for judgment [Matt. 7:13; Acts 8:20; Rom. 9:22; Phil. 1:28; 3:19]; the description is a mirror of the "man of sin," the antichrist of 2 Thess. 2:3). The Scripture alluded to is not named, but probably it is Ps. 41:9, which was cited about Judas in John 13:18.[41]

Jesus announces these things in the world as he goes to and comes from the Father. Jesus desires that the disciples may have the joy that comes from Jesus in them (see John 15:11; 16:24). So Jesus is praying for the joy that comes from residing in solid relationship to God.

This relationship now has its roots in what Jesus has given to the disciples, namely, God's word. Jesus has come to bring the message of God's way and plan. The result of their embrace of God's way is their distancing, even separation, from the world. Their reception of Jesus the Word shows that the

---

41. Acts 1:20 cites Ps. 109:8, but that is more to justify Judas's ignominious death.

disciples are not of the world, just as Jesus is not of the world (cf. John 1:13; 3:3–8; 15:19). The distance does not mean that the disciples are to be removed from the world. Jesus does not pray for that, but God is called upon to protect them from the evil one (cf. Matt. 6:13; 1 John 2:13–14; 3:12; 5:18–19; John 12:31; 14:30; esp. 16:11) as they engage the world in mission. Such protection is grounded in the fact that they are not of the world, just as Jesus is not.

So Jesus' major request is to set them apart in the truth. The request "to sanctify" them is a call to dedicate them to God's service (see John 10:36; 17:19; Jer. 1:5; Exod. 28:41). They already are taken from the world, and now they need to be equipped for the sacred duty of mission. It is their work in the truth that will make this possible. As God enables them to work in the context of the word, the mission will be effectively undertaken. The word of God about Jesus is truth and so directs them into authentic life and mission. So they are headed into the world, just as God sent Jesus into the world. John has highlighted the idea of Jesus as the sent one. Now, these disciples have become the sent ones, taking his place. They truly are his apostles.

Having requested the sanctification of the disciples, Jesus now consecrates himself "for their sake." Jesus dedicates himself to the service and sacrifice that will enable disciples to undertake their role. What Jesus is about to do in offering himself is an act of dedication to God. All the language of 17:19 points to the turning point that Jesus' death and sacrifice are, reviewing what John has said elsewhere (John 1:29, 34; 10:11, 17–18; 11:49–52; 15:13) and anticipating what he will say (John 18:11; 19:30). The "for their sake" recalls imagery like that which appears in the Last Supper and other points in Jesus' teaching (Mark 10:45; 14:24; Luke 22:19–20; 1 Cor. 11:24; also John 6:51). The roots of this consecration language resemble the sacrificial context of Deut. 15:19, 21 (cf. Heb. 9:14; 10:9–10). Jesus' dedication unto death is for others (see Rom. 5:6–11). It allows God in turn to consecrate these disciples in truth. Jesus' prayer ultimately is about how his work is part of God's plan worked out long ago. It involves disciples set apart to serve God uniquely through the provision that Jesus makes possible. The gift of eternal life leads to the life of mission in service to God. This is Jesus' request and call in this prayer.

Now Jesus turns his attention to those disciples who will come to faith through the mission of the disciples for whom he has just prayed. Jesus anticipates success in their calling despite the world's opposition. That success is grounded in the fact that Jesus' prayer here is answered, in that God glorifies the Son so he in turn can give the glory of union with God to his disciples.

Jesus' basic request calls for a spiritual union that makes all disciples one as the Father and the Son are one. That union involves not only disciples being with each other, but also their being "in us," a union with the Godhead. This is not an institutional or structural union but a visible union of spirit, grounded in disciples' mutual allegiance to God and his sent one.[42] One purpose of such a union is that the world might be challenged to believe that Jesus was sent by God.[43] So although Jesus did not pray directly for the world in 17:9, the work of the disciples is aimed very much at the world as they seek to draw others into blessing. A key means of accomplishing this mission is a genuine oneness grounded in the spiritual relationship that Christ has given to the disciples, a theme raised originally in 13:34–35.

Jesus has given the glory of this relationship to the disciples, a glory that parallels what the Father has given to and possesses with the Son (John 17:5). Christ gave this glory so that oneness would be possible. Jesus' emphasis in this climactic part of the intercession shows why both glory and unity are key themes of this prayer. It is the reciprocity of relationship and union, "I in them and you in me," that allows these disciples to be completed in oneness. The term for "being completed" in oneness in 17:23 is in the perfect tense. It looks to the attainment of a state of oneness and points its eyes eventually to the completion of the promise in the end. The disciples will be united in love, purpose, and abiding relationship with God. Jesus wants to finish well the task that they have started here. In a sense, Jesus finishes up in prayer where he started in the discourse in 14:2–3. Such unity will be a testimony and a challenge to the world to recognize and know that the Father sent Jesus into the world to redeem it and to call out a special people for his love, a love that God gives to them just as he does to his Son.

Jesus' final request is that the promise be completed one day to the point where the disciples can come and be with Jesus in heavenly glory. He asks that these disciples may behold the glory that the Father has given to Jesus in a divine love whose roots go back to the foundation of the world. Disciples are to appreciate that God's love for the sent one did not start with the incarnation, but reaches back into the divine planning made long ago. A vindicated and visible Jesus makes the truth of this claim transparent.

42. Barrett, *John*, 427, says it this way: "The unity of the church is strictly analogous to the unity of the Father and Son; the Father is active *in* the Son—it is the Father who does his works (14:10)—and apart from the Father the deeds of the Son are meaningless, and indeed would be impossible; the Son again is in the Father, eternally with him in the unity of the Godhead, active alike in creation and redemption. The Father and the Son are one and yet remain distinct. The believers are to be, and are to be one, in the Father and the Son, distinct from God, yet abiding in God, and themselves the sphere of God's activity (14:12)."

43. The structures of John 17:21 and 17:23 are quite similar. John 17:21 has three ἵνα clauses, while 17:23 has two ἵνα clauses and a ὅτι clause. In both cases, it is discussed whether the last clause is parallel to the previous two clauses or is a purpose clause following from the previous ἵνα clause. The argument of the passage and the focus on the world in the final clause in each verse leads one to see the statement of a goal produced as a result of oneness (vv. 21, 23) in each case. Morris, *John*, 650 n. 66, cites R. H. Strachan and summarizes the point: "The inward unity expressing itself in a common mission and message will alone impress the world."

Jesus' prayer closes with a statement made to the Righteous Father. Divine righteousness is noted because this is the key attribute that God exercises in the plan of salvation and the final judgment. Jesus again distinguishes between the world and the disciples. The world has not known God, but Jesus has, and so have the disciples to whom Jesus was sent. Jesus has made the character, plan, and the person of God known to them. He has made God's name known. In fact, he will continue to make it known. This ongoing work alludes especially to the Spirit's work that Jesus outlined in John 14–16. This work to come will enable the disciples to reach out in mission and claim those who will be disciples after them (see John 16:12–13; 25). The result is a love relationship that is passed on from the Father, through the sent one, and into and among the disciples. In that love is a union between Jesus and these disciples. It is the quality of this relationship and its visibility that Jesus prays for most of all. He prays because this was the plan all along, to restore people to an enduring relationship of quality with God. The idea is little different from what Paul calls being "in Christ."

J42. Jesus' Arrest in the Garden (John 18:1–12) (Aland §§330–31)

The Johannine passion account presents a very focused summary of these events. It is far more selective than its Synoptic counterparts and the tradition that those Gospels reflect.[44] John's account in John 18–19 basically has three parts: (1) Jesus' arrest and appearance before the high priest, with Peter's denials (18:1–27); (2) Jesus' trial before Pilate (18:28–19:16a); and (3) Jesus' crucifixion, death, and burial (19:16b–42). Each of these larger units has subunits. As noted, this is a much more simplified presentation than that of the Synoptics. Gone are the controversies of the last week that preceded these final events. There is no scene recording agony in the garden, nor one involving a kiss of betrayal by Judas. The meeting with Annas is new, as is the note about Roman presence at the arrest, and a concern that Roman involvement be noted.[45] In sum, John appears to have chosen to supplement what already was known with additional detail, regardless of

44. Almost all students of the Gospels believe that this passion story was one of the first sets of traditions about Jesus to be written down. For a good overview of issues tied to the Johannine material, see Beasley-Murray, *John,* 308–12.

45. It has often been the case that this more Roman note has been drawn upon to lessen the responsibility of the Jewish leadership, on the one hand, or ironically, on the other hand, to question John's historical value by arguing that he has brought the Romans in too early. Both of these responses are misguided. In a festival setting, the Romans would have been highly sensitive to any potential for extended public violence. They would have quickly made support available if the Jewish leadership had signaled a potential for danger. Only a signal from the leadership would have raised a Roman concern about Jesus. Jesus' actions, such as those in the temple or his claims to work with Israel's God, would have been matters that religious Jews, not the Romans, would be concerned about initially.

the more difficult question of whether or not he worked with the Synoptics in this section.[46] Many efforts have been made to explain certain omissions, such as Jesus' prayer and Judas's kiss in Gethsemane. No clear explanation exists except the apparent choice John made to go largely his own way, something for which his Gospel's character up to this point also has prepared us.

After his discourse and prayer, Jesus departed across the Kidron Valley into a garden. The Greek indicates that the valley has an intermittent stream that flows during the rainy season (winter) but is otherwise dry. It runs down about two hundred feet from the level of the temple's outer court. The locale was well known to Judas and the disciples; they often met there when in the city. Judas also knew that the disciples must sleep in the environs of Jerusalem on this special festival evening (see Deut. 16:5), unlike other nights, when they stayed in Bethany. So Judas gathered Roman troops ($\sigma\pi\epsilon\hat{\iota}\rho\alpha$) and other police of the chief priests (the aristocracy most threatened by Jesus) and Pharisees. Such a gathering of Roman troops was often a "cohort" of six hundred, although it could refer to two hundred troops or perhaps less from these imperial guards. Such troops would have come to Jerusalem from Caesarea to ensure that the peace was kept in the face of the large pilgrim crowds at the feast. They went prepared for anything, with torches and swords. As John 18:12 tells us, these troops were led by a commander of a cohort, $\acute{o}\ \chi\iota\lambda\acute{\iota}\alpha\rho\chi o\varsigma$.

In his summarizing way that highlights Jesus taking control and not backing down from what he is about to face, John presents Jesus stepping forward to meet his foes. Asking them whom they seek and hearing their answer, "Jesus of Nazareth," Jesus replies, "I am." The reply, coming as it does with Judas now lined up next to the arresting forces, causes the soldiers initially to draw back and fall to the ground. John notes the detail as part of the symbolism of the scene, perhaps ironic. Those who have come to arrest the one who represents the "I am" and has so described himself are initially set back when there is no resistance by the "dangerous" leader they came to arrest. He meets them only with an identification of himself, an identification that those sensitive to the name of God in John's audience will recognize. In fact, Jesus has them repeat the request to show that he fully intends to cooperate with their intentions peaceably, unlike some of his other disciples, as soon will become evident. Jesus makes one request: in arresting him, let the others go free. Jesus is thinking of the welfare of others even as he faces rejection by Israel and arrest by Rome. John notes that this request for the disciples' release fulfilled remarks that Jesus had made earlier, in John 17:12, where none but Judas is lost. In John 17:12, a remark about the fulfillment of Scripture also appears. Note how Judas, the "son of perdition"

46. Carson, *John*, 571–72, thinks that John knew one or two of the Synoptics, while Brown, *John XIII–XXI*, 787–91, argues that John worked independently of the Synoptics or their sources, though he does acknowledge traditions whose roots are old. The age and well-circulated condition of the passion material allows John to take this more independent route. He can add to what already is known.

(John 17:12), is no longer in the count in John 18:9. None are lost by Jesus. The defection has revealed that he never was really in the group (John 6:70–71).

Not everyone is content to allow Jesus to be taken into custody. Peter acts violently. Only John identifies Peter as the culprit. He strikes the high priest's servant, Malchus, on the right ear with a "dagger" (μάχαιραν).[47] If the remarks in Luke 22:35–38 are viewed as background, Peter misunderstood Jesus. When Jesus told them to procure swords now that his betrayal draws near, Peter thought Jesus wanted them to fight. Luke also mentions how Jesus healed the ear of the one struck. John lacks any mention of this detail. So Jesus stops the attempt to defend him with a command to put the sword back in its sheath. Stating it emphatically (οὐ μή), Jesus insists that he will drink the cup that the Father has given him, just as John 14–17 showed that Jesus was ready to do. In language echoing Jesus' prayer in Gethsemane (Matt. 26:39, 42; Mark 14:36; Luke 22:42), it is a cup of wrath and suffering that Jesus will drink (see Ps. 75:8; Isa. 51:17, 22; Jer. 25:15; Ezek. 23:31–33). With this, the captain of the Roman troops and the Jewish officers seizes Jesus. Jesus goes voluntarily to his divine destiny.

J43. Jesus before Annas and Peter's Denials (John 18:13–28)
(Aland §§332–34)

As we turn to these final events, I include more detail in the notes, because John often is pitted against the Synoptics in his many differences of detail. These differences are not as significant as some critics make them out to be. They do not require that one choose between the Synoptic account and John's, as some suggest (often with John coming out as less reliable). Rather, the accounts can be read as complementing one another.

Only John tells the story of this preliminary hearing before Annas. In all likelihood, this scene is omitted in the Synoptics because nothing decisive came of it, and the key hearing was the one before the Jewish council over which Caiaphas presided.[48] John includes it because it does evidence the hostility that now existed between Jesus and the leadership.

47. Brown, *John XIII–XXI*, 812, notes that the detail does not look invented, because the name Malchus is not well known. The embarrassment of the remark about Peter also is unlikely to have been invented about him.

48. More critical treatments complain about the lack of logic in this scene, but this seems to be hypercriticism. It is not surprising that Jesus is being taken to the head of the clan, Annas, nor is it surprising that in 18:19 Annas is called high priest (cf. 11:49; 18:13, 24), because he had been high priest before and still held much authority. There is precedent for such an address in Jewish materials, as other texts show (*m. Horayot* 3.1–2, 4; Josephus, *War* 2.12.6 §243). Luke also shows this pattern in his description of Annas (Luke 3:2) (Brown, *John XIII–XXI*, 820). We do the same thing today with former governors, senators, and presidents. What Josephus says about Annas and the line of high priestly appointments shows that he remained a powerful figure (*Ant.* 18.2.2 §34; 20.9.1 §198).

Annas was Caiaphas's father-in-law and head of the clan. It is likely that on this important night they were located in the same home. The reference, in Peter's denials, to a gate and a courtyard suggests that a house is in view, not a setting at the temple. John's note about Caiaphas having said that it was expedient for one man to die for the people recalls John 11:49–50 and indicates how the position of this key family with regard to Jesus was already mapped out.

Meanwhile, Peter and one other unidentified disciple follow behind to see what was taking place. The identification of this disciple is not clear. Traditionally, he has been associated with the "beloved disciple," who so often is tied to Peter and is unnamed (John 21) or called the "other disciple" (20:2, 3, 4, 8).[49] Against this identification is the suggestion that this disciple was well known to the high priest, as the description of him involves a term that would identify him as a good friend (γνωστός). Though by some coincidence this could be John, it is less than likely. The identity of this other disciple is unknown. However, he was able to secure Peter's entry into the courtyard on what John 20:18 says was a cold night that required a charcoal fire for one to keep warm. In this setting, Peter initially denies that he is a disciple.[50] It is interesting to note that Peter does not deny who Jesus is, but rather, his own attachment to Jesus and what he represents. Jesus predicted this response in John 13:37–38. Jesus stands alone (cf. John 16:32).

This interrogation by Annas proceeds in a different way from the Synoptic interrogations by the Jews.[51] Annas apparently tried to query Jesus on two issues: his disciples and his teaching. On the disciples, Jesus offers no response at all. He replies strictly in the first person about what he has taught. With regard to his teaching, Jesus responds that he has taught openly to the world. There is no "secret" teaching. Anyone who wants to know what he has taught can inquire of the Jews who have gathered in the synagogues, the temple, or other public locales where Jesus has taught. Jesus is not being flippant here, but rather is insisting on two points: (1) he should not be forced to incriminate himself, as that seems to have been against Jewish law;[52] so (2) they should find their own witnesses. If the interest really is to determine what Jesus taught, then others can

49. However, the identification has been disputed for a long time; John Calvin called it "a weak conjecture," as Morris, *John*, 666 n. 36, points out.

50. John has the servant girl asking the question using μή, which normally expects a negative reply. In this case, the interrogative is asking a "cautious" question. The woman raises the point that Peter may be a disciple with a touch of caution, perhaps not being sure why he is there. Peter goes along with the direction of the question and takes the way out that she offers.

51. The high priest asking the questions here is Annas, not Caiaphas, who is not present, as John 18:24 shows. Suggestions that John is confused here refuse to recognize the respectful title that John gives to the head of the high priestly clan.

52. Mishnah *Sanhedrin* 6.2 suggests the right of a defendant against self-incrimination: "Our true Torah does not inflict the penalty of death upon a sinner either by his own confession or by declaration of a prophet that the accused has done the deed." The law required corroborative witnesses (Deut. 19:15).

produce those facts. Jesus has been quite public about what he has done. He is not a "closet" insurrectionist, as their handling of him suggests.

The way Annas proceeds suggests that this is not a formal trial but an informal inquiry in which normal rules for trials do not apply. These initial examinations are more of a gathering of evidence to take to Rome, like a grand jury investigation.

One of the attending officers thinks that Jesus is being insolent. So he strikes him and says, "Is that how you answer the high priest?" Jesus insists that witnesses of a wrong be brought forward, replying, "If I have spoken wrong, bear witness to the wrong; but if I have spoken rightly, why do you strike me?" Jesus is arguing that his reply about teaching openly in public was true. They all knew it, so the slap was an act of injustice. It was but the beginning of such acts of disrespect toward Jesus. Annas apparently decides that he is going to get nowhere, so he binds Jesus and sends him on to Caiaphas. Annas's role appears to be that of the patriarch involving himself in the process. However, Caiaphas must be involved in anything official, since he is the high priest.

Meanwhile, at the same time, by the fire Peter is being confronted with others who sought to connect him to Jesus. The Johannine juxtaposition of the three Petrine denials with the examination of Jesus (one denial coming before and two after the Annas inquiry) is designed dramatically to underscore how Jesus stood alone at this trial. Even those closest to him did not stand up to the heat of the moment on this cold night. The two denials come in rapid succession in the narrative. First, the question is asked in a way that expects a denial or at least raises the question with caution, using the exact form of the first probe of Peter by asking the question with μή. This second query comes from the group, as "they" ask him. The impression is created that the initial question caused others to become curious and ask. But another in the audience was a relative of Malchus. He knew what had occurred. He seemingly recognizes Peter. His query expects a positive reply, in contrast to the previous two questions: "Did I not [οὐκ] see you in the garden with him?" Peter again denies the association, and the cock crows. The next thing John narrates is Jesus being brought from the house of Caiaphas, headed for the praetorium and a meeting with Pilate. It is now early in the morning. The Jews do not enter the praetorium for fear of contracting uncleanness from the Gentile setting and preventing themselves from being able to eat the "Passover."[53] Pilate would have been in Jerusalem to watch over

53. Mishnah *'Ohalot* 18.7, 9, mention that the dwelling places of Gentiles are unclean. Uncleanness was not contracted in the courtyard, among other openings in the building, or among the colonnades. It took place only if one stepped inside (Morris, *John,* 675 nn. 64–65). Morris notes that the uncleanness contracted through Gentiles lasted for a week to allow for the possibility of "death" uncleanness from Gentiles who may have disposed of aborted fetuses by tossing them down the drain. Contact with a dead body caused a seven-day uncleanness (Num. 9:7–14). In light of this, it may well be that the Jews' fear of being disqualified through uncleanness applied not only to the Passover sacrifice itself but to the entire Passover week. Regardless, in John's view, the Jews are meticulous about cleanliness in regard to the law even as they work to remove God's sent one. The de-

the celebration of the feast and to ensure that the peace was kept. It is this Roman sensitivity for order that the Jewish leadership hopes to tap.

J44. The Trial before Pilate, the Choice, and the Presentation of Jesus for Execution (John 18:29–19:16) (Aland §§336, 339–41)

Pilate, showing sensitivity to their desire to remain clean, goes out to meet the Jewish entourage. He asks them what accusation they bring. Perhaps thinking that their request for his involvement was going to be a simple matter, they issue a vague remark about Jesus "doing evil" or "habitually doing wrong." They would hand over only a man who was engaged in such activity. The charges in Luke 23:2–3 are more specific and may fit in later with John 19:7. It may be that John is summarizing here in the way the topic was introduced to Pilate, while Luke has the details. Pilate replies by suggesting that there is nothing serious here that requires his attention: "Take him yourselves and judge him by your law."

To return Jesus to Jewish jurisdiction was not good enough because only Pilate could issue an order for an execution.[54] This indicated that the Jewish leadership did mean business and desired to bring a serious charge. There would be great benefit to the Jewish leaders in a crucifixion: (1) Rome would be seen as ultimately responsible for Jesus' death; (2) death on a cross could be related to an accursed death (Deut. 21:23: "Cursed is the one who hangs on a tree"). These two factors explain why the leadership chose not to act without Rome. Jesus' death by crucifixion would fulfill what Jesus had indicated would take place (John 12:32; 3:14). His death also would procure salvation for those aligned with him (see Col. 3:1–4).

---

tail is highly ironic. Some critics sometimes argue that a reliable source for such details is not available. Others speculate that John himself went to the praetorium. Both views are speculative. The idea that the details of the examination of Jesus never spilled out assumes a level of secrecy incompatible with what was an important execution of a well-known public figure. On the other hand, nothing in the text indicates that the "beloved disciple" or any other disciple was present. Pilate normally would have resided in Caesarea, but he was here for the festival. Possibly he stayed at what was known as the "tower of Antonia" or at Herod's palace, but we do not know for sure.

54. That the right to execute at this time was exclusively Rome's is debated among scholars. However, John's point looks to be correct. See Morris, *John*, 695–97; Darrell L. Bock, *Blasphemy and Exaltation in Judaism and the Final Examination of Jesus*, WUNT 2.106 (Tübingen: Mohr, 1998), 7–12, which works through the history of this discussion and argues that the restriction is correct. A. N. Sherwin-White, *Roman Society and Roman Law in the New Testament* (Oxford: Clarendon, 1963), 36, summarizes, "The capital power was the most jealously guarded of all the attributes of government, not even entrusted to principal assistants of the governors."

Pilate decides to conduct his own inquiry. He invites Jesus in and asks whether he is "the King of the Jews." Such a title appears occasionally in Jewish settings in decidedly political contexts (Josephus: of Hasmonean kings [*Ant.* 14.3.1 §36]; of Herod the Great [*Ant.* 16.10.2 §311]). The question matches in all the accounts (cf. Matt. 27:11; Mark 15:2; Luke 23:3). This title will dominate the passion account both in John and in the Synoptics, showing up on the placard on which the charge is displayed. It is a decidedly political charge for Pilate that requires his response as one who is to protect Caesar's rights in Judea. Jesus responds by wanting to know whether the question is asked of Pilate's own accord or whether he is simply parroting a charge. The reply is neither a diversion nor evasive. If Pilate is asking from his own Roman interests, "Do you have zealot-like designs against Caesar in an alternative political kingship?" then Jesus' reply would be negative. If he is asking from a Jewish perspective, "Are you the promised Messiah?" then Jesus would respond positively.

Pilate seemingly is offended at the suggestion that he is merely parroting a Jewish charge and responds, "I am not a Jew, am I?" (μήτι expects a negative answer). Pilate then notes that the Jews have handed him over, and he simply wants to know why. He is asking Jesus to offer a defense and an explanation, giving him the opportunity to make a case for himself. Jesus uses the opportunity to explain (using a class two conditional statement) his office: "My kingship is not from this world; if my kingship were of this world [but it is not], my servants would fight, that I might not be handed over to the Jews, but my kingship is not of this world." Jesus' reply makes three points: (1) Jesus engages in no fighting; he rejected the opportunity to defend himself physically when the Jews came for him; (2) the reason for the absence of violence is that the kingdom that Jesus represents neither originates from the world nor responds as the world does; (3) Jesus does, however, have a kingdom and is a king. Here is a text that makes it clear that Jesus disavowed any attempt to act violently against Rome, even while claiming his kingship. The reply would have struck Pilate as most curious.

Pilate confirms Jesus' affirmation by noting then that Jesus actually is claiming to be a king. Jesus' reply is indirect: "You say that I am a king." It suggests a qualified agreement. In other words, "You, Pilate, say it, but probably not in the sense in which I am thinking." So he explains. For this kingship Jesus was born and came into the world, to bear witness to the truth. Jesus refers to the truth here as that which describes God's work and plan through the kingdom (cf. John 8:32). Those who belong to the truth hear Jesus' voice (see John 10:16). It is important to see that truth here is a "place" to which one can belong, showing its association with the kingdom and its benefits, and is not a mere abstract reference to concepts. Relating correctly to God and his kingdom is truth. Pilate is skeptical and retorts dismissively, "What is truth?" In doing so, Pilate indicates that he is not one who hears the voice of Jesus.

He is not one who is "of the truth." What Pilate has heard is enough for him to get a sense of what he should do.

Pilate goes out to the Jews and notes that he finds "no crime in him." Pilate's judgment is that there is nothing in Jesus worthy of a death sentence. Rome has nothing political to fear of this one who claims some other type of kingdom. Pilate hopes to secure this release with Jewish consent by offering to make Jesus the beneficiary of a custom to release a criminal at Passover.[55] He asks if they want the "King of the Jews" released. One senses that Pilate is having some fun with his Jewish neighbors. He feels no threat in the situation. The other Gospels suggest that he had thought this would end the matter (Matt 27:15–18; Luke 23:14–18). He was wrong. The group "cried out" instead for Barabbas, an insurrectionist (λῃστής). The action is full of irony because in asking for a true insurrectionist, they ask for the release of the very type of person they had portrayed Jesus wrongly to be. A substitution had taken place. An innocent Jesus was taking the place of a real criminal.

Pilate does not yet give up. He has Jesus scourged and presented to the crowd in the hope that the sight of this pathetic, whipped figure might cause the crowd to share his conclusion, "I find no crime in him" (John 19:4).[56] Adding to the scene is that the soldiers have mocked Jesus by placing a crown of thorns on his head and clothing him in a purple robe. The crown probably was an imitation of the royal crown, with spikes pointing outward by as much as a foot from the rim, possibly constructed from the common palm trees and looking more like a Native American headdress than the way this crown is popularly portrayed.[57] They continually go up to Jesus (imperfect tense verbs) and strike him, saying, "Hail, King of the Jews!" Everything about the scene is designed to show how impotent Jesus seems to be as a political threat to mighty Rome. So Jesus was presented to the crowd, whipped, and royally clothed. Dramatically, Pilate presents him to the crowd with the ironically re-

55. There is no extrabiblical confirmation of this custom, but that does not mean that it did not exist. We have little material about this era and its legal practices. See the comments of Carson, *John,* 596; Brown, *John XIII–XXI,* 854–55.

56. The timing of this whipping differs from the Synoptics, which show Jesus being whipped after the verdict with what probably was a preparatory whipping tied to crucifixion, the dreaded *verberatio* (see unit 278 above). Two suggestions exist: (1) the whipping that John mentions was an earlier, less severe beating, the *fustigatio* (Carson, *John,* 597–98; Sherwin-White, *Roman Law,* 27–28); (2) the Synoptic Gospels are not so precise among themselves on the exact timing of the scourging, but rather, each simply notes the fact of the scourging, with John giving its more precise locale (Morris, *John,* 699). There is no way to decide this for certain, given how each portrayal seems to include and omit items. The possibility of multiple whippings is not unlikely, but neither is the option that Pilate handled this delicate situation by giving Jesus a full scourging in the hope that this would satisfy the prosecutors. What is unlikely is to conclude that John or the Synoptics are in error here, given the complexity of these accounts.

57. Beasley-Murray, *John,* 336; H. S. J. Hart, "The Crown of Thorns in John 19:2," *Journal of Theological Studies* 3 (1952): 66–75.

spectful "Behold, the man!" Some have argued that this phrase sometimes is used to mean "this poor man."[58] The irony of the scene is that what Pilate mocks is presented as true by the evangelist. Jesus, even in the setting of his humble humiliation, is "the man," the chosen representative of humanity.

Pilate's effort produces the opposite result of what he intended. It does not engender sympathy for Jesus, but an insistence that the job be completed. John singles out the chief priests and officers as crying out for crucifixion. The double imperative call to crucify is emphatic. Pilate is frustrated by now and tells them derisively to take him and crucify him themselves. In effect, he wants nothing to do with this act. For a third time in John, Pilate states Jesus' innocence (John 18:38; 19:4, 6). This recalls the multiple declarations of innocence in Luke (Luke 23:4, 14–15, 22).

The leadership continues to press Pilate and now makes a more specific charge. "We have a law, and by that law he ought to die, because he has made himself the Son of God." The Jews are appealing to the law of blasphemy from Lev. 24:16, which was variously interpreted in this period but included any claim to be directly involved in actions of divine authority, as Jesus had claimed in John (John 5:18; 8:58–59; 10:33, 36).[59] Of course, this charge had come up in the council trial, which John does not narrate (see Mark 14:55–64). This may be an indication of an echo of material that John knows but does not narrate. Pilate apparently does not hear the legal, religious point but instead hears in the phrase "Son of God" a raising of the issue of Jesus being a "divine man," a person clothed with divine enablement, so common in Greco-Roman thinking (see Acts 14:8–15). This brings more fear into Pilate. This situation already was tense enough, but perhaps he had just whipped a man who had divine power and presence. After all, Jesus had just claimed to have another kingdom not of this world. Where might that leave Pilate before the gods? The whole situation made Pilate nervous, so he goes back to question Jesus again.

Pilate now queries Jesus about where he is from. The question possesses irony because Jesus already had answered it in mentioning that he was not of this world and that he had "come into the world" (John 18:36–37). Jesus remains silent (cf. Mark 14:61; 15:5; Matt. 26:63; 27:14; Luke 23:9; Isa. 53:7). He will make no defense nor offer any explanation. He will fulfill his calling. Pilate urges Jesus to speak and notes that he has the power to release Jesus or to crucify him. Jesus corrects this overstatement: "You would have no power over me unless it had been given you from above; therefore the one who delivered me to you has the greater sin." There is a cosmic drama taking place in which Pilate is a pawn, possessing no

---

58. Morris, *John*, 701.

59. For a complete discussion of the question of blasphemy in Judaism during this period, see Bock, *Blasphemy and Exaltation*. A fundamental point from this study is that the mishnaic insistence that blasphemy requires the use of the divine name (*m. Sanhedrin* 7.5) does not apply in this earlier period when Jesus was tried.

control or authority (cf. John 10:17–18; 12:27). At the same time, there is genuine human responsibility. Whatever Pilate does with these events has come from authority granted to him.[60] Pilate is in the middle of an act initiated by others. At a human level, the one who is responsible for handing him over has the greater culpability. Is this Judas or Caiaphas? It is not clear, since Judas started the whole process, as John repeatedly has noted (John 6:71; 13:21; 18:2), but Caiaphas led the delegation that actually handed Jesus over to Pilate. One suspects that all three figures (Pilate, Judas, and Caiaphas) are in view generally, but that the two Jewish figures are especially culpable for not seeing what God was doing for the nation. In a real sense, both Judas and Caiaphas have betrayed their calling. If one were to make a choice, it is Caiaphas's act that has the nation in such a precarious position and that is most responsible for placing Jesus before Pilate. The high priest's judgment was made much earlier (John 11:50).

Still, Pilate does not give up. However, those who want Jesus crucified push him more into a corner: "If you release this man, you are not Caesar's friend; everyone who claims to be a king sets himself against Caesar."[61] This charge stings. Pilate's ultimate responsibility is to protect Caesar's interests in Judea. This is the political dimension that Pilate cannot ignore.[62] So he brings Jesus out to the judgment seat (βῆματος) at a place called "The Pavement," or in Aramaic, "Gabbatha." At about the sixth hour (noon), Pilate takes the seat to judge.[63] He presents Jesus to the crowd on Passover preparation day,[64]

60. The Greek grammar here is complex. In 19:11, the phrase "had been given" does not refer merely to "authority," as the participle for "given" is neuter and the word for "authority" is feminine. The reference seems, then, to be to events as a whole. Pilate claims to be in control. Jesus denies that this is the case. Larger forces are at work.

61. On whether the term "Caesar's friend" is a technical term and whether or not we are dealing with Pilate's vulnerability because his ally and Roman "foreign minister" Sejanus is now dead, see Brown, *John XIII–XXI*, 894. We do know that Tiberius could be a ruthless administrator (Suetonius, *Tiberius* 58).

62. That Pilate thought so politically is noted in Philo, *Embassy to Gaius* 38 §302, where Pilate fears excessive scrutiny by Caesar.

63. Mark 15:25 has the crucifixion at about the third hour, or nine in the morning. Carson, *John*, 604–5, and Morris, *John*, 708, argue that both Mark and John offer approximations for this series of events in an era of sundials and astronomical charts. Late morning is meant, with each writer picking the opposite half of that time spectrum. For the grammatical question of whether Jesus or Pilate is described as sitting on the judgment seat, see Carson, *John*, 607–8, who opts for Pilate sitting there, and Beasley-Murray, *John*, 342, who makes the same conclusion. Barrett, *John*, 452–53, gives arguments for both sides before opting for Pilate.

64. For discussion about the chronological issue that this raises with the Synoptic declaration that Jesus ate the Passover meal with his disciples, something that could not be if the preparation of the Passover sacrifice is meant here, see Carson, *John*, 604. He argues that what is meant is "preparation of the Passover feast" or "Passover week." If so, no chronological problem exists between the Gospels. John keeps alluding to the Passover time frame because Jesus' death evokes that imagery, with events juxtaposed to this approaching death. Others, such as Morris, *John*, 684–95, argue that two calendars are in use and that the Gospels are referring to these different calendars. This also would remove any conflict. Barrett, *John*, 453–54, sees a conflict here.

saying, "Behold your king!" The crowd continues to insist that Jesus be crucified, even after Pilate asks them directly, placing the reference to "king" in a grammatically emphatic position. The chief priests reply that they have no king but Caesar and thus make a major theological concession (God is Israel's only king [Judg. 8:23; 1 Sam. 8:7; Isa. 26:13]).[65] Accepting Roman sovereignty, denying any eschatological hope for Israel, and denying that Jesus could be the sent one, the leaders' confession secures Jesus' crucifixion. For John's Gospel, loyalty to a world power had been embraced at the expense of God's sent one. So Pilate gives permission for Jesus' crucifixion. Nowhere does John note a sentence from Pilate. He has been backed into a corner and cowers at the political pressure. Still, as in Luke and Matthew, he is guilty of allowing one whom he saw as innocent to be sent to the cross. Roman soldiers are put in charge. Jesus heads to the cross.

J45. Jesus' Crucifixion and Death (John 19:17–30)
(Aland §§343–44, 347–48)

So Jesus takes the cross, specifically the crossbeam, and carries it out to a place known as "The Place of the Skull," or in Aramaic, "Golgotha."[66] This was the responsibility of the criminal, according to Plutarch (*The Divine Vengeance* 554 A/B; see also Eusebius, *Eccl. Hist.* 6.44). John makes no mention of Simon of Cyrene being procured to help Jesus carry the cross (cf. Matt. 27:32; Mark 15:21; Luke 23:26). What the combination of texts suggests is that Jesus began to carry the cross but was helped later by Simon, possibly because of the severity of the whipping he had received and the damage it inflicted on his strength. John chooses not to mention the aid that Jesus received here. John often omits details that could suggest human frailty for Jesus, just as he also omitted mention of Gethsemane. John is highlighting Jesus' obedience and faithfulness in enduring the cross. Noting that Jesus had help in bearing the cross was not relevant to this theme. In fact, there are many features in the Synoptics that John does not narrate.[67]

The crucifixion is told with the barest minimum of detail: "There they crucified him." There is no mention in any of the Gospels of details that one familiar with crucifixion would know. It is as if detailing such horror

65. In the national prayer the *Shemoneh Esreh*, benediction 11 reads in an address to God, "May you be our King, you alone." At the Passover, the Jews would have affirmed the unique sovereignty of God (*m. Roš Haššanah* 1.2).

66. Traditionally, the site is located inside the Church of the Holy Sepulchre.

67. Brown, *John XIII–XXI*, 914, has a list of twenty items in the Synoptic crucifixion accounts that John lacks. It is clear from such a list that John has made no attempt to reproduce what the other Gospels cover. He appears to be working primarily with independent knowledge and sources of these events, some no doubt reflecting his own experience.

is too much to present. No point is made to explain how the crossbeam was laid down on the ground along with the victim, or how the victim was then tied or hammered onto the cross, which had been joined to the vertical beam at the site. On the cross was a tiny seat (*sedecula*) that was designed to make the death even more painful by giving some aid, but not enough to help the victim breathe and support himself. To breathe, the victim had to pull his body up by pushing on his crossed legs, which were either roped or nailed together. Jesus appears to have been nailed to the cross. Hoisted up, the victim was left to hang by his own weight, dying from heart failure, muscle spasms, asphyxiation, or a combination of the three. It was such a horrific way to die that a Roman citizen could not be subjected to this form of execution. Josephus called it "the most wretched of deaths" (*War* 7.6.4 §203), while Cicero referred to it as "a most cruel and terrible penalty" (*In Verrem* 2.165). Jesus died between two others, whose crime John does not specify. Nor does he mention anything else about these other men, positive (as Luke does) or negative (as Mark does).

The crime was announced to the public by a placard that either hung around the victim's neck or was carried before him. No Gospel details how the *titulus* was taken to the scene, but all of them report the charge written on it. John has details about the placard that the other Gospels lack. He notes that the charge was written in three languages: Hebrew (Aramaic), Roman (Latin), and Greek. Anyone passing by could understand why the victim was being executed. This was fastened to the cross. John also uniquely notes the discussion about what Pilate permitted to be written: "Jesus of Nazareth, the King of the Jews." The Jews protested this, especially the chief priests, preferring that it be made clear that this was merely Jesus' claim, but Pilate, probably because he had felt so trapped in the situation, stood his ground here, stating, "What I have written stands written."[68]

There is a slight variation in the charge as noted by the Gospels, typical of the variation with which they sometimes render an expression. Matthew 27:37 has "This is Jesus, the King of the Jews." Mark 15:26 has "The King of the Jews." Luke 23:38 has "This is the King of the Jews." Only John mentions Jesus' roots in Nazareth (cf. John 18:5, 7). The three translations can explain some of this difference, but it also reflects how sometimes an evangelist chooses to give the gist of a saying, not its exact, full wording. The sayings all have one basic fact in common: Jesus died because he was convicted of claiming to be the king of the Jews.

The soldiers had the rights to Jesus' belongings. John alone notes that these clothes, which left Jesus stripped as he hung on the cross in shame, were di-

---

68. Two perfect tenses appear here, with one acting like an aorist and the other indicating that what was written will stay written. It is an emphatic way to say that nothing will change.

vided into four parts so that each soldier could have something.[69] This probably involved his belt, sandals, head tunic, and outer robe. Left was his tunic, which is described as seamless.[70] The soldiers decided to cast lots for it rather than divide it up. The entire scene reflects the fulfillment of Scripture, as John cites Ps. 22:18, where the righteous sufferer is portrayed as suffering the indignity of having his very clothes divided up as spoil. Psalm 22 also appears in the Synoptic accounts, where Jesus cries out from the cross in the language of Ps. 22:1 (Mark 15:34; Matt. 27:46). The connection not only shows how events reflect divine design, but also identifies Jesus as the righteous sufferer.

Four women stood by the cross in these final moments: Jesus' mother; his mother's sister; Mary the wife of Cleopas; and Mary Magdalene.[71] It is discussed who the second woman is and why she remains unidentified. Traditionally, she often is associated with Salome (Mark 15:40) and is seen as the mother of James and John, the sons of Zebedee, making the beloved disciple Jesus' cousin. This is quite possible. The lack of mention of her name would fit John's hesitancy to mention himself. However, the identification is not certain because the list of names in Mark is selective of a larger group of women who were present. The two lists, then, may not overlap.

More important to John is the instruction and care that Jesus gives for his mother at the cross. Jesus instructs the beloved disciple and his mother to view each other as mother and son, an instruction that almost has the feel of a family adoption. The text notes that the disciple obeys and takes Mary into his home. Here is Jesus, hanging in agony, concerned about the welfare of the mother he leaves behind. Here also is an example of how disciples relate to one another with a care that is not limited by biological connections.[72]

So John turns to Jesus' death. In a final declaration that fulfills Scripture, Jesus says, "I thirst." This appears to echo Ps. 69:21. There is irony here, as the one who earlier was declared to be the source of "living water" (John 7:37–39) is now thirsty. Here is Jesus suffering lack as he undertakes his call to die for others. From his broken body will flow rivers of living water. Other candidates for scriptural background include Ps. 22:15, 42:2, and 63:1, but John already has noted Ps. 69 in John 2:17 and 15:25. The point of the cita-

69. It is debated whether Jesus was left totally naked on the cross or whether some basic covering was left out of deference to Jewish sensitivities about public nudity (*m. Sanhedrin* 6.3). We do not know the answer to this question.

70. That this is an allusion to Jesus as a priestly figure (see Lev. 16:4; Josephus, *Ant.* 3.7.4 §161) is most uncertain because Jesus is not wearing his tunic during the scene.

71. It is sometimes proposed that the syntax can be read to refer to two or three women only, but this is unlikely.

72. It is sometimes proposed, especially in Catholic exegesis, that Mary is given a special elevation here. Brown, *John XIII–XXI*, 924–26, sees her as being evocative of "Lady Zion" here. Such a reading is most unlikely, as Carson, *John*, 617–18, and Beasley-Murray, *John*, 349–50, argue. What we see is a balanced portrayal of Jesus, the faithful son who cares for, and is concerned about, his mother even as he faces his death.

tion is that it again identifies Jesus as a righteous sufferer, much as David was. In Jesus' last moments, his very royal sonship is affirmed even as he is being executed. Those who know the pattern of Scripture can understand what really is taking place. What appears to be happening—the end of a messianic claim nailed to a cross—is not at all what is happening. The soldiers, hearing Jesus cry, offer him some common and cheap vinegar wine (ὄξος). They place it on a hyssop branch or stalk and lift it up to his mouth, where he takes it.[73]

Jesus dies righteously, completing a divine work assigned to him. This explains his closing utterance, because "it is finished" really means "it is accomplished" (note Exod. 40:33 on Moses). The perfect tense looks to the end of the road and to the completion of this work remaining in place. Having done what he came to earth to do, Jesus bows his head, like one going to sleep, and gives up his spirit (cf. Luke 23:46).[74]

J46. Jesus Is Pierced in the Side and Buried (John 19:31–42)
(Aland §§349–50)

It was now the "Day of Preparation" (i.e., Friday), and a doubly holy high day was approaching because the next day was a Sabbath and a feast day when a sheaf offering would be made (Lev. 23:11). The Jews did not want any corpses left hanging on a sacred day, and it often was the case that crucified victims could hang for days before dying. So they asked Pilate to break the legs of the victims (a practice known as *crurifragium* in Latin), hastening their death, so they could remove their bodies.[75] This act also would honor Jewish sensitivities about death, since one who was executed on a tree was not to be left out overnight (Deut. 21:22–23; Philo, *Against Flaccus* 10 §83 [body given to a relative during a festival]; Josephus, *War* 4.5.2 §317 [body removed be-

---

73. It often is debated whether a hyssop branch, being so thin, could be strong enough to lift up such a drink placed on a sponge to one hanging on a cross. Some have suggested that the symbolism is but an attempt to establish a tie to the Passover (Exod. 12:22). Another suggestion is textual: the original "on a javelin" (*hyssō*) became "on a hyssop branch" (*hyssōpō*), because the two Greek words closely resemble one another. Neither of these explanations is likely, since the detail merely for the sake of symbolism is not transparent, and the textual and historical evidence for the alternative term is weak. It is better to see a reference not just to a branch of hyssop but to a stalk that holds the sponge. It also needs to be noted that the height required to get such a drink up to a victim's mouth was not very great. See Carson, *John*, 620–21; Beasley-Murray, *John*, 318 n. q.

74. The idea that Jesus gave up the Holy Spirit here has no support from the text. It is Jesus' death alone that is in view. He dies as a real human, a point that any Docetist, whom in part John writes against, would have trouble accepting.

75. An archaeological discovery of such a corpse is reported in N. Haas, "Anthropological Observations on the Skeletal Remains from Givʿat ha-Mivtar," *Israel Exploration Journal* 20 (1970): 38–59.

fore sunset]). To leave exposed the corpse of a "cursed one" would defile the land.[76] So the soldiers broke the legs of the two criminals, but when they came to Jesus, he was already dead, so his legs remained unbroken.[77]

One of the soldiers, apparently in checking Jesus' condition, stabs him with a spear or javelin. Out comes blood and water. Two medical explanations have been given for this description: (1) a combination of blood from the heart and fluid from the pericardial sac emerges from the upper torso;[78] (2) the piercing took place lower on the torso, where such a combination of fluids more likely could emerge.[79] The second explanation is more likely to be correct, but regardless, the point is that the death was certain and confirmed by this act. There is no feigning death here, no coma. Jesus was deceased.

It is sometimes discussed whether other symbolism is part of the point here. Any sacramentalism tied to baptism or the Lord's table seems most unlikely. Most problematic is a claim to connect the water with baptism. Others mention a totally symbolic view in which ancients thought of the body being made up of water and blood.[80] More possible are suggestions that the picture is of a cleansing for life flowing from Jesus (John 6:53–54; 1 John 1:7), or that the flow of water recalls the promise of living water flowing from Jesus (John 3:5; 4:14; esp. 7:37–38). All of this possibly stands in parallelism to a well-known Old Testament scene from Exod. 17:6, where the rock provides living water. It is hard to be certain of any of these elements of symbolism for life or living water, but neither can be ruled out.

What is emphasized is that the event has the endorsement of an eyewitness, who witnesses to the truth of the details about the death and piercing and who testifies that this statement is true. The goal of the testimony is to lead the reader into more established belief. All of this testimony is underscored by scriptural support.

First, "Not a bone of him will be broken." Once again the text in view is debated. The most likely candidate comes from the Passover in Exod. 12:46 (or Num. 9:12). The bones of a Passover lamb are not to be broken. The combination of the festival being celebrated and the symbolism of Jesus' death for others favors this connection, though others argue for Ps. 34:20. If the psalm

---

76. Interestingly, *m. Sanhedrin* 11.4 argues that rebellious teachers should be executed on a feast day as an example to others.

77. In the Synoptics, some discussions appear to take place on the next day (Matt. 27:62–66). The issue there is guarding the tomb.

78. W. D. Edwards, W. J. Gabel, and F. E. Hosmer, "On the Physical Death of Jesus Christ," *Journal of the American Medical Association* 255 (1986): 1455–63.

79. A. F. Sava, "The Wound in the Side of Christ," *Catholic Biblical Quarterly* 19 (1960): 343–46.

80. Brown, *John XIII–XXI*, 947–48, rightly raises and rejects the view as not fitting John's emphasis on a real event.

is in view, it is underscoring Jesus as a suffering righteous one. Again, with John, one cannot rule out the possibility of a double conceptual allusion.

The second textual reference is not disputed. It is to Zech. 12:10 as it appears in the non-Septuagintal tradition: "They will look on him whom they have pierced." In the original context, this is a reference to God, who is pierced in reference to a representative (Zech. 13:7), creating a sense of national pain that a deliverance from exile as a penalty for the nation's sin was required. So the text points to a remorse coming some day in the future when there is a realization of what the crucifixion really was, the world's executing of God's chosen representative. John cites the text to note that this piercing has taken place, both in the nailing to the cross and in the confirmation of the death that nailing brought in the piercing of his now-dead flesh.

The point being made beyond the scriptural support is that Jesus' death was an event that thoroughly fulfilled a divine plan and that was touched on here and there throughout Scripture. Those with eyes to see are able to understand and believe. As Carson notes, the good shepherd has laid down his life for the sheep (John 10:11); with blood and water cleansing, new life, and the opportunity for the Spirit to come (John 3:5; 7:37–39).[81]

Disposing of a crucified body was not a major Roman concern. They were quite content to allow the body to sit out and rot. The remains of those convicted of sedition were not supposed to be released for any reason. Jews, however, were highly sensitive about corpses, and they had a place of burial for the body of a criminal outside of the city (Josephus, *Ant.* 5.1.14 §44; *m. Sanhedrin* 6.5). Joseph of Arimathea sought to take care of the body in a way that prevented an undignified burial (see unit 286 above). John has several additional details. Joseph was a "secret" disciple, who kept the association hidden for fear of the Jews. Although this category normally is negative for John (John 12:42–43), this account suggests that Joseph now took on some risk for his hidden commitment. He asks Pilate for the body. The fact that Pilate released it to him, given that Jesus was executed for sedition, suggests Pilate's dislike of the outcome.[82] Joseph collects the body.

Nicodemus is another figure seemingly in a similar category with Joseph. He brought a huge array of spices: myrrh and aloes weighing in at about just over sixty-five pounds, what the text calls one hundred λίτραι. His act showed his desire to give due respect to the deceased.

Skeptics have challenged this detail about the care for Jesus' body in burial on one of two grounds: (1) the profusion of the provision; and (2) in the Synoptics, the women who supposedly watched the burial also brought their own spices, suggesting that they had not seen any such provision made earlier. Both points are questionable. A large amount of aromatics for the body of a

81. Carson, *John*, 628.
82. Beasley-Murray, *John*, 358.

dignitary is supported by ancient sources. Josephus notes that five hundred slaves brought spices to Herod's burial (*Ant.* 17.8.3 §199). A later Jewish text notes what it presents as an earlier tradition involving the burial of Rabbi Gamaliel of the mid–first century. This burial included eighty pounds of spices (Talbab, *Ebel Rabbati* [or *Semaḥot*] 8.6). These spices would have existed in powdered form. If later mishnaic custom had been followed, Jesus would have been laid on sand for the Sabbath until a full tending of the body could take place after the day of rest (*m. Šabbat* 23.5 discusses permitting "shutting up" [windows] and "tying up" [breaches in a roof] so that uncleanliness from death does not pass from one house to another while a dead body is present).[83] It also is possible that this process was started but that the remainder of the spices were left behind to complete the job later. Only someone of great wealth who desired to give someone an honorable burial would go to such expense. John's point is that Jesus had a worthy burial. That the women saw where Jesus' body was laid does not mean that they observed everything that happened when Jesus was put to rest. They saw the locale, how the body was laid, and the grave closed (Matt. 27:59–61; Mark 15:47; Luke 23:55–56). In addition, nothing prevents the women from deciding to give honor to Jesus by adding their own touch of devotion in caring for his body when they return. Such devotion would be a natural way to assuage their grief and honor their king.

So the two men bound Jesus in linen clothes or strips (ὀθόνια) with the spices, according to Jewish custom. John's term for the clothes refers to linen wrappings. The use of the plural strips and the term itself are questioned by some as being different from the term used in the Synoptics (σινδών), which refers to a single linen shroud (Mark 15:46 par.; but cf. Luke 24:12). But ambiguity exists for the Johannine term, since it can be a plural of extension for one object.[84] So either "linen clothes" or a "linen sheet" could be meant. It also may just be that two generic summary terms are present. So Jesus is laid in a garden tomb that was unused. Only John tells of a locale in a garden. Given the lateness of the Day of Preparation and the near locale of the tomb, the body was placed there.[85]

The burial reflected two important realities for John. First, it brought out two formerly less visible disciples into a more open response to Jesus. Perhaps they reacted to what they thought was an injustice, as Luke 23:51 and Mark 15:43 suggest. Second, Jesus had a burial of honor worthy of his royal status. Although he was rejected by the nation and crucified, his remains received the honor due to him. Jesus' birth may have been very humble, but his burial was given with honor appropriate for a king.

83. Danby, trans., *Mishnah*, 121, esp. n. 10.
84. BDF §161; Brown, *John XIII–XXI*, 942.
85. On the possible site, see Brown, *John XIII–XXI*, 943.

J47. Resurrection Scenes at the Tomb (John 20:1–18)
(Aland §§352–53)

A discussion of how these accounts fit in relationship to the Synoptic accounts appeared in the earlier treatment of these scenes in the Synoptics (see
units 288–89 above). The sequencing is not entirely clear. The variety of witnesses who had an experience with the risen Jesus in distinct settings contributes to the complexity of the accounts. All the accounts agree that women
brought the first news. This was counter to cultural expectations, as women
normally were not accepted as witnesses (*m. Roš Haššanah* 1.8).

John mentions a trip to the tomb by only Mary Magdalene, although the next
verse says, "We do not know where they have laid him." This could suggest that
others were present, although it also could be a rhetorical "we" by which Mary describes herself. Another question is whether a woman would journey alone to the
tomb at night. Perhaps she might if the reason was strong enough. These are questions we cannot answer for certain. All the other Gospels do note that multiple
women went, with the Gospel of Mark naming three, Matthew two, and Luke
more than three. Mary Magdalene got an early start, moving toward the tomb
while it was still dark. Mark and Luke place the setting at dawn. Another option
is that multiple women went, but they may not have started out together.

In John, Mary sees that the stone has been taken away from the tomb.
There is no indication that she looked in, but upon running back and reach-
ing "Peter and the other disciple, the one whom Jesus loved," she reports,
"They have taken away the body."[86] The first possibility she works with is that

86. The first explicit mention that Mary looked in is in 20:11. One option for making sense of
all of this is that 20:1–10 is told strictly from the perspective of how Peter and John initially experienced the empty tomb. When Mary showed up, she gave her initial impression that the body was
stolen. Peter and John did not wait for any more details, but ran to the tomb. Then, in John 20:11–
18, comes what in effect is a flashback to Mary's full initial experience, complete with the angelic
sighting and then one of Jesus. Thus, in this scenario, John goes back and retells her full story even
though its real timing is earlier in the day. In this case, John 20:18 is the rest of her report to all the
remaining disciples after Peter and John had left. If the account is told in the correct sequence, which
surely is another option, then Mary's experience both of the angels and of Jesus ultimately happened
after her initial visit to the tomb and became in effect a confirmation of what had taken place earlier,
which could explain why the Synoptics lack it. What is difficult about this second option is that it
requires that an angelic announcement took place twice to two sets of women. In this second scenario, Mary still thinks that the body is stolen when the angels initially address her. This is hard to
see if the first thing that happened when the women arrived was the sighting of the angels, as the
Synoptics imply. How Mary could think the body is stolen is hard to understand if the angels appeared to the women earlier. Options here are that Mary missed that appearance by running back
instantly or that the Synoptic tradition has telescoped the angelic appearances into a tighter time
frame. For this reason, a flashback, as in our first scenario, is a real possibility, though it requires that
the Synoptic tradition did not show interest in Mary's initial encounter with Jesus, perhaps because
she stayed behind while the other women went back to make the report. If a flashback is in view in
John, then eventually she also returned to say that she had indeed seen the Lord, not just angels.

the body was stolen, as was common at grave sites. There is a recovered decree of the emperor Claudius, issued slightly later (A.D. 41–54), that orders death for those who destroy tombs or move bodies.[87] In contrast to the Synoptics, there is no initial description of an angelic appearance to the women to explain that Jesus is risen. Did Mary run as soon as she saw the open tomb, with the other women to follow later with the rest of the report? Was her initial report a skeptical one because the alternative was so unbelievable? Did Peter and John depart before she told her entire story, hearing only her initial suspicion and not all that took place? Again, there is no way to be sure.

Peter and the other disciple make a dash for the tomb. The other disciple, probably to be understood as John, reaches the tomb first. Only John notes his presence, while the Synoptics only give detail about Peter's search, although Luke 24:24 indicates that Peter was not the only one who made this trip. The other disciple glanced in, which suggests that the tomb was a burial site hewn in the rock. He saw grave clothes (τὰ ὀθόνια, the same term as in 19:40) but did not go into the tomb. Simon Peter followed. In typical Petrine style, he marched right into the tomb, and he saw the linens and the head cloth (τὸ σουδάριον), rolled up and set off from the other clothes, as if it no longer was needed. Then the other disciple went in, and he "saw and believed." The presence of two men fits the "two witness" requirement of the law (Deut. 19:15).

The empty tomb brought understanding to John, although as the text also notes, both he and the rest of the disciples did not yet appreciate how this event reflected the promise of Scripture. It is not clear which text is alluded to here. Candidates include Lev. 23:11, Hos. 6:2, or Jon. 1:17. Two of these texts mention "the third day," but interestingly, John introduces this scene not by counting three days inclusively since the crucifixion, but by noting that it was the first day of the week (Sunday). So these texts seem less likely than passages that point to exaltation, such as Ps. 16:10 (cf. Acts 2:25–31; 13:35), Ps. 118:22 (Mark 12:10), or Isa. 53:10–12. Some critics complain that this reference to not knowing the connection between Jesus' death and Scripture contradicts the fact that Jesus made predictions of his suffering according to Scripture before his death. However, John's remark should be seen to refer not to a general allusion to Scripture but to specific texts that specify what Scripture taught (spelled out also in a generic way in Luke 24:44–47; John has "the Scripture" [τὴν γραφήν] here, pointing to specific texts). Having seen the empty tomb, the two disciples head home.

This scene as a whole is told from the perspective of the beloved disciple. His mind and thoughts are present throughout the account up to 20:10.

---

87. Beasley-Murray, *John*, 371; C. K. Barrett, *The New Testament Background: Selected Documents* (London: SPCK, 1957), 15, cites the text.

There is no indication of what Peter's reaction was (but see Luke 24:12 for Peter's amazement).

John's attention now returns to Mary in what is either an account told in sequence or a flashback (see n. 86 above, where either option is held as possible). She is sitting outside the tomb, weeping, in all likelihood because the body is gone and she does not know where it is taken, as she indicates in John 20:13. Still weeping, she looks into the tomb and finds two angels in white seated where the body had been, one at the head and the other at the feet. The fact that they are in white is not unusual for heavenly agents (Ezek. 9:2; Dan. 10:5; *1 Enoch* 87.2; 2 Macc. 3:26 simply says "splendidly dressed" or "a covering of prominent glory"; glory was usually assumed to be bright or white). The body would have been set on a burial shelf, so the angels are at either end. Matthew 28:2 has a man on the outside to greet the women, while the other Gospels speak of a youth on the inside (Mark 16:5) or two men standing inside (Luke 24:4). They are described in the same way that also points to angels, as Luke 24:23 indicates as well.

They ask her why she is weeping, and she again notes her belief that the body has been stolen. Her relationship to Jesus is underscored by her reference to him as "my Lord." For some unstated reason, she turns and sees a man, whom she does not recognize as Jesus but takes to be a gardener. She responds to his question about her weeping by offering to take back the body, if the one she thinks is a gardener will give the body to her. This is not the only time a resurrection account indicates that Jesus was not initially recognizable (Luke 24 [Emmaus road]; John 21 [Sea of Tiberias]).

Finally, Jesus speaks her name. This triggers her recognition. She addresses him as "Rabboni," an Aramaic word for "teacher." The good shepherd calls his sheep by name, and they follow him because they know his voice (John 10:3–4).

Overwhelmed, Mary grabs hold of Jesus. Jesus, however, tells her to stop holding him, because he has not yet ascended to the Father. The remark has sparked no small amount of commentary because the term used is one for touching, and Thomas will be allowed to touch Jesus later.[88] Jesus' point seems to be that her desire to hold on to him now that she has seen him again is misguided. He must ascend to the Father, even as he had told the disciples in the upper room. This visit by Jesus is not a return to normal life and a resumption of the old form of ministry. She is to go to Jesus' "brothers," the disciples, and tell them that Jesus is "ascending to my Father and your Father, to my God and your God." He will resume his former intimate status in God's presence. Jesus' relationship to his Father is distinct enough to be mentioned separately from the relationship that the disciples possess. The mention of ascension to his Father also is another way to say that he is

88. For options entertained for this verse, see Carson, *John*, 641–45.

going to the Father's right hand. He will be able to do much more on behalf of the disciples there, as the upper room discourse already has explained to John's readers. His intimate status as risen Son in God's presence procures their exalted status. As Jesus will soon underscore, *my* God has become *your* God. In contrast to Mary's lack of appreciation that Jesus must be free to ascend, Thomas is graciously allowed to touch Jesus to be reassured that Jesus truly is raised, a completely different context and concern that leads to a different response.

So Mary went to the disciples as Jesus instructed and told them that she had seen the Lord. She reported what she had been told. She is the beneficiary of the first appearance of Jesus that John notes. That a woman is given such a role is a surprise culturally. It argues against this being a later creation of the church, since the cultural expectation of who would be the first witness, if the scene were created, almost certainly would have involved a man, not a woman, much less a woman such as Mary Magdalene, "from whom seven demons had gone out" (Luke 8:2). That she would be a primary witness testifies to the grace and rehabilitation of God.

J48. Later Appearances to the Gathered Disciples
(John 20:19–29) (Aland §§356–57)

Later that first day of resurrection, on the first day of the week (Sunday), the disciples were gathered, with the doors of the house shut. It is not clear whether ten (missing Judas and Thomas) are meant or a larger group. The parallel to this scene in Luke 24:36–49 suggests that this is a larger group. However, it is also possible that Jesus in giving the commission has the Eleven especially in mind. The gathered group was afraid of the Jews, although the reason is not clear. Did they fear being persecuted as Jesus was? Locking the doors probably would not stop anyone who wanted to trouble them. More likely is that they wanted their locale not to be so publicly obvious, though the text does not tell us why the doors are locked beyond their collective fear. The result is that when Jesus appears, it is clear that physical barriers did not prevent his appearing. His is an existence of another sort.

Jesus "came and stood among them and said to them, 'Peace be with you.'" This setting makes this more than a common greeting, especially since Jesus repeats it in vv. 21, 26. Jesus had promised to deliver peace to them (John 14:27; 16:33). Now he had been vindicated and had come into new life, and so he could do all that he had promised in the upper room. The new life that comes without end had been promised, and so had the Spirit. Relationship to God could now attain a new level of peace. Jesus shows them his hands and side to confirm that it really is he.[89] The disciples rejoice upon seeing him.

So, repeating the greeting, Jesus speaks now of mission (v. 21), the Spirit (v. 22), and forgiveness of sins (v. 23). As the Father sent Jesus, so now he sends them. This theme has been almost omnipresent in John. The Father's sending of the Son appears constantly (John 3:17, 34; 5:36, 38; 6:27, 57; 7:29; 8:42; 10:36; 11:42; 17:3, 8, 18, 21, 23, 25). The verb ἀποστέλλω is used here for God's sending Jesus, and the verb πέμπω is used by Jesus for sending the disciples on mission. Together they show how the momentum of God's activity aims at his disciples and their mission in the world (see 4:34; 5:23–24, 30, 37; 6:38–39, 44; 7:16, 18, 28, 33; 8:16, 18, 26, 29; 9:4; 12:44–45, 49; 13:20; 14:24, 26; 15:21, 26; 16:5, 7). They are not to be separatists. Less frequently does John have the Son send the disciples (4:38; 13:20; 17:18). God is at work through Jesus. They are sent equipped. So Jesus provides the Spirit for their labor. As in the other commissions, the Spirit and the calling to go out are noted together (cf. Matt. 28:16–20; Luke 24:44–49).

Next, Jesus bestows the Spirit. In the context of John's Gospel and the promises of the upper room, this is Jesus bringing his promise of providing the Spirit to reality. It appears to depict the provision of new life, as the language of breathing recalls both Gen. 2:7 and Ezek. 37:9 and calls forth images of providing life, even life from the dead.

The nature and timing of the event in John have caused no small amount of discussion because of its relationship to Pentecost as described in Acts 2. Both the timing and setting differ. Various explanations exist. Some argue that no harmonization is possible or should be attempted.[90] Others suggest that this is John's equivalent to Pentecost, and that it is an example of a theological event in which the biblical writers are unconcerned with chronology.[91] Others opt for a symbolic act here with the real bestowal taking place at Pentecost, especially given that no real change in the disciples is described.[92] Others speak of multiple bestowals of the Spirit as ameliorating the problem.[93] Finally, others make various distinctions between what Jesus does here and what happened at Pente-

---

89. The reference to the "hands" and "side" alludes to the wounds that would be the evidentiary marks that this was the crucified Jesus. The reference to hands includes the wrists or even the arms, which would be where nails had been driven through Jesus. Although some have doubted that victims were nailed during crucifixion during this time, there does exist an ossuary that disclosed a first-century Palestinian crucifixion victim who was nailed to a cross. On this, see Brown, *John XIII–XXI*, 1022.

90. So Barrett, *John*, 475.

91. So Beasley-Murray, *John*, 382.

92. So Carson, *John*, 649–55.

93. So Morris, *John*, 747–48.

cost.[94] The solution to this question is not clear. However, it does seem likely that this bestowal highlights the provision of life in private to the disciples, whereas Pentecost seems to emphasize a broader bestowal of the Spirit in a way that is publicly evident and that is aimed at the carrying out of, and enablement for, ministry.[95] Luke may well be highlighting how the Spirit came so visibly in public, so that Pentecost is seen as the great public event. On the other hand, John's language is too direct to be speaking merely of a symbolic display. The events are sufficiently different that they should not be equated, although it is quite correct to see their functions within John and Acts as similar.

Jesus finally speaks about forgiveness. Here the disciples as a corporate entity are in view. They have the right to forgive sins and to retain them. Since they are commissioned messengers of God's way to peace and life, this authority inevitably is bound together with their message. The perfect tenses for "they are forgiven" and "they are retained" speak of a state that remains for the one who comes under the authority of the message that these disciples now bear in Jesus' name. In sum, the way of life is to be preached, evidenced by the Spirit, and affirmed in words about forgiveness or judgment depending on how people respond to their message.

One of the Eleven, Thomas, was not present for this commission. When the disciples report that they have seen the Lord, Thomas is not impressed. He assures them that unless he sees and touches Jesus' crucifixion wounds, he absolutely will not believe.[96]

Eight days later, again on Sunday, since the ancients count inclusively, the disciples are gathered and Thomas is present. Once again the doors are shut. Jesus again appears and greets them with "Peace be with you." Everything about the scene is a virtual replay of the earlier appearance to the group of ten. However, this appearance is for the benefit of Thomas. Jesus addresses him and invites him to fulfill his wish to touch the wounds with his fingers. With the invitation comes a command: "Stop being unfaithful, and be a believer." Jesus' point is not that Thomas was not a believer (i.e., disciple) before. Rather, Thomas has not accepted the truth of all these witnesses to the resurrection. This also is the position in which the readers of John's Gospel find

---

94. Carson's discussion (*John*, 649–55) treats a variety of options. They were sprinkled with the Spirit here and saturated with the Spirit later (Calvin). There was power for life given here and for ministry later (B. F. Westcott). F. F. Bruce argues in the opposite direction from Westcott. M. M. B. Turner speaks of two comings of the Spirit, this one to fulfill John 17:17–19 and Pentecost to fulfill the Paraclete promises.

95. My preference would be close to Westcott's. However, it may be that the public versus private distinction is more important than some type of qualitative difference. In addition, if the Eleven are primarily in view here, then there may be a commissioning of them that is extended to all believers in Acts 2.

96. Note the emphatic double negative οὐ μή here.

themselves, given that they are asked to trust the witnesses of these accounts about resurrection. Thomas needs to believe that Jesus indeed is raised, as these others had claimed.

There is no indication that Thomas takes Jesus up on the offer to examine the wounds intimately. Seeing Jesus and having the invitation is enough to convince him. Thomas does not touch Jesus, but confesses to him, "My Lord and my God!" Here Thomas makes a complete reversal, uttering what surely is intended to be the decisive confession of the Gospel.[97] Here, however, the majestic respect is being given to a figure who resides in a resurrected body and is returning to the Father who sent him. Thus, it is a confession of Jesus' divine position and status. To add "my God" to "my Lord" is a statement of Jesus' equality with God, equal to other statements in the Gospel but confessed by a disciple for the first time here (cf. John 1:1 [indirectly]; 5:18; 10:33). Indeed, as a result of the resurrection, the disciples now do appreciate who Jesus truly is.

In this confessional context, Jesus' beatitude makes complete sense. Jesus notes in a rhetorical question that Thomas believes because he has seen Jesus. Most will not have that advantage. All they will have to go on is the witness to the resurrection. So Jesus says, "Blessed are those who have not seen and yet believe." By the time John writes, many already are in that category, and they are examples to anyone who hears the testimony about the raised Jesus through this Gospel. Happy are those who believe that Jesus is the sent one from the Father even though they have not seen him. Happy are those who know that Jesus resides now with the Father.

J49. The Purpose of John's Gospel (John 20:30–31) (Aland §366)

These two verses read like a conclusion to the Gospel. They state the evangelist's goal in writing his account. The Gospel really is a digest of what Jesus did, because he performed many other signs before the disciples that John did not record. Evidence for this can be seen in the many different miracles that appear in the Synoptics. It is quite likely that even combining the Synoptics with John still leaves many things unaccounted for that Jesus did, as John 21:25 suggests. John presented his selection of material for a single goal: to lead to belief about Jesus and the experiencing of life in his name.

It sometimes is debated whether John's goal was missionary-evangelistic, apologetic, or aimed at edification.[98] Sometimes the question is made to turn on

---

97. The role of this text is much like the confession of the centurion in the Synoptics; he declares Jesus to be "the Son of God" (Matthew and Mark) or "innocent" (Luke). This kind of address of respect for another's sovereignty and authority was expressed later in the century of the Roman emperor Domitian (Suetonius, *Domitian* 13).

98. Carson's commentary (*John,* 660–63) is an energetic defense of the evangelistic goal.

the textual question of whether an aorist subjunctive or present subjunctive for the verb "believe" is read in John 20:31. Both tenses have good manuscript support, as the present appears in Papyrus 66 (probably) and Codices Sinaiticus and Vaticanus, while the aorist is in Codices Ephraemi, Bezae, and Regius, and Byzantine witnesses. The slightly broader distribution favors the aorist, which also is read to allude to a more evangelistic goal, while the better witnesses contain the present. The textual problem is a virtual toss-up. However, interpreters on both sides of this debate now recognize that grammar alone cannot resolve this question, because John's usage of this verb and the variation in his use of the tenses show that he does not follow a consistent meaning with the tenses.

Other points are more important to establish that John has more than evangelism in mind. First, the goal is not simply belief, but also the life that results from belief. Thus, John is not interested in the faith decision alone, but in John 13–17 also instructs about things such as serving, the Spirit, and abiding, so that the reader may appreciate the resources that God gives to the one who enters into life as well as the character of the call to enter into life. Second, then, the nature of what is covered in the Gospel as a whole indicates that John is after a full experience of the life that Jesus gives, not merely the decision to believe.

The key confession to be embraced is that Jesus is the Christ, the Son of God. This meaning is very much what Thomas's confession in 20:28 is all about. For John, "Son of God" has for its full sense the one sent by God from heaven with a unique heavenly mission to deliver those brought into salvation. Jesus is the good shepherd in a messianic sense and is a leader-prophet, but even this messianic role is to be seen ultimately in this more cosmic role that stands at the heart of Jesus' call, even as John has pointed out from his prologue. It is Jesus sent from heaven and an appreciation of the story as given from heaven down that allow one to comprehend how Jesus can forgive sins, make judgments about the Sabbath, heal, bring life from death, be the bread of life, be the truth, send the Spirit, and thus give abundant life. An important corollary to this reading of the purpose is that faith has both an initial and an abiding quality to it. One comes to belief about Jesus, but that belief sustains itself in an ongoing relationship that leads into fullness of unending life. Both evangelism and edification are wrapped up in faith as John defines it.

J50. A Johannine Epilogue: At the Sea of Tiberias in Discussion with Peter and a Final Note (John 21:1–25)
(Aland §367)

The final chapter of John has three elements: a final appearance and a miraculous catch (21:1–14); the discussion with, and restoration of, Peter (21:15–23); and the authentication of the evangelist as witness (21:24–25). The character of this chapter has been much discussed. Was this chapter part of the original end of John, and if not, who wrote it? The reason for the discussion is that John 20 has the look of an ending, while the style and character of the John 21 event seems to some readers to suggest a later addition by someone other than the evangelist.[99] Others argue that the evangelist himself has added to the chapter, noting especially how the theme of mission is so evident in the scene, like the endings of Matthew and Luke.[100] It is hard to be certain of the answer here. If this chapter is the work of another writer, a role for the passage is to testify to John's credibility and to create a "two witness" motif for the Gospel as a whole (cf. Deut. 19:15), underscoring its fundamental integrity. This is in addition to the three key themes of the passage itself. If it is John's addition, then it especially highlights three ideas: a picture of mission, Peter's rehabilitation, and the prediction by Jesus that the beloved disciple had a destiny different from Peter's. Acknowledging that John 20 does have the feel of an ending, I think that an addendum by another is possible here to secure the testimony (perhaps by the two unnamed disciples), to mirror the evangelist's own hesitation to identity himself and provide the note of witness. However, it is just as likely that John himself made the addition to highlight mission at the end of his work as the natural extension of what the resurrection means.

Regardless of how one takes the authorship issue, two points about John 21 are certain. First, from a literary perspective, the chapter serves as an epilogue and calls the church to "catch people" as its basic task, using these seven disciples as representative. Second, the scene fits well themes noted earlier in John as the role of Peter is reaffirmed and the beloved disciple again is seen as the first to recognize Jesus. A final point to note is that although this scene often is compared to Luke 5:1–11 and seen as a variation of it, it is not the same scene. Not only are the setting and the timing different, but also the details are not the same. It may well be significant, however, that a scene that recalls their early calling in another Gospel reappears here.[101]

There also is no doubt that this event is not portrayed as the risen Jesus' initial revelation to these disciples but as a subsequent appearance (note

99. For a defense of this view with a careful look at vocabulary and style, which is not seen as decisive, see Barrett, *John*, 479–80. For another full discussion, see Brown, *John XIII–XXI*, 1077–82. Brown differs from Barrett in arguing that the later writer was sensitive to Johannine themes in making the addition, coming out of the same reservoir of Johannine tradition.

100. So Carson, *John*, 665–68. Carson notes that no textual evidence shows up to indicate that this chapter was added. What this evidence does point to is that the chapter was a part of John from very early on. Morris, *John*, 758, is almost agnostic on the point, inclining toward an addition by John but seeing the strength of the other option.

101. John does not note the parallel to the earlier calling, but a reader familiar with the Lukan account might catch the parallel with the earlier "catching people" scene, as may those who only know the saying from Matthew or Mark. The point shows the effect of reading the Gospels horizontally. It yields something of significance and is not merely harmonization. This is canonical reading.

"again" in 21:1 and "third time" in 21:14). The scene takes place at an unspecified time after Easter week, at the Sea of Tiberias. Seven disciples are present: Peter, Thomas, Nathanael, the sons of Zebedee, and two unnamed disciples. John notes that Simon Peter decides to go fishing.[102] The others join him. Working in the evening, the best time to fish, they catch nothing.

This scene should not be seen as requiring that the disciples had given up on their new role and that Peter had returned to his former vocation. There is nothing about the mission or commission of Jesus that indicates that the disciples should not obtain food.[103] So to bring a vocational element into this text is to read into it more than is there.

Early the next morning, they are still fishing. If Jesus' appearance here is like the others, then he appears suddenly on the beach, "revealing himself," according to the text. As in the Emmaus road encounter and Mary's initial encounter, Jesus is not immediately recognized by the disciples. When the query comes whether their outing has met with success, the response is that it has not. So Jesus tells them to cast the net over the right side of the boat, and there they will find fish. The point about choosing the right side of the boat is not to suggest a casting over the "lucky" side of the boat, even though in Greek culture the right side was the side of fortune. Rather, it is to highlight that Jesus knows exactly where fish are to be found, underscoring his continuing knowledge in his new resurrected state. The result is a catch so great that they have trouble hauling it in. The experience leads the beloved disciple to realize who is present: "It is the Lord!" Simon Peter takes his outer garment and wraps it around him, jumps into the water, and heads for shore.[104] Once again the beloved disciple is the perceptive one, while Peter reacts with enthusiasm. Meanwhile, the other disciples remain in the boat and drag the huge catch to shore from their locale two hundred cubits (one hundred yards) off shore.

Some question how the disciples could be in Galilee, having been commanded to remain in Jerusalem in Luke. Three of the Gospels indicate that appearances took place in the north, outside Jerusalem (Matt. 28; Mark 14:27–28; John 21). Such questions about how Galilean and Jerusalem appearances can both exist may represent an overreading of Luke. Jesus does tell the disciples to "sit" in the city until they receive power from on high, the Spirit (Luke 24:49). This command is uttered in light of the commission to preach to the nations, a mission that is going to start from Jerusalem as well. Thus, the "sitting" is not a prohibition against ever going elsewhere as much as it is a command to wait for God to launch the mission from Jerusalem. The disciples are not to return north in terms of establishing residence and a

102. In John, Peter is cited with his double name seventeen times.
103. A point well made by Beasley-Murray, *John*, 399.
104. The note in 21:7 that he was "naked" probably should be read to describe that he was clothed minimally, as Jews were offended by public nudity (Brown, *John XIII–XXI*, 1072).

missionary hub, but this need not prevent them from journeying north at all. Even the scene in Matthew where Jesus tells the Eleven to meet him on a mountain in Galilee (Matt. 28:7), where they receive another commission (Matt. 28:16–20), does not violate the idea that the mission will emanate from Jerusalem.

As the fishermen draw near to land, they find a charcoal fire with fish on it and some bread. Jesus is serving them even after his resurrection. However, there is not enough to go around, so he asks that they bring some fish from the catch. Simon Peter goes and hauls the net ashore. The number of fish caught is exactly 153. Despite the number, the net is not torn, in contrast to the earlier scene in Luke 5, where nets did tear.

Over the centuries, this number of caught fish has engendered numerous theories as to its significance.[105] Jerome, in a commentary discussing Ezek. 47:6–12, argued that according to the Greeks, there were 153 species of fish, so the catch showed the universality of the mission and its catch. Ezekiel refers to the waters of life, and Jerome speculated about what was in that water. However, only one later Greek poet (Oppion of Cilicia [ca. A.D. 180]) uses such a number. Augustine, in his commentary on John (122.8), maintains that 153 is a special number. It is the sum of all numbers from 1 to 17 (what is called a triangular of 17), and some argue that it represents the Ten Commandments plus the seven gifts of the Spirit. Cyril of Alexandria, in his work on John (12), argues that the number comprises 100 (for Gentiles), 50 (for the remnant), and 3 (for the Trinity). More modern attempts work with the numerology of locations, such as the Hebrew names En-gedi (= 17) and En-eglaim (= 153), which appear in Ezek. 47:10.[106] The array of suggestions shows that the symbolism of the number, if it exists, has been lost, as some of these proposals are anachronistic and others are not transparent. Two points remain. First, the number reflects a count made of the catch, a truly vivid detail about the event. Second, the size of the catch shows symbolically that the mission will be a full one. The catch will be large and require much labor.

Jesus invites them to have breakfast. Now they recognize that it is Jesus, but no one "dared" to ask, "Who are you?" This remark seems odd, but the point is that they made no queries to confirm the identity that they all recognized, nor did anyone probe the details of his resurrected state. The feel of the narrative here is that something amazing and mysterious is present. Who is present also is obvious, but it would be inappropriate for them to query into

105. Brown, *John XIII–XXI,* 1074–76, sifts carefully through four major options.
106. So J. A. Emerton, "The 153 Fishes in John xxi.11," *Journal of Theological Studies,* n.s., 9 (1958): 86–89, also appealing to Ezek. 47. See also the discussion in Barnabas Lindars, *The Gospel of John,* New Century Bible (London: Oliphants, 1972), 629–30, where he notes that 17 is the sum of 10 and 7, both numbers of perfection. Lindars opts for the sum of the baskets of food left over in John 6:13 (12 baskets plus 5 loaves). He goes on to say that no choice is "really convincing."

the detailed nature of the experience to dissect it with excessive chatter. So Jesus serves them with bread and fish. Some like to make a connection to the meal of John 6 and see in this scene a eucharistic aura. The early church of the first centuries after Christ seems to have done this in its art, although sometimes it is not clear whether John 6 or 21 is in view. The Scripture consistently, not just John, shows meals to be particularly significant occasions.[107] However, there is no note here about blessing the food, so an explicitly sacramental scene is not present.

John notes in closing the first part of this event that this was the third appearance where Jesus "was revealed" to the disciples. This count excludes the appearance to Mary, making the sequence: to the group of ten, to Thomas (with the others present), and to the group of seven. Mary may be excluded because the appearance to her was private, while all the other appearances involve more than one person.

Now Jesus turns to Peter. The discussion both restores and confirms a call. Three times Jesus asks Peter if he loves him, twice using ἀγαπάω and once using φιλέω. Peter replies three times, all three times using φιλέω. Because John often uses synonyms, it is best not to see any distinguishing point in the interchange of the Greek verbs for "love." In addition, in any underlying Aramaic, such a distinction would not exist. What is happening does not turn on the terms chosen; rather, it is the threefold sequence and the opening question that are key to the scene. Jesus asks, "Do you love me more than these [disciples do]?" Peter in effect had made such a claim at the last meal when he expressed his readiness to die for Jesus (John 13:38; cf. esp. Matt. 26:33). Peter had failed three times to honor the claim. The threefold questioning restores Peter to his role as one of the key members within the Twelve, now Eleven. Peter humbly refuses to answer in terms of comparison to others and relies instead on Jesus' knowledge of his heart, three times affirming, "You know I love you." That Jesus asks three times saddens Peter, but perhaps that is not merely because Jesus is repeating the question but because Peter appreciates that his earlier threefold failure is being alluded to when the question is raised the third time.

In a few verses, Peter will be told that he will get the chance to redeem his claim to be willing to die for Jesus. What Peter failed to do during Jesus' trial, the fisherman one day will do as a part of carrying out the mission, restoring the truth of his original claim, thanks to the restitution that Jesus gives here. Thus, the scene shows the transforming and recovering power of the grace that forgives and restores. In fact, that recovery will be total, because Peter will become the leader of the early church, as Acts 1–15 makes clear.

That John loves stylistic variation is seen in the way the commission is given to Peter. He is told in rapid succession: feed my lambs, tend my sheep,

107. Luke, for example, has numerous meal scenes.

feed my sheep. Peter is recalled to pastoral ministry. Nothing in the text suggests that Peter is given a position greater than others.[108] All such comparisons have been avoided in the context, even when they are initially introduced. In fact, the inclusion of discussion about the beloved disciple in what follows seems to suggest that they will work side by side in the task. Jesus simply is making it publicly clear that Peter has his commission to labor in the catch. His call will be to follow Jesus, which he will do even to the point of experiencing a similar death.[109] That such is the point is confirmed in texts such as 1 Pet. 5:1–5 and Acts 20:28, where the role as shepherd is presented not primarily in term of rule and power but in terms of service.[110]

Jesus closes his remarks to Peter with a prediction about his future. In contrast to Peter's freedom as a young man, when he girded himself and went wherever he wished, Jesus tells him that when he is old, "You will stretch out your hands, and another will gird you and carry you where you do not wish to go." The phrase "stretch out your hands" is an allusion not to hanging on a cross in crucifixion but to being forced to carry the crossbeam on the way to a crucifixion.[111] Peter will suffer a death by which he will glorify God as Jesus has done, as the parenthetical note in John 21:19 indicates. So Jesus calls to Peter, "Follow me." This is a reference to discipleship in general, to go the same path of rejection by the world and faithfulness to God as did Jesus. However, placed as it is next to the prediction, it also indicates that Peter will go this way to the same degree that was required of Jesus.

Peter then turns to see the beloved disciple, the one, John notes, who put his head on Jesus' breast at the final meal and who asked who the betrayer was. Peter asks about the fate of this other disciple, one with whom he had experienced so much. He asks, "Lord, what about this man?" Jesus' reply is

---

108. Catholic interpreters especially, linking shepherd and the idea of rule, see Peter being given a position of primacy here.

109. Tradition has it that Peter was crucified upside down. According to *Acts of Peter* 37–38, Peter asked to be crucified upside down because he did not feel worthy to experience a death exactly like that of Jesus.

110. The role of "head" in Eph. 5:22–33 operates in much the same vein, reflecting Jesus' teaching about leadership found in Mark 10:35–45. The leader serves and is not preoccupied with rank or power.

111. The objection that the order between stretching out the hands and girding is wrong for this to be a crucifixion also argues that the reference to the extended hands describes the actual death. However, if what is being described is the walk to the cross, then the crossbearing and girding are in effect simultaneous in a walk that one otherwise would rather not take. The early church connected the remark to Isa. 65:2 and saw in it a reference to the crucifixion (so *Barnabas* 12.4; Justin Martyr, *First Apology* 35; Irenaeus, *Demonstration of Apostolic Teaching* 79). As we saw, tradition said that Peter was crucified upside down, not feeling worthy to die as Jesus did. However, it is not certain that this detail is correct. Early notes of Peter's death appear in *1 Clement* 5.4; Tertullian, *Scorpion's Sting* 15; and Eusebius, *Eccl. Hist.,* 3.1.2–3, where the tradition of Peter's request for an inverted crucifixion is noted. Eusebius appears to mention Origen and his now-lost commentary of Genesis as the source of the detail.

crisp and to the point: "If it is my will that he remain until I come, what is that to you? Follow me!" Jesus makes two points. First, how Jesus chooses to use another is none of Peter's business. Second, the one thing Peter should focus on is discipleship, following Jesus. That is his priority. Hypothetically, John might get to live until the Lord's return. He might be used in a way far different from Peter. That is not Peter's concern. Walking with Jesus is. It is this singular focus on discipleship that fills many of the passages on that theme in the Gospels.

It is discussed why this scene was passed on. Was there rivalry among some Christians concerning the leadership roles of Peter and John, much like that which Paul recorded as happening concerning other leaders, including himself, in Corinth (1 Cor. 1–4)? If so, the point would seem to be that each has a commissioned role given by the Lord. There is no place for rivalry between factions or any need to "rank" the followers.

The final remark about the scene corrects a misimpression that had resulted from the saying about John remaining until Jesus' return. Some thought that Jesus had predicted that the beloved disciple would live until Jesus returned. The Gospel writer points out that this reads too much into the saying. It was a hypothetical remark, not a prediction. What the remark may imply is that John may live far longer than Peter. None of that, however, is Peter's business. Some suggest that the text indicates that John is now dead, but there is nothing textually here or in what follows that makes this evident. Even the possible reference to others testifying to John's veracity in the next verses does not require that John is now deceased, despite claims otherwise. The final resurrection scene in John ends up as a picture of mission in the large catch of fish, a reminder that Jesus is with them and still can lead and serve them. So the priority of disciples is to follow Jesus in carrying out that mission. Where Matthew and Luke close with Jesus commanding a call and commission, John pictures the call.

John's Gospel closes with a twofold witness to its integrity (cf. Deut. 19:15). The text all but identifies the beloved disciple as the author of this Gospel. It is "this" disciple, the disciple of the previous event, who is bearing witness (note the present tense) to these things. The conclusion is like a signature on a legal document, saying, "I testify that these things are so." This disciple is the one responsible for the content of this Gospel, "the one who has written these things." Others can vouch for him. Although some wish to make this an editorial "we," as may appear in John 1:14, and have John offer indirect self-authentication, it is better to see here the word of those in the church for him, adding to the note of witness here.[112] Who these additional witnesses

---

112. It is not at all clear that John 1:14 should be read as a singular reference to John's witness to Jesus' glory. Appearing as it does in the prologue, it also could affirm the witness that comes through the church about the glory that Jesus displayed.

are (the Ephesian elders, the entire church community, or some other unspecified group) is unclear. Their role, however, is to underscore the veracity of the
primary witness. "We know that his testimony is true."

The final remark notes that no one could write an exhaustive account of all that
Jesus did. If such were attempted, the hyperbole goes, the world itself could not
contain the books that would be required. The figure has precedent in ancient
writing. Ecclesiastes 12:9–12; Philo, *Posterity of Cain* 43 §144; and a minor talmudic tractate (*Soperim* 16.8) about Rabbi Johannan ben Zakkai (later first century, ca. A.D. 80) all use variations of this figure. The rabbi remarks, "If all the heavens were sheets of paper, and all the trees were pens for writing, and all the seas
were ink, that would not suffice to write down the wisdom I have received from
my teachers." John is well aware that what he has written and what others testify
to is but a piece of the total story of Jesus. Still, what John writes is sufficient to
lead to faith and the abundant life that he seeks in those who ally themselves to
Jesus. The community now is left with a calling to take that message into an often
hostile world and seek to gather others who can share in God's grace, goodness,
and greatness, which come through life in the Son.

Conclusion

John's remark about the world being too small to contain all that could be written
about Jesus is a good reminder that what we know about Jesus is but the tip of the
iceberg. The remark also is an ironic touch in that so much ink—libraries full—has
been spilt assessing the four Gospels that make up the description of Jesus. Jesus according to Scripture is a figure about whom commentary has become endless. This
has been stated most aptly perhaps in Beasley-Murray's remarks on this passage and
this Gospel, remarks that could be extended to all the Gospels:

> It may be observed that no person on earth can encompass and assimilate all
> that has been and is being written about this Gospel, which is a tribute to the
> achievement of the Evangelist, and still more to the subject of whom he wrote.
> The greatness of the revelation of God in the Logos-Son is vaster than the cos-
> mos created through him. But he sent us the Paraclete-Spirit, through whom
> the Beloved Disciple was given to grasp the revelation in a unique measure. By
> the same Spirit, and with the aid of testimony of the disciple whom Jesus loved,
> we may enter more fully into the revelation in the Son, and into the experience
> of being a disciple whom Jesus loves.[113]

What is said here of the beloved disciple is true of all the evangelists. Jesus
is a unique figure. How unique Jesus is becomes more fully appreciated when

113. Beasley-Murray, *John*, 416.

he is set against the backdrop of the first-century world into which the Father sent him. That uniqueness and the unique authority he possesses are not the product of the evangelists' writings, but are a reflection of the figure about whom they wrote. It was Jesus' life and ministry that left these four testimonies to him in their wake. It was the Word become flesh that left four testimonies to him in the scriptural word. They and he are best understood when they are read both separately and together. This is why in order to understand Jesus, one must appreciate who Jesus is according to Scripture.

Part 4
A Theological Portrait of Jesus

And the prophetic dignity in Christ leads us to know that in the sum of doctrine as he has given it to us all parts of perfect wisdom are contained.[1]

The instruction guiding the church over the centuries has been Christ's teaching and the works of apostolic reflection about God's work through him in the New Testament. In this final section, we consider a portion of that valuable deposit of divine truth, the evangelists' portrayal of Jesus' teaching. A full treatment of this theme would involve another entire book, so I limit this study to the major themes of Jesus' ministry as the Gospel writers present them. Under each key theme, I try to single out whether the emphasis is the concern of any particular evangelist or is a shared concern. I also point out any particular emphases of any evangelist within each key theme. Finally, I pay special attention to how "public" or "private" the teaching in question was as the evangelists portray it. Here we get a clue as to what Jesus said to all versus what he taught just to the disciples.

In this section the study does not proceed Gospel by Gospel, but thematically. We consider what Jesus presented as teaching or reflect on the significance of his actions. The evangelists' narrative commentary is excluded from consideration in this section. That story already has been told in our reading through the pericope units of the Gospels. Now it is time to gather together the key strands of that story that are said to go back to Jesus. What the evangelists passed on has come to us through tradition and from the choices that the given evangelists made concerning what they wished to show about Jesus. The church regards what is passed on to be the result of the active work of God's Spirit in leading the authors in what to write. Such teaching no doubt

---

1. John Calvin, *Institutes of the Christian Religion* 2.15.2 (ed. J. T. McNeill, trans. F. L. Battles, 2 vols. [Philadelphia: Westminster, 1960], 1:496).

was passed on with the conviction that it was of value to the original audiences of each Gospel. Thus, the teaching is pastoral at its core. It seeks to ground readers solidly in a walk with God. The church, in turn, recognizing the value of what was recorded for nurture in the faith, embraced these works and their portrait of Jesus as faithful expressions of what it meant to embrace Jesus and follow him. There can be no better capstone to a work on Jesus according to Scripture than to focus on the key themes of his life and ministry associated with his own teaching.

FIFTEEN

Major Themes in the Evangelists' Portrait of Jesus' Theology

*The Kingdom and the Uniquely
Authoritative One in Act and Word*

For one must reckon *a priori* with the possibility—even with the probability—
first, that in his teaching and life Jesus accomplished something new from
which the first Christians had to proceed in their attempt to explain his person
and work; second, that their experience of Christ exhibited special features not
present in any obvious analogy to related religious forms. It is simply unschol-
arly prejudice methodically to exclude from the beginning this possibility—this
probability.[1]

Jesus' teaching was unique and made unique claims. That is why understanding him and the portrait of him in the Gospels is so important. He
claims to give unique insight into God's plan, as well as the way to divine fellowship and blessing. Many of these claims are rooted in the Jewish founda-
tions to which Jesus belonged. However, Jesus' teaching on hope led to an appreciation that he was speaking about more than a plan for Israel. The nation's
calling always had been to serve as a means of blessing for the world. Jesus'
starting point involved a call to Israel to prepare for the promised completion
of what God had started with them. However, that plan, at least as far back as
Isa. 40–66 if not all the way back to Gen. 12:3, always had foreseen the inclusion of the Gentile nations within God's blessing. Jesus' teaching ultimately

1. Oscar Cullmann, *The Christology of the New Testament,* rev ed. (London: SCM, 1959), 5.

aims at this comprehensive goal of blessing extended to all the righteous of every nation. God's promise, given long ago, had affirmed that blessing would come for the righteous in all the world. We turn our attention to the major strands of Jesus' teachings and actions because through their interplay we see what his ministry was all about.[2]

This chapter focuses on Jesus' own teaching and not the theology of each Gospel as such. We also examine at points the relationship between what the Gospels present Jesus as teaching and what other portions of the New Testament proclaim.[3] Our focus is a combination of what Jesus did and what he taught as a way of summarizing how Scripture presents the promised one. As a result, one major theme that ends up not receiving development is the incarnation. The incarnation emerges as part of a reflective introduction about Jesus the Word incarnate (John 1:1–18) or as part of the emphasis in the presentation of Jesus' infancy in two of the Synoptics. In both Matthew and Luke, the emphasis is on how Jesus' birth fulfilled divine promise. In Matthew, the emphasis is on themes tied to messianic promise or the patterns of Israel's history, including themes about conflict and rejection. In Matthew's introduction, the portrait of "God with us" is the dominating note that implies the presence of the divine in Jesus. In Luke's infancy account, the note of explicit incarnation is less obvious as themes of joy and celebration in light of the fulfillment of promise accompany the account. Mark simply starts with the ministry of John the Baptist, which is where we begin our tracing of Jesus' own actions as well.

Jesus' Submitting to Baptism: Identifying with John the Baptist's Message and Being Identified by the Divine Voice

Jesus' choice to share in John's baptism meant that he was identifying with John's call to the nation of Israel to repent and prepare for the coming of God's kingdom. John's ministry is corroborated in Josephus, *Ant.* 18.5.2 §§116–119.[4] Josephus points out that many Jews saw the defeat of Herod's

---

2. This survey is not chronological but thematic. There will be points, however, where it is clear that we are dealing with events that came early or late in his ministry.

3. More critically oriented treatments of Jesus tend to highlight the differences in the scriptural portrayal and pit the theology of one writer against the other. I hope to show that there is more unity here than those approaches claim.

4. For a thorough discussion of this text, see John Meier, *A Marginal Jew: Rethinking the Historical Jesus,* 2 vols., ABRL (New York: Doubleday, 1994), 2:56–62. Meier notes in this discussion that Josephus had no desire to report the more eschatological features of John's message, such as judgment. For apologetic reasons, he also probably suppressed those issues involving Israel alone in order to avoid offending his Roman audience. Thus, this portrait of John makes him look like a good moral philosopher. Meier hints that the portrait of Luke 3:10–14 may connect with Josephus's portrait of John's ministry pointing to a call for justice.

army by the Nabatean ruler Aretas IV as divine punishment for Herod's slaying of John. Josephus notes that John urged people to receive baptism as well as to cultivate virtue and practice piety and justice. Josephus portrays this baptism as an act of purification. Herod slew John the Baptist because he feared John's persuasive power with the people.

The more eschatological elements of John's ministry, suggesting connections to Isa. 40:3, also have parallels in Judaism. The Qumran community appealed to this text for their separatism and desire to await the approach of God's redemption (1QS 8.14; 9.19–20). The Qumranians applied this text to drawing away from corrupt society and religious practices to study the law in holy preparation for God's coming.

All the Gospels connect John to this Isa. 40 tradition when introducing his ministry.[5] John's baptism makes a call for righteousness similar to the Qumranians' call but without the focus on law or withdrawal; rather, it represents an identification with the nation's and the individual's need to prepare for God's powerful coming. To submit to baptism is to share in the washing that the nation needed as preparation for God's coming. However, it was not the rite of washing that was key for John but the response of the heart ready for God to come. In fact, given Luke 3:10–14, the stress of John's call is that such a recognition of repentance will mean that the person prepared for God's coming will treat others with more compassion and integrity. As all the Synoptics make clear, there is a call to bear fruit worthy of repentance that is a part of the call to be prepared and baptized. It represents the removal of obstacles that stand in the way of God's coming (cf. Isa. 57:14). Thus, there is a community dimension to the eschatological washing. When Jesus participates in John's baptism, he is identifying with and endorsing the message of the prophet, especially in its national dimension as a community statement of Israel's need for God and his coming.[6]

Associated with the baptism is the voice from heaven. This event appears to have been a primarily private interaction between Jesus and God, given Mark's description. However, John the Baptist apparently also had access to it as a witness for Jesus, as John's Gospel affirms (John 1:29–34). The other Gospels appear to highlight the event's significance. It was at this event that God marked out his beloved Son as his unique agent.

Key to the event is not only the testimony of the heavenly voice but also the anointing by the Spirit. The voice marks out Jesus both as royal, given the allusion to Ps. 2:7, and as a Servant figure, as the use of Isa. 42:1 shows. This

5. Mark adds a connection to the idea of God's messenger sent ahead from Mal. 1, while Luke lengthens the Isa. 40 citation to extend to its outreach to all flesh, an emphasis fitting his concerns for non-Jews. These additional comments by the evangelists serve to introduce the ministry and give a context for its meaning.

6. R. L. Webb, "Jesus' Baptism: Its Historicity and Implications," *Bulletin for Biblical Research* 10 (2000): 261–309.

affirmation lays the foundational groundwork for identifying Jesus' roles. The experience of the voice and God's provision of the Spirit served as a confirmation of his call. The anointing by the Spirit confirms the call by supplying the agent of enablement who marks out Jesus as "anointed" (the Messiah-Christ), and also affirms his prophetic connection to the will of God.[7]

With this directing call behind him, Jesus now is free to move out in ministry. He picks up the message where John the Baptist left off. God's rule is approaching in the one whom God has marked to take up the call. First, however, there is an important test of his readiness.

Jesus' Temptation: Showing the Opponent and the Qualification of the One Sent as Son

All the Synoptics recount Jesus' temptations as the last event before Jesus moves into ministry. Mark tells the account in summary form, simply noting that Jesus was tempted, was with the beasts, and had angels minister to him. Mark immediately follows the account with Jesus' call that the time is fulfilled and the kingdom is approaching, and so one must repent and believe in the gospel. What is significant about Mark's version is that Jesus emerged unbowed from the test. Unlike a previous temptation (Gen. 3), there was no succumbing to the presence of evil. Matthew and Luke give details, although in different order, with Matthew apparently giving the tighter sequencing. Both these writers use the event to precede the introduction of Galilean ministry. Luke is most explicit when it comes to showing the importance of the event, because the temptations follow a genealogy that ends with the identification of Adam as "son of God." So Jesus succeeds where Adam failed and becomes the representative for humanity who is able to stand up to the devil. Jesus' success and dependence on God are not the only key points of teaching in the event. Also significant is the introduction of the devil as the key spiritual opponent to Jesus' cause. Opposition to Jesus is not merely or even primarily a matter of social or political forces. Jesus' later action in casting out demons will reinforce the point about the cosmic nature of opposition to Jesus. The event's uniform placement here before Jesus launches his ministry focuses on this "cosmic" dimension of Jesus' battle from the start.

Often it is claimed that the story of Jesus' temptation is a creation of the church. No doubt its explicit supernatural elements are responsible for such

---

7. Given the church's recognition of Jesus' divinity, such affirmation and confirmation may seem odd, especially primarily as a private experience. However, these acts represent an equipping that shows how seriously the Gospel writers took Jesus' humanity. His ministry has all the markings and more of the divine calling of any major prophetic figure (cf. Isa. 6; Ezek. 1–3; Jer. 1).

skepticism. The objection is raised that the event has no witnesses. But a better question might be, What would cause the church to remember such an event, whether in skeletal or detail form, making it multiply attested in two strands of the church's tradition (Mark and Q [= material common to Matthew and Luke])? It would seem that this had to be a story that Jesus related to his soon-to-be-gathered band of the Twelve. Its point would be to underscore that Jesus' mission was not primarily about politics or the social order. Rather, associated with Jesus' coming was a deeper spiritual battle in which unseen forces always seek to seduce people away from walking in the direction of God's call. Such a calling entailed suffering, not the kind of self-satisfaction that Satan was offering to the Son. To precede the introduction of Jesus' ministry with this shared note means that the Synoptics have underscored where the real battle for hearts and souls lies, including choices between God and self. It is what Paul would stress later when he told the Ephesians that the believers' battle is not against "blood and flesh, but against the principalities, against the powers, against the world rulers of this present darkness, against the spiritual hosts of wickedness in the heavenly places" (Eph. 6:12).

Jesus' Teaching on God as Father and His Program: The Kingdom of God as the Expression of God's Dynamic Rule and Vindication of the Righteous Both Now and Yet to Come

Clearly, the kingdom is one of Jesus' most central teachings. A look at the use of the term for God's reign, βασιλεία, shows how the concept is distributed in the Gospels:

Mark (13 times: Mark 1:15 [= Matt. 4:17]; 4:11 [Matt. 13:11; Luke 8:10]; 4:26; 4:30 [Matt. 13:31; Luke 13:18]; 9:1 [Matt. 16:28; Luke 9:27]; 9:47; 10:14 [Matt. 19:14; Luke 18:16]; 10:15 [Luke 18:17]; 10:23 [Matt. 19:23; Luke 18:24]; 10:24; 10:25 [Matt. 19:24; Luke 18:25]; 12:34; 14:25 [Matt. 26:29; Luke 22:18]—all but 4:26; 9:47; 10:24; and 12:34 have parallels in other Gospels, as shown])

Teaching material common to Matthew and Luke (9 times: Matt. 5:3/Luke 6:20; Matt. 6:10/Luke 11:2; Matt. 6:33/Luke 12:31; Matt. 8:11/Luke 13:29; Matt. 10:7/Luke 10:9; Matt. 11:11/Luke 7:28; Matt. 11:12/Luke 16:16; Matt. 12:28/Luke 11:20; Matt. 13:33/Luke 13:20)

Matthew only (27 times: 5:10, 19a, 19b, 20; 7:21; 8:12; 13:19, 24, 38, 43, 44, 45, 47, 52; 16:19; 18:1, 3, 4, 23; 19:12; 20:1; 21:31, 43; 22:2; 23:13; 24:14; 25:1)

Luke only (12 times: 4:43; 9:60; 10:11; 12:32; 13:28; 17:20a, 20b, 21; 18:29; 21:31; 22:16, 18)
John (2 times: John 3:3, 5)[8]

This is a good example of multiple attestation at a conceptual level because the idea surfaces in every strand of the Gospel tradition.[9] Often it is said that John's concept of eternal life is his equivalent for the kingdom of God, to make the idea more intelligible for a Greek audience.[10] Jesus did speak of entering life when one entered the kingdom, so the move fits with Jesus' teaching (Mark 9:43, 45; Matt. 7:14). It also is clear that Matthew especially likes to note the phrase, while Luke is more restrained (Matthew has it thirty-two times as "kingdom of heaven" and four times as "kingdom of God" [Matt. 12:28; 19:24; 21:31, 43; a fifth use in Matt. 6:33 depends on a textual variant]; Matthew has a reference in five places that Mark does not [Matt. 13:19; 18:1; 20:21; 21:43; 24:14], while Luke has it in three places where parallels with Mark lack it [Luke 4:43; 18:29; 21:31]).[11] What does this key term mean? What were its antecedents? What other concepts in Jesus' teaching are tied to it? To make these key points of Jesus' teaching clear, we cover this term in some detail and subsume other key themes to it.

Antecedents to the Term and Its Meaning: A Term with a Static Basic Meaning and Yet Variable Force

When Jesus used the expression "kingdom of God," how much of its meaning can we assume he and his audience shared? This becomes an important question because the expression itself, surprisingly, is totally absent in the Hebrew Scriptures.[12] Here is a good example of where the study of an idea involves more than the study of a specific phrase or term. Although the expression "kingdom of God" is not present in the Hebrew Scriptures, the concept

---

8. This list is adapted from Joachim Jeremias, *New Testament Theology*, vol. 1, trans. J. Bowden (London: SCM, 1971), 31. The above list adds the parallels to Mark. It is very rare for Matthew and Luke to drop a reference to the kingdom that is in Mark. Often, when it does happen, it is because of repetition with a previous line or a choice to omit a longer detail (e.g., Matt. 19:24 and Luke 18:24 lack it where Mark 10:24 has it; Mark 10:15 and Luke 18:17 have it in a pericope where Matthew lacks the verse altogether in the scene). One exception is Matt. 18:9, which lacks it where Mark 9:47 has it.

9. This point about multiple attestation holds regardless if one prefers Matthean priority for the order of the Gospels.

10. Leonhard Goppelt, *Theology of the New Testament*, vol. 1, ed. Jürgen Roloff, trans. John E. Alsup (Grand Rapids: Eerdmans, 1981), 45.

11. Outside the Gospels, reference to the kingdom in this sense is rare: 10 times in Paul, 8 times in Acts, 2 times in Revelation, and once each in Hebrews and James. This is not a common expression in the early church of the New Testament period.

12. The expression does occur in Wis. 10:10.

of God's promised rule is a prominent idea.[13] Yahweh is king (1 Sam. 12:12; Ps. 24:10; Isa. 33:22; Zeph. 3:15; Zech. 14:16–17). He rules over Israel (Exod. 15:18; Num. 23:21; Deut. 33:5; Isa. 43:15). He rules over the earth or the creation (2 Kings 19:15; Isa. 6:5; Jer. 46:18; Ps. 29:10; 47:2; 93; 96:10; 145:11, 13). He possesses a royal throne (Ps. 9:4; 45:6; 47:8; Isa. 6:1; 66:1; Ezek. 1:26). His reign is ongoing (Ps. 10:16; 146:10; Isa. 24:23). Rule or kingship is his (Ps. 22:28). It is primarily God's special relationship to Israel that is in view in these texts, as the son of David is said to sit on Yahweh's throne (1 Chron. 17:14; 28:5; 29:23; 2 Chron. 9:8; 13:8). When Israel was overrun by the nations, a longing existed that one day God would reestablish his rule on behalf of his people and show his comprehensive sovereignty to all humanity. After all, God had committed himself to David concerning a dynasty of duration (2 Sam. 7:13). It is here that the hope of a future kingdom of God, made not with hands, came to be contrasted with human kingdoms in Dan. 2 and 7. It is in the context of such expectation that Jesus used the expression "kingdom of God." What was hoped for was something that had existed in the past, but only as a mere glimpse of what had been promised: a rule to come involving total peace for God's people. In sum, as a result of the Babylonian captivity, kingdom hope is driven forward by the vision of the fullness of God's rule appearing some day. It was to this hope that Jesus preached.

Such a hope had been nurtured in some circles of Second Temple Judaism.[14] The kingdom *often* became linked to the messianic hope, but it *always* was tied to the judgment of the nations and the vindication of the saints. Some Jewish documents, content with the current arrangement, do not reflect any such hope. The concept is expressed with some variety, but central to its expression is that God will assert his comprehensive rule (*1 Enoch* 9.4–5; 12.3; 25; 27.3; 81.3). God's powerful presence will involve the removal of Satan's influence (*Assumption of Moses* 7–10). He will destroy his enemies and free his people. These enemies are described both in earthly terms, like the Romans in *Psalms of Solomon* 17–18 and *2 Baruch* 36–40, and in spiritual terms, as when Belial stands among the evil forces that will be defeated (1QS 3–4). Often the coming of the kingdom was seen as being preceded by a period of intense upheaval and tribulation (*Sibylline Oracles* 3.796–808; *2 Baruch* 70.2–8; *4 Ezra* [= 2 Esdras] 6:24; 9:1–12; 13:29–31; 1QM 12.9; 19.1–2). The cry of the prayer of 2 Macc. 1:24–29 summarizes well the hope of deliverance. The call was for God to deliver and vindicate his people. The text of *Psalms of Solomon* 17–18 gives the most detailed expression of messianic hope in all the texts, although the idea of kingdom in this period of Judaism did not

13. Chrys C. Caragounis, "Kingdom of God/Kingdom of Heaven," *DJG,* 417.
14. Michael Lattke, "On the Jewish Background of the Synoptic Concept 'The Kingdom of God,'" in *The Kingdom of God,* ed. Bruce Chilton (Philadelphia: Fortress, 1984), 72–91.

always entail a messianic hope.[15] In fact, sometimes the Messiah is seen in very earthly terms, as in the *Psalms of Solomon*, while in other texts, he clearly possesses a more transcendent power (*1 Enoch* 37–71) or seems to have a mix of the two (*4 Ezra* [= 2 Esdras] 7:28–29; 12:32–34; 13:26). Thus, associated with the consistent idea of God's coming comprehensive and vindicating rule for his people is a complex array of subthemes tied to the kingdom's coming. In Judaism, there was no unified view of the kingdom beyond the hope of God's powerful coming and vindication. It is important to appreciate that it is into this somewhat confused backdrop that Jesus preached this hope.

This complex background raises questions: Could Jesus use the phrase "kingdom of God"and really be understood? More importantly, in presenting his understanding of the idea represented in the kingdom, could he assume an understanding of the phrase by his audience? Given the paucity of Old Testament use of the phrase and the variety of details attached to the hope within Judaism, Jesus needed to explain his usage in order to be clear. It is this complexity that raises the issue of whether Jesus' use of the expression was "static" (fixed) or "tensive" (variable).[16] Norman Perrin posed these two options. Did Jesus use the expression one way all the time with a fixed referent (static)? Or was his use of the expression something that he used with symbolic force but that could not be contained in one referent alone (tensive)? In contrast to Perrin's either/or option, a third possibility seems more likely. Jesus' use operates within a fixed parameter, which he filled with a variety of detail because of the richness of the base concept that he was defining and detailing (tensive yet with a staticlike base).[17] How one approaches Jesus' terminology will impact how one reads it.

Four factors favor this third option. First, the number of, and variety within, the Gospel kingdom sayings placed alongside the paucity of older references in the Hebrew Scriptures suggests that Jesus is developing the concept along additional lines to what the Old Testament taught. However, Jesus' respect for that revelation means that he is not altering the concept but devel-

---

15. Jacob Neusner, William Green, and E. Frerichs, eds., *Judaisms and Their Messiahs* (Cambridge: Cambridge University Press, 1987).

16. This linguistic contrast was introduced by the later work of Norman Perrin, *Jesus and the Language of the Kingdom* (Philadelphia: Fortress, 1976), esp. 16–32, 127–31, 197–99. In discussing this point from Perrin, I wish to highlight the linguistic element of his discussion without embracing his language about "myth" associated with the use of the expression "kingdom of God."

17. For an incisive critique of Perrin, see Meier, *A Marginal Jew,* 2:241–43. He accuses the later Perrin of sounding like a twentieth-century Bultmannian as opposed to being attuned to a first-century Jew. Interestingly, the earlier Perrin made a similar critique about such a view of the kingdom. See Norman Perrin, *The Kingdom of God in the Teaching of Jesus* (Philadelphia: Westminster, 1963), 86, where he states, "A 'timeless' Kingdom is as foreign to 1st century Judaism as a transcendent order beyond time and space, and if Jesus held such views he singularly failed to impress them upon his followers."

oping and complementing it. The variety within his kingdom teaching validates this point. Second, the very consistency of the fundamental image within Judaism means that a basic understanding of kingdom did exist on which Jesus could build. It is *God's* kingdom and rule that are presented as the hope. The sheer number of texts that discuss judgment and vindication under this theme both in Scripture and in later Judaism shows that Jesus works with a given understanding at its base. Reflection taking place within Second Temple Judaism represented attempts to put the hope of Scripture together in terms of the details. Jesus both accepts and rejects elements of these reflections. Third, this idea that Jesus works with a rarely used Old Testament term and yet develops it by using larger categories of scriptural teaching has precedent elsewhere in his own use. Jesus does the same type of thing with the Son of Man concept. That description of a human invested with eschatological authority appears in Dan. 7 (note the conceptual overlap with the kingdom theme—Dan. 7 is a key kingdom text). Jesus takes this one image and uses it as a collection point for his christological self-understanding. In the same way, Jesus takes the kingdom concept and uses it as a collection point for both soteriology and eschatology.[18] Fourth, the very confusion of detail within Judaism of Jesus' time demanded that he take this type of approach to the kingdom of God. Here was an expression that virtually did not exist in the Old Testament. However, by Jesus' time, multiple concepts swirled around it, even though its basic meaning was well established. The expression clearly sought to summarize a major strand of Jewish hope, yet it needed defining. Its absence in the Old Testament gave Jesus room to make it a helpful synthesizing concept. Its familiarity and importance within Judaism, because of the hope it encapsulated, made it a key term to nail down. The very diversity in its contemporary usage required that Jesus explain and develop the term. Thus, as we turn to Jesus' usage, we can expect that he was referring to a hope that his audience understood in its most basic terms, but one that nevertheless needed more detail and development.

So Jesus' use of the term "kingdom" is tensive with a stable base. In each of the categories we examine, it will be shown that Jesus' use is complex and must be examined one text at a time. Choices of either/or inevitably err in narrowing the depth of Jesus' usage. To make "kingdom" a static technical term for every use is to miss the variety of nuances that he uses within the stable base meaning that he gives. The kingdom is about the presence of God's rule, the vindication of the righteous, and the judgment of the enemies of God. But what exactly does its coming involve? This raises the question of the kingdom as an apocalyptic theme.

18. I suspect that the same premise operates with Jesus' use of "the law," but with the opposite dimension. Here, the term in question is so heavily used in the Old Testament that Jesus' usage in any context must be carefully examined for its point and scope.

Kingdom as an Apocalyptic, End-Time Theme: A Remaking of the
World, a Renewing of This World in History, or Both? Is It Coming
Soon (Imminence)?

In considering Jesus' appeal to the kingdom, two questions dominate. The
first question: Did Jesus foresee a divinely remade new world or foresee a divinely wrought reorganization of the current world, and is there even the possibility that he foresaw both?[19] The second question: Did he foresee that end,
however conceived, as coming within his lifetime?

The problem concerning a remade new age or an eschaton within this
history sometimes has been highlighted by pointing out the difference in
Old Testament hope between prophetic-eschatological expectation and
apocalyptic-eschatological hope.[20] Prophetic hope is defined in terms of
God's work within history, usually tied to God's raising up a delivering
royal figure for Israel (e.g., Isa. 9). Apocalyptic hope is defined as God's
powerful work manifesting itself in an "in-breaking" from outside into normal history (e.g., Dan. 7). Apocalyptic hope entails cosmic change, the presence of a transcendent-like figure, and the backdrop of an almost dualistic
conflict with the cosmic forces of evil.[21] In sum, the Messiah represents prophetic-eschatological hope, while the "one like a son of man" represents
apocalyptic-eschatological hope.

The interesting feature in Jesus' kingdom teaching is that both strands
are present, though the more eschatological features seem to dominate.
The more apocalyptic features include the imagery of the Son of Man
coming on the clouds, drawn directly from Dan. 7:13 (Mark 13:26 par.),
along with the cosmic disturbances associated with his coming (Mark

19. The idea that Jesus did not have an apocalyptic hope, as made popular in the Jesus Seminar, is not likely. The most eloquent attempt to make this argument appears in the work of
Marcus Borg, *Jesus in Contemporary Scholarship* (Valley Forge, Pa.: Trinity Press International,
1994). For a critical assessment of this view, see Dale C. Allison, *Jesus of Nazareth: Millenarian
Prophet* (Minneapolis: Fortress, 1998), 96–129.

20. For a summary of this distinction, see Paul D. Hanson, *The Dawn of Apocalyptic:
The Historical and Sociological Roots of Jewish Apocalyptic Eschatology*, rev. ed. (Philadelphia:
Fortress, 1979), 10–12; George Ladd, *The Presence of the Future* (Grand Rapids: Eerdmans,
1974), 45–101, esp. 79–83, 93–95. Unlike many of the discussions of this distinction,
Ladd correctly sees something less than a clean distinction between these categories, not-
ing how the "apocalyptic" Daniel actually has many "prophetic" features. Ladd thus
avoids the implicit tendency of many critics to pit the two approaches against each other.
Given the "mix" in Daniel, the mix in Jesus' own presentation has precedent in the older
Scripture.

21. Rather than appealing to a genre distinction, John Collins, *The Scepter and the Star: The
Messiahs of the Dead Sea Scrolls and other Ancient Literature*, ABRL (New York: Doubleday,
1995), 11–14, argues for a distinction in the form of the messianic expectation between a royal
figure and a heavenly messianic figure. These are two of the four categories that he notes exist
in Judaism. The others are prophet and priest.

13:24–25 par.).[22] Here is divine judgment crashing the earthly party down below, an in-breaking of God's authority. This imagery is significant because it is this return that brings judgment and allows the vindicated righteous to "inherit the kingdom" (Matt. 25:34). It involves the rule of God being expressed in its coercive fullness. Here kingdom and returning Son of Man are linked. Here are standard Jewish apocalyptic themes of the kingdom. The images of a gathering up for a comprehensive judgment and of a bridegroom coming who shuts some out also have these overtones (Matt. 25:1–13, 31–46). Other imagery having a catastrophic, apocalyptic feel includes the comparisons of the judgment with the flood (Luke 17:26–27; Matt. 24:37–39) and Sodom and Gomorrah (Luke 17:28–29). The Son of Man's sudden coming is compared to lightning, revealing the "shock" of the coming (Luke 17:24; Matt. 24:27).

Other images of the kingdom in the future are harder to classify in terms of this world or a remade world. The reversal of suffering or oppression, as reflected in the promises of the Beatitudes, could fit either emphasis, as do their hopes of reward (Matt. 5:3–10). The image of the rejoicing and fellowship at the banquet table also could belong in either scheme (Matt. 8:11–12; Luke 14:15–24; 22:16–18). One text seems to indicate that Israel is still very much in view in the plan: the Twelve will judge the twelve tribes of Israel (Luke 22:30). In addition, the selection of the Twelve has been seen by many New Testament scholars as an indication that what Jesus was working for was a restoration of the nation, preparing them for the era of "regeneration" (Matt. 19:28).[23]

On the other hand, some teaching appears to shy away from the more overt apocalyptic themes of Judaism. Jesus specifically denies that signs accompany the time of the kingdom's appearing (Luke 17:20–21) although he does indicate that general signs exist in the age that should keep one watching. Such signs indicate that God is at work (Luke 12:54–56; Mark 13:1–38, esp. vv. 28–31). Jesus explicitly refuses to name an exact time for his return, precluding us from excessive calendrical calculating that often is tied to apocalyptic themes (Mark 13:32 par.).

Other texts are decidedly more eschatological and lack apocalyptic features. The parables of the sower, mustard seed, leaven, and tenants appear to

---

22. I make this point against the view of Werner Kümmel, *Promise and Fulfillment: The Eschatological Message of Jesus* (London: SCM, 1957), 104. He splits the eschatological elements from the apocalyptic ones and argues that only the eschatological elements are authentic. Although Jesus' kingdom imagery is primarily eschatological, there is no inherent reason why the key turning point in the program should not be linked to apocalyptic imagery of God's decisive in-breaking, especially if Jesus saw himself in any sense as sent by God.

23. Allison, *Jesus of Nazareth*, 101–2. Allison notes the parallels in Judaism that point in this direction: 1QM 2.1–3; 4QpIsa[d] frag. 1; *Testament of Judah* 25.1–2; *Testament of Benjamin* 10.7 (also, Rev. 21:12).

place kingdom preaching and presence as having invaded this history with no "apocalyptic" feel at all, operating more like a covert operation—so unnoticed that it is hardly appreciated as the presence of the kingdom program at all. Nevertheless, one day what has been started will reach a point of covering the whole world. These parables, explicitly presented as revealing a "mystery," show how Jesus' kingdom teaching spans more than a single catastrophic event or a given moment. It is here that Jesus makes his distinctive contribution and goes in a fresh direction in comparison to previous Jewish expressions of kingdom hope. He apparently foresees a long-running program that was declared and initiated in his teaching and work, but that one day will culminate in a comprehensive judgment. It is to this ultimate goal that the kingdom is headed. Thus, the emphasis in the kingdom teaching of the Gospels always is aimed toward this fully restorative future. In this sense, Jesus' teaching is at one with the traditional Jewish hope. The emphasis explains why the disciples, after spending years listening to Jesus teach about the kingdom, could ask him after his resurrection if now was the time he was restoring the kingdom to Israel (Acts 1:6). Nothing in what Jesus had taught them had dissuaded them from this "national" dimension of the hope. And in equally characteristic style, Jesus replied neither with a time nor a date nor a correction but with an emphasis on the current call in light of that certain future.

It is the juxtaposition of these various strands that shows how eclectic and synthetic, even creative, Jesus' kingdom teaching is. Jesus did preach a hope that Jews could recognize, but he also preached a whole lot more. He embraced strands of Jewish apocalyptic hope but did not merely parrot these themes. The sense of these texts as a whole is that Jesus works within this history and yet will reshape it one day. Again, the teaching is neither this world reorganized nor a new world created, but both in their appropriate time. But how soon, O Lord, would this fullness come?

It is here that three texts have dominated the discussion about how imminent the kingdom was in Jesus' view. Those who wish to credit Jesus with a view of imminence within a generation or so of his coming point to these three texts as decisive. On the other hand, one text within the Olivet discourse warns us not to make a judgment before all the sayings are considered. The three "imminent" texts are Mark 9:1 (which explains that before some of the disciples die, they will see "the kingdom of God come in power"),[24] Matt. 10:23 (which notes that before the disciples finish going through all the cities of Jerusalem, the Son of Man will come), and Mark 13:30 = Matt. 24:34 (which argues that "this generation" will not pass away until "all these things" take place).

24. Interestingly, the Matthean parallel in 16:28 has "before they see the Son of Man coming in his kingdom," again showing a link between Son of Man and kingdom.

Mark 9:1 often is explained by appealing to the transfiguration as the event alluded to, a moment when the inner circle saw a sneak preview of Jesus' kingdom glory. Although objectors complain that Jesus would hardly refer to an event only six days or so hence against a time frame of the disciples' death, the fact is that only "some" did see this transfiguration glimpse of glory. That event and the Gospels' juxtaposition of transfiguration with the saying seem to commend this reading. That event as a foretaste of kingdom glory justifies its association with the kingdom of the end. There is no ultimate imminence foreseen in this passage.

The case for imminence surrounding Matt. 10:23 perhaps relies on an overly literal reading. The expression "finish going through all the cities of Israel" may mean nothing more than "completing your mission to Israel." In other words, they are to continue pursuing the nation until the Son of Man returns. When he does come, they still will be engaged in that calling. As we will see in a moment, this fits with something that Jesus says at Olivet. If this reading is correct, then neither is there imminence in this second of the three texts.

Mark 13:30 = Matt. 24:34 is the most difficult saying. The initial impression that many gain from the text is that all these Olivet events are predicted to happen by the end of "this generation," so the Son of Man's return is predicted within the disciples' lifetime. However, as D. A. Carson has pointed out, to have the remark about this generation and "all these things" include the event of the return would be contradictory to earlier imagery about the coming being obvious like lightning, as well as not fitting the precursor "budding leaf" imagery of the Markan context.[25] In other words, the remarks about the Son of Man's appearing, given the seemingly obvious cosmic signs that accompany it, mark that event as excluded in the "leaf" remark of the parable. That "leaf" remark is pointing to spotting the approach of the end, not its conclusion. This would mean that "all these things" refers to those events described before the arrival of the cosmic signs. Those events would happen within a generation, and that was just how it was, given that the fall of Jerusalem in A.D. 70 is a sign of the end and is a parallel to what the end itself would look like. The fall in A.D. 70 with the temple judgment was a guarantee that the end also would come one day. It is the linkage to the A.D. 70 fall—without that being the end event—that gives this discourse its sense of imminence.

One text in the same context as the Mark 13:30 "generation" text also points to the fact that Jesus did not teach that the fullness of the kingdom would come within the generation of the disciples. It is Mark 13:10 = Matt. 24:14. Here, Jesus notes that before the end comes, the "gospel" (Mark)/

---

25. See D. A. Carson, "Matthew," in *The Expositor's Bible Commentary*, vol. 8, ed. Frank E. Gaebelein (Grand Rapids: Zondervan, 1984), 506–7.

"gospel of the kingdom" (Matthew) will be preached in all the world. Thus, a mission that would take some time seems to be in view in this remark.

So I argue that Jesus did draw on the apocalyptic-eschatological imagery of Judaism for his general portrait of the kingdom, but he also added new imagery to that portrait. Jesus' teaching stressed where the kingdom was headed in the future. It would be a time when God would vindicate his people through the Son of Man and judge the nations. However, other texts hint that this is merely the end of a much longer story. Jesus refused to predict the time of the end, nor did he preach imminence in such a way as to declare that it would come within the generation of the disciples. Signs in their lifetime would and did indicate its approach, but the times and seasons for its coming were known only to the Father.

So Jesus' teaching had roots in Judaism and drew on both strands of Jewish teaching, one arguing that the kingdom would appear in history, and the other that it would remake the world. But what else was fresh about his teaching? This brings us to the disputed topic of the timing of the kingdom's arrival.

The Kingdom's Coming: Present, Future, or Both?

C. H. Dodd's claim for a presently realized kingdom notwithstanding, the bulk of the references to the kingdom look to the future. They treat the consummation of the kingdom, the final judgment, the coming of the Son of Man, the righteous being seated at the banquet table in an era of joy and fellowship, or a period to come when the kingdom is received, inherited, or prepared.[26] The kingdom that Jesus preached was a goal of God's promise and hope that brought deliverance and vindication through the working of God's power. But key to the groundwork for that golden age was the work of one in whom and through whom God was working and would work. It is in this context that the issue of the presence of the kingdom since the time of Jesus' ministry must be raised. The kingdom as future is clear in Jesus' teaching, but is there any sense in which it can be said to have begun?

On one point almost all are agreed: Jesus' message was about the kingdom. He preached the arrival of the eschatological age and its activity of deliverance, contrasting the greatness of the kingdom era with the era of the Baptist, which seemingly had now passed (Luke 4:16–30; 7:22–23, 28 par.; 16:16; Matt. 11:12–14).

26. Jeremias, *New Testament Theology,* 32–34, cites the variety of phrasing that occurs and notes how unique Jesus' teaching within Judaism is in showing such variety of expression. Bruce Chilton, *Pure Kingdom: Jesus' Vision of God* (Grand Rapids: Eerdmans, 1996), 56–101, lays out a summary of this entire teaching along a series of coordinates of themes: eschatology, transcendence, judgment, purity, and radiance. The listing shows the scope of major subtopics that the kingdom theme covers.

Some texts highlight the kingdom's approach or proximity (Mark 1:15; Luke 10:9, 11).[27] The parable of the sower makes it clear that it is the word about the kingdom that is presently sowed (Matt. 13:19). The word is compared to seed. The image extends in other parables to include the image of a mustard seed planted. At the start, it is a tiny seed, but it ends up as a tree in which birds can nest. This cannot be a reference to the apocalyptic kingdom of the end, because that kingdom is decidedly great and comprehensive from its appearing with the Son of Man. Nor can it be a reference to the theocratic kingdom as seen in Old Testament declarations of God's rule, because that cosmic, total rule also has been comprehensive from its inception.[28] What is in view here is the launching of the eschatological kingdom, which surprisingly is "breaking in" in minuscule form. So this parable is our first clue that a "mystery" of the kingdom involves its seemingly insignificant start in the present. Jesus' announcement of its coming and his ministry are like seed going into the ground on its behalf, pointing to its inception. The parable of the leaven makes the same point in distinct imagery.

Equally suggestive about the significance of Jesus' present activity for the presence of the kingdom are the images of Jesus as a bridegroom (Mark 2:18–22 par.), a shepherd (Matt. 9:36 par.; 10:6; Luke 12:32 [cf. Ezek. 34]), and a harvester sending messengers out to reap the harvest (Matt. 9:37–38; Luke 10:1–2), all of which are eschatological images. All of this suggests that if the kingdom has not come, it is very, very close. Note how these texts permeate all the Synoptic Gospels. The kingdom is so close that what the disciples are experiencing is what prophets and kings longed to experience, a clear allusion to the arrival of the hoped-for promise (Luke 10:23–24 par.). The offer of forgiveness that Jesus declares as present is one of the great hoped-for blessings of the new era (Jer. 31:31–33; Mark 2:5; Luke 7:36–50; 19:1–10).

At the center of all of this activity was Jesus. That Jesus could interpret Torah and even explain its scope so that religious practice could change pointed to the arrival of a new era (Matt. 5:21–48; Mark 7:1–23; John 4:20–25). It is true that not all the texts that I have cited mention the term "kingdom," but most do. The other texts that do not use the term are describing the delivering and teaching activity of the one through whom the hoped-for

27. Texts such as these make it clear that whatever is being raised, it is not the universal kingdom of God that declared God's rule in a generic sense or his rule over creation (e.g., Ps. 47; 96). The approach of the kingdom in Mark 1:15 and Matt. 4:17 looks to the approach of something that has not been in place previously and that is longed for and anticipated. Thus, any attempts to make present kingdom texts in the New Testament fit into this more generic category fail. It is an eschatological kingdom that is drawing near.

28. In a sense, the coming of the promised eschatological kingdom makes visible the universal rule that God always possesses in a way that leaves no doubt that he rules. Thus what the "theocratic" Old Testament texts declare will become indisputably obvious when the promised kingdom comes.

promise comes. So one is still in the sphere of discussing the hoped-for kingdom. In Judaism, the kingdom was about the age to come or the messianic
era. Remember that in the Hebrew Scriptures, the expression "kingdom of
God" does not appear, though it is a topic of many other related themes. So
the work of the Messiah qualifies as kingdom work of the promised era, especially given teaching in the parables that the kingdom is being planted in
Jesus' teaching. The fact that this teaching is "new" or a "mystery" does not
alter the fact that it is kingdom teaching connected to the original promise
about the kingdom.

In some texts of Jesus' teaching, the kingdom also comes now, not later.
That the kingdom is not delayed because of Israel's rejection is shown in the
parable of the great banquet (Luke 14:15–24). Here, the refusal by invitees to
come to the celebration when it is announced does not lead to a postpone-
ment of the banquet but to an invitation to others to attend it. Although banquet imagery normally is looking to the future in Jesus' teaching, in this case
it is his preaching and the invitation to experience blessing starting now that
are in view. These texts show that at the heart of the kingdom is the mediating
of promised blessing and deliverance, an exercise of divine power and authority through a chosen, anointed one, who also acts with unique authority.

Among texts that talk about the presence of the kingdom, however, two
stand out: Matt. 12:28 = Luke 11:20; and Luke 17:21. It is in these texts that
two key elements of the kingdom surface, one already made obvious by our
survey, the other focusing on a key element that makes deliverance possible.

In Luke 17:20–21, Jesus declares that one need not go on a search for signs
to find the kingdom. This reinforces a point that he already has raised in his
teaching in the rebuke about being able to read the signs of the weather but
not the signs of the times (Luke 12:54–56 par.). It also parallels the warning
about the sign of his preaching being the only sign that this wicked generation
will have to respond to (Luke 11:29–32 par.). The kingdom does not come,
in this current phase, with such heavenly portents; rather, it is "in your midst."
With all due respect to the NIV, the correct rendering surely is not "within
you."[29] Although linguistically ἐντός can have such a meaning and most often
does, Jesus is not speaking of some potential within each person's heart to establish the kingdom. This reading sounds like the now mostly discredited ro-
mantic notions of nineteenth-century scholars on the kingdom in which
Jesus' work was basically one that changed hearts in a strictly individualized
way. This personalized reading is highly unlikely because Jesus' audience here
is made up of Pharisees. Such heart potential for them does not exist without

29. I also reject the reading of Caragounis, "Kingdom," 423–24, who argues for a reading
of "within you" as a basic expression of the kingdom's internal, dynamic character without requiring it refer to the Pharisees directly. However, this reading ignores who it is that Jesus is
addressing in the context and is not likely. For the linguistic elements of the debate, see the
next note below.

God's powerful work and the effect of his transforming presence. Nor is the kingdom fundamentally so individualized; rather, it is a community to which one belongs. So the point is that in Jesus the kingdom, in a sense, is right in front of their faces. It is "in their midst" or "within their reach." The object of the hunt for that which represents the kingdom's presence and authority stands before them.[30] That Jesus is speaking of the present and not the future becomes clear when the present tense of Luke 17:21 is contrasted with the future perspective of vv. 22–37. Such a reading highlights how Jesus is placed at the hub of kingdom activity, fitting all the other themes of realized promise pointing to Jesus' centrality.

In the second text, Matt. 12:28 = Luke 11:20, Jesus is defending himself against the charge that he casts out demons by the power of Beelzebul. He replies, "If I cast out demons by the Spirit of God [Matthew]/finger of God [Luke], then the kingdom of God has come upon [ἔφθασεν] you." Is Jesus noting that the kingdom has come close to overtaking them or that it has come? The key here is the aorist form of the verb φθάνω. It appears in the Gospels only in this passage. In 1 Thess. 4:15 it means "to anticipate." However, in all its other aorist uses it has the meaning of "has arrived" or "has reached" (Rom. 9:31; 2 Cor. 10:14; 1 Thess. 2:16; Phil. 3:16). It is not synonymous to the earlier declaration that the kingdom of God "has drawn near" (ἤγγικεν).[31] It says more than that the kingdom is near. Contextually, a real exercise of divine power is being defended as visibly present. The image is reinforced immediately in both contexts by the parable of a man overcoming a strong man and plundering his possessions. Jesus is describing what is taking place, not what is approaching. The point is that the miracles are a picture of God's authority and rule working through Jesus to defeat Satan. In other words, the Jewish claim that Jesus does miracles by satanic authority could not be more incorrect.

This saying is significant for a series of reasons. First, it shows that the kingdom is about divine deliverance through Jesus in the releasing of authority that overcomes the presence and influence of Satan. It is an invasion of a realm that this evil one seemingly controls. Jesus is able to exercise such authority now. Jesus' ministry means that Satan already is defeated. The arriving of the

---

30. On the question of whether Greek papyri and other texts evidence a meaning of "amongst," see Kümmel, *Promise and Fulfillment*, 33–36, esp. n. 50. This evidence—texts from Xenophon (*Anabasis* 1.10.3), Herodotus (*Histories* 7.100.3), and Symmachus's translation of Ps. 87:6—challenges Caragounis's claim of the absence of such attestation. Kümmel argues that an objection based on the audience being the Pharisees is not persuasive in arguing against "within you" because we cannot be sure that they are the original audience for this saying. I do not share his skepticism about the setting. Such a challenge to Jesus' opponents fits nicely with many other such challenges pointing to Jesus' centrality in God's work. See also Meier, *A Marginal Jew*, 2:412–23, who defends the authenticity of the saying and discusses its likely Aramaic form.

31. Again, for details, see Kümmel, *Promise and Fulfillment*, 105–7.

kingdom's presence in power is evident. Although the kingdom ultimately includes a much more comprehensive exercise of power, as the future kingdom sayings show, it is operative now in the work of deliverance that Jesus' miracles reflect. A second point also is important. The miracles themselves are not the point, but what they evidence is. A study of Jesus' ministry shows how he worked hard to deflect excessive attention being paid to the miracles. The miracles were "signs," as the Johannine perspective argues. They painted in audiovisual terms the presence of Jesus' authority and victory over Satan. They testified to the authority that Jesus brings. Such power had to be exercised and established for deliverance to take place. So here lies the third point. This passage shows the injection of an apocalyptic theme again into Jesus' kingdom teaching. The kingdom manifests itself as part of a cosmic battle, expressed in dualistic terms, in which God through Jesus is defeating Satan, who himself is doing all he can to keep humanity opposed to God. With the coming of Jesus and the kingdom inaugurated, eschatology has entered into the present. Future hope dawns as present reality, but with much more reality to come.

This account's form reveals its importance. It is a combined miracle and pronouncement account. However, it is unlike most miracle accounts, which spend most of their time on the details of the miracle and little time on the reaction. Rather, this account gives one verse to the healing and then spends all its time on the reaction. That reaction serves as a commentary on the significance of Jesus' miracles as a unit. What emerges is that the kingdom ultimately is about God's work to redeem humanity according to his promise. The kingdom is God's ultimate response to the grip that Satan has on a needy humanity. The kingdom's coming in Jesus' ministry is the inaugurating of that reversal and a manifesting of delivering power. The miracles per se are not the point, but rather, they serve as evidence for and as an illustration of a far more comprehensive deliverance that one day will extend across the entire creation. That is in part why the preaching about the kingdom also was called "good news." Jesus' ministry preached and presented a kingdom hope. That hope had made an appearance through Jesus in the exercise of divine power that served as a kind of cosmic e-mail and invitation to share in what God was doing through this chosen one.

So the kingdom teaching of Jesus involved declarations about both his present ministry and the future tied to it. A kingdom long viewed as strictly future and greatly anticipated was being pulled into the present and made initially available in an exercise of redemptive power that showed that the struggle was not merely with flesh and blood but with principalities and powers. His kingdom, again to use the language of John's Gospel, was not of this world (John 18:36), although it was breaking into this world. Although it would come in comprehensive power one day, it was invading now in Jesus.

Humanity could experience that victory over Satan, both now and in the age to come.

All of this explains a remark that John the Baptist made about "the stronger one to come." Though the remark does not invoke kingdom imagery directly, it does invoke messianic imagery and is a part of a ministry whereby he was preparing people for the coming of the Lord and the kingdom's approach. How would one know that the Messiah had come (and thus that this kingdom promise was arriving)? Luke 3:15–17 answers the question. John explains that he is not the Christ, but that the Christ's coming would be marked out by a baptism different from his own, one not with water but with Spirit and fire. So the new era would be marked by a dispensing of the Spirit, a dispersal of enablement, and a mark of incorporation into the redeemed community of God. The kingdom ultimately is future, but its formation began with the powerful preaching and work of Jesus drawing citizens to the new rule that he was in the process of establishing. But where was the kingdom to be found, and whom would it include?

The Kingdom: God's Presence, a Realm, or Both?

The texts already covered on the presence of the kingdom make it clear that the kingdom can be defined in terms of the dynamic or active presence of God's power and authority. God's rule is expressed in terms of the exercise of his authority. Thus, Jesus' miracles evidence the in-breaking of God's authority, the presence of his power. Jesus' presence as God's unique delivering representative means that the kingdom also is present. I also suggest that the promised mediation of the Spirit through Jesus is evidence of the presence of this rule, since the giving of the Spirit is a key messianic work. This idea is not explicit in the Gospel material, but it does appear in Acts and the Epistles. Most New Testament scholars accept this "dynamic" element as central to Jesus' teaching.[32]

More discussed is the issue of realm.[33] This problem is exceedingly complex because once again Jesus' use shows a variety of contexts. First, several texts indicate that Israel or activity associated with Israel are important elements in kingdom teaching. I already have noted the choosing of the Twelve (Matt. 10:2–4 par.) and Jesus' remark about the disciples sitting on the twelve thrones over Israel (Matt. 19:28–30 par.). Other texts indicate that the disci-

32. A key work arguing this emphasis is Bruce Chilton, *God in Strength: Jesus' Announcement of the Kingdom*, Studien zum Neuen Testament und seiner Umwelt 1 (Freistadt: Plöchl, 1979).

33. It often is said by older dispensational writers that George Ladd denied the presence of an idea of realm in Jesus' teaching because Ladd highlighted the dynamic force. But this characterization is wrong. Ladd simply argued that the dynamic sense was the more prevalent idea in the sayings. See *The Presence of the Future*, 195–205.

ples, after hearing all of Jesus' teaching, still expected a role for the nation of Israel. Acts 1:6 has the disciples ask if Jesus now will be restoring the kingdom to Israel. Jesus, though he does not directly answer the question of when, does not reject the premise of the question. In fact, two chapters later, in Acts 3:21, Peter makes the point that the "times of refreshing" that Jesus will bring on his return, a kingdom theme, already are described in the Scripture.[34] Thus, the eschatological dimensions of the kingdom hope emerging from the Old Testament seem to be affirmed in this Spirit-inspired speech. One final text is associated with the celebratory banquet imagery. Jesus refuses the final cup of wine at the Last Supper and notes that he will not partake of the Passover again until he does so in the context of fulfillment in the kingdom (Luke 22:16–18). Thus, Jesus looks forward to a day when the celebration will commemorate the completion of promise with a celebration rooted in Old Testament expression. Whatever additional elements there are to the kingdom realm (and there are additional elements, as we will see), they do not preclude an element involving the old Israelite expression of hope.

Other texts suggest the language of gathering that includes ethnic Israel. Luke 13:28–29 looks to people coming from "east and west" to sit at the table with the patriarchs. My only point here is that this is standard Jewish imagery.[35] Matthew 8:11–12 is the parallel. It suggests that the surprising inclusion of Gentiles is in view but not the entire exclusion of Israel. After all, the disciples represented a remnant of the nation.

Another key set of texts is Matt. 11:12 and Luke 16:16. Many treat these as parallels and point to the Matthean conflict imagery of people seeking to take the kingdom by violence as key to both texts.[36] My own suspicion is that Luke does not parallel Matthew's conflict imagery here, but points to the persuasion of preaching in his version of the image. However, this exegetical debate does not alter the key point here: the kingdom is a "thing"

---

34. It is texts like these that preclude any appeal to a "sociology of knowledge" as a way of saying that the prophets were limited in what language they could use to express what later developed in their expression of hope. Not only does this sociology view seem to affirm that the Old Testament does not mean what it appeared to mean at the time it was given, but also the question can be raised, Why limit such a hermeneutical category to the Old Testament? A denial of such an appeal means that Israel is a reference to national Israel in such texts. As a result, God's commitment for them is affirmed in such texts.

35. See Dale Allison, *Jesus of Nazareth: Millenarian Prophet* (Minneapolis: Fortress, 1998), 141–43, although he dismisses the significance of the Matthean context too easily to deny a Gentile dimension to this image.

36. In Matt. 11:12, I have in mind the second half of the verse, where people are contending over the kingdom, part of the battle motif. In the first half of the verse, the reference to βιάζεται is disputed. It refers either to the kingdom suffering violence, a reading that matches the latter half of the verse, or to the kingdom advancing. Even if the idea of advance is present, it probably still refers to the in-breaking of the kingdom moving into the world, as opposed to the idea of a continuously ascending advance.

contended over (or preached about), even in the present. The image is of a realm introduced into the world and of an object of contention (and discussion) within it.

Another unusual use is in Luke 23:42–43. Here, the thief on the cross asks to be remembered when Jesus comes into his kingdom. The request, understood in normal Jewish terms, looks to the future. Jesus' reply brings the future into the present yet again because he tells the thief that this very day he will be with Jesus in paradise. Although the reply does not use the term "kingdom," the idea of paradise is a part of that hope in Judaism. There is a sense in which Jesus reveals a current cosmic claim and dimension to the kingdom when it comes to the issue of death. This appears to be another fresh dimension to Jesus' teaching.

Finally, there is the host of texts looking to the judgment of the end, where the Son of Man carries out the eschatological assessment of humanity. I highlight one dimension of one text, the Matthean parable of the wheat and darnel (Matt. 13:24–30, 36–43). Here, Jesus notes that the field is "the world." In that world, good seed has been sown, but the evil one also has sown what has come up as "weeds." Jesus will not sort out grain from weeds until the "end of the age." My point here is that the kingdom, though present in the activity and presence of those sown by the Son of Man (i.e., Jesus), makes a claim on all humanity for which each one will be accountable in the judgment at the end. Thus, there is an aspect of the realm of the kingdom that extends beyond the believing people of God and makes a claim on all humanity in the world, even from the present "sowing" (i.e., preaching) of the kingdom.[37]

Thus, the kingdom in terms of realm operates at several levels at once, depending on the context. The realm in terms of its comprehensive presence looks to the future and the comprehensive establishment of peace and fellowship after a purging judgment. This realm appears to include hopes of old from Israel, yet it also looks to far more, a comprehensive exercise of authority over the whole of creation, including the blessing of many from outside of Israel.

However, there is also a sense in which we can talk about a realm in the present. First, an operative but invisible realm is at work in the community that Jesus is forming, as the power and presence of God is at work among those "sown by the Son of Man." I call it an "invisible" realm because, as the rest of the New Testament indicates, it is a power of God working during Jesus' absence and in anticipation of his visible return and rule. It is the community that recognizes and responds to Jesus as Lord, Son of Man, Christ. It

---

37. In other words, this text is not about some people professing Christendom within what became the church, but about the Word's work in the world and claim upon it through his preached word. Jesus' judgment will cover all people, not just those in the church or those who profess to belong to it. As such, the scope of this text goes beyond any professed Christendom. The field, as Jesus makes clear, is the world, not something that he has gathered out of it.

is the place where he is head. Second, there is a "claimed, potential realm" in that the kingdom makes a claim on the entirety of humanity in anticipation of its eventual scope.[38] That claim is the foundation for the judgment to come. It justifies extending the gospel of the authoritative Jesus to every tribe and nation. It establishes an accountability for every person before the one true God and his chosen one, so that there is only one way to God. In both the invisible presence of God's authority in the reformed community and the claimed, potential presence of divine authority in the challenge to all to respond to God, the future is pulled into the present by the preaching, presence, and challenge of the Son of Man. Responding to him brings one into this new realm, though in other contexts one can speak of entering or inheriting this kingdom later, when it is ultimately fully realized. The exceptional text with the penitent thief on the cross shows that ultimately what is at stake is eternal presence and fellowship with God in unending and renewed life. This final text represents another foretaste of the ultimate, comprehensive victory to come that will be the kingdom "fully and coercively" present, the hope that the majority of kingdom texts in the Gospels affirm.

Thus, the kingdom is about the powerful, even transforming, presence of God's rule through Christ. That rule is expressed today in the community of those whom he "planted," what became the church. But the kingdom is bigger than the church. The kingdom's presence now is but a precursor to a more substantial presence in the future. Jesus will redeem and judge what is being claimed now, when the authority of the Son of Man will judge humanity and bless those who sit with him at the table. Then the kingdom will fully show itself with traits that the Scriptures of Israel had long promised along with features of rule that Jesus himself revealed. The kingdom "invisible," "claiming and potential," and "fully and coercively" present in the future summarizes the way the issue of realm is treated in kingdom texts. In other words, kingdom texts treat Israel, the church, the world, and the cosmos as a whole—it depends on which passage is being considered. Here the "tensive" character of the term "kingdom" becomes obvious. The rest of the New Testament does much to fill in the details of what is outlined here in Jesus' teaching, especially in the eschatological texts of Paul's Epistles and in the Book of Revelation, for Jesus' teaching set certain trajectories in kingdom teaching that the rest of New Testament revelation develops.

In the Gospels, one final issue remains: the connection between righteousness and the kingdom, or what has been called the kingdom and ethics. It is to this topic that we now turn.

---

38. Note how my reading does not limit the authority here to "Christendom." The claim is far more comprehensive in scope than this. The weeds in the world are not a reference to professing Christians, but to humanity at large in the world, including those outside of the sown word that Jesus brings.

Kingdom and Ethics

In the end, the transformation associated with the in-breaking of the kingdom is not merely an abstract exercise in theology or definition. It is designed to impact life. Thus, the connection between kingdom and living or kingdom and ethics needs attention.[39] In this era, the kingdom involves the inaugural in-breaking of God's power, presence, and rule among a people that God has claimed as his own. At the center of this faith and at the core of this promise stands God's work in and through his unique sent representative, Jesus. God through Jesus is forming these disciples into a community that looks forward one day to the total in-breaking of his authority expressed throughout the world. Those who are his have acknowledged their need for God and his provision by faith alone. As a result, they have entered into an enduring relationship with God. That relationship entails a call from God on the life of the disciple. Thus, in a sense, all aspects of Jesus' teaching about discipleship involve teaching about the kingdom and ethics. In sum, what Jesus presents is the idea that the in-breaking of God's rule into one's life demands a total response to that rule. However, by means of God's grace, the disciple is enabled to move into that demand and grow in his or her experience of it. Relationship to that rule is to be more important than family, possessions, vocation, even life itself. So Jesus alludes to the fact that his family is made up of those who do God's will, says that one must hate the family for his sake, teaches that possessions are to be given to the poor, and urges the need to bear one's cross. In sum, Jesus is pointing out that no demand on a person's soul is greater than the one made by God in the context of his kingdom program. It is the greatness of the kingdom that creates the totality of its call for faithfulness.

To develop this area, I examine four themes that ultimately are also tied to the kingdom hope: faith/repentance;[40] following Jesus at all costs by responding from within; imitation in the context of reconciliation, love, and service; and reward. I introduce the themes here and develop some of them later in

---

39. This section is indebted to three studies: Perrin, *The Kingdom of God,* 201–6; Ladd, *The Presence of the Future,* 278–304; and Scot McKnight, *A New Vision for Israel: The Teachings of Jesus in National Context* (Grand Rapids: Eerdmans, 1999), 156–237.

40. I join these two terms into one because they work as equally adequate summary terms for the appropriate response to the message. However, they are not exact synonyms. Repentance looks at that response from the angle of where one starts (there is a change of direction), while faith highlights where one ends up (trusting God). Such terms overlap without being exact overlays, much like a Venn diagram in math. Thus, they can serve as equivalents for each other while focusing on distinct aspects of the fundamental response. Baptism and indwelling are similar. Baptism points to washing, while indwelling points to what results from the washing, the entering in of the Spirit. In Old Testament conceptual terms, forgiveness yields cleansing (or washing), so the Spirit may come in and indwell (Ezek. 36:24–27). God cleanses so that he can enter into a clean space. Careful attention to such lexical relationships adds depth to the text's message.

the section on the new community. Any treatment of kingdom that does not move into this area has failed to appreciate a major practical goal of the kingdom program as the Jesus of Scripture presents it.

1. The theme of faith/repentance is seen in two key elements. First, there is the preparation that John the Baptist brought in declaring that the kingdom draws near. This preparation highlighted preaching a baptism of repentance, a baptism that included a concrete call for turning expressed in practice toward others (Luke 3:10–14). This idea will be taken up more fully when we get to the theme of imitation, but its groundwork was laid in John's initial, preparatory declaration as an Elijah-like figure. His work involved a call to reconciliation in which people were implored to turn back to God. Included within this turning was a bringing of children back to their parents and the disobedient back to the wise (Luke 1:16–17). Reconciliation with God shows itself in reconciliation with others.

The second element is Jesus' teaching that to enter the kingdom one must be like a child (Matt. 18:2–4). Here there is a humility and dependence that is invoked. That humility may well include a "humiliation" that involves suffering and sacrifice. In fact, it is humility that defines "greatness" in the kingdom.[41] In this context, it is clear that it is not the kingdom in the future that is addressed, because the whole of the chapter is looking at relationships in the newly formed community (see Matt. 18:17). Such faith in God extends to a recognition that even daily needs are in his hands and that he will care for his own (Matt. 6:11, 25–34; Luke 11:3; 12:22–31). Faith ultimately is a humble recognition that one needs God and so moves to trust him, relying on his rule and provision. John's Gospel expresses this idea in terms of eternal life and of knowing God and his sent one (John 17:1–3). This knowledge of him takes place in a context in which the world rejects Jesus and the disciples who know him (John 17:4–26). It is in the context of relying on God's provision that the gospel message also moves in a direction that we are most familiar with through the Pauline emphasis on the work of the cross in relationship to sin. However, one should not forget that alongside God's fundamental provision of forgiveness comes an enablement of provision and power through the Spirit that changes one's identity and allows the disciple to live in a way that honors God and reflects a connection to him as his child. In fact, Paul's burden in Rom. 1–8 is to make this very point about the gospel.

2. Following Jesus at all costs by responding from within raises the issue of how demanding Jesus' call to discipleship was. It was a cost to be fully counted and not entered into lightly or unadvisedly (Luke 14:25–35), to borrow a

41. It is probably this note of humility that explains Jesus' focus on reaching out to those on the "fringe" of society, the poor and the tax collectors. Here are people who, as seeming "outsiders," more easily understand their need for God. It is clear that Jesus focused his message toward such people (Luke 4:16–19).

phrase from the initiation of another important relationship. Thus, it is noted in the calls of disciples how they left their nets or tax collection booths to follow Jesus (Mark 1:16–20 par.; Luke 5:28). Jesus expresses it as hating or leaving mother and father for his or the kingdom's sake (Luke 18:29; Matt. 10:37; 19:29). It means hating mammon (Matt. 6:24; Luke 12:14–21; 16:13). It involves carrying the cross, even daily, even at the risk of life (Matt. 10:38–39; Luke 9:23). The assumption in all of this is that the way will not be easy, nor is the road one of powerful triumph. Victory comes through suffering and rejection like that which Jesus himself would experience. Jesus sought to reveal the whole program to the multitudes. He desired that they understand what was involved in the relationship with God that they were entering into. God's rule is not selective; it makes claims on the whole of life. So Jesus defines the members of his family as those who do God's will (Mark 3:31–35 par.; 10:29–30 par.). Sons and daughters respond to the Father. They "seek his kingdom" and rest by faith in his care (Luke 12:31), what Matthew's Gospel calls seeking "first his kingdom and his righteousness" (Matt. 6:33).

Where Mark emphasizes the readiness to serve and suffer by following after Jesus (Mark 10:35–45), Matthew focuses on a practical righteousness that reflects a life of integrity, as the Sermon on the Mount reveals (Matt. 5–7). Luke also has a practical turn, but his emphases focus on the compassionate treatment of enemies (Luke 6:27–36), a concern for the poor (Luke 4:16–18; 7:22–23; 14:12–14), and avoiding the danger of materialism (Luke 8:14; 12:13–34; 16:19–31; 18:18–30; 19:1–10). John's teaching on how disciples might glorify God in faithfulness before a hostile world belongs here (John 14–17).

This following of Jesus also entails a response from within. Mark 7:1–23 shows this clearly when Jesus defines defilement in terms that look at "what is inside" the person. The list highlights those acts that defile as primarily associated with relational categories. The six antitheses of the Sermon on the Mount press the law in this inward direction. It is not just murder but also anger, nor is it just adultery but also lust, that violates God's righteous standard (Matt. 5:21–48). This internal feature stands at the heart of kingdom spirituality[42] and is central to what goes into spiritual formation. That formation is spiritual because God calls and goes to work on the inner person, on our spirit, through the Holy Spirit. This also is not mere triumphalism, as Paul makes clear, since we groan for the completion of redemption in the salvation to come (Rom. 8). In the meantime, the call is to be faithful and walk by the Spirit.

42. For a fine discussion of this theme in light of the Sermon on the Mount, see Dallas Willard, *The Divine Conspiracy: Rediscovering Our Hidden Life in God* (San Francisco: HarperSanFrancisco, 1998).

3. The following of Jesus leads naturally to the theme of imitation. The child is to be like the Father. One dimension of this concept is the theme of reconciliation. We noted reconciliation as a defining quality of a "prepared" people for God. In responding to the Baptist, people were accepting the call of God to be a reflection of him and his holiness. What God would provide through the Messiah, as John noted, would be a greater baptism of the Spirit, one of the great provisions of the new era. That Spirit, by his grace, enables the transformation that God's kingdom calls for from those who trust God to provide for their spiritual well-being and deliverance. Jesus makes the same point in the upper room (John 14–16). So Jesus issues a call to love and serve that is an imitation of God's own character (Luke 6:27–36). This extends even to loving one's enemies. Jesus holds up his own life as the example to be imitated (Mark 10:41–45; John 13:1–17). Such a character is revealed in the Beatitudes (Matt. 5:3–13; Luke 6:20–23). In fact, it is character like this that is salt and light in the world, reflecting the call of what the kingdom citizen is to be (Matt. 5:14–16). So the disciple is to show mercy (Luke 10:29–37). This is why Jesus identified the Jew who quoted the two great commandments of loving God and loving one's neighbor as someone "not far from the kingdom" (Mark 12:28–34). It is also why the commandment to "love one another" was the sign that would identify Jesus' disciples (John 13:34–35). A major goal of the kingdom was to produce children in kind, which is why the standard for character is so high and the demand of the kingdom so great (Luke 6:36; Matt. 5:48).

4. The kingdom is not without its rewards. Chief among them is vindication in judgment and unending relationship with God, as represented in the image of the banquet table. The Father sees the sacrifice and honors it. Such is the promise of Jesus to an uncertain Peter who desperately asks about who can be saved, in the midst of a longer discussion about who can be saved if the rich are not able to enter the kingdom (Luke 18:18–30, esp. 23–30). Jesus' reply assures Peter and those he represents. Jesus summarizes the reward that accompanies participation in the kingdom, saying, "I tell you the truth, no one who has left house or wife or brothers or parents or children for the sake of the kingdom of God will fail to receive many times as much in this age, and in the age to come eternal life." The Markan parallel, which speaks of the gospel and not the kingdom—showing the inherent relationship between the two—adds the note that what is received in the present age is "houses, brothers, sisters, mothers, children, and fields, and with them, persecutions." Matthew 25:31–45 shows that the Son of Man's return in his glory brings with him the vindication of those who have reached out to him. The reward noted in the Beatitudes also underscores that although there is suffering and sacrifice now, there will be great reward. Here again an appreciation for what the future brings impacts how we see ourselves in the present and calls us to live in light of what the future will bring. The future calls on us in the present to re-

flect as light what we are becoming and will be. The meek will inherit the earth, but they also are to illuminate it. With our security resting in God's power, presence, and hope, the rule of God can bring us to be what God made us to be and redeemed us to become. This is precisely why one of the more important parables about the kingdom pictures God's word about the kingdom as a seed that is planted and takes root in good soil and whose goal is to produce fruitfulness (Matt. 13:1–9, 18–23 par.). Viewed from the human perspective, it is the goal of the kingdom to produce sons and daughters of God who are fruitful for him.[43]

One other dimension of reward is less clearly developed and is of lesser significance in Jesus' preaching than the theme of vindication and eternal reception. It is the idea of the future exercise of responsibility for a faithful stewardship. Only a few passages hint at this idea. It is suggested by the note of expanded responsibility in the parable of the talents (Matt. 25:14–30) and the idea of having responsibility over cities in Luke 19:17, 19. The rewarded servants are "set over much" for their faithfulness. The images are specific to the construct of the parable, but they seem to indicate something about reward for stewardship. The reward for the blessed servant in Luke 12:43–44 points in a similar direction. This theme may also be indicated in the note about whether to entrust more to a steward who is irresponsible, in Luke 16:11–12. The sum of this teaching suggests a period when the kingdom will still be at work in the exercise of its rule, themes that may relate to the idea of an intermediate earthly kingdom (or millennium) before the eternal state comes.

It is time to pull together much of what has been said. So now I review the description of the kingdom, noting especially what other terms intimately connect to it. This section is important because it provides a bridge to the rest of the New Testament teaching on the kingdom and the effect of Jesus' life and ministry. So in the next subsection, I treat these implications and note some of the key links to the rest of the New Testament.

Implications of the Kingdom: Messiah, Spirit, Son of Man, Salvation, Gospel, Overcoming Satan, and Sin

One of the difficult things about working with a concept is being confident that the conceptual association made with a biblical term is legitimate. In this section, I want to suggest other issues that connect to the kingdom of God theme. The effect of this is to expand the texts that relate to the kingdom theme, but the justification for doing so needs attention because some argue that tying the kingdom to the Messiah or to the present era reads into the text rather than from it.

---

43. In Pauline terms, this is expressed in terms of the work of God's grace, in the key mission passage of Titus 2:11–14 (see also Eph. 2:10).

The inclusion of the work of the Messiah within the scope of kingdom teaching is challenged by those who note how infrequently the two ideas are juxtaposed in the Gospels or by those who emphasize a definition of the kingdom in terms of its future coercive rule. However, it is Luke who makes the connection by associating the explicit teaching of John the Baptist, as he proclaims the nearness of the kingdom, to remarks that he makes about recognizing when and on what basis the Christ comes (Luke 3:15–17). To his Jewish audience, this association of messianic work with kingdom work and presence would be entirely natural. Jesus' submission to John's baptism means that he embraced John's basic message and connection. One of the signs of the kingdom, or the eschaton, would be the superior baptism that would indicate that the Messiah had come. The allusion here for John the Baptist, given that he speaks as one picking up the prophetic hope, would be the promise of the new covenant. Here, forgiveness and a work of God from within are promised. Jesus says as much in John 3 to Nicodemus. The imagery reflects the images of purity from Judaism. Only a washed and clean vessel can be a place that God inhabits. So the provision of forgiveness and the washing that is pictured in it cleanses the vessel so that God may enter in. It is in this sense that John "prepares" the people for the Lord's coming

It is precisely this promise with this conclusion that Peter preaches in the great sermon at Pentecost (Acts 2:14–41). It is also back to this base event that Peter refers to determine that Gentiles are rightly included in the community by God (Acts 10:34–43; 11:13–18).[44] This baptism marks a definitive sign of the Messiah's work and the presence of eschatological hope. The Spirit came to be seen as the down payment on God's further kingdom work, representing his presence and rule, what Paul simply calls "our inheritance" (Eph. 1:13–14). It is in this cluster of concepts that one can find the connection between not only Messiah and eschaton but also salvation and gospel.

Paul's preaching on the Spirit's work as a part of new covenant realization and Hebrews' emphasis on the forgiveness of sins coming through the promised Messiah fit in here (2 Cor. 3–4; Heb. 1; 8–10). Here is the inaugural era of promise, which Jesus described as kingdom. Here is why Paul could describe the gospel as that which was promised to come through the Son of David in Scripture (Rom. 1:2–4). It is also why Paul called the gospel the "power unto salvation" in Rom. 1:16–17, as an introduction to Rom. 1–8. That book presents the exalted Son's work in terms of forgiveness, filial connection, and Spirit enablement. This combination is the essence of the gospel, a reversal of the penalty and power of sin. It is what Paul calls elsewhere a rescue "out of the authority of darkness" and a transfer "into the kingdom of

---

44. Note the allusion back to Luke 3:15–17 in Acts 11:16, as the indication of promise realized. This emphasis is clearest in Lukan theology and the development of it in Luke-Acts, but the roots go back to themes in Jesus' message.

[God's] beloved Son" (Col. 1:13). Here the work of Jesus as the Christ brings pardon, deliverance, and adoption-citizenship, all royal works of messianic authority.

The kingdom, both in its inception, where rescue takes place, and at its culmination, when victory becomes complete, is part of a great cosmic battle and reversal against sin and Satan. That this kingdom program over which Christ currently is ruling (1 Cor. 15:25; Rev. 1:5–6) is tied and related to the ultimate realization of the kingdom is seen in 1 Cor. 15:26–28, where Paul describes the ultimate giving over of this same kingdom to the Father at the end. Seen in a larger theological context, this victory represents the reversal of the fall's effects and evidence of a cosmic battle introduced in Gen. 3. It is why the imagery of Rev. 21–22 and the new heaven and new earth looks back to the Garden of Eden and forward to the New Jerusalem. The Book of Revelation is about the completion of the kingdom program. In the return, the kingdom of the world has become the kingdom of "our Lord and his Christ" (Rev. 11:15).

This return includes setting up an intermediate kingdom before the new heaven and earth, because of the way Rev. 20 describes this period. In that intermediate kingdom fit the things said about Israel and its future role in a rule existing in the midst of the nations within this history. The promise of God from both Old and New Testaments meets full realization here. It is here as well that Jesus' mix of apocalyptic imagery comes to fruition. Some things involve Israel in this history, while others involve a remade world of the new heaven and earth.

However, for two reasons, much less of this national role for Israel is made in the New Testament than in the Old. First, Israel's role is assumed as a given, having already been revealed and treated in detail in the Hebrew Scriptures, which the church embraced. Acts 3:19–21 points back to Moses and the prophets for "the rest of the story." So the New Testament does affirm that the story about the future has details in it from the Old Testament. Second, the more comprehensive New Testament concern is the eventual total victory that Jesus brings to the whole of humanity and the creation. This relativizes to a degree the importance of national Israel's role in the plan.

Still, it makes more hermeneutical sense for the theological unity of Scripture that the New Testament complements what God already has committed himself to in the Old. Maintaining a role for national Israel within the kingdom program seems to make the most coherent sense of Paul's argument in Rom. 11, where Israel is not a reference to the church, but is treated in distinction from the current structure through which blessing is preached. This approach, known as premillennialism, sees a hope for national Israel (as well as for the nations), with Christ functioning as Israel's Messiah in the future kingdom program. At the same time, this approach affirms the fundamental unity of Jew and Gentile in Christ. This view is a comprehensive approach to the difficult unity-diversity question that plagues debates about eschatology.

There is soteriological unity (all are one in Christ and share in one unified plan), while there is structural distinction in the different dispensations of God's administration (period of Israel ≠ period of the church ≠ period of the consummated kingdom moving to the new heaven and earth). Such an approach is a better synthesis than merging Israel and the church, as much contemporary New Testament theology does, so that the promises made to national and ethnic Israel cease to operate for these original recipients of God's covenantal promise of grace. Such a covenantal merger conflicts with God's faithfulness, which Paul wishes to defend in Rom. 9–11. The apostle maintains hope that one day all Israel will be saved, in contrast to Israel's current rejection of Jesus and the current blessing of many more Gentiles.[45] What God has started in bringing Jew and Gentile together, he will complete one day for both groups.

So, on the future end of the kingdom calendar is the work of the returning Son of Man to be the vindicating "judge of the living and the dead" (Acts 10:42; cf. Matt. 25:31–46). He is the one who welcomes his own into the "prepared-for-you kingdom," in which is found not only fellowship, but also "eternal life" (Matt. 25:34, 46). It is toward this great vindicating moment that the kingdom always is aimed, so that the concept always is looking to that bright future that is the kingdom come in full.

It is this cluster of concepts around the kingdom on which the Epistles draw as they make the point that the era of our rule with Christ has not yet come (1 Cor. 4:8). For example, the author of Hebrews notes that all things are not yet submitted to the feet of humankind as God had promised in Ps. 8:5–7. Nevertheless, he extols that we do see Jesus through the suffering of his death crowned with glory and honor, looking for the completion of what God has begun (Heb. 2:5–9). It is also why Peter, using the language of Ps. 110:1, argues that Jesus, as a result of that exaltation, already is "at the right hand of God, with angels, authorities, and powers made subject to him" (1 Pet. 3:22). Who is right? Is there an incompleteness to what Jesus has done, as Hebrews presents? Or is there an already-extant cosmic subjection, as Peter claims? As with the other tensions noted in the discussion of the kingdom, this is not an either/or, but a both/and. The victory is obtained already, but the full manifestation of that victory is yet to come.[46]

---

45. This paragraph outlines my view on a major debate in eschatology that has been a part of the evangelical scene for a long time. See the discussion between Craig Blaising (premillennialism), Robert Strimple (amillennialism), and Ken Gentry (postmillennialism) in *Three Views on the Millennium and Beyond,* ed. Darrell L. Bock (Grand Rapids: Zondervan, 1999). For more on this question, see Darrell L. Bock, "Why I Am a Dispensationalist with a Small 'd,'" *Journal of the Evangelical Theological Society* 41 (1998): 383–96.

46. A now-famous illustration of "already but not yet" compares the idea to D-Day. The allies "won" the war with that invasion. After that event, victory was inevitable and a matter of time, but the full victory occurred later, when full peace finally came.

The God of the Kingdom: The Father Who Knows, Seeks, Vindicates, Judges, and Is Uniquely the Father of the Son

There is no doubt that Jesus emphasized the sovereignty of the God who brings the kingdom.[47] He is a God who can be trusted and knows the needs of his people (Matt. 6:25–34; Luke 12:22–32). He knows the time of the end (Mark 13:32). For Luke, he is the designer of what "must be" (δεῖ) in the plan of salvation (Luke 4:43; 24:7, 26, 44). The basis of Jesus' suffering and that of the disciples is that the Father knows what is ahead and will provide and protect in the midst of the experience. Jesus' prayer at Gethsemane resolves itself on this point, as does his teaching in the Olivet discourse about how disciples can endure persecution. So God is a God who knows.

But God's great power does not make him distant. It is here that Jesus' teaching on God is its most distinctive. God is "Father" to those who are his (Matt. 6:9; Luke 11:2). Jesus' use of this form of address for God appears in all the Gospel strata.[48] Jesus used this form especially in his prayers (Mark 14:36; Matt. 6:9 = Luke 11:2; Matt. 11:25–26 = Luke 10:21; Luke 23:34, 46; John 17:1, 5). This form of addressing God does not appear in the Old Testament. In Judaism, God often is addressed with his name Yahweh or in light of his promise as the God of Abraham, Isaac, and Jacob, as in benediction 1 of the Jewish community prayer known as the *Shemoneh Esreh*. It is rare as an address in intertestamental Judaism as well (Sir. 23:1, 4; 3 Macc. 6:3, 8; Wis. 14:3). Yet Jesus taught his disciples to appreciate the fact that there is only one who is Father to them (Matt. 23:9).

Even more significant is Jesus' address to God as Father in Mark 14:36 and in Matt. 26:39, 42 ("my" Father). Here, in the tensest moment of his life, as he faces death, Jesus rests in God's tender care, submitting as Son to the sovereign Father. It is in "my Father's kingdom" that Jesus looks forward to the day of full realization (Matt. 26:29). Here is a point of connection between kingdom, God, and Son, resting in an intimacy affirmed even at Jesus' baptism with the divine voice's address of the "beloved Son" and in the recognition that the relationship between Father and Son is unique (Matt. 11:27; Luke 10:21; John 5:17–20). It is in this appreciation of his unique relationship to the Father that the bridge is made to a full understanding of who Jesus is ("my" Father texts: Matt. 7:21; 10:32–33; 11:27; 12:50; 16:17; 18:10, 14, 19; 20:23; 25:34; 26:39, 42, 53; Luke 10:22; 22:29; 24:49; plus 22 occurrences in John). Source levels here include unique Matthean material, unique

---

47. For this section, see George Ladd, *A Theology of the New Testament*, rev. ed. (Grand Rapids: Eerdmans, 1974), 79–88.

48. Jeremias, *New Testament Theology*, 62. In Mark 14:36 (Mark); Matt. 6:9 = Luke 11:2; Matt. 11:25 = Luke 10:21a; Matt. 11:26 = Luke 10:21b (Matthew-Luke teaching material); Luke 23:34, 46 (Luke); Matt. 25:34; 26:42 (Matt.); and John 11:41; 12:27–28; 17:1, 5, 11, 21, 24–25 (John).

Lukan material, and some Matthean-Lukan texts (= Q). The expression is multiply attested.

God also is a God who invites and seeks. This is especially brought out in the parables of Luke 15 and in the nature of Jesus' mission to and befriending of tax collectors and sinners, whereby Jesus sees himself called by God to be a physician to the sick (Mark 2:15–17; Matt. 9:9–13; Luke 5:27–32). The extent of Jesus' initiative to seek the sinner reveals the heart of the God of the kingdom and was unprecedented within Judaism in its emphasis.

The God who invites and fellowships is portrayed above all in the image of the banquet table where many are present, including some who might not be expected to be there (Matt. 22:1–14; Luke 14:15–24; cf. Matt. 8:11). Such associations brought a charge against Jesus that he was a friend of the wrong type of people (Luke 15:1; Matt. 11:19 = Luke 7:34). God's grace extends to those outside the community and is a model for how true "children of God" should act (Matt. 5:45; Luke 6:35–36).

However, that God is gracious does not prevent him from exercising his vindicating judgment. Taking up where John the Baptist left off (Matt. 3:12; Luke 3:7–9), Jesus also affirmed a reckoning with God, a reckoning in which the "Son of Man" would have a key role (Matt. 10:32–33; 11:22–24; 18:6; 23:33; 25:34, 41; Mark 3:29; Luke 10:14–15; 12:4–12). Even Israel and its capital would not be spared for its unfaithfulness in a judgment that was a sign of the coming of the end (Matt. 23:37–39; 24:15; Mark 13:14; Luke 13:34–35; 19:41–44; 21:20–24; 23:27–31). The clearest text is the parable of the judgment of the sheep and the goats (Matt. 25:31–46). In the end, the God of the kingdom will sort out who belongs there from among the nations on the basis of their response to him as seen in their care of those who are his (a view like Gen. 12:3 of Israel). The coming of the kingdom is an opportunity to be blessed and experience God's grace, but it also means that a separation is coming one day to which all will be accountable (Matt. 13:24–30, 36–43). Of all the Gospels, Matthew makes an emphasis of this point.

Summary on the Kingdom

The treatment of Jesus' teaching on the kingdom shows how comprehensive a concept it is for him as well as how it laid the groundwork for much of what we see in the rest of the New Testament. Here was God's promise coming to fruition now in reforming and gathering the righteous to God through the announcement, call, and work of God's unique representative. He was the promised one, bearing the promise and Spirit of God's presence. What Jesus announced and started in almost hidden fashion, he would complete one day in a return when God's rule would decisively enter this history in judgment and prepare the way for a new world. In the meantime, those who allied themselves with Jesus are called to a life of integrity and service as they in faith embrace the hope that Jesus offered and await the completion of the promise.

One final note needs reaffirming about Jesus' kingdom teaching. The discussion of Jesus' teaching on the kingdom has been plagued by an either/or posing of various problems associated with his teaching in the Gospel tradition. Did Jesus declare an apocalyptic or prophetic hope of the kingdom? Did he teach a dynamic presence or discuss a realm of rule? Did his teaching on the kingdom declare its presence already or its coming in the future? As a rule, what this survey has shown is that each way of posing the question risks missing a dimension of Jesus' teaching by forcing a choice. Although one element may receive more emphasis than another in each of these contrasts and in particular texts, Jesus' teaching reflects a depth that encompasses all of these elements.

In Jesus' teaching there is not only a focus on what Jesus preached about the kingdom of God, but also on who the proclaimer of the kingdom is. It is to that matter that we now turn.

Jesus' Titles, Teaching, and Actions: Who Is Jesus?

In modern studies of Jesus, it is much debated how he saw himself. Categories such as a Cynic-like philosopher, charismatic leader, prophet, sage, or messiah are all paraded as the possibilities. The debate is a reflection of how skeptically many view the portraits in the Gospel accounts.[49] My survey of this question seeks to summarize the scriptural data. However, it should be noted that except for the Gospel of John, the key to assembling this portrait of Jesus is not found primarily in the ways Jesus refers to himself. Rather, it is found in what he does and in what those actions both individually and as a group represent. I divide this section into titles and acts, but note that except for the title "Son of Man," the key to the portrait is seen in what Jesus does and what he says about what he does rather than in self-confession.

Titles

Rabbi-Teacher. The term "rabbi" was not a self-designation of Jesus but a way of addressing him used by others who respected his teaching. Thus, Mark

49. In thinking of discussions of the historical Jesus that closed out the twentieth century, we see that the spectrum of options is rather full: the Cynic-like philosopher of Crossan, to Hartmut Stegemann's charismatic leader, to Witherington's sage, to the prophetic reforming figure of Sanders, to Allison's millenarian prophet, to the probably messianic figure of Meier, to Wright's messianic reformer who has a central role in God's program in fulfillment of God's promise to return to Zion and save Israel and reach the world in line with covenant promise. See Mark Allan Powell, *Jesus as a Figure in History: How Modern Historians View the Man from Galilee* (Louisville: Westminster/John Knox, 1998).

uses it in 9:5; 10:51; 11:21; 14:45. John has it in 1:38, 49; 3:2, 26; 4:31; 6:25; 9:2; 11:8; 20:16. In Matthew, only Judas in the midst of his act of betrayal calls Jesus "rabbi" (Matt 26:25, 49). Luke opts for the term "teacher" four times (7:40; 11:45; 12:13; 19:39), probably in deference to his non-Jewish audience. Luke never has disciples call Jesus this, but those who observe him. He prefers the term "master" from those who follow Jesus (5:5; 8:24 [twice], 45; 9:33, 49; 17:13). Mark also uses the alternative title "teacher" ten times in the form of an address, with everyone from opponents to disciples addressing Jesus this way (Mark 4:38; 9:17, 38; 10:17, 20, 35; 12:14, 19, 32; 13:1). John also notes this alternative from both believers and observers (1:38; 3:2; 8:4; 11:28; 13:13–14, with a reference to "lord" as well; 20:16). The address of Jesus in this way shows how important his teaching was to his ministry, but the preferred expression in Luke from the disciples makes it clear that there was an authority represented here that made this description only an aspect of his identity. The observation that Jesus taught with an unusual authority also points in this direction, especially when that teaching also is tied to acts such as exorcism (Mark 1:27 [tied to exorcism]; Matt. 7:29 [not as one of the scribes]). The personal authority embedded in Jesus' teaching is expressed clearly in the image of the man who builds his house either on the sand or on the rock because it is *Jesus'* teaching that the wise person responds to and the fool ignores (Matt. 7:24–27; Luke 6:46–49).

Prophet. The idea that Jesus was a prophet apparently was the most common way for the unresponsive populace to view him (Matt. 16:14; 21:11; Mark 8:28; Luke 7:16; 9:19; 24:19). The combination of his teaching and public activity made them think of Jesus as more than a teacher. Whether he was compared to Elijah (Mark 6:15; Luke 9:8) or to the return of John the Baptist, or to a prophet in general, there was a recognition that God was involved in his message. In Luke, Jesus does not discourage this association. In the unique scene of the synagogue message (Luke 4:16–30), Jesus speaks of himself in these terms, comparing himself to a "prophet without honor" in his hometown as well as to Elijah and Elisha. That text also mixes in potential messianic imagery in the invocation of the Servant portrait from Isa. 61:1–2 and its tie to Jesus' earlier anointing at the baptism. Much of Jesus' activity, especially as he travels to Jerusalem in Luke, has this prophetic feel. However, it is more in the sense of a leader-prophet like Moses, a category that borders on royal-political emphases.[50] Hints of this exist when Jesus declares John to be the last of the great prophets (Luke 7:26; 16:16; Matt. 11:11–15) and then speaks of the coming of the kingdom. Jesus as a prophet announces and leads

---

50. David Moessner, *Lord of the Banquet: The Literary and Theological Significance of the Lukan Travel Narrative* (Minneapolis: Fortress, 1989); Scot McKnight, "Jesus and Prophetic Actions," *Bulletin for Biblical Research* 10 (2000): 197–232, contains a full taxonomy on Old Testament prophetic actions, those of Moses, and those of first-century popular-movement prophets.

into the kingdom era, but in leading the way to the new era, he shows himself to be far more than a prophet. He is greater than Jonah the prophet or Solomon the royal sage (Matt 12:40–42; Luke 11:29–32). John pointed to the eschaton; Jesus brings its inauguration.

Son of David. The infancy material of both Matthew and Luke makes a major point of Jesus' association to David and his messianic position, but in this section we focus on Jesus' own teaching and the events of his ministry. This heading includes not only texts tied to the naming of "Son of David" but also the use of the royal psalms with reference to Jesus. As such, this category takes on a significant place in teaching about Jesus and overlaps with the reference to the Messiah in the next subunit. It is here that the heavenly voice at Jesus' baptism marks him out as "Son," using Ps. 2, one of the great royal psalms of promise and regal affirmation.

Interestingly, it is especially people in Jesus' audiences, who no doubt long for God's deliverance, that use this title of him. So a blind man cries out for the Son of David to give him sight (Mark 10:46–52; Matt. 20:29–34; Luke 18:35–43). This linkage of Jesus' kingship and healing as Son of David may reach back to traditions about Solomon as exorcist and healer (Josephus, *Ant.* 8.2.5 §§45–46; Wis. 7:17–22, presented as Solomon speaking; of David himself: Pseudo-Philo, *Biblical Antiquities* 60.1–3). The title or image is raised in the voices of the disciple-pilgrims who enter Jerusalem (Mark 11:10 [kingdom of our father David]; Matt. 21:9, 15 [Son of David]; Luke 19:38 refers only to "the king"). Matthew highlights the title in describing Jesus (1:1; 9:27; 12:23; 15:22; 21:9, 15).

The key text, however, is Mark 12:35–37a (= Matt. 22:41–46; Luke 20:41–44). Here, Jesus raises a question about the significance of the name "Son of David" and ties it to a discussion of David's addressing this one as "Lord," through appeal to Ps. 110:1. The passage's point again shows how "Son of David," though a messianic title to be accepted, is not as important as the recognition that this one is acknowledged by his father David as "Lord." Jesus poses the dilemma of how in a patriarchal society a son can possess such authority over a father. The riddle is left unanswered except to suggest that "Son of David" is a title of lesser significance than the authority even an ancestor grants to the king to come. Once again an acknowledged description is accepted but also is shown as ultimately inadequate.

Messiah, King of the Jews. The title "Christ" is one that all the Gospels use within their narratives (Matt. 1:16; 2:4; 11:2; Mark 1:1; Luke 2:11, 26; 4:41; 23:2; 24:26, 46; John 1:17; 1:41; 3:28; 4:29; 7:26–42; 10:24; 11:27; 12:34; 17:3; 20:31). The titulus on the cross marking Jesus out as "King of the Jews" moves in this direction as well (Mark 15:26, 32; Matt. 27:37; Luke 23:38; John 19:19).[51]

---

51. The nature of Jewish messianic expectation is discussed in chapter 4 of my *Studying the Historical Jesus* (Grand Rapids: Baker, 2002).

Seven scenes here are key. First is Peter's confession at Caesarea Philippi, where the Synoptics share the christological core of the key disciple's confession. Jesus accepts this utterance, especially as it stands in contrast to the populace's view of him as being only a prophet. However, Jesus also redefines the confession quickly in terms of his approaching suffering, so that the term is not merely one of glory but takes on overtones of the Servant who suffers as well (Matt. 16:13–23; Mark 8:27–33; Luke 9:18–22). The need to explain who he is leads Jesus here and in several other places to restrict making a point of the title publicly (Mark 1:25 = Luke 4:35; Mark 1:34; 3:12 = Matt. 4:16; Mark 1:44 = Matt. 8:4 = Luke 5:14; unique to Mark: 8:30; 9:9 [the Lukan parallel in Luke 9:36 notes only that they said nothing but does not explain why]).

Second is the Pharisees' attempt to get Jesus to rebuke his disciples for their confession of him as king, a scene unique to Luke (19:39–40). Here Jesus refuses to stop them and says that if they did not speak, creation would.

Third is the scene at Jesus' examination before the Jewish leadership (Matt. 26:57–68; Mark 14:53–65; Luke 22:66–71). Here the question about whether Jesus is the Christ eventually evokes a positive, though qualified, response from Jesus in terms of exaltation, appealing to the Son of Man image and the picture of one at God's right hand from Ps. 110:1, another royal psalm. This affirmation not only of Jesus' messianic authority but also of his exaltation to authority at the side of God, implying his shared equality, is judged to be blasphemous. Thus, the public acknowledges Jesus' claim of a messianic role by the end of his ministry.

Fourth is the emphasis that emerges at the examination by Pilate, whether one works with the Synoptics or John (Matt. 27:11–14; Mark 15:2–15; Luke 23:2–5; John 18:29–38). These accounts all focus on the discussion that Jesus was "King of the Jews," a point reinforced by the charge on the placard attached to the cross. The discussion makes sense, since Pilate would not be interested in a religious dispute over Jesus' claims, but if they had political overtones, then as governor he would need to protect the interests of Caesar. Jesus accepts the title, although with an affirmation that suggests that he views it differently from Pilate (Mark 15:2 = Matt. 27:11 = Luke 23:3). In this context, the confession is virtually messianic.

As we turn to examples from John, Jesus is more direct. Fifth is the discussion in John 4, where Jesus reveals himself as the Messiah to the Samaritan woman. Sixth is the discussion with the blind man and his family in John 9, where the confession of Jesus as the Christ has yielded a reaction from officials to expel those who make the confession. Seventh is Martha's confession of Jesus to be the Christ, the Son of God, who comes into the world (John 11:27). This is her response when Jesus raises the issue of his authority over resurrection. The Johannine texts all are ways of affirming Jesus as the unique and promised sent one of God.

Other Titles: Servant, Holy One, Shepherd. These remaining titles can be treated more briefly because their explicit use is not that common. The title "Servant" comes only in narrative remarks (Matt. 12:18 in its use of Isa. 42:1–4). However, aspects of the description of the Servant appear as allusions in several key texts. The voice at the baptism calls Jesus "the Beloved" in allusion to Isa. 42:1 (Matt. 3:17; Mark 1:11; Luke 3:22), a remark repeated at the transfiguration (Mark 9:7; Matt. 17:5; Luke 9:35). The death of Jesus is associated with sacrifice in language that looks at Isa. 53 in the Last Supper, in all likelihood in the ransom saying (Matt. 20:28; Mark 10:45), and in Jesus being reckoned among criminals at his death (Luke 22:37). Again, the title is not one that Jesus himself confesses but is tied to actions that raise the imagery.[52] Many connect the emphasis on the idea of Jesus having to suffer as the Christ with this image of the Servant who suffers.

The Johannine equivalent of Caesarea Philippi is Peter's confession at the end of John 6 that Jesus is "the Holy One of God" who has the words of eternal life (John 6:68–69). This is another way to say that he is the promised one who brings the life of deliverance. Mark and Luke also use this title in the confession by demons (Mark 1:24; Luke 4:34). Again, the description is found on the lips of one trying to affirm who Jesus is and by cosmic enemies.

A key image of a leader-king of the people is "the Shepherd." One can think of 2 Sam. 7:8, where the hope of Davidic kingship is introduced. One can also reflect on the role of leader of the people in the rebuke of Ezek. 34, which leads to the declaration that God will shepherd his people one day and give them a royal shepherd of righteousness (Ezek. 34:11–12, 23–24). It is this image that stands behind Matthew's observation that what motivated Jesus was that he saw people who were like sheep without a shepherd (Matt. 9:36). It also is key to the imagery of John 10, where Jesus refers to himself as the good shepherd. This is a role that Jesus views as central to his call.

Thus, these three titles are other ways to refer to Jesus as the unique one sent by God, the promised Christ.

Lord. This title was key in the early church, but it appears less prominently in the Gospels. Often it is merely a vocative of address (like "sir"), a title of respect where the person's exact view of Jesus is unclear (Matt. 15:27; 18:21; Mark 7:28; Luke 7:6; 9:59; 11:1; 12:41). It also appears frequently in Luke as a narrative description for Jesus (Luke 7:13, 19; 10:1; 13:15, 23; 17:5; 18:6;

---

52. On the importance of this imagery, see William H. Bellinger and William R. Farmer, eds., *Jesus and the Suffering Servant: Isaiah 53 and Christian Origins* (Harrisburg, Pa.: Trinity Press International, 1998). Note especially in that volume the essay by Otto Betz, "Jesus and Isaiah 53," 70–87. Betz argues for the backdrop of Isa. 52:14 and 53:1 in the remarks that Jesus makes at his anointing by the woman at Bethany in Matt. 26:13 and Mark 14:9, as well as in John 12:32–38 in the idea of the Son of Man being lifted up. The first of these allusions is less than clear. More solid are appeals to Jesus' allusion to Isa. 53 in Mark 10:45 and 14:22–24. Betz defends the authenticity of these sayings while making his case.

24:3). The last example in Luke is important because it and 24:34 show that this title became associated with Jesus' resurrection. It is the Lord who was raised.

In other texts, it is clear that the title points to Jesus' stature, but just what it confesses is unclear. So when Peter bows before Jesus to confess himself as a sinful man, it suggests Jesus' holiness and association with God as a revealing agent (Luke 5:8). In Matt. 7:21, those who confess Jesus as Lord but fail to do what he commands are rebuked. In Matt. 21:3 = Mark 11:3 = Luke 19:31, the man supplying the donkey for the entry into Jerusalem is told, "The Lord has need of it." Again, exactly how Jesus is seen is unclear.

Two Synoptic texts are more important. One is the already-discussed treatment of "Son of David" versus "Lord" in Matt. 22:45 = Mark 12:37 = Luke 20:44. Here it is clear that Jesus intends "Lord" to be a key title and that it is associated with the exalted imagery of Ps. 110:1, where this figure sits at God's right hand. This imagery became connected with the resurrection-ascension in the early church. As a result, Jesus' lordship became associated with his position at God's side. The other text is Mark 2:28 = Matt. 12:8 = Luke 6:5, where Jesus is "Lord of the Sabbath." Here as well the title points to a comprehensive kind of authority that extends even over the commanded day of rest. The implications of this kind of act will be developed in the section on Jesus' actions.

The title "Lord," though rarely used in the context of Jesus' ministry in the Synoptics, suggests the presence of one with divine authority and one who is close to God. Interestingly, John's Gospel has a similar thrust. In the three uses in John 1–19 (4:1 [variant reading]; 6:23; 11:2), it is simply a narrative remark from the evangelist. In addition, others address Jesus as "Lord," but in most cases in a way that is not clear as to exactly what is meant (John 4:11, 15, 19, 49; 8:11; 9:36, 38 [in connection with confession of Jesus as Son of Man]; 11:3, 12, 21, 27 [tied to confession of Jesus as Christ and Son of God], 32, 34, 39; 12:21; 13:6, 9, 13–14, 37; 14:5, 8, 22). Like the use of "Lord" in Luke, John also focuses frequently on this title in discussing the resurrection. It appears fifteen times in two chapters, more than half being descriptions of Jesus, not addresses of respect to him (John 20:2, 13, 18, 20, 25, 28; 21:7 [twice], 12). None is more important than when Thomas cries out, "My Lord and my God!" upon seeing the risen Jesus. Here the term takes on its full meaning, a sense that it clearly also had in the early church. What is amazing is how restrained this usage is within the events of Jesus' life for a tradition that many critics argue is full of later Christology inserted into the Gospel tradition. The restraint may well suggest that the Gospels do not express Christology as anachronistically as some critics argue.

Son of God. The term "Son of God" is full of ambiguity because of its potential royal implications through the imagery of 2 Sam. 7 and the royal psalms, such as Ps. 2. As such, the term is a good bridge term, as we will see with "Son of Man." In the Synoptics, Jesus does not use this full phrase for himself, although he does speak of himself as "Son" in several texts. The title appears nine times in John's Gospel: 1:34 (a confession by John the Baptist); 1:49 (part of a confession by Nathanael in a messianic context); 3:18 (a narrative remark); 5:25 (in a major discourse on the Father-Son relationship); 10:36 (a cause for Jesus being accused of blasphemy); 11:4 (the recipient of glory to come from Lazarus's illness); 11:27 (part of a confession by Martha); 19:7 (a reason for Jewish leaders wanting to kill Jesus); 20:31 (a narrative remark).

More frequent in the Gospels is the designation of Jesus by others as "Son" or "Son of God." It comes in a variety of settings and from a variety of sources. We already have noted its use by the divine voice at Jesus' baptism and transfiguration. Luke 9:35 uniquely notes that this means that Jesus is the one who "stands chosen." "Son of God" also is the major title of focus at the temptations (Matt. 4:1–11; Luke 4:1–13). Demons also confess Jesus as the Son of God (Matt. 8:29 = Mark 5:7 = Luke 8:28 [Mark and Luke speak of the "Son of the Most High God"]; Luke 4:41). The Luke 4:41 text is significant because it ties the title to Jesus' messianic position as the Christ in an explanation unique to his account. Sometimes the suggestion is made that the Son of David or the Messiah is an earthly authority, while the Son of God is more cosmic and tied to spiritual forces.[53] However, texts such as Luke 4:41 or the healing of the blind man by Jesus as Son of David make such a clear distinction unlikely. What is more likely is that the title "Messiah," which could be understood in strictly earthly terms, is raised to new levels in its association with sonship in the way Jesus eventually discusses it. Interestingly, the only person to call Jesus "Son of God" in Mark is the centurion at the cross (Mark 15:39), a note that Matthew also shares (Matt. 27:54).[54]

Jesus also uses "Son" as a major self-designation. A key text is Matt. 11:25–27 = Luke 10:21–22. Jesus as Son is the unique revelator of God, giving knowledge of the Father of which only he can be the mediating source to others. This use of the title is saved for the disciples until later in Jesus' ministry. This use of the term is like the one so prominent in John's Gospel, where John calls Jesus the "Word" and also speaks of his key role in revealing the way of the Father in several texts (John 3:14–36; 5:9–27; 6:40; 8:36; 14:13; 17:1). In fact, John 5 presents the Father and the Son as inseparable in will and action. In contrast to the Synoptics until the last week of Jesus' ministry, John has Jesus speak of himself explicitly as Son throughout his ministry.

53. This appears to be suggested in remarks by Goppelt, *Theology of the New Testament,* 200.

54. Mark lacks a reference to Jesus as "Son of God" at Caesarea Philippi that Matt. 16:16 has. Matthew also has the title uniquely as a confession by the disciples at the stilling of the storm (14:33) and in the mocking of Jesus by the passersby, chief priests, and scribes while he hangs on the cross (27:40, 43).

A second key Synoptic text is the imagery involved in the parable of the wicked tenants (Matt. 21:33–41 = Mark 12:1–12 = Luke 20:9–19). Here it is the leadership's rejection of the Son that is prominent. He is the last and the highest figure in a line of servants (prophets) whom God has sent to Israel to look for fruit from the nation. However, even his unique status as Son does not protect him. He is slain. Here, Jesus goes public in the capital with his claim of sonship and notes that it has not been accepted. Yet the force of the remarks assumes that he has portrayed himself this way already, for otherwise Jesus' allusion to himself as the "beloved son" (Mark and Luke) or "heir" (Matthew) does not make sense. Yet vindication comes for the Son; the Father will judge the rejection, a point that Jesus makes by appealing to Ps. 118:22 in a sense that portrays Israel's leadership as enemies of God.[55]

Of course, Jesus' language of God as "my" Father also belongs here. These notes about sonship have multilayered attestation, appearing in Markan, Matthean-Lukan, Matthean (confessions by others only at this level), and Johannine material.

A final key text is the one at Jesus' examination by the Jewish leadership. They ask Jesus whether he is the "Son of the Blessed One" (Mark 14:61) or "Son of God" (Matt. 26:63, where Matthew uses a more direct reference to God). Luke has this question in his trial scene in a slightly later spot during the interrogation (Luke 22:70). In all three Synoptics, the title appears to be a synonymous appositive to "Christ" in this scene, but that conclusion is not entirely certain. Jesus' reply is qualified in Matthew and Luke but is basically positive. The qualification appears to suggest that Jesus is affirming the title but with a different, more significant meaning than the question from the leadership suggests. In Mark, the reply comes as a simple yes. Jesus' larger response makes it clear how comprehensively he views the term. In the context of all three replies comes Jesus' affirmation that he will be at the right hand of God, reinforcing his claim to authority as Son. Luke's summary has the confession as a confirming remark, while Matthew and Mark use it as an introduction to the allusions to Ps. 110:1 (Jesus to be seated at the right hand) and Dan. 7 (Son of Man [all]; coming on the clouds [Matthew and Mark]). It is this reply that leads the leadership to regard Jesus to be blaspheming. Sonship at the side of God was something they could not see as possible for Jesus and a claim that had to be totally rejected. It is the issue of Jesus' authority and proximity to God that eventually was the affirmation that led to his death. Thus, although "Son" and "Son of God" are used restrictively in the Synoptics, their appearance both in the Synoptics and in John gives rise to much controversy about Jesus. The combination of royal role and divine intimacy wrapped up in the references make "Son of God" an important title, but the most significant title of all for Jesus is the last one we examine, "Son of Man."

---

55. The reversal of the past reading, in which Israel was on the blessed side of the psalm, shows how transforming a decision about Jesus is. A similar reversal shows up in the church's use of Ps. 2 in Acts 4.

The titles "Son of God" and "Son of Man" are important in understanding Jesus. As a result of the resurrection-ascension and what that exaltation means for who Jesus is, the early church developed an understanding of Jesus early on as sharing in the divine identity.[56] He was not only "son" functionally; he really was the only Son. Texts that point to Jesus' absolute authority (Phil. 2:5–11; 1 Cor. 8:6; Rom. 9:5; Heb. 1:5–14; Eph. 1:21–22; Rev. 4–5) or that speak of him as Son in connection with the Father and the Spirit (Matt. 28:19–20) reflect this acknowledgment of the total authority of the one who is the Son. In these texts, what was implied in Jesus' life and activity in being the Son and carrying a unique authority becomes explicit. The bridge now fully crossed through the divine vindication that raised the Son to God's side shows that John's explicit prologue is a natural conclusion about who Jesus was and is.

Son of Man. This title represents Jesus' favorite self-designation. In fact, this title is prevalent in a variety of ways. First, it is almost always on the lips of Jesus. Of its 82 appearances in the Gospels, only John 12:34 has it on someone else's lips. The term appears 30 times in Matthew, 14 times in Mark, 25 times in Luke, and 13 times in John. Apparently, there are 51 different sayings involved in this number,[57] with 14 of them rooted in Mark, 10 involving Matthean-Lukan teaching material, 8 peculiar to Matthew, 7 peculiar to Luke, and 13 found in John.[58] Matthew has several texts on his own (Matt. 10:23; 13:37, 41; 16:28; 24:30, 39; 25:31; 26:2). Luke has several as well (Luke 12:8; 17:22; 18:8;

56. For a presentation of this emphasis on Jesus sharing the divine identity as part of a very early high Christology in the early church, see Richard Bauckham, *God Crucified: Monotheism and Christology in the New Testament* (Grand Rapids: Eerdmans, 1998). This study has some important corrections to offer on how New Testament Christology is handled by many in New Testament studies. The importance of what the resurrection-ascension taught the early church is well balanced in Bauckham's approach, as is his emphasis on how suffering connects to the divine identity.

57. I use the term "apparently" because there is debate about which sayings are parallel and which are unique. Here is the list of texts where "Son of Man" appears: Matt. 8:20; 9:6; 10:23; 11:19; 12:8, 32, 40; 13:37, 41; 16:13, 27, 28; 17:9, 12, 22; 19:28; 20:18, 28; 24:27, 30 (twice), 37, 39, 44; 25:31; 26:2, 24 (twice), 45, 64; Mark 2:10, 28; 8:31, 38; 9:9, 12, 31; 10:33, 45; 13:26; 14:21 (twice), 41, 62; Luke 5:24; 6:5, 22; 7:34; 9:22, 26, 44, 58; 11:30; 12:8, 10, 40; 17:22, 24, 26, 30; 18:8, 31; 19:10; 21:27, 36; 22:22, 48, 69; 24:6–7; John 1:51; 3:13, 14; 5:27; 6:27, 53, 62; 8:28; 9:35; 12:23, 34 (twice); 13:31.

58. Jeremias, *New Testament Theology*, 260. Jeremias later (pp. 262–63) reduces the number of authentic sayings by arguing that thirty-seven of the fifty-one Gospel sayings have parallels in which the term is missing or has "I" in its place. Jeremias argues by using the sequence of Markan priority as key. But even if this is the order of the Gospels, matters are not so simple. Is it not more likely that a Gospel writer would remove or simplify the reference to a title that has fallen out of use than to introduce it into the tradition to give it an archaic feel? Furthermore, even if Jeremias is right on some of the examples, turning a direct reference to Jesus into a Son of Man saying or omitting the title still makes the same conceptual point. It still leaves us in touch with Jesus' historical teaching because the ideas were synonymous, given that Jesus was the Son of Man. For these reasons I question his reducing the number of these sayings that go back to Jesus, even if some of the sayings have differences with some of their parallels at this point. All that these differences might show is that in some texts the title "Son of Man" was lacking, but not necessarily what the concept indicated.

19:10; 21:36; 22:48; 24:6–7). This means that the expression has multiple attestation. All of John's 13 sayings are unique to his Gospel.

These sayings in the Synoptics have been divided up into three subclasses: sayings about Jesus' present ministry (17 passages total), sayings about his suffering (26 passages total), and sayings about his role in the end, called apocalyptic sayings (27 passages total).[59] Each type is well distributed across each Gospel, but with varying emphasis, depending on the Gospel. Matthew has 7 present-ministry sayings, 10 suffering sayings, and 13 apocalyptic sayings. Mark, known for emphasizing Jesus' suffering, has 3 present-ministry sayings, 9 suffering sayings, and 3 apocalyptic sayings. Luke has 7 present-ministry sayings, 7 suffering sayings, and 11 apocalyptic sayings. For John, the subdivisions are different in terms of topic. He has 4 sayings that speak of the coming and going of the Son of Man, 6 sayings that treat crucifixion and exaltation, 1 that names him as judge, and 2 as salvation bringer.

The key to this title and Jesus' use of it is the imagery from Dan. 7:13–14, where the term is not a title but a description of a figure who rides the clouds and receives authority directly from God in heaven.[60] This Old Testament background to the title does not emerge immediately in Jesus' ministry, but is connected to remarks made to disciples at the Olivet discourse and Jesus' reply at his examination by the Jewish leadership. The title is appropriate because of its unique fusion of human and divine elements. A "son of man" is simply an expression that describes a human being. In contrast to the strange beasts of Dan. 7, this is a figure who is normal, except for the authority he re-

59. Some of these classifications for a particular saying could be debated or in a couple of cases reflect a mixture of categories so they count a couple of times, leading to the extra number of passages. Working with sayings units, not counting total references, Ladd (*Theology of the New Testament,* 148–49) has a useful chart of the Synoptic Son of Man sayings. His count: 10 earthly (2 Markan; 3 Q [= material common to Matthew and Luke]; 2 M [= material unique to Matthew]; 3 L [= material unique to Luke]); 9 suffering (3 Markan; 1 Q; 1 Mark-Luke; 4 Mark-Matthew); 18 apocalyptic (3 Markan; 3 Q; 7 M; 5 L). Ladd offers a good discussion of these titles on pp. 143–47, with bibliography.

60. For more on this background, see discussions of Mark 13:26 = Matt. 24:30 = Luke 21:27, and Mark 14:62 = Matt. 26:64 = Luke 22:69. The bibliography and debate surrounding this title is immense. For two other discussions surveying this background and debate, see Darrell L. Bock, "The Son of Man in Luke 5:24," *Bulletin for Biblical Research* 1 (1991): 109–21; idem, *Blasphemy and Exaltation in Judaism and the Final Examination of Jesus,* WUNT 2.106 (Tübingen: Mohr, 1998), 224–30, which defends the authenticity of the key Son of Man saying at the Jewish examination of Jesus. Some critics try to divide the sayings up into classes and then challenge them, as well as reject the more biblically explicit texts tied to Dan. 7 as being products of the early church, on the premise that they are too developed to be authentic. However, given the evidence that Jesus used the title so extensively, it is hard to believe that he did not root it in a biblical backdrop. The rejection of these sayings is hypercritical, taking a "divide and conquer" approach to an expression that is solidly multiply attested. Key here also are two Jewish texts: *1 Enoch* 37–71 and *4 Ezra* (= 2 Esdras) 13. They also foresee a figure who exercises judgment in the end, showing that the concept was "floating around" in or near this period.

ceives. In riding the clouds, this man is doing something otherwise left only to the description of divinity in the Old Testament (Exod. 14:20; 34:5; Num. 10:34; Ps. 104:3; Isa. 19:1). In addition, the title was in Aramaic an indirect way to refer to oneself, making it a less harsh way to make a significant claim. Despite its indirectness, the nature of Jesus' consistent use of the term makes it clear that he was referring to himself, not someone else.

All this data shows how widespread this concept was for Jesus, covering the entire realm of his present and future ministry. In his earthly ministry, the Son of Man has authority to forgive sins (Mark 2:10 par.), is Lord of the Sabbath (Mark 2:27 par.), comes eating and drinking in lifestyle (Matt. 11:19 = Luke 7:34), and has nowhere to lay his head (Matt. 8:20 = Luke 9:58). A word against him can be forgiven (but forgiveness is not available to one who blasphemes the Spirit's testimony about him [Matt. 12:32 = Luke 12:10]). He sows good seed (Matt. 13:37), but persecution results from his presence (Luke 6:22). He comes to seek and save the lost (Luke 19:10). When Judas betrays Jesus with a kiss, it is the Son of Man who Jesus notes is being betrayed (Luke 22:48).

The suffering Son of Man appears most in passion predictions that he will suffer (Mark 8:31; 9:12, 31 [delivered into human hands]; 10:33 [delivered and condemned]; 14:41 par.; Matt. 12:40 = Luke 11:30 [three days in the earth]). Silence about the transfiguration is commanded until the Son of Man is risen (Mark 9:9). The Son of Man came to serve and give his life as a ransom for many, stated in a key text that may well also allude to Isa. 53, thus combining Son of Man and Servant references (Mark 10:45 = Matt. 20:28). He is betrayed to sinners (Mark 14:41 = Matt. 26:45).

The apocalyptic sayings highlight his coming with the angels, on the clouds, or seated at God's side, all focusing on the heavenly authority that he possesses (Mark 8:38 par; 13:26 par.; 14:62 par.; Matt. 13:41). He comes at an unknown time (Luke 12:40 = Matt. 24:44). Like lightning, he comes illuminating all (Luke 17:24 = Matt. 24:27). Like the flood in the days of Noah, he comes suddenly and catastrophically (Luke 17:26 = Matt. 24:37). He comes with angels (Matt. 13:41), on a throne (Matt. 19:28), with the heavens shaking (Matt. 24:30), and in glory (Matt. 25:31). It is in these terms that the powerful coming in judgment is described (Matt. 24:39; Luke 17:30). The mission to Israel will not be done before the Son of Man comes (Matt. 10:23). Yet some will not die before they see the Son of Man in glory (a reference to the transfiguration as a precursor to the final glory [Matt. 16:28]). The Son of Man will acknowledge before the angels those who acknowledge him (Luke 12:8). But there will be enough delay that the question remains whether the Son of Man will find faith by the time he comes (Luke 18:8). The disciples' prayer is to be that they will prove faithful in the face of all of these things so that they can stand before the Son of Man (Luke 21:36).

The Johannine statements, even though they take a different form from the Synoptic Son of Man statements, are not as distinct as one might think. The promise that a disciple will see the heavens open up and see the angels ascending and descending on the Son of Man resembles the remarks about Jesus coming in glory or with the angels (John 1:51). The idea that the Son of Man has authority to judge is inherent in the apocalyptic sayings (John 5:27). The association of the Son of Man with a death that glorifies may well combine ideas expressed in the suffering and apocalyptic sayings (John 12:23; 13:31). Here is an example of the Gospel of John's emphasis pointing to what Christ does in the present as tied to things normally associated with what he will do in the future. Although the language of being "lifted up" is new, the imagery of the Son of Man suffering is like other predictions of his suffering (John 3:14; 8:28). Three of the texts are simply questions about the Son of Man, one asked by Jesus (John 9:35) and another asked by the crowd in association with discussions about the promise of the Christ (John 12:34 [twice]).

Four texts are more distinctive in emphasis, though two of them on closer consideration overlap with Synoptic emphases. The idea of no one having ascended into heaven except the one who descends, the Son of Man, highlights John's focus on Jesus as being sent from heaven (3:15), like the image of the Word become flesh (1:14). Similar to this is the prediction made to grumbling disciples that they should not take offense at Jesus' remarks, for they may see the Son of Man ascending to where he was before (John 6:62). In the next verse, Jesus emphasizes himself as the giver of the Spirit in his teaching. This fits with an earlier remark that Jesus as the Son of Man gives food that endures to eternal life and does not perish (John 6:27). So John highlights the teaching of Jesus. This is similar to the idea of the Son of Man sowing good seed (Matt 13:37). The most distinctive text is John 6:53, which has Jesus say to the Jews that if they do not eat the Son of Man's flesh and drink his blood, they have no life in themselves. Here Jesus compares himself to a sacrifice consumed at table, even with the hyperbole of consuming his blood. It is a roundabout way of saying that they must identify with his coming suffering and partake of it. Although expressed in uniquely picturesque imagery, the point is not unlike the suffering Son of Man saying in which the idea of Jesus as a ransom is set forth (Mark 10:45).

The Son of Man sayings summarize Jesus' ministry as the uniquely empowered eschatological agent of God, a human saturated with divine authority. And yet he is one who gives himself for the people that he one day will vindicate in glory. A survey of the scope of the usage of "Son of Man" helps us to see why Jesus chose it as his favorite way to speak of himself. As Ladd aptly says of the title, "Jesus laid claim to a heavenly dignity and probably to pre-existence itself and claimed to be one who would one day inaugurate the glorious kingdom. But in order to accomplish this, the Son of Man must become the Suffering Servant and submit to death."[61]

God. All of this leads to the very rare use of the simple title "God." In John 1:1, it is found in the narrative remark about Jesus: "the Word was God," or "the Word was divinity." This saying involves a reflection about Jesus in John's prologue, not an event in Jesus' life or ministry. A similar remark appears in John 1:18 about Jesus as the "only-begotten God." The one text in the life, ministry, and resurrection of Jesus that uses this title is the remark of Thomas in John 20:28, when he exclaims, "My Lord and my God!" after seeing the risen Jesus.

Interestingly, what is far more common is the charge that Jesus by his actions is impinging upon space or prerogatives unique to God. So when he forgives the sins of the paralytic in Mark 2 (also Matt. 9 and Luke 5) or of the sinful woman in Luke 7, the leadership complains that he is claiming to do something only God can do. When Jesus claims to work alongside the Father on the Sabbath in John 5, he is claiming to make himself equal with God. Jesus' opponents appear to appreciate the significance of his actions and what they ultimately mean. So, with the awareness that Jesus' acts were highly controversial and that they could teach theology and Christology, we turn to his teaching and actions.

Teaching and Actions

To truly appreciate Jesus, it is imperative to understand his acts and their scope. Nothing illustrates the importance of this section more than a text such as Matt. 11:2–6 = Luke 7:21–23. When Jesus is asked straight out by messengers of John the Baptist to confess whether he is "he who is to come," Jesus does not reply with an affirmative confession. Rather, he points to the acts that God is working through him to give his affirmation, appealing to the language of the prophet Isaiah in the process (Isa. 29:18; 35:5–6; 42:18; 26:19; 61:1). So we look to eleven different elements of Jesus' ministry that serve to testify to who he is and saw himself to be.

Association with Tax Collectors and Sinners. We begin with one of the more relational and controversial aspects of Jesus' ministry: the way he opened himself up to the fringe of society, especially those marked out as unrighteous. Jesus' actions here stand in stark contrast to the community at Qumran, for

---

61. Ladd, *Theology of the New Testament,* 156. As Goppelt (*Theology of the New Testament,* 186) notes, "It is very probable, therefore, that Jesus himself made use of the Son of man concept as a model and filled it in such a way that it became a central expression of his mission." He goes on to note later in his discussion (pp. 190–99) how the association of death with the Messiah is unprecedented in Judaism, so the idea was not derived from Jesus' Jewish roots. He also speaks of Jesus' appropriation of Isa. 53 and that Mark 10:45 and Mark 14:24 = Matt. 26:28 belong to the oldest strata of the tradition, suggesting their authenticity.

example. That separatist society restricted access to God on the basis of ritual washings and a strict community code, including a long probationary period. Only those who rigorously kept the Torah could sit in God's presence. The Pharisees, though not as radical in their separatism as the Qumranians, also held to very restrictive access. And in the Old Testament, access to the temple was restricted in such a way that those who were lepers or handicapped were denied.

In contrast, Jesus sought out or was responsive to the unrighteous as well as the "impure." Numerous texts note his controversial associations. His associations or positive examples in stories included tax collectors (Mark 2:17 par.; Luke 18:13; 19:7), a sinful woman (Luke 7:34, 37, 39), Samaritans (Luke 10:29–37), and even Gentiles (Matt. 15:21–28 = Mark 7:24–30). His going to a banquet held by the tax collector Levi/Matthew (Matt. 9:9–13 = Mark 2:13–17 = Luke 5:27–32) led to him responding in terms of his mission of outreach as a physician coming to heal and call the sick. Luke adds the note that the call is to repentance. Jesus notes that his controversial associations have led some to reject him (Matt. 11:19 = Luke 7:34). The parables of Luke 15 make a similar point, again explaining the associations in terms of seeking the lost. Jesus' initiative to Zacchaeus (Luke 19:1–10) also belongs here. Jesus' willingness to encounter lepers and the blind also is a part of this ministry emphasis. This portrait of Jesus is multiply attested and expresses one of the fundamental values of his ministry. God was gracious in opening up access to those who would recognize their need for God and trust in him for spiritual care, like the way one might go to a doctor for physical care. He took the initiative in doing this and made the point emphatically by not requiring any formal restitution like the Qumranian probationary periods for becoming a full member of the righteous community.[62]

No story summarizes the difference in perspective as well as the story of the anointing of Jesus by the sinful woman in the house of Simon the Pharisee (Luke 7:36–50). The Pharisee makes the judgment that Jesus' willingness to associate with the woman disqualified him from being a prophet. In contrast, Jesus argues that the potential of God forgiving a huge debt of sin drove him to reach out to her, so she could experience God's forgiveness.

This feature of Jesus' ministry challenged the portrait of who could belong to the community of God and also transformed how righteousness was seen to be gained. Did one earn it, or did one receive it by grace? Was full transformation in practice required before entering into God's presence, or was this personal transformation a response of gratitude for having experienced God's

---

62. Although perhaps overdrawn in his criticism of other views that stressed grace alone as the issue, E. P. Sanders, *Jesus and Judaism* (Philadelphia: Fortress, 1985), 204–8, puts stress on the absence of any restitutionary requirements for entry in conjunction with repentance, a point that may well be correct.

grace? In contrast to the Jewish officials around him, Jesus emphasized access to God in the context of a gracious forgiveness available even to the most unrighteous. This acceptance of God's kindness was the ground for divine provision and transformation. So Jesus defined by his own authority who it was that God accepted. Such a definition of access to God by grace alone and the claim of authority over righteousness that it represented became an irritant for the Jewish leadership about Jesus' ministry.

Forgiveness of Sins. As much as Jesus' associations were an irritant to the leadership, his claim to be able to forgive sins was one of the major objections they had to his ministry. Here, two passages are key. One is the text of the sinful woman anointing Jesus (Luke 7:36–50). The other is the healing of the paralytic (Matt. 9:1–8 = Mark 2:1–12 = Luke 5:17–26). In both cases, the declaration of forgiveness of sins brings a reaction from the observers. They either believe that blasphemy has taken place in Jesus' assuming a prerogative that is God's alone (Mark 2:7 par.), or they raise a question about who he is because he speaks words of forgiveness (Luke 7:49). Although Jesus does express the declaration with a passive idea ("your sins are forgiven" [presumably by God]), his remarks are exceptional in that there is no declaration that God is responsible for this utterance, as in the case of Nathan to David in 2 Sam. 12:13 ("The Lord has taken away your sin"). Nathan, speaking as a prophet for God, can make the remark, but he explicitly gives the credit for the declaration to God.[63] Jesus' declaration is less explicit about this connection and thus more direct, making it more offensive to the leadership. The question posed in Luke 7:49, then, is precisely that which the Scripture wishes to raise: "Who is this who even forgives sin?"[64] The question is posed but not answered at the literary level to allow reflection about the text. The scriptural portrait of Jesus makes forgiveness of sins one of the major irritants in the Jewish officials' reaction to Jesus. To them, he was claiming an exclusively divine prerogative. The irony of the text is that their observation about the significance of Jesus' act is accurate even as they reject it.

Sabbath Incidents and Healings. The issue of Jesus' healing on the Sabbath or of his disciples' breaking the Sabbath in other ways also produced contro-

---

63. Discussion about whether a person can forgive sin in Judaism surrounds one Qumranian text, 4QPrNab 1.4 (= 4Q242), where forgiveness is noted. If this text declares that an exorcist forgave sin, then it is an exception to the rule in Judaism. No rabbinic texts make such an association. Whether this Qumran text refers to a declaration of forgiven sin ("an exorcist forgave my sin") or is a shorthand way to describe the effect of what the healing shows ("No one gets up from his sickbed until all his sins are forgiven" [*b. Nedarim* 41ᵃ]) is not clear due to the fragmentary nature of the text.

64. What is important to remember about this question contextually is that the possibility of Jesus being a prophet already had been raised and rejected, so it looks as if some other role is implied by this question.

versy and raised the question of Jesus' authority to act and interpret. Jesus is claiming authority over holy time and the divine calendar, with a promise rooted in the commandments. The key passage is a paired set of controversies in the Synoptic tradition that link the incidents of the plucking of grain on the Sabbath and the healing of the man with the withered hand (Mark 2:23– 3:6 = Matt. 12:1–14 = Luke 6:1–11). The pairing of these two Sabbath events appears to belong to the early part of the tradition, because the healing of the man with the withered hand seems to confirm Jesus' remark that the Son of Man is Lord of the Sabbath, said in order to defend his disciples. In addition, Luke notes two other Sabbath healings (Luke 13:10–17 [crippled woman]; 14:1–6 [man with dropsy]). John also notes healings on the Sabbath (John 5:1–18 [man with paralysis]; 7:22–23, looking back to John 5; 9:1–17 [man born blind]). So this kind of healing appears in three distinct layers of the Gospel tradition. Interestingly, the only two miracles that John's Gospel has in Jerusalem proper are these two Sabbath miracles.

Some challenge the authenticity of such events. They argue that there was no set Jewish tradition about Sabbath healing activity, that Jesus performed no real action in healing in the Mark 3:1–6 account (where he only speaks), and that the idea of Pharisees following Jesus and his disciples around in Galilee in the plucking of grain incident is far-fetched.[65] Key to this authenticity discussion and the reaction it brings is the recognition that the opposition to Jesus did not surface on the basis of this one set of Sabbath actions only. In other words, Jesus was performing many actions, such as forgiving sins and forgoing some traditional purity practices, that represented a challenge to the range of Jewish practice. The more Jesus made distinct challenges, the more each challenge became a part of the polemical environment that was forming. Part of the point of grouping all of Jesus' actions together in this section is to highlight at how many levels Jesus challenged current practice. Once he was viewed with suspicion and as the actions piled up, each action, no matter how seemingly minor initially, would be brought into the argument that Jesus was altering normal sacred customs. The authenticity challenge to Sabbath healing is possible only when critics again attempt to reject the evidence through

---

65. For such arguments, see Sanders, *Jesus and Judaism*, 264–67. More circumspect is Meier, *A Marginal Jew*, 2:681–85, who doubts historicity and simply says that the case cannot be proved one way or the other, using many of the same arguments. The point about no set Jewish tradition is correct in that the Essenes of Qumran were stricter on Sabbath restrictions, not even allowing animals in desperate circumstances to be helped (CD 11.13–14), than were the Pharisees or the Sadducees (see *m. Šabbat* 18.3, where such help is permitted to animals except on a feast day). In the Jewish view of the healings, since no life-or-death situation existed, the move to heal could wait a day (cf. Luke 13:14). Jesus' view was that a day given over to contemplating God was the best day for such a healing. See the discussions of the specific Jewish passages in the earlier units on these specific Synoptic texts.

a type of divide-and-conquer argument. A good case can be made for these scenes' authenticity.[66]

So what is the point of such incidents? What do they tell us about Jesus? Witherington summarizes well: "The categories of teacher or prophet are inadequate to explain such a stance: We have here either a lawbreaker or one who stands above the law and uses it to fit his mission and the new situation that results from that mission."[67] The fact that the topic swirls around one of the Ten Commandments underscores Jesus' claim to authority even more. For who has the authority to adjudicate over divinely authorized Torah commands? Although part of Jesus' answer in these disputes looks to the legal-ethical issues of the scope of the law in the face of acts of compassion or need, the final remark in the plucking of grain incident is a self-claim about Jesus' role. So Jesus' claim to be "Lord" over the Sabbath is not the innocent remark of a prophet but a claim to be the restorer of the kingdom presence of God and divine authority over how God's commands operate in that rule. In this way it is like the claim that the Son of Man also has authority to forgive sins (Mark 2:10).[68] Thus, the portrait in John 5 that sees such an event as implying blasphemy is correct. Here is another act that was extremely irritating to those who read the law differently.

Exorcisms. The texts discussing exorcism include the casting out of the demoniac in the synagogue (Mark 1:21–28 = Luke 4:31–37), the Gerasene demoniac (Mark 5:1–20 = Matt. 8:26–39 = Luke 8:26–39), the Syrophoenician woman's daughter (Mark 7:24–30 = Matt. 15:21–28), and the epileptic boy

66. Ben Witherington III, *The Christology of Jesus* (Minneapolis: Fortress, 1990), 66–73, defends the authenticity of the plucking of grain account. First, Witherington argues that the setting connected to Abiathar, a controversial reference, does not look like a created detail. Second, the fact that the controversy of the grain is about the disciples, not Jesus, also is against a "made up" account, as such a fictitious account, if it existed, would be about Jesus directly. Third, there is no explicit development of the David-Jesus connection, so the alleged later Christology is too understated to be late. See also Graham Twelftree, *Jesus the Miracle Worker: A Historical and Theological Study* (Downers Grove, Ill.: InterVarsity, 1999), 295–97. With regard to Mark 3:1–6, Twelftree specifically challenges the claim that no work was done on the Sabbath in this healing by noting that the issue is not about an action that Jesus performs but that he acts to heal at all, by whatever means. Twelftree also notes that the saying by itself makes no sense without the event that gives it contextual meaning. There also is no indication that healing on the Sabbath was an early church debate around which a story like this would be created. Most on target is the refutation by N. T. Wright, *Jesus and the Victory of God* (Minneapolis: Fortress, 1996), 390–96, who challenges Sanders's view directly and notes that the Pharisees were not "thought police," but more like self-appointed guardians of the Jewish culture. Texts such as Philo's *Special Laws* 2.46 §253 and Jesus' kingdom claims and the prophetic nature of his ministry make his situation different in significance from the general practice of those who lived in Galilee. The Pharisees would have paid careful attention to him. Once Jesus was not seen as an ordinary Jew but as a threat, his actions would have been carefully watched.

67. Witherington, *The Christology of Jesus*, 69.

68. So, correctly, Robert Gundry, *Mark: A Commentary on His Apology for the Cross* (Grand Rapids: Eerdmans, 1993), 144–45.

(Mark 9:14–29 = Matt. 17:14–20 = Luke 9:37–43). Interestingly, John's Gospel has no exorcisms. The exorcism accounts are reflected in the Markan strand of the tradition, with Matthew and Luke each using three of these accounts, but not the same three.[69] Numerous other texts assume such a ministry (Matt. 12:24 = Luke 11:15 and Mark 3:22; Luke 13:32; Mark 9:38–40 = Luke 9:49–50).

However, a final key text is a part of the Matthean-Lukan teaching tradition (Matt. 12:28 = Luke 11:20). Matthew 12:24 = Luke 11:15 makes it clear that this healing of a mute man also is seen as an exorcism. The opponents claim that Jesus heals by the power of Beelzebul, but Jesus explains it in a completely different way. This text is important because it explains the significance of such healings in terms of the arrival of kingdom rule and authority. Jesus says, "If I cast out demons by the finger [Luke]/Spirit [Matt.] of God, then the kingdom of God has come upon you." This is followed in both accounts by a parable where the house of a strong man (Satan) is plundered by a stronger man (Jesus), pointing to his victory over the forces of evil. Thus, the exorcisms are graphic acts by Jesus to demonstrate that he has come to overturn the presence and authority of evil. More important than any theological debates that he may have with the Jewish leadership is his battle to overturn the hidden presence of evil that shows itself in tearing down people. The exorcisms portray this battle in the most direct way. They also raise the question of who has the authority to exercise such power.

The Scope of Jesus' Miracles. In discussing miracles, we already have noted Sabbath healings and exorcisms. However, the array of Jesus' miraculous activity also should receive attention. There are nineteen miracle accounts in Mark alone, with a few summaries added to the list.[70] To this number Matthew adds two more, the healing of the official's son (Matt. 8:5–13) and the catch of the coin in the mouth of the fish (Matt. 17:24–27).[71] Luke also has twenty miracles stories and three summaries. Two of his miracles he shares with the Matthean tradition of teaching (Luke 7:1–10; 11:14), and six miracles are unique to his Gospel (large catch of fish [5:1–11]; raising of the widow of Nain's son [7:11–17]; crippled woman healed on the Sabbath [13:10–17]; man with dropsy healed on the Sabbath [14:1–6]; ten lepers cleansed [17:11–

---

69. For a defense of the historicity of this class of texts, see Twelftree, *Jesus the Miracle Worker*, 282–92. One should recall that even the Jewish materials recognized that Jesus performed such works, calling them "sorcery" (*b. Sanhedrin* 43ª).

70. Twelftree, *Jesus the Miracle Worker*, 57. The texts are Mark 1:21–28, 29–31, 32–34 (summary), 40–45; 2:1–12; 3:1–6, 7–12; 4:35–41; 5:1–20, 21–43; 6:30–44 (two miracles present), 45–52, 53–56 (summary); 7:24–30, 31–37; 8:1–10, 22–26; 9:14–29; 10:46–52; 11:12–14 with 20–26. I count nineteen miracles here, while Twelftree says there are twenty accounts.

71. Ibid., 102.

19]; replacement of the severed ear of the high priest's servant [22:51]).[72] John has eight miracles (water changed to wine [2:1–12]; healing of the official's sick son [4:46–54]; healing of the paralytic at the pool [5:1–18]; feeding of the five thousand [6:1–15 = Mark 6:32–44 = Matt. 14:13–21 = Luke 9:10–17]; Jesus walking on the water [6:16–21; like Mark 6:45–52 = Matt. 14:22–33; Mark 4:35–41 = Matt. 8:23–27 = Luke 8:22–25]; restoring of sight to the man born blind [9:1–7]; raising of Lazarus [11:1–57]; large catch of fish [21:4–14; like Luke 5:1–11]).

Besides exorcisms and healings that took place on the Sabbath, Jesus' healing miracles include healing paralytics, giving sight to the blind, curing lepers, raising the dead, curing fever, stopping a hemorrhage, making a deaf-mute speak and hear, reattaching a severed ear, and curing a man of dropsy. Nature miracles of another sort include two examples of a large catch of fish, catching a fish with a coin for tax, stilling a storm, feeding a multitude on two occasions, walking on water, turning water into wine, and withering a fig tree (the only miracle of judgment in the list). No other biblical figure has this scope of miraculous activity. The only other figures and periods that are close are the time of the exodus with Moses and the period of high apostasy with Elijah and Elisha. Only there do we see a combination of healing and exercise of authority over the elements. What these older parallels show is that the human figures could perform any one of these classes of miracle, although in the Old Testament no one ever gives the blind sight. However, what is impressive is the scope of Jesus' activity, which involves the creation, the healing of the blind, the cleansing of lepers, and the power to raise from the dead. In this variety we see an authority that is unique in scope, a figure who is Moses' equal and much more.

When given the chance to confess who he is, Jesus points to the miracles as his "witness" and explanation. Six texts are important here.

In Matt. 11:2–6 = Luke 7:18–23, when John the Baptist sends a message asking if Jesus is "he who is to come," the miracle worker replies that John should be told what is being done: "The blind see, the lame walk, lepers are cleansed, the deaf hear, the dead are raised, and the good news is preached to the poor." Jesus replies in the language of the hope of Isaiah's prophecies about the period of God's great work of salvation. The period points out his identity and mission.

The second and third texts come from John's Gospel, where Jesus' works attest to his claims (John 5:36; 10:38). They represent the work of the Father giving attestation to the claims and person of Jesus. These Johannine texts that attest to the Son are fundamentally in agreement with Jesus' reply to John the Baptist.

72. Ibid., 144.

The fourth text is associated with Jesus' nature miracles. Here the question is raised after the stilling of the storm, "What sort of man is this that even the winds and the sea obey him?" The question is raised because the creation was seen to be in the hands of God (Job 40–42; Ps. 107:23–29). For a similar miracle in Matt. 14, where Jesus walks on the water, the resulting confession combined with worship is, "Truly you are the Son of God."

The fifth text is tied to Jesus' power over life itself. This is most dramatically developed in the story of Lazarus, in which Jesus is portrayed as the resurrection and the life. Other resuscitation texts are Jairus's daughter (Matt. 9:18–26 = Mark 5:21–43 = Luke 8:40–56) and the widow of Nain's son (Luke 7:11–17). Being the source of life is yet another divine prerogative.

Finally, there is a sequence of texts in Mark 4:35–5:43 = Luke 8:22–56. Here the scope of Jesus' miraculous power is summarized in a linked series of four miracles: calming of the sea, exorcism, healing of a woman with a hemorrhage, and a raising from the dead. This sequence covers the whole scope of Jesus' power, from creation to supernatural forces, human well-being, and life itself. It shows that Jesus has the power to deliver, and to do so comprehensively. It also raises the question of what human being is like this.

Thus, the scope of the miracles indicates the comprehensive extent of Jesus' authority. The power over life, demons, and the creation indicates a scope of authority in one person that can exist only because he shares in divine power. Again we summarize from another study of the topic. Graham Twelftree concludes his study of Jesus' miracles with this note: "In short, for Jesus and the gospel writers, a miracle performed by Jesus is an astonishing event, exciting wonder in the observers, which carries the signature of God, who, for those with the eye of faith, can be seen to be expressing his powerful eschatological presence."[73]

Purity and Other Practices. This issue involves mainly two texts (Mark 7:1–23; Matt 15:1–20). These are the only Gospel texts where the question of what is "common" or "profane" (κοινός [i.e., unclean]) comes up. What is disputed is the disciples' failure to keep "the tradition of the elders." They fail to wash their hands to prevent uncleanness in their handling of food.[74] Other texts address Jesus' practice in relationship to fasting or point to Jesus' critique of the religious practices of the Jewish leaders (Luke 5:33–39; 11:37–54; Matt. 23). These texts do not so much challenge purity practices as reprioritize them, making true piety a reflection of more than one's ability to follow detailed practices.

In Matthew, Jesus replies in kind, noting that the tradition of the Pharisees and scribes breaks the ethical side of the law by violating the command to

---

73. Ibid., 350.
74. For discussion of the Jewish practice here, see Roger Booth, *Jesus and the Laws of Purity: Tradition History and Legal History in Mark 7,* JSNTSup 13 (Sheffield: JSOT, 1986), 155–87.

honor mother and father. He then goes on to assert that it is not what goes into a person that defiles but what comes out of the mouth. When the disciples note that the Pharisees were offended by his statements, Jesus drives the point home: "Every plant that *my* heavenly Father has not planted will be rooted up." Then he calls the Pharisees blind guides. Jesus' final remark on the topic is that what comes out of the mouth and out of the heart is what defiles, "but to eat with unwashed hands does not defile."

Mark goes a similar route, even describing the custom for his Gentile audience in 7:3–4. When asked, Jesus challenges them for their hypocrisy with regard to honoring mother and father. Then he tells the crowd that what defiles is not what comes from outside but what comes out of a person. Mark stresses that defilement comes from what emerges from the heart. He alone also adds the implication of Jesus' remarks (although this was not immediately recognized): Jesus "declared all foods clean."

All of this tradition was developed from Lev. 15, where being made unclean by a discharge required a washing. Although the body was still considered unclean for a time after the washing, a rinsing rendered the hands clean.

What Jesus responds to, then, is the tradition about uncleanliness, not the Torah per se. Jesus' response makes it clear that he rejected the use of oral law in this way. However, when Jesus goes on to elaborate his response, he does comment on matters of "defiling" that Torah does treat. Here he opts for a priority on the ethical dimensions of the law in terms of personal behavior. Both the rebuke that confronts them on how parents are dishonored and the emphasis on defiling coming from the heart show this focus on the law as it relates to one's interpersonal actions. When Mark adds the narrative comment that the effect of Jesus' remarks was to make all foods clean (Mark 7:19), the import is that Jesus, by the emphasis he gave, has reconfigured how the law is seen and prioritized it. Reading Matthew gives one the same sense, but to a lesser degree. The emphasis on the interpersonal relationships is still there, but the explicit statement of foods being declared clean is lacking.

Jesus' comments are not merely those of a prophet commenting on the law, nor are they the work of a scribe interpreting the law. Rather, the point is that Jesus, in light of his authority, has the right to comment and even prioritize on matters tied to purity. Ben Meyer speaks of an "eschatological ethic" at work here as the arrival of the new age brings a fresh look at the law and its priorities because a new standard of righteousness is being more effectively worked out in conjunction with the promise of the new era.[75] Jesus' remark in defense of his lack of fasting—that new wine requires new wineskins—makes the point explicitly (Mark 2:22 = Matt. 9:17 = Luke 5:38).

75. Ben Meyer, *The Aims of Jesus* (London: SCM, 1979), 138–39. He goes on to say, "Jesus was not a rabbi but a prophet and, like John, 'more than a prophet.' He was the unique revealer of the full final measure of God's will" (p. 151).

This kind of supersession also must point to the revealer. As Meyer states, "Since the Mosaic code was conceived to have been divinely revealed, any code claiming to supersede it had somehow to include the claim to be equally revealed—indeed, to belong to a superior revelation."[76] This also had implications for the revelator. Who could emphasize and reveal the scope of the law and practice that God gave through Moses? It is someone through whom God brought a time that transcended that of Moses and who transcended Moses himself. Here, Jesus did not claim to go up to the mountain to get the revelation of God as Moses had. Rather, he spoke directly of what "*my* Father" would do and what he requires. Thus, these acts inherently present a claim of authority and divine insight.

Law Issues. In one sense, this section is an extension of the previous ones. There, we looked at issues tied to the Sabbath and to purity, which are legal matters. Also relevant are matters tied to the temple. However, that discussion is important enough on its own terms to be covered separately later. This subunit considers all other matters related to the law not found in the other subunits treating legal questions.

The portrait of the law in the Gospels varies in emphasis depending on the Gospel in question.[77] The term "law" (νόμος) nevers appears in Mark, but is used eight times in Matthew (5:17, 18; 7:12; 11:13; 12:5; 22:36, 40; 23:23), four times in Luke 10–24 (10:26; 16:16, 17; 24:44) plus five times in Luke 2 (vv. 22, 23, 24, 27, 39), and fifteen times in John (1:17, 45; 7:19 [twice], 23, 49, 51; 8:5, 17; 10:34; 12:34; 15:25; 18:31; 19:7 [twice]).

Mark's handling of the law appears to be the most radical in that he develops Jesus' break with the law in the most explicit terms, as is seen in his unique remark about how Jesus declared all food clean in Mark 7:19. Matthew and Luke are more restrained. They share with Mark texts that show Jesus following the law in several places (e.g., Matt. 8:1–4 = Mark 1:40–45 = Luke 5:12–16), while also noting the tension of prioritization of ethical dimensions over the cultic in his remarks and acts of Sabbath healing (in remarks unique to Matthew, Matt. 9:13; 12:7; Matt. 12:1–8 = Mark 2:23–28 = Luke 6:1–5; Matt. 12:9–14 = Mark 3:1–6 = Luke 6:6–11; so also John 5:23). In the Sabbath healings, actions by David not in line with the law and the shewbread specifically are raised. The temple is discussed in a way that both implies its removal (John 2:19–22) and looks to its role as a place of prayer not to be defiled (Matt. 21:12–13 = Mark 11:15–18 = Luke 19:45–46; Matt. 5:23–24; 23:16–22). John's Gospel tends to portray the period of the law as past and its feasts as realized in Jesus (John 1:17). John also often cites the law as testifying to what Jesus is experiencing, as a text where the mission of Christ is dis-

---

76. Ibid., 152.
77. For this area, see William R. G. Loader, *Jesus' Attitude toward the Law*, WUNT 2.97 (Tübingen: Mohr, 1997).

cussed or attested, or as a text that explains how Jesus should be treated (John 1:45; 8:17; 12:34; 15:25; 18:31; 19:7). Luke and Matthew also have remarks that go in this direction, where the period of the kingdom follows that of the law and prophets as its fulfillment (Matt. 11:13; Luke 16:16). Outside of these generalized texts, two passages are especially important: (1) the text about the greatest commandment (Mark 12:28–34 = Matt. 22:34–40 [like Luke 10:25–28 and Luke 18:18–20, where the relational dimension of the Ten Commandments is discussed in response to a question about how to receive eternal life]) and (2) the six antitheses (Matt. 5:21–48), a text unique to Matthew.

The ethical prioritization noted in the discussion on purity shows up in the "great commandment" text. Here the law is distilled to love for God and love for one's neighbor. Certain Jewish texts made similar comments.[78] Here Jesus upholds the law in its relational emphasis, making the point that our relationship to God should impact how others are treated as well. Matthew 22:40 expresses it by saying that the law and the prophets hang on these emphases, like hinges that make a door workable. Jesus, in Matt. 23:23, rebukes the failure of the Pharisees to apply the law in this relational way. Their error is that they treat the law simply as a string of commands. John 13:34 seems to go in a similar direction with a "new commandment" to love one another. This focus is what Jesus highlights at his last meal with the disciples.

More revealing are the antitheses. Sometimes it is argued that Jesus is merely rejecting oral law in his "you have heard it said, but I say to you" remarks. This argument does not work. The antitheses intensify each command, pressing it in terms of its internal intent. So the issue is not just murder but also anger that leads to murder. The issue is not just adultery but also lust that leads to adultery. The issue is not thinking through how one can get out of marriage, but taking one's vow seriously in order to keep it, recognizing also that God is involved in bringing a couple together. The issue is not how an oath is worded, but the integrity that makes oath taking unnecessary. The issue is not eye-for-eye retribution, but a kind of nonretaliation that keeps the spiral of violence from spinning out of control.[79] This example is particularly revealing, showing Jesus' emphasis on the relational dimension of the law and a refocus on a fresh hub for it, so that relationships do not break down. Absence of retribution again is the point in Jesus' stepping back from the call to hate one's enemy. The standard may not be what is "fair" or "equal," but what

---

78. Some of these texts are disputed as having been influenced by Christian interpolations (*Testament of Dan* 5.3; *Testament of Issachar* 5.2; 7.6). However, Philo, *Special Laws* 2.15 §63, makes a similar emphasis. The roots of this are in the prophets (Mic. 6:8; Isa. 33:15–16; cf. Ps. 15). Rabbi Hillel taught, "What seems to you to be hurtful, do not to your neighbor; that is the whole Torah. All the rest is commentary" (*b. Šabbat* 31ᵃ)

79. Note how this antithesis simply cites Exod. 21:24 or Lev. 24:20. There is no oral law here.

goes beyond the call of normal duty to reverse the cycle that causes relation-ships to be destroyed. The outcome is that the standard of righteousness that Jesus' reading of the law calls for exceeds that of the scribes and Pharisees, op-erates at a standard greater than that which the world lives by, and reflects the character of God in the process.

It is also in this light that Jesus' remarks about coming to fulfill the law in Matt. 5:17–20 must be read. Here, Jesus is not discussing a casuistic reading of legal detail and scribal ruling, but a reading that looks at the scope and inner goal of the law to enhance relationships and reflect God's gracious character and righteousness.

All of this raises the question of who has the authority to open up the inner character of the law in this way, discerning what is to be kept and what is less important, as well as when certain legal limitations apply and when they do not. Again, a quotation from Witherington pulls all the strands of this section together:

> Jesus seems to assume an authority over Torah that no Pharisee or Old Testa-ment prophet assumed—the authority to set it aside. What is striking is that his response in the authentic material seems varied. Sometimes he affirms the validity of some portions of the law. Sometimes he intensifies the law's de-mands (e.g., portions of the Sermon on the Mount), a point of view that does not violate the law but goes beyond it. Sometimes he adds new material, appar-ently of juridical force to the law (e.g., his teaching on adultery and divorce in Mark 10/Matthew 19). Sometimes he sets aside Torah as he does in Mark 7:15. In short, he feels free not only to operate with a selective hermeneutic but also to add and subtract from Scripture. All of this suggests that Jesus did not see himself as a Galilean Hasid ["holy man"] or another prophet, even one like Eli-jah. He saw himself in a higher or more authoritative category than either of these types familiar to Jewish believers.[80]

This summary is well stated and correctly surfaces the question of what kind of person Jesus saw himself to be that he could arrogate to himself such au-thority. Jesus had no doubt that he could serve as the revelator of God, speak-ing and revealing the divine way and will. He and the Father were one when it came to understanding what law and divine will required. Jesus' response in John 5 to the "breaking" of the Sabbath proceeds in exactly this way. Once again John's Gospel is shown to be parallel in its conception to what the Syn-optics reveal, even though the form of expression differs. Jesus' attitude to the law set a direction that later was taken up in the early church's insistence that circumcision was not required for Gentile believers even though it had been so central a sign in the law. It took a while for this emphasis to make itself clear to them, as Acts 10–15 testifies. In the meantime, two other points are

---

80. Witherington, *Christology of Jesus*, 65.

clear from Jesus' teaching: (1) compassion and character are what the law was designed to help form and serve; (2) Jesus' reading of the law shows his authority over it. If I may paraphrase, it shows that the Son of Man is not simply Lord of the Sabbath; he is Lord over the reading of the law. In this, Jesus reveals not only his authority, but also his wisdom as the interpreter of the law par excellence.

Redesigning Liturgy. Underscoring what has been said about the law is how Jesus handles sacred liturgy rooted in the law as evidenced in the Last Supper (Matt. 26:17–30 = Mark 14:12–26 = Luke 22:7–23). What appears to be a Passover meal is reinterpreted in terms of Jesus' approaching death (Mark 14:2; Luke 22:15). At the least we have a meal offered during Passover season that evokes the establishing of a new relationship with God on terms that Jesus creates. The connection to Passover imagery is likely, given that they are eating the meal as Jerusalem pilgrims there for Passover, even if we cannot be absolutely sure that a Passover meal was the occasion.[81] A sacred meal, or at least imagery tied to a sacred event, the exodus, is reshaped into a message about the new era of eschatological deliverance.[82]

So what does this recasting in terms of sacrifice and covenant mean about Jesus? The remarks about the meal clearly present Jesus as a sacrifice who opens up the way to the new covenant relationship with God. He is the means through which forgiveness is given. That this result is associated with the kingdom is clear from Jesus' remark about not drinking of the cup again until he drinks it anew in the kingdom of God. The bread and cup imagery emphasizes the issues tied to what Jesus provides through his death (covenant, forgiveness). Jesus then stands at the hub or base of a new era and makes provision for the establishment of a fresh way of relating to God in a fresh context of forgiveness. Both the bread and the cup picture what Jesus offers "on your behalf." The blood pictures what is "poured out for many" (Matt. 26:28 = Mark 14:24). Here Isa. 53:12 stands in the background, while the Passover

---

81. There is debate whether a Passover meal is at the base of the Last Supper, although this does seem likely. Even if it is not, the event took place so close to Passover that the associations would exist. The classic work arguing for a Passover meal is Joachim Jeremias, *The Eucharistic Words of Jesus,* trans. N. Perrin, 2d ed., New Testament Library (New York: Scribner, 1966). In contrast stands the thesis of Bruce Chilton, who argues that the Passover connection is anachronistic and favors seeing the meal in terms of Jesus' view of cultic purity and his practice of forgiveness as seen in his meals and associations (*The Temple of Jesus: His Sacrificial Program within a Cultural History of Sacrifice* [University Park, Pa.: Pennsylvania State University Press, 1992], 148–54). This approach seems to me to ignore the background inevitably raised by the festal occasion, regardless of what we can or cannot know exactly about the form of a Passover meal at the time. To speak of a death at Passover time in the context of a work of deliverance naturally would lead to this association. Thus, a Passover backdrop is still more likely here. So Goppelt, *Theology of the New Testament,* 215.

82. For other details about the event, see unit 264 above. Here our concern is the import of the event.

stands as the illustrative event. The meal was a promise that what Jesus was to do would provide a context for a new relationship with God that had been promised long ago.[83]

That Jesus could take sacred exodus imagery and refill it speaks to his view as interpreter of both the law of God and the plan of God. It also points to his ability to take on a creative role in that plan, to author and perfect a traditional act of worship. He acts as the unique sent revelator of God. It is like the authority he exercised over the law. It is also like the authority he asserts in the temple. Jesus is expanding and reforming most of the major images of Judaism. The question that is raised by all of this activity is, What sort of person is this that he is able to recast old sacred rites?[84] Jesus is not merely establishing a new rite; he is modifying one of the most sacred rites of Israel. To believe that he can do this shows how in tune Jesus was with God's way and will.

Temple and Temple Cleansing. Jesus displayed a mixed relationship to the temple in his various remarks and activities associated with it. In many ways, that mix is much like his approach to issues of law in general. Some things are affirmed, while other remarks show that the temple would not remain the center of activity that it had been.

It is debated whether Jesus' act in clearing out the temple's money changers was a call of cleansing reform for the temple or a symbolic picture of its destruction (John 2:13–22; Matt. 21:12–13 = Mark 11:15–17 = Luke 19:45–46).[85] In favor of a symbolic act picturing destruction are (1) the following fig tree incident; (2) the remarks of John 2:19, which suggest a concern about another temple more important to God's plan than the physical temple; and

83. When one adds the portrait of John's Gospel here, the results are interesting. John does not depict the Last Supper with its bread and cup, but what he does highlight is the announcement of the coming of the Paraclete (the Holy Spirit), yet another key dimension of the new covenant promise. John's role in supplementing well-known tradition is seen here.

84. Goppelt, *Theology of the New Testament*, 220, says it this way: "Jesus now vouchsafed forgiving fellowship by giving himself as the One who died for the benefit of all others. It is not a heavenly body, not a pneumatic substance, that was given, and also not only an atoning power, but Jesus as the One who died for all."

85. For the destruction view see Wright, *Jesus and the Victory of God,* 413–28; for that of destruction with the expectation of a renewed temple, see Sanders, *Jesus and Judaism,* 61–76; for the view "more probably" of a symbolic cleansing as a messianic act tied to entry, see Witherington, *The Christology of Jesus,* 107–16. As the above studies show, even more disputed is why the cleansing/destruction was required. Was it for economic reasons (Sadducees taking unfair economic advantage), purity reasons (sacrifices did not really belong to the worshiper but merely were purchased, or sacrifices were moved into the holy space of the court of the Gentiles), both, or the temple as a national symbol for Israel's nationalism? This is less than clear, although I prefer the option that both economic and worship ideals were being compromised by the recent move of the money changers into the court. See earlier discussion of the passage. Meyer, *The Aims of Jesus,* 197, rightly calls it several things: a demonstration, a prophetic critique, a fulfillment event, and a sign of the future. The temple cleansing pledges the "perfect restoration of Israel" (p. 198).

(3) Jesus' predictions in the Olivet discourse of the temple's coming destruction (Matt. 24 = Mark 13 = Luke 21:5–37). However, in support of a cleansing reform are the remarks about the temple being either a place of prayer (Matt. 21:13) or a place for the nations (Mark 11:17). This appears to foresee a time when the temple will continue to function. In addition, the early church kept its attachment to the temple, so that any idea that it ceased to have value or was totally obsolete appears not to have been adopted by the church. The Jewish background that the temple would be part of what would be renewed in the last times also is part of the backdrop of Jesus' action, pointing slightly more to a cleansing (*1 Enoch* 90.28–30, 40; Zech. 14:21; *Shemoneh Esreh,* benediction 14). These factors appear to suggest that the temple was being cleansed with a prophetic-like call to the nation to behave appropriately in the temple. No doubt that if covenantal unfaithfulness continued, then judgment would come (Mark 13:2 = Matt. 24:2 = Luke 21:5–6). However, it is better to see Jesus acting as a messianic claimant. He is making his statement about the need for reform of the temple to prepare for the new era. This is like the prayer in benediction 14 of *Shemoneh Esreh,* which links together messianic hope and the temple, just as the later inquiry of Jesus before the council moves from temple to messiahship. The fact that this is Jesus' first act after entering the city as a messianic claimant also makes this view likely. If this claim meets with rejection, then the nation stands culpable.

Again, to make such a move by itself could have been seen as merely prophetic, but placed alongside the eschatological claims of Jesus and his other actions that touched on the law, a more messianic claim is present with implications for the arrival of the kingdom. Jesus is challenging holy space by what he does here. To see oneself as having the authority to exercise judgment over the central religious symbol of the nation was to perform an act that assumed a claim to divinely connected authority. This is precisely why the cleansing raises the leaders' question after the event about the source of Jesus' authority (Matt. 21:23–27 = Mark 11:27–33 = Luke 20:1–8). It was exactly the right question to raise. Even the way Jesus plays with the "temple" image, fusing his body as temple with the physical temple, suggests a level of holiness associated with his presence that links it to God's presence (John 2:19). So, like the handling of the law, the treatment of the temple suggests an authority over the most sacred of Israel's sites, the very place where God dwells. He is the Messiah and, more than the temple, functions as the hub of what the promise brings in needed restructuring.

Suffering and Cross. In this section we consider what Jesus had to say about his rejection and suffering. The narrative depictions of the cross do not fit in here, since they are presented in terms of the evangelists' understandings of the event. In general, these depictions portray Jesus as a righteous sufferer, along the lines of the psalms, or as an innocent who is sent to his death even though the one judging him (Pilate) is not truly convinced of his guilt. Luke emphasizes this innocence theme, and it is present also in Matthew and John.[86]

The passion predictions speak of the necessity of Jesus' suffering or of fulfilling Scripture (Mark 8:31 = Matt. 16:21 = Luke 9:22; Mark 14:21 = Matt. 26:24; Luke 18:31; 22:22). In particular in Mark, Jesus suffers as the Son of Man. The idea of Jesus being handed over (παραδιδόναι) appears to recall Isa. 53:6, 12 (Mark 9:31 = Matt. 17:22 = Luke 9:44; Mark 10:33 = Matt. 20:18).[87] This probably represents a fusion of exalted Son of Man background with the suffering of the righteous and the Servant images.[88] Also important is the imagery of Zech. 9–14, in which the shepherd is struck and the sheep are scattered (Mark 14:27).[89] Important to recognize in these predictions are three basic elements: (1) rejection as seen in the delivering over, (2) death, and (3) vindication in a quick resurrection.

The theme of rejection-vindication also is seen in the use of Ps. 118:22, which appears in two contexts, one tied to the parable of the wicked tenants (Matt. 21:42 = Mark 12:10–11 = Luke 20:17) and another associated with Jesus' warning about Israel's coming desolation (Luke 13:34–35). Here the rejected stone becomes the exalted stone, which also is a stumbling stone. Similar in implication is the appeal to Ps. 110:1, which comes to be read as a vindication of the judged Jesus because he ends up at God's right hand despite being sentenced to death (Matt. 26:64 = Mark 14:62 = Luke 22:69). In other words, most of the Gospel texts concentrate on the fact that Jesus as a righteous one was unjustly crucified, but that God would reverse the injustice into exaltation and victory. The reversal is seen as divine substantiation for Jesus' claims.

Yet the theme of Isa. 53, though its presence here has been debated, is not absent.[90] Four texts are especially important when placed in a backdrop that

86. In Matthew, Pilate washes his hands and is warned by his wife after she has a dream. As in the infancy material, dreams play a major role in Matthew, showing God's involvement in the events. See John 18:38; 19:4.

87. Joel Marcus, *The Way of the Lord: Christological Exegesis of the Old Testament in the Gospel of Mark* (Louisville: Westminster/John Knox, 1992), 193–94.

88. On the background and authenticity of these suffering Son of Man sayings, see Darrell L. Bock, *Luke 1:1–9:50*, BECNT 3A (Grand Rapids: Baker, 1994), 952–55; Hans Bayer, *Jesus' Predictions of Vindication and Resurrection: The Provenence, Meaning and Correlation of Synoptic Prediction*, WUNT 2.20 (Tübingen: Mohr, 1986). The key texts here appear to be Ps. 118, Isa. 53, and the suffering righteous in the Psalter, appealing to passages such as Ps. 22, 31, and 69, which show up in Jesus' utterances on the cross. In this portrait, the utterances of Jesus in Mark and Matthew have a note of lament through Ps. 22:1, while Luke has a note of trust and hope of triumph in the use of Ps. 31:5. All the Gospels, including John, have imagery from Ps. 69. Texts speaking to the vindication of the righteous may also have a role (Old Testament: Ps. 3; 8; 9; 18; 27; 32; 56; Jewish texts: Wis. 2:12–20; 5:1–7).

89. Marcus, *The Way of the Lord*, 157.

90. The debate is reflected in the essays in Bellinger and Farmer, eds., *Jesus and the Suffering Servant*. The essay by Morna Hooker argues against such a connection, while essays by Otto Betz and Rikki Watts argue for it.

argues that all of Isa. 40–66 is important to Mark's understanding. They are Mark 9:12, about suffering and being despised, appealing to Isa. 53:3; the passion predictions as a group, appealing to Isa. 53:8 (on judgment) and 53:6, 12 (on being handed over); Mark 10:45, with the concept of ransom tied conceptually to Isa. 53:12; and Mark 14:22–24, about bearing the sins of many with poured-out blood, appealing to Isa. 53:12b (also Matt. 26:27). Again, most of these texts simply describe the circumstances of rejection. However, the reference to ransom and to blood being poured out for many begins to describe how forgiveness is achieved. Mark 14:22–24 set in the backdrop of Passover also underscores this sacrificial context. Luke 22:37 also appeals to language of the Servant portrait in Isa. 53:12 to describe the depth of the rejection. This righteous one is viewed as a "lawless" one, a transgressor.

These texts show Jesus portraying the experience of the cross in many dimensions. He is rejected and regarded as unrighteous, yet he is an innocent sufferer. The actual descriptions of Jesus' death on the cross and the Scripture he cites from the cross point to this portrait. The injustice of the cross will be vindicated when Jesus is raised up like the rejected stone of Ps. 118. John's Gospel also gets at this idea when it speaks of the Son of Man being lifted up. Here the cross is seen not as a defeat, but as the means of glorification for the Son (John 3:14; 17:1–5). Not much time is spent describing how forgiveness comes through Jesus' work, but those texts that do treat it view his death as a sacrifice opening up the way to a new covenant. In a larger context, this opens up the way for the coming of the Spirit, the sign of the new age (John 14–16).

Thus, in terms of Christology, Jesus' suffering and cross mark him out as one whom God vindicates even as he suffers an unjust and heinous death born out of rejection. He suffers primarily as the Son of Man, but the portrait is drawn from righteous sufferer and Servant texts. That his sacrifice is worthy of establishing a new covenant also speaks to the greatness of his person, as does the nature of the vindication that God gives to him. Who else is worthy to sit at the right hand of God but one who shares divine status and authority? Thus, we turn to the final act that identifies who Jesus is: the resurrection.

Vindication in Resurrection, Ascension, Provision, and Judgment to Come. The significance of resurrection is developed by Jesus in the Gospels at his Jewish examination, in the very moment when he is being condemned to the cross. The moment of seeming defeat is the very moment of disclosure of how God will bring him victory. When Jesus appeals to Ps. 110:1 upon being asked if he is the Christ, he is claiming that rather than being the defendant before the council, he one day will be their judge, operating from the very side of God.[91] One day,

91. The detailed explanation and defense of the historicity of this scene is the burden of Darrell L. Bock, *Blasphemy and Exaltation in Judaism and the Final Examination of Jesus*, WUNT 2.106 (Tübingen: Mohr, 1998). The North American edition of this book is *Blasphemy and Exaltation in Judaism: The Charge against Jesus in Mark 14:53–65*, Biblical Studies Library (Grand Rapids: Baker, 2000).

they will see the Son of Man seated at the right hand of the Father. Matthew and Luke intensify this remark, noting that "hereafter" (Matthew) or "from now on" (Luke) they will see this exercise of authority.

What does Jesus mean besides referring to the fact that he will possess judgment authority one day and gather his elect for their final redemption (the apocalyptic Son of Man texts, esp. Matt. 24:29–31 = Mark 13:24–27 = Luke 21:25–28; Matt. 25:31–46)? In Acts, this becomes the theme that God has appointed one to be the judge of the living and the dead (Acts 10:42; 17:31). In John's Gospel, this is expressed in the authority of Jesus' words that will be the basis of judgment one day (John 12:48 [like Matt. 7:22]; 5:24–29; 11:25–26). The reaction to Jesus is the basis of this judgment in a text that probably is a narrative comment (John 3:18–19). In John's Gospel, Jesus' central role is depicted less in the picture of him as the one who judges and more in terms of how response to him determines how that judgment resolves itself.

So clearly, Jesus' authority is seen in the role that he has in relationship to final judgment. Is that authority seen anywhere else? It is here that the promise of provision of the Spirit as evidence that the Christ is present (Luke 3:15–17) in the new era (Luke 24:49; Acts 1:4–8; John 14–16) is so important. Acts 2 explains the significance of what Jesus declared by pointing to the distribution of the Spirit as a sign of messianic authority and the arrival of divine promise. Jesus' questions about Ps. 110:1 and his initially cryptic claim for vindication at his trial are resolved in Acts 2. The early church's teaching is reflected in Peter's speech. Resurrection-ascension made it clear what Jesus' allusion to Ps. 110:1 implied. Peter's speech in Acts 2 explains that here is evidence, along with the distribution of the Spirit, that Jesus is Lord and Christ, the bearer of a new era with its long-promised benefits.

In sum, the resurrection leads to Jesus' being given a place at the side of God. His resurrection not only means that there is life after death and a judgment to come, for which all people are accountable to him, but also it points to the identity of the one who brings the promise of life and the Spirit. He is the one qualified to share the very presence of God, distribute the blessing of God, and execute the judgment of God. As we have seen throughout this section on Christology, the stress is not on seeing who Jesus is through his verbal claims; the key is to appreciate what his array of acts tells us about his unique human-divine identity as the Son of Man.

Summary of Events and Acts of Jesus. It is the scope and ultimate unity of all of these acts that point to Jesus' uniqueness. Taking most of these categories one by one, we see that parallels with activity by other human divine agents can be found. Moses worked with the creation. Prophets revived the dead. Elijah ended a drought. However, no one attempted or achieved the combination of acts that Jesus performs. It is the scope of these acts that establishes his uniqueness. The directness of his involvement with salvation—in the forgiveness of sins, the sacrificial provision for life, and the giving of the Spirit—tells us that Jesus is more than a human agent commissioned with divine authority. The Gospels argue that the full array of Jesus' acts explain that Jesus the promised Messiah is also the divine Lord. So Jesus shares not only in divine authority but also in divine personage. The crucifixion is the ground from which God builds his plan of redemption through a uniquely worthy sacrifice. The miracles, and especially the exorcisms, show the scope of Jesus' authority and against whom he is battling to bring victory. The reconfiguring of imagery tied to feasts shows that a new era has come.

Confirming all of this are some sayings that highlight Jesus' unique authority at the hub of divine activity.[92] Numerous texts declare the authority that Jesus has to judge and acknowledge others before God (Matt. 10:32–33; Mark 8:34–38; Matt. 10:40; Mark 9:37) or that blessing comes from not being offended at him (Matt. 11:6). The apocalyptic Son of Man sayings fit here as well. Jesus stands at the center of divine blessing in several "I" sayings that show his authority (Matt. 11:28 [over rest]; 5:17 [over law]; Mark 2:17 [over forgiveness]; Luke 19:10 [over the lost]; 12:49 [to bring fire]). He is greater than Abraham (John 8:58), than Jacob (John 4:12–14), and than Solomon and Jonah (Matt. 12:38–42 = Luke 11:29–32). He is greater even than the temple (Matt. 12:6). In sum, Jesus is unique as the revelator of God standing in the middle of divine deliverance.

The resurrection-ascension is the ultimate vindication of these claims. The judgment to come is the ultimate proof that Jesus possesses absolute authority. However, in the current era, it is the provision of the Spirit as the enabler of his children that points to this uniquely authoritative Jesus. His seated position at the side of God shows that he shares completely in divinity. He is the one who is both Lord and Christ. He has brought the promised new era of God and with it a new community filled with new promise. So what does this new community of the new era look like? To that question we now turn our attention.

Jesus' Community of the New Era: The Calling of Those Who Respond

The Gospels are somewhat enigmatic when it comes to defining the new community that Jesus' ministry forged. On the one hand, Jesus preached to Israel and called for reform in fulfillment of the arrival of the new era. His actions, as well as those of the Baptist, appear to call for repentance and a re-

92. Robert H. Stein, *The Method and Message of Jesus' Teachings*, rev. ed. (Louisville: Westminster/John Knox, 1994), 122–24, mentions two categories of sayings here: (1) the totalitarian claims of Jesus, and (2) Jesus comparing himself with Old Testament saints. This paragraph reflects these sections.

newed walk with God in line with long-established hopes. At this level, Jesus looks like a specially endowed "charismatic" figure whose authority and claim of a special relationship to God produced a following and new social group within Judaism.[93] On the other hand, he called out a special group of followers and formed the most important group into a band of twelve to lead this new community and to picture the renewal of the nation in a fresh teaching and leadership structure. The term "church" (ἐκκλησία), which this group eventually evolved to become, is rarely used in the Gospels, appearing only three times (Matt. 16:18; 18:17 [twice]). Its basic meaning of "assembly" could be the meaning in these passages, although Jesus' reference to "my" assembly in Matt. 16 makes it clear that he does have in mind something fresh and distinct from what currently exists. Thus, there is an inherent complexity in the way the presentation of Jesus in Scripture handles this question of community.

As important as its structure are the community's character and calling. In fact, Jesus spends much more time here than on questions of its form. Those who ally themselves to Jesus and the community built around him and his teaching are called to take on a certain lifestyle in relationship to the world, others, and life. Jesus' teaching on discipleship and discussion of ethical values as a means of testimony to God belong to this theme. So we consider in this section the forming of community in the call to discipleship and the calling of that community in terms of Jesus' ethical teaching and ministries of service and mission. This section will alternate between themes tied to the formation and structure of a new community and its ethical commitments.

Response to Grace: Repentance and Faith

This theme we have examined already in the discussion on kingdom. However, it needs to be noted here and supplemented because it is the base of re-

---

93. The term "charismatic" is used here in a technical sociological sense of an appealing, publicly powerful leader figure. Some like to argue that Jesus was such a figure with no "institutional" goals. In other words, he had no interest in forming a new community or structure. This often is summarized in the view that Jesus came to reform Israel but what came instead was a church that he never intended to create. Such a dichotomy between Jesus as a charismatic and as an institutional founder is rightly challenged by John Meier, "Dividing Lines in Jesus Research Today: Through Dialectical Negation to a Positive Sketch," *Interpretation* 50 (1996): 366–68. Those who argue for Jesus as charismatic but not an institutional founder argue that having apocalyptic goals, Jesus would not be interested in founding a new community when the nearness of the end is so emphasized. However, Meier correctly observes that the Qumran community was apocalyptic in its worldview and yet formed an entirely restructured community as they anticipated the arrival of the end. The evidence that Meier gives for Jesus' institutional concerns include his forming of an inner group of disciples, the circle of the Twelve, the role of baptism among his followers, and, subsequently, the formation of a prayer for his disciples and the institution of a unique symbolic fellowship meal. All of these elements are multiply attested in the Gospel tradition.

lationship from which Jesus builds and from which he defines his own mission. The calling of Levi/Matthew and the controversial relationships with outsiders it represented led Jesus to make a mission statement that he, like a physician, had come to call the sick, that is, sinners (Matt. 9:10–13 = Mark 2:15–17). Luke, in commenting on this same scene, adds the note that the calling is to repentance (Luke 5:32). Similar in thrust is a text unique to Matthew (Matt. 4:17), where the summary of Jesus' message is "Repent, for the kingdom of heaven is at hand." Those who would enter the kingdom of God must appreciate their need for his direction and rule in their lives. They must acknowledge their need for God and for coming to him on his terms. Luke, in a passage unique to his Gospel (Luke 13:1–5), makes the same point in discussing fatal tragedy. Rather than discussing whether tragedy is the result of a worse type of sin, Jesus warns that without repentance his audience likewise will perish. Still another evidence of Luke's emphasis on this theme is Luke 15:7, 10, which notes how heaven rejoices when a sinner repents, as an explanation for why Jesus associates with sinners. A final uniquely Lukan text (Luke 24:47) highlights Jesus' commissioning of a message for the newly emerging community: "repentance for the forgiveness of sins is to be preached to all the nations, beginning from Jerusalem." This message is a realization of teaching expressed in the Old Testament (Luke 24:44–47).

Failure to repent will lead to judgment (Matt. 11:20 = Luke 10:13; Matt. 12:41 = Luke 11:32). Thus, this repentance theme is multiply attested. It expresses the response from the standpoint of its starting point. To come to Jesus is to have a change of perspective and direction about God from the path that one previously was traveling. To come to him as to a physician is like coming to God for healing from a spiritual disease.

A second key term of response is "faith," which most often appears in the Gospels as a response and expectation that God can act, often through Jesus. Here we find faith affirmed in the centurion (Matt. 8:10, 13 = Luke 7:9), the friends of the paralytic (Matt. 9:2 = Mark 2:5 = Luke 5:20), the woman with the hemorrhage (Matt. 9:22 = Mark 5:34, 36 = Luke 8:48), the healing of the boy with the unclean spirit (Mark 9:23–24), the healing of two blind men (Matt. 9:28–29, similar to the commendation of Bartimaeus in Mark 10:52 = Luke 18:42), the Gentile woman (Matt. 15:28, where the Markan parallel does not mention faith), the parents of the girl who has died (Luke 8:50), and the sinful woman (Luke 7:50). Jesus exhorts the disciples to have faith in their prayers and life (Matt. 17:20 = Luke 17:5–6; Matt. 21:21–22 = Mark 11:22–24; Luke 22:32; discourse not using the term "faith" but describing such trust: Matt. 6:25–33 [like Luke 12:22–34]).

Interestingly, the term "faith" is rarely used as a technical term for entry into the community. Faith reflects an attitude that God honors with his gracious response involving acts of deliverance through Jesus. In this way the term pictures the more technical theological usage that the attitude came to have in the early church. However, more technical uses of "faith" as the response to Jesus' message do appear. In Matt. 18:6, the verb is used to summarize the defining characteristic of a child of God as a "little one who believes" (= Mark 9:42). In addition, in Mark 1:15, it is used as a summary term of response to Jesus' call to believe the gospel of the kingdom, where both "repent" and "believe" appear. In Matt. 27:42, the verb is used ironically by taunters who say they will believe if Jesus comes down from the cross (= Mark 15:32). The idea of believing also is a summary term for what Satan prevents in the Lukan version of the parable of the seed (Luke 8:12; a reference to short-lived faith is present in 8:13). The lack of believing response also causes Jesus' rebuke of the two men of Emmaus (Luke 24:25).

In John's Gospel, the noun "faith" is not used. However, it does show up in its verbal form as the summary response term. In fact, John's use of the act of believing parallels the Epistles' use of the term "faith" as a summary term (John 1:7, 12; 2:11, 23; 3:12, 15, 16, 18, 36; 4:39; 5:24, 46; 6:29, 35, 40, 47, 69; 7:31, 38; 8:24, 31 [short-lived faith]; 9:38; 10:25–26, 42; 11:25–27, 48; 12:11, 36, 42, 44, 46; 14:1, 10–12; 16:27, 30–31; 17:8, 20–21; 19:35; 20:8, 25, 29, 31). No text highlights the importance of faith and its dynamic ongoing character more than John 6:60–68, where Peter confesses for the disciples that they will not walk away from Jesus, because he has the words of life. The concept of abiding in Jesus' word has its roots in a response like this (John 15:1–11). Here is a response term that looks at reception in terms of where it ends up. It trusts in God and his work through Jesus.

Calling Disciples and the Twelve

Five texts are prominent when it comes to picturing the calling of disciples. When Jesus walks by some fishermen cleaning their nets, they drop what they are doing and leave everything behind to follow him (Mark 1:16–20 = Matt. 4:18–22). The call here is to become "fishers" of people. Similar is a scene that confirms this call with the miraculous catch of fish (Luke 5:1–11). The additional element here is the surfacing of Peter's exemplary attitude whereby he obeys Jesus in casting the nets despite the seeming futility of the instruction. Peter confesses his sinfulness, a humility that Jesus can work with because Peter is responsive to him. There is the call of Levi, showing Jesus reaching out to the "rejected" of society (Matt. 9:9–13 = Mark 2:13–17 = Luke 5:27–32). We previously noted the mission statement about Jesus' call to sinners that this event produced. There is another set of discipleship call texts, in which the priority of putting this response above everything else, including the family requirement to bury a father, shows it to be the single most important decision one makes (Matt. 8:19–22 = Luke 9:57–62). Finally, Luke 14:25–35 makes it clear to the multitudes that the cost of discipleship must be counted. Jesus wanted the crowds to know what the walk entailed before they started into it. Kingdom parables pointing to the value of being in the kingdom make the same point while picturing a related concept (Matt. 13:44–46).

The formation of the Twelve also shows Jesus' intent to build a community around people whom he expects one day to lead his new community (Matt. 10:2–4 = Mark 3:16–19 = Luke 6:13–16).[94] It is these twelve whom he sends out into mission to call Israel to the kingdom and repentance. Jesus gives them ability to illustrate the coming of God's rule with miraculous authority (Matt. 10:1–15 = Luke 9:1–6). To the leader of these twelve, he says that he will build his church, after hearing Peter's messianic confession (Matt. 16:13–20). To them Jesus promises a kingdom and the right to sit over the twelve tribes of Israel (Luke 22:29–30 = Matt. 19:28). Jesus intentionally is restructuring the people of God around a community that he forms. Interestingly, he does not count himself as one of the Twelve, for he stands distinct and above them in authority.

When it comes to forming a new community, the formation of the Twelve shows an intentionality about Jesus. He is forming a community grounded in humble dedication to God as an expression of a renewal and realization of Israel's hope. The choice of the Twelve shows that Jesus consciously seeks to parallel Israel and make a claim on Israel. The mission of the Twelve is to call others into this new relationship, which connects to Israel's hope but is distinct from some current structures in Israel. The emphasis and priorities of those who see their need for God and his rule as Jesus represents it will be different from those of current Judaism, with its focus on Jewish identity markers tied to the law. This leads us into the theme of discipleship and the inherent reaction that such a calling evokes from the community needing reform out of which it emerged.

Discipleship

We previously noted five texts in which a calling to follow Jesus takes place.[95] They highlight how the call to mission led the disciples immediately to leave their vocational tasks to take up with Jesus. A prominent theme in all the Gospels is discipleship and referring to those who embrace Jesus as disciples. The noun "disciple" (μαθητής) appears frequently in each Gospel and

94. For a full development of this theme and a defense of its fundamental historicity, see Scot McKnight, "Jesus and the Twelve," *Bulletin for Biblical Research* 11 (2001): 203–31.

95. There were the two accounts of the call to the four fishermen, the call of Levi, the miraculous catch of fish, and the urgent call to discipleship. For this section, see Richard N. Longenecker, ed., *Patterns of Discipleship in the New Testament,* McMaster New Testament Studies (Grand Rapids: Eerdmans, 1996), 1–97.

refers to a "learner." It appears seventy-two times in Matthew, forty-six times in Mark, thirty-seven times in Luke, and seventy-eight times in John. The term is not used again in the New Testament outside of the Book of Acts. Thus, this is a term associated with Jesus' ministry.

What discipleship involves is a total commitment. All other relationships take a backseat to discipleship, including caring for one's parents in death, a category that Jesus selects because it was considered to be one of the highest familial duties (Luke 9:59 = Matt. 8:21–22). No one pursuing discipleship is to pause to inform family, an image that stands in contrast to Elijah's calling of Elisha (Luke 9:61–62; cf. 1 Kings 19:19–21). In fact, the choice to follow Jesus could well split families (Matt. 10:34–39 = Luke 12:49–53).

Discipleship involves a struggle to grasp all that it requires, and so progress can be difficult. One of the unique elements in Mark's Gospel is how it portrays the disciples as stumbling and bumbling their way through their walk with Jesus during his lifetime. Luke 9 also portrays many missteps, but Jesus treats the disciples with patience because their desire is to follow him.

Discipleship is to be entered into with forethought lest one embarassingly not complete the assignment (Luke 14:25–35). However, it also should be entered into with an awareness that one is not stronger than God. So one should not oppose him. Thus, discipleship is to come first, ahead of all other allegiances and relationships, including to one's own life (Matt. 10:37 = Luke 14:26; Matt. 16:25 = Mark 8:35 = Luke 9:24; Luke 14:33). Discipleship also entails suffering, a taking up of the cross, which Luke further notes is taken up daily (Matt. 16:24 = Mark 8:34 = Luke 9:23). It means an unsettled life (Matt. 8:19–20 = Luke 9:57–58). For Luke, the disciple will appreciate that separation from the world means a different attitude toward possessions (Luke 12:13–21; 16:10–13; Matt. 6:24).

For John's Gospel, discipleship means facing rejection from the Jews and a separation from the world (John 9:22; 12:42; 16:2; 17:14–16). We saw that in John's Gospel, believing in Jesus is central to defining who a follower of Jesus is. To be a disciple is to know the Father and the Son (John 6:69; 17:3). It is to be a member of Jesus' personal flock, which recognizes his voice (John 10:7–18). The disciple bears fruit (15:1–7), loves (15:12–13), and serves (13:14–16).

The character of the disciple also is a topic of concern. The theme of the disciple's love shows up in the Synoptics (Matt. 22:34–40 = Mark 12:28–31 [like Luke 10:25–28]). Forgiveness also is a characteristic of the disciple, as the Lord's Prayer points out, and as is dramatically demonstrated in a parable unique to Matthew (Matt. 18:21–35). Leadership is to be exercised not in acts of power, as is done among the Gentiles, but in service (Matt. 20:25–28 = Mark 10:42–45 = Luke 22:24–27). The disciple also is called to mission (Matt. 5:14–16; 28:18–20; Luke 24:47).

Many of the parables pick up themes tied to discipleship. They emphasize the need to heed what Jesus teaches (house on the rock [Matt. 7:24–27 = Luke 6:47–49]), to forgive (two debtors [Luke 7:41–44]; unforgiving servant [Matt. 18:23–35]), to respond to the word (the sower [Mark 4:1–20 = Matt. 13:1–23 = Luke 8:4–15]), to love one's neighbor (good Samaritan [Luke 10:29–37]), to pray (bold neighbor [Luke 11:5–8]; nagging widow [Luke 18:1–8]), to be generous (rich fool [Luke 12:13–21]; rich man and Lazarus [Luke 16:19–31]), to be accountable to God and alert to him (watchful servant [Luke 12:35–48]; ten virgins [Matt. 25:1–13]; pounds/talents [Luke 19:11–27, like Matt. 25:14–30]; fig tree [Luke 21:29–33]), to be humble (seats at the banquet [Luke 14:7–14]; Pharisee and tax collector [Luke 18:9–14]), to be totally committed to God (tower and warring king [Luke 14:25–33]), to serve as a matter of duty (uncommended servant [Luke 17:7–10]), and to be useful (salt [Matt. 5:13, like Luke 14:34–35]).

Jesus was concerned that those who follow him be prepared for the task and appreciate what a calling to walk in God's way involves. These themes also are multiply attested, appearing at all levels of the Gospel tradition. Much of his practical instruction and ethical emphasis shows up in discourses on discipleship or in parabolic teaching. We will return to some of these themes tied to expressed righteousness when we consider how Jesus calls on his followers to relate to the world.

The Role of Parables

The parables, so prominent in discipleship teaching, were also a veiled form of teaching that reflected a judgment on those who did not wish to embrace Jesus (Matt. 13:10–17 = Mark 4:10–12 = Luke 8:9–10). They were mysteries through which the kingdom and the calling were revealed.[96]

The parables cover far more than issues of discipleship and spiritual life. The parables divide up into the following themes: now is the new day of salvation (Matt. 9:14–17 = Mark 2:18–22 = Luke 5:33–38; Mark 4:21–25 = Luke 8:16), the call to pay attention to the light (Matt. 6:22–23 = Luke 11:34–36), the invitation to the banquet (Matt. 22:1–10; Luke 14:15–24), the mercy of God for sinners and lost disciples (sinners: Luke 7:41–43; 15:11–32; 18:9–14; disciples: Matt. 18:10–14), the great assurance of access to God (Luke 11:5–8; 18:1–8), the kingdom and its growth (Matt. 13:31–33 = Luke 13:18–21), the imminence of catastrophe or judgment (Matt. 25:31–

---

96. This area is one of the more prominent aspects of Jesus' teaching. I can only very simply summarize its contribution to show the breadth of its usage. For more detail, see Craig Blomberg, *Interpreting the Parables* (Downers Grove, Ill.: InterVarsity, 1991); Simon Kistemaker, *The Parables of Jesus* (Grand Rapids: Baker, 1980); Joachim Jeremias, *The Parables of Jesus*, trans. S. H. Hooke, rev. ed., New Testament Library (Philadelphia: Westminster, 1963).

46; Luke 12:16–21, 49–53; Matt. 10:34–36 = Luke 12:51–53; 13:6–9), it may be too late (Luke 13:6–9; 14:15–24 = Matt. 22:1–14), the need to listen to and obey Jesus (Luke 6:47–49 = Matt. 7:24–27; Luke 11:24–26 = Matt. 12:43–45; Luke 12:58–59), accountability as a matter of faithful serving (Luke 16:1–9; 17:7–10; Matt. 25:14–30 = Luke 19:12–27; Matt. 21:28–32), care for the poor and warnings about wealth (Luke 12:13–21; 16:19–31), the call to love (Luke 10:25–37), the call not to worry (Matt. 6:25–34 = Luke 12:22–32), the way is narrow (Matt. 7:13–14 [like Luke 13:23–24]), the return (Matt. 24:45–51; Luke 12:35–40), the kingdom in general (Matt. 13 = Mark 4 = Luke 8:1–15; Luke 13:19–21), the equality of grace (Matt. 20:1–16), and the rejection and exaltation of the Son in the face of wicked tenants (Matt. 21:33–46 = Mark 12:1–12 = Luke 20:9–19).

The use of these instructional stories was one of the most basic elements of Jesus' teaching. The bulk of the parables treats themes tied to describing the kingdom, the return and its associated judgment, or the behavior of disciples.

Community: Israel, Expansion to Gentiles, and Worship

One of the oddities for a modern reader of the Gospels is how focused Jesus' mission was on Israel. However, it is too often forgotten that Jesus' program was a realization of promises originally made to that nation. It was the program of the God of Abraham, Isaac, and Jacob. Nothing in Jesus' activity indicates that he diverted from these roots in terms of the focus of his own program, although there also are hints that Jesus foresaw a day when his effort would reach out to the nations.[97]

Several texts point to Jesus' concern for Israel, with the concentration of such texts tied to Jesus' remarks appearing in Matthew's Gospel.[98] In the mission of the disciples, Jesus sends them out only to "the lost sheep of Israel," specifically excluding a mission to Gentiles or to Samaria (Matt. 10:5–6). He sees this mission to Israelite towns as continuing until the Son of Man comes

97. Two recent approaches to Jesus have emphasized how in line with Israel and its hopes this story was. Both G. B. Caird, *New Testament Theology*, compl. and ed. L. D. Hurst (Oxford: Clarendon, 1994), 350–66, and Wright, *Jesus and the Victory of God*, saw this to be the central, defining feature of Jesus' message. Jesus declares the end of Israel's spiritual exile in the offer of the kingdom. For an assessment of Wright's approach, see Carey C. Newman, ed., *Jesus and the Restoration of Israel: A Critical Assessment of N. T. Wright's Jesus and the Victory of God* (Downers Grove, Ill.: InterVarsity, 1999). A classic work discussing these themes is Joachim Jeremias, *Jesus' Promise to the Nations*, trans. S. H. Hooke, rev. ed. (Philadelphia: Fortress, 1982).

98. In fact, Mark does not even raise this theme in any detail, probably because of his Gentile audience. Matthew has seven relevant texts (Matt. 2:6; 10:6[J], 23[J]; 15:24[J], 31; 19:28[J]; 27:42), while Luke has seven, but most of his texts are in narrative remarks (Luke 1:54, 68; 2:25, 32, 34; 22:30[J] [= Matt. 19:28]; 24:21). The letter *J* by a verse means that Jesus is portrayed as speaking.

(Matt. 10:23). When confronted by a Gentile, Jesus specifically says that he was sent only to the lost sheep of the house of Israel (Matt. 15:24; interestingly, Mark lacks this specific response). The success of his ministry means that the God of Israel receives the glory (Matt. 15:31). Eschatologically, Israel is still in view, as one day the twelve apostles will judge the twelve tribes of Israel (Matt. 19:28 = Luke 22:30). Narrative remarks point to this focus as well. The citation of Mic. 5:2 leads to a description in Matt. 2:6 of Jesus as one who will govern God's people Israel. The taunting on the cross causes some to joke about Jesus as "King of Israel" (Matt. 27:42; Mark 15:32). The births of John and of Jesus lead to a mission for Israel in line with covenant and prophetic hope (Luke 1:16, 54, 68). Simeon's welcome to Jesus is that of a faithful Jew who was looking for "the consolation of Israel" (Luke 2:25). According to Simeon, Jesus comes as "glory for your people Israel" and one who will be "set for the fall and rising of many in Israel" (Luke 2:32, 34). The two disciples on the road to Emmaus had hoped that Jesus would be the "one to redeem Israel" (Luke 24:21). In John's Gospel, the witness of John the Baptist is that Jesus received the confirmation of heaven at the baptism "that he might be revealed to Israel" (John 1:31). Both Nathanael and the crowds that greet Jesus' entry to Jerusalem hail him as "King of Israel" (John 1:49; 12:13). Jesus' forming of the Twelve points to an intent to reform Israel, as previously noted.

Jesus' pronouncement of judgment on the nation also shows his national concern. Here, the Olivet discourse is prominent (Matt. 24 = Mark 13 = Luke 21), but so are earlier remarks about Israel or Jerusalem's coming fate and the image of the withered fig tree (Luke 13:6–9, 34–35; 19:41–44; 23:27–31). Some of these texts hold out hope that this judgment is not final, that one day the "times of the Gentiles" will be done; Israel's house is desolate until they cry out, "Blessed is the one who comes in the name of the Lord" (Luke 21:24; 13:35). So much of Jesus' concern for Israel is seen also in how he handled issues of law and purity (treated earlier in this chapter). His goal was to instruct and reform Israel in its walk with the God of promise. The condition of Israel and the arrival of the new era called for such reform, as John the Baptist's ministry also suggested.

However, it would be wrong to suggest that the portrait of Jesus in the Gospels ignored the potential inclusion of the nations in Jesus' mission.[99] Three of his more prominent miracles involved Gentiles (the centurion [Matt. 8:5–13 = Luke 7:1–10]; the Gentile woman's daughter [Mark 7:24–30 = Matt. 15:21–28]; the Gadarene demoniac—probably Gentile, as this Decapolis area

99. There is another class of texts that show how Jesus used the Gentiles as a negative example of how the world operates. In these passages the Gentiles become the measure of how not to act (Matt. 5:47; Matt. 6:32 = Luke 12:30; Matt. 20:25 = Mark 10:42; Luke 22:25). The tone of these texts shows how deeply Jewish Jesus is in his teaching perspective.

was predominantly Gentile and pigs are involved in the miracle [Mark 5:1–20; Matt. 8:28–34 = Luke 8:26–39]). Even though Jesus' initial response to the Gentile woman asking him to heal her daughter is a reply about the exclusive focus of his call, he moves to honor her request. Jesus also drew from Gentile areas, as the summaries of the location of his work and the sources of the crowds before the Sermon on the Mount make clear (Matt. 4:13–15, 24–25). Jesus' ministry of bringing justice and hope to the nations in line with the call of the Servant is expressed in a narrative note in Matt. 12:18–21. Luke also strikes this note. In the synagogue sermon in Luke 4:25–27, Jesus suggests that Israel's lack of response will produce a time like that of Elijah and Elisha, when blessing came only to Gentiles, a remark that sparks the Jewish audience's anger. In addition, the work of John the Baptist and the one who comes after him represent the time when "all flesh will see the salvation of God" (Luke 3:6).

Other texts explicitly have Jesus teaching that those included in the banquet at the end will involve many coming from north, south, east, and west, but some of Israel will be excluded (Matt. 8:11–12; Luke 13:28–29). John 4 and 12 present Jesus in dialogues with Samaritans and Greeks, while Luke 9:51–56 has Jesus sending a mission into Samaria. Luke 17:11–19 has Jesus commending the faith of a foreigner. In Mark 11:17, the temple is to be a place of prayer for the nations, probably looking to a day in the future when the nations will stream to Jerusalem to pray and worship (citing Isa. 56:7; see also Isa. 2:2–4; 19:23–25; 42:6; 49:6; 66:19–20; Mic. 4:1–2; Zech. 14:16 [all rooted in Gen. 12:1–3]).[100] Jesus explicitly mentions how the mission of the disciples involves going out into all the world (Matt. 24:14 = Mark 13:10; Matt. 26:13 = Mark 14:9). The vineyard, lacking fruit from Israel, will be given to another nation bearing fruit (Matt. 21:33–46 = Mark 12:1–10 = Luke 20:9–19). Jesus gives commissions to this effect at the end of his ministry (Matt. 28:18–20; Luke 24:44–47; Acts 1:8). The Book of Acts makes it clear that the import of these instructions to go to all the nations, running so counter to the focus of Jesus' own earthly ministry, took time to sink in for the disciples. However, nothing in Jesus' ministry, even as it focused on Israel, precluded the inclusion of the nations. In fact, a look at how the relationship of Jew and Gentile plays itself out underscores what Paul said later about the gospel being "to the Jew first and also to the Greek" (Rom. 1:16). All of this emphasis is in line with the prophetic hope, except that Jesus' teaching lacks any notes of retribution against the nations as such. As we will see, the vindication that God brings in judgment will be directed at the wicked, whoever they may be. God will move to gather the righteous who have welcomed Jesus and those associated with him (Matt. 25:31–46). The kingdom's authority and reach will extend out over the entire world (Matt. 13:37–43).

100. For this theme, see Jeremias, *Jesus' Promise to the Nations,* 57–73.

When it comes to religious practice and worship, Jesus also is at points very Jewish. He goes to the synagogue and ministers (Luke 4:16–30 = Matt. 13:53–58 = Mark 6:1–6; Matt. 12:9–14 = Mark 3:1–6 = Luke 6:6–11; Luke 13:10–17). He sends a healed leper to the priest in obedience to the law (Mark 1:40–45 = Matt. 8:2–4 = Luke 5:12–16). He teaches in the temple courts and is concerned for the well-being of the temple, as the cleansing incident shows. In this way, he is typically Jewish.

However, other acts show a conscious effort by Jesus to be distinct. He is not particularly sensitive to some issues of purity tied to hand washing or to the touching of lepers or the dead (Luke 7:11–17; 11:37–41; Mark 7:1–23 = Matt. 15:1–20). He is willing to create a prayer that is distinct for his disciples (Luke 11:1–4). His remarks at the Last Supper lead to the institution of a meal of remembrance and affirmation by his disciples. Interestingly, Jesus says nothing about the form of worship. What he calls for is integrity in worship, whereby one who approaches the altar does so without having anything against a brother or sister (Matt. 5:21–26), and whereby those who tithe also should remember justice, love, mercy, and faith (Matt. 23:23–24 [like Luke 11:42–43]). Worship is to be in spirit and in truth (John 4:24). Matthew, and Luke in particular, have Jesus praying regularly and exhorting with respect to prayer as well as acts of charity (Luke 3:21; 11:1–13; Matt. 6:1–18; 7:7–11). The vulnerable position of those whom he seeks to serve is pictured in the image of the flock or the picture of lost sheep (Matt. 9:35–38; 10:6; 15:24; Mark 14:27; Luke 12:32; 15:3–7). This is why the community needs to hear the voice of the shepherd sent from God (John 10:1–18). Clearly, the community that Jesus forms is to be in healthy, dependent communion with God, living a life of righteous character, which brings us to the next topic concerning community.

The Character of the Disciple and the Relationship to the World

Here we consider five major areas: love-mercy, righteous integrity, possessions and the world, suffering, and service-mission.

Love and Mercy. At the base of the ethical call of Jesus stands the command to love and the call for mercy. Several texts make this point. The most dramatic text is Mark 12:28–34 = Matt. 22:35–40 (like Luke 10:25–28). Here, a question about the primary commandment invokes the Shema of Deut. 6:4 and then immediately follows it with the call to love one's neighbor as oneself. In other words, love for God will translate into sensitive care and concern for others. Discipleship is not only about relationship with God but also about how that relationship makes for better relationships with others. The concluding remark is that all the law and prophets depend on this. A similar answer to the same question is commended by Jesus in the Luke 10:25–28 passage. Yet another passage emphasizes this ethical base: Matt. 19:16–30 = Mark 10:17–31 (like Luke 18:18–30). Here the issue is the reception of eternal life. The initial reply comes in terms of the commands of the second half of the Ten Commandments, the portion treating human relationships. The rest of the answer later comes in terms of allying oneself to Jesus and his cause, but the two ideas should not be disconnected. To ally oneself to Jesus and follow him means that God will be loved and that one's neighbor will be treated with love and integrity as well. That is part of the practical result of what turning to God in the call of Jesus involves. Luke sets up this point in the ministry of John the Baptist, where the prophet's work and call to repentance also realigns relationships to God and others (Luke 3:7–14). Luke also highlights this theme in the parable of the good Samaritan, which underscores what a good neighbor is while also making the point that neighbors can come from surprising places, just as Samaritans were not respected by those of Israel. Luke and Matthew make the point again in texts that call for love of enemies (Matt. 5:43–48; Luke 6:27–36). In Matthew, vengeance and retaliation specifically are ruled out, as Jesus heightens the call of God.

Matthew has two additional texts that focus on the question of mercy, something that Luke already has pointed to in the call to imitate the mercy of the Father in Luke 6:35–36. The debate over Jesus' associations with tax collectors and sinners along with a Sabbath incident generate remarks about God desiring mercy, not sacrifice (Matt. 9:9–13; 12:1–8). The character of Jesus' ministry to those on the fringe, especially highlighted in Luke, also points to this theme. In John, this call is present in two key texts. The exchange over the woman caught in adultery shows how Jesus introduces sinners to forgiveness while calling them to righteousness (John 7:52–8:11). Mercy first is extended to the woman. The tone of Luke 7:36–50, with its commendation of the anointing by the sinful woman, is similar. The second Johannine text is the "new" commandment, whereby a premium is put on the disciples' love for one another as a testimony to being followers of Jesus (John 13:34–35). It is this call and standard that in part leads Jesus to call for disciples to have a righteousness that exceeds that of the Pharisees or to be "perfect" as the Father is perfect. It also is a concern for this standard that produces a unity in the community that drives Jesus' prayer in John 17, where such a response expresses knowing God and experiencing eternal life (John 17:3, 13–26). As John will put it later in one of his letters, "We love because he first loved us" (1 John 4:19). Paul expresses the same idea in teaching that we have been designed to walk in love and unity (Eph. 4–5). The other dimension of that call is Jesus' call for a walk of integrity of heart, as also seen in the antitheses of Matt. 5:21–48.

Righteous Integrity. The disciples' character also is a focus of Jesus' teaching. The disciples should live as lights and honor God (Matt. 5:14–15). Jesus' exposition of the law in Matt. 5:21–48 intensifies the Torah into an exhortation for what the citizen of the kingdom should be like from the heart. Here the issues are not just murder but also anger, not just adultery but also lust, not divorce but faithfulness to a commitment, not oath taking but truthfulness, not retaliation but serving vulnerably, not hatred or selective love but unconditional love and prayer. Life is to be lived in a way that is distinct from the way Gentiles live, in which one gives love only to those from whom love is received. It is this integrity of character that mirrors God (also Luke 6:35–36). The emphasis on what comes from the heart also appears when Jesus speaks of what truly defiles (Matt. 15:10–20 = Mark 7:14–23). The negative counterexample of this call to integrity is seen in Jesus' rebuke of the scribes and Pharisees in the woes that he gives to them in two different texts: Matt. 23 and Luke 11:37–52. Here, the negative example to avoid is hypocrisy. Jesus' emphasis on the fruit of the disciple also fits in here. Fruit is the goal of his ministry when seed is sown or a vineyard is planted (Matt. 13:23 = Mark 4:20 = Luke 8:15; Matt. 12:33–37 = Luke 6:43–45).

Possessions and the World. Jesus has much to say about devotion to the world and to possessions. His warning, encased within the parable of the sower, is about the threat to fruitfulness (Matt. 13:22 = Mark 4:19 = Luke 8:14). Jesus' call to trust God makes the point that God's care means that one does not need to be anxious about such concerns (Matt. 6:25–34 = Luke 12:22–32).

Several other texts make the point strongly that possessions can be an obstacle to God and can create a hard heart toward others. So in the exchange with the rich man, Jesus points out how difficult it is for a rich man to enter the kingdom (Matt. 19:23 = Mark 10:23 = Luke 18:24). Numerous parables in Luke likewise underscore this concern and warning. Jesus' concern about material things and their use appears in the parable of the rich fool (Luke 12:13–21) and in the parable about stewardship with its following remarks (Luke 16:1–13). Luke 16 is not just about money, but about any form of possession, as the term "mammon" indicates. Ethically, the point about hardheartedness and its spiritual risks surface in the scene involving the rich man and Lazarus (Luke 16:19–31). In contrast stands Jesus' praise of the widow who in offering her meager copper coins gives of her very life to God (Mark 12:41–44 = Luke 21:1–4). Another positive example is the repentant rich man Zacchaeus. He serves as a model for handling wealth because he now is generous with his possessions and fully rights the wrongs that he previously committed (Luke 19:1–10).

In one sense, the problem with attachment to possessions is that it reflects independence from God and excessive union with the world, which is an affront to God. To gain the world but lose the soul is a tragedy (Matt. 16:26 = Mark 8:36 = Luke 9:25 [like John 12:25]). John's Gospel makes this point by noting that the world's hatred of Jesus will carry over to his disciples and that his disciples are not of this world (John 7:7; 8:23; 15:18–19; 16:20, 33;

17:14). The world does not understand Jesus or what he represents (John 14:17). Jesus has taken them out of the world. They are his special objects of prayer as he calls them to face rejection in the world rather than isolate themselves from it (John 17:6, 9, 14–19). This leads into the next subtheme: suffering.

Suffering. In the world, to bear the cross is the mark of the disciple. Jesus did not teach a triumphalism of victory in the current era. Vindication and triumph await his return. Now, the disciples' call is to share in the rejection that Jesus met. The texts just noted in John's Gospel make this point. However, the clearest text on suffering appears just after Peter confesses Jesus to be the Christ at Caesarea Philippi. Here, Jesus turns immediately to preach his impending suffering and to call the disciples to be prepared to share in that road of shame and rejection (Matt. 16:24–27 = Mark 8:34–38 = Luke 9:23–26). Luke speaks of "counting the cost" of this discipleship, which will not be easy (Luke 14:25–33). In other texts, Jesus speaks of how the decision for him may split families (Matt. 10:34–39 = Luke 12:51–53). He offers encouragement by revealing that fearing God and acknowledging the Son of Man will lead to the disciple being acknowledged before God (Matt. 10:26–33 = Luke 12:1–12). In the Olivet discourse, Jesus notes that the persecution to come and the Spirit's enablement will allow disciples to testify on the gospel's behalf (Matt. 24:9–14 = Mark 13:9–13 = Luke 21:12–19). One whose trust is in God will endure (Luke 21:19).

Service-Mission. This ethical call to suffering and the risk that it includes do not mean that disciples are to withdraw from the world as the community at Qumran did. Jesus has sent disciples out into the world to serve it as an example, being like salt and light that draw attention to God's goodness (Matt. 5:13–16; John 17:11, 15). Whether it is seen in the mission of the disciples during Jesus' ministry (Matt. 10; Luke 9:1–6; 10:1–23) or in the commissions that conclude Matthew and Luke or begin Acts (Matt. 28:18–20; Luke 24:44–49; Acts 1:8), the call of the disciple is to take the message of the deliverance of God and forgiveness, along with the message of how one should live before God, into all the nations (Mark 13:10; 14:9). It is parallel to Jesus' call to enter into rest and give life's heavy burden to him (Matt. 11:28–30). In addition, the example of Jesus' general compassion to outsiders shown in his healing ministry also indicates that acts of compassion serve as a testimony to the caring character of God.

Summary. Jesus defines his mission as that of the Servant who calls out to the captives to experience release (Luke 4:16–19). Everything about the character of Jesus' ministry wedded together words and deeds of compassion and showed the love of God standing behind his preaching of divine forgiveness and mercy. But the presence of the offer of forgiveness and mercy does not mean that salvation is automatic for everyone. Jesus formed a new community of those who wished to walk in what soon became known as "the way" (Acts

9:2; 18:25; 19:9). It was to be made up of Jews and eventually Gentiles who came to Jesus in a faith that had turned them to God out of a sense of spiritual need for deliverance and forgiveness. In embracing God and his love, they took on a commitment to love God and their neighbor, taking the message of this fresh walk into eternal life to a needy but rejecting world, with all the risk of suffering that this entailed. But not everyone would respond, and the suffering would be great. When would God resolve the need for justice to be dispensed? So here surfaces the final major theme of the vindication to come.

The Vindication to Come: Warning to Israel, Inclusion of Gentiles, and the Return of the Son of Man to Judge the World

Judgment texts can be divided into two types: (1) those that speak of judgment in general, and (2) those that describe the activity of the Son of Man. This theme is a major component of Jesus' teaching, as a textual listing shows.[101]

Mark: 3:28–29 (= Matt. 12:31–32 = Luke 12:10); 4:24 (= Matt. 7:2 = Luke 6:38); 4:25, 29; 6:11 (= Matt. 10:14 = Luke 9:5); 8:38 (= Matt. 10:32–33 = Luke 12:8–9); 9:43–49 (like Matt. 5:29–30); 10:25 (= Matt. 19:24 = Luke 18:25); 10:31 (= Matt. 19:30); 12:1–12 (= Matt. 21:33–46 = Luke 20:9–19, 40); 13:4, 13, 20, 24–27 (with parallels in Matt. 24 and Luke 21); 14:62 (= Matt. 26:64; like Luke 22:69)

Teaching material common to Matthew and Luke (i.e., Q): Matt. 7:1–2 = Luke 6:37–38; Matt. 7:13–14 (like Luke 13:23–24); Matt. 7:22–23 (like Luke 13:25–27); Matt. 7:24–27 = Luke 6:47–49; Matt. 8:11–12 (like Luke 13:28–29); Matt. 10:14 = Luke 9:5; Matt. 10:15 (like Luke 10:12); Matt. 10:28 (like Luke 12:4–5); Matt. 10:32 (like Luke 12:8–9); Matt. 10:39 (like Luke 17:33); Matt. 11:6 = Luke 7:23; Matt. 11:21–24 (like Luke 10:13–15); Matt. 12:27 = Luke 11:19; Matt. 12:32 = Luke 12:10; Matt. 12:41–42 = Luke 11:31–32; Matt. 19:28 (like Luke 22:28–30); Matt. 23:34–36 (like Luke 11:49–51); Matt. 23:37–39 (like Luke 13:34–35); Matt. 24:37–39 (like Luke 17:26–29); Matt. 24:40–41 (like Luke 17:34–35); Matt. 24:45–51 (like Luke 12:42–46); Matt. 25:11–12 (like Luke 13:25); Matt. 25:14–30 (like

101. For a comprehensive study of this theme minus Son of Man texts, see Marius Reiser, *Jesus and Judgment: The Eschatological Proclamation in Its Jewish Context,* trans. Linda M. Maloney (Minneapolis: Fortress, 1997). In the list that follows, the description that a text is "like" another indicates that it is not clear that the passage is a true parallel. It may only be a text with a similar theme.

Luke 19:11–27); Luke 11:30 (like Matt. 12:40); Luke 14:16–24 (like Matt. 22:2–14)

Matthew only: 5:4, 7, 22; 7:19, 21; 8:29; 12:36–37; 13:24–30, 36–43, 47–50; 15:13; 18:14, 23–35; 21:43; 23:33; 25:31–46

Luke only: 6:21, 24–26; 10:20; 12:48–49, 58–59; 13:2–5, 6–9; 14:11; 16:1–8, 19–31[102]

Clearly, the theme of judgment is widely distributed in the Gospel material. While Jesus' general remarks about judgment often serve to warn national Israel of its risk, the Son of Man sayings move in a more comprehensive direction. I treat these themes in this sequence.

Many of Jesus' general remarks about judgment are designed to challenge Israel to respond to the promise he offers by reversing expectations that they had about who would receive blessing. Thus, in Matt. 12:41–42 = Luke 11:31–32, there is Jesus' remark that the Queen of the South and the people of Nineveh will rise up at the judgment and be witnesses against the nation of this generation and condemn it for failing to see that one greater than Solomon or Jonah is present. Two features are important in this warning. First is that Gentiles are portrayed as being more responsive than Jews (a similar theme appears in Luke 4:24–27). Second is that the issue of a lack of responsiveness focuses on the person of Jesus, not just on what he teaches. His person should be embraced because he is greater than the king of wisdom (Solomon) and is more important than a prophet like Jonah.[103]

Similar in tone is a second text. In Matt. 11:21–24 = Luke 10:13–15, Jesus notes that the judgment will be more tolerable for the wicked Gentile cities of Tyre and Sidon than for Chorazin and Bethsaida, while Capernaum will be brought down to Sheol. In favor of the authenticity of this saying is that Chorazin is an obscure town that appears nowhere else in the Gospel tradition. If the saying were a later creation of the church put onto Jesus' lips, why would it highlight a town of no significance? In Matthew, Jesus goes on to note that even a place like Sodom would have responded to such an opportunity to repent. Hard-heartedness about Jesus' call to repent will meet with judgment. So, both well-known and obscure towns are included in Jesus' warning about the consequences of rejecting his message.

102. Reiser, *Jesus and Judgment*, 303, says that this comprises 37 verses in Mark (or 22 percent of Jesus' discourse material in this Gospel), 76 verses of Q (or 35 percent of Q material), 60 verses of Matthean special material (64 percent of Matthew's discourse material), and 37 verses in Luke's unique material (28 percent of Luke's special material). My list does not match Reiser's numbers exactly because I note parallel texts more fully, but the figures are generally on the mark. They reveal how important this theme is for Jesus, in contrast to the Jesus Seminar's claim that Jesus did not teach about judgment.

103. Reiser, *Jesus and Judgment*, 219–20, defends the authenticity of this saying, including its open but indirect Christology, which he argues would not be the approach of a text created by the church.

A third warning to Israel with the provocative note of Gentile inclusion appears in Matt. 8:11–12 = Luke 13:28–29. Here the image is of people coming from east and west (Luke adds north and south) to sit at the banquet table of the kingdom while the "children of the kingdom" (Matthew) or "you yourselves" (Luke) are thrust out into "outer darkness" (Matthew), where there is weeping and gnashing of teeth.[104] Again the warning is to Israel for its refusal, with the disturbing note that Gentiles, even many of them, will fare better.

A fourth text with the same themes is the parable of the rejected invitation to the feast in Matt. 22:2–14 = Luke 14:16–24. It sometimes is disputed that the new invitees include an outreach to Gentiles. However, the pattern of these texts as a group argues in favor of an allusion to them. Here it is the fringe plus the Gentiles that are seen as "in," while those originally invited miss the banquet, which comes now and is not postponed until later. To miss the invitation now and not respond is to miss the blessing of kingdom.

That repentance is important for escaping judgment is explained in Luke 13:1–9. Here the issue is whether a judgment through a social tragedy or a natural disaster is indicative of the presence of judgment on "worse" sinners. Jesus does not answer that question, but instead warns that without repentance all will perish. This warning to individuals then is made more corporate by a parable in which a fig tree, picturing Israel, fails to yield fruit. The parable argues that the nation has only a short time left to respond. The image of the separating judgment in John the Baptist's teaching and in Jesus' kingdom parables makes a similar point (Matt. 3:7–12 = Luke 3:7–9, 16–17; Mark 4:29 = Matt. 9:37 [like Luke 10:2]; Matt. 10:14).

Finally, that Israel is a focus of this judgment also is seen in Matt. 19:28 (like Luke 22:28–30), where Jesus' chosen disciples sit as judges over Israel. These texts underscore the fact that Jesus had a special ministry to Israel and held that nation especially accountable for how it reacted to him, even at times trying to shame its people with the prospect that the hated Gentiles would fare better in the judgment to come. The issue in these texts is a proper response to Jesus and his message in turning to God and embracing the kingdom that Jesus brings in a way that leads to the bearing of fruit. So people had better get their accounts sorted out with God (Luke 12:57–59), and also, as beneficiaries of grace and forgiveness, be ready to show the same to others (Matt. 18:23–35).

More comprehensive in scope are the Son of Man judgment texts and the judgment imagery emerging from the kingdom parables, especially several unique parables in Matt. 13.

---

104. Both expressions, outer darkness and weeping and gnashing of teeth, are figures associated with being rejected in judgment (Reiser, *Jesus and Judgment,* 236–39). On darkness, see *1 Enoch* 10.4; 10.8; *Jubilees* 7.29; *Psalms of Solomon* 14.9; 15.10.

These kingdom parables make it clear that although Israel is a focus (Mark 12:1–12 = Matt. 21:33–46 = Luke 20:9–19), the ultimate scope of Jesus' rule extends across the entire earth (Matt. 13:24–30, 36–43).[105] In the crucially important parable of the wheat and darnel, Jesus makes it clear that kingdom authority extends to "the field" of the "world." Thus, kingdom judgment is comprehensive and comes at the "end of the age." The executor of the judgment is the Son of Man, who carries it out in the presence of the angels. The result is a dividing of humanity into the righteous, who shine as light in the kingdom, and the evildoers, who are cast into fire, where there is weeping and gnashing of teeth. The point is made again in less elaborate detail in the parable of the net (Matt. 13:47–50).

The judgment rotates around two themes: the performance of righteousness, tightly linked to the recognition of the Son of Man. Whereas the kingdom parables speak of the doing of righteousness, the Son of Man sayings tend to highlight the embracing of the Son of Man, although the theme of judgment tied to righteousness also appears (Matt. 16:27 = Mark 8:38 = Luke 9:26). Matthew alone highlights the judgment's attachment to the standard of "according to one's deed." It is a decision about the Son of Man that looks to be in view here as "the deed." Mark and Luke speak of "being ashamed of [Jesus]." The point may well be that response to Jesus leads to righteousness.[106] A key text here is Matt. 10:32–33 = Luke 12:8–9. To acknowledge the Son before humanity (i.e., to embrace and testify to him) is to receive the promise that the Son of Man will acknowledge the respondent before the angels in judgment. The linkage between the idea of righteousness and responding to Jesus is seen most vividly in the parable of the judgment of the nations (Matt. 25:31–46). Here it is the treatment of those tied to Jesus with acts of service and compassion that allows one to be a "sheep" and enter into the kingdom. The assumption in the parable is that embracing Jesus leads to a change of heart and of behavior that God will honor. This is not unlike the emphasis that one sees in John the Baptist as one who prepared the way (Luke 1:16–17; 3:10–14). This same emphasis is also assumed in the Sermons on the Mount and on the Plain (Matt. 5–7; Luke 6:20–49).[107]

The apocalyptic Son of Man sayings tend to surface toward the end of Jesus' ministry. The eschatological discourse material is key here (Matt. 24–25; Mark

105. Reiser, *Jesus and Judgment*, 238–39, points out how Jesus' imagery of judgment deals not with a transcendent kingdom hope but one expressed on this earth and history. This point is well made. Reiser's failure to treat Son of Man texts leads, however, to an inadequate appreciation of the comprehensiveness of Jesus' claim to judge the world, as well as an understatement of the nature of hope of Gentile inclusion anticipated in these texts.

106. In Paul, Rom. 6 and 8 make this linkage emphatically.

107. The same point was made above in the subsection "Kingdom and Ethics."

13; Luke 17:22–37; 21:5–38).[108] The judgment will come suddenly. Other texts speak of it as a thief in the night (Luke 12:39; Matt. 24:43), coming at an unexpected hour (Luke 12:40; Matt. 24:44), appearing instantly like lightning (Luke 17:24; Matt. 24:27), or coming as in the days of Noah and Lot, suddenly in the midst of everyday life (Luke 17:26–30; Matt. 24:37–41). Beyond general signs of religious, political, and natural chaos, Jesus gives no calendrical detail. Rather, these texts stress the point that the judgment's uncertain timing and the accountability it brings require that one be alert, faithful, and always prepared (Luke 12:35–48 [like Matt. 24:43–51]; Matt. 25:1–13). It may well take longer to come than they might hope (Luke 17:22). This coming leads the nations to mourn, for it is a judgment that extends over the entire earth, with the unrighteous and unresponsive headed for condemnation (Matt. 24:30 = Mark 13:26 = Luke 21:27). The vindication involves the Son of Man coming with divine judgment authority, as indicated by his association with riding the clouds, an image from Dan. 7.

Another key text is Jesus' reply at the Jewish examination of him (Mark 14:62 = Matt. 26:64 [like Luke 22:69]). Key to this description of vindication is the declaration of total divine authority to judge even the Jewish leadership. Jesus makes this claim as one who is to be seen at God's right hand and coming on the clouds with final judgment authority. This theme also appears in John, but with less emphasis. John 5:27 has Jesus speak of being given authority to judge because he is the Son of Man. Here as well the judgment to come is based on both righteousness and response to Jesus (John 5:24, 28–29). Jesus also speaks of his words being a judge on the last day, underscoring the authority of his teaching (John 12:48). A narrative remark in John also focuses the judgment on how one responds to Jesus' message (John 3:18–19).

The picture of the Son of Man as judge does not detail the timing, other than the fact that judgment comes in association with return and the end of the age.[109] More important for Jesus is the idea that judgment and eschatolog-

108. The theme here is the final judgment, but it should be recalled that this discourse is a "pattern" prophecy in which the judgment on Israel and the destruction of the temple (predicted for A.D. 70) are seen as a microcosm of the way final judgment proceeds. After all, it is Jesus' observation about the temple's destruction that triggers the discourse. That A.D. 70 is not the only event referred to here is seen in the remarks about unprecedented tribulation in the Matthean and Markan versions of the discourse, which show that their Gospels are highlighting the end judgment in contrast to Luke, who highlights the nearer type. Also, the theme of gathering together those who believe precludes an exclusive refernce to A.D. 70. See the detailed discussion of these passages in chapter 11, units 245–53.

109. In considering the doctrine of the "end times," issues of timing are addressed through consideration of other texts, both in the Old and New Testaments, that detail the contents of this consummative era. Thus, Peter speaks of the return of Jesus leading to the completion of all that the Old Testament already had taught (Acts 3:18–21). The christological point in judgment is that God has appointed one (Jesus) to be the judge of the living and the dead, a message that Luke shows is the way the gospel was summarized to Gentile audiences that did not know the Old Testament (Acts 10:42–43; 17:31) and could not appreciate who the Son of Man is.

ical hope show that everyone is accountable to God and must be ready to settle accounts with him. No theme shows the centrality of Jesus' person and authority more than the fact that he is responsible for the final judgment. Here, Jesus' favorite title, Son of Man, comes into play, drawing on the imagery of Dan. 7 to make the point that the one whom God promised would have such authority. In fact, the Son of Man has come both in ministry and to suffer, as his earthly ministry shows. Of course, it is the journey to the cross and what resulted from the resurrection that indicate that Jesus assumed such a role in God's plan. It is to the events and teaching of this crucial last week that we now turn to conclude this study.

Jesus' Final Week: A Dispute over Authority Leads to the Cross, Resurrection, and Seating with Authority at God's Right Hand

This survey of Jesus' theology and ministry closes by focusing attention on the crucial last week of his ministry as the Gospels present it. This sequence of key events leads to Jesus' arrest, trials, conviction, and crucifixion. There is a unity to the story at this point that magnifies the importance of these events. By this time, the Jewish leaders have made their own assessment of Jesus' claims and have rejected them. They had been exposed to much of the teaching that informs the earlier portions of this chapter and had rebuffed Jesus' claims to unique authority. The last week does not happen in a vacuum. What already has taken place leads to the strong reaction of the leadership during this crucial week. In turn, Jesus reacted to the leadership's assessment with pronouncements about the nation. At the center of the dispute stood Jesus' claims of authority as the unique representative of God. On top of all this stood ultimately the empty tomb and the events tied to it. It is here that Jesus ceased to be a failed dead prophet and was revealed to be far more to his disciples. To understand the importance of the resurrection and the claims associated with it, one must appreciate the debate of the final week of Jesus' life. This overview of the key elements of the week starts with the entrance of Jesus into Jerusalem.

Jesus entered the city on a donkey, evoking a claim of kingship through the disciples' praising God's work and the hope of kingship (Matt. 21:1–9 = Mark 11:1–10 = Luke 19:28–40 = John 12:12–16). Although John's Gospel is clear that the significance of this event in terms of Zech. 9:9 is something that the disciples came to appreciate only later, the entry was a declaration of the arrival of the promised figure and a time of hope. It was the offer to the nation of its king, but with an air of humility that paralleled the larger suffering and service character of Jesus' ministry. Thus, Jesus entered the city not merely as a pilgrim or even as a prophet, but as a messianic claimant. All the Gospels underscore the eschatological notes of the entry. Luke and John note in different ways how the Pharisees reacted to this event. In Luke, they make an effort to get Jesus to stop this proclamation of praise, but Jesus refuses. In John, the emphasis is how popular Jesus is. They sense the threat of his claims.

As Luke alone notes, Jesus enters the city quite aware that the leadership will not accept him, precluding the mass of the populace from embracing him. Weeping at the tragedy of it all, he declares that the nation, epitomized by the city, will be judged because "you did not know the time of your visitation" (Luke 19:41–44).

The next event underscores Jesus' sense of call and identity as he moves into the temple to act against it symbolically by challenging the money changers (Matt. 21:12–13 = Mark 11:15–17 = Luke 19:45–46). The act was significant because the temple was the central place of worship for Judaism, the sacred space of the nation. It also was believed that in the last days a cleansing of the nation would accompany the messianic times. In a sense, the end of spiritual exile would come with the arrival of the cleansing of the holy city. In effect, this is what Jesus was claiming to do. So the act was an inherent claim for authority to reform Judaism, even down to its most sacred spaces.

The first in a series of controversies underscores this point. The Jewish leadership asks Jesus where he received the authority to do such things as cleanse the temple (Matt. 21:23–27 = Mark 11:27–33 = Luke 20:1–8). Jesus replies with a question of his own about the authority of John the Baptist. His question in effect asks whether God can work through someone from outside the socially constituted leadership of the nation. The expected reply is that God can and did do this in the case of John. So Jesus' authority is like that of John. It is rooted in God. Everything about the last week centers around whether or not Jesus is sent from God.

To drive home the point, Jesus tells a parable about wicked tenants, picturing the Jewish leadership as unfaithful in their response over a long period (Matt. 21:33–46 = Mark 12:1–12 = Luke 20:9–19). Just as they rejected the prophets before him (the sent servants), so now they are about to reject "my beloved son." Here, Jesus makes a public claim of his unique relationship to God. No one before or since has occupied this position, and yet those given stewardship over the people of God will move to kill this unique one. That will result in judgment and the care of the vineyard passing on to others. In other words, Jesus is the rejected cornerstone that will be exalted by God regardless. Once again the point is a dispute about authority.

Other disputes follow about taxes and resurrection. However, the final dispute is a question to ponder (Matt. 22:41–46 = Mark 12:35–37 = Luke 20:41–44). Why does the patriarch David call his son "Lord" in a society in which respect goes to the ancestor, not to a son? Using Ps. 110:1, Jesus makes the point that the Messiah is not merely David's son, but really is his Lord. The title again raises the note of authority.

Jesus' eschatological discourse predicting both the destruction of the temple and the return of the Son of Man to redeem his own and judge the world also points to the issue of Jesus' authority (Matt. 24–25 = Mark 13 = Luke 21:5–37). This teaching, although given privately, points to the comprehensive scope of Jesus' relationship to God. He is the one who gives the final judgment. All are accountable to him.

Jesus' authority shows itself again privately when at the Last Supper he alters a sacred meal and gives it an interpretation tied to his upcoming rejection and death (Matt. 26:26–29 = Mark 14:22–25 = Luke 21:14–23). Here Jesus compares his upcoming work to a sacrifice that makes the new era possible by providing an efficacious offering for those who acknowledge him. The uniqueness of his calling and person is underscored here.

These claims, many of which were made in public, led the leadership to arrest Jesus. For both political and religious reasons, the leadership wanted Jesus stopped. The issue at his trial ended up still being about authority. After failing to get secure charges tied to Jesus' remarks about destroying the temple, as Matthew and Mark make clear, the issue became Jesus' messianic role (Matt. 26:57–62 = Mark 14:53–60). The goal here was to devise a charge that could be translated into political terms against which Rome would have to react. The failure of the temple charge led into the question about whether Jesus was the Son of God, probably meant messianically, given that the question is about the Christ (Matt. 26:62–66 = Mark 14:60–64 [like Luke 22:66–71]). In an event whose importance cannot be overestimated, the messianic question to Jesus becomes an occasion for him to claim authority over his questioners. God would vindicate him one day soon in a way that they could see. His claim was that he would be exalted to a place at God's right hand and one day would come on the clouds like the Son of Man of Dan. 7. At the Jewish examination of Jesus, what he said either was a rightful claim to be exalted by God or was blasphemy. There was no middle road. The issue at the trial was whether Jesus was who he claimed to be. The claim in Jesus' reply was that he was the Messiah and more. Not only was he the Christ, but also the Son of Man, who has the right to sit permanently in God's very presence and exercise final judgment. The Jewish leadership regarded this religious claim as blasphemy. It also allowed them to take a political charge to Pilate that Jesus claimed to lead a kingdom competing with Rome. Jesus was crucified because of the role he claimed to possess. He even supplied the testimony that led to his own conviction. His death was no accident but was purposed even as he chose to enter into the path of suffering and substitution that God had set before him.

The trial before Pilate rotated around the political issue of a claim for kingship because the Romans did not care that Jesus made more transcendent claims (Matt. 27:11–26 = Mark 15:1–15 = Luke 23:1–25). This note of Roman skepticism on Jesus' greater claims comes through in the account of John 18:28–38. Pilate appears initially to desire to let Jesus go, not regarding him as a true threat to Rome or having done anything deserving death. The pressure of the Jewish leadership induces him finally to agree to Jesus' death, despite his declarations of Jesus' innocence, a point that Luke 23 makes several times. Thus, Jesus dies unjustly as a result of human blindness and hard-heartedness. He dies as an innocent. According to the placard hung on the cross, Jesus dies of the charge of claiming to be "the King of the Jews." For his Jewish opponents, Jesus was killed because he made this claim, but even more for the comprehensive authority that he claimed to possess as that figure. They heard blasphemy in his claim to sit with God. They regarded that claim as an insult to the unique integrity of God and his honor. In their view, his death would bring an end to this error.

It is in this light that the Gospel portraits of the resurrection must be understood. The resurrection is seen as a divine vindication of Jesus' claims that he has the right to sit at God's side. As a vindication of these claims, the resurrection, with its assumed exaltation, means not only that Jesus is alive and that there is life after death, but also that he is shown to be who he claimed to be, given that God has exalted Jesus into his presence in heaven. The theological development of this understanding of the event is shown in Matt. 28:18. As Jesus notes, God has given all authority in heaven to him. Divine vindication is affirmed in how the ministry and church mission are linked as connected to a divine plan revealed in Scripture, in Luke 24:44–49. It is affirmed in Peter's claim that the arrival of the Spirit is evidence of God's vindication of Jesus as Lord and Messiah and is evidence of the arrival of the new era (Acts 2). Divine vindication also surfaces in the teaching that Jesus was resurrected so that there is one ordained to be the judge of the living and the dead (Acts 10:39–42). All these texts fill in what Jesus claimed during the Jewish examination: one day the leadership would see evidence of God's exaltation of him. For the Gospels, the evidence for Jesus' authority includes the empty tomb, the resurrection, and the place where Jesus ended up as a result of being raised from the dead. Jesus' announcement of exaltation points to who he is. Exaltation means resurrection to God's side, confirming Jesus' divine authority. It is Jesus' authority and the origin of it that are the most important topics of the last week of Jesus' ministry.

The oldest creed of the church that we have is the old Roman form of the Apostles' Creed, dating from the late fourth century.[110] It states well a summary of what was confessed about Jesus by the early church of that period:

---

110. Philip Schaff, *The Creeds of Christendom*, 3 vols., 6th ed. (1931; reprint, Grand Rapids: Baker, 1977), 1:21–22. The oldest form of the creed that we possess dates to c. A.D. 390, but it is referred to by earlier church fathers (see ibid., 1:16–20).

I believe in God the Father Almighty.
And in Jesus Christ, his only Son, our Lord; who was born by the Holy Spirit
    of the Virgin Mary;
Was crucified under Pontius Pilate and was buried;
The third day he rose from the dead;
He ascended into heaven; and sits on the right hand of the Father;
From there he shall come to judge the quick [living] and the dead.
And in the Holy Spirit;
The Holy Church;
The forgiveness of sins;
The resurrection of the body.

Here we see clearly the church's understanding that the events of the last week
led Jesus to assume a position of unequaled authority at God's side to share
in the divine prerogative of judgment and salvation. Jesus is more than a
teacher, more than a prophet, and more than a Messiah. He is the uniquely
authoritative revelator of God. He is the unique Son of God.

Conclusion: Jesus, the Uniquely Authoritative Revelator of God

The thrust of Jesus' teaching was that he brought the promised new era of
the rule of God. As prophet and as the one hoped for, Jesus both explained
the divine program and embodied divine presence and authority. His mission
began with and focused on Israel, but his ultimate goal was to bring the presence and promise of God to the world. The kingdom presence that he inaugurated opened the way for the victory of God and the Spirit of God because
forgiveness was made possible along with the hope of everlasting life. Opening
up access to the grace of God, Jesus made possible a way of life that honored
God. It was a way of life that reflected God's character and will. Jesus' ministry
started on the premise that here was a mission to a nation and a world that
needed this message of hope. Jesus understood that the renunciation of self-
focus bound up in his call to turn to God meant that many in the world would
not accept the invitation to be a part of God's people. To accept God's gift of
grace meant to acknowledge one's own need and limitations. Whether expressed as faith or repentance, the blessing of the kingdom comes only to
those who embrace their need for life in the way God has established it.

At the center of this newly announced divine program stood the person of
the one who makes its presence and sustenance possible. Jesus portrayed himself as the Son of Man, a human being who possessed divine authority because
he also was divine, as is shown by the fact that he has the right to sit in God's
very presence in heaven. Jesus according to Scripture is far more than a

prophet. He is far more than a king who promised deliverance. He is the revealer and explainer of God's plan, as well as the bridge of access to God. As the unique revelator of God and as the Son of Man, Jesus is what the Synoptics and John portray him to be, whether the story is told from the earth up or from heaven down. For the Synoptics, Jesus is the Messiah-Lord, who possesses divine authority clothed in humanity. John's Gospel says it much more simply: Jesus was the Word of God, and was God—God in the flesh (John 1:1, 14).

The painting on the jacket of this book shows two men staring at Jesus. They represent the evangelists, who, having experienced Jesus, tell us about him. Beyond the evangelists, two types of people tend to inquire about Jesus. One type searches for who he is. The other, having discovered where he can be found, tries to appreciate the depth of his message even more. The premise of this book is that our glimpse of Jesus is far clearer when he is seen according to Scripture rather than viewed in the reconstructions that pick and choose from the four portraits we have of Jesus. Our study has tried to show Jesus from the earth up (Synoptics) and from heaven down (John). In the end, the two portraits are not as diverse as they might initially appear—if one keeps the first-century Jewish context in view and allows the portraits a degree of dialogue with each other. That an ultimate unity emerges from these portraits has been the burden of this final chapter.

Jesus' challenge, which he set out from Scripture and through his sayings and acts, was that God's long-promised and longed-for kingdom rule had broken into creation through his ministry. God's promise of hope and life, the provision of the Spirit, forgiveness, and a vindicated rule had come in him. Jesus according to Scripture is a powerful figure who makes what people think of him and his mission the primary question that one must face in life. The question of Jesus is primary because it asks of us not only who Jesus is, but also who we are as God's creatures. If one seeks to know oneself or find life, one must measure oneself against the Creator and his plan. Jesus never is assessed alone, as if his identity were a historical or academic curiosity or merely a matter of private opinion. For what we think of Jesus reveals what we think of ourselves, our capabilities, and our needs, given the way that Jesus presented our need for God and Jesus' own role in that plan. Even as Jesus is the revelator of God, he also is the revelator of our hearts before God.

John's Gospel poses the issue this way: "The law was given through Moses; grace and truth came through Jesus Christ. No one has ever seen God; the only Son, who is in the bosom of the Father, he has made him known" (John 1:17–18). Later, John cites Jesus' own words in prayer and adds, "And this is eternal life, that they know you, the only true God, and Jesus Christ whom you have sent" (John 17:3). This is why understanding that Jesus never claimed to be one more religious great among others is so important even though that is how our world prefers to present Jesus. Jesus never allowed such a domesticated option for who he is. Jesus claimed to be unique in his authority as the Son of Man and the unique bearer of the hope of God's rule. As the revelator of God, Jesus according to Scripture argues that knowing God means being related to him as well. And in coming to know him, we will come to know ourselves and our Creator—and in the process find everlasting life.

Selected Bibliography

The following bibliography is confined to key commentaries, general studies on Jesus, and basic resources for Jewish studies. Other important works referred to in the book are cited in full on first mention in each chapter.

Key Commentaries on the Gospels

Matthew

Blomberg, Craig L. *Matthew*. New American Commentary. Nashville: Broadman, 1992.

Carson, D. A. "Matthew." In vol. 8 of *The Expositor's Bible Commentary*, ed. Frank E. Gaebelein, 1–599. Grand Rapids: Zondervan, 1984.

Davies, W. D., and Dale Allison. *Matthew*. 3 vols. International Critical Commentary. Edinburgh: Clark, 1988–97.

Hagner, Donald. *Matthew*. Word Biblical Commentary. Dallas: Word, 1993–95.

Keener, Craig. *A Commentary on the Gospel of Matthew*. Grand Rapids: Eerdmans, 1999.

Mark

Cranfield, C. E. B. *The Gospel according to St. Mark*. Cambridge Greek Testament Commentary. Cambridge: Cambridge University Press, 1959.

Evans, Craig A. *Mark 8:27–16:20*. Word Biblical Commentary. Nashville: Nelson, 2001.

France, R. T. *Commentary on Mark*. New International Greek Testament Commentary. Grand Rapids: Eerdmans, 2002.

Guelich, Robert. *Mark 1:1–8:26*. Word Biblical Commentary. Dallas: Word, 1989.

Gundry, Robert. *Mark: A Commentary on His Apology for the Cross*. Grand Rapids: Eerdmans, 1992.

Hooker, Morna D. *The Gospel according to Saint Mark*. Black's New Testament Commentaries. Peabody, Mass.: Hendrickson, 1991.

Lane, William. *The Gospel according to Mark*. New International Commentary on the New Testament. Grand Rapids: Eerdmans, 1973.

Marcus, Joel. *Mark 1–8*. Anchor Bible. New York: Doubleday, 2000.

Witherington, Ben, III. *The Gospel of Mark: A Socio-Rhetorical Commentary*. Grand Rapids: Eerdmans, 2001.

Luke

Bock, Darrell L. *Luke 1:1–24:53*. 2 vols. Baker Exegetical Commentary on the New Testament. Grand Rapids: Baker, 1994–96.

Fitzmyer, Joseph A. *The Gospel according to Luke*. 2 vols. Anchor Bible. Garden City, N.Y.: Doubleday, 1981–85.

Green, Joel B. *The Gospel of Luke*. New International Commentary on the New Testament. Grand Rapids: Eerdmans, 1997.

Marshall, I. Howard. *Commentary on Luke*. New International Greek Testament Commentary. Grand Rapids: Eerdmans, 1978.

Nolland, John. *Luke*. 3 vols. Word Biblical Commentary. Dallas: Word, 1989–93.

Stein, Robert H. *Luke*. New American Commentary. Nashville: Broadman and Holman, 1992.

John

Barrett, C. K. *The Gospel according to St. John*. 2d ed. London: SPCK, 1978.

Brown, Raymond E. *The Gospel according to John*. 2 vols. Anchor Bible. Garden City, N.Y.: Doubleday, 1966–70.

Carson, D. A. *The Gospel according to John*. Pillar New Testament Commentary. Grand Rapids: Eerdmans, 1991.

Morris, Leon. *The Gospel according to John*. Rev. ed. New International Commentary on the New Testament. Grand Rapids: Eerdmans, 1995.

Works on Jesus

Allison, Dale C. *Jesus of Nazareth: Millenarian Prophet*. Minneapolis: Fortress, 1998.

Blomberg, Craig. *Jesus and the Gospels*. Nashville: Broadman and Holman, 1997.

Bock, Darrell L. *Blasphemy and Exaltation in Judaism and the Jewish Examination of Jesus*. Wissenschaftliche Untersuchungen zum Neuen Testament 2.106. Tübingen: Mohr, 1998.

Bockmuehl, Marcus. *This Jesus: Martyr, Lord, Messiah*. Edinburgh: Clark, 1994.

Bornkamm, Günther. *Jesus of Nazareth*. New York: Harper & Row, 1960.

Casey, P. M. *From Jewish Prophet to Gentile God: The Origins and Development of New Testament Christology*. Louisville: Westminster/John Knox, 1991.

Chilton, Bruce. *Rabbi Jesus: An Intimate Biography*. New York: Doubleday, 2000.

Crossan, John Dominic. *The Historical Jesus: The Life of a Mediterranean Jewish Peasant*. New York: HarperSanFrancisco, 1991.

Dunn, James D. G. "Messianic Ideas and Their Influence on the Jesus of History." In *The Messiah*, ed. James Charlesworth, 365–81. Minneapolis: Augsburg Fortress, 1992.

Ellis, E. Earle. "New Directions in Form Criticism." In *Prophecy and Hermeneutic in Early Christianity*, 237–53. Tübingen: Mohr, 1978.

Evans, Craig A. *Jesus and His Contemporaries: Comparative Studies*. Leiden: Brill, 1995.

Fredriksen, Paula. *From Jesus to Christ: The Origins of the New Testament Images of Jesus*. New Haven, Conn.: Yale University Press, 1998.

———. *Jesus of Nazareth, King of the Jews: A Jewish Life and the Emergence of Christianity*. New York: Knopf, 1999.

Hengel, Martin. *Studies in Early Christology*. Edinburgh: Clark, 1995.

Jonge, Marinus de. *Jesus, the Servant-Messiah*. New Haven, Conn.: Yale University Press, 1991.

Kinman, Brent. *Jesus' Entry into Jerusalem: In the Context of Lukan Theology and the Politics of His Day.* Arbeiten zur Geschichte des antiken Judentums und des Urchristentums 28. Leiden: Brill, 1995.

McKnight, Scot. *A New Vision for Israel: The Teaching of Jesus in National Context.* Grand Rapids: Eerdmans, 1999.

Meier, John P. *A Marginal Jew: Rethinking the Historical Jesus.* 3 vols. New York: Doubleday, 1991–2001.

Osborne, Grant. *The Resurrection Narratives: A Redactional Study.* Grand Rapids: Baker, 1984.

Sanders, E. P. *Jesus and Judaism.* Philadelphia: Fortress, 1985.

Stein, Robert H. *The Method and Message of Jesus' Teachings.* Rev. ed. Louisville: Westminster/ John Knox, 1994.

Stuhlmacher, Peter. *Jesus of Nazareth—Christ of Faith.* Peabody, Mass.: Hendrickson, 1993.

Theissen, Gerd, and Annette Metz. *The Historical Jesus: A Comprehensive Guide.* Minneapolis: Fortress, 1998.

Vermes, Geza. *Jesus the Jew: A Historian's Reading of the Gospels.* 2d ed. New York: Macmillan, 1983.

Webb, Robert L. *John the Baptizer and Prophet: A Socio-Historical Study.* Sheffield: Sheffield Academic Press, 1991.

Witherington, Ben, III. *The Christology of Jesus.* Philadelphia: Fortress, 1990.

Wright, N. T. *Jesus and the Victory of God.* Minneapolis: Fortress, 1996.

Works on Jewish Literature

General Works

Cowley, A. *Aramaic Papyri of the Fifth Century B.C.* Oxford: Clarendon, 1923.

Evans, Craig A. *Noncanonical Writings and New Testament Interpretation.* Peabody, Mass.: Hendrickson, 1992.

Grisby, Bruce H. "A Proposed Guide for Citing Rabbinic Texts." *Journal of the Evangelical Theological Society* 24 (1981): 83–90.

Jastrow, Marcus. *A Dictionary of the Targumim, the Talmud Babli and Yerushalmi, and the Midrashic Literature.* 1903. Reprint, New York: Judaica, 1992.

Levy, J., H. L. Fleischer, and L. Goldschmidt. *Wörterbuch über die Talmudim und Midrashim.* Darmstadt: Wissenschaftliche Buchgesellschaft, 1963.

Mulder, M. J., ed. *Mikra: Text, Translation, Reading, and Interpretation of the Hebrew Bible in Ancient Judaism and Early Christianity.* Philadelphia: Fortress; Assen: Van Gorcum, 1988.

Neusner, J. *Introduction to Rabbinic Literature.* New York: Doubleday, 1994.

———. *The Study of Ancient Judaism.* 2 vols. New York: Ktav, 1981.

Rost, L. *Judaism outside the Hebrew Canon: An Introduction to the Documents.* Nashville: Abingdon, 1976.

Stemberger, Günther. *Introduction to the Talmud and Midrash.* Trans. Marcus Bockmuehl. 2d ed. Edinburgh: Clark, 1996.

Hebrew Bible and LXX

Dos Santos, E. C. *An Expanded Hebrew Index for the Hatch-Redpath Concordance to the Septuagint.* Jerusalem: Dugith, [1974].

Elliger, K., and W. Rudolph, eds. *Biblia Hebraica Stuttgartensia.* Stuttgart: Deutsche Bibelgesellschaft, 1997.

Hatch, Edwin, and Henry A. Redpath. *A Concordance to the Septuagint and the Other Greek Versions of the Old Testament (Including the Apocryphal Books)*. 2d ed. Grand Rapids: Baker, 1998.

Le Boulluec, A., and P. Sandevoir, eds. *La Bible d'Alexandrie*. Paris: Editions du Cerf, 1989.

Muraoka, Takamitsu. *Hebrew/Aramaic Index to the Septuagint (Keyed to the Hatch-Redpath Concordance)*. Grand Rapids: Baker, 1998.

Rahlfs, Alfred, ed. *Septuaginta: Id est Vetus Testamentum graece iuxta LXX interpretes*. Stuttgart: Deutsche Bibelgesellschaft, 1935.

———. *Septuaginta*. 2 vols. Stuttgart: Württembergische Bibelanstalt, 1935.

Septuaginta: Vetus Testamentum Graecum. 20 vols. to date. Göttingen: Vandenhoeck & Ruprecht, 1931–.

Taylor, Bernard A. *The Analytical Lexicon to the Septuagint: A Complete Parsing Guide*. Grand Rapids: Zondervan, 1994.

Samaritan Pentateuch

Macdonald, John, ed. and trans. *Memar Marqah: The Teaching of Marqah*. Beihefte zur Zeitschrift für die alttestamentliche Wissenschaft 84. Berlin: Töpelmann, 1963.

Old Testament Apocrypha and Pseudepigrapha

Black, Matthew. *The Book of Enoch or I Enoch: A New English Edition*. Studia in Veteris Testamenti Pseudepigrapha 7. Leiden: Brill, 1985.

Charles, R. H., ed. *The Apocrypha and Pseudepigrapha of the Old Testament in English*. 2 vols. Oxford: Clarendon, 1913.

Charlesworth, James H., ed. *The Old Testament Pseudepigrapha*. 2 vols. New York: Doubleday, 1983–85.

Denis, A.-M. *Concordance Grecque des Pseudépigraphes d'Ancien Testament*. Louvain-au-Neuve: Université Catholique de Louvain, 1987.

Hollander, H. W., and M. de Jonge. *The Testaments of the Twelve Patriarchs: A Commentary*. Studia in Veteris Testamenti Pseudepigrapha 8. Leiden: Brill, 1985.

Jacobson, Howard. *The Exagoge of Ezekiel*. Cambridge: Cambridge University Press, 1983.

Kee, Howard Clark. *The Cambridge Annotated Study Apocrypha: New Revised Standard Version*. Cambridge: Cambridge University Press, 1994.

Knibb, Michael A, ed. *The Ethiopic Book of Enoch*. Oxford: Clarendon, 1978.

Lechner-Schmidt, Wilfried. *Wortindex der lateinischen erhaltenen Pseudepigraphen zum Alten Testament: Texte und Arbeiten zum neutestamentlichen Zeitalter*. Ed. K. Berger, F. Vouga, M. Wolter, and D. Zeller. Tübingen: Francke, 1990.

Sparks, H. F. D., ed. *The Apocryphal Old Testament*. Oxford: Clarendon, 1984.

Tromp, Johannes. *The Assumption of Moses: A Critical Edition with Commentary*. Studia in Veteris Testamenti Pseudepigrapha 10. Leiden: Brill, 1993.

Uhlig, Siegbert. *Das äthiopische Henochbuch*. Jüdische Schriften aus hellenistisch-römischer Zeit 5.6. Gütersloh: Mohn, 1984.

Wahl, C. A. *Clavis Librorum Veteris Testamenti Apocryphorum Philologica*. Graz: Akademische Druck, 1972.

Dead Sea Scrolls

Allegro, John. *Qumran Cave 4 I (4Q158–4Q186)*. Discoveries in the Judaean Desert of Jordan 5. Oxford: Clarendon, 1968.

Charlesworth, James H. *The Dead Sea Scrolls: Hebrew, Aramaic, and Greek Texts with English Translations.* Vol. 1, *Rule of the Community and Related Documents.* Tübingen: Mohr (Siebeck), 1994.

Davies, P. R. *The Damascus Document: An Interpretation of the Damascus Document.* Journal for the Study of the Old Testament Monograph Series 25. Sheffield: JSOT Press, 1983.

Discoveries in the Judaean Desert of Jordan. 34 vols. to date. Oxford: Clarendon, 1955–.

Dupont-Sommer, A. *The Essene Writings from Qumran.* Trans. Geza Vermes. Gloucester, Mass.: Smith, 1973.

García Martínez, Florentino. *The Dead Sea Scrolls Translated: The Qumran Texts in English.* Trans. Wilfred G. E. Watson. 2d ed. Grand Rapids: Eerdmans, 1996.

García Martínez, Florentino, and Eibert J. C. Tigchelaar. *The Dead Sea Scrolls Study Edition.* 2 vols. Leiden: Brill; Grand Rapids: Eerdmans, 1997.

Knibb, Michael A. *The Qumran Community.* Cambridge Commentaries on Writings of the Jewish and Christian World 200 B.C. to A.D. 200, vol. 2. Cambridge: Cambridge University Press, 1987.

Maier, Johann. *Die Qumran-Essener: Die Texte vom Toten Meer.* 2 vols. Uni-Taschenbücher 1862–63. Munich: Reinhardt, 1995.

Vermes, Geza. *The Dead Sea Scrolls in English.* 3d ed. London: Penguin, 1987.

Josephus

Thackeray, H. St. J., Ralph Marcus, Allen Wikgren, and L. H. Feldman, trans. *Josephus.* 10 vols. Loeb Classical Library. Cambridge, Mass.: Harvard University Press, 1926–65.

Whiston, William, trans. *The Works of Josephus.* New ed. Peabody, Mass.: Hendrickson, 1987.

Philo

Colson, F. H., G. H. Whitaker, J. W. Earp, and R. Marcus, trans. *Philo.* 10 vols. plus 2 supplementary vols. Loeb Classical Library. Cambridge, Mass.: Harvard University Press, 1929–53.

Yonge, C. D., trans. *The Works of Philo.* New ed. Peabody, Mass.: Hendrickson, 1993.

Midrash

Bietenhard, Hans. *Midrasch Tanhuma B.* Judaica et Christiana 6. Bern: Peter Lang, 1982.

———. *Sifre Deuteronomium.* Judaica et Christiana 8. Frankfurt: Peter Lang, 1984.

Braude, William G., trans. *The Midrash on Psalms.* 2 vols. Yale Judaica Series 13. New Haven, Conn.: Yale University Press, 1959.

———. *Pesikta Rabbati.* New Haven, Conn.: Yale University Press: 1968.

Finkelstein, Louis. *Siphre ad Deuteronomium.* Corpus Tannaicum: Siphre d'be Rab 3.2. Berlin: Gesellschaft zur Forderung der Wissenschaft des Judentums, 1939. Reprint, New York: Jewish Theological Seminary of America, 1993.

Freedman, H., and M. Simon. *The Midrash Rabbah.* 3d ed. 10 vols. London and New York: Soncino, 1983.

Goldin, Judah, trans. *The Fathers according to Rabbi Nathan.* Yale Judaica Series 10. New Haven, Conn.: Yale University Press, 1955.

Hammer, Reuven. *Sifre: A Tannaitic Commentary on the Book of Deuteronomy.* New Haven, Conn.: Yale University Press, 1986.

Horovitz, Saul. *Siphre ad Numeros adjecto Sipre zutta.* Corpus Tannaiticum: Siphre d'be Rab
3.1. Leipzig: Frock, 1917. Reprint, Jerusalem: Shalem, 1992.

Kuhn, Karl G. *Der tannaitische Midrasch, Sifre zu Numeri.* Rabbinische Texte: Tannaitische
Midraschim 2/3. Stuttgart: Kohlhammer, 1959.

Lauterbach, Jacob Z. *Mekilta de-Rabbi Ishmael.* Philadelphia: Jewish Publication Society,
1933–49.

Neusner, J. *Midrash in Context: Exegesis in Formative Judaism.* Philadelphia: Fortress, 1983.

———. *Sifra: An Analytical Translation.* Brown Judaic Studies 140. Atlanta: Scholars Press,
1988.

———. *What Is Midrash?* Philadelphia: Fortress, 1987.

Porton, G. G. *Understanding Rabbinic Midrash.* Hoboken, N.J.: Ktav, 1985.

Saldarini, Anthony J. *The Fathers according to Rabbi Nathan: Aboth de Rabbi Nathan Version
B.* Studies in Judaism in Late Antiquity 11. Leiden: Brill, 1985.

Schechter, Solomon. *Aboth de Rabbi Nathan.* New York: Feldheim, 1945.

Townsend, John. *Midrash Tanhuma, Genesis: Translated into English with Introduction, Indices,
and Brief Notes* (S. Buber Recension). Hoboken, N.J.: Ktav, 1989.

Winter, Jakob, and A. Wünsche. *Mechiltha: Ein tannaitischer Midrasch zu Exodus.* Leipzig:
Hinrichs, 1909.

Targums

Diez Macho, Alejandro. *Neophyti 1: Levitico.* Textos y Estudios. Madrid: Consejo Superior de
Investigaciones Cientificas, 1971.

———. *Neophyti 1: Numeros.* Textos y Estudios. Madrid: Consejo Superior de Investigaciones
Cientificas, 1974.

Grossfeld, Bernard. *A Bibliography of Targum Literature.* 2 vols. Bibliographica Judaica 3 and
8. Cincinnati: Hebrew Union College; New York: Ktav, 1972–77.

———, trans. *The Targum Onqelos to Genesis.* Aramaic Bible 6. Wilmington, Del.: Glazier,
1988.

———. *The Targum Onqelos to Exodus.* Aramaic Bible 7. Wilmington, Del.: Glazier, 1988.

———. *The Targum Onqelos to Leviticus and the Targum Onqelos to Numbers.* Aramaic Bible
8. Wilmington, Del.: Glazier, 1988.

———. *The Targum Onqelos to Deuteronomy.* Aramaic Bible 9. Wilmington, Del.: Glazier,
1988.

Harrington, Daniel J., and Anthony J. Saldarini, trans. *Targum Jonathan of the Former Prophets.* Aramaic Bible 10. Wilmington, Del.: Glazier, 1987.

Maher, Michael, trans. *Targum Pseudo-Jonathan: Genesis.* Aramaic Bible 1B. Collegeville,
Minn.: Liturgical Press, 1992.

McNamara, Martin, Ernest G. Clarke, and Shirley Magder, trans. *Targum Neofiti 1: Numbers
and Targum Pseudo-Jonathan: Numbers.* Aramaic Bible 4. Collegeville, Minn.: Liturgical
Press, 1995.

McNamara, Martin, Robert Hayward, and Michael Maher, trans. *Targum Neofiti 1: Exodus
and Targum Pseudo-Jonathan: Exodus.* Aramaic Bible 2. Collegeville, Minn.: Liturgical
Press, 1994.

———. *Targum Neofiti 1: Leviticus and Targum Pseudo-Jonathan: Leviticus.* Aramaic Bible 3.
Collegeville, Minn.: Liturgical Press, 1994.

Nickels, P. *Targum and New Testament: A Bibliography Together with a New Testament Index.*
Rome: Pontifical Biblical Institute, 1967.

Mishnah and Tosefta

Blackman, Philip, ed. *Mishnayoth*. 7 vols. London: Mishna, 1951–56.

Danby, Herbert, trans. *The Mishnah: Translated from the Hebrew with Introduction and Brief Explanatory Notes*. Oxford: Oxford University Press, 1933.

Herford, R. Travers, ed. *Pirke Aboth: The Tractate "Fathers," from the Mishnah, Commonly Called "Sayings of the Fathers."* 3d rev. ed. New York: Jewish Institute of Religion Press, 1945.

Neusner, J. *Mishnah*. New Haven, Conn.: Yale University Press, 1988.

Taylor, Charles. *Sayings of the Jewish Fathers: Sefer Dibre Aboth Ha-Olam Comprising Pirque Aboth in Hebrew and English with Critical Notes and Excursuses*. Amsterdam: Philo, 1970.

Zuckermandel, M. S., ed. *Tosefta*. Jerusalem: Sifre Vahrman, [1970].

Talmuds

Epstein, I., ed. *The Babylonian Talmud*. 35 vols. London: Soncino, 1936–48.

Goldschmidt, Lazarus. *Der babylonische Talmud*. 8 vols. Berlin: Calvary, 1897–1909. Reprint, Haag: Nijoff, 1933–35.

Hengel, Martin, Jacob Neusner, Peter Schäfer, Hans-Jürgen Becker, and Frowald Gil Huttenmeister, eds. *Übersetzung des Talmud Yerushalmi*. 16 vols. Tübingen: Mohr (Siebeck), 1975–.

Neusner, J. *The Talmud of the Land of Israel: A Preliminary Translation and Explanation*. 35 vols. Chicago: University of Chicago Press, 1982–89.

Schäfer, Peter, and Hans-Jürgen Becker. *Synopse zum Talmud Yerushalmi*. Tübingen: Mohr, 1991–.

Jewish Mysticism

Schäfer, Peter, and Hans-Jürgen Becker, eds. *Übersetzung der Hekhalot-Literatur*. 4 vols. Texte und Studien zum antiken Judentum 17, 22, 29, and 46. Tübingen: Mohr (Siebeck), 1987–.

Index of Subjects

Index of Modern Authors

Index of Scripture and Other Ancient Writings

Old Testament

New Testament

Page numbers in bold type indicate unit-level discussion.

Old Testament Apocrypha

Old Testament Pseudepigrapha

Mishnah

Tosefta

Talmuds

Targums

Other Rabbinic Writings

Qumran / Dead Sea Scrolls

Papyri

Josephus

Philo

Classical Writers

Early Christian Writings